THE
RENAISSANCE
IN ROME

THE RENAISSANCE IN ROME

Charles L. Stinger

INDIANA UNIVERSITY PRESS
BLOOMINGTON AND INDIANAPOLIS

This book is a publication of

Indiana University Press
601 North Morton Street
Bloomington, IN 47404-3797 USA

www.indiana.edu/~iupress

Telephone orders 800-842-6796
Fax orders 812-855-7931
Orders by e-mail iuporder@indiana.edu

First paperback edition 1998
© 1985, 1998 by Charles L. Stinger

Manufactured in the United States of America

Stinger, Charles L., date,
The Renaissance in Rome.

Bibliography: p.
Includes index.
1. Rome (Italy)—Civilization—15th century.   2. Rome
(Italy)—Civilization—16th century.   3. Renaissance—
Italy—Rome.   4. Papacy—History—1447–1565.   I. Title.
DG812.1.S75   1984   945'.63205   83-49337
ISBN 0-253-33491-8 (cloth) — ISBN 0-253-21208-1 (paper)
3 4 5 6 02 01 00

To Owen and Kate

Contents

I. Introduction   1

II. *Urbs Roma*   14

Topography and Urban Realities, 14; Rome of the Pilgrims, 31; Liturgy and Ceremony, 46; The Ancient City, 59; The Subterranean and the Super-Terrestrial, the Demonic and the Celestial, 76

III. The Renaissance Papacy and the *Respublica Christiana*   83

The Renaissance Popes, 83; Italian Politics, 96; Europe and Crusade, 106; Church Administration and Spiritual Power, 123; Theological Developments, 140

IV. The Primacy of Peter *Princeps Apostolorum* and the *Instauratio Ecclesiae Romanae*   156

Papalism vs. Conciliarism, 158; Humanists and the *Primatus Petri*, 166; Moses, *Typus Papae*, 201; Solomon and the Temple, 222; Paleo-Christian Antiquity in Ecclesiastical Architecture and in Patristic Scholarship, 226

V. The *Renovatio Imperii* and the *Renovatio Romae*   235

The Roman *Imperium* and the Pope as Caesar, 238; Augustus and Constantine, 246; The Capitol Renewed, 254; The Vatican Rebuilt, 264; The Vatican Library and Classical Studies, 282

Maps & Illustrations

Maps

Illustrations

PREFACE TO THE FIRST EDITION

The cultural world of Renaissance Rome first drew my attention nearly a decade ago. At that point, as I was putting the finishing touches to my book on the patristic revival in early fifteenth-century Florence, I began to investigate to what extent the humanistic study of the Church Fathers, initiated by Ambrogio Traversari, continued after his death. What soon became clear to me was that by the middle of the fifteenth century, Rome had supplanted Florence as the leading center for furthering Renaissance patristics. Why should this have been the case? Did the impetus to these studies there stem from any special concern for early Christianity and its relevance for contemporary issues? How did an interest in Christian antiquity relate to the other intellectual aspirations of the humanists active in Rome, and how did this fit into the overall cultural and intellectual life of the Eternal City? From these initial questions, this book eventually germinated.

To answer my initial queries satisfactorily meant, in fact, to come to grips with the whole movement of the Renaissance in Rome. The revival of Christian antiquity, I quickly discovered as I read more extensively in the writings of the Roman humanists, formed only one aspect of a larger program of restoration and renewal. Indeed, I became convinced that a distinctively *Roman* Renaissance had occurred. A shared outlook, a persistent set of intellectual concerns, similar cultural assumptions, and a commitment to common ideological aims bound Rome's humanists and artists to a uniquely Roman world, different from Florence, Venice, and other Italian and European centers.

Gradually the outlines of a book took shape. It should probe for the basic attitudes, the underlying values, and the core convictions that Rome's intellectuals and artists experienced, lived for, and believed in from the time of Pope Eugenius IV's definitive return to the Eternal City in 1443 to the Sack of 1527. Moreover, to analyze in any meaningful way the emergence and development of the Renaissance in Rome would require taking into account the particular political, social, and economic conditions within which the cultural world of Rome existed.

The time seemed ripe for such a work of synthesis to appear. The old multi-volume studies of Ferdinand Gregorovius and Ludwig von Pastor, invaluable as they remain for many aspects of Rome's political life and for the diplomatic and ecclesiastical affairs of the papacy, seemed increasingly inadequate in their accounts of cultural history. For Gregorovius, in fact, the period from the Great Schism to the Sack represented merely the last chapter in the long medieval history of Rome. Pastor's real subject, on the other hand, was a history of the papacy from the end of the Middle Ages. He tended to see the age of the Renaissance as marked by corruption and torpor in the Church, and where he did discuss cultural developments he imposed the distorting lens of a presumed dichotomy between a "true, Christian Renaissance" in service to the Church and a "false, pagan Renaissance" symptomatic of the period's moral and religious decay. In reality, the humanists in Rome strove to reconcile classical values and Christian truths.

Early in this century, the French scholar Emmanuel Rodocanachi did direct numerous studies to Rome's Renaissance culture, particularly to festivals and pageantry. Following Burckhardt, however, he, like Gregorovius, viewed the Renaissance in almost wholly secular terms as the revival of ancient paganism. In so doing he neglected any serious consideration of the religious dimension in Roman thought and values.

Renaissance Rome had suffered, too, from the long shadow Reformation historiography had cast over it. As scholars dwelled on the corrosive effects of a "corrupt" Renaissance papacy, or alternatively tried in certain measure to exculpate it, they considered the Renaissance world of Rome less for its own sake and in its own terms than for what it implied for the coming of Protestantism and post-Tridentine Catholicism.

Historians of the Italian Renaissance, on the other hand, continued to be preoccupied with Florence and, to a lesser extent, Venice. Florence, it seemed, was the creative source of all that was characteristic of the Renaissance as a whole. Here the basic humanistic commitments had first taken root, and from here they gradually were diffused elsewhere. Analyzing the political, social, economic, cultural, and religious features of Florence thus dominated the scholarship produced over the last quarter-century, to the neglect of other Italian cities—a point Amedeo Quondam has recently stressed.

Still, important elements of the intellectual and cultural life of Renaissance Rome had come to light in contemporary scholarship, particularly John O'Malley's studies of Giles of Viterbo and John Shearman's work on the Vatican stanze and on Raphael's tapestry cartoons for the Sistine Chapel. Several younger historians were also writing theses or dissertations, which eventually reached published form, on Roman topics. These included John McManamon's study on funeral oratory from the papal court, Egmont Lee's work on the humanists of Sixtus IV's pontificate, John D'Amico's investigation of a group of humanists at the Roman Curia in the early sixteenth century, and Melissa Bullard's biography of Filippo Strozzi, who was so active in the fiscal affairs of the two Medici popes.

A fresh, overall approach to the Roman Renaissance world these scholars were each elucidating in part thus seemed desirable. Such a book would offer to non-specialists a discernible portrait of a major Renaissance center. At the same time scholars would benefit from the comprehensive presentation of existing research, and perhaps see more clearly where further reflection and research were required.

Realizing this project nonetheless proved far more demanding and time-consuming than I could have imagined at the outset. The Roman Renaissance was the creation not of one towering intellectual leader nor of a single, identifiable group. Rather it embodied the aspirations of dozens of figures, variously active in an eighty-year period. Many of their writings remain unpublished, and even the more influential Roman humanists, such as Flavio Biondo and Platina, lack modern monographs. The problem is not lack of relevant source materials. Rome's libraries and archives present an almost bewildering richness of pertinent sources, which threaten to swamp any investigator, no matter how intrepid. Existing scholarship and newly published studies, notably Massimo Miglio's articles, did provide invaluable guidelines for my own research in the Vatican and other Roman libraries, and contributed immensely to my historical understanding. In this respect, John O'Malley's new book on humanist oratory at the papal court proved indispensable. Using these as a starting point, I attempted to read for myself all the humanist works I judged relevant to revealing the general aims and character of the Roman Renaissance.

At the same time I worked to master the scholarship on such matters as Rome's retarded economic development, the papacy's increasing entanglement in Italian politics, papal preoccupation with crusade against the Ottomans, and the effects of papal fiscal and administrative practices. Denys Hay's book on the Italian Church, Felix Gilbert's study of the fiscal affairs of Julius II and Agostino Chigi, and, particularly, Kenneth Setton's detailed analysis of the Renaissance papacy's crusading ventures were among the newly appearing studies that shaped my own thinking.

Consideration of economic, social, and political forces does assume a certain place in this study. These help explain persistent tendencies and the recurrence of certain issues. Nonetheless, I am convinced these developments recede in importance before the cultural history of the period. Only in the context of the ideological and cultural commitments advanced in the writings of the humanists and reflected in the works of artists and architects do we fully understand the motivation for papal policies. Reality, for most Renaissance Romans, took on intelligibility only in the light of Rome's mythic destiny, and what was most real transcended the human bounds of mundane politics and society. Therefore, the cultural world of Rome is, I would argue, what we must understand first if we are to reconstruct adequately anything else about the city and its inhabitants, and before we can look more closely at institutions, policies, or the careers of individual pontiffs, humanists, and artists.

Essentially, then, this book fits the genre of cultural history. Mood, myth, image, and symbol as manifested in liturgy, ceremony, festival, oratory, and art denote key elements of Rome's Renaissance aspirations. Moreover, these aspirations centered upon a persistent constellation of fundamental themes: the image of the city of Rome, the restoration of the Roman Church, the renewal of the Roman Empire, and the fullness of time. A topical rather than a chronological organization seemed the most appropriate way of analyzing the content, meaning, origin, and implication of these central ideas, and that is the structure I have given to this book.

Nonetheless, this book adheres to a certain chronological logic. Before everything else, both in longevity and in priority, stands the city of Rome itself. Grasping its essential characteristics and manifold guises must come first. Next follows an analysis of the Renaissance papacy, of papal administration of temporal and spiritual power, and of theological developments in Rome. Distinctive features in each of these areas prevailed through most of the Renaissance period, and they set this era of Church history apart from both the medieval and Counter-Reformation epochs.

With both Rome and the Roman Church thus presented in their salient features, one can then turn to the general issue with which the first generation of Roman humanists was most concerned: the reaffirmation of papal primacy and the restoration of the Roman Church. The humanists discovered in paleo-Christian and Hebraic antiquity important precedents for underscoring the religious centrality of the papal office, and they affirmed the unique sanctity of the city of Rome, particularly the Vatican region, from earliest times.

These ideological claims persisted in the later fifteenth and early sixteenth centuries, but increasingly they were joined to a second general theme: the renewal of the Roman Empire. Under Popes Julius II, the "new Julius Caesar," and Leo X, the "new Augustus," the Renaissance in Rome reached its apex. During their pontificates, Roman culture accentuated, too, the eternal character of the city of Rome, and the fulfillment there of the loftiest aims of both civilization and Christianity.

As this book unfolds, then, the chronological focus tends to move forward in time from the middle decades of the fifteenth century to the opening decades of the sixteenth. Nonetheless, within each chapter revealing developments throughout the whole period of the Roman Renaissance are included. To help compensate for what difficulties in comprehension this may create, and to aid readers in orienting themselves to the period, I have included in the Introduction a short sketch of papal history during the Renaissance.

The purpose and scope of this book will prove useful, I hope, to Renaissance—and to Reformation—scholars. In its demonstration of the interconnectedness of basic themes, in its analysis of the recurrent tendencies in Roman Renaissance thought, and in its documentation in original and secondary sources, it should serve both as an overall interpretation of the Roman Renaissance and as a point of departure for further thinking and investigation.

But in writing this book, I meant to make it accessible, too, to more general readers, non-professionals who may know something of Rome, who perhaps have grown fascinated with it as I have, and who may wish to learn something more about one of its most creative and influential periods. May they see come alive in their mind's eye the extraordinary world that was the Renaissance in Rome.

Research in Rome for this study was made possible by grants from the State University of New York Research Foundation and from the American Council of Learned Societies. A sabbatical leave from SUNY at Buffalo greatly aided the completion of a first draft. I am grateful also for the aid and kindness extended by the following institutions: the Biblioteca Apostolica Vaticana, the Biblioteca Hertziana in Rome, the Biblioteca Berenson at Villa I Tatti in Florence, the Rare Book and Inter-Library Loan departments of Lockwood Library, SUNY at Buffalo, and the library of Christ the King Seminary, East Aurora, New York. The maps were prepared by the Cartographic Laboratory of the Department of Geography, SUNY at Buffalo, and I wish to acknowledge the help of its Director, Mike O'Neill.

In the research and writing of this book, I have enjoyed the generosity, advice, and encouragement of many Renaissance scholars. Among these, I wish especially to thank John D'Amico, John McManamon, Clare O'Reilly, Donald Kelley, Elisabeth MacDougall, Eugene Rice, Deno Geanakoplos, Lewis Spitz, and Charles Trinkaus. For matters involving music, I benefitted from the knowledge of Edmond Strainchamps, musicologist and my colleague in Renaissance studies at SUNY at Buffalo. The superior command of Greek and Latin that my wife, Pat, possesses helped me through some perplexing passages, and her perceptive criticisms clarified my thinking and my prose. Her encouragement was instrumental at each stage of this undertaking. Above all, I am deeply indebted to John O'Malley. He supported my project from the outset, shared unstintingly his unequalled knowledge of Roman humanist thought, emboldened me to overcome doubts, and in reading the text enabled me to sharpen my analysis and saved me from errors. The defects and mistakes that remain are, naturally, my own.

Some dozen years, slightly more than the length of a typical Renaissance pontificate, have passed since this book's first appearance. Historical inquiry into Renaissance Rome, fitful when I began my research in Rome a quarter century ago, has since then produced a torrent of new scholarship with no signs of abating. There is now even a journal, *Roma nel Rinascimento*, published annually (beginning in 1984) by the Istituto Storico Italiano per il Medio Evo in Rome. At this point we know much more about the cultural, political, and social life of the Eternal City during the fifteenth and sixteenth centuries than when I composed this book. Indeed, a thoroughly revised text, were I to undertake such a project, would require reassessment, refinement, and even in some instances revamping of what appears here.

In particular, I would devote more attention to developments in the 1520s and 1530s and to the impact of the Sack. In the Epilogue I sketched out what I viewed as having occurred. New studies, discussed below, would now allow a fuller and more nuanced account. The Sack did have a shattering impact, I remain convinced. Yet the mythic images of Rome, which had figured so prominently in Renaissance intellectual and artistic conceptions of the city and of its destiny, continued to inform religious and cultural aspirations into the middle decades of the sixteenth century, and even beyond. Granted, these themes of triumph, eternity, and transcendence were modified and transformed in response to religious and political conflicts, particularly the great movement of Catholic reform. Still, that humanist ideas and images persisted forms part of what is significant about the history of the Renaissance in Rome.

I would have wished to be more attentive, too, to the ways in which the cultural and ideological aspirations of the humanists at the papal court, with which this book is most concerned, met resistance and required negotiation, both within the Vatican itself and especially with the civic world of the "other Rome" on the opposite side of the Tiber. I remain persuaded, however, that the particular notions of regeneration, renewal, rebirth, and fulfillment explored here constituted a distinctly *Roman* Renaissance. Much recent work in fact serves, as I see it, to further validate and extend that fundamental conclusion. It therefore seems warranted to reissue the text as originally published.

In an effort, however, to make this book more useful to new readers, I attempt in the following bibliographic overview to acknowledge the significant new scholarship which has appeared since I completed my text. I emphasize works of cultural and intellectual history, though even here my discussion cannot be regarded as exhaustive. Also, while I have been attentive to contributions in Italian and other European languages, I have been particularly concerned to mention works in English, much of it produced by an extraordinarily talented new generation of American scholars.

No new comprehensive study of the Renaissance in Rome has appeared, but a good place to assess the current state of scholarship is Sergio Gensini, ed., *Roma Capitale (1447–1527)* [Centro di Studi sulla Civiltà del Tardo Medioevo San Miniato, Collana di Studi e Ricerche, 5] (Pisa: Pacini Editore, 1994). In this large volume are published the contributions, including extensive bibliographic references, of the two dozen Italian, North American, and British scholars active in research on all aspects of the city's Renaissance history who participated in the 1992 international conference at San Miniato. Similarly sweeping in its portrayal of the Roman world, if more restricted chronologically, is Massimo Miglio et al., eds., *Un pontificato ed una città, Sisto IV (1471–1484): Atti del convegno (Roma 3–7 dicembre 1984)* [Studi storici, fasc. 154–62] (Rome: Istituto Storico Italiano per il Medio Evo, 1986). An important collection of essays by Vincenzo De Caprio, a leading Italian authority, explores many aspects of Roman humanism: *La tradizione ed il trauma: Idee del Rinascimento romano* (Manziana: Vecchiarelli, 1992).

With regard to liturgy and ceremony, Hans Belting, *Likeness and Presence: A History of the Image before the Era of Art,* trans. Edmund Jephcott (U. of Chicago Pr., 1994) identifies the historical circumstances, and in the appendix provides excerpts of relevant texts, related to the various sacred icons and images in Rome and their cults. These include the Veronica, and the images of Christ and the Virgin involved in the annual ceremonies on the Feast of the Assumption. For an overview of the ritual significance of papal processions, see Peter Burke, *The Historical Anthropology of Early Modern Italy: Essays on Perception and Communication* (Cambridge U. Pr., 1987), Ch. 12: "Sacred Rulers, Royal Priests: Rituals of the Early Modern Popes," pp. 168–82. Claudia Rousseau, "The Yoke Impresa of Leo X," *Mitteilungen des Kunsthistorischen Institutes in Florenz,* 33 (1989): 113–26, explicates the mythical and symbolic allusions in this pope's personal device, which figured so prominently during his pontificate. There is much pertinent discussion about the mythology of Leo X in Janet Cox-Rearick, *Dynasty and Destiny in Medici Art: Pontormo, Leo X, and the Two Cosimos* (Princeton U. Pr., 1984). I re-examine Leo X's Capitoline festivities of 1513 in Charles M. Rosenberg, ed., *Art and Politics in Late Medieval and Early Renaissance Italy: 1250–1500* (U. of Notre Dame Pr., 1990), pp. 135–56. For a comprehensive consideration of theater, spectacle, and festival in Renaissance Rome, see Fabrizio Cruciani, *Teatro nel Rinascimento, Roma 1450–1550* (Rome: Bulzoni, 1983). Note also on a favorite papal pastime: Jeremy Kruse, "Hunting, Magnificence and the Court of Leo X," *Renaissance Studies,* 7 (1993): 243–57.

Relatively little work has been devoted to the administrative history of the Renaissance papacy, but several recent books make fundamental contributions. Peter Partner's *The Pope's Men: The Papal Civil Service in the Renaissance* (Oxford: Clarendon Pr., 1990) indicates how the staffing and recruitment of the papal curia increasingly reflected the entrenched interests of Italian elites. Thomas Frenz, *Die Kanzlei der Päpste der Hochrenaissance (1471–1527)* (Tübingen: Max Niemeyer Verlag, 1986) clarifies the structure and complex bureaucratic procedures of the papal chancery. Barbara McClung Hallman, *Italian Cardinals, Reform, and the Church as Property* (Berkeley and Los Angeles: U. of California Pr., 1985), like Partner, stresses how the Roman Curia became the focus for investment by Italian elites and how the nepotism and patronage networks thus engendered thwarted attempts at fiscal and administrative reform.

Two recent books look at the canonist and scholastic defenses of papal authority: P. Ulrich Horst, O.P., *Zwischen Konziliarismus und Reformation: Studien zür Ekklesiologie im Dominikanerorden* (Rome: Istituto Storico Domenicano Santa Sabina, 1985), and David V. N. Bagchi, *Luther's Earliest Opponents: Catholic Controversialists, 1518–1525* (Minneapolis: Fortress Pr., 1991). The final two volumes of Kenneth M. Setton's monumental study of papal initiatives toward the Muslim east appeared only after the completion of my text. See now *The Papacy and the Levant*, Vol. 3: *The Sixteenth Century to the Reign of Julius III;* and Vol. 4: *The Sixteenth Century from Julius III to Pius V* [Memoirs of the American Philosophical Society, 161–62] (Philadelphia: American Philosophical Society, 1984).

As for the careers and policies of the Renaissance popes themselves, the only new book-length study is Christine Shaw, *Julius II: The Warrior Pope* (Oxford: Blackwell, 1993). Shaw deftly exploits many new archival sources, especially from outside Rome, to analyze this pontiff's diplomatic and political ambitions, but she insists that Julius did not envision himself as a second Julius Caesar. Largely neglected, too, are the Renaissance cardinals, except in D.S. Chamber's *A Renaissance Cardinal and His Worldly Goods: The Will and Inventory of Francesco Gonzaga (1444–1483)* [Warburg Institute Surveys and Texts, 20] (London: The Warburg Institute, 1992), which profiles one of the most influential collectors of antiquities in fifteenth-century Rome, and Claudia Märtl's *Kardinal Jean Jouffroy (d. 1473): Leben und Werk* [Beiträge zür Geschichte und Quellenkunde des Mittelalters, 18] (Sigmaringen: Thorbecke, 1996), a comprehensive treatment of this leading diplomat and humanist patron, who delivered the funeral oration for Pope Nicholas V. For the Latin text of this oration and an analysis of its themes, see Laura Onofri, *"Sicut fremitus leonis ita et regis ira:* Temi neoplatonici e culto solare nell'orazione funebre per Niccolò V di Jean Jouffroy," *Humanistica Lovaniensia*, 31 (1982): 1–28. Especially relevant for papal self-images are the numerous inscriptions placed on buildings and monuments, for which see now Iiro Kajanto and Ulla Nyberg, *Papal Epigraphy in Renaissance Rome* (Helsinki: Academia Scientiarum Fennica, 1982).

The outlook and characteristic interests of Roman humanism form a central core of my study. Much important new scholarship on Rome's humanists has since appeared. A good overview is James Hankins's essay "The Popes and Humanism" (pp. 47–85) in Anthony Grafton, ed., *Rome Reborn: The Vatican Library and Renaissance Culture* (New Haven and London: Yale U. Pr., 1993), the sumptuously illustrated volume which accompanied the 1993 exhibition of Vatican manuscript treasures at the Library of Congress. Grafton's essay in the same volume, "The Ancient City Restored: Archaeology, Ecclesiastical History, and Egyptology" (pp. 87–123), surveys the humanists' persistent archaeological interests in Rome's classical and Christian past. Hankins's remarkable *Plato in the Italian Renaissance,* 2 vols. (Leiden: E. J. Brill, 1990) contains in Part III (pp. 161–264) important new assessments of the Platonism of Cardinal Bessarion and of his controversies with George of Trebizond. A significant work of the late John F. D'Amico, whose sudden untimely death in 1987 deprived humanist scholarship of a major figure, appeared after I had completed my text. His "The Progress of Renaissance Latin Prose: The Case of Apuleianism," *Renaissance Quarterly,* 37 (1984): 351–92, provides further context to the Ciceronianism of the curial humanists, which D'Amico so masterfully elucidated in his 1983 monograph, *Renaissance Humanism in Papal Rome.* For important new information on Nicholas V's Vatican library project and an up-to-date inventory of the Latin manuscripts (superseding Müntz and Fabre, *La Bibliothèque du Vatican . . .*), now consult Antonio Manfredi, *I codici latini di Niccolò V: Edizione degli inventari e identificazione dei manoscritti* [Studi e Testi, 359] (Vatican: Biblioteca Apostolica Vaticana, 1994).

Valuable new studies of individual Roman humanists have also been undertaken. Notable is the continued attention given to Lorenzo Valla, whose significance for Renaissance humanism as a whole of course transcends his relations to Rome. For the Roman aspects, note the recent discussion of Valla's celebration, in the *exordium* to his *Elegantiae,* of Rome's cultural *imperium:* Alan Fisher, "The Project of Humanism and Valla's Imperial Metaphor," *Journal of Medieval and Renaissance Studies,* 23 (1993): 301–22. In "Lorenzo Valla: A Symposium," in the *Journal of the History of Ideas,* 57 (1996): 1–86, there are important new assessments of Valla's diatribe against the Donation of Constantine, including essays by Salvatore J. Camporeale and Riccardo Fubini, and Ronald K. Delph elucidates what Agostino Steuco, the learned papal librarian and defender of papal authority during the 1530s and 1540s, regarded as the philological and textual critical shortcomings of Valla's tract. Also part of the Symposium is Charles Trinkaus's "Lorenzo Valla on the Problem of Speaking about the Trinity," which includes new suggestions about the impact of Valla's encounter with the Neapolitan Inquisition.

The career and works of Pietro Marsi, protégé of Pomponio Leto and a popular sacred orator, are examined in Marc Dykmans, S. J., *L'humanisme de Pierre Marso* [Studi e Testi, 327] (Vatican City: Biblioteca Apostolica Vaticana, 1988). Dykmans includes the Latin text and an extended discussion of an oration that Marsi delivered in honor of the Virgin Mary in 1499 as part of the ceremonies at S. Maria Maggiore marking the Feast of the Assumption; in the oration Marsi points to various ancient Roman religious practices as precedents for contemporary devotions. Fundamental for the whole tradition of humanist funeral oratory, including those of Marsi and other Roman humanists such as Tommaso Inghirami, is John M. McManamon, S.J., *Funeral Oratory and the Cultural Ideals of Italian Humanism* (Chapel Hill: U. of North Carolina Pr., 1989). For Inghirami, see now Lucia Gualdo Rosa, "Ciceroniano o cristiano? A proposito dell'orazione *De morte Christi* di Tommaso Fedra Inghirami," *Humanistica Lovaniensia,* 34A (1985): 52–64. The works of Nagonius, the obscure poet who celebrated Julius II as a second Julius Caesar, are discussed by Paul Gwynne, "'*Tu alter Caesar eris*': Maximilian I, Vladislav II, Johannes Michael Nagonius and the *renovatio Imperii*," *Renaissance Studies,* 10 (1996): 56–71. I re-examined the humanist patristic scholarship in Rome as part of an essay, "Italian Renaissance Learning and the Church Fathers," in Irena Backus, ed., *The Reception of the Church Fathers in the West: From the Carolingians to the Maurists* (Leiden: E. J. Brill, 1996), pp. 473–510. For Lilio Tifernate, the translator of Philo, see now Ursula Jaitner-Hahner, *Humanismus in Umbrien und Rom: Lilius Tifernas, Kanzler und Gelehrter des Quattrocento* [Saecula spiritalia, Bd. 25–26], 2 vols. (Baden-Baden: Valentin Koerner, 1993).

A great deal of new work on the image and idea of Rome in the Renaissance has appeared. I return to this subject in my contribution, "Roman Humanist Images of Rome," published as part of the *Roma Capitale* conference proceedings previously mentioned. A brief overview by a leading architectural historian, stressing how the popes in their urbanistic projects embued the city with an imperial aura, is Christoph L. Frommel, "Papal Policy: The Planning of Rome during the Renaissance," *Journal of Interdisciplinary History,* 17 (1986): 39–65. Especially notable is Charles Burroughs, *From Signs to Design: Environmental Process and Reform in Early Renaissance Rome* (Cambridge: MIT Pr., 1990), which examines Nicholas V's urbanistic and artistic projects with special attention to the distinctive topographical and symbolic character of Rome's physical space. Burroughs deploys insights from current cultural theory in insisting that rather than an arena where papal ideological values were coherently realized, Rome was the setting for a play of signs and codes between competing interests, and that Nicholas's pontificate was particularly sensitive to local concerns. This is an important book filled with rich details and astute insights. In more recent articles Burroughs explores later Roman Renaissance projects. His "The Building's Face and the Herculean Paradigm: Agenda and Agency in Roman Renaissance Architecture," *Res,* 23 (1993): 7–30, points out how references to Roman legends of Hercules are woven into various architectural undertakings, including Peruzzi's Palazzo Massimo alle Colonne and Michelangelo's Campidoglio. Note also his "Michelangelo at the Campidoglio: Artistic Identity, Patronage, and Manufacture," *Artibus et Historiae,* 28 (1993): 85–111. In his "The 'Last Judgment' of Michelangelo: Pictorial Space, Sacred Topography, and the Social World," *Artibus et Historiae, 32* (1995): 55–89, Burroughs adduces Paul III's revival of traditional processions—including that of the Assumption, which had fallen into abeyance after the Sack—as constituting a deliberate policy of resanctifying Rome. Burroughs also sees allusions to the sacred topography of Rome in the representations of the Virgin and of the martyr saints in Michelangelo's fresco.

Recent scholarly work on Raphael's projects in Rome have also insisted upon their relation to papal aspirations to renew the city's status as *caput mundi.* This is a persistent theme in C. L. Frommel, S. Ray, and M. Tafuri, *Raffaello Architetto* (Milan: Electa, 1984); note especially the essay of the late Manfredo Tafuri, "'Roma instaurata': Strategie urbane e politiche pontificie nella Roma del primo Cinquecento," pp. 59–107. Tafuri returned to various urbanistic projects in Renaissance Rome in his *Ricerca del Rinascimento: Principi, Città, Architetti* (Turin: Einaudi, 1992). Note also for papal urbanism Hubertus Günther, "Das Trivium vor Ponte S. Angelo: Ein Beitrag zur Urbanistik der Renaissance in Rom," *Römisches Jahrbuch für Kunstgeschichte,* 21 (1984): 165–251. For Sixtus IV's transfer of bronze statuary from the Lateran to the Campidoglio, see now Tilman Buddensieg, "Die Statuenstiftung Sixtus' IV. im Jahre 1471," in *Römisches Jahrbuch für Kunstgeschichte,* 20 (1983): 33–74, and for the likely role intended for the Villa Madama as part of the ceremonial entries into Rome, see in the same issue John Shearman's "A Functional Interpretation of Villa Madama": 313–28.

Another architectural historian, Philip Jacks, in his *The Antiquarian and the Myth of Antiquity: The Origins of Rome in Renaissance Thought* (Cambridge U. Pr., 1993) draws upon an extensive body of unpublished guidebooks and topographical and other antiquarian materials in assessing humanist exploration into, and perceptions of, the origins and development of the Eternal City. Jacks provides important new material on the revival of the Palilia, the festival of the birthday of the city, and on the antiquarian studies of the mid and late Cinquecento. For a more extensive look at one of the figures Jacks treats in his book, see his "The *Simulachrum* of Fabio Calvo: A View of Roman Architecture *all'antica* in 1527," *Art Bulletin,* 72 (1990): 453–81. Relevant also is Brian Curran and Anthony Grafton, "A Fifteenth-Century Site Report on the Vatican Obelisk," *Journal of the Warburg and Courtauld Institutes,* 58 (1995): 234–48, which publishes a text of the humanist Angelo Decembrio.

Annio da Viterbo, whose ardent celebration of golden-age Etruscan Italy involved the forging of antiquarian texts, has been the subject of several recent studies, including C. R. Ligota, "Annius of Viterbo and Historical Method," *Journal of the Warburg and Courtauld Institutes,* 50 (1987): 44–56; Walter Stephens, *Giants in Those Days: Folklore, Ancient History, and Nationalism* (Lincoln: U. of Nebraska Pr., 1989), Ch. 3 "Annius of Viterbo, the Flood, and a New Universal History," pp. 98–138; and Anthony Grafton, *Defenders of the Text: The Traditions of Scholarship in an Age of Science, 1450–1800* (Cambridge: Harvard U. Pr., 1991), Ch. 3 "Traditions of Invention and Inventions of Tradition in Renaissance Italy: Annius of Viterbo," pp. 76– 103. Another influential text, Chrysoloras's *Comparison of Old and New Rome,* appears in complete English translation as an appendix in Christine Smith, *Architecture in the Culture of Humanism: Ethics, Aesthetics, and Eloquence, 1400– 1470* (New York: Oxford U. Pr., 1992), and the author provides a perceptive discussion of how humanists used ekphrasis and the rhetorical values of the second sophistic in their depictions of the built environment.

A number of new studies have focused on the Roman cultural world of the early sixteenth century. Two revealing poetic descriptions of Agostino Chigi's Villa Suburbana (the present Villa Farnesina), which incorporate mythic images of Eternal Rome, were published with incisive analysis by Mary Quinlan-McGrath, "Aegidius Gallus, 'De viridario Augustini Chigii vera libellus': Introduction, Latin Text, and English Translation," *Humanistica Lovaniensia,* 38 (1989): 1–99, and "Blosius Palladius, 'Suburbanum Augustini Chisii': Introduction, Latin Text, and English Translation," *Humanistica Lovaniensia,* 39 (1990): 93–155.

The leading contemporary scholar of the intellectual and artistic world of Julian and Leonine Rome is Ingrid Rowland. Her "'Render unto Caesar the Things Which Are Caesar's': Humanism and the Arts in the Patronage of Agostino Chigi," *Renaissance Quarterly,* 39 (1986), probes the mythic image projected by this fabulously wealthy Siennese financier, who played so influential a role during the pontificates of Julius II and Leo X. Her "Abbacus and Humanism," *Renaissance Quarterly,* 48 (1995): 695–727, illuminates further Egidio (Giles) da Viterbo's key role in articulating the intellectual and religious vision of Julian Rome. For a persuasive analysis of how Raphael's Stanza della Segnatura reflects similar inspiration, see her "The Intellectual Background of the School of Athens: Tracking Divine Wisdom in the Rome of Julius II," in Marcia Hall, ed., *Raphael's "School of Athens"* (Cambridge U. Pr., 1997), pp. 131–70. Rowland's "Raphael, Angelo Colocci, and the Genesis of the Architectural Orders," *Art Bulletin,* 76 (1994): 81–104, adduces new evidence of the humanist Colocci's role in the composition of Raphael's famous letter to Leo X regarding the project for an archaeological reconstruction of ancient Rome, and shows how in a larger sense this project aimed at renewing the aesthetic and urbanistic ideals of imperial Rome in the papal capital. Due out shortly after this writing is Rowland's book-length study *The Culture of High Renaissance: Ancients and Moderns in Sixteenth-Century Rome* (Cambridge U. Pr., 1998). For another view of how the intellectual and cultural commitments of Julian

Rome are represented in this pope's artistic commissions, see Mary D. Garrard, "The Liberal Arts and Michelangelo's First Project for the Tomb of Julius II (with a Coda on Raphael's 'School of Athens')," *Viator,* 15 (1984): 335–404.

Fundamental to understanding the increasing vulnerabilities of Roman humanist culture in the 1520s and the traumatic impact of the Sack is Kenneth Gouwens's *Remembering the Renaissance: Humanist Narratives of the Sack of Rome* (Leiden: E. J. Brill, 1998), which explores how four humanists at the court of Clement VII—Pietro Alcionio, Pietro Corsi, Jacopo Sadoleto, and Pierio Valeriano—responded in different ways to the shattering events of 1527. Note also Gouwens's "Ciceronianism and Collective Identity: Defining the Boundaries of the Roman Academy, 1525," *Journal of Medieval and Renaissance Studies,* 23 (1993): 173–95; "Life Writing and the Theme of Cultural Decline in Valeriano's *De Litteratorum Infelicitate*," *Sixteenth Century Journal,* 27 (1996): 87–96; and "Discourses of Vulnerability: Pietro Alcionio's Orations on the Sack of Rome," *Renaissance Quarterly,* 50 (1997): 38–77. For Valeriano's lectures on Catullus at the University of Rome, begun during the last days of Leo X's pontificate but then a casualty of Adrian VI's anti-humanist austerities, see Julia Haig Gaisser, *Catullus and His Renaissance Readers* (Oxford: Clarendon Pr., 1993), Ch. 3. Note also her consideration of humanist sodalities in the cultural life of early sixteenth-century Rome: "The Rise and Fall of Goritz's Feasts," *Renaissance Quarterly,* 48 (1995): 41–57. For the feast of the "talking" statue Pasquino, with its often licentious jibes at contemporary pontiffs, see now Anne Reynolds, "Cardinal Oliviero Carafa and the Early Cinquecento Tradition of the Feast of Pasquino," *Humanistica Lovaniensia,* 34 (1985): 178–208. For Carafa's involvement in the intellectual and cultural life of Renaissance Rome, note also Reynolds's "The Private and Public Emblems of Cardinal Oliviero Carafa," *Bibliothèque d'Humanisme et Renaissance,* 44 (1982): 271–84.

T. C. Price Zimmerman, *Paolo Giovio: The Historian and the Crisis of Sixteenth-Century Italy* (Princeton U. Pr., 1995) provides the first comprehensive study of the life and works of this humanist biographer and historian, whose outlook was shaped in the congenial humanist milieu of Leo X's pontificate, and whose masterpiece, the *Vita Leonis X* of 1548, helped fix the idea of a Leonine Golden Age. Price Zimmerman's engaging and thoughtful account includes many astute observations about the cultural world of papal Rome from the pontificate of Leo X to that of Paul III.

There is much still to learn about popular culture in Renaissance Rome, but several works point in new and fruitful directions. For the significance of portents, prodigies, and prophetic signs in the popular preaching of early sixteenth-century Rome there is much pertinent information in Ottavia Niccoli (trans. Lydia G. Cochrane), *Prophecy and People in Renaissance Italy* (Princeton U. Pr., 1990) and in her "High and Low Prophetic Culture in Rome at the Beginning of the Sixteenth Century," in

Marjorie Reeves, ed., *Prophetic Rome in the High Renaissance Period* (Oxford: Clarendon Pr., 1992). This volume also contains important essays by Nelson H. Minnich, Cesare Vasoli, Roberto Rusconi, William Hudon, and others about the persistent apocalyptic expectations for an Angelic Pope. Revealing glimpses into what they call the "vernacular" culture of mid-sixteenth Rome appear in the trial transcripts (in English translation) and commentary of Thomas V. Cohen and Elizabeth S. Cohen, *Words and Deeds in Renaissance Rome: Trials before the Papal Magistrates* (Toronto and Buffalo: U. of Toronto Pr., 1993). The authors deploy insights from cultural anthropology and the methods of microhistory to explore the social, cultural, and religious outlook and practices of servants, prostitutes, urban households, shepherds, and village communities. Another use of civic records, in this case customs registers, provides a fascinating look at what might be called the Roman consumer market for souvenir images, art objects of all sorts, and building materials both newly quarried or ransacked from ancient sites such as Ostia: see Arnold Esch, "Roman Customs Registers, 1470–80: Items of Interest to Historians of Art and Material Culture," *Journal of the Warburg and Courtauld Institutes*, 58 (1995): 72–87.

A revealing new study of Altieri's *Li nuptiali* as a key to the outlook of Rome's civic patriciate, a class whose existence and identity I overlooked, is Stephen Kolsky, "Culture and Politics in Renaissance Rome: Marco Antonio Altieri's Roman Weddings," *Renaissance Quarterly*, 40 (1987): 49–90. The noble Porcari family, including Stefano, executed by Nicholas V as the ringleader of an anti-papal conspiracy, is now the subject of a comprehensive study: Anna Modigliani, *I Porcari: Storie di una famiglia romana tra Medioevo e Rinascimento* (Rome: Roma nel Rinascimento, 1994).

The remarkable artistic and architectural undertakings of Renaissance Rome have continued to stimulate scholars, producing an art historical literature too extensive to treat adequately here, but some important works, beyond those such as Rowland and Burroughs mentioned previously, provide important insights into the cultural context of Renaissance Rome. A good starting point by one of the leading art historical authorities, and informed by considerations of the ideological and cultural outlook of the papal court, is Loren Partridge, *The Art of Renaissance Rome, 1400–1600* (New York: Harry N. Abrams, 1996). The recent restoration of Michelangelo's Sistine Chapel ceiling and of his "Last Judgment" focused renewed attention on the function, purpose, and meaning of the decorations to this papal chapel in the Vatican. An impressive overview is the collection of essays in Carlo Pietrangeli, ed., *The Sistine Chapel: The Art, the History, and the Restoration* (New York: Harmony Books, 1986), especially John Shearman's discussion of the role of papal liturgies in "The Chapel of Sixtus IV" (pp. 22–91) and John O'Malley's judicious exploration of theological meaning in "The Theology behind Michelangelo's Ceiling" (pp. 92–148). Perceptive considerations of the sibyls and of the ancestors of Christ appear in Creighton

Gilbert, *Michelangelo: On and Off the Sistine Ceiling* (New York: Braziller, 1994). John Monfasani, "A Description of the Sistine Chapel under Sixtus IV," *Artibus et Historiae*, 7 (1983): 9–18, points out a contemporary humanist source that implies a revised dating for the chapel's construction and decoration. Rona Goffen identifies aspects of Franciscan theology as suggestive sources for the typological emphasis on Moses as a prefiguration of Christ in her "Friar Sixtus IV and the Sistine Chapel," *Renaissance Quarterly*, 39 (1986): 218–62. Less convincing, to my mind, is Carol F. Lewine's claim in her *The Sistine Chapel Walls and the Roman Liturgy* (University Park: Pennsylvania State U. Pr. 1993) to have discovered a forgotten Lenten liturgical scheme as the framework for the biblical narratives contained in the wall frescoes, but her monograph does explicate revealing details in 'the frescoes. Both Loren Partridge's extended interpretative essay in *Michelangelo— The Last Judgment: A Glorious Restoration* (NY: Harry N. Abrams, 1997) and Bernardine Barnes, *Michelangelo's 'Last Judgment': The Renaissance Response* (Berkeley and Los Angeles: U. of California Pr., 1998) see this work as reflecting the doctrinal concerns of the papacy, and Barnes emphasizes that we should be attentive to the distinct religious and intellectual outlook of the audience that attended papal liturgies in the Sistine Chapel.

Recent work on Raphael has also clarified how his Roman projects relate to the ideology of Julian and Leonine Rome. In addition to the studies of Tafuri and Rowland cited above, note Philipp P. Fehl, "Raphael as a Historian: Poetry and Historical Accuracy in the Sala di Costantino, *Artibus et Historiae*, 28 (1993): 9–76, who argues that the Arch of Constantine is an important historical source for the representation of the Vision of Constantine in this last of the Raphael *stanze* in the Vatican, and includes further substantiation that the site of the Emperor's vision in the fresco is that of the basilica of St. Peter's in the Vatican. The latest consideration of Raphael's Stanza d'Eliodoro further elucidates how the room's fresco decoration elaborates the theme of the providential destiny of the papacy: Michael Rohlmann, "*Dominus mihi adiutor:* zu Raffaels Ausmalung der Stanza d'Eliodoro unter den Papsten Julius II. und Leo X." *Zeitschrift für Kunstgeschichte*, 59 (1996): 1–28. Bernice F. Davidson, *Raphael's Bible: A Study of the Vatican Logge* (University Park: Pennsylvania St. U. Pr., 1985) reveals the many connections to the intellectual and religious outlook of Leo X's pontificate in this Raphael project in the Vatican. Christoph Luitpold Frommel, "Il Palazzo Vaticano sotto Giulio II e Leone X: Strutture e funzioni," in *Raffaello in Vaticano* (Milan: Electa, 1984), pp. 118–34, suggests (at p. 127) that it is probably Bramante's construction of the Logge, begun towards 1508–1509, that is represented in the left background of Raphael's "Disputà" (not the Cortile del Belvedere, as I speculated). Frommel's "St. Peter's: The Early History," in Henry A. Millon and Vittorio Magnago Lampugnani, eds., *The Renaissance from Brunelleschi to Michelangelo: The Representation of Architecture* (NY: Rizzoli, 1994), pp. 399–423, considers the project for the new St. Peter's and reviews the various designs from Bramante to Michelangelo, including Raphael's plans.

Earlier artistic projects have also received new attention. For further explication of the Egyptological themes in the "Room of the Saints" in the Borgia Apartment in the Vatican, see now Claudia Cieri-Via, *"Characteres et figuras in opere magico:* Pinturicchio et la décoration de la *camera segreta* de l'appartement Borgia," *Revue de l'Art,* 94 (1991): 11–26. Filippino Lippi's frescoes of St. Thomas Aquinas in the Carafa Chapel in S. Maria sopra Minerva are fully explored for the first time in Gail L. Geiger's *Filippino Lippi's Carafa Chapel: Renaissance Art in Rome* [Sixteenth Century Essays & Studies, v. 5] (Kirksville, Missouri: Sixteenth Century Journal Publishers, 1986). Geiger elucidates how characteristic Roman humanist themes emphasizing classical prefigurements of Christian sacrifice and triumph inform both the architectural setting of the chapel and Filippino's paintings, including notably the ceiling frescoes of the sibyls, among whom the Cumaean Sibyl occupies the central position over the altar.

Cardinal Alessandro Farnese had a role in the many of the most important artistic and architectural projects of mid-sixteenth-century Rome, including the Farnese Hours, the Villa Farnese at Caprarola, the Farnese Gardens on the Palatine Hill, and various programs of palace and church decoration. The cultural and religious attitudes shaping his patronage are analyzed in Clare Robertson, *'Il Gran Cardinale': Alessandro Farnese, Patron of the Arts* (New Haven and London: Yale U. Pr., 1992). For the development of the grand architectural gardens of sixteenth-century Rome, including the Villa d'Este at Tivoli and the Villa Lante at Bagnaia, one should now consult Claudia Lazzaro's superbly illustrated *The Italian Renaissance Garden: From the Conventions of Planting, Design, and Ornament to the Grand Gardens of Sixteenth-Century Central Italy* (New Haven and London: Yale U. Pr., 1990).

James S. Ackerman, dean of Renaissance architectural historians, whose research first identified significant Roman imperial themes as informing the Cortile del Belvedere and the building projects on the Capitoline Hill, republished these seminal essays along with an updated bibliography and postscripts stating his subsequent thinking in *Distance Points: Essays in Theory and Renaissance Art and Architecture* (Cambridge: MIT Pr., 1991)

The religious developments in Italy during the middle decades of the sixteenth century, touched on in my "Epilogue," have attracted ever-increasing scholarly attention. For the revealing thought of Agostino Steuco, whose defense of the splendor of papal liturgies and emphasis on the religious centrality of Rome echoed many of the images, myths, and aspirations of earlier Roman humanists, see now the important series of articles by Ronald K. Delph, including "Polishing the Papal Image in the Counter-Reformation: The Case of Agostino Steuco," *Sixteenth Century Journal,* 23 (1992): 35–47; "From Venetian Visitor to Curial Humanist: The Development of Agostino Steuco's 'Counter'-Reformation Thought," *Renaissance Quarterly,* 47 (1994): 102–39; and "Valla Grammaticus, Agostino Steuco, and the Donation of Constantine" (pp. 55–77) in the *JHI* Symposium on Valla mentioned above. Helpful orientations to the whole issue of the Italian Reformation by two of the leading authorities are Anne Jacobson Schutte, "Periodization of Sixteenth-Century Italian Religious History: The Post-Cantimori Paradigm Shift," *Journal of Modern History,* 61 (1989): 269–84, and Massimo Firpo (trans. John Tedeschi), "The Italian Reformation and Juan de Valdés," *Sixteenth Century Journal,* 27 (1996): 353–64. Elisabeth G. Gleason's *Gasparo Contarini: Venice, Rome, and Reform* (Berkeley and Los Angeles: U. of California Pr., 1993) judiciously assesses the religious and intellectual cross-currents at work in the Rome of Pope Paul III. The new image of Rome as *Civitas Sancta* in the sacred oratory of later sixteenth-century Rome is now fully explored in Frederick J. McGinness, *Right Thinking and Sacred Oratory in Counter-Reformation Rome* (Princeton U. Pr., 1995). For a superb treatment of the urban character of Rome at the height of the baroque, see Laurie Nussdorfer, *Civic Politics in the Rome of Urban VIII* (Princeton U. Pr., 1992).

Buffalo, New York
March 1, 1998

THE RENAISSANCE POPES

Name	Dates	Family Name	Place of Origin
Martin V	11 Nov. 1417–20 Feb. 1431	Colonna	Rome
Eugenius IV	3 Mar. 1431–23 Feb. 1447	Condulmer	Venice
Nicholas V	6 Mar. 1447–24 Mar. 1455	Parentucelli	Sarzana
Calixtus III	8 Apr. 1455–6 Aug. 1458	Borja	Játiva (Spain)
Pius II	19 Aug. 1458–15 Aug. 1464	Piccolomini	Siena
Paul II	30 Aug. 1464–26 July 1471	Barbo	Venice
Sixtus IV	9 Aug. 1471–12 Aug. 1484	Della Rovere	Savona
Innocent VIII	29 Aug. 1484–25 July 1492	Cibo	Genoa
Alexander VI	11 Aug. 1492–18 Aug. 1503	Borgia	Játiva (Spain)
Pius III	22 Sept. 1503–18 Oct. 1503	Piccolomini	Siena
Julius II	21 Oct. 1503–21 Feb. 1513	Della Rovere	Savona
Leo X	11 Mar. 1513–1 Dec. 1521	Medici	Florence
Adrian VI	9 Jan. 1522–14 Sept. 1523	Dedel	Utrecht
Clement VII	18 Nov. 1523–25 Sept. 1534	Medici	Florence
Paul III	13 Oct. 1534–10 Nov. 1549	Farnese	Rome

THE
RENAISSANCE
IN ROME

I

Introduction

> This city Rome, head of the world, through your
> singular beneficence, Sixtus [IV], . . . is so entirely
> restored [*instaurata*] and adorned that it seems
> almost founded anew.
>
> —AURELIO BRANDOLINI, *Laudes Sixti IV*.

Rome in the early fifteenth century belied its traditional claim to be *caput mundi* (head of the world). Long abandoned as the papal residence in favor of Avignon, then further neglected during the chaos of the Great Schism and the Conciliar period, the decayed city gave domicile to a papacy weakened both in spiritual authority and in temporal power. Distanced from the mainstream of intellectual and artistic renewal taking place in Tuscany and in northern Italy, the city on the Tiber remained a cultural backwater.

But by 1500 so much had changed. Once more a true capital, the home of Roman pontiffs restored to ecclesiastical primacy and powers to be reckoned with in Italian and European affairs, the Eternal City also had emerged as the setting and focus for a distinct cultural world. Ceremony, ritual, spectacle, intellectual vitality, and artistic efflorescence celebrated the city's reborn centrality to the sacred destiny of Christendom and attested to the renewal of its civilizing mission.

The particular nature of Rome's restoration acquired its main outlines from three key influences specific to the Roman cultural scene. Foremost was the city of Rome itself. The peculiar realities of the actual city on the Tiber—its topography and physical setting, its role in ritual and ceremony, its economic circumstances, the basic nature of its society and governance, and its function as papal residence—go far to explain the dominant assumptions of the cultural outlook that emerged there. Rome meant, too, the ancient city, the vast ruins surviving from both classical and Christian antiquity that protruded everywhere and still dominated much of the cityscape. The ruins intrigued Roman humanists and artists, encouraged their explorations of the classical and paleo-Christian worlds, and provided many of the keys for their imaginative

reconstruction of the city's past. The imposing presence of the ruins helps
to explain also why Roman humanism tended to dwell on an archeological
treatment of antiquity, rather than emphasizing a politico-historical or
literary approach. Above all, Rome existed as concept and image, the
stimulus to so much of the city's thought and art. As idea, Rome never
strayed far from the thoughts of the humanists and artists who lived in the
Eternal City, and as myth and mystique it pervaded the ideology of the
period.

Closely tied to the meaning Rome held for its Renaissance inhabitants was the meaning of the Roman Church, the second main element
determining the central features of the Roman Renaissance. For contemporaries, the Roman Church connoted first the Roman Catholic Church,
that is, the basic institutions and doctrines of Latin Christianity, as they
had been transmitted from the Middle Ages. These ecclesiastical structures and theological beliefs remained fundamental. But in the Renaissance period, this Church, founded by Christ on Peter, and governed by
the Apostle's successors, in fact became more "Romanized." Administrative and legal power gravitated toward Rome, and the Roman Curia
increasingly dominated the affairs of the Church as a whole. In a further,
and more self-conscious, sense the Church became more Roman for the
humanists and artists of the period: The ideology of the Roman Renaissance accentuated the Church's Roman foundations; it imparted special
significance to Rome as its enduring capital; and it stressed the ties
between the Roman Empire's historical import and the Church's divine
charge.

The third decisive force in fifteenth and early sixteenth-century
Rome was the Renaissance itself—that intellectual and cultural movement, dominated by humanists and artists, which focussed attention on
rediscovering antiquity, which found there inspiration for its own creative achievements, and which saw in its resuscitation a powerful impulse
to revive the contemporary world in light of its accomplishments. The
Renaissance movement took hold earliest not in Rome, but in Florence. In
Rome, however, basic Renaissance notions that had first emerged elsewhere acquired distinctive characteristics. For instance, the aspirations of
empire, not the ideals of republics, were uppermost in Roman minds.
Moreover, the relevant past included Hebraic and Christian, as well as
classical, antiquity. When seen in these contexts, Rome and the Roman
Church both assumed an enlarged significance. Finally, in Rome the idea
of rebirth meant not just an intellectual and artistic revival, but more
fundamentally the restoration (*instauratio*) of the Roman Church and the
renewal (*renovatio*) of the Roman Empire.

Roman Renaissance ideology assumed written form in the treatises,
oratory, poetry, letters, translations from the Greek, and other literary
works, almost exclusively in Latin, produced by humanists in Rome or in

close proximity to the papal court. These figures should be designated Roman humanists, even though few were actually native Romans. Most came from other parts of Italy, and many, especially in the middle decades of the fifteenth century, had direct contact with Florence first. Nonetheless, in Rome their work tended to acquire Roman characteristics, thus justifying calling them, during their careers in the Eternal City, "Roman" humanists.

At the same time one could usefully describe these writers as Curial humanists. What prompted their coming to Rome was, primarily, prospects of papal patronage. Increasingly, these hopes for appointment and advancement depended on taking holy orders. As clerics, and in terms of the extent to which their Roman careers involved them with the papal court, the term "Curial" humanist seems appropriate.[1]

Humanists were not the only intellectuals contributing to Renaissance Rome's cultural world. Lawyers and theologians did so, too. But humanists held pride of place over these professionals, whose disciplines stemmed from medieval developments. Lawyers and theologians occupied influential positions within the Roman Curia, where they remained central to the definition of doctrine and to the implementation of papal policy. But they tended to do this within the ideological considerations elaborated by the humanists. It was the humanists who designed the festivals, created the pageantry, delivered the sermons and orations, and wrote the histories of the period. They gave the city its characteristic style and taste, and expressed its cultural ideals.

The central themes of the Roman Renaissance found enduring expression not just in words. Painting, sculpture, and architecture embodied many of the same ideological aspirations. In fact, Renaissance Romans tended to see words and the visual language of the arts as both employing an "optical" vocabulary to serve the same ends. This was especially true of the spoken words belonging to the revived epideictic genre of classical rhetoric. The fundamental importance of epideictic rhetoric for Roman humanism will be examined fully later.[2] Briefly, the orator dealt with matter that can be visualized; he was expected to create within his address an extended visual image; and his intent was to move his audience to "look," to "view," and to "gaze upon" the works and deeds his words evoked. Both oratory and the arts, then, produced pictorial images, and these images were meant to induce devotion, veneration, and praise.

That art should serve such a rhetorical purpose is set forth in a chapter of Paolo Cortesi's *De Cardinalatu* (1510), devoted to cardinals' palaces. Here the Roman humanist advises the commissioning of paintings having "ingenious subjects" and "erudite" content, citing as models the wall frescoes of the Sistine Chapel and the decoration of the Carafa Chapel in S. Maria sopra Minerva. Such learned paintings, he argues, by exciting our visual attention stimulate the imagination and arouse the intellect, which in turn inspire us to imitate the admirable deeds depicted.[3]

The extent to which Roman humanists actually designed erudite iconographic programs for painting, sculpture, and architecture in the Eternal City is another matter. In the later sixteenth century, humanists clearly did so. Surviving correspondence plainly reveals, for instance, the collaboration of Onofrio Panvinio (1529-68), the Roman historian and antiquarian, in creating the program for the Room of the Farnese Deeds, frescoed by Taddeo Zuccaro in the Farnese villa at Caprarola in the early 1560s.[4] No documentation from earlier decades is so explicit. Nevertheless, circumstantial evidence suggests that some Roman humanists of the Renaissance period did participate, to a certain extent, in such undertakings. Platina, for instance, composed the Latin inscriptions for the fresco cycle of Sixtus IV's life, painted in the Ospedale di S. Spirito in Rome; Lilio Tifernate seems to have been aware of the discussions surrounding the scenes of Moses' life to be included in the Sistine Chapel wall frescoes; Giannozzo Manetti is our principal source for what Nicholas V envisioned in rebuilding the Vatican; and a number of humanists were clearly enlisted to design pageantry for festivals, notably Tommaso Inghirami's work on the Capitoline ceremonies of 1513.[5]

Where humanism and the arts seem closest in Renaissance Rome, however, is in the similarity of ideological themes. The wall frescoes of the Sistine Chapel, Michelangelo's ceiling, the Raphael tapestries, the Vatican stanze, the Julius tomb, and the new St. Peter's reveal the same set of ideas put forth in the works of the Roman humanists. As "learned" visual images, they advanced similar notions of Rome's twin apostolate, the meaning of its imperial vocation, and the mission of the Roman Church. Detailed discussions of these connections will follow in due course. One particular point merits attention now. Both sacred oratory and religious painting evoked the same Biblical subject matter, even alluding to the same key passages from Sacred Scripture. Thus, for example, two favorite "architectural" metaphors from 1 Peter 2 and Ephesians 2 appear repeatedly in humanist remarks on the meaning of the Church's foundation, and these same texts reveal themselves in Raphael's *Disputà* and in his tapestries for the Sistine Chapel.[6]

Moreover, a similarity of approach to Scripture seems to inform both modes of "seeing." Within the spectrum of Biblical exegesis, emphasis tended to fall more toward the literal and historical end rather than toward the allegorical. Cortesi, for instance, favored the painting of historical narratives, whereby the "lessons of history" could be brought to life.[7] Biblical narrative nevertheless contained for Renaissance Romans a "prophetic" meaning. That is, Old Testament history foreshadowed New Testament events, and both could be interpreted as "unfolding" the inner meaning of present historical developments. The relation of past to present was, then, a "typological" or "figural" one. The present had an antetype in the past, and the past prefigured significant patterns in the present. Thus Moses, whose career and powers prefigured Christ's, served for Renaissance Romans as *typus papae*, and Jerusalem as sacred capital foreshadowed Rome.[8]

Not just sacred history, but the *res gestae* of the "Gentiles" revealed such "signs" as well. The deeds of Rome's early rulers, Romulus and Numa, pointed forward to the acts of the Renaissance pontiffs. So did the accomplishments of the Caesars. Indeed, such notions tended to underpin what Renaissance Romans perceived as the "providential" destiny of Rome from its inception. In this way the purpose and meaning of Rome's history, in which divine will stood revealed, remained aloof from the vicissitudes of time.

Reborn Rome was seen, in fact, as "fullfilling" all of human history that had gone before, and the "empire" of the Roman Church transcended even global limitations to embrace the whole cosmos. Both time and space thus centered on Rome.

The continuous elaboration of such ideas in the thoughts of the humanists, in the subject matter and design of art and architecture, and in the elements of pageantry and ceremony comprise the distinguishing characteristics of the cultural world that emerged in Rome during the last half of the fifteenth century and the early decades of the sixteenth. These intellectual and cultural manifestations delineate what the Renaissance meant in Rome, and it is the persistence of these ideological themes that sets this age apart as a distinctive period in the history of the Eternal City. These overarching ideas developed, nonetheless, within a particular historical context and in response to specific historical challenges. Definition of these requires a brief discussion.

For the Renaissance to emerge in Rome, two conditions needed fulfillment. First, a reunited papacy, generally accorded recognition as the spiritual head of the whole of Latin Christendom, had to be established once again in the Eternal City. This seemed accomplished when Martin V, elected pope at the Council of Constance, entered Rome in 1420. With the exile in Avignon ended and the scandal of the Great Schism resolved, the undivided papacy once more took up residence at the Apostolic See. Yet the little headway this Colonna pontiff had managed to make toward reviving the nearly moribund city almost came undone during his successor's decade-long absence from Rome. Only in 1443 did Pope Eugenius IV, survivor of the Council of Basel's assaults on papal sovereignty, at length arrive back in the city on the Tiber. This time the papacy stayed permanently in the capital of Christendom.[9]

The second condition involved the humanists. They had to be present in Rome in sufficient numbers and with enough support from prelates within the Curial hierarchy to make their intellectual and cultural influence felt. The popes early recognized the value of the humanists' expertise in Latin for the secretarial and diplomatic needs of the papal court. In the opening years of the Quattrocento, during the Schism, several prominent young humanists found employment with the papal Curia in Rome. These included Poggio Bracciolini and Leonardo Bruni, both fresh from the intellectual stimulation of Florence, Antonio Loschi from Milan, Pier Paolo Vergerio from Capodistria, and the Roman Cencio de' Rusticci. Strongly influenced by the humanistic ideas of the Florentine Chancellor Coluccio Salutati and the Byzantine classicist Manuel Chrysoloras, this group did not however develop any distinctively Roman intellectual commitments. Moreover, the Council of Pisa (1409) and the Council of Constance (1414–18) soon dispersed this humanist circle. Leonardo Bruni, for instance, went back to Florence in 1415, and Poggio, following trans-Alpine travels and a sojourn in England, returned to Rome only in 1423. Martin V's Rome, as a humanist center, remained undistinguished, at least in comparison with Florence of the 1420s.[10]

Eugenius IV, a Venetian, proved more sympathetic to humanism than Martin V, and his lengthy stays in Florence in the mid-1430s and again during the Council of Florence (1439) meant renewed contact with the unrivalled intellectual and artistic capital of Italy.[11] When Eugenius journeyed back to Rome, accompanying him were a group of Curial humanists—either Florentines (like Alberti) or others newly inspired by contact with Florentine culture during the papacy's residence in the city on the Arno (like Biondo)—who made decisive contributions to the cultural formation of the early Roman Renaissance. Already committed to the humanist outlook, these humanists nevertheless fell powerfully under the spell of the Eternal City, and for the first time Roman humanism developed notions that went beyond an echo of the Florentine outlook. Characteristic is Biondo's influential *Roma instaurata*, which dates from the last, Roman, years of Eugenius's pontificate.[12]

The year 1443 thus appears again as the most suitable date for marking the beginnings of the Roman Renaissance. At this point, too, the papacy, while it had managed to return to Rome in that year, still remained shaken from the effects of the conciliar challenge. Formulating an ideological defense of papal authority thus continued to absorb most of the energies of papal theologians and canon lawyers. Such an agenda concerned the Roman humanists also, but for them the assertion of papal prerogatives involved articulating the nature of Rome's spiritual and cultural centrality. In this way, the *instauratio Ecclesiae Romanae* emerged as a key ideological theme for the first generation of the Roman Renaissance.[13]

These incipient notions, first expressed in Eugenius's last years, received confirmation under Nicholas V, the Tuscan humanist elected to succeed the Venetian pontiff in 1447.[14] From the 1420s, the future Pope Nicholas had maintained close contact with Florentine humanist circles; from them he received plaudits for his discoveries of classical and patristic texts. He attended the Council of Florence, and there witnessed for himself the critical contributions made by humanistic study of the Greek Church Fathers to the efforts to resolve long-standing theological differences between Catholic and Orthodox doctrines. With these experiences, it is not surprising that Nicholas V made the assembling of a first-rate classical and patristic library a first priority, nor that he paid handsomely for leading humanist scholars to produce Latin translations of major texts in Greek classics and patristics. But Nicholas's efforts to revive Rome and to make it a major Renaissance center went further. He proclaimed 1450 a Jubilee Year, thus underscoring the spiritual prestige of the pilgrimage to Rome. He promoted a more dignified and beautiful celebration of liturgical solemnities. He began the rebuilding of Rome's ancient churches, and conceived ambitious ideas for the remaking of the Vatican as a new sacred city. In each of these ways he inaugurated trends that continued to influence the culture of the Roman Renaissance through to the end of the period.

Overshadowing this work of renewal, during Nicholas's last years, was the dramatic fall of Constantinople to the Ottoman Turks in 1453. Byzantium's extinction shocked Latin Europe generally, and papal Rome in particular. With Italy seemingly imperiled, crusade against the Infidel became Nicholas's primary concern. Indeed, the Ottoman threat influenced papal policies and the outlook from Rome for the next century and more, continuing beyond the Renaissance and extending well into the Counter-Reformation period. More immediately, hopes for a crusade explain the election of the elderly Spaniard, Alonso de Borja, as successor to Nicholas V.

Calixtus III[15] made war against the Infidel his first priority. He was austere by nature and had little interest in Renaissance culture, and his expenditures for war reduced papal patronage of humanism and the arts to parsimonious levels. In consequence, many humanists who had been prominent in Nicholas V's Rome departed for Naples and other places where prospects were more promising than they were in Rome. Their dispersion left Nicholas's more ambitious projects stillborn.

Calixtus occupied St. Peter's chair for only three years, however, giving way in 1458 to Pius II, a humanist with a European reputation.[16] Pius, too, devoted much of his energy to plans for crusade, and expenditures on rebuilding his home town, Pienza, diverted attention from Rome. Yet, as a humanist, he renewed support for the ideological aims first articulated under Nicholas V. Classical and patristic studies received reinvigorated patronage, the new sacred oratory of papal liturgies acquired added emphasis, and building projects resumed in the Vatican. Above all, the ceremonies accompanying the reception of the relic of St. Andrew's head, in 1462, reinforced the historical meaning of Petrine primacy and accentuated the place of St. Peter's basilica in the Vatican as the pivotal sanctuary for the whole of Christendom.[17]

Paul II, [18] the nephew of Eugenius IV, mounted the papal throne in 1464. Long a resident of Rome before his election, he used the resources of the papacy to add to his already impressive collection of ancient gems, cameos, and other artifacts and to create the imposing Palazzo di S. Marco complex in the center of Rome. Here, for the first time, new construction consciously imitated the designs of imperial Roman architecture. A promoter of augmented liturgical splendor in papal ceremonial, Paul also reorganized the Roman Carnival, making it an occasion of pageantry and spectacle. He thus contributed in significant ways to the ideology of Rome's renewal, despite his notorious suppression of Pomponio Leto's Roman Academy in 1468.

Paul's quarrel with the humanists of Leto's circle did not spring from any general antipathy to humanism or to classical studies; in fact, he patronized humanist study of the Church Fathers and the ancient histo-rians. Friction with the Academicians arose instead as a consequence of Paul's reform of the Curia, which eliminated posts in the College of Abbreviators, where a number of humanists had found attractive sine-cures. Among those whose posts were suddenly eliminated was Bartolom-meo dei Sacchi, called Platina, who in reaction bitterly criticized the pope, even threatening an appeal to a general council of the Church. Raising the specter of conciliarism was a dangerous folly on Platina's part, and Paul moved quickly to arrest him and the other Academicians, even going so far as to obtain Leto's extradition from Venice, to which he had departed some time before events came to a head in Rome. Imprisoned for a year, the Academicians were subjected to a series of interrogations, before at length charges were dropped and they regained their freedom. Both Leto and Platina remained in Rome, continuing as influential lead-ers of Roman humanism; Platina's most significant contributions, in fact, came after this point, during the pontificate of Paul's successor, Sixtus IV. Sixtus also permitted the revival of the Roman Academy in 1478, this time constituted as a religious *sodalitas*. The long-term effects of the 1468 suppression thus proved negligible, as humanism remained central to the culture of the Roman Renaissance. What seems most to have provoked Paul II's anger were the secrecy and cult overtones of the Academy's activity. The pope suspected republican conspiracy, sexual immorality, and pagan irreligion in what the youthful members of Leto's circle would instead have called a passion for Rome's classical past (perhaps carried to the point of eccentricity), belief in an intimate teacher-disciple rela-tionship (probably innocent of any overt homosexuality), and the disgruntled anti-clerical murmurings provoked by Curial retrenchment. The suppression may have encouraged Rome's humanists to temper their neo-classical enthusiasms, accommodating them more closely to Rome's restoration as a Christian capital; Sixtus IV's policies, in fact, promoted just that, as Platina and other Academicians assumed prominent Vatican posts. Overall, however, the suppression of the Roman Academy proved a brief interlude, not a turning point in the Roman Renaissance.[19]

For the ideology and culture of the Roman Renaissance, Sixtus IV's long pontificate was the most significant since Nicholas V's.[20] In many respects, Sixtus took up Nicholas's legacy, resuming projects left partially in abeyance. Nicholas's zeal for book collecting and for classical and patristic studies thus found affirmation in Sixtus's enduring arrangements for the Vatican Library, the plans of Sixtus's predecessor for the Vatican Palace bore fruit in the Sistine Chapel, and the emphasis on Rome as a religious capital was underscored in the Jubilee of 1475 and in Sixtus's rebuilding of many ancient churches. It is a measure of humanism's dominance that this non-humanist pontiff (he was a member of the Franciscan Order and was trained in scholastic theology) should so actively have promoted its cultural values. Only thus could Rome fulfill Sixtus's ambitions to have it rival Florence as a cultural capital, and thus be restored to its ancient prominence.

Sixtus left his mark in other ways. Nepotism reached unprecedented levels, as the Della Rovere and Riario moved into key positions in Rome, in the Curia, and in the Papal States. Sixtus also pursued aggressive policies in Italian affairs, prompted largely by the temporal ambitions of his nephew, Girolamo Riario. As a result, Sixtus's last half dozen years found the papacy nearly continually at war with other Italian states. At the same time, the Ottoman advance in the Mediterranean reached a high-water mark with the capture of Otranto on the Italian mainland in 1480.[21]

Innocent VIII succeeded Sixtus in 1484. A weak individual, and in poor health for much of his pontificate, Innocent's personal impact on Rome's cultural life was nearly negligible. Even a cipher in the Vatican could not at this point, however, significantly disrupt the world of Renaissance Rome. The intellectual and cultural trends within the Eternal City had acquired a life of their own—in the liturgy and sacred oratory of the papal chapel, in the practices and the procedures of the Curia, in the tastes and styles of papal entertainments at the Vatican Palace, in the antiquarian and literary interests pursued in the scattered *vigne* of informal Roman academies, and in the humanistic, musical, and theatrical undertakings in the lavish, new cardinals' palaces. Indeed, perhaps the most influential patrons in Rome of the 1480s were Cardinals Giuliano della Rovere, Raffaele Riario, and Oliviero Carafa.[22]

By 1492 another powerful cardinal, Rodrigo Borgia, was poised at last to win the papacy. Named Vice-Chancellor by his uncle Calixtus III,

Borgia had held this central post in papal administration for more than thirty years, amassing enormous wealth in the process. An insider's knowledge of the Curia, a reputation for political acumen, attested administrative skill, a personal magnificence given expression in the sumptuous entertainments of his splendid palace, and the backing of Spain proved unbeatable assets, and he emerged victorious from the conclave, choosing the name Alexander VI.[23] Like Sixtus before him, but with more dramatic successes, the new pope pursued dynastic ambitions. Borgia designs on creating a permanent Romagnol duchy for Alexander's son Cesare gained feasibility from the altered political circumstances of Italy. The massive French invasion under King Charles VIII in 1494 put an end to the balance-of-power politics established with the Peace of Lodi in 1454 and carefully nurtured by Lorenzo de' Medici's statesmanship. In rapid-fire order, power changed hands in Florence, in Naples, and then in Milan. The Kingdom of Naples entered on its long period of foreign subjugation, first to the French, then definitively to the Spanish, and these two powers competed for the upper hand in Lombardy. Florence found its room for maneuver and its real power sharply curbed, while Savonarola's millenarianism exacerbated internal tensions in the wake of the Medici ouster. Only Venice and the papacy emerged from the first decade of European intervention relatively unscathed. With a French army at his disposal, Cesare scored stunning victories in the Romagna, in Umbria, and in Tuscany as Borgia fortunes reached their zenith in the years 1498-1503.

Military victories and the growing temporal power of the papacy contributed to the changing tone of the Roman Renaissance. Triumph, glory, and imperial dominion replaced martyrdom and holiness as themes for praise in humanist writings, and Rome's populace witnessed ever grander and more lavish spectacles. Rome's artistic and intellectual communities similarly increased in numbers, in significant achievements, and in Italian—and even European—influence. The Rome of 1500 had supplanted Florence as the cultural capital of the peninsula. Only some of this can be credited to Borgia patronage. Alexander did support the rebuilding of the Sapienza, Rome's university; he employed Pinturicchio, his favorite artist, in numerous commissions; and he advanced the careers of several key humanists, most notably Adriano Castellesi, a leading Ciceronian stylist, who became private secretary to the pope and then a cardinal.[24] Alexander was no intellectual, however, and Rome's cardinals and its growing foreign colonies perhaps mattered just as much as the Vatican to the city's accelerating *renovatio*. Thus Michelangelo sculpted the *Pietà* in St. Peter's for a French cardinal during his first Roman sojourn, 1496-1501, and his *Bacchus* from the same period came out of the classical studies cultivated in the humanist circle about Cardinal Raffaele Riario.[25] Bramante, too, who came to Rome just before 1500, received his first important Roman commission—the cloister of S. Maria della Pace—from Cardinal Oliviero Carafa, and he designed the Tempietto of S. Pietro in Montorio for the Spanish crown.[26]

Alexander VI's character, demeanor, and policies did not escape criticism, even in Rome. To many, his nepotism, his fiscal rapacity, his blatant family dynasticism, the sordid stories of licentious entertainment in the Vatican, and Cesare's responsibility for the brutal murder there of his sister Lucrezia's second husband—all revealed the rampant excesses of a tyrant, whose vices defiled St. Peter's throne.[27] In reaction, the cardinals chose as Alexander's successor Cardinal Francesco Todeschini-Piccolomini, nephew of Pius II, a humanist Maecenas, and a churchman with a reputation for personal virtue and as a supporter of ecclesiastical reform.[28] The newly elected Pius III served as Roman pontiff for less than a month.

From the conclave that followed Pius III's death, Giuliano della Rovere emerged as Pope Julius II.[29] A nephew of Sixtus IV, Giuliano, like Rodrigo Borgia before him, had long been a power in Rome, carefully setting the stage for his own advancement to the papacy. As a cardinal, Giuliano had also sustained many of the same cultural aspirations promoted during his uncle's pontificate. As pope, he was in a position to pursue these aims more vigorously. During his pontificate, and during that of his successor, Leo X, the Renaissance in Rome reached its apogee.

No Renaissance pontiff left a more forceful impression on his contemporaries than Julius II. His daemonic energy, his fierce *terribilità*, his Jove-like fulminations, and his ability to overcome seemingly insuperable obstacles imparted a more-than-human aspect to his persona. As the European powers continued to compete for the upper hand on Italian soil, this warrior pope struggled to recover the papal patrimony and to drive the French "barbarians" from the peninsula. He led his armies in person, yet he saw his conquests as enlarging the *imperium* of the Roman Church, not the personal fortunes of the Della Rovere. His policies did, in fact, augment the territorial power of the papacy.

The clamor of war did not drown out those voices devoted to the arts of peace. In fact, no Renaissance pope before him left a greater imprint on the face of Rome. Under him, Bramante conceived the vast enlargement of the Vatican palace and the colossal new St. Peter's basilica. Michelangelo went to work on the Julius tomb, then on the Sistine Chapel ceiling. Raphael began his fresco decoration in the Vatican stanze. Animating these extraordinary projects, as well as his temporal and spiritual policies, was Julius's determination to fulfill what he saw as the Roman Church's imperial mission. As heir to the civilizing achievements of the Roman Empire—and destined to surpass them in universality—renewed Rome and the restored Roman Church could find only in the classicism of imperial Rome the forms suitable to express these overarching ambitions.

An ideology of heroic classicism, grand synthesis, and triumphal culmination thus underlay the art and architecture of Julius's pontificate, and
these same notions run through the writings of the humanists active then
in Rome.

If Julius II was the second Julius Caesar, then Leo X was the new
Augustus.[30] Contemporaries looked to this second son of Lorenzo the
Magnificent to restore peace to war-torn Italy and to end the schism
provoked by the French-backed *conciliabulum* of Pisa and Julius II's
answering Fifth Lateran Council. These accomplished, a Virgilian
Golden Age of intellectual and artistic efflorescence would ensue. During
Leo's first years as pope, these hopes seemed destined for fulfillment.
Central Italy did enjoy a brief respite from the upheavals of war; Leo did
resolve the schism with the French; and Rome's poets, orators, musicians,
and artists found papal largesse unstinting. The Fifth Lateran Council,
meeting until 1517, further confirmed Rome's place as capital of the
Christian world. Spectacle reached unprecedented levels of theatricality
in Leo's coronation, the Capitoline festivities of 1513, and the Carnival of
1514. Neo-Latin poetry and antiquarian studies flourished in the humanist academies, which met in charmingly evocative classical settings on the
Quirinal and on the slopes of the Capitoline.

By the end of the decade, however, the mood had changed. The
costly War of Urbino (1516–17), provoked by Leo's ambition to seize that
duchy for his nephew Lorenzo, brought the return of war to central Italy.
At the same time, the sudden Ottoman conquest of Syria and Egypt
alarmed Rome again as to the dangers of the "Turkish peril." Crusade
once more became a watchword of papal policy. Danger lay closer to
home, too. In 1517 a conspiracy against the pope's life was uncovered.
The rather inept plot never jeopardized Leo, but he was shocked to find
that a disaffected cardinal was the instigator and that other cardinals,
including the then elderly Raffaele Riario, were in some sense involved.
Several executions followed, including that of the ringleader, Cardinal
Petrucci; the implicated cardinals, including Riario, were stripped of
their red hats; and to ensure a College pliant to his policies Leo named
thirty-one new cardinals, an unprecedented number for a single Consistory.

More intractable in the long run, and with much graver consequences for Christendom as a whole was yet another development of
1517: the first stirrings of the Reformation in Germany. While it was at
first dismissed as a "monks' quarrel," by 1521 even papal Rome had come
to recognize the seriousness of this renewed religious challenge from
beyond the Alps.

In the conclave that followed Leo's sudden death in December 1521,
Cardinal Giulio de' Medici, Leo's cousin, was the leading candidate, but
he failed to garner enough votes for election. At length the cardinals

settled on an elderly and little-known Dutch cardinal with close ties to the Holy Roman Emperor Charles V. At the time of his election Adrian VI was residing in Spain, and he did not arrive in Rome until the end of August 1522, nearly eight months later. Adrian, the only Northerner among the Renaissance pontiffs, found much of Renaissance Rome repugnant. Unsympathetic to the cultural aspirations of Julian and Leonine Rome and determined to eradicate corruption, he alienated humanists and artists. To Romans his parsimony stood in particular contrast to Leo's profligacy. Adrian survived in Rome for just a year, however, so that his pontificate meant more a temporary disruption than a decisive break.[31]

The conclave following Adrian's death lasted some fifty days, by far the longest in the Renaissance period, until the persistent Giulio de' Medici finally gained the crucial votes. He chose the name Clement VII. Romans rejoiced, looking to this second Medici pontiff to return the days of Leo X. Such was not the case. As the French and Imperial struggle for Italy continued unabated, the papacy lost its room for maneuver. This downward spiral in the papacy's political fortunes in the end produced the catastrophic Sack of Rome in 1527. At the same time the tide of the Reformation advanced in trans-Alpine Europe and Rome's imperial ambitions ebbed. The traumatic experience of the Sack irrevocably altered Rome's cultural world. In the later 1530s Paul III did make efforts to breathe new life into the fading Roman Renaissance. Nevertheless, the religious controversies engendered by the Reformation increasingly dominated papal policy decisions and absorbed Rome's intellectual energies. By the middle of the sixteenth century the Renaissance had given way to the Counter-Reformation. Rome remained a cultural center, but both the city and the world had changed.[32]

II

Urbs Roma

Messer Maco da Siena: In short, Rome is the *coda*
mundi [tail of the world].
·Sanese: *Capus* [capon] you mean.

—Pietro Aretino, *La cortigiana*,
rev. version, Act I, Sc. 1, ll. 1-2.

Mastro Andrea: What brings you to Rome?
Sanese: To see the *Verbum caro* [Word in
the flesh] and the Jubilee.

—*La cortigiana*, orig. version,
Act I, Sc. 2, ll. 9–10.

TOPOGRAPHY AND URBAN REALITIES

Early autumn of 1460 found Pope Pius II en route to Rome. For more
than a year and a half he had remained away from the Eternal City,
occupied first with the Congress of Mantua he had convened in hopes of
promoting a crusade against the Turks, then delighting in a spring and
summer spent amidst the "smiling hills" about his native Siena. Only with
reluctance did the pontiff leave southern Tuscany. There the Consistory
and papal tribunals had met in spring-fed groves of laurel and ilex,
evocative of the bucolic landscape this classicist pope so cherished. There,
too, the village of his birth, renamed by him Pienza, was becoming
transformed through his wishes into an ideal Renaissance city. Designed
in accordance with Albertian architectural principles, Pienza's new
palaces, cathedral, and central piazza imparted a rational order to the
urban space; human-scaled, these buildings seemed nevertheless to command the surrounding countryside. Yet seductive as the pleasures of
building and the humanized prospects of Tuscany were, Pius could no
longer delay his return to Rome. During his absence an unruly band of
young barons had abducted a bride on her wedding night, staged a night
assault on the convent of Sant'Agnese, and committed other acts of
mayhem. Repeated efforts of the papal governor to curb their violence

had proved ineffectual, a clear reminder of how precarious papal grip on the Christian capital remained. Furthermore, the papacy had been itinerant long enough. For as the pope remarked, "[papal] letters seem to have no weight unless they are dated from St. Peter's at Rome."[1]

Pius's journey south to Rome had its dangers and discomforts. The route along the ancient Via Cassia passed by ominously fortified hill towns and dilapidated summer residences built by medieval popes; brigands roamed the countryside; and the condottiere Jacopo Piccinino, whom reports placed somewhere in the vicinity, posed a threat. Beyond Viterbo, the volcanic terrain, scarred by deeply eroded gorges, became increasingly barren, while the poverty of this sparsely inhabited district accentuated its inhospitable aspect. A late start from Viterbo found evening overtaking the papal party in the narrow, depressing valley at the foot of Monte Cimino. There the pope had to put up with cramped lodgings in a derelict palace. The next day, to avoid the fiefdoms of the Orsini and the Colonna, with whom he was at odds, Pius chose a less frequently travelled route, spending the last night of his trip at Formello, fourteen miles north of Rome. No preparations had been made for his reception. The Cardinal of Avignon, travelling separately, took lodging in the pope's stead at the Orsini castle at Campagnano, and there the cardinal's entourage consumed the banquet intended for the pope. Almost within sight of Rome, Pius was thus reduced to a meager supper fare of bread and onions obtained from peasants. The next afternoon, as he approached the Eternal city, an advance party of civic authorities and Roman nobility intercepted him, and, from the sixth milestone, the *Conservatori* and other leading citizens joined the escort. In their company he at length safely reached the monastery of S. Maria del Popolo, located just inside the ancient Porta Flaminia, where he stayed the night. The next day, 7 October, in contrast to the privations and indignities of his journey, Pius received the honors due his office, and made "a kind of triumphal progress through the city to St. Peter's," where he "knelt and weeping did reverence to the relics of the Holy Apostles."[2]

The alien character of the region Pius encountered outside Rome did not impose itself on him alone. Unlike Tuscany, where a landscape intensely cultivated with grain, olive, and the vine revealed the benign and productive activity of human hands, the Roman Campagna in the fifteenth century was a lonely region of marsh, pasture, and abandoned villages. An occasional posting-station provided the only sign of the renewed pilgrimage traffic to the Eternal City. Here was the domain of vast feudal possessions, such as those of the Orsini centered at Lake Bracciano or the Colonna at Palestrina; while at the opposite end of the social spectrum from these barons with their castle strongholds and private armies was an impoverished peasantry, adversely affected by seigneurial depredations during the chaotic period of the Great Schism.

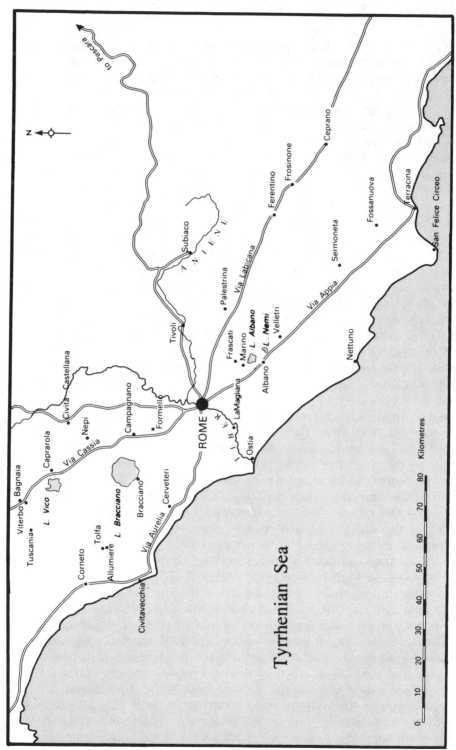

The Roman Campagna and surrounding region

The declining agricultural productivity of this region, which had once sustained the wealth of Tarquinia, Cerveteri, and other Etruscan city-states, did not go unrecognized by fifteenth-century observers. The *cuniculi* and other Etruscan drainage and land-reclamation works had, of course, long since fallen into ruin, but several Renaissance popes enacted legislation intended to promote increased farming. In 1478 Sixtus IV authorized anyone who proposed to cultivate the land to appropriate one-third of any holdings abandoned to pasturage, even if the landlord was ecclesiastical. To the same end Julius II decreed stern measures against the barons' impeding the marketing of grain produced in the Campagna, and Clement VII reissued his predecessors' measures. Yet agriculture continued to decline in the face of stock-raising. Indeed the popes themselves pursued contradictory policies, for the rights and privileges of transhumance shepherds were regularly protected and extended. The reason for this is not hard to find. From vast stretches of land—approaching ninety percent in the districts of Civitavecchia and Tuscania—which the Apostolic Chamber controlled, the papacy derived a lucrative income from the renting of pasturage. More importantly, this income, and the equally lucrative head-tax on all livestock entering the Papal States, provided a consistent, and therefore calculable, source of annual revenue, in contrast to the wildly fluctuating fortunes of the harvest. The result was an underdeveloped rural economy and a deserted countryside, the abandoned solitude of which still appealed to the romantic sensibilities of Goethe in the eighteenth century.[3]

South of Rome the terrain was much the same. Gaspare da Verona, a humanist who held the chair of rhetoric at the University of Rome and who composed a biography of Pope Paul II, spent the summer of 1468 at Sermoneta as a guest of its lord, Onorato Gaetani. Gaspare praised the herbs, wild fruits, melons, mushrooms, and fishponds of the region, but he also mentions the wild water buffalo and the devastated village of San Felice on Monte Circeo, a casualty of the Angevin-Aragonese struggle for the throne of Naples.[4] Other contemporaries likewise found the region desolate and impoverished—Flavio Biondo remarks in his *Italia illustrata* how different it was from Strabo's description.[5] Chronic feudal warfare had destroyed the ancient drainage works and malaria had done the rest.

The most deadly malarial region was the Pontine Marshes. Among its victims was the papal condottiere Roberto Malatesta, who succumbed from fever three weeks after his spectacular victory over an Aragonese army at Campomorto in August 1482.[6] At various points in the fifteenth century there was talk of draining the marshes, including Sixtus IV's request to Ercole d'Este, Duke of Ferrara, to send a hydraulics expert (the Este Dukes had employed such engineers in numerous irrigation, drainage, and land-reclamation projects in their low-lying Po delta principality).[7] Nothing came of this, however. Nor was anything more accom-

1. Ninfa. The ruins of an abandoned medieval village in the Pontine Marshes, typical of the desolate character of the region during the fifteenth and six-teenth centuries. (Photo: by the author)

plished when Leo X briefly engaged Leonardo da Vinci on the project. The costs involved, both for the drainage works themselves and for indemnification of owners, proved prohibitive, and not until the end of the sixteenth century were efforts resumed.[8] In this respect, too, the Papal States lagged behind the successful ventures of Milan and Venice in making agriculturally productive the drained lands of the Lombard plain and the Po delta.[9]

Indicative also of the Roman region's economic underdevelopment was foreign exploitation of the alum deposits found in 1461 at Tolfa in the mountains inland from Civitavecchia. Alum, a chemical used as a mordant in the dyeing of wool cloth, was essential to the textile industries of Florence, Venice, and the Low Countries. Before the Tolfa discovery, the West drew its supply from the mines of Phocaea on the Gulf of Smyrna in Asia Minor. For two centuries Genoese merchants had monopolized this source. When the Ottomans conquered Phocaea in 1455, the enormous profits of alum export fell into infidel hands—Pius II pegged their annual value at a much exaggerated 300,000 gold ducats—and subsequent disruptions in supply and a steep rise in price led to a frantic search for a new source. From about 1460 Giovanni da Castro, a Genoese merchant-banker, had been prospecting for mineral and metallurgic wealth in the region northwest of Rome. When he discovered vast deposits of high-grade alum at Tolfa, in an amount more than sufficient to supply all the West's needs, Pius greeted the find as providential. The pope determined that proceeds from its sale should be placed in a special crusading account (the *Depositeria della Crociata*) to be expended only for war against the Infidel, and he interdicted Christian merchants from importing Turkish alum. His successor, Paul II, went further. He attempted to create a papal monopoly, stipulating that Christian merchants could market only Tolfa alum. To reinforce this measure, he also decreed that any interference with pontifical alum was a sin of extreme gravity unabsolvable by any ordinary confessor.[10]

Using spiritual power to promote a monopoly proved simple enough, but actual production and marketing were problems of a different order. Initially, Pope Pius conceded to Giovanni da Castro and his wealthy Genoese and Pisan partners the rights to extraction and smelting. The Apostolic Chamber then sold a small amount of this refined alum direct to buyers, primarily in Venice. To market the rest, the papacy turned to the Medici Bank, the firm with the most extensive commercial network in Europe. After deductions for shipping, warehousing, and other overhead expenses, the Medici received one-third of the profits, the papacy two-thirds. Later contracts reduced the Medici rate of profit and set ceilings on production, since the initial euphoria of discovery had led to a glut on the European market and a crisis of oversupply in the 1470s. Nonetheless, the Medici clearly benefitted handsomely from the "providential" find. Papal net income from the Tolfa mines exceeded 25,000 gold ducats per year during the first decade after discovery, dipped to below 7,000 in the mid-1470s, then levelled off at about 11,500 over the next four decades, an amount equivalent to about five percent of total papal income.[11] This was not an insignificant amount, but financial dependence on foreign bankers provides a telling sign of the papacy's "colonial" relationship to the more economically advanced parts of Italy.

The most revealing picture of the Tolfa enterprise comes from the tenure of the Sienese merchant-banker, Agostino Chigi. In 1500, he gained from Alexander VI exclusive control over mining, production, and sales, in exchange for a fixed annual rent—a basic arrangement that persisted until his death in 1520. During this period, Chigi constructed the village of Allumiere, complete with church, to house the miners and smelters, purchased Port'Ercole from Siena to serve as a re-export site for alum initially shipped from Civitavecchia, and established agencies for sales throughout Europe and the Mediterranean. No Roman rivalled the entrepreneurial scale of Chigi's undertakings, and with a fortune derived essentially from alum he became one of the city's wealthiest individuals. His lavish villa, later called the Farnesina, constructed on the bank of the Tiber near the Vatican, provides eloquent testimony to his vast fortune, as do the huge loans he made to the papacy, including notably the 75,000 ducats he advanced to cover the costs of Leo X's coronation pageantry.[12]

Thus, as Jean Delumeau has observed,[13] profits from one of the largest mining enterprises in fifteenth and sixteenth century Europe (Tolfa employed some eight hundred men around 1550) failed to be used as capital for commercial or industrial investment. Instead, Tolfa revenues remained in foreign hands or helped pay for papal wars and pontifical splendor.

Lonely, wild, and forbidding in ordinary circumstances, the Roman Campagna in the Renaissance period held further natural and human terrors. Pius II describes a violent storm which lashed the papal party camped in tents during an excursion to Ostia, and which drove them naked into the howling night.[14] In the *Facetiae*, Poggio Bracciolini recounts a similar tempest that tumbled down an abandoned castle, blew the roof off a country tavern, and levelled a church tower. Two herdsmen, witnesses of this last destruction, claimed to have seen at the height of the storm the recently deceased papal condottiere, Cardinal Vitelleschi, clasping the *campanile* in his arms and smashing it to the ground. Vitelleschi, widely feared for his cruelty, had died in Castel Sant'Angelo of wounds received when he was arrested for suspected treason against Pope Eugenius IV. Thus, one must presume, he was a likely candidate for venting his post-mortem fury on the Roman countryside.[15]

Cover for bandits and marauders existed everywhere in the Campagna. A still more ominous threat was Saracen pirates, who could lurk undetected in such havens. Gaspare da Verona reports Muslim galleys landing near Civitavecchia, where their crews surprised the inhabitants and made off with a number of them.[16] In 1516, rumors, which proved false, reached Rome that Leo X himself had been captured by Saracens raiding the same port city.[17] Cellini, the obstreperous goldsmith, relates a similar incident of being attacked by buccaneers as he was collecting pebbles and seashells along this same deserted stretch of shoreline.[18]

On the other hand, the abandoned land abounded in game. Girolamo Riario, Sixtus IV's nephew, hosted a splendid stag hunt for the visiting Duke of Saxony in 1480, which took place in the Campo di Merlo along the Tiber a few miles southwest of the Porta Portese.[19] This area continued to be a favorite hunting ground well into the sixteenth century. Indeed, here, at La Magliana, a succession of Renaissance popes beginning with Innocent VIII created an increasingly magnificent hunting lodge. Saracen corsairs plundered the site in a raid in 1511, but not even this underscoring of the dangers of La Magliana's exposed position succeeded in dampening papal enthusiasm for continued construction there. Leo X, in particular, found it a favorite outlet for his passionate devotion to the chase. Wealthier cardinals emulated papal practice. In *De cardinalatu*, Paolo Cortesi recommended hunting as a suitable recreation for the princes of the Church, and at Bagnaia and Caprarola near Viterbo, and at Bagni di Tivoli, Cardinals Raffaele Riario, Alessandro Farnese, and Ippolito II d'Este created extensive hunting parks, called *barchi*. The importance of hunting to the style of life cultivated by the Renaissance cardinals is reflected, too, in Cardinal Adriano Castellesi's *Venatio*, a lengthy Latin poem composed in the early years of Julius II's pontificate. In the poem, the goddess Diana conducts a hunt of stags, boars, and other wild beasts in the marshlands below Tivoli, there follows a splendid outdoor banquet served to the participants who recline, in ancient Roman fashion, on couches, and the work concludes with the destruction of the pagan deities and Diana's praise of the emergent Christian God.[20]

Once safely within the walls of the Eternal City, the mid-fifteenth-century traveller saw before him a cityscape not remarkably different from the countryside he had just traversed. The Aurelian Walls, built for a population in excess of one million, still defended the city, but vast stretches (the *disabitato*) were given over to gardens, vineyards, and orchards, and much simply lay overgrown and abandoned. The clusters of buildings around the distant basilicas of S. Maria Maggiore and St. John Lateran formed separate settlements connected to the rest of the city by the remnants of ancient Roman streets and to each other by winding dirt paths. The Roman Forum was known as Campo Vaccino, because it served as a cow pasture, the Tarpeian Rock on the Capitoline was called Monte Caprino, for there goats foraged, and the Castrum of

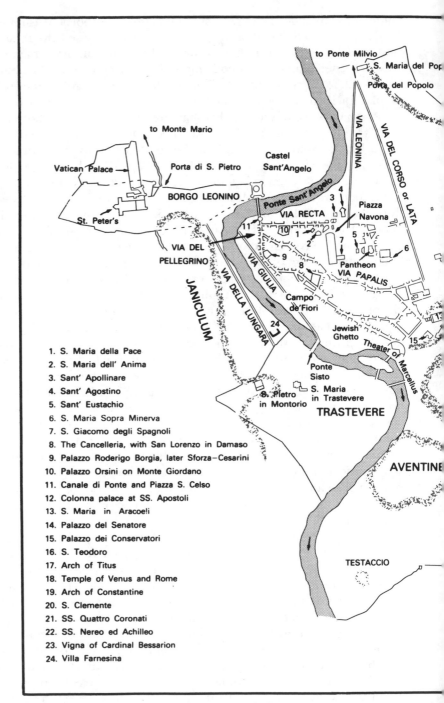

1. S. Maria della Pace
2. S. Maria dell' Anima
3. Sant' Apollinare
4. Sant' Agostino
5. Sant' Eustachio
6. S. Maria Sopra Minerva
7. S. Giacomo degli Spagnoli
8. The Cancelleria, with San Lorenzo in Damaso
9. Palazzo Roderigo Borgia, later Sforza–Cesarini
10. Palazzo Orsini on Monte Giordano
11. Canale di Ponte and Piazza S. Celso
12. Colonna palace at SS. Apostoli
13. S. Maria in Aracoeli
14. Palazzo del Senatore
15. Palazzo dei Conservatori
16. S. Teodoro
17. Arch of Titus
18. Temple of Venus and Rome
19. Arch of Constantine
20. S. Clemente
21. SS. Quattro Coronati
22. SS. Nereo ed Achilleo
23. Vigna of Cardinal Bessarion
24. Villa Farnesina

The City of Rome in the Renaissance period

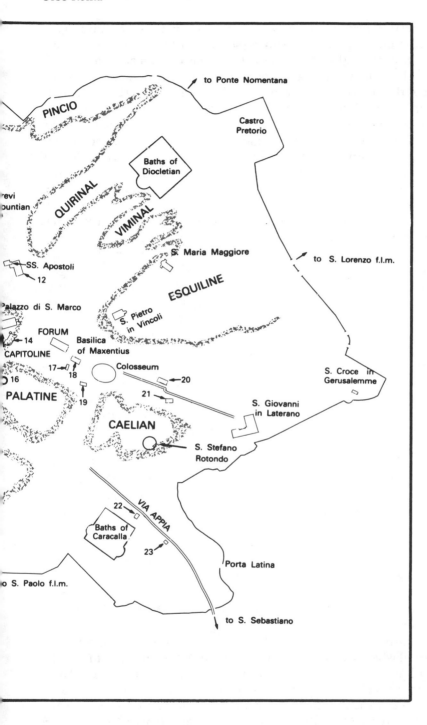

to Ponte Nomentana

PINCIO

Castro
Pretorio

Baths of
Diocletian

QUIRINAL

revi
puntian

VIMINAL

S. Maria Maggiore

to S. Lorenzo f.l.m.

SS. Apostoli

ESQUILINE

12

Palazzo di S. Marco

S. Pietro
in Vincoli

FORUM

14

Basilica
of Maxentius

CAPITOLINE

17

18

Colosseum

20

S. Croce in
Gerusalemme

16

21

S. Giovanni
in Laterano

PALATINE

19

CAELIAN

S. Stefano
Rotondo

22

VIA APPIA

Baths of
Caracalla

23

Porta Latina

o S. Paolo f.l.m.

to S. Sebastiano

the Praetorian Guard near the Baths of Diocletian was, around 1500, made into a hunting preserve.[21] During severely cold winters wolves came over the ramparts, and several were killed in the Vatican gardens early in the fifteenth century.[22] In 1450 nothing had changed significantly the prospect of the city Petrarch, a century before, had seen stretched before him from a perch atop the ruins of Diocletian's Baths. There, after fatiguing explorations of the classical sites in the immense expanse of the ancient city, he had often ascended; and in that airy silence and "votive solitude," his gaze surveying the melancholy enormity of the ruins, he was prompted, he recalls, to leave behind all his private and public cares and to ponder more deeply ancient history and the origins of human knowledge.[23]

In the fifteenth century not only the Viminal from which Petrarch had contemplated the city, but also the other *monti*—the Quirinal (called Monte Cavallo from the ancient statues of the "horse-tamers" there, i.e., the Dioscuri), the Pincio, Caelian, Aventine, and Palatine—were largely uninhabited. Of the eleven ancient aqueducts that had supplied water to the hills, only the Aqua Virgo, which brought water to the Campus Martius, continued, haltingly, to function, though the impressive arches of the Aqua Claudia and portions of others still marched across the city. Under Nicholas V's direction, Leon Battista Alberti restored portions of the underground passages of the Aqua Virgo where it passed beneath the Pincio, and its waters emptied into a modest outlet, where the Trevi Fountain is now.[24] Its conduits received further repairs during Sixtus IV's pontificate, but not until the late sixteenth century were other ancient aqueducts again utilized, and only from then did numerous public fountains delight visitors to Rome.

The problem of water supply meant that the majority of Rome's meager population (63 percent of the 54,000 inhabitants in the 1526–27 census, and probably at least that percentage of an estimated 25,000 to 30,000 in the mid-fifteenth century) huddled in squalor in the low-lying area within the bend of the Tiber, where water-carriers could supply public needs directly from the river.[25] But this district also proved prone to recurrent devastating floods. One inundation, in December 1480, after twelve days and nights of steady rain, cut off the Vatican from the rest of Rome. Nevertheless, conditions did not become so severe, the diarist Gherardi remarks, as four years earlier, which was the worst flooding in sixty years.[26]

This district along the Tiber had the aspect of a medieval village—*Roma turrita*, which Flavio Biondo glimpsed in the evening light from the distance of Marino in the Alban Hills, where he had accompanied Cardinal Prospero Colonna on a hunting expedition.[27] Numerous crenellated baronial towers, such as the Orsini complex on Monte Giordano, or the fortified Theater of Marcellus owned by the Savelli, thrust above a warren

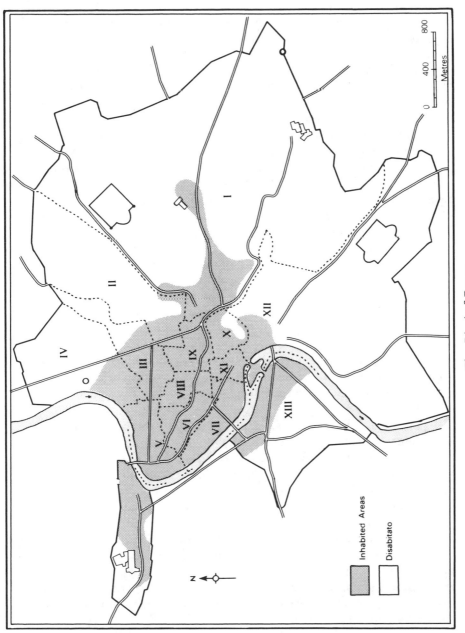

The *Rioni* of Rome

of narrow, unpaved streets and alleys. Wooden balconies, porticoes, and exterior stairways protruded into the public passages and encumbered movement. At points two horsemen could not pass one another. Only the providential action of rains removed the offal of the butchers and fishmongers and other refuse and filth, which was simply thrown into the streets.

Such conditions stimulated papal action, especially during Sixtus IV's pontificate. Besides improved public hygiene, such efforts also promised better police control (by facilitating troop movement) and, more important, presented to pilgrims and other visitors a more decorous city. During the fifteenth century, the medieval communal officials in charge of public works, the *magistri stratarum*, first came under papal jurisdiction, then were made subject to papal appointment, then finally became salaried officials of the Apostolic Chamber. Papal statutes of 1452, and a more comprehensive version of 1480, issued by Sixtus, stipulated a host of regulatory measures: the demolition of structures projecting into public thoroughfares; fines for violators of sanitation provisions; the paving and regular cleaning of the three major streets that converged at Ponte Sant'Angelo and of the public markets in Piazza della Rotunda, Piazza Navona, and Campo de' Fiori; and prohibitions against the private holding of any towers on the walls of Rome.[28] An incident during Sixtus's pontificate shows that these enactments of urban renovation did not remain merely pious hopes. The pope noticed, upon returning to the Vatican after an outing in the city in March 1482, that ancient porticoes near Ponte Sant'Angelo had not been removed. Their owner objected that tearing them down meant the destruction of his shops. But Sixtus ordered his imprisonment and stood by while the structures were demolished.[29]

In the end, nevertheless, what is striking is not the enactment and enforcement of such provisions, many of which merely repeat medieval edicts, but rather what this legislation reveals about contemporary conditions in the city and how ineffectual public attempts to control the urban environment had been. In this respect, too, Rome remained two centuries behind the more advanced city-states of northern and central Italy.[30]

Contributing further to the general impression of decay and backwardness that confronted the fifteenth-century visitor was the unfocussed diffuseness of the city. The Capitoline Hill had symbolized the ancient city and functioned as its religious and ceremonial center. During the Middle Ages and Renaissance the communal government met there, but the Palazzo del Senatore was oriented away from, rather than toward, the Roman Forum, and it had to compete with the Franciscan church of S. Maria in Aracoeli for visual dominance of the hill. The Campidoglio stood, moreover, at the edge of the medieval city's populated area, and though an open-air market drew crowds to its western slopes (until 1477, when the market moved to Piazza Navona), the hill remained in many ways peripheral to patterns of daily life. Removed similarly from ordinary urban functions was the Borgo Leonino, the Vatican area that contained St. Peter's basilica and the Vatican Palace. Indeed, this district did not lie within the walls of the classical city, but instead had gradually grown up around the Constantinian church of the Prince of the Apostles. Originally fortified by Pope Leo IV (847–55)—hence its name—to protect the tomb of the Apostle, which had been sacked by Saracen raiders in 846, the Borgo Leonino formed a separate sacred precinct, an appendage to the city, rather than its topographic center and urbanistic focal point. As such, Rome lacked the visual linkage of sacred and secular power which the Duomo–Palazzo della Signoria axis gave to Florence and the S. Marco–Doge's Palace complex gave to Venice. Lacking, too, was the carefully planned spatial organization and the spirit of geometric regularity Florentines had imposed on their monumental center. These made it, in Leonardo Bruni's image, the mid-point (*umbelicus*) from which radiated outward in ever-widening concentric rings the urban walls, the villa-dotted suburban hills, and the walled towns and castles of the subjugated mountains.[31]

Just as fifteenth-century Rome presented a medieval visage, so did this disordered urban space give home to a society still basically medieval. Unlike Florence or Venice, whose cosmopolitan patriciates derived their economic and political power from a shrewd calculation of the profits international markets offered, Rome fell prey to a feudal nobility whose factional politics, parochial outlook, and ready recourse to armed violence differed little from the motives and ambitions of their thirteenth-century counterparts. The military campaigns Alexander VI launched against the Gaetani, the Colonna, and the Orsini, followed by Julius II's political defeat of the nobles in 1511 began to curb baronial *prepotenza*. Yet the Colonna assault on the city in 1526 forced Clement VII to seek refuge in Castel Sant'Angelo, and the destruction wrought seems trivial only in comparison to the Sack of the following year. Decline in the barons' political power, in short, occurred only gradually, and not until the late sixteenth century had their subsequent economic ruin become apparent.[32]

What distinguished Rome, however, from the feudalized Kingdom of Naples and from the other smaller Italian feudal principalities was the presence of the papacy. Since the Avignonese period, the administrative, judicial, and fiscal functions of the Church had become increasingly centralized in the papal Curia. There was a steady growth in the number of personnel of the various offices and tribunals that comprised the papal bureaucracy; by the early sixteenth century it and the papal household proper—whose numbers had quadrupled from Pius II's pontificate to Leo X's—employed nearly two thousand people. The volume of business generated and the sheer scale of the papal court's domestic maintenance consequently exerted significant economic leverage on the city, as Pius II himself observed.[33] Among other things this meant that hotels were more numerous and better than in any other Italian city, and corresponding numbers of *osterie, taverne,* and artisans' shops catered to the luxury demands of a wealthy international clientele.[34] Prostitutes, too, flourished in a city where there were sixty men for every forty women.[35] By the late fifteenth century, the emergence of the courtesan to a prominent place in the city's social and cultural life added a yet more exotic note to this service-oriented character of the Roman economy.[36]

The most lucrative sources of income in papal finance, such as the treasuries of the various Curial departments and of the regions of the Papal States, continued to be monopolized, however, by foreign merchant-bankers. Firms from Genoa and Augsburg were among the *mercatores Romanam Curiam sequentes* serving the financial needs of the papacy. But through most of the Renaissance period Tuscan bankers controlled these fluid forms of capital. Especially conspicuous were the twenty-five to thirty-five Florentine banks, most of them located in the block-long Canale di Ponte, the financial district of Rome, situated across the Tiber from Castel Sant'Angelo. The Florentine community in Rome also included the innkeepers, butchers, tailors, and other members of service industries stimulated into being by the needs of the merchant-bankers. Clustered along the east bank of the Tiber opposite the Vatican and near the site where later would stand the church of S. Giovanni de' Fiorentini that Michelangelo designed in 1559–60, this sizeable Florentine colony was granted legal recognition as a "nation" by Leo X in 1515 and gradually acquired other extraterritorial privileges, concessions, and exemptions. The Archconfraternity of S. Giovanni Battista de' Fiorentini also emerged as a focus for spiritual and charitable needs, and June 24th, the feast of the patron saint of Florence, John the Baptist, provided an occasion for lavish festivities attesting to the loyalty these Florentines still felt for their native city.[37]

The Florentine community in Rome provided a congenial atmosphere for the numerous Tuscan artists who flocked to Rome in the late fifteenth and early sixteenth centuries. Otherwise, however, it did not contribute significantly to creating a specifically Roman Renaissance culture. An international body that did, and that evinces the pre-eminently aristocratic character of Rome's society, was the College of Cardinals. Increasingly drawn from the princely families of Italy, such as the Gonzaga, Este, and Medici, or raised to the purple by uncle popes, Renaissance cardinals viewed themselves as Senators of the *respublica Christiana* with an obligation to emulate the secular splendor of their classical forebears. Indeed, as early as 1438 Lapo da Castiglionchio the Younger, a secretary to Pope Eugenius IV, had argued that for cardinals the life of apostolic poverty now was past and that cultivation of splendor and magnificence had become the appropriate way to gain men's allegiance.[38] Paolo Cortesi's *De Cardinalatu*, the 1510 guide to all aspects of the ideal cardinal's bearing and conduct—hence, comparable to Castiglione's handbook for the courtier—also assumed the necessity of great wealth in stipulating the details of princely elegance and the standards of cultural patronage essential to the cardinal's dignity.[39]

Most cardinals expected to reside in Rome for much of their careers, making a palace proper to their status a requirement. Rodrigo Borgia's new structure, compared by Pius II to the legendary magnificence of Nero's Golden House,[40] and Pietro Barbo's Palazzo di S. Marco (the present Palazzo Venezia) set the trend. But from Sixtus IV's pontificate onwards, new palace construction for cardinals featured prominently in the Roman cityscape.

The first criterion for these palaces was space, for cardinals' households were indeed princely in scale. Upwards of two hundred *familiares* and servants—squires, chamberlains, stewards, chaplains, notaries, secretaries, a physician, grooms, tailors, butchers, and cooks—proved not uncommon, and even the rather modest household of Francesco Gonzaga (1444–83), named cardinal by Pius II in 1461, consisted, when he began his career in Rome, of eighty-two people and fifty-four animals.[41] Storage rooms, stables, a garden, a chapel (or church incorporated within the palace as S. Marco was in Palazzo Venezia and S. Lorenzo in Damaso in the Cancelleria), reception rooms, a library, servants' quarters, and the cardinal's personal suite all had to be included.

Until about 1480, the cardinals' palaces evoked in style the basic features, though regularized, of baronial complexes. Large rectangular blocks marked by corner towers, their façades made of brick or of rubble faced with stucco, they reserved classical elements only for details. In thus preserving continuity with the seigneurial architecture native to late medieval Rome, the cardinals expressed their desire to accommodate their positions to local conceptions of aristocratic power. Yet, with exteriors oriented towards streets and piazzas, and with the simple, but assertive, geometry of their interior layout, these new palaces imposed a measure of authority on the surroundng urban space. In this sense their design exemplified Renaissance notions. As such, architecture served to emphasize the dignity and magnificence of the cardinals' position in Roman society and the results contrasted with the irregular and defensive character of the barons' towers.[42]

More distinct classical forms first appeared in the courtyard loggia of Barbo's Palazzo di S. Marco, while in the design of Raffaele Riario's palace (the present Cancelleria), dating from the late 1480s and '90s, the medieval baronial qualities disappeared altogether. Architects turned, at this point, directly to Roman imperial architecture for inspiration—a

measure of the self-confident assertiveness of the Roman imperial renewal that was becoming fundamental to the Roman Renaissance as a
whole. This projection of mighty opulence had the further advantage,
according to Paolo Cortesi, of dazzling the ignorant multitude and thus
restraining their temptation to plunder. Yet Cortesi warned also of the
necessity to provide for the armed defense of the cardinal's palace against
the riots of the urban rabble, and he advised, too, of the desirability of
secret peepholes from which the demeanor of waiting visitors could be
scrutinized.[43] Imposing buildings thus continued to mask a certain pre-
cariousness in the cardinals' position in Roman society.

From the pontificate of Sixtus IV, who substantially enlarged the
College of Cardinals, some twenty-five or thirty cardinals, each with his
more or less sizeable household and palace complex, lived at any one time
in Rome. The city was dotted, then, with scattered foci for artists and
architects, humanists and musicians, libraries and collections of antiquities, theatricals and other entertainments—in short, with small courts,
each reflecting the individual tastes and cultivated patronage of the
cardinal-prince, but each intended to reveal the opulent magnificence
that was the expected standard for all.[44]

This gradual replacement of feudal stronghold by Renaissance
palace became possible in a city otherwise jealous of its propertied prerogatives through measures promulgated by Sixtus IV. His decree of
1480, which we have seen set forth general principles of urban renewal,
also stipulated the forced sale, for just compensation determined by the
Cardinal Chamberlain and the *magistri stratarum*, of abandoned or neglected housing, provided the new owner intended to enlarge or construct a palace. Indeed, evictions were even authorized, including cases
where the owner was ecclesiastical.[45] An earlier bull, from 1475, also gave
an important incentive to palace building. This measure exempted members of the papal court from the rule stipulating that the property of
clerics dying in Rome devolved upon the pope: such an exemption was
granted provided that income from benefices and curial offices had been
invested in buildings.[46] Together these bulls provided the financial inducement and the legal means to clear away the medieval underbrush,
which would have inhibited construction or distracted from the proper
splendid setting.

The urban reality of fifteenth-century Rome might be summed up,
then, as the gradual transformation, both topographical and social, from
medieval alley and tower to Renaissance street and palace. Through
papal leadership, a spasmodically functioning urban organism, tainted
still with an ominous aura of ruin and decay, exposed to the baleful effects
of the scirocco and malaria, and subject to endemic violence, began once
more to show signs of new vitality. Economically, however, the city and
the region remained underdeveloped and basically pastoral. Foreigners

dominated commerce and banking, industry aside from the building trades remained virtually non-existent, and the lavish construction projects of the popes and cardinals depended for their financing upon the fiscal resources of the Church at large and the more effective taxation of the Papal States.

Conspicuous by their absence from the refined aesthetic and intellectual sensibility that formed so fundamental an aspect of the Roman Renaissance ideal of daily life were the bourgeois values of sober domesticity, attentive nurturing of the family, and astute husbanding of patrimonial resources. Tuscan Renaissance art, and literature, created for bourgeois audiences, included these as subject matter. Merchants, artisans, and peasants are missing, however, from contemporary self-portraits of Roman life; and the resulting gap between the gilded leisure of Rome's elite and the humble world of work had important consequences, as Delumeau has suggested,[47] both for the future economic vitality of the Eternal City and for the responsiveness of the Roman Church to the spiritual concerns of the laity.

ROME OF THE PILGRIMS

Yet all capitals, Fernand Braudel observes,[48] are in some measure parasites, and in this respect Rome proved no different from sixteenth-century Madrid or seventeenth-century Paris. What in the end becomes clear about Rome is the inadequacy of economic and social analysis to account for its significance; for indeed more influential in determining the overall character of the city than the sophisticated, cosmopolitan, and courtly culture of the cardinals' palaces were, paradoxically, the transient crowds of pilgrims, whose lodgings, far from palatial, were often no more than the porticoes next to St. Peter's. There they slept on beds of straw purchased from the straw-dealers (*paliarii*), who plied their wares in the piazza, jostling the fruit-vendors and souvenir-hawkers, and disputing with the canons of the basilica as to what was public space.[49]

The ebb and flow of pilgrim crowds accompanied the rhythms of the Roman liturgical year. Rising for Lent and Holy Week, they reached a crescendo during the Jubilee Years, when their numbers probably surpassed 100,000.[50] Their physical needs and spiritual expectations also altered the spatial features of the city. Sixtus IV's urban renewal legislation of 1480, for instance, had pilgrims mainly in mind in its plans for creating a more commodious urban setting. Rome, the bull begins, is the city consecrated to Christ through the glorious blood of the Apostles Peter and Paul, and has been made by the Most High head of the Christian religion and seat of His vicar. This *civitas sacerdotalis et regia* (royal and priestly city) is *caput mundi*, and in consequence draws multi-

tudes of the faithful from all parts of the earth to visit the basilicas of the
Apostles and to gain indulgences, especially during Jubilee Years. For
these reasons, a more decorous and beautiful city was vital.[51]

At times swelling crowds of pilgrims did simply overtax the con-
gested medieval passages through the city. In 1450, Ponte Sant'Angelo,
the only bridge then connecting the Vatican with the rest of Rome,
became jammed one evening with pilgrims returning from St. Peter's. A
stubborn mule blocked movement on the narrow span, and in the ensuing
crush more than a hundred persons died—some were trampled, others
were forced into the river where they drowned.[52]

To prevent a recurrence of this disaster, Sixtus IV constructed,
before the Jubilee of 1475, the Ponte Sisto, which gave alternative access
to the Vatican. Circulation of crowds within the Borgo Leonino similarly
improved with the creation of the Via Sacra, begun in 1475 and completely paved by 1483. Its route approximated the present Borgo
Sant'Angelo.[53] The same motives prompted Alexander VI, before the
Jubilee of 1500, to enlarge the piazza in front of Castel Sant'Angelo and to
connect this to Piazza S. Pietro by means of another new street, the Via
Alessandrina (since disappeared in the creation of the Via della Con-
ciliazione in the 1930s).

Julius II had more ambitious plans. With Bramante as architect, he
created the Via Giulia, a rectilinear artery connecting his uncle Sixtus IV's
Ponte Sisto to a projected new Ponte Giulio, which would have crossed the
Tiber directly to the Vatican at the site of the ruined Pons Triumphalis,
known also as the Neronian Bridge. This Ponte Giulio, with its suggestive
echoes of imperial grandeur, never was built, but the Via Giulia did
become the widest thoroughfare then existing in Rome. Palace construction along it added further to the street's prominence and magnificence.[54]

Two other arterials appeared in these opening decades of the sixteenth century. Julius II's Via della Lungara cut straight through Trastevere from the Vatican to the Via Aurelia, and probably there were plans
to extend it to the port at Ripa Grande. Besides thus improving pilgrim
access it would have served the more mundane purpose of facilitating
transport of commodities to the Vatican. Concern to improve access to the
Vatican from the north explains the other new street, the Via Leonina
(the present Via di Ripetta). Built under Leo X, as its name suggests, it cut
more directly from Piazza del Popolo to Ponte Sant'Angelo than the older
circuitous route along the Via del Corso.

The urban topography of the Renaissance city that emerged from
its medieval and feudal predecessor gained its form, then, primarily from
Rome's real constituents, the pilgrims. Their impact can be measured,
too, in the increased number of pilgrim hospices. Usually these consisted
of a dormitory, which also doubled as a hospital, the national church, and
a cemetery. Among the largest of these complexes was the German

foundation of S. Maria dell'Anima, but by the end of the fifteenth century the Spanish, Portuguese, French, Bretons, English, Scots, Flemings, Swedes, Bohemians, and Hungarians all had such hospices in Rome.[55]

Rome as the focus of pilgrimage did not, of course, originate in the fifteenth century. From the early centuries of the Christian era pilgrims had sought the city, and in the Middle Ages the pilgrimage *ad limina Apostolorum* had ranked with those to Jerusalem and to the shrine of St. James at Compostela for sanctity of purpose and efficacy in expiating sinfulness.[56] The pilgrimage Ercole d'Este, Duke of Ferrara, made to Rome in 1487 in fact reflects just these notions. Originally he expressed the desire to fulfill the intention his father had stated early in the century to visit Compostela. But when Ercole reached Milan, papal officials persuaded him to come to Rome instead. Not an ordinary, nameless penitent, the Duke made his devotional entrance in the company of an entourage 380 strong, all with costumes created expressly for the occasion. Elaborate, too, was the choreography of his reception, as municipal and papal officials greeted him in stages from Ponte Milvio to Porta del Popolo, and from there the whole body moved in ceremonial procession to St. Peter's.[57]

The impulse that drew Ercole and thousands of humbler people to Rome stemmed, as it had for centuries, from the desire for immediacy of contact with the more than earthly heroism of the Apostles and martyrs. Here pilgrims could behold directly the places where the saints had remained steadfast in their faith in the face of such spectacular tortures. Here, too, they could gaze upon scenes where so many miraculous signs of divine intervention had been manifested. In pilgrim eyes the Eternal City became in fact a vast repository of sacred relics. To the devout visitor, these did not exist merely as symbols or commemorative tokens. They retained the spiritual potency of the Apostles, martyrs, and saints, and their power proved tangibly real. Just as Pope Gregory the Great had testified in the sixth century to the horrible deaths of those who inadvertently had tampered with the bones of St. Paul and St. Lawrence,[58] so Maffeo Vegio, the humanist canon of St. Peter's, reminded his mid-fifteenth century readers of the miracles, visions, and cures caused by the living presence of St. Peter within his basilica, at that point undergoing major renovation in accordance with Nicholas V's rebuilding plans.[59]

In a similar echo of medieval practice, Vegio also provided the funds to construct a new marble tomb in the church of Sant'Agostino for St. Monica, St. Augustine's mother. Her body had come to light in the cathedral of Ostia during Martin V's pontificate, and subsequently had been translated into Rome in a ceremony of Palm Sunday 1430. Vegio credited St. Monica with primary responsiblity in causing her famous son's conversion to Christianity, and thus did much to promote her cult. He wrote a hagiographical portrait of her, drawn from Augustine's

Confessions, composed a liturgical office in her honor, and arranged for his own burial in the same chapel in Sant'Agostino where her relics had come to reside.[60]

Persisting, too, from the Middle Ages, when a continuous demand existed for some part of Rome's hoard of relics, whether procured by agreement, stealth , or theft,[61] were the entreaties for these holy treasures. In 1483, Sixtus IV, while present at the election of municipal officials, was upbraided "in the name of the Roman people" for permitting relics of the saints to be exported. In defense of his action, the pope replied that the relics in question had been sent at the urgent request of King Louis of France, then dying. The king's gifts to the Lateran, Sixtus went on, testified clearly to his piety, and as a further justification there was precedent for such papal decisions in the deeds of Gregory the Great.[62]

New occurrences of the supernatural testified, also, to Rome as the domain of the sacred and miraculous. About 1480 a venerated painting of the Madonna was struck by a stone and began to bleed. Sixtus IV, an ardent supporter of Marian piety, honored the miracle by constructing at the site of this occurrence a new church. At the conclusion of a peace treaty with Naples in 1482, this took the designation S. Maria della Pace.[63]

Earlier miracles received renewed attention as well. Masolino used the dramatic new resources of linear perspective to depict, in an altarpiece commissioned by Martin V for S. Maria Maggiore, the miraculous summer snow that fell, according to legend, on the Esquiline in a pattern indicating the ground plan for the basilica.[64] A new statue of St. Michael the Archangel, installed atop Hadrian's tomb (Castel Sant'Angelo) by Nicholas V, referred to another miracle. This was the vision that appeared to Gregory the Great of St. Michael standing on the mausoleum and sheathing his sword, a sign that the pope's prayers and intercessory procession had been heeded and that the plague ravaging the city would cease. In this case, in fact, there was a double significance; for the previous statue of St. Michael, destroyed in 1379, in bowing in obeisance to an image of the Virgin Mary carried in intercessory procession, had signalled the end of the Black Death in Rome.[65] Restoring the statue permitted Nicholas V to emphasize the renewal of sacred leadership exemplified in the deeds of his great sixth-century forebear, and encouraged pilgrims approaching the Vatican to recall this historical testimony to divine mercy and miraculous deliverance.

These pilgrim perceptions of Rome as a world apart gained reinforcement in the pamphlet-sized guidebooks to the city, which were first published in the 1470s and proliferated in succeeding decades. The most popular such work was the *Indulgentiae ecclesiarum Urbis*, forty-four Latin editions of which appeared between 1475 and 1523, in addition to twenty editions in German and lesser numbers in Italian, French, Spanish, and Flemish. This guide indicated the major relics and the indulgences

2. Masolino, *The Founding of the Church of S. Maria Maggiore.*
Naples, Museo Nazionale. (Photo: Alinari/Art Resource,
NY)

attached to them in, first, the seven major basilicas (St. John Lateran, St. Peter's, S. Paolo f.l.m., S. Maria Maggiore, S. Lorenzo f.l.m., S. Sebastiano, and S. Croce in Gerusalemme), then in some eighty other churches grouped in several itineraries. The book included a list of Roman stations and, in some editions, a chronological listing of the popes.[66] The *Mirabilia Urbis Romae*, the medieval guide to the wonders and miracles of Rome, also received numerous printings, and thus continued to affect pilgrim impressions.[67]

These ways of seeing Rome influenced not just the simple, the naïve, and the credulous. Fra Mariano da Firenze, a Florentine Franciscan and administrator of Franciscan monasteries in Tuscany, wrote, following his visit to the Eternal City in 1517, an *Itinerarium Urbis Romae*. He intended his work as a comprehensive guide to the "miracles, sacred places, relics, and indulgences of the city," which those with ardent souls should wish to know about and see during a visit of eight or ten days. Mariano gives some treatment to classical Rome and its surviving monuments, and each of the six itineraries he describes starts from the Roman Forum. But legends from the *Mirabilia* frequently crop up, such as the encounter of Augustus and the sibyl or the fall of Simon Magus, and he concentrates on the churches, their relics, and the years of indulgences to be acquired. One such was the Franciscan church of S. Maria in Aracoeli on the Campidoglio, where Mariano specifies that plenary indulgences could be obtained on the feasts of the Nativity, the Circumcision, all the feasts of the Virgin, and the feasts of Sts. Antony of Padua and Bernardino of Siena.[68]

Even the worldly wise Florentine merchant Giovanni Rucellai, who commissioned Alberti to design the Palazzo Rucellai and the facade for S. Maria Novella in Florence, looked at Rome in a different way when he went there in 1450 to gain the Jubilee "pardon." Rather than a functioning city with a coherent topographic unity, he saw it as a congeries of nodal points, denoted by talismans of the sacred. These observations appear in the notes he recorded during the evenings of his nearly month-long stay in Rome. Each morning he went by horseback to visit the four principal basilicas, as required in obtaining the Jubilee indulgence; then, after the midday meal, he remounted, traversing the city to look at antiquities.

Giovanni made some effort to grasp the physical dimensions of the places he visited: St. Peter's he judged to be about the size of S. Croce in Florence, while the Baths of Diocletian had once covered an area about half that of the prato of Ognissanti—"a marvellous thing." But what held most fascination for him were lists of relics, such as those in the Lateran complex: Aaron's rod, the tablets of the Law which God had given to Moses, the table where Christ ate the Last Supper with the Apostles, the heads of Peter and Paul, and, shifting to classical relics, the gigantic bronze head and arm with a bronze ball, and the bronze she-wolf. *Mirabi-*

lia wonders appear in his notes, too, such as the "Templum Pacis" (actually the Basilica of Maxentius). This, Giovanni records, was held to be a temple of idols, which the Romans said would endure until a virgin gave birth, and which collapsed into ruins the night Christ was born. Another wonder was the "*bocca della verità*," a round stone with a face in relief, that "in ancient times had the power to show when a woman played false to her husband."

Some sense of Rome's contemporary reality does intrude here and there in Giovanni's account. He notes that walls, gates, towers, and bridges were inferior in magnificence to the marvels he had related. But the only item suggesting any recognition of the city as an economic actuality is the number of hostelries in Rome during the Jubilee Year— one thousand twenty-two with signboards, and an additional large number without.[69]

Humanists were not immune to the spell of pilgrim perceptions either. Pier Paolo Vergerio (d. 1444), the most ardent supporter of Salutati's revival of the civic ethos of the Roman Republic in the 1390s and an early advocate of the *vita activa civilis*,[70] saw, during his first trip to the Eternal City in 1398, a Rome altogether different from what these political commitments might have suggested to him. He had, he writes, anticipated dire effects from his visit, for it was common belief that cities ruined by violence or abandoned by the times contained unhealthy air, as indeed was the case in Ravenna and Aquileia. Certainly Rome, once *caput orbis*, was now that in name only, while other cities had more claim to it in fact. Yet, to his surprise, his health had not suffered, and far from fulfilling the proverb that one seeking Rome a dog returned a wolf, he had on the contrary experienced—he hoped he could say without arrogance—some improvement in his soul. But who would not be similarly inspired to self-examination of sinfulness, he asks, when confronted by so many sacred places, so many temples, so many relics of the saints, so many monuments of true religion—all frequented with so much the greater devotion since the popes had granted to these visitations indulgences for total or partial "remission of sins?"

Vergerio then indicates the principal sacred sites of the city: the basilica of St. Peter, *princeps apostolorum*, where was preserved the *sudarium*, the cloth of Veronica miraculously imprinted with Christ's facial features as He made His way to Calvary; the basilica of St. Paul, *vas electionis*, which to the shame of the Roman clergy and populace was nearly roofless, and the nearby fountains that sprang up from the spilling of Paul's blood, when he was decapitated on Nero's orders; St. John Lateran, formerly seat of the papacy, which possessed the heads of Peter and Paul; the place outside the gate on the Via Appia where the fleeing Peter, confronted by Christ, asked, "*Quo vadis?*" and then returned to face martyrdom; the chapel within Porta Latina where St. John the Evangelist was immersed in boiling oil, but from which through divine virtue he emerged unharmed; S. Lorenzo with the bodies of that saint and St. Stephen; S. Maria Maggiore, whose location derived from a miracle, and which possessed the manger in which the Christ child was laid; the Franciscan church of S. Maria in Aracoeli which marked the spot where the sibyl showed the Emperor Augustus the altar of heaven; the "wondrous" Pantheon, built by Agrippa and formerly dedicated to the goddess Cybele and other demons, but now dedicated to the Virgin Mary and other saints. These and similar sights suffice by themselves to arouse the soul, Vergerio declares, but besides these Rome possesses the majesty of the papacy with its powers of binding and loosing souls, and, above all, the splendor of religious ceremonies.

Compared to these vivid impressions of Christian Rome, the classical city proved elusive to Vergerio, lost as it was in legends and fables. But the sheer scale of the ruins and the scattered fragments of columns and statuary of marble, porphyry, and alabaster suggested the "miraculous" nature of the city where so many "divine geniuses" had flourished. These vestiges of ancient glory were fast disappearing, however, as Rome's present-day inhabitants out of ignorance and avarice destroyed the memory of their past by casting marble into lime kilns, just as they destroyed precious manuscripts in making souvenir paintings of the *sudarium* to sell to pilgrims.[71]

To the Renaissance pilgrim, surrounded by Rome's plethora of relics and miracles, which held most meaning? Some penitents sought certain shrines because of their specific recompense. Gherardi describes a "pious spectacle" having all the character of a joyous spring outing: on Sundays in May, he states, crowds of all ages, both sexes, and all social classes walk in procession out the Via Appia to the basilica of S. Sebastiano, dedicated to the victim of Diocletian's persecution. The purpose of their festivity brings one face to face, however, with the somber realities of the fifteenth century; for the devout commend themselves piously to the saint, he remarks, so that they might be safe from the plague.[72]

Despite such precautions, bubonic plague repeatedly struck Rome, as it did other cities during the early modern period. During one serious outbreak, in August 1522, Castiglione, the author of *The Book of the Courtier*, reports that some Romans went in procession to the principal churches of the city, carrying the head of St. Sebastian and an image of St. Roch. Some young children, nude from the waist up, marched while beating themselves and crying for God's mercy. Miracles occurred. A young woman, carrying an infected baby in her arms, went in procession to Sant'Agostino, and after placing him on the altar of Our Lady found he was suddenly cured. Nevertheless, Castiglione himself chose to remain isolated from the plague-ridden city in the remote security of the Vatican Belvedere.[73]

If Romans found in St. Sebastian an ally to combat the contagion of the plague, so, too, did Roman piety generate a means of protection against the terrors of tempests and floods. The specific in this case was the *Agnus Dei*, wax discs stamped with the image of the Lamb of God, which the popes distributed each Wednesday after Easter. Not surprisingly, the demand for these was always intense.[74]

Outside of such remedies for crisis, however, the most venerated relics of Renaissance Rome were those that brought the suppliant directly into contact with the redemptive mysteries of Christ's life and death, with the miraculous events connected with His mother, the Virgin Mary, and with the spiritual power of Peter. Desire to be in touch with the humanity of Christ and to participate vicariously in His life and Passion corresponds to the trend toward piety that was everywhere in evidence in the late medieval world.[75] In this regard primacy of place among the Roman relics went, as it had already in the thirteenth century, to the Veronica, miraculously imprinted with the features of Christ's suffering countenance.[76] Flavio Biondo lists it first among the sacred objects which drew pilgrims to Rome from the ends of the earth.[77] Maffeo Vegio calls it the most singular treasure of the whole world.[78] Preserved in its own chapel in St. Peter's, the relic was exposed by the pope for veneration from the Loggia of Benediction on Easter, Ascension, and Christmas, and on every Sunday and additional feast days during Jubilee Years.[79] The Veronica served in fact as the chief symbol of the Roman pilgrimage. Simple woodcut depictions of it appeared in the pamphlet guides to Rome, souvenir copies were sold to pilgrims, and even Albrecht Dürer, though he never went to Rome, made an engraving of it in which it was held up by two adolescent angels.[80]

Another image of Christ, believed to be an exact likeness, was the "Image of Pity" preserved in the subterranean chapel of the basilica of S. Croce in Gerusalemme, the earth paving of which had been brought from Golgotha. This mosaic icon of Christ as the Man of Sorrows is probably Byzantine in origin, dating from the late thirteenth or early fourteenth century, and it appears to have reached Rome in the late fourteenth century by way of Mt. Sinai. By the late fifteenth century, however, the image was connected with a legendary mass of Pope Gregory the Great during which a vision of Christ appeared. The pope ordered an image to be produced in accordance with his vision, so it was said, and the "Image of Pity" was venerated as that image.[81]

In the late fifteenth century yet another image of Christ reached Rome. This was the *Vera effigies*, an emerald cameo from the Treasury of Constantinople which Sultan Bajazet II gave to Pope Innocent VIII, probably about the same time as his gift of the Holy Lance in 1492. The head of Christ on the jewel was reputed to be of great antiquity and was reproduced in a number of Roman Renaissance bronze medals. It also furnished the model for Raphael's depiction of Christ in his tapestry cartoon of the *Miraculous Draft of Fishes* for the Sistine Chapel.[82]

The preservation of objects giving tangible contact with the humanity of Christ went farther. There was the manger where He was placed as a newborn babe (in S. Maria Maggiore), swaddling clothes and even the foreskin from the Circumcision (in the chapel known as the Sancta Sanctorum at St. John Lateran), the Scala Sancta or stairway to Pilate's *praetorium* in Jerusalem where Christ had stood to be sentenced (also at the Lateran), and numerous remnants of the Cross on which He was crucified.[83] Among these was the wooden sign affixed to the Cross with its inscription in Latin, Greek, and Hebrew "Jesus of Nazareth, King of the Jews." This relic came to light during the course of restorations to S. Croce in Gerusalemme on the same day as news of Granada's capitulation to Ferdinand and Isabella reached Rome. So extraordinary an event seemed to contemporaries not mere coincidence but rather to portend divine significance, particularly since the titular cardinal of the basilica was the Primate of Spain.[84]

In the same year Pope Innocent obtained from Sultan Bajazet the Holy Lance of Longinus, which the Roman centurion had used to probe Christ's side while He hung on the Cross. Its arrival in Rome occasioned an elaborate ceremonial entrance, despite the reservations of some cardinals, who noted that both Nuremberg and Paris claimed to possess the true lance.[85] The lance nevertheless became one of the most celebrated relics of St. Peter's, and was customarily revealed along with the Veronica from the Loggia of Benediction.[86]

Revealing, too, of the attention accorded Christ is the prominence of the annual Feast of Corpus Christi. The pope, seated beneath a baldacchino, carried the consecrated Host—the body of Christ—in ceremonial procession from the Vatican Palace to Castel Sant'Angelo and then back to St. Peter's. The procession made possible a splendid display of the Roman clergy ranked in hierarchical order from the lowest (the secular clergy from the city's parishes) to the highest (the papal secretaries and chamberlains) with serried orders of various Curial notaries, auditors, abbreviators, and other officials in between, whose relative importance is indicated by the sliding scale of fines for absenteeism noted by Burchard.[87]

The most spectacular Corpus Christi celebration during the Renaissance took place not in Rome, however, but rather when Pius II was in Viterbo in 1462. Arches of broom, myrtle, and laurel lined the processional route as did dramatic scenes sponsored by the cardinals. These included representations of the Last Supper, of St. Thomas Aquinas administering the sacrament, and (in the scene provided by the Vice-Chancellor Rodrigo Borgia) of five kings magnificently attired who at first barred the Pope's way, then because of the sacrament he carried proclaimed him Lord of the World. Wine fountains, choruses of singing boys, and the sounding of trumpets and other musical instruments added to the spectacle. When the procession reached the piazza of the town hall, there appeared a model of the Holy Sepulchre and a dramatic representation of the Resurrection. In the piazza before the cathedral, the tomb of the Virgin Mary had been constructed and high above it God the Father was seated in majesty surrounded by companies of angels. After Mass the climax of the whole festival came in the dramatic representation of the Assumption of the Virgin: a young girl rose from the tomb to heaven, where she was greeted by "Christ" and presented to the "Father" who seated her at His right hand.[88]

Relics of the Virgin Mary were not so conspicuous in Rome as those of her Son, though Biondo mentions a small vessel of her milk "of wonderful whiteness" preserved in the Sancta Sanctorum,[89] and various miracles such as those of S. Maria Maggiore and S. Maria della Pace testified to her divine intervention. Marian piety nevertheless was strongly evident in the city. Sixtus IV, who promoted devotion to the Immaculate Conception and the cult of the Rosary,[90] made it a practice to go every Saturday to S. Maria del Popolo to pray before an image of the Madonna attributed to St. Luke.[91] Under Sixtus, too, a new main altar to hold this icon was commissioned; it was executed by the sculptor Andrea Bregno in 1473. Subsequent creation of tomb chapels for the Della Rovere, Borgia, Chigi, and others, and architectural and decorative interventions of Pinturicchio, Bramante, and Raphael made S. Maria del Popolo one of the most prominent Renaissance churches in Rome.[92]

Marian feast days occupied a major place also in the Roman liturgical year. On the Feast of the Purification of the Virgin (2 February), the pope distributed candles to the assembled cardinals and other dignitaries.[93] More elaborate was the Feast of the Annunciation (25 March). In the late fifteenth and early sixteenth centuries, this observance normally included a papal Mass at S. Maria sopra Minerva, after which the pontiff gave a papal benediction, pronounced a plenary indulgence, and bestowed dowries on a number of poor girls in attendance. In 1497 a dramatic representation of the Annunciation entertained the papal entourage en route to the Minerva.[94]

The Feast of the Assumption (15 August), too, offered an occasion for dramatic spectacle. On the eve of the feast, Roman guild members marched in procession to the Sancta Sanctorum of the Lateran, where they removed a miraculous icon of Christ, known as the *Acheropictos*, because of the tradition no human hand had painted it. They then carried the image in torchlit procession along a specified route to S. Maria Maggiore, and there placed it next to an image of the Virgin. Throughout the night mother and Son beheld the rapt veneration of the faithful. En route to the basilica a ceremonial washing of the icon's feet took place with the precious water dispersed over the crowd. The cortege also passed, by design, through the Arch of Constantine, which Albertini in describing this festival remarks was "now used in the triumph of the Savior."[95]

The picturesque, domestically human, and perhaps even sweetly pathetic piety evident in the Roman celebrations of the Feasts of the Annunciation and the Assumption appears most strikingly in the cult of the Holy House of Loreto. According to legend, officially promulgated in Julius II's 1507 bull *In sublimia*, the Casa Santa was the actual house in Nazareth in which the Virgin Mary was conceived and nurtured. There the Angel Gabriel announced her divine maternity, and there Christ became incarnate by the Holy Spirit. Following the extinction of the Crusader States in Palestine at the end of the thirteenth century, the Holy House was miraculously transported first to Dalmatia, and then across the Adriatic to the Marche. Loreto seems not to have been prominent as a pilgrimage site early in the fifteenth century, but from the pontificate of Paul II, who began the rebuilding of the basilica that encloses the shrine, Renaissance pontiffs, especially Sixtus IV, Julius II, and Leo X lavished attention there. Major Renaissance artists and architects worked at Loreto, including Melozzo da Forlì, Luca Signorelli, Giuliano da Sangallo, Andrea Sansovino, and Antonio da Sangallo the Younger. Under Julius II's patronage, Bramante planned both the basic architectural arrangement of the basilica, piazza, and Apostolic Palace, and the design of the marble structure that encased the house itself.[96] By the early sixteenth century, no shrine in Italy was more venerated. Julius II himself celebrated Mass there on the Feast of the Nativity of the Virgin (8 September) 1510, while en route from Rome to Bologna and the war zone during his struggle against the French.[97] Even the libertine Cellini judged it worth his while to make his devotions there.[98]

The cult of Loreto appeared in Rome, too. In 1507 there began construction in Trajan's Forum of a new church, a domed, central-plan temple characteristic of Renaissance sacred architecture, dedicated to S. Maria di Loreto.[99] Consecrated to the same veneration is Raphael's remarkable Cappella Chigi in S. Maria del Popolo.[100]

Renaissance Rome possessed powerful indications of the sacred presence of Christ and His mother, but above all it was the city of St. Peter. For the Renaissance pilgrim a succession of sacred sites brought tangible contact with Peter's life and martyrdom. One was the basilica of S. Pietro in Vincoli, where were preserved the chains that had bound the Apostle in prison in Jerusalem, and from which an angel had miraculously released him (Acts 12: 1–19). The chains, brought to Rome during the fifth century through the aegis of the Byzantine Empress Eudoxia—according to the tradition Biondo attributed to the Venerable Bede[101]—were provided in 1477 with a new gilded reliquary depicting scenes from Peter's life. The patron of this project was Cardinal Giuliano della Rovere, the future Julius II, who held as his titular church S. Pietro in Vincoli, and who also completed in this same period the rebuilding of the basilica and constructed the adjoining cardinal's palace.[102]

Rebuilt also in the late fifteenth century, through the patronage of the Spanish crown, was the church of S. Pietro in Montorio on the Janiculum. At this site, according to some Renaissance Romans, Peter was crucified, and in the first decade of the sixteenth century Bramante built in the attached courtyard his famous tempietto, a *martyrium* to Peter that marked the presumed exact spot of his execution.[103]

Most sacred of all, of course, was Peter's tomb, commemorated throughout the Middle Ages in the Constantinian basilica of S. Pietro in Vaticano. Nicholas V began its renovation in the mid-fifteenth century, and then half a century later Julius II razed it to make way for an entirely new structure.[104]

The pilgrim perception of Rome—forcefully reasserted in the Renaissance period by the renewal and elaboration of particular cults and devotional practices, and affirmed in prestige and spiritual significance by the increasing multitudes of the pilgrims themselves—proved of utmost importance in shaping cultural and intellectual proclivities in the city. For pilgrims, Rome existed not as a city in the sense of a human community, but rather as a vast, mysterious, and potent sanctuary, a gateway to the heavenly world. Contemporary reality paled before the visionary splendors of the eternal kingdom, as human dimensions of space and time gave way to mystical celestial links, unfathomable to rational inquiry. Such attitudes received reinforcement from the fact that the benefits of pilgrimage applied not so much to one's present life, but rather to one's status in the life beyond death. The proper attitude of perception was, therefore, not with the eyes of the mind, but instead with the eyes of the soul—not seeing, analyzing, understanding, but rather beholding, contemplating, venerating, praising.

These attitudes reached their culmination in the celebration of the Jubilee Years. The history of these events dated back to Pope Boniface VIII, who proclaimed 1300 a "year of indulgence," during which any pilgrim who made devotional visits to the basilicas of Sts. Peter and Paul for the prescribed period (thirty consecutive days for inhabitants of Rome, fifteen for foreigners) obtained plenary remission of temporal punishment due to sin. Boniface intended such opportunities to be renewed only every hundred years, but in the fourteenth century the period between Holy Years was shortened first to fifty, then to thirty-three years (the lifespan of Christ), and visits to St. John Lateran and S. Maria Maggiore became added requirements. The chaotic conditions of the Great Schism hampered its renewal, but Martin V seems to have proclaimed a Holy Year after his return of the papacy to Rome.[105]

Few penitents attended Martin's Jubilee, however, and restoration of the Holy Year to a central place in pilgrim devotion and in the religious life of Rome came about only with Nicholas V's proclamation of 1450 as a Jubilee Year. The Jubilee bull specified that such times of remission should occur every fifty years, citing the Old Testament precedent (Leviticus 25: 8-55) of a year of jubilee held at fifty-year intervals during which slaves were to be freed and land bought for a price returned to it original owner. But, the bull goes on, what in the Old Testament conception of the mystery of the Jubilee Year belonged to the remission of the world and the restitution of properties is to be understood by Christians in a spiritual manner. Thus all people, even those guilty of the most serious sins, provided they are truly repentant, have confessed, and have visited the four major basilicas in Rome, should receive a plenary indulgence for their sins. The bull affirms, too, that the authority to proclaim a Jubilee Year derives from St. Peter, on whom Christ had conferred full powers of binding and loosing. Peter's successors, the Roman pontiffs, similarly exercise such power; and as dispensers of the mysteries of God, they had chosen certain times in which the streams of divine mercy should flow more plentifully for the faithful, just as God at certain times—by the Flood, by circumcision, by the Law, and finally by the Incarnate Word— had renewed for the better the fallen state of mankind.[106]

Despite the strength of the Old Testament precedent for fifty-year intervals, Paul II set 1475 as the next Holy Year. The reason, according to the antiquarian Andrea Fulvio, who presented his *Saecularis sive Iubilaeus annus*, a hexameter poem on the origins and history of the Jubilee, to Pope Clement VII in 1525, was the brevity of human life.[107] Following 1475, Jubilee Years continued, in fact, to be celebrated every quarter century. In his poem, Fulvio, besides pointing out the ancient Hebraic practice referred to in Nicholas V's bull, a text also cited by other Roman humanists, remarked that the ancient Romans used to celebrate the first year of each century with *ludi saeculares*. As in other aspects of Roman Renaissance culture, a contemporary development was thus seen as renewing features of both sacred traditions—Hebraic and Roman—from which Roman Christianity had taken root.

In the popular mind, procuring the spiritual benefits of the Jubilee Year meant passing through the "holy doors" of the major basilicas. One tradition, reported by the Nuremberger Nikolaus Muffel, who visited Rome in 1452, spoke of the far right door of St. Peter's as the "Golden Gate" of Jerusalem through which Christ had passed on Palm Sunday. This, it was believed, Titus and Vespasian had brought back to Rome after their conquest of the Jewish capital. At one time, according to Muffel, this hallowed entrance to the Vatican basilia had always stood open, and if any sinner walked through, even one who had committed murder, his sin was remitted. To avoid tempting God, however, a later pope had ordered the door bricked up. Muffel mentioned, too, as did many pilgrim guide-books, the existence of a similar door at the Lateran, this one brought from Pilate's palace in Jerusalem. Through this door, also, Christ had walked, in the course of His Passion, and passing through it similarly freed a person from his sins.[108]

These pilgrim legends acquired a fixed place in official ceremony through Alexander VI's actions at the beginning of the Jubilee of 1500. Stonemasons opened what was presumed to be the ancient walled-up door to St. Peter's, though in fact no door existed there, and a passage through the broken wall simply led into the back of the Chapel of the Veronica. As workmen cleared away the rubble, the papal entourage sang music composed for the occasion, which described the door as the "portal of Justice," the "*porta Domini*," by means of which the Just would enter the Lord's house. Then Alexander, dressed in pontifical robes and adorned with the triple tiara, walked through—on pain of death no one was to precede him—and all the papal court followed. At the same time, "holy doors" were opened in the other three basilicas, and all the bells of the city resounded.[109]

Doors as key religious symbols drew reinforcement from other occasions. In 1480, Florentine ambassadors came to Rome seeking absolution from the ecclesiastical censures Sixtus IV had imposed in the wake of the Pazzi Conspiracy. The pontiff received the Florentines before the closed bronze portals of St. Peter's, where they prostrated themselves, kissed the pope's foot, knelt in confession, and implored pardon. Then followed the reading of the instrument of absolution, the ambassadors swore an oath of obedience, the pope reproved their former disobedience but then touched them lightly on the shoulder with the rod of the *penitentiarius*, and blessed them. Thus they were restored to the community of the faithful, the gates of the basilica swung open for them, and all filed into the church, proceeding to the high altar to hear Mass.[110]

Relics, tombs, miracles, holy doors—these sacred objects and divine signs constituted the essential attributes of the pilgrims' Rome. Only gradually, with the creation of the Vatican as a governing center and the construction of new arteries in the city, did the coherent topographical image of Rome as the restored imperial capital begin to rival the penitents' outlook. For them, the Eternal City consisted of those sacred sites, scattered at random through the decayed ruins of the ancient city, which divine initiative, not human decision, had chosen to sanctify. A tenuous network of horizontal connectives, continually fashioned by ritual processions of pilgrims, joined together these tangible testimonies to celestial power and purpose. As a mystical sacred arena, however, in which ritual served as the means to restore the right relationship between the *respublica Christiana* and divine providence, more fundamental than the horizontal space was the vertical dimension. Along this axis the sanctuaries of the saints and their suppliants became mysteriously joined to the heavenly kingdom. In Rome, in short, ceremony and liturgy were the most significant human actions. Ritual possessed a transcendent power and purpose, making insubstantial by comparison the circumscribed limits of merely human space and time. Resonant with such sublime import was the solemn moment each Christmas, Easter, and Ascension when the pope, the Vicar of Christ, ascended with the Veronica and other holiest relics to the Loggia of Benediction, the marble triple portico giving entrance to the sacred precinct of St. Peter's basilica, which Pius II had started to build. From this gateway to Peter's hallowed sanctuary, the successor to Peter's powers of binding and loosing souls bestowed on the multitude gathered below in the piazza his apostolic blessing *Urbi et orbi.*[111]

LITURGY AND CEREMONY

The Roman pontiff, blessing the crowds in Piazza S. Pietro, served as the sluice gate by which the streams of divine mercy were channeled downward to the pilgrim Church. In accord with this same perpendicular emphasis, Renaissance preachers in the sermons delivered during the papal liturgies urged the ordered ranks of the papal court, assembled in the Sistine Chapel, to "look up" to the heavenly court as its perfected image and examplar and as its final destiny.[112] Paris de Grassis, the papal Master of Ceremonies under Julius II and Leo X, in fact, saw the quadrangular formal seating arrangements for public meetings of the Consistory and for the papal chapel—in both of which the papal dais with its throne formed one side with the cardinalitial orders assigned to the other three—as the earthly reflection of the throne of God and of the twenty-four thrones for the elders, described as the setting for celestial liturgies in Revelations 4.[113] From this anagogical perspective, the way in which earth could most truly conform to heaven was, as Jean Jouffroy asserted in his funeral oration for Nicholas V, in the beauty and splendor of liturgical ceremony.[114]

A more impressive and lavish celebration of the divine cult formed, indeed, for Pope Nicholas himself one of the principal accomplishments of his pontificate. The pontiff states this in his "last testament" to the College of Cardinals, preserved by his biographer Giannozzo Manetti, and in the same *Vita* Manetti praises Nicholas for devoting his whole mind to spiritual matters and for the remarkable care with which he observed ecclesiastical ceremonies. The pope, to increase the admiration of the Christian people, and thus to inspire them to more diligent devotion, used sumptuously bejeweled and decorated vestments and church plate. When people saw divine offices everywhere so beautifully and worthily performed, they were seized with so much admiration, wonder, and devotion, Manetti claims, that they recognized clearly revealed to them in the Church Militant the image of the Church Triumphant.[115]

Nicholas did not stand alone in emphasizing observance of the divine service. Similar views on ritual as the heart of Rome's sacredness were repeatedly set forth in the reports of the reform commissions appointed by Pius II, Sixtus IV, and Alexander VI.[116] Even after the outbreak of the Lutheran controversy, they continued to be propounded. Indeed, the Curial humanist Zaccaria Ferreri (d. *ca.* 1525) in his *De reformatione Ecclesiae suasoria*, addressed to Pope Adrian VI in 1522, placed primary emphasis on preservation of the divine cult in his program for reform: "The earthly Golden Age and holy times will return/ Pious Rome, if to these rites you hold fast."[117]

Beyond such attentiveness to ritual function, the Renaissance proved an active period, too, for issuance of liturgical and ceremonial works. Petrus Burgensis (Pedro Gundisalvi de Burgos), Clerk of Ceremonies from 1445 to 1469, in fact produced for Nicholas V a new version of the *Liber caeremoniarum*. This handbook to the liturgies and ceremonies of the papal court preserved substantially unaltered the practices of the thirteenth and fourteenth centuries, and thus was consciously conservative in purpose. Yet some changes or additions, in the form of marginal notations, made their way into this text.[118]

More important innovations appeared in *De caeremoniis Curiae Romanae libri tres* (1488), which Agostino Patrizi and Johannes Burchard, the curialists in charge of ceremonies for Innocent VIII, compiled for the Cibo pope; and besides a new Ceremonial, they also provided a new version of the Pontifical (1485). Despite these changes, to be considered shortly, Burchard, too, was anxious to preserve a continuity with past tradition. Restoration, not novelty, guided his work, and to this end he systematically collected liturgical texts written over the previous two centuries. He also preserved records of important ceremonial occasions, such as the canonizations of St. Catherine of Siena (1461) and St. Bonaventure (1482). The same zeal for liturgical scholarship appears in the miscellaneous notes and documents he gathered later in his career regarding the conclaves and other public events of Alexander VI's and Julius II's pontificates.[119]

Other aspects of liturgy came under scrutiny as well. Leo X, for instance, ordered Zaccaria Ferreri to revise the Roman Breviary according to the standards of humanistic eloquence. Ferreri continued the work under Adrian VI, and in 1525 this new manual for daily offices and prayers was ready for publication. Held up for revisions, in the end it never appeared. In the same year, Ferreri did, however, publish *Hymni novi ecclesiastici*, a gathering of hymns to be inserted in the offices for Sundays and other feast-days, a project also inspired by Pope Leo and connected to the reform of the Breviary. The hymns were to be composed in classical Latin meters and according to the poetic demands of classical genres. The completed hymns also included allusions to classical gods and goddesses, such as Bacchus, Circe, and Venus, and contained other classical *topoi*.[120]

Attesting to the increased importance accorded liturgy in the Renaissance period is the rise in status of the officials in charge of ceremony—normally there were two, performing senior and junior roles—from mere clerks to the more dignified "master" (*magister*). Moreover, both Burchard, *Magister Caerimoniarum* from 1483 to 1506, and Paris de Grassis, who held the same office from 1504 to 1528, ended their careers as bishops, the aspiration of all Curial careerists, and both, to judge from the detailed diaries they kept to serve as a record of ceremonial events and as a guide for their successors, became not only intimates of the popes but also were much in evidence on ceremonial occasions.[121]

At times increased attention to liturgy went beyond mere revision and the augmented esteem accorded its experts. For Nicholas V, proper performance of ceremony formed the crux of efforts to restore the dignity of the Roman See and of its authority in the Christian world. Initially, too, he envisioned a more comprehensive program of liturgical renewal, centering on the revival of the Roman "stations."

The Roman "stations" consisted of a solemn papal procession to, and the celebration of a papal Mass at, some forty specified Roman churches on eighty-seven days of the year—mainly Lent and Holy Week, but also during the Christmas season, and on Pentecost and other feast days. Renaissance Romans attributed the origin of the Roman "stations" to Pope Gregory the Great.[122] Actually their development preceded his pontificate, but Gregory had preached on these occasions, and the survival of these cycles of sermons, added to the prestige of his authority for the early Church, contributed to the mid-fifteenth century conviction that revival of the "stations" would serve as a means to restore the paleo-Christian conception of Rome's sacredness.

During the Jubilee Years of 1450, Nicholas and the College of Cardinals, according to Platina's testimony, did attend the "stations,"[123] and in his "last testament" the pope himself states that the physical rehabilitation of the station churches formed part of his comprehensive plan for rebuilding the city of Rome.[124] Nevertheless, completion of such an undertaking proved beyond Nicholas's resources, especially since major projects were initiated simultaneously for the Vatican and St. Peter's. Repairs and alterations did manage to be made to Sto. Stefano Rotondo, the distinctive, central-plan church on the Caelian, to S. Teodoro, also a central-plan church, and to several other station churches. Subsequent fifteenth-century popes, particularly Sixtus IV, and a number of cardinals followed Nicholas's lead, and in consequence a dozen station churches received some repair, while major reconstruction was accomplished at several more, including S. Marco, S. Pietro in Vincoli, and S. Lorenzo in Damaso.[125]

The tradition of the Roman "stations" gained renewed attention, too, in the pilgrim guides to the city, which included Albertini's *De Urbis stationibus et reliquis*. In the same spirit, the humanist and antiquarian Pomponio Leto wrote a Latin poem describing the succession of Lenten "stations" according to the Roman missal.[126]

Occasionally later fifteenth-century popes actually attended station masses at the designated station church, as Alexander VI did the second Wednesday in Lent 1493, when he went in formal procession to S. Maria Maggiore.[127] Nonetheless, the celebration of the Roman stations, stipulated in Petrus Burgensis's newly issued Ceremonial, normally was honored in the breach. In fact, a fragmentary diary, probably also the work of Burgensis, which covers ceremonial events for the years 1451–53, indicates that the station masses were celebrated in the choir of St. Peter's basilica or else in the chapel (*capella magna*) constructed in the Vatican Palace by Nicholas III in the thirteenth century.[128] The latter represented the practice that had evolved at Avignon, where many of the papacy's ceremonial functions came to be performed in the huge *capella palatina* constructed in the papal palace under Clement VI.

This more courtly aspect of papal liturgy eventually triumphed under the Renaissance papacy as well, and this was what Patrizi's and Burchard's Ceremonial codified. Indeed, the requirement for a more suitable chapel in the papal palace for the Mass *coram papa* celebrated during the Sundays of Advent and Lent led Sixtus IV to build the Sistine Chapel. Another liturgical development contributed further to the courtly demeanor of papal ceremonials: the popes no longer preached. Instead, sermons for Advent and Lent were delivered by members of the mendicant orders (by Sixtus IV's time according to a prescribed regular succession), and for the ten other occasions of the liturgical year in which solemnities entailed sermons, the Master of the Sacred Palace, the Dominican who served as the pope's official theologian, selected the preachers.[129]

In other ways, the papal liturgy of the later fifteenth century acquired an ever more courtly character. Preliminary events to the papal Mass, such as the vesting of the pope and the obedience sworn by the cardinals, became more prolonged and elaborate, the center themselves of spectacle.[130] At the same time the convening of Consistories, the sending of legates *a latere*, and the reception of kings, princes, and foreign envoys—testimonies to the regal rather than the priestly powers of the pope—assumed greater ceremonial importance.[131]

One such political ceremony accruing added splendor during the Renaissance was the Neapolitan ambassador's yearly presentation to the pope on the Feast of Sts. Peter and Paul (29 June) of white horses, the annual tribute that signified the feudal allegiance of the Kingdom of Naples to the Roman pontiffs. The gift of the white horse, a symbolic act traced back to Constantine's Donation to Pope Sylvester I, embodied, from the papal point of view, the proper relationship of secular princes to the papacy.[132]

Another annual rite, prompted often by political motivations, was the papal bestowal on a chosen secular ruler of the Golden Rose. The Rose—actually a spray of roses made of gold and embellished with diamonds and sapphires—was ceremonially presented each year on the fourth Sunday in Lent.[133] In 1500, Alexander VI accorded the Golden Rose to his son, Cesare Borgia, in recognition of his recent conquest of Imola and Forlì,[134] while in 1519 Leo X granted the Golden Rose to Frederick the Wise, the Elector of Saxony, in hopes of influencing his involvement in the Lutheran controversy and in the impending imperial election in Germany.[135]

Non-observance of the Roman Stations, combined with the more regal nature of papal ceremonial, meant that annual liturgical processions were reduced in number, but those that remained, such as the Feast of Corpus Christi, became more spectacular. The same development can be seen in the celebration of the Feast of St. Mark (25 April). On this occasion, the pope, cardinals, and Curial clergy marched in procession from St. Peter's to the church of S. Marco, where after Mass the clergy of the city of Rome joined them in a further procession. Later the pope was treated to a banquet at the adjoining Palazzo di S. Marco, hosted by the resident Venetian cardinal. In 1504 Julius II witnessed at this event a dramatic spectacle staged in his honor, "neither tragedy nor comedy," reports Burchard, "but a kind of invention in praise of the pope and his glory, in which a boy, six years old or so, was Mercury."[136]

Associated also with this feast day was Pasquino, the battered remnant of a classical statue thought to represent Hercules, but now believed to depict Menelaus with the body of Patroclus, or Ajax with the body of Achilles. Discovered in 1501 during the course of renovations to Cardinal Oliviero Carafa's palace located near Piazza Navona, the cardinal ordered it placed on a pedestal by the palace, next to a spot where the clergy of S. Lorenzo in Damaso erected a portable altar for processions connected with the Festa di S. Marco. The custom quickly developed of dressing the statue with costumes alluding to contemporary events. In 1510 it assumed the guise of Hercules striking off the Hydra's head—an allusion to Julius II's successful War of the League of Cambrai against Venice. In 1512 Pasquino appeared as Mars, again in reference to Julius's martial exploits, while in 1513 the statue, dressed as Apollo, acclaimed the newly elected Leo X. Anonymous epigrams and poems, known as *pasquinate*, also came to be affixed to the statue or to the adjoining wall. Barbed or satirical in nature, they frequently targeted the pope and papal policies as the object of their invective.[137] Thus a day on which the ceremonial splendor of the Roman clergy appeared conspicuously in Roman streets became also a day in which papal panoply received a popular riposte.

Christian ritual as political spectacle was not, of course, unique to Rome during the Renaissance period. The elaborate festivities by which Florentines celebrated the Feast of John the Baptist, their patron saint, or the Ascension Day "wedding" of Venice and sea functioned as ritualized expressions of political power. Florence's Epiphany Festa de' Magi provided a suitable outlet for the Medici to appear in regal splendor,[138] as similarly the Venetian Scuole Grandi assumed a central role in that city's commemoration of Corpus Christi. In both cities, too, crises, whether natural or political—though both often were regarded as divinely ordained—generated intercessory processions. Richard Trexler has shown, for instance, how the icon of the Virgin kept at Impruneta served as a rain deity for Renaissance Florentines.[139]

Yet, other responses to the realities of the Renaissance world developed in both cities. At the same time that Gregorio Dati was extolling the splendor of Florence's festival in honor of the Baptist, he also participated in the *pratiche*, the political deliberations which Gene Brucker has shown became increasingly sophisticated in their political and historical analysis of Florentine policies.[140] In Venice, too, impulses towards ceremonial display on the part of the Scuole Grandi were checked by the rival demands that their funds be expended instead on the practical problem of poor relief.[141]

Pageantry and ritual seem, in the final analysis, more fundamental to Rome than to other Italian cities. This stems in part from the economic underdevelopment of both the city and the region, which, as we have seen, bordered on semi-colonial dependency, and on the weakness of secular political life. Indeed one of the successes of the Renaissance papacy was the suppression of republican sentiments, and the effective emasculation of Roman city government as a rival to papal power.[142] But the conspicuousness of the ceremonial in Roman life is explained also by its function as the capital of Christendom, and by the stress the Roman humanists increasingly placed on its mythic past and supernal destiny. In certain ritual activities, in fact, Roman topography seemed to function as a microcosmic arena of the geo-political world of Latin Christendom as a whole, and ceremonial activity served to confirm or even induce the desired course of events.

Two examples, one celebrating victory, the other propitiatory in the face of catastrophe, can serve to elucidate this. When news of the Spanish conquest of the Kingdom of Granada reached Rome in early February 1492, the great bell on the Campidoglio pealed in jubilation, bonfires were lit, and a papal procession made its way from the Vatican to S. Giacomo degli Spagnoli, the recently constructed Spanish national church. Following Mass there, a sermon praising God for the victory, and the singing of the *Te Deum*, a bullfight (in which five bulls were killed) was held by the Spanish Cardinal, Rodrigo Borgia, in an arena built in the courtyard of his palace. Two weeks later, in connection with the Roman Carnival, more bullfights and games took place in Piazza Navona, including a mock battle depicting the fall of Granada. A triumphal car drawn by four white horses then circled the piazza carrying representations of the King and Queen of Spain and the Moorish king in chains at their feet. Later Cardinal Raffaele Riario presented at his palace a dramatic spectacle, composed in Latin by the papal secretary Carlo Berardi, of the fall of Granada.[143]

The Ottoman Sultan Selim's conquests of Syria and Egypt in 1516–17 brought a different response. Leo X launched a variety of initiatives to bring peace to Europe and to take war to the Turks, culminating in his publication of a crusade bull in early March 1518. On three successive days supplicatory processions then traversed Rome: from Sant'Agostino to S. Maria in Aracoeli, from S. Lorenzo in Damaso to S. Maria del Popolo, and from St. Peter's to S. Maria sopra Minerva. Leo himself walked this last route barefoot, with cardinals, prelates, and monks accompanying him in like manner. The icon of Christ from the Sancta Sanctorum, the image of the Virgin from S. Maria Maggiore, the head of John the Baptist, and other sacred relics joined the marchers, and all implored God to free Christendom from the Ottoman threat. Following Mass at the Minerva, the papal secretary Jacopo Sadoleto, famed for his eloquence, preached the necessity of holy war. Crowd noise made much of his speech inaudible, but the gist of his remarks—according to Francesco Novello, a contemporary Roman and one of the *Conservatori*, who includes these actions as among the most noteworthy events of Leo's pontificate in his *Compendium vitae Leonis Papae X*—was that a crusade was needed "to drive the barbarians from the neck of Italy."[144] No Christian crusade ensued, but Selim's unexpected early death in 1520 was attributed by at least one sixteenth-century observer, the Roman antiquarian and papal biographer Onofrio Panvinio (1529–68), to the efficacy of these ritual supplications.[145]

Roman responses to the fall of Granada and to Ottoman conquests in the Levant—to which many other examples could be added, such as the three days of procession through the Borgo Leonino ordered by Sixtus IV when news of Mehmed the Conqueror's death reached Rome at the end of May 1481,[146] or the three-day festivity climaxed by the Feast of St. Thomas, the Apostle to India (21 December), arranged by Julius II in 1507 to acclaim a series of Portuguese victories in the Indian Ocean[147] —made of the Eternal City's terrain the sacral space in which humanly initiated ritual action could celebrate (or alternatively hope to propitiate) God's intentions for the *respublica Christiana*.

A similar traversing of Rome's topography as a ritualized means of proclaiming political and spiritual purpose was central to papal coronation rites. With the conclusion of the actual consecration ceremony in St. Peter's, the newly crowned pope marched in procession to St. John Lateran, the cathedral church of Rome. This ceremonial passage was known, significantly, as the *possesso* (literally, taking "possession"). Originating in the ninth century, the *possesso* had been gradually embellished in the course of the Middle Ages, reaching high points of pomp and splendor in the coronations of Innocent III and Boniface VIII.[148] Even during the Great Schism the *possesso* continued to be performed by the popes in Rome, but from Nicholas V on, and particularly in the coronations of Alexander VI and Leo X, it became ever more elaborate in its pageantry, and more purposeful in articulating the ideals, expectations, and intentions of individual popes.

The route of the *possesso*, known as the Via Sacra or Via Papalis, went from Piazza S. Pietro to Castel Sant' Angelo, then crossed Ponte Sant'Angelo to Monte Giordano, passed close to the southern end of Piazza Navona, proceeded to the church of S. Marco, traversed the Capitoline Hill, threaded through the Roman Forum, marched past the Arch of Constantine and the Colosseum, then ran uphill past S. Clemente and S. Quattro Coronati to the Lateran. The cortege, the exact composition of which was specified in the Ceremonial books, acquired added splendor in the course of the fifteenth century. Papal servants, the captains of the *rioni* of Rome each with the flag of his district, representatives of the Knights of St. John and other military orders, the Roman barons, papal secretaries, the papal singers, non-Roman clergy, abbots from the city's monasteries, the cardinals, and the heads of the various papal tribunals and other members of the Curia—all had their designated places in the hierarchically arranged order of procession. Near the front the consecrated host was carried on a white horse surmounted by a baldacchino. The pope, coming near the end, also was borne on a white horse, and his presence, too, was dignified by a baldacchino. The sacramental real presence of the Body of Christ and the person of the Vicar of Christ thus were accorded equal treatment and marked the focal points of the procession. In addition, the colorful garb of men and horses, the fluttering standards, the glittering gold of the processional cross and thuribles, and the dazzling jewels of the papal triple tiara—all contributed to the overall sense of splendor.[149]

At several points on the ceremonial route to the Lateran, ritualized acts, also specified in the Ceremonials, occurred. The first was the meeting of the pope with the leaders of Rome's Jewish community at Monte Giordano (though Burchard states that to avoid possible anti-Jewish riots this took place within the confines of Castel Sant'Angelo). The Jewish leaders offered to the pope the Torah, asking him to adore it, and to approve and confirm it. The pope, holding the Hebrew text, responded that he commended the Law, but condemned the Jews' understanding and observance of it on the grounds of their refusal to recognize in Jesus Christ the Savior promised by the prophets. Then he allowed the Torah to fall to the ground.[150]

This curious rite seems to have served several functions. First, it comprised a formal recognition by the papacy of the Roman Jewish community, which existed in the ghetto located in an area bounded by the Tiber and the Via delle Botteghe Oscure. This recognition seems to have been understood as a basic legal agreement, extending papal protection to the community. Second, in a religious sense, the pope as Vicar of Christ in condemning the Jewish Torah asserted in a dramatic way the supplanting of the old dispensation by the new. Third, as the Florentine humanist Jacopo Angeli da Scarperia pointed out to the Byzantine classicist Manuel Chrysoloras in a letter describing the *possesso* of Gregory XII (1405), ancient Roman custom obliged subject peoples to submit to a newly chosen Emperor by commending themselves to his protection and by presenting to him their law. If, Angeli remarks, such peoples avoided the imperial presence, the Emperor might not wish to spare them, but on the account of the law, which the Caesars rarely scorned, he might be inclined to compassion.[151] In performing a similar act, the popes thereby emulated a Roman precedent for imperial government.

At Monte Giordano also, and at three other designated spots en route to the Lateran, including the church of S. Marco, an official of the papal household tossed coins to the crowd. Jacopo da Scarperia again likened this to acts of the ancient Roman Emperors, and noted that during his stay in Constantinople he had seen the Byzantine Emperor do the same thing.[152] When Julius II celebrated a triumph in Bologna in 1506 following papal conquest of the city, he arranged, prompted by the same imperial precedent, for the tossing of gold and silver coins to the throngs lining the processional route. Indeed, the coins were newly minted for the occasion and contained an appropriate legend.[153] Not to be outdone, Leo X, when he made his ceremonial *entrata* into his native Florence in 1515, ordered the exact same monetary amount (3000 ducats) of coins to be flung to the Florentines as Julius had expended in Bologna.[154]

Once the pope reached the Lateran basilica, he sat in an ancient marble seat in the portico of the church known as the *sedes stercoraria*. It was thus called, according to the Ceremonial books, inasmuch as when the cardinals honorably lifted him from it these words could truly be said: "he lifts up a poor man from the dust, and a pauper from dung, so that he may sit with princes and possess the throne of glory." Then, standing next to the *sedes stercoraria*, the pope threw three fistfuls of coins to the crowd, saying "gold and silver are not mine; what I have I give to you."[155]

Inside the Lateran complex, the pope was conducted to another

ancient seat, a double one made of porphyry. Sitting in the right side, the
new pontiff received from the Prior of the Lateran a rod "as a sign of rule
and correction," and the keys to the Lateran basilica and palace "signify-
ing the power of closing and opening, binding and absolving." The pope
then shifted to the other seat, where a girdle of red silk with an attached
purple purse containing precious stones was placed around him. The
Lateran clergy then kissed his feet, and the pope again threw coins to the
crowd, saying "he distributed, he gave to the poor, his justice will abide
forever and ever." Afterwards the pope went into the Sancta Sanctorum
to pray, and then followed a banquet. At length the pontiff returned, in
the evening, to the Vatican.

These ritual elements of the *possesso*—meeting the Jewish leadership, tossing coins, the Lateran formalities—were traditional ones dating back to the Middle Ages, though the detailed account Burchard
provides indicates their continuing significance for the Renaissance papacy. Moreover, a number of the ceremonial actions were more closely
tied to Roman imperial precedent, following the general pattern of Roman Renaissance culture. With the later Renaissance popes, however,
especially Leo X,[156] the procession itself, rather than specific rites, increasingly occupied center stage. Sumptuous costumes bedazzled observers, and the temporary triumphal arches lining the Via Papalis became
ever more elaborate.

Leo X was elected pope on 11 March 1513 and crowned eight days
later, but his *possesso* was delayed until 11 April, partly to avoid conflict
with the ceremonies of Holy Week, but also to allow ampler time to be
devoted to preparations. The date chosen was, significantly, the Feast of
St. Leo (Pope Leo I), the Medici pontiff's great fifth-century namesake,
but it also happened to coincide with the anniversary of Leo's capture the
previous year at the Battle of Ravenna, when his fortunes had fallen to
their nadir. The eleventh day of the month was auspicious for Leo: one of
the triumphal arches, in fact, showed eight scenes from his life with an
explanatory inscription noting that all the most decisive events, including
his birth, the day he was named a cardinal, his forced departure from
Florentine territory during Charles VIII's invasion, his capture at Ravenna, his election as pope, and now his *possesso*, had all occurred on that
day.

As for the costumes, perhaps the most splendidly dressed members
of the papal retinue were the musicians—fittingly so, since Leo proved to
be a great musical patron. Dressed in Leo's livery of white, green, and red
velvet, they sported gold-lace embroidery on their chests, embellished by
a diamond, and white, green, and red feathers with the word SEMPER (a
well-known Medici motto dating back to the time of Cosimo *Pater Patriae*).
On their backs appeared a yoke with the word SVAVE, an allusion to the
impresa Leo had chosen as cardinal, with its echo of the Gospel phrase:

"*Jugum meum suave est, et onus meum leve*" (My yoke is easy, and my burden is light. Matthew 11:30).[157]

Diamonds and golden balls (*palle*) were familiar Medici devices, and both appeared in profusion along the route to the Lateran. Lions also abounded on the triumphal arches, suggestive not only of Leo's name and of regal qualities, but more particularly of the messianic sense of Revelation 5:5: "*Ecce vicit Leo de tribu Juda, radix David*" (Behold the lion from the tribe of Judah, the scion of David).

Various personages from both sacred and secular history appeared on the arches, too, as exemplars for Leo's pontificate. These included Aaron (with the admonition that scrupulous attention to the liturgical cult would restore religion) and Moses (constant adherence to divine will would bring defeat to the enemies of Christ), as well as Numa and Antoninus Pius (identified as Romans who had spared the shedding of blood and thereby had earned the "trophy" of peace).

Numerous classical gods and goddesses likewise made their appearance, especially Apollo, a reference to the hoped-for patronage of letters and the arts under Leo. Similarly, a large frieze on the arch sponsored by Agostino Chigi bore the inscription: "Venus had her time [referring to the amorous proclivities of Pope Alexander VI]; Mars had his time [an allusion to Julius II's wars]; now Pallas Athena has her time." Another arch showed Astraea, the goddess of justice and the last deity to leave earth at the end of the Golden Age, holding a sword in her right hand and a ball in her left; the inscription stated: "At length I have returned from heaven." Paired with this was a figure of Christ with the keys in hand and the words "I give to you the kingdom of heaven and earth." Hailed in other arches as the sustainer of virtues and eradicator of vices, Leo here was seen as restoring divine justice to a troubled world. Other inscriptions heralded a reign of peace in which the Golden Age would return, and with all the arts, both mechanical and intellectual, restored to their proper prominence in human society, "Rome will be golden."

Repeatedly, the theme recurs of a new time breaking in, of the celestial world manifesting itself on earth through the actions and policies of "*Leo X Pontifex Optimus de Coelo*." One arch proclaimed him as "the new star of longed-for tranquillity;" on another painted display he was depicted in heaven surrounded by palm branches, with Sts. Peter and Paul at his right hand while on his left an angel sounded a trumpet from which a banner with the papal arms unfurled. Below appeared a rainbow (the goddess Iris) and beneath it mountains, streams, and plains, luxuriant foliage, and men and women, with the inscription: "The world is opened, and the King of Glory comes forth."

Pageantry in Leo's *possesso*, prepared by Leo himself in collaboration with Paris de Grassis,[158] functioned on many levels. Ancient rites, solemnly performed, offered living testimony to the continuity of papal sanctity and to the sacredness of Rome, which served as stage and backdrop to their enactment. At the same time, the dazzling splendor of the procession and decorations affirmed the wealth and power of the new pontiff, and in their poetic allusions and elaborate artistic conceits revealed the extraordinary creative talents Renaissance Rome could call upon. Beyond this beckoned the fulfillment of time, seemingly imminent in the triumphal promise of Leo *de tribu Juda*.

Rome, then, provided the stage upon which the newly elected pontiffs ritually established the fundamental nature of their authority. In a similar way, the city functioned as an arena in which pent-up demands for sport, violence, and play could find a stylized and controllable outlet. During the days before Ash Wednesday, the city was given over to the licensed games and frivolities of Carnival.

Medieval Rome had celebrated these last days of feasting before the privations of Lent with tournaments, hunts, and races at Monte Testaccio, the hill outside Porta S. Paolo formed from the sherds of broken amphorae—the refuse from the centuries of alimentary supply to the capital.[159] Paul II transformed the Roman Carnival by shifting most of the races to the Via del Corso, where he could conveniently view their conclusion from his Palazzo di S. Marco, by adding to their number, and by introducing masquerades, allegorical floats, and elaborate public banquets.[160] A regular schedule of races and other festivities came to be established, lasting ten days in all. Among these were the races of the Jews, young men, old men, donkeys, buffalo, and horses—held as much to provide opportunities for betting as for the competition.

Some events continued at Testaccio, including the attaching of pigs and bulls to carts, then launching them down the hill. At the bottom the hurtling carts smashed to pieces and the waiting mob slaughtered the animals—a practice preserving, it seems, an echo of the medieval ritual sacrifice there of a bear, bullocks, and a cock, symbols of demonic temptations and fleshly urges to be subdued in the weeks before Christ's Resurrection. As in other aspects of Roman popular culture, humanists wondered if these practices could be traced back to antiquity. Flavio Biondo mentions in *Roma instaurata* that while watching the bull sports at Testaccio, the Roman lawyer Lelio della Valle asked him if Varro had recorded the ancient Romans holding the same spectacle. Now, Biondo states, he is able to answer that they did hold so-called *ludi taurii* in the last days of February, but that in fact these were the *equiria*, the horse races held in honor of Mars run in the Campus Martius.[161]

The Renaissance celebration of Carnival incorporated other Roman sites, too. Hunts of bulls took place in Piazza del Campidoglio (and later in Piazza di S. Pietro also); masquerades, tournaments, and processions (the *Festa di Agone*) were staged in Piazza Navona; and, with the shifting of the papal residence permanently to the Vatican, many of the races were run

from Campo de' Fiori across Ponte Sant'Angelo to Piazza S. Pietro, or
were held in the Borgo itself. Alexander VI even added a race of the
Roman whores.

What in the Middle Ages had been essentially an expression of the
Roman populace thus became increasingly in the Renaissance a spectacle
dominated by the papal court. True, the municipal magistrates remained
in charge of the program for Carnival and of its execution, but papal
approval was necessary, and papal funding was provided. The cardinals,
splendidly costumed—several on one occasion masqueraded as Mamelukes, a suggestive inversion of their roles as princes of the Church—also
formed a center of attention. Private theatrical entertainments, lavishly
staged, became more prominent, too. For the Sunday evening (6 March)
of Carnival in 1519, Ariosto's play *I suppositi* was performed in the Vatican
Palace before the pope, the papal court, and the ambassadors. The
scenery, designed by Raphael, showed a perspective scene of Ferrara, and
upon the pontiff's entrance the torches by the stage spelled out LEO X
PONTIFEX MAXIMUS.[162]

The pageantry of procession in the *Festa di Agone* similarly acquired
added magnificence, and a changing character. In the fifteenth century,
the floats depicted Olympian deities or recreated such spectacles as the
triumph of Vespasian and Titus. Under Julius and Leo processions more
pointedly lauded papal virtues and accomplishments. The *Festa di Agone*
of 1513, held in the waning months of Julius's life, served in fact as an
apotheosis of his pontificate. The parade, which proceeded along the new
Via Giulia in following the route from Piazza del Campidoglio to Piazza
Navona, included the governor of the city, the *Conservatori*, the *Caporioni*,
and other municipal magistrates and officials, followed then by members
of various Roman guilds, each of which sponsored a *carro trionfale*.
Among these was one showing a map of Italy with mountains, cities, and
regions, a palm tree above it, and the explanatory caption, "Italy liberated." Another bore an obelisk with inscriptions in Latin, Greek, Hebrew,
and "Egyptian hieroglyphs" proclaiming "Julius II, liberator of Italy and
expeller of the schismatics." Both floats alluded to the pope's anti-French
policy, while other *carri*, depicting the Romagna, Bologna, Reggio in
Emilia, Parma, and Piacenza, represented cities and regions recovered by
the papacy since the formation of the anti-French Holy League (1511).
Other allusions to the same theme were a temple of Apollo from which
the god had destroyed giants with his arrows, an angel cutting off the
Hydra's heads with a sword, a mounted St. Ambrose driving out heretics
(the patron saint of Milan was thus to expel the French from that city), and
an oak tree (symbol of the Della Rovere, Julius's family) with the pope and
other members of the Holy League seated in its branches. A large snake
with a flayed Turk in its mouth and the inscription "Moses raised up the
serpent" (a reference to Numbers 21: 7–9) and another float showing

Aaron sacrificing at an altar presented the two Old Testament "types" of religious leadership combined in the person of the pope.[163]

The 1514 *Festa di Agone*, designed by Tommaso "Fedra" Inghirami, who specialized in the production of spectacles for Leo X, was perhaps even more lavish. Eighteen triumphal cars formed the procession, each representing an attribute of Leo's pontificate. "Mildness" showing a docile lion, "Obedience" displaying women with a yoke and a horse, "Prudence" indicated by diamonds and a woman with two faces, and "Justice" depicted by an open hand with *palle* included familiar Medici devices. The other ascriptions were hope, friendship, mirth, liberty, magnanimity, liberality, peace (oxen plowing), magnificence (a triumphal arch), truth (a nude woman covered with a black veil), fortitude, temperance, fortune (a wheel), felicity (a mountain surmounted by a Victory), and finally eternity (two lions drawing a triumphal chariot).[164]

THE ANCIENT CITY

If contemporary Rome functioned as a potent setting for the manipulation of reality by ritualistic or symbolic means, protruding everywhere into that scenographic space was another Rome, the half-buried ruins of the ancient city. Abandoned and overgrown for a millennium, the ruins in one sense formed part of the natural landscape, or served as convenient foundations for medieval construction. Thus the Arch of Septimius Severus in the Forum was abutted by the church of SS. Sergio e Bacco, until its demolition in 1536, and in 1600 a defensive tower still rose from atop the monument.[165]

Other ancient buildings were continually ransacked for building materials or converted by lime-burners into mortar. At the very time, in fact, when Renaissance humanists strove to improve their understanding of the origin and function of the classical buildings, the pace of their destruction accelerated in response to the quickening pulse of Renaissance building activity. In a famous letter to Leo X, probably composed on Raphael's behalf by his friend Castiglione, the artist laments how many monuments and buildings had disappeared even during his own brief stay of less than a dozen years in the city.[166] The Colosseum, in particular, proved too tempting a quarry of travertine blocks for repeated prohibitions against pillaging it to remain in effect. The Ponte Sisto, among other projects, used material from the Colosseum, [167] and even popes, like Pius II, who were sympathetic to the preservation of the classical city licensed the removal of building stone.[168]

Still, no matter how frequently plundered or how often parasitically built into or upon, the ancient ruins proved simply too vast to be ignored. The gigantic scale of imperial Roman buildings contrasted sharply with

3. The ruins of a Roman quadrifront triumphal arch, with bushes, grass, and other foliage growing from the bricks and dislodged marble blocks of its half-destroyed cone-shaped crown. From the *Sketch-book* of Giuliano da Sangallo, containing drawings of ancient monuments, particularly from Lazio and Rome, which the Florentine architect observed during travels 1485–1514. BAV, ms. Barb. lat. 4424, fol. 36ᵛ. (Photo: Biblioteca Apostolica Vaticana)

the medieval village that Rome had become, and their presence provided inescapable reminders to early Renaissance humanists of the feebleness of contemporaries compared to the achievements of the ancients. Yet, at the same time, their destruction also suggested the ultimate futility of relying on human effort alone to stem the ravages of time.[169]

This nostalgic and moralizing mood marks the opening pages of Poggio Bracciolini's De varietate fortunae, begun around 1431 but presented to Nicholas V finally in 1448. As such, it provides a useful touchstone for early Renaissance perceptions of the ancient city. Poggio sets his work toward the end of Martin V's pontificate, when the pope for reasons of health had withdrawn to Tuscolo. Taking advantage of the temporary freedom from public business, he and Antonio Loschi, a colleague in the papal secretariat, had wandered on horseback, exploring the ancient ruins. At length, they ascended the Campidoglio, and dismounted at the Tarpeian Rock, where a grand prospect of the ruined capital lay before their eyes. Anguished by the sight, Loschi remarks that far from golden as Virgil had described the city (Aeneid, VIII, 348) it now was squalid, full of thorns and brambles. No greater evidence of the cruelty of fortune could exist, he argues, than the present condition of Rome, denuded of all beauty, lying prostrate like a giant decaying corpse, unrecognizable to any of its former inhabitants. Magnificent structures, which their builders thought to be beyond the power of fate, had been levelled to their foundations. The Capitoline Hill itself, once head of the Roman Empire and citadel of the whole world, where kings and princes had trembled, where so many emperors had ascended in triumph, adorned with the gifts and spoils of so many peoples, now lay desolate and destroyed. Vines had succeeded to the seats of the senators, and transformed from former gold, all had become a receptacle for filth and refuse.[170]

Nostalgic in its evocation of ancient splendor, and moralizing in its emphasis on the destructive power of fortuna, Poggio's dialogue nevertheless marks a new departure. In it he included detailed descriptions of the ancient temples, baths, triumphal arches, pyramids, theaters, amphitheaters, palaces, gates, and other classical monuments. Importantly, too, he abandoned the magical and fabulous outlook of the medieval Mirabilia, instead regarding the ruins as vestiges of a human civilization, long-vanished but discoverable through intellectual inquiry. To this end, he incorporated into his work results from two lines of investigation. The first involved a more careful probing of neglected classical texts. One such was De aquis Urbis Romae of Frontinus, who had charge of the city's water-supply under Nerva (A.D. 97). Recently, Poggio states, he had found a manuscript of Frontinus's work in the monastery at Montecassino, and from it he had learned the names, locations, and extensive nature of the ancient aqueduct system.[171]

Poggio's second new method made use of epigraphic evidence. He had begun to compile a volume of inscriptions copied from ancient monuments, he mentions in passing, and he expresses surprise that Petrarch could subscribe to the popular error that the pyramid by the Porta Ostiense was the tomb of Remus, when the inscription on it showed it belonged to Cestius.[172]

Through such diligence, Poggio pioneered the way to reconstruct in historically accurate terms the topographical reality of the ancient city. Decades of residence in the Eternal City as papal secretary made these initiatives possible, and frequent sojourns to nearby hill-towns enabled exploration also of the surrounding region. A two-weeks' stay in the Alban Hills in September 1430, while the pope kept summer retreat at Grottaferrata, for instance, allowed Poggio to explore the ancient villas in the vicinity of Tusculum and to conjecture which might have been Cicero's.[173] Two years earlier he had braved the mid-day September heat to climb a vine-covered gate tower at Ferentino to read the nearly obliterated ancient lettering—an exploit made easier, he admits, by the attentive stares of two attractive adolescent girls.[174]

When Eugenius IV returned to Rome in 1443, after the lapse of nearly a decade, Poggio's fellow Apostolic Secretary, Flavio Biondo, also took up permanent residence in the city, and became the most impassioned student of ancient Rome in the middle decades of the century. Moreover, for him the ruins of Rome represented not the poignant remnants of a destroyed civilization but rather invaluable sources for repristinating ancient Roman culture and values. He expressed this point of view in his *Roma instaurata*, begun in 1444 and presented to Eugenius IV in 1446. What impelled him to compile this topographical description of the ancient city, he writes in the preface, was his realization that not just the ignorant multitude but also the cultivators of learning defiled and defamed the extant remains of classical buildings with false and barbarian appellations. The resultant damage had serious consequences, he charged, for hidden in the structures themselves was that Rome which was "the progenitor of genius, student of virtues, model of renown, acme of praise and glory, and seedbed of good things for the whole world."[175]

Archeology, then, provided the key to the humanistic enterprise of recovering the wisdom of ancient Rome, and critical to archeological research was correct identification and classification of the ancient buildings. What follows in the body of Biondo's work is a topically organized account of the gates, obelisks, baths, theaters, amphitheaters, circuses, temples, columns, and other monuments, in which his aim was not merely to describe and identify them but also to explain their function and purpose. Thus in discussing theaters, Biondo includes both the architecture of the buildings and the basic elements of classical performance of tragedy, comedy, and pantomime.

Besides studying the ruins themselves, Biondo also carefully combed classical texts for clues to Roman topography. Livy's history, Pliny the Elder's letters, and Varro's *De lingua latina* were obvious sources, and he studied them intensively, but he also scrutinized newly discovered manuscripts of Tacitus and Frontinus, and of the "regionaries," topographical descriptions of the city's regions compiled in Constantine's era. Biondo found an illustrated codex of such a work during a visit to Montecassino, and his list of city gates follows closely the compendium of Festus Pompcius, an illustrated manuscript of which the humanist Pietro Donato discovered at Speyer in 1436.[176]

Biondo did not actually engage in any archeological digs—no Renaissance archeologist did—but he stayed alert to evidence which might accidentally be unearthed. Such a chance discovery enabled him to pinpoint the location of the atrium of Pompey's theater, where from Suetonius and Ovid he had learned that Julius Caesar had been assassinated. A Roman lawyer, deepening his wine cellar in the vicinity of the church of S. Lorenzo in Damaso uncovered in the course of digging a large dressed-stone block with cubit-high letters reading *"Genius theatri Pompeiani."*[177]

In methodology and use of textual sources Biondo established a tradition that lasted well into the sixteenth century, and the archeological, antiquarian, and topographical exploration of ancient Rome stimulated by his and Poggio's work was sustained over the next eighty years by a succession of Roman humanists. Among the major studies in this vein there could be singled out Pomponio Leto's revisions, emendations, and interpolations to the *Notitia regionum Urbis*, the distillation of material gathered while guiding humanistic tourists through the ancient ruins over the course of the last third of the fifteenth century; the *De Urbe Roma*, compiled shortly after 1495 by Bernardo Rucellai, son of the 1450 pilgrim, Giovanni; and Andrea Fulvio's massive compendium *Antiquitates Urbis*, which appeared in the spring of 1527, only a few weeks before the Sack.[178]

More striking, though, than any single work of scholarship is the persistent level of scholarly activity, and the zealous, and often ingenious, exploitation of sources. Humanists followed up Poggio's interest in inscriptions, for example, by systematically compiling sylloges of classical, and later also paleo-Christian, inscriptions from Roman buildings. Deciphering the meaning of these much-abbreviated and often elliptical texts offered an enjoyable intellectual pastime for Roman humanists, but as classical epigraphy emerged as a separate branch of scholarship its serious historical, linguistic, and literary significance became apparent.[179] This taste for classical Latin lettering carried over, too, into manuscript production, where, for instance, inscribed triumphal arches appeared as favorite motifs for title pages among the Roman miniaturists.[180] Similarly,

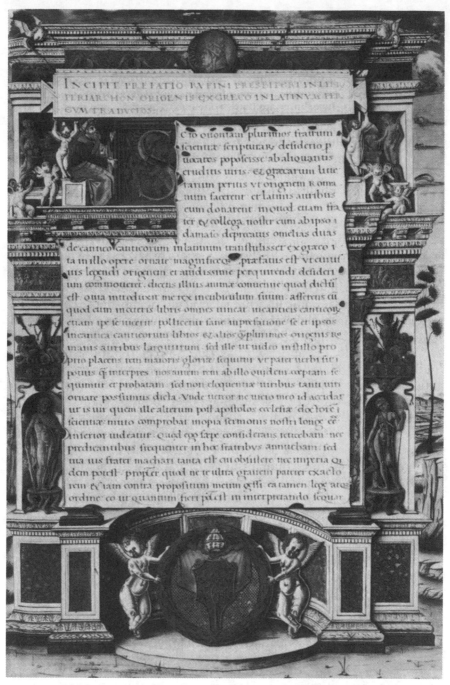

4. Frontispiece of Rufinus's Latin translation of Origen's *Peri Archon*, BAV, ms. Vat. lat. 214, fol. 1ʳ, painted by Giorgio Culinović, called Lo Schiavone. This manuscript was written and decorated for Sixtus IV c. 1474–80. The triumphal arch architecture, the antique moldings, the sculptural embellishment, and the classical lettering typify the classicizing taste in Roman miniatures of the period. Below appear the triple tiara, crossed keys, and oak tree and acorns of the Della Rovere pontiff's papal shield, while above, the bust portrait of Sixtus IV in the medallion reproduces the obverse of Sixtus's coronation medal. (Photo: Biblioteca Apostolica Vaticana)

classicizing inscriptions proliferated on the tombs of Renaissance prelates buried in Rome's churches. They also remain conspicuous on the walls of the Sistine Chapel and in the entrance to the Cortile del Belvedere.[181]

Collecting ancient statues, bronzes, coins, medals, cameos, and gems became a passion, too, of the Roman humanists, and even more of their wealthy patrons. Paul II proved to be a notable early collector, but by the early sixteenth century no cultured cardinal or curialist could neglect decorating the garden of his villa with ancient statuary and his study with other suitable antiquities.[182] On one level, such collecting represents fashionable taste, but on another it indicates a passionate attachment to these objects as manifestations of classical culture; and to those with antiquarian acumen, they became a source of knowledge as well as fascination. Coins, for instance, with their portraits of emperors, served as aides in identifying sculpture, and by early sixteenth century numismatics, like epigraphy, had emerged as a scholarly discipline. Like classical lettering, coins also were adopted as decorative motifs in works of art, and the popes issued new coins and commemorative medals imitative of ancient Roman practice.[183]

The research into ancient weights and measures, undertaken by Angelo Colocci, shows how attentive study of disparate material contributed to a factual understanding of ancient Roman life. Colocci, a humanist and curialist, whose *vigna* on the Quirinal became a favorite gathering place for Roman humanists early in the sixteenth century, purchased from an antiquarian an ancient bronze sphere marked with letters, which he eventually came to realize was a Roman weight. Later, examining a tomb of an ancient architect near the aqueduct of the Aqua Virgo, he discovered depicted among various architectural instruments the measure of a Roman "foot." Afterwards, he also found the same measurement on a column near the Lateran and on a block built into the façade of a shop in the Jewish ghetto.[184]

Archeological and antiquarian research formed, then, one main tendency in the humanists' rediscovery of the ancient capital. Measurement, surveying, and architectural and engineering investigations constituted another. Donatello and Brunelleschi, according to Brunelleschi's biographer, Antonio di Tuccio Manetti, made measurements and scaled drawings of ancient Roman buildings and examined engineering details of their construction during visits to the Eternal City early in the fifteenth century.[185] The humanist Ciriaco d'Ancona also made drawings and measurements of Roman buildings while visiting the city in the 1420s and again in 1433, when he acted as guide to the antiquities for the Holy Roman Emperor Sigismund. Rome thus was added to the other ancient sites Ciriaco entered into his sketchbook, the compilation of years of travel throughout the Mediterranean.[186]

More systematic and searching were the investigations of the poly-

math Leon Battista Alberti. Like Biondo and Poggio, Alberti belonged to
the papal secretariat, and like them he came with the Curia to Rome in
1443. Alberti's improved grasp of the purpose and design of Rome's
classical buildings owed such to his study of Vitruvius's *De architectura*, the
text of which Poggio had found during his travels to Switzerland in 1414.
Though not entirely unknown to the Middle Ages, Vitruvius's account of
the architectural and engineering enterprises of the Augustan Age, filled
as it is with technical matters and obscure terminology, proved fully
comprehensible only to one, like Alberti, who actually practiced
architecture and who could study the monuments existing in Rome.
Moreover, like Biondo, Alberti aimed not just at understanding ancient
Rome but also at restoring it. The result was his *De re aedificatoria*, presented to Nicholas V in 1452. Here he presented the "rules" of classical
construction, the modular system of Roman architecture, and a coherent
theory of aesthetics. These, to Alberti's mind, constituted the basis upon
which Roman architecture in theory and practice could be renewed.[187]

In this approach to the ruins of ancient Roman buildings as sources
both of aesthetic values and of engineering concepts for use in contemporary construction, Alberti had followers in Bramante and in other
papal architects of the early sixteenth century. Among these was Giuliano
da Sangallo, who in 1513 made detailed measurements of the
Colosseum.[188]

As an engineer, Alberti's skills involved him in another mid-
fifteenth-century project. Cardinal Prospero Colonna employed him to
raise the large state barges dating from imperial Roman times that lay
submerged in Lake Nemi in the Alban Hills. Stringing a row of empty
barrels to form a sort of bridge from which he suspended windlasses,
Alberti succeeded in raising the hull of one of the barges high enough for
its prow to be revealed and thus its nature ascertained. To extract it,
however, proved beyond his means.[189]

A more successful application of technology to archeology was the
astrolabe-like surveying disk that Alberti used to determine the polar
coordinates of ancient monuments as sighted from the Campidoglio. The
measurements, published in his *Descriptio Urbis Romae* of the 1440s, enabled the placement of the walls, bridges, aqueducts, and other ancient
monuments in their correct corresponding relationship to one another.
For the first time a comprehensive and coherent grasp of the horizontal
dimensions of the city became possible. Alberti's mapping work drew
upon the revival of the cartographical and geographical interests of
Ptolemy, whose *Geography* Manuel Chrysoloras and Jacopo da Scarperia
translated from Greek into Latin in the early fifteenth century. The
precision of Alberti's surveyed coordinates and the revived Ptolemaic
notion of a map as a proportioned depiction of actual surface measurements lay behind the naturalistic and perspective views of Rome that

began to appear in the later fifteenth century. Instead of the elliptical or circular views of the city, still adopted, for instance, by Taddeo di Bartolo for the image of Rome in the Palazzo Comunale in Siena in 1413–14, post–1450 plan-views, such as the panoramic archeological view made by Alessandro Strozzi, accurately portrayed the perimeter of the Aurelian Walls and showed the placement of monuments in correct perspective disposition, both within and outside the walls.[190]

Nevertheless, topographical accuracy did not yet exist as an end in itself. Strozzi's plan-view, in fact, left out many features of the Roman cityscape. Rather such "mappings" aimed at presenting an imposing visual representation of the city, rendered in up-to-date artistic terms, which allowed places of historical and spiritual significance to be readily identified.[191] Indeed, as late as Marco Fabio Calvo's *Antiquae Urbis Romae cum regionibus simulachrum* (1527)—the end result of Raphael's plan to produce a topographic map of ancient Rome, a project interrupted by the artist's death—schematic diagrams represented the city's appearance during various epochs. Romulus's Rome thus took the form of a quadrilateral enclosing four ovoid hills, Augustus's city became a circle divided into sixteen segments, each with a single monument, and Rome at the time of Pliny the Elder also assumed a circular shape, with thirty-two gates identified, six bridges over the Tiber indicated, and a couple dozen of the major monuments outlined.[192]

Not until 1551 did the first true ichnographic map (vertical projection showing ground plan of buildings) appear. The person responsible was Leonardo Bufalini (d. 1552), a military engineer and surveyor, who used the skills of his profession to measure precisely and to depict with fidelity the topographical features of the city. Only with Bufalini's work did concern for geographical precision supplant the encomiastic and didactic intentions of earlier views.[193]

By the early sixteenth century, three generations of humanists, artists, and architects—by clambering over the ruins, measuring their dimensions, drawing their main features, studying the relevant texts, and using their accumulated knowledge in an attempt to imaginatively recreate the ancient city—had produced a vastly more accurate understanding of Rome's classical buildings and monuments. The baths, for instance, were recognized for what they were, and not regarded as ruins of palaces (the view of the *Mirabilia*). Similarly, the "Septizonium" on the Palatine, still in the early fifteenth century looked upon as the seat of the seven sciences or a temple of the sun and the moon (according to the *Mirabilia*), came to be identified correctly as the palace of Septimius Severus.[194] The Colosseum, believed by many in the Middle Ages to be a temple of the sun, now was rightly perceived as an amphitheater, and Biondo had provided lengthy discussions of the gladiatorial games held there.[195] The bronze equestrian statue at the Lateran (moved in the 1530s to the

5. View of Rome, by Pietro del Massaio. Miniature in a manuscript of Jacopo da Scarperia's Latin translation of Ptolemy's *Cosmographia*, produced for the humanist Niccolò Perotti in 1469. Ms. BAV, Vat. lat. 5699, fol. 127ʳ. Massaio's sketch-plan reveals some interest in providing topographical accuracy, though for the most part only the major monuments appear, such as the Colosseum, the Campidoglio, and the Pantheon. The Borgo Leonino, at the right, is presented in greater detail, including Castel Sant'Angelo, the Leonine Wall, and Old St. Peter's. (Photo: Biblioteca Apostolica Vaticana)

Campidoglio), which medieval Romans were convinced depicted Constantine, received a number of new identities—Septimius Severus by Poggio, Antoninus Pius by Bernardo Rucellai. Platina, however, in the 1470s hit correctly upon Marcus Aurelius.[196]

Limits existed, nonetheless, to the knowledge accumulated by Renaissance archeologists, particularly in judging artistic style. Thus the statues of the "horse-tamers" on the Quirinal, while no longer said to represent the two "philosophers," Phidias and Praxiteles (so the *Mirabilia* claims), were still regarded in the early sixteenth century as the creations of these two most prominent names among Greek sculptors.[197] Similarly, it took the discernment of a Raphael to recognize that the reliefs on the Arch of Constantine came from different periods.[198] Revealing, too, is the number of humanists taken in by Annio da Viterbo's faked antiquities and forged classical texts.[199]

More significant than such lapses or inadequacies in aesthetic judgment, however, were the limitations inherent in the antiquarian approach to the Roman past. For many, antiquarian lore proved an end in itself, and they remained content to describe, compile, and collect, rather than analyze. Classical artifacts were often, indeed, for the Roman classicist what relics were for the Roman pilgrim: talismans of a more potent spiritual power. Those who probed deeper, such as Leto, the guiding light for Roman antiquarians in the late fifteenth century, still stopped short of seeing archeology as a means to uncover the historical origins and development of a civilization.

Leto, who affected antique Roman dress, and who made his home on the Quirinal in the midst of ruins and a collection of inscribed marble, in fact made of Roman antiquity a cult, immersing himself in the sublime memories of the ancient city which the ruins evoked. The surviving *Excerpta* of his guided walks through the ancient city highlight such sites sacred to its former inhabitants as the spot in the Forum where the mounted Curtius, in obedience to the oracle and to save Rome, leaped into the chasm which suddenly opened, and the Lupercal, the cave on the Palatine where the she-wolf suckled Romulus and Remus. The bizarre and fantastic seems especially to have appealed to him. In describing the Quirinal, he gives an extended account of the punishment meted out to a Vestal Virgin guilty of unchastity: she was placed in an artificial cave carved near one of the gates, her sacred garments were stripped from her body by the priests, and then the populace buried her alive.[200]

Leto's fascination with ancient Roman religious rites and practices, reflective perhaps of the Christian city where ritual use of Rome's sacred space was so vital, reveals a fundamentally a-historical approach to classical Rome. What intrigued Leto, and Biondo, too, were the timeless manifestations of Roman civilization.

Biondo was almost certainly the most original historian among the

Roman humanists. His *Decades*, completed in 1453 after some fifteen years of work, traces the history of the West, with increasing emphasis on Italy in the later periods, from the collapse of the Roman Empire to 1441, and in so doing he created medieval history.[201] Yet, when he turned again to classical Rome, he wrote not a history, but rather *Roma triumphans* (begun probably in 1453, completed 1459), a topically arranged discussion of the institutions and practices of Roman religion, public administration, military organization, private life, and public festivals. Ancient Rome's greatest achievement, for Biondo, lay in the dissemination of the arts of civilized living to all other nations, an accomplishment whose benefits, he declares, "seemed rather the work of gods than men." It was not the ancient Rome of any particular historical period Biondo wished to evoke, nor a human society shaped by historical processes, but instead "that flourishing city, the mirror, exemplar, image, and principle of all virtue and of good, holy, and propitious living, which Blessed Augustine desired to see triumphant."[202]

Caught up in admiration for classical Rome's accomplishments, how readily Biondo overlooked the fundamental Augustinian distinction of the earthly and heavenly cities, the city of the world and the city of God! But Biondo was not alone. In the opening initial of a contemporary manuscript of Augustine's *De civitate Dei* made for Aeneas Silvius Piccolomini, the future Pius II, there appears a view of Rome—its Christian temples and classical monuments both given prominence—as the terrestrial realization of the heavenly Jerusalem.[203]

The *speculum* (mirror) motif became, in fact, one of the most frequently evoked images of the city. Thus Bernardo Rucellai, in the preface to his *De Urbe Roma*, stresses that whoever proposes to build a noble city must take Rome as "pattern and exemplar." To facilitate this, and in particular to enlighten his fellow Florentines, plunged into debate as to the proper nature of the city in the wake of the expulsion of the Medici in 1494, Rucellai set forth a detailed analysis of Rome's ancient topography and monuments.[204]

Wonder and stupefaction, not measured judgment, were, in short, the emotions to be inculcated among beholders of ancient Rome's splendor and majesty. Though different in specific content, such an attitude was not unlike the medieval *Mirabilia*. Indeed, in the early sixteenth century, the most popular guide to ancient Rome was Francesco Albertini's *Opusculum de mirabilibus novae et veteris Urbis Romae* (1510). As Albertini indicates in his preface, he intended his work precisely as an updating of the *Mirabilia*, "shorn of its fables and nonsense," and giving equal attention to the new wonders produced since Sixtus IV "began to restore (*instaurare*) the city."[205] The same outlook emerges in another Albertini work, *Septem mirabilia orbis et Urbis Romae et Florentinae civitatis*, which, as its title suggests, describes the seven wonders of the ancient world, then the seven wonders of both ancient and modern Rome—including the Aqueduct of Claudius, the Baths of Diocletian, the Forum of Nerva, the Pantheon, the Colosseum, Hadrian's Tomb, the Lateran complex, St. Peter's, S. Maria Maggiore, S. Maria in Aracoeli, the Palazzo di S. Marco, and the church and palace of SS. Apostoli. For good measure Albertini then added seven wonders of his native Florence.[206]

This emphasis by the Roman humanists on the timeless aspects of ancient Rome's achievements and on the exemplary mode of causation stands in striking contrast to the preoccupations of the Florentine humanist tradition. In the work of the civic humanists, and again in Machiavelli, investigation of Roman history proved a critical intellectual task precisely because this enabled understanding of the political forces at work in secular society. For Leonardo Bruni study of Republican Rome served as the means to transcend the mythic and symbolic treatments of Florence's past and to discover what psychological and political conditions were conducive to the development of republics. For Machiavelli, the Roman Republic provided the crucial historical experience from which one could deduce the laws governing political behavior. Although their aims differed, for both men historical analysis was decisive, and the Republic, not the "degenerate" age of the Roman Empire, represented the acme of civic ethos.[207]

Renaissance Rome, however, did not create a climate conducive to republican values. In fact, to defend republicanism as an ideology was fraught with danger, as the Porcari conspiracy showed. Stefano Porcari, a Roman noble whose attachment to republican ideals is manifest in the orations he delivered in Florence during a stint there as Capitano del Popolo in 1427, during the heyday of Bruni's civic humanism, became increasingly dismayed with the Roman populace's loss of civic *libertas*. The rapacity and injustice of papal governance prevented, he charged, the restoration of *gravitas* and the other civic virtues of Republican Rome. When Porcari's outspoken remarks were linked to a public tumult during the Carnival games of 1451, Nicholas V exiled him to Bologna, and from there he plotted to return to his native city, seize the pope, and proclaim a republic. Porcari managed to return in secret to Rome, but just as he was formulating his final plans the conspiracy was uncovered. Arrested, he readily confessed his responsibility, and was beheaded in Castel Sant'Angelo in January 1453.[208]

Papal aspirations to control Rome, the political power of the barons, and the absence of a commercially based economy had all inhibited, even in the medieval age of communes, the development of self-governing civic institutions in the Eternal City. Porcari's grim fate served as a further effective reminder to Roman humanists not to indulge in vain dreams of re-establishing the classical Republic, and this helps, too, to explain the neglect of historico-political analysis in their thought and writings. But

more decisive in shaping Roman humanist views was their perception of
the city not as a human community, not as a political society where
classical notions of the *polis* and the ethico-political values of citizenship
forged purpose and meaning, but rather as the capital, the *urbs terrarum
orbis* (global city) and *arx omnium gentium* (citadel of all peoples), as Biondo
said, citing Cicero.[209] Sacred to both civilization and Christianity, Rome's
foundation and destiny transcended human comprehension. Such an
outlook meant that ritual, ceremony, and myth overwhelmed rational
inquiry. And archeology, rather than history, provided the means by
which the Roman humanists made tangible the grandeur and mystique of
the ancient capital.

Where these attitudes entered into the public life of the city was,
characteristically, in a ceremonial way. On 20 April 1483, Pomponio Leto
and members of the Roman Academy re-established the ancient Roman
custom of celebrating the Palilia (or *Parilia*), the "birthday" of the founding of Rome. Initially, the festival consisted of an oration by a member of
the humanist sodality followed by a banquet.[210] By 1501, when Burchard
describes the event, the setting had shifted to the Capitoline Hill, the
Senator, the *Conservatori*, and other civic magistrates, as well as members
of the Papal Curia, attended, the papal choir sang for Mass in S. Maria in
Aracoeli, the banquet took place in the Palazzo dei Conservatori, and a
Latin comedy was performed. In fact, the festival that year had to be
postponed until 2 May because the drama required additional preparation time. The oration celebrating Rome, however, still remained
central.[211]

Roman humanist oratory, moreover, both for celebrating the Palilia
and for numerous other ceremonial occasions, established a panegyric
tradition, which in ever loftier and more cosmic terms elaborated the
mythic destiny of Rome. Renaissance eulogists inherited from the Middle
Ages various sublime attributes associated with the city. Principal city of
the world (*caput orbis* or *mundi*), a royal and priestly city (*civitas sacerdotalis
et regia*), the center of the Christian faith (*caput fidei* or *caput Christianae
religionis*), the common fatherland of all peoples (*patria communis*), the
source of law (*mater legum*)—all found expression in medieval praises of
Rome;[212] and a string of such laudatory ascriptions appears in one of the
earliest Renaissance celebrations of the city, the *Descriptio Urbis Romae
eiusque excellentiae*, written around 1430 by Niccolò Signorili, a Roman
citizen and civic official, and addressed to Martin V. Signorili's remarks,
however, were merely prefatory to the more mundane task of listing for
the pope the contents of various registers relating to tributes and *censi*,
papal temporal and spiritual jurisdictions, and administrative and ceremonial procedures. Damaged or lost during the occupation of the city by
King Ladislas of Naples two decades earlier, archives containing this
information now had to be compiled anew.[213]

The attributes summed up in Signorili's *Descriptio* continued to have a place in Renaissance praises of Rome, but the humanists managed to exploit, in addition, newly discovered classical sources and the reacquired tradition of classical rhetoric. The earliest panegyric meeting humanist expectations is the *Laudatio Urbis Romae et Constantinopolis*, composed in Greek by Manuel Chrysoloras following a visit to Rome in 1411, and translated into Latin some thirty years later. In this work, the Byzantine scholar emphasizes the glory and sacredness that link Rome to the "New Rome" (Constantinople), and which in turn bind together Latin Christendom and Byzantium. Recognition of this would induce, he hoped, western aid to the beleaguered eastern capital. For Chrysoloras's readers among the Roman humanists, this general idea mattered less than a particular theme he advanced in praising Rome. Rome, he claimed, belonged not to earth, but rather formed part of heaven.[214]

As his source for this assertion, Chrysoloras cited "that sophist." In all likelihood, his unnamed classical orator was Aelius Aristides, an influential Hellenistic rhetorician of the "Second Sophistic," who delivered his "Roman Oration," composed in Greek, in the Eternal City, in, probably, A.D. 143. Writing at the height of the Roman Empire in the second century, Aristides stressed the *aeternitas* of imperial Rome, and the creation under the Antonine emperors of an ideal state—indeed, a Roman cosmos—in which a divinely established order of peace and justice transcended the forces of human history.[215]

Aristides' panegyric suggested to Roman humanists key themes for celebrating Rome. Poggio, for instance, in his *De varietate fortunae*, remarks that Rome once was so beautiful and magnificent that the ancients held it to be "*non urbem, sed quasi quandam caeli partem*" (not a city, but almost a part of heaven)—a phrase he wrongly attributed, however, to Libanius, another late Hellenistic rhetorician.[216] Just as important, Aristides' "Roman Oration" belongs in form to epideictic oratory, one of the principal branches of classical rhetoric. The function of epideictic, the *ars laudandi et vituperandi*, was praise and blame, attributions particularly appropriate to ceremonial occasions. In praising, the orator sought not to persuade a deliberative body to a particular point of view from which would ensue certain decisions and actions (the purpose of judicial and political rhetoric), but rather to impress on his hearers feelings of wonder, awe, admiration, and love.[217]

The humanist rediscovery of epideictic oratory became fundamental, as O'Malley has recently shown,[218] to the intellectual character of the Roman Renaissance. Not only was it increasingly cultivated in the sacred oratory of the papal court, where many Roman humanists had opportunities to preach, but it also contributed to a characteristic state of mind. To admire, love, and praise meant not to think but to gaze upon. Indeed, the use of ekphrasis—the detailed visual description, often of buildings or works of art, which the revived epideictic took over as a prominent stylistic device from Hellenistic and Byzantine rhetorical traditions—aimed at bringing about "seeing through hearing."[219] Concomitant was a movement from the cerebral to the visual, and a suspension of critical inquiry in favor of beholding a more than human world.

Chrysoloras's *Laudatio* exemplifies these characteristics of epideictic rhetoric. Moreover, many of the specific elements of praise contained in his work reappear repeatedly in later humanist panegyrics. This being the case, the *Laudatio* merits a closer look at this point.

Like Aristides, Chrysoloras celebrates the splendor, wealth, magnificence, power, and dignity of the imperial capital. True, all now lies in ruins, partly through the accidents of time, partly through violation by human hands. But the very ruins suggest the magnitude and beauty of the Roman achievement. Especially evocative are the numerous triumphal arches, testaments to Roman victories over the barbarians—and suggestive of Chrysoloras's pressing concern as Byzantium strove to preserve its civilization before the Ottoman threat. In fact, the Roman monument to which Chrysoloras devoted the most detailed visual account—a prime instance of ekphrasis—was the Arch of Constantine.[220]

What nevertheless makes Rome truly part of heaven, and more celestial in his own time than in classical antiquity, despite the ruinous appearance of the city, is, Chrysoloras asserts, the accumulated treasure of the relics of the saints. Above all, Rome possesses the remains of "those two wholly heavenly suns," Peter and Paul, whose dignity cannot be sufficiently admired, and the preservation of whose memory prompted, in large part, his writing the *Laudatio*. Behold, he urges us, the crowds of pilgrims flowing into Rome from Europe, Greece, and Asia, overcoming enormous difficulties and hardships to venerate and to give thanks to the two great Apostles, the two "suns," who after so many years of darkness had liberated mankind from error and revealed the glory of immortal God. These pilgrims come, animated by the same holy fervor as possessed the great Greek Church Father, John Chrysostom. Inspired by the Holy Spirit he had expressed his desire to see Rome and to behold the bodies and tombs of the Apostles. Moreover, extensive as Roman imperial jurisdiction and administration, emanating outwards from the capital, had been, it must accede, Chrysoloras insists, to the even greater amplitude of spiritual authority exercised by the Church of Rome. From a yet loftier vantage point, the "gathering in" to the Temple of the Apostles (St. Peter's basilica) of so many peoples from such distant lands, speaking so many different languages, fulfills the prophesied vision of the twelve Apostles judging the twelve tribes of Israel. But indeed it transcends even that vision, for from Rome the Roman Church judges the whole globe.

Rome as the capital of a global empire and part of the heavenly kingdom appear as key themes in Biondo's *Roma triumphans*, in Domenico

de' Domenichi's "*Oratio in laudem civitatis et civilitatis Romanae*," and in the
orations of Giles of Viterbo and Cristoforo Marcello, which will be examined closely later. As the fifteenth century turned into the sixteenth,
what one perceives overall in these paeans, however, is the growing
crescendo of exultant and triumphant praise.

The Roman humanists contributed to the public life of Rome, then,
a ceremonial occasion—the Palilia—and an encomiastic tradition. Yet the
public world could not become wholly the province of Roman humanist
activity. Excluded from the process of political decision-making, the
Roman humanists were unable to exercise the public authority wielded by
the succession of humanist chancellors of Quattrocento Florence. Rather
than in the public sphere, it perhaps was in the private literary leisure of
the Roman villa where the Roman humanists succeeded most in recreating the actual experience of Roman antiquity.

From the early fifteenth century the rustic country *vigna*, a simple
house set amidst vineyards and orchards either within the *disabitato* or just
outside the city walls, had provided a summer retreat for members of the
papal Curia. Poggio, for example, has the participants in his dialogue, *De
avaritia*, share their thoughts during the post-prandial pause from official
duties in the country house near the Lateran that belonged to his fellow
papal secretary, Bartolommeo da Montepulciano.[221] What such a *vigna*
may have been like can be imagined from the so-called Casino of Cardinal
Bessarion, located on the Via Appia just within the walls a short distance
from Porta S. Sebastiano.[222] In choosing a villa setting for his dialogue
Poggio was also, of course, imitating the example of Cicero, many of
whose philosophical works had suburban settings. Other Roman humanists, too, recognized how pleasurable ancient Romans had found gardens,
and they were quick to liken contemporary *vigne* to them. Biondo, for
instance, in *Roma instaurata* praised Cardinal Prospero Colonna for restoring to the Quirinal the cultivated and cultured humanistic ambience
which Horace had praised in the gardens of Maecenas. Virgil, too,
according to Donatus, had lived on the Quirinal, Biondo went on to note,
and Pliny, besides praising the gardens of Maecenas, had described the
even more luxurious nearby gardens belonging to Sallust.[223] In *Roma
triumphans*, Biondo provided a more extensive treatment of ancient Roman villas. Varro's and Cato's remarks on the sites suitable for villas are
duly noted, as are their comments on the requisite structures. Also discussed is Cicero's villa at Tusculum, and Biondo describes the present
appearance of the site.[224]

In the later fifteenth century, Leto's home on the Quirinal combined
the *vigna* with an impressive collection of antiquities, thereby providing
the antiquarian discussions of the Roman Academy with a particularly
evocative setting.[225] By the early sixteenth century more elaborate villa-
garden complexes had begun to emerge. Among these was one belonging

to Johann Goritz (Corycius), situated between Trajan's Forum and the
Campidoglio. In 1525 Giles of Viterbo praised its "Parnassan" beauty.
Equally famous was the garden Angelo Colocci created during Leo X's
pontificate on the slopes of Monte Cavallo. Contemporaries regarded it as
renewing the ancient *Horti Salustiani*; and its amenities were enhanced by
numerous ancient sculptures, including one of Socrates embracing Alci-
biades, and by a splendid library of Latin and Greek classics. Colocci's
garden also featured a sleeping-nymph fountain, fashioned out of an
arch of the Aqua Virgo and by diverting some of its water.[226]

What Roman humanists and poets sought in such villas, and what
their more successful fellow classicists, like Sadoleto,[227] aimed at in their
own *vigne*, was an escape from the demands of the papal court. Roman
villas, unlike the Venetian villas Palladio designed, were not working
farms; they were for pleasure and restorative leisure, which the Roman
humanists associated with the Ciceronian ideal of *otium*. The literary
world of the Roman villa lacked, too, the intellectual intensity and philosophic commitments of Marsilio Ficino's Florentine Academy. Nor did
Roman academies consider contemporary public issues, as occurred in
the debates at Bernardo Rucellai's Orti Oricellari in Florence; there
history and politics provided the focus of discussion, and there
Machiavelli developed his reflections on Livy into the *Discorsi*.[228] Roman
poets and antiquarians by contrast sought in villa life an asylum from the
political world. On the slopes of Rome's sparsely inhabited *monti*, surrounded by classical artifacts, they were free to indulge their classical
tastes and to cultivate the Muses far from the conflicting passions of court
and marketplace and removed from the economic and political realities
of the city spread below them.

THE SUBTERRANEAN AND THE SUPER-TERRESTRIAL, THE DEMONIC AND THE CELESTIAL

One of the marvels of new Rome celebrated in verse by early sixteenth-
century Roman humanists was the dining loggia Agostino Chigi created
c. 1511 at the edge of the Tiber on the grounds of the Villa Farnesina.
Beneath this open-air, arcaded pavilion opened an underground grotto,
reached by an outside stair, where water from the Tiber filled a basin.
There fish swam, and bathing could be enjoyed. A bench surrounded the
pool, and a hole in the vault allowed a dim light to filter in from above.[229]

Renaissance Romans were fascinated by caves, whether artificial like
Chigi's or natural. Pius II, for instance, during a visit to the Alban Hills in
1463 explored at the monastery of S. Maria Palazzuola a large natural
grotto, shady till noon, from which a spring gushed forth. The monks
used the cave for summer dining, as did more illustrious refugees from

Rome's summer heat, including Cardinal Isidore of Kiev.[230] Spring-filled grottoes, often rusticated, became a regular feature, too, of early sixteenth-century Roman gardens, such as the *Orti Blosiani* created by Blosio Palladio during Leo X's time;[231] and fountains placed in wooded groves, like the nymphaeum of the Villa Madama set into a cleft of Monte Mario,[232] were characteristic of Roman villas. The Villa Madama (begun for Giulio de' Medici, later Clement VII) seems also to have been embellished with eight statues of the Muses, discovered at Hadrian's Villa at Tivoli during Alexander VI's pontificate,[233] and fountain-grottoes with statues of nymphs, Venus, or Apollo and the Muses became common elements in the garden decoration of later Renaissance Roman villas.[234] Such cool and shady nooks enhanced the mood of poetic reverie or nostalgic evocation of pastoral simplicity, but the deliberate contrast of nature and artifice and the pleasurable sense of wildness in the overgrown vines and dripping water formed part of the appeal. In the same way Renaissance Romans were attracted to the wild desolation of the Roman campagna and to the haunting silence of the abandoned ruins.[235]

Deeper than the dim recesses of caves and grottoes lay the shadowy underworld of the buried ancient city itself. One of the most enticing glimpses of the imperial past was the ruins of Nero's extravagant Domus Aurea, beneath the Esquiline. The scene of the spectacular debaucheries reported by Suetonius and Tacitus (and deplored by Biondo[236]) Nero's Golden House began to be probed around 1480 by the group of Tuscan artists Sixtus IV called to Rome to work on the Sistine Chapel wall frescoes. Graffiti carved on the walls mark their explorations, while elements of the Domus Aurea's decoration began to appear in what contemporary artists conceived for their Roman commissions. Pinturicchio, in particular, seems to have been fascinated by the gilded stucco ornamentation and geometrical compositions of the ceiling designs, and he incorporated these motifs, as well as grotesques (derived from the word grotto) in his many Roman pictorial cycles. Raphael, too, took inspiration from the Domus Aurea. His Vatican Loggia shows the influence of the Neronian palace's cryptoportico, and his Vatican *stufetta* for Cardinal Bibbiena with its *all'antica* illustrations of myths associated with the goddess Venus similarly bears the imprint of attentive observation of the underground paintings.[237]

In another part of the Domus Aurea, which had been incorporated into Trajan's Baths and was known as the Sette Sale, there was unearthed in 1506 the celebrated ancient sculpture of the *Laocoön*.[238] Other ruins yielded their ancient treasures, too, in the Renaissance period. Among many such works were the head and limbs of a marble colossus found during Innocent VIII's pontificate near the Basilica of Maxentius,[239] and a huge sculpture of Hercules on a hill holding a bull by the horns (the famed *Farnese Bull*), uncovered in the Baths of Caracalla in 1545–46.[240]

The find which seems most to have astounded Renaissance Romans, however, was the exhumation near the Via Appia in 1485 of an undecomposed body of an ancient Roman girl. Transferred to the Campidoglio, crowds came to view the prodigy, and speculations as to who she may have been ranged from a Scipio, to one of Cicero's family, to Poppaea, Nero's wife. All were amazed by her freshness and the appearance of life, which imparted the sense of tangible contact with the classical inhabitants of the city. After exposure to the air, however, the cadaver quickly began to decay, and to put an end to what he regarded as an inappropriate pilgrimage Innocent VIII arranged for the body to be secretly removed.[241]

Christian Rome was not neglected either in the Renaissance probing of the subterranean city. As early as 1432 Franciscans began organizing visits to the catacombs of S. Callisto. But as reminders of the dangers, travail, and early ritual experience of primitive Christianity the catacombs exerted the greatest attraction on Pomponio Leto and fellow members of the Roman Academy. In his life of Calixtus I, Platina mentions that he and his friends had visited the catacombs *religionis causa*," and had seen there the ashes and bones of the martyrs and the underground chapels.[242] There, like the visitors to the Domus Aurea, the Academicians also left graffiti.[243]

If underground Rome increasingly drew Renaissance Romans into its depths, the space above ground came to be invaded as well. There was the elevated *passetto*, created by Alexander VI atop the Leonine Wall in order to connect the Vatican and Castel Sant'Angelo; down this Clement VII was forced to flee when imperial forces broke into the city in 1527. Within the interior of what had once been Hadrian's mausoleum, labyrinthine stairs and passageways led from the helicoidal central ramp to storerooms and to dank dungeons, excavated out of the solid masonry of the drum. Atop the structure, the early sixteenth-century popes created several levels of courtyards, loggias, guardrooms, audience halls, council chambers, a bath, a chapel, and papal apartments—in effect, a small aerial city, secure from any undesired intrusions.

Under Paul III another aerial route joined Palazzo Venezia and the Capitoline Hill.[244] In the same vein, Michelangelo, according to Vasari, planned at one point to connect Palazzo Farnese to the Villa Farnesina across the Tiber by means of a bridge, as part of a grandiose concept that would have joined piazza, palace, river, gardens, and villa into one magnificent perspectival compositon.[245] Most famous of all these aerial structures was the elevated corridor of Bramante's Cortile del Belvedere, which drew inspiration from the palace passageway Nero had built between the Palatine and Esquiline Hills.[246]

By delving into the ruins and catacombs and by constructing aerial passages, Renaissance Romans managed to descend beneath or ascend above the earth-bound surface world of the city. Just as readily the human-scaled measure of reality succumbed: Renaissance Roman construction is characterized by the colossal (e.g., the new St. Peter's) and by the miniature (e.g., S. Pietro in Montorio).

In a similar way the image of Rome was made the subject of wit and caprice. In the later Renaissance Villa d'Este at Tivoli, the famous Fountain of Rome depicted on a miniature scale the Tiber, the Seven Hills, and the notable monuments of the ancient city, though unsuspecting visitors might be soaked by hidden water tricks.[247] Earlier, around 1515, Baldassare Peruzzi transformed the main salon of the Villa Farnesina into the illusionistic Sala delle Prospettive. The room appears to be a sumptuous belvedere, open on all sides, from which the city and the surrounding countryside can be glimpsed beyond elegant purple-columned loggias. All this is painted artifice, however, and as an added fillip to this witty display of the painter's craft the Villa Farnesina itself appears.[248]

If, moving perpendicularly, the circumscribed limits of mere earthly existence could so easily be evaded, if the city itself could assume such manifold guises, then it is not surprising that the human plane should be penetrated by superhuman forces and that Renaissance Romans should sense both the nearness of heaven and the powerful proximity of the demonic.

No insurmountable distance separated Rome from the heavenly world. Not only did Rome's panegyrists proclaim it part of the celestial kingdom, not only did preachers urge the papal court to "look up" in order to behold its heavenly image and exemplar, but the imagery of triumphal procession also suggested the nearness of the ingress to heaven,[249] and the elaborate ceremonies for the canonizations of Bernardino of Siena (1450), Bonaventura (1482), and Francesco di Paola (1519) made tangible and immediate that entrance.[250] Passage from heaven to earth occurred just as easily. Miracles, indulgences, and the pope's Easter blessing were clear signs for Renaissance Romans of the benevolence with which God chose to favor their city. Providentially elected by God in His eternal wisdom, Rome was identified as the *civitas Dei*. Moreover, for speakers at the Fifth Lateran Council, the Roman Church, gathered in synod under the pope (the *vicarius Christi* to whom had been given the power of opening and closing heaven) was the new, holy Jerusalem descending from heaven which St. John the Evangelist saw (Rev. 21: 2). By contrast the rival *conciliabulum* of Pisa was the tower of Babel.[251]

In a dream-vision, written in Latin hexameters by the humanist Zaccaria Ferreri and addressed to the newly elected Leo X in 1513, Rome departs altogether from its earthly moorings and becomes wholly celestial. Ascending through the heavenly spheres, the dreaming poet encounters Dante, and rising together to the sphere of Jupiter, they enter a luxuriant landscape of gardens and flowering fields. In the distance they

see a lofty palace surrounded by high walls. Dante discloses to Ferreri that
this splendid sight is the Mons Vaticanus with its papal residence. Climb-
ing to reach a better vantage-point, they then behold the walls of the
Borgo Leonino, the Tiber, Hadrian's tomb, the Capitoline, Aventine,
Caelian, and other hills, the amphitheaters and circuses, columns, the
Pantheon, the sites of the *naumachiae*, the obelisks, and the other distinctive monuments of Rome. They find the city in the midst of a joyous
celebration, by reason of Leo's election; and as "Dante" elucidates the
arcane symbolism of the Medici *stemma*, praises the pope's Medici forebears, and celebrates the previous Pope Leos to whose virtues and
achievements Leo X is heir, they enter the gates to join the throng in
Piazza S. Pietro acclaiming the new pontiff.[252]

To Renaissance Romans, the Roman pontiffs, Jove-like in their
command over heaven and earth, embodied as well the excellence of
monarchical rule and formed the font of just law that Dante, in *Paradiso*,
XVIII, had set forth in his majestic vision of Jupiter's orb. (Conveniently,
Ferreri neglected Dante's tirade at the end of this canto against the
"buyers and sellers in the temple" that was built with the blood of the
martyrs, and who "trample the vineyard" Peter and Paul died for). Indeed, in the opening years of the sixteenth century, the Vatican began to
be transformed into a new image of imperial capital and sacred city—an
urbanistic projection of the "cosmic" dignity of Rome and the papacy
Ferreri exalted.

Not everyone shared this vision. In reaction to the wholesale
changes in the Vatican these new projects entailed, there appeared in
Rome in 1516 the satiric dialogue, *Simia*, written by Andrea Guarna. In
this work, Bramante, the recently deceased architect Julius II had put in
charge of the Cortile del Belvedere and the new St. Peter's, and who in the
process gained the opprobrious nickname "*maestro ruinante*," appears
before St. Peter at the gates to heaven. The heavenly gatekeeper upbraids
the architect for demolishing his earthly basilica, but Bramante in turn
complains that the way from earth to heaven is too arduous in its ascent.
In its stead he proposes to erect a commodious winding staircase (like the
famous "*chiocciola*" he built in the Belvedere), then offers to tear down
Paradise to its foundations and construct it anew, thereby providing the
Blessed with a more cultivated and agreeable habitation. (This latter is
Guarna's apparent jibe at Bramante's razing of Old St. Peter's to make
way for the new colossal temple—an apt satiric thrust inasmuch as the
atrium of the Constantinian basilica was known as the "Paradisus").
Should Peter not agree to these plans, Bramante threatens to go straight
on to Pluto, Lord of the Underworld, where he knew for certain his
services would be in demand. Indeed an entirely new hell was required,
for the present one was tumbling to pieces and partially consumed by the
eternal flames. The upshot, however, is that Peter condemns Bramante to

remain waiting at the gates of Paradise until the new St. Peter's is completed.[253]

Less indirect in its attacks on contemporary admiration for the ancient imperial city and on ambitions for its renewal is the 1518 oration in praise of Rome delivered by the Florentine Dominican, Zanobi Acciaiuoli (d. 1519). The occasion for Acciaiuoli's remarks was the triennial Chapter General of his Order, which traditionally closed with a speech in praise of the host city. For the Dominican, only Christian Rome, however, deserved praise, whereas the ancient capital merited condemnation. There were indeed two sharply divergent Romes, one earthly, the other heavenly, one the work of Cain, the other of Abel. No one, he argues, should regret the destruction of the former seat of the Roman Empire nor wax nostalgic over its ruins: beneath these, in fact, lies the devil. Nor did Acciaiuoli look kindly on the enthusiasm of contemporary artists for exploring Nero's Domus Aurea. Ancient Rome was not golden, but rather was the consequence of iron war and ruthless rapine. Only Christian Rome was founded on true virtue, and its holy power provided a spiritual bridge for the elect to gain access to heaven. Not bacchanals, chariot races, gladiators, and other sinful excesses, but rather the veneration of the *sudarium* and of the Holy Lance mark the virtuous nobility of Christian Rome.[254]

As Guarna's and Acciaiuoli's remarks indicate, if Romans thought their city was close to heaven, so, too, was it close to hell. No longer current, it seems, was the *Mirabilia* legend that the mouth of hell itself once yawned in the Roman Forum (in the vaults which provided supports for the Palatine palaces), until the heroism of St. Sylvester closed it.[255] But Fra Mariano da Firenze did point out to his readers the place in the Forum where Peter and Paul by means of prayer brought Simon Magus, borne by the devil through the air, plunging to his death.[256] The Roman diarist Infessura mentions, too, that for the Feast of Peter and Paul in 1473 there was a *sacra rappresentazione* of Christ's Resurrection and the despoiling of hell, by which "all men, whether famous or obscure, triumphed."[257]

Other signs of the demonic were not difficult to detect. Giovanni Rucellai records among the relics preserved in St. Peter's the rope by which Judas hanged himself after betraying Christ,[258] and many believed that the malevolence of Nero (regarded in the Middle Ages as a demon or even as Anti-Christ[259]) still afflicted the region around S. Maria del Popolo or haunted the nearby "tower of Nero."[260] Leto, on his guided tours through the ancient city also pointed out the "tower of Maecenas" from which Nero had watched Rome burn.[261]

Rome's detractors continued to refer to it as Babylon,[262] and Bernardino Carvajal in his oration to the College of Cardinals in preparation for the election of a successor to Innocent VIII depicted the city as awash in every form of carnality and licentiousness: "Who doubts but that the city of Rome is that notorious sinner [Mary Magdelen]? Would that God would cast out the multitude of demons from her as he cast out the seven from that evangelical woman [Mark 16: 9; Luke 8: 2]!"[263]

At one point, too, Pius II, exasperated with the treachery, sacrilege, and heresy of Sigismondo Malatesta, Lord of Rimini, threatened to enroll him among the citizens of hell (in a kind of reverse canonization); and he did subsequently burn him in effigy on the steps of St. Peter's.[264]

The Colosseum also, which Biondo described as having incited ancient Romans to every form of luxury and vice, especially the cruel pleasure in bloodshed,[265] still seemed sinister to many. This remained the case despite the Archconfraternity of the Gonfalone's presentation there each Good Friday (from Innocent VIII's time on) of a *sacra rappresentazione* of Christ's Passion. Normally performed in antique Roman dress, in 1520 it was newly produced in the form of a "tragedy."[266] Nevertheless, it was to the Colosseum that Cellini went, at night, accompanied by a necromancer, to conjure devils. So successful were the incantations, uttered in Hebrew, Greek, and Latin, that "legions" of demons appeared. Terrified by this specter, the goldsmith's apprentice befouled his pants (the stench from which helped to keep the devils at bay). Yet as they made their way home after the hour of Matins to the Via dei Banchi, he kept crying that two demons he had seen in the amphitheater were leaping ahead of them over the roof-tops of the city.[267]

Diabolical, malevolent, sinful, and sinister, yet also civilized, splendid, miraculous, and holy—these were the alternate faces of Rome that stirred the fears and hopes, nightmares and dreams, of its Renaissance beholders. Just, too, as the many strata of this palimpsest city loosened its inhabitants' grasp on present realities; so, in the same way, did Janus-headed Rome, heir to the myths of its two-thousand-year past and divinely destined to a transcendent future, mesmerize its adherents with seductive visions of supernal glory. The result was the extravagance in praise (and blame), and the related tendency to the grandiose, to which Renaissance Romans seemed all too prone.

III

The Renaissance Papacy
and the *Respublica Christiana*

> . . . in Rome, where they believe that the blood of
> the Apostles and Martyrs is very sweet, and at
> their expense is a nice life.
>
> —LUDOVICO ARIOSTO, *I studenti*, Act III,
> sc. 4, ll. 1022–24.

> Who lies here? The Sixth. Which Sixth? The one who
> by guileful craft confounded sea with sky and sky with earth;
> Who now molests more cruelly the Tartarean shades;
> and from whom savage Megaera, fettered, retreats.
> Why is this structure so huge? Because here are stored
> thefts, deceits, frauds, wars, greed, and lust.
>
> —PAOLO BELMESSERI, *Epitaphium Alexandri
> sexti pontificis*, ll. 1–6.

THE RENAISSANCE POPES

On the night of 5 March 1447, the cardinals, meeting in conclave in
S. Maria sopra Minerva[1] to elect a new pope, had retired to their respective cubicles. Tommaso Parentucelli, Bishop of Bologna for a little over
two years and named a cardinal only the previous December, drifted off
to sleep, turning over in his mind the matter of the election. Suddenly
there appeared to him a vision of the recently deceased Pope Eugenius
IV, splendidly adorned in full pontifical garb. The dead pontiff began to
divest himself of his raiment, and indicated that Parentucelli should also
disrobe. Then he proceeded to dress the cardinal with his own vestments,
thus presaging Tommaso's election as his successor. At that moment,
Parentucelli awoke, and recalling vividly his dream began to laugh. When
his servants inquired what had occasioned his mirthful outburst, he
jocularly repeated his experience to them.

The next morning, "against any evident hope, and contrary to the opinion of all prudent and reasonable men, he was raised to the summit of the papacy, in accordance with the ways of God rather than men." So concludes Giannozzo Manetti (1396–1459), the Florentine humanist who served Nicholas V as Apostolic Secretary in the years 1453–55, and who records this whole episode in his *De vita ac gestis Nicolai Quinti Pontificis*, composed within a few months of the pope's decease. For Manetti, Parentucelli's vision was "not a human dream but instead a true oracle from omnipotent God."[2]

Parentucelli's election did indeed surprise contemporaries. But Aeneas Silvius Piccolomini, the future Pius II, who witnessed the proceedings of the 1447 conclave, provides a different explanation for the course of events. In a report to the Holy Roman Emperor Frederick III, composed some two months after the election, Aeneas Silvius relates that in the first two ballots of 5 March Cardinal Prospero Colonna had received ten votes (two short of the necessary two-thirds majority of the eighteen cardinals present). Strong opposition to Colonna's election was mounted, however, by those closely associated with Eugenius's administration, including the dead pope's nephew, Cardinal Francesco Condulmer, and Cardinal Giovanni Berardi, who had represented Eugenius at the Council of Basel. Berardi, moreover, as a relative to the Orsini, the traditional Colonna rival, had in this a further motive for opposing Prospero's election. And both cardinals were well aware of the adverse consequences for their own positions of a new Colonna pontificate, since Eugenius, to gain control of the Papal States, had had to wrest holdings from his Colonna predecessor, Martin V. To break the deadlocked conclave, Berardi proposed Parentucelli, who besides his neutrality in Roman and Italian politics also had the virtue of being a staunch anticonciliarist, a position on which all the Italian cardinals agreed. Berardi's suggestion won quick approval, and on the third ballot, held the morning of 6 March, Parentucelli was chosen.[3]

Human considerations would thus seem to have been prominent in the 1447 conclave. Nevertheless Manetti's account should not be dismissed as mere rhetorical invention or *ex post facto* hagiography. For the Florentine, the dream of 5 March was not, significantly, an isolated supernatural event, but part of a recurrent pattern discernible in Parentucelli's life from the beginning, "so that he seemed not to have been born according to the common and ordinary law of nature but rather was created or elected by omnipotent God."[4] The first sign of Tommaso's portentous future was the dream experienced by his mother, sick with grief over the grave illness of her ten-year-old son. In her dream there appeared a figure, clad in dazzlingly white priestly garments, who bade the sorrowing mother not to despair for her son's health, since, in accordance with divine foreknowledge, he would ascend before he died to the loftiest levels of priestly dignity. If she wished greater certainty with regard to this, she should promise that at the opportune time Tommaso would become a priest.[5]

Following Parentucelli's election as pope, two further oracular dreams came to him. The first occurred in the third year of his pontificate, when he again lay seriously ill. Eugenius IV once again appeared to him, declaring he would recover, but would die in the eighth year of his reign (a prophecy that proved true). In the last dream, Stefano Porcari, leader of the attempted coup, materialized, brandishing a rod with which he seemed to strike the pope's arm, but in such a way that no injury was sustained. This premonitory vision, Manetti relates, came to the pope while he slept in the Vatican, just a few days before Porcari's conspiracy came to light.[6]

Inclusion of prophetic dreams in the lives of important public personages had been recommended by classical rhetorical theory (e.g., Quintilian, *Orat. inst.*, III, 7). Moreover, Manetti aimed not so much at producing a comprehensive biography as at providing a laudatory sketch—a distinctive classical genre discussed by Quintilian and illustrated, for example, in Plutarch's *Lives*.[7] Nevertheless, divine intervention in the lives of the popes proved to be recurrent in the Renaissance period: Nicholas V was far from alone in experiencing through dreams, prophecies, and other miraculous signs supernatural confirmation of divine office. Calixtus III, his successor, remained unshaken in his trust in Vincent Ferrer's prophecy he would become pope—and one of Calixtus's first acts as pontiff was to canonize Vincent.[8] A half century later, contemporaries similarly regarded Giovanni de' Medici's election as Leo X as a clear manifestation of divine will. What might have seemed the bizarre twists of fate—such as his capture by the French at the Battle of Ravenna in April 1512, a harrowing experience that preceded by just eleven months his election as pope—were understood instead as signs of God's providential intention. Thus, as Cristoforo Marcello argued in his "*Oratio ad Leonem X Pont. Max.*" (written some six months after Leo's election), the choice of the Medici pope proved that God always looked after human affairs: If at times He desired the bark of the Church, established by Himself, to be tossed about, He never permitted it to be submerged, but instead gave succor to it at the moment of its direst need. No one could now doubt, Marcello concludes, that Leo's election constituted a sign of divine benevolence. As such, it was an event to silence any adherents of the "depraved and detestable sect" of ancient philosophers, led by Democritus and Leucippus, who asserted all things happened by chance. Leo, whose authority derives from God not from man, and who as administrator of divine things is like another God on earth, "was chosen not according to the ways of men but by the judgment of God."[9]

At first glance, such a divine aura seems entirely absent from Pius

II's election. In his own graphic account of the 1458 conclave (expurgated from early printed editions of the *Commentarii*), motives of personal advantage, political expediency, and pursuit of power predominate: the cardinals meet stealthily in the privies in quest of votes and to divide the spoils, while Aeneas Silvius himself buttonholes one cardinal after another warning of the danger of a French pope (Guillaume d'Estoute-ville, Cardinal of Rouen, was the leading candidate).[10] Yet half a dozen years earlier, while Piccolomini was accompanying Frederick III to Rome for the imperial coronation, the monarch had drawn him aside as they rode past Viterbo and predicted that he would become a cardinal and that the chair of St. Peter awaited him. To Aeneas Silvius this prophecy seemed all the more solemn, since after the imperial coronation Frederick reported to Nicholas V a dream he had experienced some years before, the night after Parentucelli had left Vienna (where as Bishop of Bologna he had been sent on legation). In the dream, the emperor saw himself in Rome, being crowned by Parentucelli's hands. This caused him to marvel, he stated, and to wonder at the validity of the coronation, inasmuch as it was performed by the Bishop of Bologna, not the Bishop of Rome. After awaking, he dismissed the dream as insignificant, only to learn subsequently from Aeneas Silvius's letters that Parentucelli had become a cardinal and then pope. These developments convinced him that the dream of his coronation would prove prophetic. In response to these remarks, Nicholas V replied that the dreams of rulers often come true.[11]

Of all the Renaissance popes, it was Sixtus IV who enjoyed the most remarkable variety and number of dreams and portents prophetic of his election. The humanist Platina (1421–81), whose incomplete life of Sixtus is the last of the papal biographies in his *Liber de vita Christi ac omnium pontificum* (presented to the pope in 1475), describes a dream Francesco della Rovere's mother experienced before the future pope's birth. In the dream, St. Francis and another Franciscan seemed to bestow upon an infant the tunic, hood, and cord of the Franciscan habit. In response to the dream, and to honor this saint, Platina goes on, the newborn child was given the name Francesco. Immediately miraculous signs appeared. As the midwife was bathing the newborn, he raised two fingers, as if blessing the water. Then, having been held too long in the water, he seemed for a moment to stop breathing. His mother, mindful of her dream, vowed in thanks for his safe recovery from this episode that within six months he would be dressed in the habit of the Franciscans. The time elapsed, and Francesco's mother failed to fulfill her vow. At that point, the infant became ill, and recovered only when the vow was reiterated. Later also, when his parents were persuaded that perhaps they had been guided by superstition and that so austere a life should not be chosen before their son came of age, Francesco again broke out in fever, and became well only with the renewal of the vow. At length, at the age of nine, Francesco did enter the Franciscan Order, and he eventually became its head.[12]

Other contemporary accounts of Sixtus's early life enhance even more the role of the supernatural. Venturino de Prioribus (c. 1430-after 1482), a humanist from Sixtus's native Savona, in one of the series of Latin poems he wrote in honor of the pope—inspired by his hopes, ultimately dashed, to become a papal court poet—changes the incident of the bath to a second dream of Francesco's mother. In this, her infant son blesses the waters of a beautiful sea. Anxious to know what the dream portended, she went to her confessor. After puzzled mulling, at length he was moved, we are told, by divine impulse to affirm, "he will be high-priest of the city of Rome."[13]

Similarly, Robert Flemmyng (1415–83), an Englishman connected with the papal court since Pius II's time, mentions in his *Lucubraciunculae Tiburtinae*, presumably composed while the papal court sojourned at Tivoli in the summer of 1473, that as Francesco's nurse carried him in her arms across the main piazza of Savona, he raised his right hand in a gesture of blessing. Flemmyng also states that as a youth Francesco had fallen into the sea while walking along a seawall at Savona, and being unable to swim was rescued by Sts. Francis and Antony of Padua.[14]

The guiding presence of these two saints at critical moments in Sixtus's early life and their role in his election as pope were not just the myth-making flattery of courtiers. Their sacred intervention formed a key element in Sixtus's own projection of his pontificate. His coronation medal, in fact, shows Sts. Francis and Antony of Padua crowning him pope, the inscription explaining: HEC DAMVS IN TERRIS. AETERNA DABVNTVR OLIMPO.[15] A bull of 12 March 1472, seven months after Sixtus's election, which granted indulgences to the church of St. Antony in Padua, similarly states that through the merits of this saint, and of St. Francis, the pope, from a tender age, had been brought to the sanctity of the religious life, was sustained by them in his education as a theologian, and at length elevated to the papacy. More explicit is the bull issued six months later (3 October 1472), which made the feast of St. Francis a holy day of obligation. In this bull Sixtus states that when, as a baby, he wavered between life and death, he was brought back to health through St. Francis's intercession. In gratitude, he will wear the Franciscan habit to the end of his life and will promote the saint's teachings.[16]

Both Franciscan saints were still on Sixtus's mind on 8 December 1479, when he issued a bull regarding his burial chapel in St. Peter's. The bull specifies that the chapel is to be dedicated to the Virgin Mary and to Sts. Francis and Antony, "through whose merits and intercession," God not only had brought him to the Franciscan Order, the honor of the cardinalate, and the apex of the papacy, but also continued unceasingly to

6. Coronation medal of Sixtus IV, made by
Lysippus the Younger, 1471. The obverse
reads: SIXTVS.IIII.PONT.MAX.SACRICVLT[OR].
Washington, D. C., National Gallery of Art,
Samuel H. Kress Collection. (Photo: National
Gallery of Art)

concede His grace to His vicar on earth. To honor further these intercessors, the bull continues, and to encourage the devotion of the faithful, to
all Christians truly penitent and confessed, who visit annually the chapel
on the feast day of the Conception of the Virgin and on the feast days of
Sts. Francis and Antony, there will be granted plenary remission and
indulgence of all their sins.[17] This proclamation received visual reinforcement in the apse fresco of the *Capella Sixti IIII*, completed by Perugino
before the pope's death. The painting, no longer extant, showed the
Virgin and Child surrounded by angels and adored by Sixtus IV. St.
Peter, in turn, presented the pontiff to mother and son, as Sts. Paul,
Francis, and Antony of Padua bore witness.[18]

A more extensive visual treatment of these same themes focussing
on divine intercession appears in the lengthy series of frescoes devoted to
key events in Sixtus's life, painted in the Ospedale di S. Spirito in Sassia.
This major charitable institution, situated in the Borgo near Piazza
S. Pietro, gave refuge to the infirm and the destitute. In 1471 it burned,
and Sixtus in rebuilding it made it into one of the principal new monuments of restored Rome. The cycle, to which Platina contributed the
explanatory Latin inscriptions, begins with the hospital's foundation
under Innocent III. The first scenes show the sin of infanticide—mothers
tossing their newborns into the Tiber—and Innocent then dreaming of
fishermen drawing up drowned babies in their nets. This dream proves
all-too-true, and the pope orders construction of the hospital, the actual
site pointed out to him by an angel appearing in a vision. The depiction of
Sixtus's life begins with Sts. Francis and Antony of Padua appearing in his
mother's dream before her giving birth, with Francis holding out the
Franciscan habit and Antony the cord to a baby who kneels in prayer
before them. Then, in succession, follow Sixtus's birth, his baptism, his
brush with death while his nurse bathes him, his mother's renewed vow
that her son would become a Franciscan, the marvel of his raising his hand
in blessing as his nurse carries him across the piazza of Savona, his
mother's second renewal of her vow, his rescue by Sts. Francis and Antony
after falling into the sea, and his becoming a Franciscan at the age of nine.
After this appear five frescoes of Sixtus's accomplishments before his
election as pope, and then twenty more of his deeds as pontiff. The
penultimate scene shows him arrayed in his gold robe and triple tiara,
kneeling in judgment before God, with the Virgin Mary and St. Francis
serving as the pope's intercessors. Angels hold up in the foreground a
model of the Ospedale di Santo Spirito, while in the background other
angels display the Ponte Sisto, and the churches of S. Maria del Popolo
and S. Maria della Pace—all prominent Sistine constructions. In the last
fresco, St. Peter unlocks the door to Paradise and conducts Sixtus within.[19]

Pointed as these works, both poetic and artistic, might seem in their
stress on Sixtus's divine election, they are surpassed in their claims by the

De laudibus et de rebus gestis Sixti IIII Pont. Max., a poetic encomium composed by the Florentine humanist Aurelio Brandolini, who came to the papal court around 1480 and won such renown for his extemporaneous versifying that he became a papal intimate. Brandolini's poetic tribute originated apparently at Naples, before his transfer to Rome, was issued in a first version around 1481, and gained final form only after Sixtus's death, probably in the later 1480s, as part of a larger collection of prose and poetic praises of Sixtus presented to the deceased pontiff's nephew, Giuliano della Rovere (the future Julius II). As such it belongs to the same eulogistic motives that prompted Giuliano to commission Pollaiuolo to create his monumental bronze tomb for the Della Rovere pope.[20]

Brandolini's poem begins with omnipotent God surveying the cosmos from His throne on the heights of Olympus. Scrutinizing the ways of men, He discovers them immersed in the evils of war, attached to luxury and other vileness, and in continuous violation of human and divine laws. Determined to eradicate these wrongs, God wrathfully threatens the destruction of the human race. At this point the Virgin Mary tearfully intercedes for sinful humanity, and proposes that a lover of peace and a cultivator of virtue and probity be sent to earth to occupy Peter's see so that he can submit the necks of the savage human race to God's yoke. God is won over by this appeal, and agrees to create a man endowed with such wisdom, judgment, and virtue that as the good shepherd he will be able to watch over His flock and rule land and sea, wielding the divine scepter "as another God on earth." But who will preserve and guide this redeemer of the human race during his tender years? St. Francis volunteers to do so, and promises also to be a perpetual guardian of his life and labors. God assents and solemnly creates Sixtus's soul, endowing him with all His promised virtues and powers, and bestowing on him the name Sixtus, since through divine will he is to be given the power to hold firm (*sistere*) the tottering world.[21]

When one recalls the Della Rovere pope's morally dubious role in the Pazzi Conspiracy, his launching of dynastic wars, and his other all too human failings, Brandolini's claims seem at the least ingenuously myopic, if not blatantly blasphemous. But in Catholic doctrine, one must be reminded, the papacy is not a secular institution. Sacred doctrine affirmed its divine establishment by Christ through Peter, the Prince of the Apostles, and historical experience attested to the continuing presence of the Holy Spirit in the election of the Roman Pontiffs.

Nonetheless, the mystique of divine election came more often to be evoked for the surprise choices or the compromise candidates. Appeal to divine decision occurred, too, when expectations for reform, and therefore for a true spiritual leader, ran especially high, as in the conclave from which Leo X emerged. For popes like Paul II, Alexander VI, Julius II,

Clement VII, and Paul III, whose Roman careers made them prominent and whom contemporaries regarded for some time as *papabile*, emphasis on divine intervention proved less necessary. In the same way, newcomers to the Roman scene, like Nicholas V and Sixtus IV, once elected pope, needed most to affirm their authority and consolidate their power by underscoring divine guidance in their promotion and in their decisions. The enhancement of papal monarchical powers during the Renaissance period—powers exercised both in the ecclesiastical and secular arenas and in the spiritual office of binding and loosing souls—helps to explain, also, the intrusion of the divine. Emphasis on such claims to divine choice may well reflect, too, the peculiar nature of the Eternal City, where the merely human was so circumscribed by multiple manifestations of divine wonders, by the mythic potency of a glorious past, and by expectations of a transcendent future.

An evocation of the accomplishments of illustrious forebears and reference to other such symbols laden with historical and mythic prestige are apparent, in fact, in the names the Renaissance popes chose. Nicholas V, it is true, rather modestly commemorated the memory of his mentor, Cardinal Niccolò Albergati, whom he had served for twenty years as humanist secretary, and whom he succeeded as Bishop of Bologna;[22] and Sixtus IV was content to honor the martyr saint, Pope Sixtus II (257–58), on whose feast day the conclave that elected him commenced, though contemporaries were quick to recognize in him the virtues of all three previous pontiffs of that name.[23] Pius II, however, inspired by the Virgilian line, "*Sum pius Aeneas—fama super aethera notus*" (*Aeneid*, I, 378), chose a name that identified his given name (Aeneas) as that of the Trojan progenitor of the Roman people and suggested a similarly august acclaim for the new ruler of Rome.[24]

Julius II, not so poetically allusive, encouraged those who proclaimed him a second Julius Caesar, though he also promoted the cult of the fourth-century pope, Julius I, by pronouncing a plenary indulgence for those who venerated his recently discovered relics, displayed in S. Maria in Trastevere.[25]

Pierre d'Aubusson, Grand Master of the Hospitallers of Rhodes, hailed Alexander VI's election with the hopes that like his namesake, Alexander the Great, the Borgia pontiff would conquer the East, freeing it from barbarian tyranny; and in Johannes Tinctoris's motet the new pontiff is similarly celebrated as surpassing, by merit of his own virtues and by the celestial nature of his office, the achievements of the Macedonian.[26]

Even more remarkable are the attributes indulged in by Leo X. His *possesso*, as we have seen, coincided with the feast day of St. Leo (Pope Leo I), and he appears in the guise of the same pope in repelling Attila from the gates of Rome in Raphael's fresco in the Vatican Stanza d'Eliodoro. In the adjacent Stanza dell'Incendio, as Pope Leo III he crowns Charlemagne, while as Leo IV his benediction miraculously quells a fire in the Vatican Borgo and he gives thanks to God for the tempest that wrecked a Saracen fleet menacing Ostia. Allusions to lions were similarly culled for imagery of praise. On one of the papal coins minted during his pontificate, a lion as a symbol of vigilance—medieval lore held that lions slept with their eyes open—lies at the foot of the Mons Vaticanus as guardian of the new St. Peter's; on another a lion in profile is crowned by a Victory, and the inscription, VICIT LEO DE TRIBU JUDA, like the triumphal arch inscription of Leo's *possesso*, alludes to the messianic "lion, from the tribe of Judah, the scion of David," who is deemed worthy to break the seven seals and thus usher in the final time of apocalyptic fulfillment. The same Biblical passage is cited by Simon Kožičić Begnius, the principal speaker of the first session of the Fifth Lateran Council convened after Leo's election, and this Croatian bishop extends the image, hailing Leo as the longed-for savior raised up by God, who will free His people from the hands of their enemies (i.e., the Turks).[27]

Recognition of divine will and the use of names that conveyed mythic potency did not, however, preclude entirely discussion of the human qualities and moral character that should distinguish papal candidates. The orations "Concerning the Election of the Pope," delivered during the Mass of the Holy Spirit just before the cardinals entered into conclave, consistently emphasized that popes should possess the virtues of justice, piety, clemency, and humility, as well as wisdom joined to eloquence by which to persuade Christians to peace and concord and to moral life. The pope should, in short, by his nature and wisdom be a mirror to his flock and thus foster the art of good and holy living (*bene beateque vivendi*). These are princely virtues, as John McManamon points out,[28] and despite their commonplace generality the assumptions reflected in this mirror-of-popes literature are important. The pope is viewed as a ruler of an organic community—the Church—and his leadership role in its moral rejuvenation, the preservation of its liberty, the cultural renewal of its capital Rome, the establishment of *pax et concordia* among its members, and its defense against the Turks required involvement in the world. The values of the cloister—poverty, chastity, and obedience—whereby monks sought sanctity in withdrawal from the world were not appropriate to the Renaissance perception of the papacy's mission.

While recognizing that popes must in some sense be worldly, these same preachers still found much to reproach in their moral failures, particularly the rampant abuses of nepotism and simony, and many advocated as the most urgent need of the Church the complete reform of the Roman Curia. Openly condemnatory is the oration Alexis Celadoni delivered before the conclave to elect a successor to Alexander VI. He censures the flagrant corruption of the Borgia pope, who virtually "procured" the papacy, and who in choosing the name Alexander revealed his intentions to be like Alexander the Great and to subjugate the whole Christian world in pursuit of novel power in which he regarded neither human nor natural laws nor God Himself as denying him anything. Even though the pope had been favored by the force of the fortuitous in human affairs ("what the ancients called fortune, but what we should call by the pious designation *permissio Dei*"), and had survived shipwreck, pestilence, and a concussion resulting from when a lightning bolt caused part of the roof of the Vatican to collapse around him ("thus he overcame the perils of water, earth, and sky"), still what really marked Alexander's pontificate, Celadoni concludes, were the evils of war-mongering and wasteful luxury. Indeed, the Borgia pope preferred to be feared rather than loved, whereas the cardinals' responsibility must be, Celadoni warns, to give to the Church a spouse, not a pimp, a pastor, not a wolf. When entering into conclave, the cardinals must be electors, not candidates, he reminded, and setting aside political machinations and heeding only God and their consciences they must select not someone ambitious for the office, but rather one who would delight in "feeding his sheep."[29]

Whatever one's judgment of the Borgia pontiff, Celadoni's remarks on the qualities desired for the Vicar of Christ could hardly provoke disagreement. Celadoni's vehement moral condemnation, however, glossed over the nearly insuperable difficulty of finding combined in one man both the capacity to inspire religious renewal and the ability to maintain the political position of the Church in Rome, in Italy, and in the Latin Christian world. The choices actually made, in fact, show an oscillation between hopes for a genuine spiritual leader (Nicholas V, Sixtus IV, Pius III, Leo X, Adrian VI) and demands for a proven administrator (Paul II, Alexander VI, Clement VII). In Julius II, the Renaissance papacy came closest to finding a leader who was both. Resisting the temptations to family aggrandizement, he exercised his commanding authority on behalf of the Church, or at least what he understood as the Church's responsibilities and domain. Yet he, too, lacked the deep religious commitment and charismatic zeal of a Gregory the Great or Innocent III, which was needed for the Roman Church to rise above the maelstrom of Italian politics and to respond to the pressing spiritual anxieties of Latin Christendom.

A scrutiny of the occupants of St. Peter's chair in the Renaissance period reveals other important human characteristics. In the first place, they were overwhelmingly Italian. Indeed, of the fifteen pontiffs elected between 1417 and 1534, only three did not have Italian origins. Of these, two were the Borgia popes, Calixtus III and Alexander VI. Both came from Spain, but much of Calixtus's career before becoming a cardinal in 1444 had been spent in service to King Alfonso V, first in Aragon and

then in Naples. He thus had well-established Italian connections.[30] Even
more clearly was this the case for his nephew, Rodrigo, whose long career
as Vice-Chancellor brought him enormous wealth and influence at the
papal court, and whose numerous commendatory abbeys and other Italian benefices were shrewdly positioned on the strategic routes leading
north and south from Rome.[31]

The other non-Italian, Adrian VI, a Dutchman, owed his election to
a deadlocked conclave, his close ties to the Holy Roman Emperor Charles
V, whom he was serving as regent of Spain at the time of his election, and
the growing concern over the danger of schism in Germany. As it turned
out, he held the pontificate for only twenty months, just the last twelve of
which found him actually residing in Rome.[32]

Of the dozen Italian pontiffs, however, only Martin V and Paul III
were Romans, and only Martin, a Colonna, belonged to the powerful
baronial clans of Rome that had so dominated the papacy in the thirteenth century. The other Renaissance popes all came from northern
Italy: five Tuscans, three Ligurians, and two Venetians. What this reflects,
nevertheless, is not geographical affinity, but instead family power. By the
later fifteenth century, the papacy belonged increasingly to men whose
uncles had, as popes, promoted them to the purple. Besides Alexander
VI, this was true also of Paul II, Pius III, and Julius II—to which group
should be added Clement VII, named cardinal by his cousin, Leo X.
Borgia, Della Rovere-Riario, and Medici partisans thus became increasingly decisive in papal elections, displacing the older dominance of
the Colonna and Orsini factions.

This quasi-dynastic succession to the papal throne reached its apex
under the Medici, whose twenty-year control was but briefly interrupted
by Adrian's pontificate. Leo X's election, moreover, meant the capture of
the papacy not by someone made cardinal on the strength of his own
merits—Giovanni de' Medici was only thirteen in 1489, when Innocent
VIII promised a red hat for Lorenzo's second son—but rather because of
his link to one of the ruling houses of the Italian peninsula. This trend
actually began when Pius II nominated the first Gonzaga cardinal. By the
end of the fifteenth century, the Sforza and Este also had representatives
in the College of Cardinals, as did the Aragonese Kingdom of Naples.
Throughout the period Venice, too, never lacked its cardinals. These
politically motivated appointments indicate, in fact, the changing composition and nature of the College. Until Sixtus IV, the popes respected
the conciliar decree of Constance limiting the College's size to twenty-
four, and though Italians dominated (eleven of the eighteen cardinals in
the conclave which elected Nicholas V, nine of the eighteen from which
Pius II emerged pontiff), other European nations had representation.
Their numbers, moreover, included such distinguished theologians and

churchmen as Nicolaus Cusanus, Juan de Torquemada, Domenico Capranica, and Bessarion. These four had died by 1473, and Sixtus IV's
thirty-four creations, including six nephews, not only enlarged the College but stemmed in the main from political considerations. Men of
learning did not disappear entirely from the College in the later Renaissance period. One could point to Oliviero Carafa, Bernardino Carvajal,
Cajetan, and Giles of Viterbo. But clearly the cardinalate had become
more worldly—and overwhelmingly Italian (twenty-seven of the thirty-
eight in the conclave which chose Julius II, eighteen of the twenty-five in
Leo's conclave, thirty-four of the thirty-nine in Clement VII's).[33]

For Giles of Viterbo, Sixtus IV's pontificate marked the turning-
point of the papacy's descent into an advanced stage of corruption,
venality, and nepotism.[34] Actually, however, nepotism had become a
fixture of the Renaissance papacy before Sixtus's succession. Of the 820
appointments recorded during Pius II's reign, 122 (14.9 percent) involved papal relatives or Siennese compatriots, and an additional 71 (8.6
percent) can be tied directly to influence exercised by other ecclesiastics or
by secular rulers. In fact, similar papal favoritism long predated the
fifteenth century.[35]

Sixtus's experience is instructive, nevertheless, in taking the measure of the human realities of papal office. His rise within the Church was
owed to his prominence as a theologian and to his reforming administration of the Franciscan Order. Neither attainment provided a training
ground for experience in wielding the temporal power of the papacy.
Family origins in provincial Savona of modest mercantile means, and the
fact that his recent elevation to the cardinalate meant he had not yet
developed a strong party in the College or within the hierarchy of the
Roman Curia, proved further handicaps. Dynastic ambitions aside, inevitably he turned to family members to help administer the Church and
to govern Rome and the Papal States.

As pope, Sixtus promptly named his nephews Giuliano della Rovere
and Pietro Riario cardinals, and Pietro was granted vast sums to create the
brilliant court entertainments the Renaissance judged necessary for successful diplomacy. The Prefecture of Rome was secured for another Della
Rovere, Lionardo, while Girolamo Riario became Captain General of the
Church and received a power base in the Romagna. In his thirteen years
as pope, Sixtus appointed, in addition to the six family members raised to
the purple, each lavishly endowed with pluralities of benefices, at least
four other Della Rovere as provincial treasurers. Moreover, dynastic
considerations, inspired by Girolamo's ambitions, did come to the fore
during the last half dozen years of Sixtus's pontificate. Weakness of
character may explain some of Sixtus's excesses, but the political realities
seem more fundamental. Machiavelli, in fact, praised Sixtus for his cour-

age in recognizing the political obstacles that confronted the effective
exercise of papal temporal power. But, he remarked, characteristically,
that neither *fortuna* nor the pope's *virtù* sufficed to overcome them.[36]

ITALIAN POLITICS

Sixtus IV's predicament derived in large part from the consequences of
decisions made half a century before his accession. In the early fifteenth
century, the opinion held nearly universally among Latin Christians was
that to resolve the scandal of the Great Schism the papacy, again reunited,
needed to be returned to Rome. During the chaos of the Schism, however,
the popes had lost political control of central Italy, first to the mercenary
companies, then to the territorial aggrandizement of Gian Galeazzo Visconti of Milan followed by Ladislas of Naples. Ladislas, in fact, remained
arbiter of Rome from 1408 until his death in 1414, and his occupation of
the city became the prime cause prompting Pope John XXIII's agreement to attend the Council of Constance.

That Council's selection of Oddo Colonna represented a level-
headed recognition of the political realities confronting restoration of the
papacy to the Eternal City. At the time of Martin's election in 1417, Rome
was in the hands of the Perugian condottiere Braccio da Montone, who
had managed to carve a state out of nominally papal territories in Umbria.
A show of force against Braccio, then negotiations to gain the allegiance
of other *signori* delayed the Colonna pontiff a year and a half in Florence,
until finally in September 1420 he rode into Rome. Gradually wresting
control of the Papal States from illegitimate usurpers required much of
the remainder of his pontificate. But the means used—reliance on the
baronial power base of the Colonna—could not readily be transferred to
Martin's successor. Indeed, Colonna reluctance to hand over their strongholds to the Venetian, Eugenius IV, provoked war. This in turn permitted the intrusion of the *condottieri* Niccolò Piccinino and Niccolò Forte-
braccio. Their menacing of Rome aroused the rebellion of the Roman
populace in 1434, which forced Eugenius to flee from the city in a
rowboat, disguised as a monk. Florence provided refuge, and he spent
most of the next decade there and in Bologna.

The point was clear. No pope could reside safely in Rome unless he
controlled the city politically and militarily, and this in turn depended
upon effective government of the surrounding Papal States. The cruel
campaigns of Cardinal Vitelleschi succeeded eventually in pacifying
Latium, and when Eugenius in 1443 shifted from the Angevin to the
Aragonese cause in Naples—an acquiescence to Alfonso V's battlefield
supremacy—the path at last became clear for the papacy to come back to
Rome.[37]

Eugenius was the last Renaissance pope forced to flee Rome because of popular revolt, and Stefano Porcari's failed plot against Nicholas V was the last republican challenge to papal dominance of local government. The independent Roman commune, capable of overturning papal policy, was no more; and by the end of the fifteenth century not only had control of urban planning and public works come under papal control, but all other key positions in urban administration also had become subject to papal jurisdiction. Urban finances were integrated into the Apostolic Chamber, and the papal Vice-Chamberlain became the effective governor of the city. Moreover, many other key positions of local power switched from lay to ecclesiastical incumbency—this was the case, for instance, of the *castellano* of Castel Sant'Angelo from 1464 onward. This meant a more pliant adherence to papal will.[38]

The Roman citizenry thus found its access to real power slowly eroded. In its place, Roman citizenship became channeled into such festive outlets as the *Festa di Agone* of the Roman Carnival, took its meaning from assimilation to the mystique of ancient Roman glory (as in the collection of antique bronzes Sixtus IV gathered on the Capitoline), or, as was the case with so much of Roman Renaissance culture, expressed itself primarily in ceremonial display.

The most elaborate such public spectacle was the two-day long pageantry of September 1513, held to honor Leo X's brother, Giuliano, and nephew, Lorenzo, with Roman citizenship. This event, underwritten by the Roman civic officials, the *Conservatori*, took place in a sumptuous temporary theater, constructed expressly for the occasion on the Capitoline Hill. Two Roman Academicians, Tommaso Inghirami and Camillo Porzio, had been enlisted to create the various elements of the spectacle, and they used the revived tradition of the Palilia, the celebration of the anniversary of Rome's founding, as a vehicle to glorify the magnificence of both Rome and the Medici. The gilded wooden architecture of the theater, which seated more than a thousand dignitaries, had an appropriately classical design, including a triumphal arch entrance. Painted scenes devoted to subjects from ancient Roman history also filled the intercolumnar spaces of the walls. These stressed the intimate connections that had existed between the Etruscan and Roman civilizations, and implied their renewal in the restored link between Tuscan Florence and Rome accomplished by Leo's election as pope. One scene, in which an Etruscan soothsayer showed how to interpret omens, and another, in which an Etruscan priest instructed his Roman counterpart in the proper performance of ritual sacrifices, celebrated the new high priest from Tuscany who now presided over the sacred rites of the Roman Church.

The pageantry itself consisted of the arrival of Giuliano and his entourage (Lorenzo remained behind in Florence); his reception by the *Conservatori* and other Roman magistrates; a solemn Mass; an oration by a young Roman disciple of Pomponio Leto; the actual presentation to Giuliano of the document proclaiming him a Roman citizen, punctuated by the sounds of trumpets and artillery; a banquet of more than twenty courses enlivened by music and buffoons; a series of dramatic representations, allegorical in nature, in which various gods, nymphs, and human figures celebrated in speech, dance, and song Giuliano and the pope; and, on the next day, another allegorical sketch, richly costumed, followed by a performance in Latin of Plautus's play *Poenulus*.

Through all the dramatic *rappresentazioni* threaded a persistent theme: the resurgence of Rome's glory under Medici rule meant that augmented dignity and honor had devolved upon the city's citizenry. The third skit of the first day's spectacle, in particular, centered upon this notion. From a door in the back of the stage appeared the *Mons Tarpeius*, with the Capitol at its summit. Upon reaching the middle of the proscenium, this device opened, revealing the ancient *Deus Capitolinus* himself, supporting on his right shoulder the temple of Jupiter Capitolinus and against his chest the refuge of Romulus. Marvelling at the public festivity before him, then realizing the reason for such joy, he proceeded to divest himself of his hoary beard and unkempt hair, and emerged as a handsome youth—just as the Capitoline Hill itself had been rejuvenated in the construction of the theater and in the unfolding pageantry.

Then followed a recitation in Latin verse, in which the repristinated *Deus Capitolinus*, struck with wonder at the pomp of the festivities, declared them to surpass in splendor the triumphs of antiquity, when victorious Roman commanders mounted the Capitoline to the tumultuous acclaim of the Roman people. For time out of mind, however, the Hill had lain deserted, deprived of glory. Now at last was fulfilled Jove's declaration that the Fates would bring as benign benefactor that supernal issue of the Medici, Giuliano. In antiquity the Capitoline had preserved the *fasci* of the Consuls and borne the weight of the world, witnessing distant, barbarian peoples made subject to Roman rule. Now it is for Giuliano, spurred on by the same "pious glory," to take the Romans as his comrades and to assume the defense of Rome's citizenry:

> In you is my hope, and in Leo X, who is the splendor of the world, and whom Rome, now preserved, calls Father; the Senate and the People applaud you. . . . Live felicitously, and if these last words of our mouth move you, Rome, through you, will reassume the curule chairs; Italians, freed from care, will return to their standards; and the ancient Campus Martius will renew its rights of suffrage. Thus, as true physicians [Medici] your name will mount to the stars and the fame of your race will be celebrated eternally.[39]

By such carefully choreographed means were Roman citizens enticed to submerge their will in the exultant vision of the Renaissance papacy.

Rome, then, gradually submitted to papal rule. Indeed, by the end of Nicholas V's pontificate this process was well under way. In the 1440s, too, the emerging pattern of peninsular politics, which persisted until the French invasion of 1494, proved favorable to the papacy's interests in consolidating central Italy into a territorial state. Alfonso of Aragon's victory over his Angevin rival for the throne of Naples lessened opportunities for independent action by ambitious *condottieri* in that vast feudalized kingdom bordering Rome so closely to the south. At the same time, Cosimo de' Medici's *de facto* rule of Florence and the success of his old ally, Francesco Sforza, in seizing the Duchy of Milan in 1450 brought to an end the more than half-century long series of conflicts between the Florentine Republic and the Visconti with their inevitable repercussions on papal dominions in Umbria and the Romagna. The Peace of Lodi of 1454, signed by Venice, Milan, and Florence, and enlarged the following year into a general Italian League with the addition of Naples and the papacy, confirmed the great power stability in Italy.[40]

There was, moreover, an important economic, in addition to political, incentive to extending papal temporal power in central Italy. This involved the changed nature of papal revenues, yet another legacy of the Great Schism. Under Gregory XI (1370–78), the last pope before the divided papacy, no more than twenty-five percent of total papal income came from the temporal proceeds of the Papal States. During the Schism, however, and particularly during the Council of Constance, European rulers took advantage of the weakened and split papacy to reduce taxes. Under Martin V this "spiritual" income from the Church at large— annates, first fruits, common services, and tenths—amounted to only one-third of its pre-Schism total, and the drawn-out struggle between Eugenius IV and the Council of Basel reduced yet further these older ecclesiastical revenues. Increased and more systematically collected direct and indirect taxes on Rome and the Papal States partially compensated for this reduced spiritual income. Indeed this "temporal" income, owed to the pope not because he was head of the Church, but because he was ruler of central Italy, approached fifty percent of Martin's annual income, and in Sixtus IV's budget for 1480–81 was calculated at nearly sixty percent. The Papal States, in short, formed the most readily expandable source of revenue for the Renaissance papacy, and the rationalized territorial administration Martin V developed to exploit the fiscal possibilities of the papal dominions continued to be enlarged by his successors.[41]

Besides motives of security and fiscal interests, yet another reason prompted papal determination to hold on stubbornly to the Papal States. These territories, the popes believed, constituted the "patrimony" of Peter. That is, they belonged to the saint himself, and therefore to the Roman church. The popes thus had a sacred duty to prevent their falling into alien hands. Religious mystique served in this way to reinforce political and economic ambitions in the shaping of papal policy.[42]

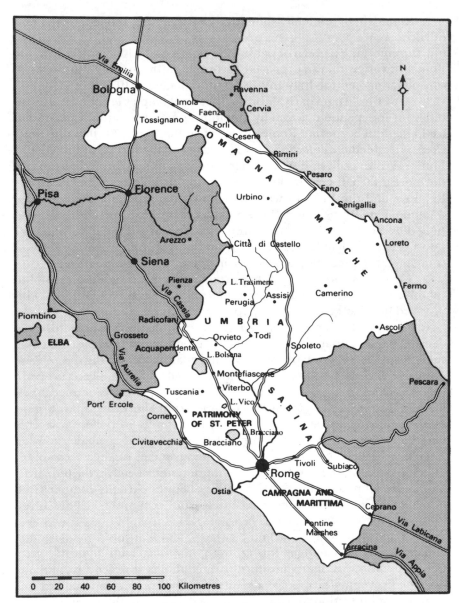

The Papal States in the late fifteenth century

Circumstances, both geographical and political, nonetheless continued to thwart papal efforts to manage central Italy as effectively as the Florentines governed Tuscany or the Venetians controlled eastern Lombardy and the Veneto. In the first place, the Papal States did not form a coherent geographical entity. Straddling both sides of the Apennines, and extending to both the Tyrrhenian and Adriatic Seas, papal territory was a collection of disparate regions. Provincial agents and fiscal officers of the Apostolic Chamber might compete with some measure of success against baronial power in the Roman District or in the Patrimony of St. Peter in Tuscany, which extended northwest of Rome to the towering *rocca* at Radicofani, the border of the Siennese state, but the farther one went from Rome the more tenuous became papal authority. Through to the end of the fifteenth century, the Montefeltro Dukes of Urbino controlled all the key Apennine passes between Rome and the northeast, and equally free from papal rule remained the Sforza of Pesaro (also in the province of the Marche). From here, in fact, Francesco Sforza managed to catapult himself to the Duchy of Milan. Ancona, the chief Adriatic port of central Italy, was brought under direct papal rule only in 1532. Yet even then it served as entrepôt not for Rome but instead for commercially developed Florence, and the Florentine axis had been responsible for its earlier economic growth. Both Perugia and Bologna, too, each of which rivalled Rome in population and surpassed it in economic power, stayed effectively independent under local tyrants for most of the fifteenth century.[43]

Clearly the most refractory region, however, was the Romagna. Since the fourteenth century a constellation of petty principalities ruled by local *signori* had existed in Ravenna and in the small cities along the Via Emilia from Rimini to Imola. Appointment as papal vicars hardly disguised the reality of their independence from papal rule, as Pius II's exasperations with Sigismondo Malatesta attest. Until Cesare Borgia's campaigns, these *signori* could fall behind in their annual *censi* (the tax owed the Apostolic Chamber) with impunity. Even more troublesome, the Romagna provided Italy's best soldiers and its ablest *condottieri*, and often as not they served the popes' rivals. Moreover, Florence, Milan, and especially Venice had ambitions in the region. The Venetians acquired a protectorate over Ravenna in 1441, came near to seizing Ferrara in 1482–84, occupied key ports in Apulia in 1495, thus threatening Ancona, and with the collapse of Cesare Borgia's state in 1503 gained control of Rimini and Faenza. Julius II's War of the League of Cambrai finally reversed Venetian Romagnol expansion. Peace did not ensue, however, as French and Spanish ambitions for dominance of the peninsula made this strategic region a major battle ground, notably in the bloody Battle of Ravenna on Easter Sunday of 1512. Nonetheless, Julius's actions in re covering the Romagna laid the foundations for its eventual integration into a centrally administered state.[44]

A sign of this incipient consolidation appears in Adrian VI's notion to subject the whole of the Papal States to uniform direct taxation, a goal achieved with Paul III's institution in 1543 of the "Triennial Subsidy," which in reality was a permanent tax. Oppressive fiscality became truly the accomplishment only of the later sixteenth century, however. In 1600 the papal dominion provided three times the revenues it had contributed a century before and represented nearly eighty percent of total papal income. To this same period belongs, too, the final reduction of the remaining independent enclaves within the Papal States. Papal seizure of Ferrara in 1598, for instance, brought to an end four centuries of Estensi rule in that city.[45]

State-building, in short, despite clear fiscal advantages to the Apostolic Chamber, proved a laborious process. The Renaissance papacy gained substantial headway, but also encountered repeated reverses, and completion of the task lies beyond our period. Fundamental to grasping the nature of the Renaissance papacy, however, is the recognition of how much pursuit of temporal power diverted papal energy from other concerns and tended to distort papal authority in monarchical directions.

In the first place, territorial consolidation obligated the popes to very substantial military expenditures. Contemporary estimates pegged the cost of Sixtus IV's mercenary armies at one hundred thousand ducats a year, almost sixty percent of the temporal income from the Papal States.[46] The importance of military power to the papacy, and the esteem accorded victorious accomplishments, is exemplified, too, in this same pontiff's jubilant procession to S. Maria del Popolo in celebration of Roberto Malatesta's defeat of Neapolitan forces at the Battle of Campo Morto in August 1482. When Malatesta died a few weeks later of disease, probably dysentery, contracted in the Pontine Marshes during the campaign, he was accorded a funeral in St. Peter's befitting a cardinal, and Sixtus arranged for a marble sepulcher with a sculpted relief of the mounted condottiere to be placed conspicuously in the basilica along with an epitaph commemorating Roberto's exploits.[47]

Castle construction similarly testifies to the prominence of military affairs in the minds of the Renaissance popes. The imposing remains of Pius II's *Arx Pia* at Tivoli and of the Borgia castle at Civita Castellana guarding the Tiber crossing forty miles north of Rome remind us how security-conscious they were. Not only did the popes fortify extensively, but the designs employed were also among the most innovative in providing defense against the increasing effectiveness of siege artillery. The *rocca* Giuliano della Rovere built at Ostia in 1482–86 was the most advanced fortress of its time, while similarly current in design, and costly, was this same cardinal's fortifying of Grottaferrata in the Alban Hills,

7. *Rocca* at Ostia, built for Cardinal Giuliano della Rovere, 1482–86, by the architect Baccio Pontelli. The adjacent church of S. Aurea, seen at the right, was also designed by Pontelli. (Photo: by the author)

which he held as commendatory abbot.[48] Repair of the dilapidated Aurelian Walls formed a key element in Nicholas V's plans for rebuilding Rome,[49] and his fortification of the Ponte Milvio and the Ponte Nomentana on the outskirts of the city can still be seen.[50] The successive modernizations of Castel Sant'Angelo under Nicholas and Alexander VI, Nicholas's system of defensive walls and great round tower in the Vatican, and the projecting battlements of the Sistine Chapel reveal that military considerations penetrated even into the ceremonial heart of the Borgo Leonino.[51]

The 1527 Sack showed that there was good reason for such precautions, but it also showed how inadequate Rome's defenses were for the new age of artillery. The fresh memory of the disasters of the Sack, plus the ominous mooring of the Ottoman fleet off the Tiber estuary, encouraged Paul III, shortly after his accession, to envision the complete modernization of Rome's defensive circuit. In fact, the initial proposal amounted to a halving of Rome's long defensive perimeter by extending a new wall across the sparsely inhabited *monti*. This new line was to include eighteen powerful, double-flanked bastions, spaced some five hundred meters apart and supported by intermediate gun emplacements. Of this vast plan, only the bastion at Porta Ardeatina reached completion, under Antonio da Sangallo the Younger in 1542. This was among the most respected works of military architecture produced anywhere in the sixteenth century, but its enormous cost—slightly more than Sixtus V later spent to move the Vatican obelisk, though but a sixth of what he expended on the Aqua Felice—made continuation of the project seem prohibitively expensive. There was the further drawback, too, that the new wall would have left outside both the Lateran and S. Maria Maggiore. The outmoded Aurelian Wall thus continued to provide later sixteenth-century Rome with its first line of defense.[52]

In their concern for military priorities, the Renaissance popes echoed the policies of Europe's secular rulers. Pursuit of the politics of power is evident, too, in the dynastically motivated marriages of papal relatives. This is yet another development traceable to Sixtus IV (i.e., Girolamo Riario's marriage to Caterina Sforza), but illustrating best the cynical exploitation of family members in the furthering of papal temporal policies are Lucrezia Borgia's marriages. Before her father's accession as Alexander VI, she was betrothed to an Aragonese count, but soon after his accession, her engagement was broken and a new match, with Giovanni Sforza, Lord of Pesaro, was made. By this means Alexander sealed Sforza's adherence to the League of St. Mark; and it had the added benefit of winning for papal service an able military commander, who was also a potentially recalcitrant papal vicar in the Marche. Despite the pomp of a wedding in the Vatican—Innocent VIII had set the precedent of such public celebrations of the nuptials of papal offspring—the political value of Lucrezia's marriage proved nil almost from the outset. Papal policy shifted to the Neapolitan connection, and Lucrezia's first marriage ended in annulment after four years, when political pressure from Milan at length forced Giovanni to an ignominious public acknowledgment that he had failed to consummate the marriage.

Lucrezia's second marriage, to Alfonso, Duke of Bisceglie, the illegitimate son of Alfonso II of Naples, ended even more disastrously. Following another diplomatic *volte-face* by which Alexander abandoned Naples, Alfonso was murdered in the Vatican, on the orders of Lucrezia's brother Cesare.

In 1501 Lucrezia married for the third time. Still only twenty-one, she was betrothed to Alfonso d'Este, heir to the Duchy of Ferrara. This was a more prestigious match than any previous papal dynastic arrangement, and brought Borgia influence into the most stable and respected of Italian principalities. Wedding festivities extended over the last week of December 1501 and the first week of January 1502. Alexander ordered the Carnival moved up to coincide with this event, and balls, banquets, games, bullfights, and dramatic representations provided a ceaseless round of spectacle and entertainment. The *Festa di Agone* parade of floats celebrated the triumphs of Hercules and Julius Caesar (alluding to Alfonso's father, Ercole d'Este, and to Cesare Borgia), and the pageantry staged the evening of 2 January similarly lauded these two figures. This began with *Virtus* and *Fortuna* discussing which was superior, but then Glory arrived in a triumphal chariot with the world under her feet and the identifying inscription GLORIA DOMUS BORGIE. She announced her preference for virtue over fortune, since both Caesar and Hercules had defeated fortune's power by the exercise of virtue. This served as a point of departure for Glory to recount many of Cesare Borgia's noble deeds. Hercules then fought Fortune (sent to oppose him by Juno), and vanquished her, but at length agreed to set her free on condition she would bring no harm to Cesare or to the House of Borgia. The skit concluded with Juno's blessing of Lucrezia's marriage. This time, despite the eclipse of Borgia fortunes—or perhaps because of it—Lucrezia's marriage lasted until her death in 1519, and as Duchess of Ferrara she gave birth to Ercole II, who eventually succeeded Alfonso as Duke of the Este principality in 1534.[53]

Dynastic marriages provided one way to promote family ambitions; resort to war was another. Again, Borgia actions—Cesare's campaigns to conquer Tuscany and the Romagna—seem most blatant. Crusading funds, sale of offices, proceeds from the Jubilee indulgence, and outright confiscations—all were resorted to in order to keep Cesare's army in the field.[54] What proved unusual about Borgia ambitions, however, as P.J. Jones has pointed out,[55] was neither their purpose nor their unscrupulousness, but rather that they succeeded, as long as Alexander lived at least. After all, Sixtus IV earlier had purchased Imola for his nephew Girolamo Riario, and then acquired Forlì for him by force. Girolamo's growing power in the Romagna became one of the factors leading to deteriorating relations with Medicean Florence, and Sixtus at the very least failed to put a halt to the plot—the notorious Pazzi conspiracy—by which Girolamo intended to rid the city on the Arno of his Medici rivals. The upshot was Giuliano de' Medici's murder at the high altar of the Florentine cathedral, while Lorenzo barely escaped the same fate by fleeing into the sacristy. The ensuing war with Florence, and the subsequent rapid succession of wars with Naples and Ferrara, then with Venice—all likewise stemmed from Sixtus's pursuance of Girolamo's interests. In the end, short-fused Forlivesi assassinated Girolamo in 1488, and his widow, Caterina Sforza, became one of the victims of Cesare Borgia's conquests.[56]

Lorenzo de' Medici's son, Pope Leo X, despite the negative precedent of Girolamo Riario, and despite the hopes his election raised for

bringing peace to Italy, also used war as an instrument of family aggrandizement. The costly War of Urbino (1516–17) wrested the Duchy of
Urbino from Francesco Maria della Rovere, nephew of Leo's predecessor
Julius II, and placed it in the hands of Leo's nephew, Lorenzo. But the
enormous military expenditures nearly bankrupted the papal treasury,
further exacerbated the fragile basis of political stability on the peninsula,
and in the end proved fruitless, since Lorenzo's early death in 1519 left no
other legitimate or marriageable family member alive to succeed to the
Duchy.[57]

Papal wars inspired by dynastic motives were not unique to the
Renaissance, of course. One could point to Boniface VIII's promotion of
Caetani fortunes in the years around 1300, or to Urban VIII's War of
Castro (1641–44), which vainly attempted to supplant Farnese rule, consolidated a century earlier under Paul III, and to replace it with the
Barberini.[58] Nevertheless, for the Renaissance papacy, effective territorial
administration, astute maneuvering in the kaleidoscopic world of Italian
politics, and gaining the military upper hand were seen as essential means
for maintaining the prestige, independence, and authority of the Roman
see. More often than not—Julius II is the obvious exception—this meant
relying on trusted family members as the main instruments of policy and
the inevitable primacy of dynastic interests. The elective nature of the
papal office, which meant the vulnerability of any gains to spoliation by an
embittered successor (the case of Cesare Borgia under Julius II) only
compounded the internal contradictions of the situation. So, too, did the
relatively brief span of time papal incumbents could expect to occupy the
papal throne. Renaissance popes served on average about nine years:
Eugenius IV's sixteen years was the longest, Pius III's twenty-six days the
shortest. Many were already elderly when elected. Calixtus III was
seventy-six, Julius II and Paul III in their sixties, while the exceptional
youth of Leo X, thirty-seven, should be discounted by Medici tendencies
to early death. This only increased the sense of urgency to achieve
dynastic successes before death intervened.[59]

EUROPE AND CRUSADE

The parochial politics of Italy, though always a factor in shaping papal
policies and frequently the dominant one, could not hold exclusive sway.
The popes, after all, had responsibilities for Latin Christendom as a
whole, and these generated countervailing pressures against a single-
minded pursuit of Italian temporal power. As spiritual heads of the
respublica Christiana, the Roman pontiffs addressed a whole range of
religious issues—appointments, reform measures, efforts to combat
heresy—that brought awareness of the European scene into the confines

of the Vatican Palace, and the frequent arrivals and departures of legations to and from the Eternal City promoted the same recognition of a larger Christian world.

Several Renaissance popes, notably Nicholas V and Pius II, also acquired considerable experience of trans-Alpine Europe gained firsthand from extensive journeys made before their accessions. Pius, especially, possessed a keen eye for landscape and local custom, and his geographical interests are apparent both in his *Commentaries* and in his unfinished *Historia rerum ubique gestarum*, which Columbus studied closely.[60]

Geographical awareness even extended beyond Christian boundaries. In early sixteenth-century Rome, several Roman humanists cultivated Arabic studies, and there for a time, after his capture by pirates in 1517, lived the Arab traveler and geographer Leo Africanus. His *De totius Africae descriptione* gave Europeans a much improved grasp of North Africa and of the Muslim world generally.[61]

Within the sphere of European politics as such, Rome also reclaimed a place of prominence. After the Peace of Lodi, the Eternal City became the nerve center of the emerging Italian diplomatic system, and all the Italian powers maintained resident ambassadors there. The European states, first Spain (by 1480), then France, the Holy Roman Empire, and England (after 1494), followed suit. As a diplomatic corps, these ambassadors attended the papal court, formed an audience for the lavish entertainments so readily available in the city, and reported to their respective governments the various rumors and intrigues that circulated through this listening post of Europe.[62]

The restored prestige of papal Rome as the hub of international politics acquired yet more luster from visiting heads of state. Among such luminaries were Christian I, King of Denmark and Norway, Nicholas Ujláky, King of Bosnia, and Charlotte of Lusignan, ex-Queen of Cyprus—all commemorated in the frescoes of the Ospedale di Santo Spirito that depicted highpoints of Sixtus IV's pontificate.[63]

Similarly, one of the great events of Nicholas V's pontificate, for contemporary observers, was the coronation in Rome of the Holy Roman Emperor Frederick III. The German ruler adhered precisely to the ceremonial route of imperial entry from Monte Mario to the Vatican and other elements of the coronation rite scrupulously observed medieval tradition.[64] After the lapse of two centuries, the twin heads of Latin Christendom thus seemed to reassume their proper roles. With hindsight, however, this last imperial coronation in Rome seems hopelessly anachronistic. Gone were the days of a Frederick Barbarossa or Frederick II, when the German emperors surpassed in power all the other secular rulers on the continent and battled popes and communes for control of northern and central Italy. Unlike Frederick III (or Maximilian), Charles

V, the last Holy Roman Emperor to be crowned by papal hands (by
Clement VII, in Bologna in 1530), did possess real power in Italian
affairs. But in reality his coronation testified to the hegemonic might of
Spain. Not Germany, but rather the Aragonese inheritance formed the
basis of Charles's dominance in Italy, and the Iberian kingdoms were the
key to his Habsburg empire.[65]

Equally anachronistic, too, at first glance, seem the repeated papal
calls, made throughout the Renaissance period, for crusade against the
Infidel. Holy Wars to wrest Jerusalem and the other holy places of
Palestine from Muslim hands—those sanctified expeditions that had so
inflamed the martial zeal and fired the spiritual imagination of the Christian nobility—were characteristically medieval impulses. Yet from Pope
Urban II's famous speech at the Council of Clermont in 1095, which
launched the First Crusade, wars against the Infidel had provided opportunities for underscoring papal headship of a Christian *imperium*, united
in sacred purpose, and the popes had ensured the religious merit of the
crusades by granting indulgences and other spiritual benefits to their
participants.[66]

Promotion of crusade enabled, then, the Renaissance popes to re-
evoke the memory of these stirring medieval feats, made possible a direct
appeal to the consciences of Latin Christians, and in both respects provided a means of reasserting papal leadership of the *respublica Christiana*.
But proclamations of crusades were not just an exercise in nostalgia. The
apparently inexorable Ottoman advance in the Balkans, in central
Europe, and in the eastern Mediterranean during the fifteenth and
sixteenth centuries posed a real threat to Latin Europe. To serious-
minded Christians, the popes should assume responsibility for responding to this challenge. Indeed, in the sermons for the elections of the
popes, speakers repeatedly declared to the cardinals that war against the
Turks constituted a prime religious task for any pontiff, and one integral
to religious reform.[67]

Reform and crusade form linked causes, too, in Giles of Viterbo's
celebrated inaugural address to the Fifth Lateran Council. Corruption,
spiritual weakness, and dissension have permitted the power and dominion of Muḥammad to increase, Giles argued, and Julius II's mission,
following the example of Moses, must be to use the true weapons of the
Church—piety, devotion, prayers, and offerings—to launch an assault
against the Turks. The shield of faith, the arms of light, and the golden
cloak of the burning spirit provided the means by which the Church
conquered Africa, Europe, and Asia. When, Giles declared, these were
exchanged for the iron weapons of mad Ajax much of the empire of the
twelve Apostles was lost. Religion and sanctity, not war and iron, are the
keys to victory.[68]

Here Giles enjoined direct papal recourse to arms, but on other occasions he showed fewer scruples, exhorting the popes to take up themselves *pia arma* and to lead the *pia bella* against the Turks. Like Peter, the pope should use the sword against "Malchus, the slave of the Prince of this World."[69] Deeply disturbed by the ominous implications of the Turkish advance, Giles seems to have felt that the crisis justified papal conduct of war, if that proved the most expeditious means to initiate the *sancta expeditio*.[70]

Giles did not stand alone among the speakers at the Fifth Lateran Council in stressing the need for crusade. Speech after speech warned of the Turkish peril, Ottoman atrocities were repeatedly recited, and the pope was urged to use both the spiritual and temporal swords to save Christendom. Among the most fervent addresses is that of Simon Begnius, whose Croatian see was besieged by the Turks. "Fetter the enemies who persecute us," he exhorts the newly elected Leo X, "set free the tabernacle of your spouse [i.e., the Church], which the hands of the impious have polluted, so that just as the Christian people venerate you as the only true pope, the enemies of the Christian name will stand in fear of your religious power and tremble before your might."[71]

Still more impassioned is the Latin poetry Johannes Michael Nagonius addressed to Julius II. This figure, who declares his designation by public decree as a Roman citizen and poet laureate, but who seems otherwise little known, composed his poetic exhortations in the flush of the extravagant praise that greeted Julius following his conquest of Bologna in 1506. Aspire, Nagonius urges this second Julius Caesar, to the more sublime, immortal, and eternal triumph, praise, and glory to be earned in recovering the Holy Land and all the East from barbarian servitude. Have mercy on the most holy city of Jerusalem. The enslaved city, dressed in mourning and flowing with tears, asks particularly for your help, your protection, your power, your military expertise. Who, except Julius, Nagonius queries, could presume to extricate Antioch, Ptolemaic Alexandria, and Jerusalem—the "workshop" (*officina*) of our salvation—from the teeth of the barbarians? Who but Julius would dare to carry the sign of the Cross to the Euphrates and the Tigris, and restore to Mesopotamia the Christian name? "Therefore rejoice Julius II! There exists no people so barbarous, so uncivilized, so alien as to prevent your attainment of glory, fame, praise, and eternity!"[72]

Prefacing Nagonius's volume is a full-page miniature depicting Julius, adorned with golden cloak, crowned with the triple tiara, and riding in a triumphal chariot in the guise of a classical *triumphator*. At his side, dressed in antique helmet and military garb, is Francesco Maria della Rovere, who accompanied his uncle on the 1506 Bologna campaign. Bound captives lie below, while above an angel unfurls a banner with the words HIERVSALEM MISERERETVR. The explanatory text reads: "*Hierusalem syonque tuus pater ecce triumphat. Julius expulsis hostibus atque nepos*."[73]

8. Julius II as *Triumphator*. Frontispiece to volume of Latin poetry addressed
to Julius II by Johannes Michael Nagonius. BAV, ms. Vat. lat. 1682, fol. 8ᵛ
(Photo: Biblioteca Apostolica Vaticana)

In another poem, this time in Italian *terza rima*, Girolamo Bardoni has Jerusalem herself address Rome and Leo X. "*O alma augusta et trium-phante Roma*," she says, "awake! I, the poor damsel, whom the Arab and Mameluke have raped and despoiled, implore your help on bended knee." Rehearsing the victories after victories achieved by the ancient Romans, she urges Rome to send "your true sons born of Mars." Remind-ing Rome of her temples made into mosques, her sacred mount deserted, her sanctuaries and sacred relics laid prostrate before the barbarians, she declares she will never find peace unless "the fierce lion from the tribe of Judah" rises up. Delay no longer the unfurling of the sails of the Apostolic Roman bark, she urges. Delphic Apollo foresees good fortune to the end, whether on sea or land. If the Greeks to recover the daughter of Leda (Helen)—a single woman—spilled so much blood that Turkish soil is still vermilion, what should be done in response to a thousand times greater provocation? If Leo fulfills his destiny to vindicate our dishonor, she declares, "I will make of all nations one flock and you the shepherd, monarch, and commander." He is that great Lion, celestial man and mortal god, worthy of eternal name, whose roar makes earth, sea, heaven, and hell tremble. Time is short! To horse![74]

Such crusading sentiments were not the preserve of Rome alone. One could point to Philip the Good of Burgundy, whose chivalric zeal to fight the Grand Turk single-handedly formed the emotional climax to the famous "Vows of the Pheasant" made in 1454.[75] Forty years later, among the prophecies stemming from the French court of Charles VIII as he prepared to invade Italy, was one in which the king, having conquered the peninsula, would cross over to the East, wrest Jerusalem from the Infidel, and there in his thirty-fifth year receive an angelic crown on the Mount of Olives.[76]

At the base of these persistent longings lay the reluctance to distin-guish the zeal to recover the Holy Sepulcher, ennobled by medieval tradition, from the strategic planning necessary to confront Ottoman expansion. Containment of the "Turkish peril" required the mobilization of western military power on a different basis from the old chivalric motives of piety and knightly heroism implied in the term crusade. The disaster at Nicopolis (1396), where the Franco-Burgundian nobility was decimated, confirmed what had become increasingly apparent over the previous century: the tactical futility of the frontal charge of heavily armored knights. This mode of attack, enshrined in chivalric honor, had been the key to the growth of Latin power in the Mediterranean during the High Middle Ages.[77] But the Ottoman Empire—with its ghazi troops converted to regular cavalry; its Janissary infantry levied from the formerly Christian Balkans, trained as professional soldiers, and made fanatically loyal to Islam and the Sultan; and in possession of gunpowder artillery used to devastating effect in the conquest of Constantinople—

was in command of military might overwhelmingly superior to any single expedition of Christian knights.[78] The utter defeat of the Crusade of Varna—the venture launched by Eugenius IV in fulfillment of pledges made to the Byzantine Emperor at the Council of Florence—on the shores of the Black Sea in 1444 served as a clear demonstration of the pointlessness of such campaigns, and it was the last crusade based on the medieval model.[79]

Yet the fall of Constantinople to Mehmed the Conqueror in 1453 made urgent some form of military response to this dramatic show of strength. Despite long standing western awareness of the Byzantine capital's jeopardy, its capture was profoundly shocking. For Rome, this extinction of "one of the two lights of Christendom"[80] seemed especially ominous since reports reaching Nicholas V from the Levant warned that Mehmed boasted he would soon be on his way to the Eternal City.[81] With the ensuing loss of the Morea to the Ottomans in 1460, and the steady erosion of Venetian power in the Aegean—Venetian defeat in the long, debilitating war of 1463–79 meant the decisive shift in eastern Mediterranean naval supremacy to the Turks—Rome's position seemed even more precarious. Italy, in fact, stood at the frontier, and in a striking display of Mediterranean power the Ottomans followed up their defeat of Venice by simultaneously besieging Rhodes and seizing Otranto (in Apulia).[82]

Papal response to the Turkish danger took a variety of forms. Nicholas V's initial reaction to the fall of Constantinople was to summon all Christian rulers to a crusade, to solicit their financial assistance, and to convene a congress of Italian powers to meet in Rome in order to establish a peninsular peace. This congress, which deliberated from November 1453 to March 1454, failed to settle Italian conflicts, but in April 1454 Venice and Milan suddenly ended hostilities in the Peace of Lodi, and within a year all the major Italian powers had become signatories to an Italian League and were pledged to a twenty-five year peace.[83]

Circumstances in Italy thus seemed propitious for establishing the united front to counterattack the Ottomans. Securing trans-Alpine support, however, proved another matter. Growing resentment at what many perceived as papal misuse of crusading taxes for other purposes was one reason—although until Sixtus IV's pontificate revenues from the sale of indulgences were actually expended on crusade.[84] More fundamental were the weakness of the Holy Roman Empire, conflicting political ambitions (such as the French crown's support of the Angevin claim to Naples), and the higher priority accorded state building.

Competing state interests afflicted Italy, too. They prevented, for instance, any effective co-ordination of Venice and Naples, the two Italian states in the best position to use their Mediterranean sea power to counter the Turkish advance. Each, however, realistically feared giving the other an advantage in Italian affairs. Repeated papal proclamations of crusade and a continuous stream of cardinal legates thus produced no effective response.

Nor did Pius II's Congress of Mantua, convoked in June 1459 as a meeting of all European powers to prepare for a Turkish campaign. Pius waited months for trans-Alpine representatives to arrive, and even the Italian states proved dilatory in appearing. After eight months of delays, haggling, and recriminations, Pius left Mantua with no firm commitments for united action.[85]

Similarly inconsequential were Leo X's anxious efforts following Selim's conquest of Egypt in 1517 to promote European peace and a crusade. Neither the report of a cardinals' commission nor the sending of legates to the Christian powers nor the proclamation of a five-year truce accomplished anything.[86]

No matter how eloquent papal ambassadors might be, no matter how vehement the language of crusading bulls, papal diplomacy invariably failed to establish a united Latin Christian effort. And, however noble in impulse, Pius II's personal taking of the Cross in St. Peter's in 1464 must be judged the quixotic action of a frustrated and dying pope.[87]

More realistic than European congresses and grand schemes of an overall Christian alliance were military subsidies, drawn from the Tolfa alum receipts and other sources, to the Christian rulers most immediately threatened by the Ottoman expansion. Among the most successful resistant leaders was the Albanian, Scanderbeg (d. 1468). Exploiting the geographical advantages of his mountainous native land, the determination of his people to escape Turkish enslavement, and the tactics of surprise assault, he managed for a quarter century to defeat numerically superior Turkish forces.[88] Similarly, aid to Hungary, particularly if combined with alliance to the naval power of Venice—the strategy pursued by Paul II—was a feasible policy. But Hungarian energies were frequently diverted from the Turkish struggle to conflict with the Habsburgs, and other opportunities were missed in desultory campaigns to expunge the Hussite heretics from Bohemia.[89]

Pragmatic as this strategic juncture of local resistance, Mediterranean naval power, and central European land forces might be in theory, sustaining this grouping for the long term and effecting tactical coordination over the enormous distances involved proved unmanageable. Moreover, even within these groupings of confrontation states, rivalries undermined concerted action. Paul II, for instance, kept a desperate Scanderbeg waiting two months in Rome in the winter of 1466–67 for a promised subvention, which in the end never materialized. Paul feared that aid to Scanderbeg would release Venetian forces to seize advantage of Milan's momentary vulnerability following the death of Francesco

Sforza.[90] In short, the successes of papal inspired and subsidized military alliances were limited to administering merely temporary reverses to the Ottoman surge.

Intensive European diplomacy and financial support for active combatants were not the only alternatives pursued by the papacy in confronting the Turkish peril. Calixtus III, who vowed to devote all his energies as pope to the recovery of Constantinople and to the destruction of the Turks, expended the huge sum of 150,000 ducats during the first year of his pontificate to construct and equip a papal navy. Naval warfare in the Mediterranean in the fifteenth century was based on rowed galleys, essentially the same instrument of war that had been used in antiquity. Not until the late sixteenth century did galleys give way to the broadside sailing ship.[91] Calixtus's fleet of sixteen galleys was built in Rome itself at an arsenal created on the Vatican side of the Tiber, and shipwrights and carpenters were brought in from other parts of Italy. The papal squadron spent some eighteen months in the eastern Mediterranean, under the command of Cardinal Ludovico Trevisan, engaging the Turkish fleet off Lesbos and briefly occupying the Acropolis at Athens. The fleet was supposed to be joined by Neapolitan galleys, but to the fury of the pope, King Alfonso instead used them to attack Genoa. At Calixtus's death the papal galleys sailed home, were moored in the Tiber, and there allowed to rot away. By the time Pius II had committed himself to personal leadership of a crusade, in 1463, the papal fleet had to be outfitted again from scratch.[92]

Later fifteenth-century popes followed Calixtus's example in sporadic fashion. Sixtus IV contributed a number of galleys to a large Venetian-Neapolitan-papal fleet which harried the coast of Asia Minor in the summer of 1472. Unopposed by the Ottoman navy, the crusaders burned the harbor area of Satalia and sacked Smyrna, but did not dare to venture into the Dardanelles. The papal galleys re-entered Rome in January 1473, bringing with them some Turkish prisoners and part of the harbor chain of Satalia, which was mounted as a trophy of war over the main portal of St. Peter's.[93]

The shock of the Ottoman sack of Otranto in the summer of 1480—the first Turkish assault on the Italian mainland and the high-water mark of Mehmed's western advance—again spurred papal naval initiatives. Sixtus, immersed in the Tuscan War, which was the aftermath of the Pazzi Conspiracy, concluded hostilities. He then made hasty arrangements to assemble a crusading fleet, contributing twenty-five papal galleys. Before this enterprise could embark, news reached Rome, on 2 June 1481, of Mehmed's death. At S. Maria del Popolo, Sixtus gave thanks for God's deliverance, and three days of jubilant celebration followed. With high hopes the papal fleet prepared to part for Apulia at the end of the month. The Roman chronicler Gherardi describes the pageantry of the setting late in the afternoon of 30 June, the day after the Feast of Sts. Peter and Paul, as the pontiff and cardinals went to the fleet anchored in the Tiber alongside S. Paolo f.l.m. Sixtus addressed the sailors, exhorting them to place their hope in Our Lord, "who will not allow the bark of Peter to be engulfed," then solemnly blessed the fleet. Swords were brandished, clamorous shouts invoking the pope's name were raised to the heavens, cannon thundered, trumpets blared, and an infectious joy raced through the crowd.[94]

The fleet did participate in the recovery of Otranto, but the outbreak of plague there and dissension in the ranks forestalled a follow-up attack on Valona, the key Turkish naval port on the opposite Albanian coast. The Turks, nevertheless, had been driven from Italian shores, and Sixtus went in person to Civitavecchia on 20 October to welcome the returning fleet.[95]

Julius II continued his uncle Sixtus's development of papal naval power. In 1508 he decided to strengthen the port of Civitavecchia to serve as a naval base and to provide improved coastal defense against Muslim pirates. Bramante furnished the design for the massive *fortezza a mare*, the pope himself presided over the laying of the foundation stone, and work continued there under Antonio da San Gallo and Michelangelo during much of the first half of the sixteenth century.[96] Leonardo da Vinci, in his Roman sojourn of 1513–16, also spent time at the port city and was able to reconstruct the plan of the ancient port facilities, originally built under the Emperor Trajan.[97]

Papal galleys continued to be constructed and manned through the first three quarters of the sixteenth century. Pope Paul III provided twenty-seven galleys for the fleet of the Holy League of Venice, Spain, and the papacy, which was formed in response to the Ottoman navy's attack on Corfu in 1537 and to the simultaneous cavalry raid into Apulia. Once again, as in 1480, Italy seemed on the verge of full-scale assault, but despite the defeat of the Holy League's fleet, under the command of Andrea Doria, at Prevesa in September 1538 and the Venetian separate peace of 1540, Italy once again was spared. The Ottoman Empire's war with Persia and the contest with Portugal for control of the Red Sea and the Indian Ocean diverted Turkish military power away from the Mediterranean.[98]

A generation later, in 1571, a dozen papal galleys under the command of Marcantonio Colonna formed part of the great fleet of more than two hundred war galleys of the Holy League (again comprised of Venice, Spain, and the papacy), which won the spectacular victory over the Ottoman navy in the Gulf of Lepanto.[99]

Despite participation in such "glorious feats," direct papal involvement in sea warfare proved largely inconsequential in curbing Turkish ambitions. As a second-class power, the papacy simply lacked the re-

9. Medal of Sixtus IV, commemorating the liberation of Otranto from the Ottoman Turks in 1481, made by Andrea Guacialoti. On the reverse stands the nearly nude figure of Constancy, holding a long staff in her right arm and resting her left elbow on a fluted column. Turkish prisoners with captured pennons kneel at her feet, and ships at harbor appear in the background. The inscription reads: PARCERE.SVBIECTIS. ET.DEBELLARE.SVPERBOS. ("to spare the conquered, and vanquish the proud": Virgil, *Aeneid*, VI, 853). Washington, D.C., National Gallery of Art, Samuel H. Kress Collection. (Photo: National Gallery of Art)

sources in the extravagantly costly arena of galley warfare to mount by itself anything more than raiding expeditions, which as often as not resulted in the scandal of piratical attacks upon Christian commercial shipping.[100] More telling for the fortunes of Latin Christendom than any papal naval activity was the steady shrinking of Venice's Aegean Empire. Representative of Christian retreat in the Mediterranean, too, is the history of the Knights of St. John, whose Grand Master, as we have seen, had looked to the second Borgia pope as a new Alexander the Great, who would conquer the East. Instead the Knights were pushed westward. Heroic defenders of Rhodes in 1480, they were driven from the island in 1522 in one of the first campaigns of Suleyman the Magnificent (1520–66), whose long career of conquests was as daunting to sixteenth-century Christendom as Mehmed the Conqueror's had been to the fifteenth. Withdrawn to Malta, the Knights were assaulted there by the full force of Ottoman might in 1565, and only the most stubborn resistance enabled them to survive.[101]

In the end it was imperial Spain, exploiting all the economic resources of an Italy firmly under her command, which produced a stand-off in the central Mediterranean. Indeed, as the sixteenth century—the age of "gunpowder empires"—wore on, the destiny of the Mediterranean, including Italy, turned on the policies of the imperial powers—France, Spain, and the Ottoman Empire. With the alliance of Francis I and Suleyman, and the resulting joint operations of the French and Turkish navies—including the wintering of the Ottoman fleet at Toulon in 1543–44—struggle for control of the Mediterranean depended less on any remaining crusading impulses and latent dreams of a united Latin Christendom than on the geo-political strategies of the great powers.[102]

Rome could witness various victories and defeats. The Eternal City celebrated, for instance, the Emperor Charles V's conquest of Tunis in 1535 with a triumph in the classical mode, staged during the monarch's visit to the city the following year. Paintings on the temporary triumphal arches evoked the memories of Rome's victories over Carthage, and Charles was hailed as a third Africanus, equal to the two Scipios.[103] But just as seizure of the African city proved ephemeral—Don John of Austria used enormous forces to recapture it in 1573, only to have it retaken by the Ottoman fleet a year later[104]—so did Rome's participation in Charles V's victory prove irrelevant to the realities of Mediterranean power politics.

At least as important as any western action, moreover, were the internal dynamics and imperial designs of the Ottoman state. The succession struggle that followed Mehmed's sudden death in 1481, for instance, gave Latin Christendom an unexpected and sorely needed reprieve. Indeed, the loser in the struggle, Jem Sultan, escaped to the West, and eventually lived six years as a prisoner of the popes until his death in 1495.

While alive, Jem posed a continual threat to Sultan Bayezid's throne, a danger which Innocent VIII and Alexander VI exploited to divert (partially) the contest with the Ottomans into diplomatic channels.[105] From the Ottoman perspective, furthermore, expansion into central Europe and into the Aegean and Ionian Seas was only one direction of conquest. Selim I (1512–20) focused Turkish energies on seizing Syria and Egypt from the Mamluks, and in the mid-sixteenth century Suleyman was much preoccupied with wars to the East, against the Shiite Safavi Empire.[106]

Negligible, in the final analysis, as direct papal involvement in war against the Turks might be in any military sense, its implications for the nature of the Renaissance papacy were far from inconsequential. In the first place, preparations for belligerency against the Ottoman infidel, like the pursuit of temporal power in Italy, kept the papacy on a war footing. Crusade expenditures had the result, too, of further distorting the papal budget toward military priorities, which in turn contributed to the popes' tendencies to see themselves not so much in the succession of Aaron as in that of Moses (or Joshua). Over time, too, as so many proclamations of crusade, so many diplomatic missions, so many congresses, so many abortive campaigns failed to eradicate, or even come to grips, with the Ottoman menace, the currency of crusade became devalued.[107] When crusading tenths became part of the normal income of the Spanish crown (and spent in Italian wars), when Alexander VI made overtures to Bayezid for assistance against the Italian invasion of Charles VIII of France in 1494, when the same pontiff sanctioned the partition by France and Spain of the Kingdom of Naples in 1501 as being in the interests of the crusade and diverted crusading funds to finance Cesare's campaigns in the Romagna, then the whole notion of crusade became just another negotiable item in the tangled skein of international politics.[108]

By the later fifteenth century, in sum, increasing cynicism marked the papal calls for crusade. But throughout the Renaissance period there was an entirely different perspective from which some Romans considered the Turkish peril: the impending eschatological *dénouement* of human history. For George of Trebizond, the *émigré* Greek scholar, Mehmed's conquest of Constantinople ushered in the final days. The Ottoman sultan was "King of Kings" and destined to rule the whole world; his seizure of Rome was imminent, and he would soon rule from Britain to Ceylon. But Mehmed's world empire would be but the prelude to the reign of terror of Gog and Magog, unless, like Constantine, he converted to Christianity and thus created of the whole *oikoumene* one religion and one empire with its capital at Constantinople. Indeed, within a month after news of Byzantium's fall reached Rome, George had written a treatise addressed to Mehmed urging him to emulate Constantine and showing how Islam and Christianity might be reconciled; and for the next decade he attempted to persuade both the popes and the kings of

Naples (in whose services he was employed) to send him to Constantinople to attempt in person to convert the Ottoman emperor. In 1465 Paul II seems to have acceded to George's insistent entreaties, and he spent some months in Istanbul in the winter of 1465–66, without however ever meeting Mehmed. En route home, his convictions still unshaken, George wrote another treatise, *On the Eternal Glory of the Autocrat and his World Empire*, in which he underscored the Sultan's role in the apocalyptic fulfillment of human destiny. This, added to the fervent admiration of the Ottoman ruler and the eagerness to enter his service that George frankly expressed in his letters to Mehmed, strained Paul II's patience too far. Returned to Rome, George found himself clapped into Castel Sant'Angelo, where he remained for a four months' stint, until released through papal clemency.[109]

George of Trebizond's eschatological fervor proved exceptional among fifteenth-century Romans, but other thinkers did share his hopes that the "way of conversion" might be the solution to Christendom's plight and that such a development might bring mankind into a new age of peace and stability. Nicolaus Cusanus, for instance, who served as Vicar-General of Rome while Pius II attended the crusading Congress of Mantua, composed in that period his *Cribatio Alcorani*, which argued the basic concordances existing between Islam and Christianity. Cusanus's irenicism had a precedent in the *De mittendo gladio divini Spiritus in corda Saracenorum*. This treatise, the work of Juan de Segovia, a missionary preacher to Muslim North Africa who furnished Cusanus with a Latin translation of the Koran, advanced ideas of Muslim-Christian rapprochement. Segovia intended to dedicate his tract to Nicholas V, but was dissuaded when the pope made clear his determination to pursue the path of crusade. Cusanus's ideas, in turn, influenced a remarkable letter that Pius II composed in the fall of 1461. In this *"Epistula ad Mahumetem,"* which, it seems, he never actually sent to Mehmed II, the Piccolomini pontiff attempted to show the superior reasonableness of Christianity to Islam. From this cultural superiority stemmed a superior civil order and a stronger moral force, which the pope saw as a more stable structure for human society than the force of arms. Like Constantine, Mehmed should recognize this, and his conversion, like the fourth-century Roman emperor's, would provide the basis for a new world community. Pius thus saw his own role as that of another Pope Silvester (the pope who had converted Constantine to the True Faith), and as late as March 1462 Pius was consulting the humanist Domenico de' Domenichi regarding the authenticity of Silvester's baptism of Constantine. Pius's letter (any discussion of which he expunged from his *Commentaries*) was a response of desperation to the failed crusading conference at Mantua, and it preceded the equally desperate decision to lead a crusade in person.[110]

Yet the dream of such a conversion persisted. In December 1518

Paolo Giustiniani, the Camaldulese hermit and earlier author of a program of ecclesiastical reform presented to Leo X, addressed a letter (again probably never sent) to the *Turchorum imperator* (Selim). In this he argued that the sultan should not seek to emulate Caesar or Alexander the Great, whose world-empires it was reported he wished to rival, but rather Constantine; for in converting to Christianity Selim would quickly gain the world dominion he so desired.[111]

In the early sixteenth century there was articulated anew, also, a more developed eschatological framework for considering the Turkish problem. But the dire forebodings of George of Trebizond's outlook were counterbalanced—in the views of Giles of Viterbo—by the import of recent Spanish and Portuguese accomplishments, especially the voyages of discovery.

From the time of Eugenius IV, Renaissance popes had, in fact, taken cognizance of Portuguese oceanic exploration. By 1455 Nicholas V had granted to the Iberian kingdom possession of Madeira, Cape Verde, and the Azores, a concession which had its basis, at least in part, in the principle utilized since the eleventh century and traceable ultimately to the Donation of Constantine that all islands fell under papal jurisdiction.[112] Subsequent papal decrees, including Alexander VI's famous bulls of 1493 that conceded the islands found by Columbus to the Spanish crown, emphasized also that along with rights of possession went the responsibility to propagate the Gospel to the inhabitants of new-found lands. As such, these papal enactments drew on the conception, developed in the canonist tradition of the late Middle Ages, of papal responsibility for the care and governance of the whole of mankind, both Christian and infidel. As universal shepherd, the pope had spiritual responsibilities even for the unbaptized, who were not yet in the fold, since one day there would be only one flock and one shepherd (John 10: 16).[113]

For early sixteenth-century Romans, the extension of Christianity to newly discovered regions of the world, along with the wresting of the Kingdom of Granada from the Muslims (1492) and the Spanish capture of several outposts along the North African littoral (e.g., Bugia, modern Bougie or Bejaïa, in 1510), seemed to reverse the shrinkage of Christendom in the face of Ottoman advances.[114] Particularly dramatic was the news which King Manuel I of Portugal (1495–1521) sent to Julius II in the fall of 1507. The Portuguese kingdom had just achieved three startling successes in the Far East: the discovery of Madagascar, the placing of Ceylon under tribute, and the naval victory over the fleet of the Zamorin of Calicut. Julius responded, as we have seen, by proclaiming three days of thanksgiving, culminating in the solemn celebration in St. Peter's of the Feast of St. Thomas, the Apostle to India. Giles of Viterbo furnished the oration for the occasion, and afterwards, at the pope's request, prepared a longer, written version, which was sent to King Manuel. The central theme of this discourse, the dawning Golden Age, will be explored more fully later. But in terms of the Turkish challenge, Giles emphasized that the expansion of the Christian *imperium* beyond anything previously known constituted a clear sign of the impending union of all mankind in peace and concord. At last the time was propitious for a crusade. Once Antichrist (the Ottoman infidel) was defeated and the holy places in Jerusalem and Palestine recovered for Christendom, then the Johannine promise of one shepherd and one sheepfold would be fulfilled.[115]

An even more hopeful eschatology characterizes Giles's *Historia XX saeculorum*, written during Leo X's pontificate and dedicated to him. In this work, Giles linked the discovery of the New World and what he saw as a firmer determination to defeat the Turks with the intellectual accomplishments of the Renaissance as indications of the emerging tenth age under Leo X. He felt, too, that the ecclesiastical renovation these signs portended might be completed during the pope's lifetime.[116]

More somber in tone is Giles's *Scechina*, his Christianizing interpretation of the cabala, begun in 1530 at Pope Clement VII's request, but dedicated instead to the Emperor Charles V. The horrors of the Sack of Rome in 1527 convinced Giles that a period of tribulation and upheaval, in which purgation would be accomplished only by bloodshed, had now begun. Significantly, too, he now saw the emperor, not the pope, as the key charismatic figure. Just as it was Charles's ships that had sailed to new lands, so it would be his armies that would conquer the Turks. He would be the shepherd who would gather all into one sheepfold and thereby be the true king of Jerusalem.[117]

In yet another way did the Turkish peril influence developments in Roman Renaissance culture. The conquest of Constantinople signified not just the demise of the great eastern Christian capital, but meant also, as Aeneas Silvius Piccolomini put it, "the second death for Homer and for Plato, too."[118] The Ottoman sack of the city, in short, threatened the calamitous loss of classical Greek literature and thought just at the point when Italian humanists were beginning to exploit these sources of learning.

Preservation of Greek wisdom thus became one of Rome's urgent tasks, and this cultural mission contributed to the renewed sense of Rome's pivotal role as a world capital. In this regard, it is revealing that in the *Strategicon adversus Turcos*—ostensibly an analysis of the weapons, tactics, and military organization of the Ottomans and how best to combat them, composed by the Lombard humanist Lampugnino Birago (d. 1472) and presented to Nicholas V within eighteen months of the fall of Constantinople—the author found military value in the promotion of Greek culture and learning the pope so actively cultivated. Love of learning, Birago argued, would contribute to the wisdom and authority of the

western princes, who in Themistocles and other ancients would find
models for inspired military and political leadership. To help fulfill the
cultural mission he advocated, Birago while in Rome translated into Latin
various works of Plutarch and Xenophon, and provided a Latin version of
the whole of Dionysius of Halicarnassus's *Antiquitates Romanae*, dedicated
to Paul II.[119]

The link between Greek studies and crusade was stressed also by the
Greek cardinals, Bessarion (d. 1472) and Isidore of Kiev (d. 1463). Isidore, in fact, barely escaped capture during the Ottoman sack of Constantinople and his was among the first accounts of the destruction of Greek
libraries in the looted city.[120] Not only were both cardinals ardent supporters of war against the Ottomans—Bessarion headed a number of legations to trans-Alpine nations, in attempts to rouse support for crusading
expeditions—but both also made of their Roman households informal
academies for Greek scholarship. Young Italian humanists with an interest in Greek studies were able to find positions on the cardinals' staffs
or in other ways found them supportive patrons. Francesco Griffolini
(1420-after 1470) of Arezzo, for instance, first found a place in Rome with
Isidore, and while in the Eternal City translated works of the Greek
Church Fathers and parts of the Homeric *corpus*.[121] Similarly, the young
Roman Cristoforo da Persona (d. 1485) joined Isidore's *familia* in the
1450s and through his patronage was named (in 1456) Prior of the
Roman monastery of S. Balbina on the Aventine. Like Griffolini, Persona
was a translator of Greek patristics, and he also made Latin versions of
Procopius's and Agathius's histories of the Gothic Wars.[122]

Beyond patronage of Greek studies, the Greek *émigrés* made Rome
the arena for one of the major intellectual controversies of the fifteenth
century: the debate over Plato and Aristotle. The dispute had its origins in
Byzantium before the fall of Constantinople, was continued in the polemical exchanges among Greek refugees in Italy during the 1450s, and
reached its climax with the fusillades traded between the Platonist Bessarion and the Aristotelian George of Trebizond in the period 1467–72.
Until this last stage of the controversy, the language of disputation was
Greek, which meant that even though Italian humanists' loyalties were
roused to either side, the actual content of the debate had little direct
impact on humanist thought. Nevertheless it did bring into the limelight
important works of Greek classical thought, and brought onto center
stage as a serious task of philosophic inquiry a detailed confrontation
between Plato's and Aristotle's philosophic systems. Moreover, while the
controversy raged, Rome was the setting for the impassioned
arguments.[123]

The extinction of Constantinople, then, stimulated in a variety of
ways scholarly and intellectual activity in Rome, and thus a back-handed

consequence of the Turkish advance was a furtherance of the cultural renewal of the Eternal City.

CHURCH ADMINISTRATION AND SPIRITUAL POWER

The demands of temporal power had a decided influence in shaping the character and policies of the Renaissance papacy. But these dramatic developments should not obscure the equally fundamental role of ecclesiastical power. Indeed, since administrative practices and theological decisions affected Latin Christendom as a whole, and were more apt to impinge upon Christians in their daily lives, they perhaps had even greater significance in determining contemporary perceptions of the papacy and of Rome. Increasingly, Rome was the place where appointments to ecclesiastical office were made, legal disputes argued, cases of conscience resolved, and spiritual favors gained. These functions enhanced Rome's position as capital, elaborated in additional ways the monarchical and courtly definition of the papacy, and offered important career opportunities and financial inducements for humanists at the papal court. But the administrative intricacy and financial aspects of papal practices also proved disillusioning, even to many in Rome, who found their implications for papal religious authority too worldly. Clearly, too, they added to the mistrust and suspicion outsiders harbored for Rome as Babylon, and widened the gulf between Rome and the Church at large.

The administrative history of the Renaissance papacy has yet to be written, leaving uncertain many details of the jurisdiction, function, and procedure practiced by the various papal organs and tribunals.[124] Nonetheless, it is clear that the Renaissance popes continued the tendency begun by the Avignonese papacy towards centralization and bureaucratization.[125] One result was the dramatic growth in numbers of Curial officials. During the itinerant pontificate of Eugenius IV, the papal entourage numbered just over one hundred fifty people, and this included both the palace staff and the officials of the main administrative departments of the Curia.[126] Under Pius II, the papal court was still so few in numbers that the Signatura could meet in the chestnut groves of Monte Amiata and the pope's affixing of his seal could be interrupted by hounds chasing a stag.[127] This bucolic image disappeared, however, by the end of the fifteenth century, as the papal court recovered its Avignonese size of between five and six hundred, while by the 1520s, if largely honorific venal offices are counted, its numbers surpassed two thousand.[128]

A distinction had developed, moreover, between the papal *familia*, with its increasing numbers of domestic servants and honorary courtiers, and the Curial staff, who had gone "out of court." Chancellery officials, for instance, performed many of their duties during Rodrigo Borgia's headship in his palace across the Tiber from the Vatican, and the Chancellery remained there under his successor. So pressing had need for office space become by the early sixteenth century, particularly with the demolition of older Vatican buildings to make way for the new St. Peter's, that Julius II envisioned constructing a vast Palazzo dei Tribunali, situated on his new Via Giulia. This huge complex would have housed the various courts of justice, in addition to the Datary and the Apostolic Chamber. The project never reached beyond ground-floor construction, but enough of Bramante's design survives to indicate he conceived this monumental *"forum Julium"* as a visual embodiment of the implacable authority and imperial majesty projected by the Renaissance papacy at the height of its powers.[129]

The increase in numbers of Curial officials, their permanent residence in Rome, and the extension of their jurisdictional competence contributed to the increasing prestige and status of a post in the Roman Curia. Like all bureaucracies, there developed as well an acute awareness of rank within the hierarchy and of the perquisites that went with it. Rancorous disputes about precedence, such as whether protonotaries or bishops had the right to be closer to the pope in the great ceremonial processions, marred a number of Roman religious spectacles. Beyond dispute, however, was the pre-eminence of any Curialist over the ordinary ranks of the Roman clergy.[130]

One important effect of this increasingly centralized bureaucracy was its contribution to papal income. In this respect the most revealing development is the growth of the Datary, an office established by Martin V, but which reached its maturation as the key organ of papal finance and administration only with Sixtus IV. By then it was entrenched as the mechanism by which all supplications, including appointments to most benefices, as well as requests for dispensations and indulgences reached the pope. As the source of venal offices, it was the linchpin, too, of financing the papal debt. Its name comes from the fact that the dating of the papal *concessum* or *fiat* gave the granting of the favor legal effect, but, as will be seen, dating was often neither an obvious nor straightforward matter.[131]

To grasp the Datary's role in papal appointments to ecclesiastical office, one must be reminded of the ways by which such appointments had come under papal control and the various subtleties of the benefice system. Two practices, both stemming from the thirteenth century, had brought most clerical offices out of the control of local bishops, cathedral chapters, or lay patrons, and into papal hands. These were papal provision—the right of the pope to confer a benefice without the concurrence and even against the will of the local authority—and papal reservation—

offices reserved for appointment exclusively by the pope.[132] Already by the Avignonese period, provision was the normal means of access to a bishopric. In the Renaissance period provision to bishoprics and other of the most important Church positions took place in Consistory, the formal meeting of pope and cardinals. One reason was the occasion this offered for cardinals to earn "tips" (*propina*) for advancing candidates.[133] Then followed an elaborate series of bureaucratic steps to prepare the appropriate forms, after which all taxes and fees had to be paid to the papal banker before the sealed bull of appointment was released, permitting the appointee to take up office.[134]

Papal reservation, however, because it covered so much wider a range of Church offices, is a more revealing indicator of how the appointment process worked. As with provisions, the Avignonese papacy had already widely used reservation, but Martin V went a step further by instituting the practice of "papal months," six to eight months out of the year in which any benefice that fell vacant was filled by papal appointment.[135] Frequently also connected to appointments at this level were requests for papal dispensations permitting pluralism, non-residency, or occupying "incompatible" benefices. This last meant holding offices, such as a parish and a priory, where obligations of both secular and regular clergy were entailed. The term used to describe this practice was *unio* or *incorporatio*, and unions in perpetuity required the payment of half the annual value of the benefices to the Datary.[136]

The Datary was the key cog in the appointments process at the non-Consistorial level for other reasons. In the first place, various legal devices, each requiring action by the Curia and with financial implications for the Datary, were used to favor certain candidates. One such, the promise of a benefice not yet vacant, was called an "expectative favor" (*gratia expectativa*), and had been used extensively by the Avignonese papacy, particularly to fill canonries.[137] Expectatives continued as a common practice in the Renaissance period, but other methods developed with regard to vacating benefices. The incumbent could resign his benefice but reserve part of its revenues as a pension; he could resign but with the right to reassume the office (the right of "regress"); or he could resign in favor of some designated person (*resignatio in favorem*).[138] Each was tinged with simony, and each entailed action by the Curia and payments to the Datary, but it was the *resignationes in favorem* which produced the most serious abuses. A revealing instance is the poet Ariosto's effort (the subject of his second *Satire* on the greed and ambition of the Roman Curia) to obtain the resignation of the parish church of S. Agata sul Santerno (worth three hundred ducats) in the diocese of Faenza, a benefice held by an aging friend. Leo X granted Ariosto's request in 1513, even though Ariosto was not a priest, but not until the incumbent finally died in 1527 did the poet realize any return on his investment.[139] Even more flagrantly corrupt was a practice resorted to by unscrupulous procurators in Rome to leave blank both the name of the person in whose favor the benefice was to be vacated and the date. When the incumbent died, the procurators solicited bids for the benefice, the name of the highest bidder was filled in, and the document back-dated to precede the previous incumbent's death.[140]

This practice in particular led critics of the Roman Curia to charge that everything was for sale, and back-dating was one of the prohibitions included in the proposals for Curial reform made by Alexander VI's 1497 reform commission.[141] Nevertheless, manipulations of dates persisted, and Rome continued to be the arena for the "chase" for benefices.

A helpful guide to the intricacies of this hunt is the memorandum of a Spanish cleric, Juan Páez de Castro, one of the *familia* of the Cardinal of Burgos. Páez's notes, composed in Rome, were addressed to a fellow Spaniard unfamiliar with Curial practices. They are thus unusually detailed in their explanations, and though they date from just past our period (1550–52), they still reflect Renaissance usages since the reforms of the council of Trent had not yet been implemented.[142]

Páez stresses that when an incumbent dies, of utmost importance is the speed with which the request to succeed him is made. This was because priority went to the candidate whose supplication to the Datary had the earliest date. If, therefore, the benefice has sufficient value, and if for certain it is reserved for papal appointment, a special courier should be hired to go to Rome, despite the expense. An arrangement should be made with him, too, Páez suggests, not to deliver any other letters until two or three days after his arrival in the Eternal City. But, he warns, the supplicant must be careful to avoid benefices where rights of resignation, regress, or expectatives are involved. Even in these cases, provided the claimant has not yet received the bull of appointment or actually taken possession of the benefice prior to the former holder's decease, there are ways to nullify the resignation. Nevertheless, these are highly litigious matters, he cautions, requiring the greatest skill and diligence. Critical, too, is determining that a benefice falls under papal rights of reservation. To this end, Páez provides a lengthy list of types of beneficies which fulfill this requirement. Detailed knowledge was sometimes required. For instance, benefices given to any Curial official or member of the papal household during his term of appointment are reserved, but not those gained later. Complicating matters were certain gray areas, such as papal reservation gained by the failure of the ordinary to make an appointment within six months (reservation by "devolution") or in which simony, usury, or *incompatibilia* are involved.

Obviously what Páez's memorandum shows is that timing, shrewdness, and detailed knowledge of the rules and procedures of the Roman Curia were the ingredients for success. Rome was no place for the naïve or the uninformed. And insiders, or those with inside connections, had decisive advantages.

Compounding further the difficulties any outsider confronted in his dealings with the Datary was the matter of payment. Initially, the *Datarius* charged no set fees, on the grounds that levelling a tax for granting a papal favor would mean spiritual benefits were for sale, a simoniacal situation. Instead the supplicant and the *Datarius* were to agree on a sum, known as "composition," intended for use as alms for some pious purpose, such as public charity or church construction. The funds gained through compositions increased so rapidly, however, that by the end of the fifteenth century they were simply viewed as another form of papal revenue and were funneled through the Apostolic Chamber for general expenditure. In response to the scale of requests for favors, and to avoid increasing complaints about arbitrary charges, some rationalized fee schedule also proved necessary, despite the stigma of simony, and by the early sixteenth century customary fees for various categories of favors had been established.[143]

The Datary generated revenues from office-holders in yet another way: through the creation and sale of venal offices. From the early fifteenth century, offices in the Roman Curia had been sold, a not uncommon practice of *ancien régime* governments where office as property and office as public service were not clearly distinguished, and where such sales proved an attractive fiscal expedient.[144] By the end of the fifteenth century, all Curial offices were venal, and beginning with Sixtus IV whole colleges of new offices had been created, most with fictitious duties, as a means of floating the papal debt. The purchase price of the office was, in effect, a form of invested capital and the "salary" of the office, equivalent on average to an 11% annual return on the investment, a form of interest. The offices were called *vacabilia*, because they were vacated at the death or promotion of their owner and then became available for resale. Thus no hereditary class of office-holders, like the *noblesse de robe* of *ancien régime* France, developed in papal Rome.

The system of venal offices, which began with Sixtus IV's new colleges of notaries and solicitors (called in popular parlance colleges of Mamelukes, Stradiots, and Janissaries), was enlarged by Innocent VIII and Alexander VI, but reached its greatest extension under Julius II and Leo X. Among Julius's creations was a college of 101 *Scriptores Archivii Curiae Romanae* (sold for a total of 70,000 ducats) and another of 141 *Praesidentes Annonae* (supposed overseers of the provisioning of Rome) that brought in 90,000 ducats. Leo enlarged this latter college to 612 members, created colleges of *cubicularii* (chamberlains) and *scutiferi* (shield-bearers), which generated 202,000 ducats in sales, and capped this by establishing in 1520 the *Milites S. Petri*, 401 titles of which were sold for 1,000 ducats apiece. To pay the salaries of this vastly inflated officialdom,

revenues were assigned both from the temporal income of the Papal
States and from fees derived from transactions at the Curia. In 1525 such
salaries amounted to over 140,000 ducats a year, or about 32 percent of
total papal income.[145]

Moreover, the burden of paying these non-functional office-holders
offered enormous resistance to any efforts to simplify the bureaucratic
processes of the Curia or to eradicate the fees and taxes they involved.
The inertial force of this vast administrative apparatus, representing
enormous financial investment, clearly formed an effective obstacle to
any reform of the Church *in capite*. In the end this made stillborn the
repeated proposals of papal reform commissions for eradicating Curial
abuses in the bestowing of benefices. Report after report, from the draft
reform bull of Sixtus IV, to the reform commission of 1497, to the reform
bull of the Fifth Lateran Council, to the *Consilium de emendanda Ecclesia* of
1537 stressed that the abuses involved in resignations, rights of regress,
incompatibilia, and expectatives should cease immediately, but none led to
any fundamental change.[146]

Creating venal offices formed one response to the need for funds,
but the pressures to borrow continued to grow. This eventually led
Clement VII in 1526 to adopt an expedient long resorted to by Venice
and Florence: the creation of a *monte* (literally "mountain" of indebted-
ness), shares in which were sold as bonds. By such a means, the papacy
could tap the commercial wealth of Italy and even beyond. So advan-
tageous did Clement's *Monte della Fede* prove that the papacy created
more than forty separate *monti* by the end of the sixteenth century. Shares
in these were sold according to fluctuating market prices, and could be
bequeathed to heirs or had to be "vacated" on the death of their owner, in
which case they bore higher rates of interest. In the later sixteenth
century, the market price of papal *monti* shares frequently exceeded their
face value, a testimony to their attractiveness as investments, and to the
reliability of the excise tax revenues from the city of Rome upon which
interest payments were pledged. One must also take into account, of
course, the inflationary price rise of the period. Popular as the *monti* were,
the popes still resorted to the formation of new venal colleges of officials.
Paul III, for instance, established two hundred *Cavalieri di S. Paolo* in
1540, and six years later added the "Knights of the Lily" (a reference to
the Farnese family emblem).[147]

Processing appointments and selling offices and *monti* shares were
not the only revenue sources for the Datary. This was also the agency for
granting dispensations and indulgences. Among the most frequent dispensations, and the most lucrative for the papacy, were marriages within
the forbidden degrees of consanguinity or affinity. Other dispensations
included commutation of the vows to go on pilgrimage to Rome, Jerusalem, or Compostela (compoundable according to the person's rank,

what he would have spent on the journey and as an offering, and his conscience, but reducible at the will of the *Datarius*); no mention of a person's illegitimacy in papal documents, making him eligible to hold a benefice (100 ducats); permission for a bishop to conduct a visitation for purposes of reform in his diocese (compoundable according to the value of the see); and absolution for committing a homicide in the Papal States (25 ducats for each murder). Beyond these fees owed the Datary, in most cases charges were due the Apostolic Chamber and the Chancellery as well; murderers, for instance, owed two hundred ducats if the person killed belonged to the nobility, one hundred if he was a commoner.[148]

Indulgences fell into a category of their own. Composition for permission to issue plenary indulgences fell to the determination of the *Datarius* and in the fifteenth century amounted to one-third of the offerings gained. By the early sixteenth century this had risen normally to one-half, and payment had to be pledged against the security of a designated bank. One type of indulgence allowed members of a confraternity or other collegial organization the privilege to eat cheese, eggs, or milk products on fast days. For these "butter letters" the fees varied from 50 to 300 ducats, depending on the fertility and wealth of the country involved. Another type of indulgence gave the purchaser the merit of having performed the Roman Stations, or the same spiritual benefits in his own church or chapel as would have been gained by visiting various sacred sites in Rome. The usual fee for these was 100 ducats per person, but substantial group discounts were available for ten or more.[149]

The dramatic growth of the Datary's fiscal importance to the papal treasury can be measured by comparing the papal budgets for the years 1480–81 and 1525. Under Sixtus IV the income of the Datary was figured at 37,000 florins—12,000 from compositions, 15,000 from the sale of venal offices, 10,000 from indulgences and other fees gathered by apostolic collectors. This represented about one-third of the "spiritual" income of the papacy and about 13% of total papal income. In Clement VII's 1525 budget, income from the Datary is reckoned to have reached 144,000 ducats, approximately two-thirds of the "spiritual" revenues and one-third of total papal income. Both budgets, moreover, stress the elasticity of this income. By taxing vacant offices more strictly and distributing dispensations more generously, the 1480–81 budget notes that 60,000 florins more could be taken in. The 1525 budget remarks that with regard to compositions and vacancies of office the revenues "are more or less according to what needs to be made."[150]

By the early sixteenth century, the papacy was once again, as in the Avignonese period, drawing substantial revenues from the Church. But instead of annates and other taxes distributed over the ecclesiastical landed wealth of Latin Christendom, the Renaissance papacy derived income chiefly from fees and favors of the Roman Curia, from dispensations and indulgences, and from those who for prestige or investment value purchased offices at the papal court. The subtleties of the benefice system, venal offices, and the *monti* made Rome a center of high finance and fiscal speculation.

This image is brought into even sharper focus by the essential role in papal finance played by the papal banker, called the Depositor General. Since papal expenditures, whether for the court, the rebuilding of Rome, or war, were normally made in anticipation of receipts, much of papal finance consisted of credit transactions. The actual cash flow stayed in the hands of the great international banking firms, like the Medici in the fifteenth century or the Fuggers in the sixteenth. Only they possessed the financial resources and the necessary expertise to make possible the advance of large sums to the popes, the receipts of fees owed papal collectors from trans-Alpine benefices along with their transmittal in the form of bills of exchange or letters of credit to Rome, and the resolving of the accompanying currency-exchange and balance-of-payments problems. Such banking operations were extremely lucrative. Raymond de Roover, the historian of the Medici Bank, calculates that the Rome branch of the bank yielded a return of 30 percent or more in relation to invested capital, and profits from its operation at times amounted to over 50 percent of total Medici banking income. Speed, efficiency, and the credit resources of the great international banks justified for the papacy profits of these dimensions. At the same time they reveal the lack of fiscal planning and the erratic spending policies endemic to the Renaissance papacy.[151]

For critics of Rome, this deepening involvement in a capitalist banking economy corroborated their suspicions that at the papal court liturgical and sacramental actions were performed, as Giles of Viterbo charged, not for the sake of sacred divinity but for money (*non numinis sed nummi gratia*), not for spiritual health but for pleasure. Or, as Baptista Mantuanus asserted, "everything is for sale—temples, priest, altars, . . . prayers, heaven, and God."[152] To a considerable extent the Renaissance papacy was indeed mortgaging the spiritual direction of the Church as a whole to the fiscal demands of the papal court. Such funds enabled the remarkable scale of investment in building, pageantry, and cultural patronage, but the perceived rapacity of the system had a corrosive effect on lay confidence outside of Italy. This can be seen, for instance, in the long lists of grievances (*gravamina*) against the innovations of the Roman Curia presented to the German imperial diets, or in Martin Luther's *Appeal to the German Nobility*, where he charged that the house of the *Datarius* was a den of iniquity, and that "the Romanists traffic in livings [benefices] more disgracefully than the Gentiles under the Cross trafficked with Christ's garments."[153]

Clearly, a basic source of tension between the papacy and an increasingly critical laity was the benefice system itself. In effect, the income or property value of ecclesiastical office was separated from the spiritual charge of cure of souls. This split stemmed in part from the way church office was defined by the canonists,[154] but it also reflects the strains of trying to accommodate the increasingly outmoded land-based and feudal assumptions of the medieval Church to the new economic realities of the commercialized and urbanized world of the Renaissance and to new forms of lay piety.

One economic reality of the fourteenth and fifteenth centuries was that population decline and the resultant economic retrogression were particularly disadvantageous to landlords. In southern Italy, where the large number of bishoprics, dating from Roman times, already exceeded population needs (Italy had more sees than the rest of Latin Christendom combined, and more than half the Italian bishoprics were in the south), this meant the sharp erosion of episcopal income. The median assessment, for imposition of common services, of these impoverished south Italian sees was less than 200 florins, in contrast to the nearly 900 florins for northern Italy, and 4000 florins for England and Wales.[155] A certain rationale existed, then, for the papacy to use the bishoprics of Calabria, Apulia, and Basilicata, along with those in Corsica and Sardinia, to provide additional salaries for papal secretaries and other Curial officials.[156] This entailed, of course, the abuse of non-residency, but neither revenues nor population justified maintaining so many bishops in their sees.

Italian urban monasteries were another casualty of changing economic and spiritual realities. In the thirteenth century, they had been the chief beneficiaries of lay philanthropy. But in the fifteenth century, hospitals, lay confraternities, and other more specialized agencies of organized charity had supplanted the social welfare functions of the monasteries, while monastic corporate prayer no longer corresponded to the more individual piety characteristic of civic Christianity.[157] Again, therefore, the assigning of such monasteries *in commendam* to cardinals, thereby making their accumulated wealth available for palace construction or princely patronage, suggests that the "abuse" of non-residency in some instances served to make obsolete institutions fund new expectations.

An even better case in defense of papal practices regarding the disposition of benefices could be made for canonries. The canons' ecclesiastical function as episcopal electors had become vestigial, since, as we have seen, most bishops were provided by the papacy. Obsolete, too, just like that of the monks, was the canons' daily round of corporate prayer, at least in terms of the changing nature of lay piety. These well-endowed cathedral posts thus became sinecures for local elites. It is difficult to quarrel, then, with the papal practice, frequent since the Avignonese period, of assigning canonries as a form of stipend to support non-resident young clerics in the long years of university studies necessary for advanced degrees in theology and canon law. In this way, the Church provided itself with essential professional expertise, and at the same time extended a ladder of opportunity to the bright but impoverished. Patronage of achievement in arts and letters worked the same way. A variety of canonries and an archdeaconate enabled Petrarch, for instance, to enjoy the *vita contemplativa* of poet and classicist, for only occasionally did he actually perform any of the duties involved in these offices.[158]

Pluralities and non-residency, papal provision and reservation, though clearly susceptible to corruption, did give, then, the papacy a means to recruit and reward talent. As such, these practices were preferable, it could be argued, to appointment through local favoritism or spoliation of church revenues by secular authorities.

In the Renaissance period, as the number of posts in the Roman Curia proliferated, the benefice system came to be exploited more thoroughly to serve papal interests. Aspiring humanists were among the beneficiaries, and for provincial Italians with intellectual and administrative ambitions the papal court beckoned as a mecca. Several generations of the Maffei family of Volterra, for instance, became curialists.[159] Similarly, Flavio Biondo of Forlì, who first entered the Curia under Eugenius IV, was able to obtain posts for several of his sons.[160] More meteoric was the career of Giannantonio Campano, who from peasant background near Naples became court poet and classicist companion to Pius II. The pope rewarded him first with the bishopric of Crotone in Calabria (assessed at 50 florins), then transferred him to the richer see of Teramo in the Abruzzi (300 florins). Campano later held a series of Umbrian governorships under Sixtus IV, but then, while governor of Città di Castello, he foolishly supported the local tyrant, Niccolò Vitelli, whom Sixtus was determined to oust, and Campano spent his last years in disgrace in his see at Teramo.[161]

Most spectacular of all, perhaps, was the career of Adriano Castellesi. Born in relative obscurity in Corneto (modern-day Tarquinia), he came to Rome during Sixtus IV's pontificate, gained access to intellectual and Curial circles, and made the most of English connections cultivated during a stint there as papal emissary in 1489–91. Innocent VIII's annulment of a contracted early marriage paved the way for higher church office. Alexander VI made him protonotary, then private secretary, and finally in 1503 a cardinal. Castellesi then began a lavish palace on Alexander's new Via Alessandrina in the Vatican, continued to exploit his English ties, and pursued humanistic and theological studies. Embroiled in monetary disputes over his English revenues, he abruptly fled Rome in 1507 for Venice, where he stayed until Leo X's election. But then he had the poor judgment to become implicated in the cardinals' plot against

Leo, fled once again to Venice, was deprived of his offices, and died while returning to Rome to take part in the conclave to elect Leo's successor.[162]

As these examples suggest, appointments of curialists to canonries, archdeaconates, and bishoprics gave the Renaissance papacy sources of income to supplement officials' salaries, and perhaps just as important served as an informal *cursus honorum*. As one rose in the hierarchy of the Roman Curia so did one's clerical status. To become a bishop was the ambition of all curialists, and then one could aspire to rise from a less distinguished to a more important see, or even, like Castellesi, to become a cardinal. Higher church office meant, too, a more dignified place in the increasingly prominent ceremonial life of the papal court. All this explains why the Roman Curia, including the secretaryships, was by the later fifteenth century almost exclusively staffed by clerics. In Julius's or Leo's Rome no layman was as influential as Biondo or Poggio Bracciolini had been earlier. Moreover, for these Curial humanists of Leonine Rome, 90 percent of whom were Italians, but only 11 percent of Roman origin, a beneficed position at the papal court was the key to influence and prestige in what had become the cultural capital of the peninsula.[163]

If the benefice system served well the increasingly courtly and clerical character of the Renaissance papacy, it clearly served much less well the pastoral needs of the laity, as the reform commissions repeatedly declared. Ecclesiastical office in becoming so completely divorced from spiritual charge separated still further the way affairs were perceived in Rome from the outlook of the rest of Latin Christendom. This split is readily apparent in the career of Jacopo Sadoleto. Son of a Ferrarese jurist and Estensi civil servant, he succeeded, on the basis of achievements as a classicist and elegant Latin stylist, in being named to the papal secretariate by Leo X in 1513. Four years later he was rewarded with the bishopric of Carpentras in Provence, and with his new-found affluence was able to purchase a *vigna* on the Quirinal. There he presided in leisure moments over a literary circle that included his fellow secretary Pietro Bembo, Castiglione, and Raphael. Only after 1527, when Sadoleto resided for a decade in his Provençal see, did the issues raised by the Reformation force him to take seriously his pastoral duties as bishop.[164]

Yet even before the benefice system came to be so thoroughly exploited by the later Renaissance papacy, the internal contradictions were telling. A striking mid-fifteenth century example is the career of Piero da Monte (d. 1457), whom we shall meet again in the next chapter as an important early humanist defender of papal authority.[165] Following completion of legal studies at the University of Padua in 1433, he briefly attended the Council of Basel as a member of the Venetian delegation, then was appointed papal collector to England. There he was responsible for receiving the various taxes and fees owed to the pope, and there also

he energetically defended papal primacy against the rival claims of the
Council of Basel. During his stay he encountered sharp criticism of the
venality of the Curia, which prompted, on his return to the Curia in 1440,
his addressing a list of abuses to the Cardinal Chamberlain, Ludovico
Trevisan. Among these were the indiscreet granting of expectative
favors, through which, Piero asserted, benefices were bestowed on unworthy men; the indiscriminate issuance of dispensations without regard
to reason or merit, but only for the revenue they generated; and the evils
and scandal resulting from disputes between canonically elected office
holders and those provided by the Apostolic See. But Piero's real motives
for returning to the Curia, then located in Florence, were to gain a more
secure livelihood and to pursue Greek studies in the congenial humanistic
atmosphere of the city on the Arno.

Piero's first desire was met when Eugenius IV named him in 1442
Bishop of Brescia, an important see in the Venetian *terra firma* assessed at
700 florins. This was not a depopulated south Italian village, but a thriv-
ing Lombard urban center. Before Piero's provision, the Brescian city-
council, objecting to the practices of the previous absentee bishop, whom
they accused of despoiling the Brescian church, had sought the appointment of one of their own citizens. Even after Piero was awarded the see,
the council continued its opposition, and the Venetian Senate supported
the case on the grounds the pope had not sought the Brescians' approval
before naming Piero bishop. Piero's three-year stint as papal legate to
France forestalled an immediate collision, but in 1445, when he made his
ceremonial first entry into Brescia, angry crowds disrupted the procession.

As a resident bishop, Piero worked on behalf of the civic needs of the
community: he obtained, for instance, a papal dispensation permitting a
hospital to be built on land belonging to canons regular. But he also
opposed the return of Jews to the city, whom the council wanted as
licensed money-lenders able to make small loans at lower interest rates
than Christian pawnbrokers. Other disputes with the city council over
episcopal prerogatives continued to mar his tenure.

In 1449, the Roman Curia demanded that Piero pay 1400 gold
florins, which it claimed he owed from monies collected in England and to
settle previous debts of the bishopric of Brescia. Piero travelled to Rome,
the better to defend himself, and in early 1450 the case was settled with his
payment of 1100 florins. While in Rome, he explored opportunities for
his own return to the Curia. In the meantime the Brescian council accused
Piero of abandoning the spiritual guidance of the citizenry and demanded his immediate return. The following year, Nicholas V named
him Governor of Perugia, and in 1454 Piero obtained his wish to return to
the Curia, securing an appointment as *referendarius*, a post he held until

his death. Despite his non-residency, he remained Bishop of Brescia, and continued to draw income from the episcopal revenues.

Rancor, suspicion, and litigation thus marked Piero's experience in his Brescian see, and despite his clear intellectual and spiritual qualifications as a bishop, it is hard to believe either his talents or the spiritual needs of the Brescian laity were well served in the process. This erosion of bishops' spiritual and administrative responsibilities for their dioceses came to be reversed only with the Counter-Reformation. To combat the Protestant threat, the Roman Church at the diocesan level needed to become a bulwark. In Gian Matteo Giberti, a humanist who left his Curial post as *Datarius* to Clement VII in 1528 in order to reside in his bishopric at Verona, the new age found an exemplary model. More important, the mid-sixteenth century popes and the Council of Trent were determined to restore the episcopate, and they did so by returning to bishops real administrative powers and by requiring residency.[166]

Just as the functioning of the benefice system centralized power in Rome and eroded local responsibilities, so was this the case, too, with ecclesiastical justice. The Eternal City, with its various legal tribunals, was the focus for the vast and complex system of canon law and Church courts. During the Renaissance period, the legal competence of papal judicial bodies encroached ever further upon local prerogatives, resulting in a corresponding increase in the volume of cases acted upon in Rome.

The oldest papal judicial body was the Apostolic Penitentiary, which was responsible for issuing absolutions and stipulating penances in cases of conscience reserved for the pope. Certain sins—twenty in all, according to the canonist Andreas de Escobar, whose manual of reserved cases was printed a number of times during the fifteenth century—were of such a nature that when confessed neither priest nor bishop could absolve them, but only the pope. Among these were crimes against the property and authority of the Church, such as burning churches, falsifying papal letters, violating religious vows or obligations, or associating with those excommunicated by the pope. Also included were crimes against the person of the clergy. To these broad categories had been added specific cases, such as preventing pilgrims from going to Rome, trafficking in arms or military supplies with the Infidel, piracy, and tampering with a corpse by the burning or boiling of bones.[167]

Not all of these cases were actually heard by the Apostolic Penitentiary, since certain confessors, normally members of the mendicant orders, had been empowered by the papacy to pronounce absolution in such matters. Yet, even so, the Roman caseload increased, requiring a large staff to handle it. The tribunal's prestige is indicated, too, by the fact it was headed by a cardinal, and by his salary, which equalled the lucrative stipend of the Vice-Chancellor.[168] Indicative of the importance financial considerations could have in choosing a Grand Penitentiary is that during the critical decade of the 1520s Lorenzo Pucci occupied this post. A curialist since the days of Innocent VIII, Pucci had served Julius II as *Datarius*, been made a cardinal by his fellow Florentine Leo X in 1513, and, according to Guicciardini, was responsible for Leo's policy of widely disseminating indulgences. At his death, Leo owed Pucci 150,000 ducats, and it was Pucci six years later who found himself handling the explosive matter of Henry VIII's divorce.[169]

More rapidly expanding, and therefore more revealing of papal centralization of justice, was the Sacred Rota, the court of appeals for cases in canon law initiated at the diocesan level throughout Latin Christendom, and the court of first instance for civil cases from the Papal States involving sums greater than five hundred ducats. The Rota had emerged as a separate entity during the Avignonese period, but the number of its judges, called Auditors, was finally fixed at a dozen only with the reorganization of the court by Sixtus IV in 1472. The Auditors served under the Vice-Chancellor, and in turn supervised a large staff of notaries.[170]

During the Renaissance period, local cases were much more routinely transferred to Rome, enlarging the Rota's volume of legal business, and generating substantial fees for the numerous solicitors and procurators connected to the papal court. Like other early modern monarchies, the papacy used the processes of justice as a source of revenues, but an appeal to Rome, from the point of view of affected laity, entailed an expensive, time-consuming, and often mystifying process. Typical is the reaction of the German humanist Jacob Wimpheling, who charged in 1515 that cases were transferred to Rome on trivial pretexts and that this infringed upon the rights of imperial and episcopal jurisdiction. Similarly, the *gravamina* presented at the Diet of Worms in 1521 complained that too often cases involving inheritances, mortgages, and other secular matters were subject to a summons to be heard in the first instance in Rome.[171]

Yet even in the less rapacious days of Pius II, pursuing a legal case in Rome could be an expensive and exasperating experience. There survives the remarkably detailed record of a Lübeck canon, Albert Krummediek, which provides an accounting of all the expenditures involved in an appeal to Rome. In 1461 Krummediek travelled to Rome seeking a papal bull to settle the jurisdictional quarrel between the city of Lübeck and nearby monasteries. The legal business consumed six months, with our canon eventually forced to follow Pius's itinerant court first to Viterbo, then to southern Tuscany during the summer of 1462. Besides food and lodging for himself, a chaplain companion, a servant, and their three horses, Krummediek made continual disbursements—for tips to prominent Sienese prelates to facilitate obtaining a papal audience, for messengers to and from Rome (where Cardinal Cusanus, who had an interest in the case, was governor), and for fees and taxes required in the preparation, transcription, and recording of the requisite drafts and other legal papers. Krummediek's hopes alternately waxed and waned, but in the end his persistence won out and his mission reached a successful conclusion—an accomplishment doubtless facilitated by his knowledge of Curial practices gained during an earlier stint as a notary of the Rota. But his total expenses for the ten-month round-trip came close to 1000 ducats, of which, by my count, about 135 ducats were spent on taxes and fees and more than 350 on tips and gifts.[172]

Like the Datary, the Rota was continually a subject for proposed reform, even from insiders within the papal administration. Cardinal Lorenzo Campeggio, for example, whom Adrian VI appointed to head the *Signatura justitiae*, charged in his *De depravato statu Ecclesiae* of 1522 that the Rota was an area where the distinction of spiritual and temporal had been obliterated and that as a court of justice it needed urgent reform. Only men of learning, sanctity, and justice should be appointed to it, he insisted, and unless respect for it were restored, Rome could not presume to hold its rightful place as a source of justice.[173]

The supreme tribunal of the Roman Curia was the *Signatura*. Like the other judicial organs, its business also increased rapidly—so much so that late in the fifteenth century it was divided into the *Signatura justitiae*, presided over by a cardinal, and the *Signatura gratiae*, headed by the pope himself. The former resolved conflicts of jurisdiction within the various legal bodies of the Roman Curia; the latter permitted the pope's personal intervention in responding to appeals or supplications.[174] Under Julius II, the *Signatura gratiae* met in the room of the Vatican Palace now known as the Stanza dell'Incendio. The ceiling, painted by Perugino around 1508, relates to the room's function. Its four *tondi* depict the *Pantocrator*, Christ as *Sol justitiae*, Christ between personifications of justice and grace, and the transmission from Christ to the Apostles of power over remission and retention of sins (John 20: 21–22). The ceiling thus illustrates, as Shearman suggests, the "integrity, plenitude, and spiritual grace of divine justice, and its transmission to the institution of the Church through its head."[175] As such it presented the authoritative basis of papal justice and served as a reminder of the divine context in which justice was to be enacted. Yet one function of the *Signatura gratiae* in practice was to provide a streamlined way of accomplishing certain Curial business. The price list of compositions Francesco Collucci compiled in 1519 indicates that with regard to provision to a consistorial monastery or to particular forms of resignation by abbots of such monasteries, the *Signatura gratiae* provided an alternate route, which, though its fees were higher, was quicker and avoided the nuisance and anxiety involved in handling these matters through the Consistory.[176]

Papal Rome became the catch basin, then, for the ever larger flood of cases in canon law. But papal legal power flowed the opposite direction, too, in the form of excommunication and interdict, which potentially could isolate any sinful member of Latin Christendom. Moreover, these were important weapons in the pontifical political arsenal. The most notorious example, perhaps, is Sixtus IV, in the wake of the vengeance wreaked on the Pazzi conspirators, excommunicating Lorenzo de' Medici and placing Florence under interdict. This meant both the suspension of the sacraments, with the accompanying potential for increased spiritual anxiety in the Arno city, and the exposure of Florentine merchants to sequestration of their goods—a potent economic threat to Florence's commercial livelihood. Indeed, the papacy seized Medici holdings in Rome and repudiated its debts to the Medici Bank. Even though the Florentine government held that the papal censures were illegal, their prolongation during the ensuing war presented a clear danger to the Medici regime, particularly since Sixtus implied that the interdict was Lorenzo's fault and that his acquiescence to papal will would result in the lifting of the ban.[177]

Lorenzo's astute Neapolitan diplomacy and the repercussions of the Ottoman landing at Otranto led to a compromise settlement, concluded, as we have seen, with Sixtus's absolution of Florentine penitents before the gates of St. Peter's in 1480.

A more effective use of excommunication as a political weapon, also involving Florence, was the anathema Alexander VI proclaimed against Savonarola in 1497. In the pope's mind, the Dominican firebrand was the major obstacle to the Florentine Republic's joining his anti-French Italian League, and thus needed to be silenced. Charging Savonarola with defiance of his previous order against preaching and disseminating pernicious doctrine, the pope excommunicated him and all who listened to him preach or who gave him support. The result was a steady erosion of the friar's popular approval, which in turn led to Savonarola's fateful decision to resume preaching despite the ban. Alexander countered by threatening to confiscate Florentine goods in the Papal States and to imprison Florentine merchants. As the pressure mounted between the Roman pontiff and the prophet whose jeremiads called for the unseating of one who was neither pope nor Christian, deepening rifts divided the Florentine populace. The upshot was the famous ordeal by fire, that in the end never came off, the ensuing attack on S. Marco, Savonarola's arrest and interrogation under torture, his confession to Roman commissioners that he was a false prophet, their conviction of him as a heretic and schismatic, and his execution by Florentine authorities and the burning of his body.[178]

The Borgia pope subsequently used spiritual weapons against the papal vicars of the Romagna as the overture to Cesare's campaigns,[179] and Julius II adopted the same course against the Bentivoglio of Bologna.[180] In the War of the League of Cambrai against Venice, Julius likewise placed Venice under interdict and excommunicated the Senate on the grounds both of Venetian usurpations in the Romagna and the Republic's resistance to papal disposition of Venetian benefices.[181]

These practices prompted Giucciardini's tirade against the Renaissance popes, who, he charged, used the terror of spiritual weapons only as an instrument of princely rule.[182] But papal use of ecclesiastical censures for the ends of temporal power in Italy in fact had a long history. The Holy Roman Emperor Frederick II spent much of his long career excommunicated, and Florence had been placed under interdict eight times in the thirteenth century and at least eight times again in the period 1300–75.[183]

Nevertheless, papal censures and excommunications seem clearly to have multiplied in the fifteenth and sixteenth centuries. The *gravamina* presented to the 1521 Diet of Worms complained that excommunications were used indiscriminately by the Church as a means of recovering debts or of collecting legal expenses entailed in cases before ecclesiastical courts.[184] For the laity, such excommunications had the added complication of falling into the category of reserved sins, meaning that they required absolution through the Penitentiary.[185]

From the papal point of view, however, headship of the *respublica Christiana* meant directing human society to salvation. All other concerns of secular society were subordinate. In a sinful and often refractory world the spiritual weapons of excommunication and interdict were of necessity employed to defend the sovereignty of the Church and to protect its legitimate rights from encroachment by secular powers.[186] To this end the Renaissance popes exerted considerable energy to recover the position of the papacy in Rome and in Italy and thus to avoid the dire straits experienced during the Great Schism. They saw this as defending the "liberty" of the Church. Excesses might occur, and the popes were reproached for their human failings, but it did not occur to Roman thinkers that there should be fundamental institutional change. In the last analysis, moreover, as Giles of Viterbo remarked, "the papacy does not belong to men; it was created by God, to whom belongs the power to examine and judge it."[187]

Still, the papacy did appear to act more often in a jurisdictional than in a spiritual role; and spiritual authority, such as the power of excommunication, frequently became a negotiable element in the pursuit of political ends. What existed, then, was an unresolved tension between theory and practice. In practice, the papacy, like other early modern monarchies, responded, though often inconsistently and without enthusiasm, to fiscal and bureaucratic pressures for centralized financial and bureaucratic powers. Thus the activities of the Datary, control of the benefice system, resort to venal offices, and the credit machinery of the *monti* and the Depositary. In theory, by contrast, the popes as Vicars of Christ and heir to His spiritual headship should, contemporaries felt, be inspired to act according to the virtues of love and charity exemplified in Christ's life and in the works of the Apostles and saints. The uneasy compromises the Renaissance papacy resorted to, such as the fiction of compositions, tended merely to paper over these opposing assumptions, leaving the papacy exposed to charges of hypocrisy and corruption.

Indeed, the unwillingness to confront openly the impact of changing administrative functions and procedures inhibited adopting standards of rational efficiency, exacerbating still further the actual situation. Rather than reform plans for rationalization and standardization, critics more often appealed, nostalgically, to the simplicity and poverty of the Apostolic Church. Wealth, invariably tainted by avarice, seemed suspicious in itself, or at least to be disdained, yet the amenities of cultured life in Rome that wealth made possible were admired and cultivated. Nor was Paolo Cortesi alone in urging *magnificentia* as a virtue all cardinals should cultivate.

Poggio Bracciolini alone of the Curial humanists, in his *De avaritia*, attempted to reassess medieval commonplaces and to affirm the essential link between wealth and civilization. Later Curial humanists made no such creative efforts. This neglect seems attributable, at least in part, to the humanists' courtier-like status at the papal court with its concomitant exclusion from real exercise of power; to the absence of a tradition of political analysis fostered by the republican setting of Florence (and later true, too, of Venice); and to the economic underdevelopment and "colonial" dependency in financial terms of Rome and the Papal States, which left Romans outside the inner circles of emergent financial capitalism. Giles of Viterbo's reaction to early sixteenth-century Rome was to uphold the eremitical ideal and to long for the unsullied Church of caves and forests. Yet at the same time he wanted for the Church the splendor that only vast riches could sustain. Giles's humanist contemporaries harked back, too, to what they regarded as the pristine practices of former times, instead of sponsoring any concrete program of reform appropriate to contemporary realities. Curial reform thus remained a moral stance, not a coherent policy.[188]

THEOLOGICAL DEVELOPMENTS

Past treatments of Renaissance Rome have tended to assume that the Eternal City, the presumed seedbed of religious corruption, and home to popes whose ambitions appeared to center on secular aggrandizement, could only be theologically barren. An exception should perhaps be made, these older works sometimes suggested, for Lorenzo Valla, whose Biblical scholarship and evangelical concerns marked new departures in humanist thought. In fact, however, Valla's theological impact in Rome, for reasons that will be explored later, was relatively slight; his real religious heir was instead Erasmus.

If even Valla falls outside the mainstream of the Roman Renaissance, this does not, nevertheless, confirm the impression of theological sterility. Rome's intellectuals actually contributed in significant ways to at least three key theological developments of the Renaissance period. In the first place, Roman humanists participated extensively in the patristic revival. These studies were directly connected to the humanists' overall concern for the *instauratio* of the Roman Church, the subject of the next chapter. Exploration of this topic should therefore be put aside for now, and looked at instead in that context.

A second development, also involving the humanists, stemmed from their rhetorical approach to the Bible, particularly in their sermons. This approach has broad implications for the general nature of the Roman Renaissance, and for several specific topics, such as the figure of Moses examined in Chapter III, and the meaning of Creation treated in Chapter V. Briefly, humanistic rhetoric, as applied to Scripture, involved exegetical repercussions, namely, a newly recovered appreciation for the literal or historical-prophetic meaning of the text over against the allegorical. Quotations from Scripture and allusions to Biblical precedent abound in Roman humanist writings, as will be seen. The humanists' departure from medieval allegory helped shape their conclusions regarding the nature of the papacy and the Roman Church and their views of the central mysteries of the Christian faith.

The third area in which Renaissance Rome made a theological contribution lay in the field of scholastic theology. The revival of Thomism, an important general trend of mid-sixteenth century Catholic theology, had its origin here, during the middle decades of the fifteenth century, earlier than has generally been recognized. This development merits attention at this point, since it leads first to a consideration of the institutional settings in Rome where the formal study of theology took place and, second, to several doctrinal decisions with important implications both for the nature of the papal office and for the relation of Rome to the laity of Christendom. In this context it should be remembered that the pope was the final arbiter in matters of doctrine; and while prevailing attitudes held that doctrinal innovation was to be avoided, some key enactments had important consequences.

As the locale of theological studies, the papal court in the Middle Ages never approached the distinction achieved by trans-Alpine centers of learning, notably the universities of Paris, Oxford, and Cologne. The same held true in the Renaissance, but Rome did possess several institutions for theological study. First, there was the University of Rome (the *Studium Urbis* or Sapienza). Founded by Boniface VIII in 1303, Rome's University had preserved a tenuous existence during the Avignonese period, and in 1406 Leonardo Bruni, at the behest of Pope Innocent VII, the pope of the Roman obedience, drafted a proposal to resuscitate it from its nearly moribund state.[189]

The real renewer of the Sapienza, however, was Eugenius IV. In 1431 he provided a solid financial base by earmarking for university expenditures the revenues derived from a surcharge on the tax levied on imported wine sold in Roman taverns. At times the Renaissance popes allocated the resources of this *gabella studii* for other purposes: Sixtus IV, for instance, diverted funds, augmented by the proceeds from the influx of Jubilee pilgrims frequenting Roman wineshops, to pay for repairs to the Aqua Virgo and to build the Ponte Sisto. Generally, however, the papacy favored the university as a focal point of Roman intellectual life. At the end of the fifteenth century, Alexander VI even began the reconstruction of its deteriorated facilities, which were located near the church of Sant'Eustachio in the region of the Pantheon. A number of important humanists, including Valla and Leto, held chairs of rhetoric at the *Studium Urbis*, and other classical studies were cultivated there, too, as exemplified in the appointment of Johannes Argyropoulos to the chair of Greek studies. Similar to other Italian universities, however, the faculties of law and medicine vastly outnumbered their colleagues in the humanities and in philosophy. Theology also lacked strength in numbers (there were two positions in 1473–74, three in 1482–84), but among those teaching at the Sapienza were such eminent figures as Cajetan and Prierias.[190]

Besides the *Studium Urbis*, theology formed part of the curriculum at several small colleges and seminaries founded during the fifteenth century by scholarly-minded cardinals, among them Domenico Capranica and Stefano Nardini.[191] But the other main center for theological study in Rome was the *Studium* of the Roman Curia. This pontifical university, in existence since the thirteenth century, had accompanied the papal court to Avignon and then returned with the papacy to Rome following the end of the Schism. The leading theologian at the papal *Studium*, situated in the Vatican, was the Master of the Sacred Palace. This personage, who became increasingly influential in the Renaissance period, always came from the ranks of the Dominicans. His responsibilities as the pope's official theologian included choosing preachers for the papal liturgies and supervising the content of the sermons delivered on these ceremonial occasions. Noteworthy occupants of this post were Juan de Torquemada, Cajetan, and Prierias.[192]

Besides being Dominicans, these three theologians were all prominent Thomists. In fact, from Torquemada's time in the mid-fifteenth century a steady influx of Thomistic theologians occupied posts in the Eternal City. These exponents of Aquinas included Jacobus Gil (Master of the Sacred Palace, 1452–72/73), Domenico de' Domenichi (not a Dominican, but a favorite theologian of Paul II in particular), Ludovico da Ferrara (he taught at the Sapienza in the 1490s) and Vincenzo Bandello (elected master general of the Dominicans in 1501).[193]

Thomism, indeed, had better and more influential representation in Renaissance Rome than any rival scholastic tradition. Ockhamism and other *via moderna* schools are conspicuous by their relative neglect, even though both the Franciscan and Augustinian Orders, from whose ranks many nominalists came, were well-placed in Rome's religious life. What commended Aquinas to Rome's scholastic theologians, and many humanists as well, was not so much his authority as *the* Dominican theologian as the basic nature of his theology itself. Aquinas's emphasis on the harmony between nature and grace, and on wisdom, both divine and human, imparting order to nature and to human governance, found favor at the papal court, which clearly valued hierarchy, order, and harmony. A number of Renaissance Rome's theologians, in fact, drew heavily on Thomistic thought in elaborating pro-papalist, anti-conciliar views of ecclesiology—a matter to be looked at closely in the next chapter. Upholder of papal primacy, defender of the Church against the Fraticelli, refuter of Greek Orthodox "errors," Aquinas was also systematic, comprehensive, and clear, in contrast to the Terminist subtleties of nominalist logic.[194]

Perhaps the best indicator of the general esteem accorded St. Thomas in Renaissance Rome is the liturgical prominence of his feast day (7 March), commemorated annually in the Dominican church of S. Maria sopra Minerva. These solemnities were marked by the participation of the College of Cardinals, by the added liturgical dignity of the singing of the Creed (an honor otherwise accorded only the four Latin Church Fathers, and which in effect made Aquinas equal to them as a Doctor of the Church), and by the delivery of a sermon in his praise. This sermon took place *inter missarum solemnia*, that is, during the Mass after the singing of the Gospel, rather than either before or after the divine service. This gave it a special dignity, matching the practice for sermons delivered during the papal liturgies. Chiefly responsible for creating this Roman *festa* to honor Aquinas was Pope Nicholas V. This pontiff's veneration for the great scholastic theologian derived in part from the identity of their baptismal names (Tommaso) and also from the fact that his election as pope came the day before St. Thomas's feast day.[195] But Nicholas devoted extensive study to Aquinas's theology, and his portrait, along with those of Sts. Ambrose, Augustine, Jerome, Gregory the Great, Leo the Great, Athanasius, and John Chrysostom, adorned Nicholas's chapel in the Vatican, frescoed by Fra Angelico.[196]

Aquinas's feast day remained an important ceremonial occasion after Nicholas's death. The panegyrics for the *festa*, for instance, were delivered by some of Rome's most prominent humanist orators, including Giannantonio Campano, Aurelio Brandolini, Tommaso "Fedra" Inghirami, and Lorenzo Valla. Valla's 1457 encomium is the most famous, but it is atypical. In effect, he composed an anti-panegyric. While praising Thomas's sanctity, he pointed out as theological shortcomings the medieval scholastic's excessive reliance on Aristotelian philosophy and his non-existent Greek. Nor was the oration well received. According to Gaspare da Verona, everyone agreed with Cardinal d'Estouteville's remark that Valla had spoken nonsense. The other encomiasts praised Aquinas's learning as well as his holiness. For them no sharp dichotomy separated scholastic from humanistic modes of theology—at least so far as doctrinal content was concerned—and Aquinas had the great virtue of being orthodox beyond reproach.[197]

Rivalling Nicholas V as a promoter of Thomism in Renaissance Rome was Oliviero Carafa, Cardinal-Protector of the Dominican Order from 1481 to 1511, and himself a reader of Aquinas as well as a patron of Dominican Thomists, most notably Cajetan. Carafa staunchly supported the feast day of Aquinas, and he also commissioned for his own funerary chapel in the Minerva a large fresco of the *Triumph of St. Thomas Aquinas*. In this painting, the work of the Florentine Filippino Lippi, who frescoed the whole chapel during the years 1488–93, Aquinas, accompanied by personifications of philosophy, theology, rhetoric, and grammar, sits enthroned within a triumphal arch, victorious over Averroes, who lies prostrate at his feet. Vanquished, too, are the heretics Arius, Sabellius, Apollinare, Photinus, Eutyches, and Manichius—all deniers of orthodox Trinitarian doctrine—and their writings lie strewn on the ground before St. Thomas's throne.

The note of triumph and the use of triumphal arch architecture echo a major theme of Roman Renaissance culture, but in the fresco the Roman motif, through background particulars, receives special emphasis. To one side of the triumphal arch appears, in the distance, the ancient equestrian statue of Marcus Aurelius, situated in front of the Scala Sancta of the Lateran (where it stood before its removal to the Campidoglio under Paul III); on the other side one glimpses the Roman port of Ripa Grande on the Tiber, probably meant as an allusion to the papal crusading fleet that embarked from there under Carafa as admiral and that successfully assaulted Satalia in 1472. St. Thomas's "triumph" thus takes place within a contemporary Roman setting. Indeed, the fresco suggests an image of the triumphant Roman Church, upheld through Thomistic orthodoxy and defended by the church militant.

Carafa himself appears in the *Triumph*, and also in the altar painting, an *Annunciation*, where Aquinas presents the kneeling cardinal to the Virgin Mary. The chapel, dedicated to the Virgin and Aquinas, acquired a particular significance, moreover, during the solemnities of 7 March honoring the saint's feast day. After Mass, the cardinals filed from the

10. Filippino Lippi, *Triumph of St. Thomas Aquinas*. Rome, Carafa Chapel in S. Maria sopra Minerva. (Photo: Alinari/Art Resource, NY)

nave of the church into the chapel to pray and to receive the indulgence
Alexander VI had provided.[198]

No other theologian—not even St. Augustine—was honored with a
liturgical recognition anything like that given to Aquinas, nor does there
survive any body of encomia as substantial as that for the great Dominican
doctor.[199] Even Paolo Cortesi, a relentless Ciceronian in his Latin Classicism, turned to Aquinas, not to one of the Church Fathers, as his chief
theological authority in preparing his theological textbook, the *Liber
sententiarum* (1504). Intended as a comprehensive treatment of Christian
doctrine, Cortesi adopted the format of a commentary on Peter Lombard's *Libri quattuor sententiarum*, the text used by three centuries of
scholastic theologians in their university training. Cortesi undertook this
project because he was convinced that theology should form an essential
component of humanistic studies. Theological truth must nevertheless be
joined, he held, to eloquence, the *eloquium romanum*. Thus Cortesi
eschewed the technical language of the scholastics, replacing its nonliter-
ary terminology with a Ciceronian vocabulary. Aquinas, of course, was
unclassical in his Latin, but Cortesi admired his lucid treatment of such
matters as God's omnipotence, which avoided the excessive speculation of
the later scholastics. This, combined with his orthodoxy and his intellec-
tualistic, as opposed to voluntaristic, views, made St. Thomas Cortesi's
most respected theologian.[200]

A similar dependency on Aquinas marks Raffaele Maffei's *De institutione Christiana* (1518), also a theological textbook intended for humanists.
Indeed, Maffei's work owes its general outline and much of its doctrinal
exposition to Aquinas's *Summa theologiae*. Aquinas was not the only scholastic Maffei knew, but like Cortesi he regarded St. Thomas as the clearest
and most dependable expositor of doctrine. In particular, he avoided the
contentiousness, the "sophistry," and the pointless subtleties that for
Maffei marred the later scholastics' discussions of topics like predestination and the Eucharist.[201]

Valla stood almost alone, then, in his negative assessment of
Aquinas's theology. Nor did Roman intellectuals, again with the exception of Valla, see in humanism an impulse for doctrinal reform or innovation. Humanist theology in Rome, whether expressed in treatises or
sermons, was consciously conservative in intent.[202] A *theologia rhetorica*
provided the means to highlight and affirm perennial truths; it was not
intended to create new ones, and in fact controversial subjects were
explicitly to be avoided in the sermons delivered during papal liturgies.[203]
Nevertheless, the new sacred oratory, based as it was on the rhetorical
culture of antiquity, tended to present Christian verities in a less ascetic
and cerebral context. The world and man's actions in the world came
more to the fore. In the same way the concordistic and conciliatory
impulses of the new rhetoric allowed the perplexingly technical problems

dear to the nominalists— the relationship of God's uncreated sovereignty and human contingency, of election and free will, of faith and reason, of theology and philosophy—to recede into the background. The religious outlook of the Roman humanists affirmed the beneficence of God, the wonder of creation, and the dignity of man made in God's likeness. To probe the precise nature of these matters was to indulge in oversubtle speculation, or at least in speculation improper for oratory. The doctrinal assurance manifested in the *theologia rhetorica* of Renaissance Rome distinguishes it sharply from trans-Alpine Christendom. Spiritual anxiety, increasingly evident north of the Alps on the eve of the Reformation, did not trouble the Eternal City. Instead Romans had confidence they possessed the essential verities, and were convinced that classical and Christian traditions, humanism and Thomism, spoke to the same human and divine truths.[204]

This tendency to incorporate the stabilized content of *via antiqua* scholasticism into the humanistic form of revived classical rhetoric has a counterpart in the tomb of Sixtus IV. This large, free-standing bronze monument, created by the Florentine Pollaiuolo in the years shortly after the pontiff's death, shows the deceased pope recumbent and surrounded by representations of the virtues and the liberal arts. The latter—eight in all, the science of optics being added to the usual medieval trivium and quadrivium—appear as lithe young women, each involved in the intellectual activity peculiar to her "art," and identified by an appropriate inscription taken from a classical or medieval text. These eight intellectual disciplines form the foundation for the study of philosophy and theology, representations of which appear at the head of the tomb. "Philosophy's" inscriptions quote the opening lines of Aristotle's *Metaphysics* and *Physics* (in William of Moerbeke's thirteenth-century Latin translations), while "Theology," strikingly presented as a nearly nude, reclining Diana, the moon goddess, who peers into and is illumined by the dazzling sunburst of the Trinity, is accompanied by an angel holding open a book inscribed with the opening lines of the Vulgate version of Genesis 1 and John 1.[205]

Sixtus IV was a theologian, indeed the only true theologian among all the Renaissance popes, and before his election had participated in perhaps the most heated theological controversy of the Roman Renaissance—whether Christ's blood, shed in His Passion and reassumed in His Resurrection, remained united to His divinity during the three days His body was in the tomb, and therefore deserved the *cultus* owed divinity proper. Dominicans upheld this, Franciscans opposed it. In an effort to resolve the dispute, Pius II, during the Christmas season of 1462, held a formal disputation on the subject in Rome, with Francesco della Rovere defending the Franciscan cause.[206] Pius leaned to the Dominican side, but made no formal pronouncement, and the future Sixtus IV re-affirmed his arguments in a treatise, *De sanguine Christi* (1467). In this work, which

11. Antonio Pollaiuolo, Tomb of Sixtus IV, detail. Bronze relief sculpture of "Theology." Rome, St. Peter's. (Photo: Alinari/Art Resource, NY)

employs scholastic methods of disputation, Francesco argued that the Dominican viewpoint made too literal a connection between the blood of animals sacrificed according to Hebraic rites and Christ's blood shed on the Cross. Mankind, he asserts, was saved by Christ's death, not by His blood.[207]

The issue, while it provoked impassioned debate, was hardly of momentous consequence for Christian doctrine as a whole. More important was the question of the Immaculate Conception of the Virgin Mary, where again Dominicans and Franciscans held opposing views (the former opposed, the latter in favor). This doctrine had, in fact, been promulgated at the Council of Basel in 1439, but since the Roman See did not recognize the legitimacy of the later sessions of the Council the question remained open. As pope, Sixtus IV favored the Franciscan position, but did not proclaim it a doctrine of the Church. He did, however, grant special indulgences to all who attended services on the Feast of the Immaculate Conception (8 December), and he commemorated the feast himself by celebrating Mass in the new chapel in St. Peter's, which he had built to house his tomb.[208]

By such actions Sixtus conservatively furthered tendencies firmly grounded in late medieval piety and theology. In instituting the Feast of the Visitation, promoting devotion to the Rosary, and building or rebuilding a number of Roman churches dedicated to the Virgin (S. Maria del Popolo, S. Maria della Pace, and the Sistine Chapel, consecrated to the Assumption), Sixtus similarly elaborated aspects of Mariology. None of this was particularly controversial, nor was his canonization of the Franciscan theologian Bonaventura (in 1482),[209] nor his extension of the privileges of the Franciscans over and against the secular clergy in such matters as last rites, funerals, and legacies.[210] Even a Franciscan theologian as pope thus avoided theological departures from established consensus.

Sixtus did promulgate one doctrine, however, which though it, too, seemingly meant only the conservative extension of doctrinal precedents, was fraught with unanticipated consequences. His Bull *"Salvator Noster"* (3 August 1476) extended, by intercession (*per modum suffragii*), the remission of satisfaction gained by indulgences to the dead in purgatory. What the pope claimed was that the Church, through its head the pope, could reduce purgatorial punishment for those already dead by issuing indulgences, purchasable by living friends or relatives and applied on the deceased's behalf.[211]

To grasp the significance of this measure, it is necessary to recall the late medieval conception of the sacrament of penance. This sacrament provided the means by which the baptized sinner, having relapsed into mortal sin (the ordinary experience for all but the saints), is restored to a state of grace and thus made acceptable to God. Three steps constituted the process. In the first place, the sinner must feel genuine sorrow, increasingly defined as guilt and remorse, for his sins. Late medieval teaching varied, however, as to the degree and nature of sorrow required. The "attritionists," especially those who followed Duns Scotus, held that repentence based on imperfect sorrow (sometimes described as fear of God's righteous punishment) was sufficient; others, the "contritionists," argued that the sinner should reveal a more intense sorrow, informed by grace and motivated by a loving respect for God. Whether love, or merely fear, was required depended in large part on how one regarded the next step, sacramental confession and absolution by a priest. The attritionists stressed the *ex opere operato* efficacy of priestly absolution, that is, that it depends not so much on the interior disposition of the penitent as on the power inherent to it from its institution by Christ. In the increasing sacramentalism of the late Middle Ages, this view tended to predominate. The forgiveness of sins, won by Christ, was channelled to Christians through the sacrament of penance; only sacramental confession achieved the remission of sins, and only the absolution of the priest applied the merits of Christ to the individual sinner. From this perspective, penance—rather than baptism or the Eucharist—tended, in effect, to become the central Christian sacrament.[212]

Nicholas V thus adhered strictly to contemporary understanding of doctrine in his discussion of the sacraments, the first topic of the oral testament he delivered to the cardinals at his deathbed. The sacraments, Nicholas states, were instituted by Christ and the Apostles as the remedy for all transgressions and as the means for acquiring the glory of eternal life. Leaving aside matrimony and divine orders, which are voluntary, five sacraments of the "new and evangelical law" are necessary for human salvation. Baptism and confirmation, being non-repeatable, do not, the pope suggests, require discussion. Of the remaining three—penance, the Holy Eucharist, and extreme unction—it is penance that occupies his attention. He notes the many theological distinctions, *quaestiones*, and ambiguities involved in doctrinal treatments of this sacrament, but these remain irrelevant to his purpose, which is to stress that through the ineffable grace of omnipotent God, the infinite mercy of Jesus Christ Our Savior, and the immense clemency of the Holy Spirit penance sustains mankind's fragile existence. As the certain means for the abolition of sins, it is not only useful but essential. Indeed, Nicholas concludes, theologians have rightly called it the "second plank" (baptism being the first) by which we are rescued from the maelstrom. From the shipwreck of our transgressions we are delivered cleansed and purified to the safety and tranquillity of the port of our salvation.[213]

Confession and priestly absolution did not, however, conclude the penitential process. There remained the third step, "satisfaction" of the temporal punishment due for sins. In order to preserve the justice of God the sinner must recompense God for his unloving, sinful deeds. Prayers, fasting, pilgrimage, alms, or works of charity provided the various penitential means by which such compensation could be offered. Sins that remained uncompensated for at death had to be recompensed in purgatory.[214]

But an alternative was available. Satisfaction could be remitted by indulgences. Indulgences as the commutation for acts of satisfaction originated as papal spiritual favors made available to crusaders, then became one of the spiritual benefits extended by Boniface VIII to pilgrims who came to Rome during the Jubilee Year of 1300. During the fourteenth century, opportunities to gain indulgences proliferated, as their doctrinal basis became elaborated. Clement VI's bull *"Unigenitus"* of 1343 stated that as a result of Christ's sacrifice on the Cross, and of the saintly deeds of the Virgin Mary and all the elect, the Church had acquired a "treasure of merits," dispensable by the popes as successors to Peter, the bearer of the keys to the Kingdom of Heaven.[215]

Various reasons explain the attractiveness of indulgences and their proliferation in the late Middle Ages and Renaissance. Clearly, the papacy gained financial advantage from them, whether to help underwrite the cost of crusades, or to provide funds for church construction, or simply, as became the case in the late fifteenth and early sixteenth centuries, as a readily expandable "spiritual" revenue funnelled through the Datary and available for general expenditure.

But indulgences appealed, too, to some of the rigorists among the composers of confessional manuals. As Thomas Tentler has pointed out,[216] indulgences enabled the arduous penances prescribed in the early medieval Penitential Canons (the general rule was seven years of penance for each mortal sin) to be preserved, while accommodating the tendency to leniency and the emphasis on guilt and remorse. Strictly speaking, the time value in days and years assigned to the indulgences was to correspond precisely to the time periods of penance stipulated in the Canons.

Moreover, despite the charges of hucksterism with which papal indulgences came to be labelled from Chaucer onwards, many laity found indulgences a source of spiritual consolation and certainty, particularly in dealing with anxiety over death. Representative is the pious, nouveau-riche silk merchant of Florence, Gregorio Dati (d. 1435). The death of his third wife, Ginevra, in childbirth, sorely tried him, he writes in his diary, but she remained lucid at the time of her death and received all the sacraments: confession, communion, extreme unction, and a papal indulgence "granting," he claimed, "absolution for all her sins." This Dati's brother, Lionardo, the General of the Dominicans, had obtained from Pope Martin V, and it comforted Ginevra greatly, Dati adds.[217]

Increased emphasis on indulgences had consequences for the outlook of the Renaissance in Rome also, since this contributed to the enhancement of the papacy's spiritual power and augmented the sacred character of the city of Rome. It was during the Jubilee Years, it should be recalled, when the popes made available plenary indulgences, that the pilgrimage to the principal basilicas in the Eternal City acquired its most potent spiritual value. In at least one instance, too, the spiritual opportunities of the Jubilee Year more directly influenced Roman intellectual life. The Umbrian humanist, Lilio Tifernate, indicates in his dedication to Nicholas V of his Latin translations of John Chrysostom's homilies *De poenitentia* and the Ps.-Chrysostom sermons *In iustum et beatum Job de patientia* that the approach of the Holy Year proclaimed by the pope had inspired his labors. The Greek Father's subject matter was particularly suited to this occasion, Tifernate remarks, inasmuch as this was a time first to be willing to suffer patiently, and then to do penance for human afflictions, thereby obtaining the remission and indulgence of sins made available during the Jubilee.[218]

Indulgences, added to the pope's jurisdiction over an increasing number of "reserved" sins, meant, furthermore, that the Roman pontiff's most important spiritual functions involved the penitential forum, rather than, for example, preaching or teaching. And the pope's role in the penitential process was to heal and purify. These priestly functions, in fact, the later Renaissance popes saw directly before them, while seated in the papal throne in the Sistine Chapel. There, in Botticelli's fresco of the *Healing of the Leper*, appears the Jewish High Priest, a "type" of the pope, performing the ritual cleansing in accordance with the rite described in Leviticus 14:1–32, a passage interpreted as a "figure" of the sacrament of penance. That this Hebraic rite of cleansing the leprous body should be allegorically understood as the prefigurement of the Christian pontiff's purification of the sinful soul of the penitent is made more pointed in the fresco by the background depiction of the Temple in Jerusalem in the guise of Old St. Peter's in Rome.[219] Directly below Botticelli's fresco hung Raphael's tapestry of the *Healing of the Lame Man*, a miraculous cure performed by St. Peter before the Beautiful Gate of the Jerusalem Temple. This, too, symbolized the pope's power of binding and loosing in the penitential forum, for by the power of the keys the Roman pontiff, successor to Peter as the *claviger coeli*, gives repentent sinners access to heaven.[220]

This same theme of the pope's healing power prompted increasing reference to the pope as *Christus medicus*. Thus Cristoforo Marcello in his address to the fourth session (10 December 1512) of the Fifth Lateran Council exhorts Julius II, now that Italy has been freed from tyranny through the pope's just wars, to turn from arms and bodily matters to spiritual laws and the cure of souls. Like Peter, the pope should attend to his bride, the Church, restoring its dignity and beauty. He should see to the spiritual food required to feed the flock committed to his care, so that it might live. He should eradicate the disease invading the whole globe,

12. Botticelli, *Healing of the Leper.* Wall fresco from the Sistine Chapel (before restoration). (Photo: Alinari/Art Resource, NY)

strive to prevent drought from withering the fruits entrusted to his cultivation, and aim to make one sheepfold out of a divided Christendom. Let the port of salvation illumine the tossing bark (of Peter) agitated by dire winds on the deep. Take care, Marcello urges, for the health, life, and spirit you have given us, lest we lose it. "For you are shepherd (*pastor*), physician (*medicus*), helmsman (*gubernator*), cultivator (*cultor*)—in short, another God on earth."[221]

Prominent already, this *Christus medicus* theme became pervasive under Julius's successor, Leo X. His family name (Medici) offered irresistible opportunities for word-play, and after the tumult of Julius's wars contemporaries looked to Leo to apply the *medicina Dei* to the ills of society, thereby bringing in the peace and unity for which they so deeply yearned.[222]

Late medieval and Renaissance views of the sacrament of penance, then, and especially the increased emphasis on indulgences, accentuated the unique priestly powers of the pope, acting from the sanctuary of Rome. Yet the proliferating practice of indulgences did not go unopposed. Maffeo Vegio, the humanist canon of St. Peter's, complained in his historical description of the basilica, written in the 1450s, that the popes had become too lax in granting the grace of indulgences. They thereby squandered this most precious heavenly treasure.[223]

More controversial—and at length we return to Sixtus IV's Bull "*Salvator Noster*"—was the extension of papal powers of jurisdiction over the Church Militant so that it included the souls in purgatory. Gabriel Biel, for instance, had argued before 1476 that the pope's powers were limited to the living; otherwise he could empty purgatory simply by issuing plenary indulgences for the dead there. After the promulgation of "*Salvator Noster*," however, Biel accepted the papal assertion to jurisdiction over purgatory and explained that the pope could not empty it since he could only liberate those for whom a work of piety had been performed.[224]

Despite Biel's acquiescence, papal claims regarding penance and indulgences contributed to the questioning of papal powers as such, an issue resumed with renewed fervor in the debate over the legitimacy of the French-sponsored Council of Pisa (1511–12). Thus Jacques Almain, the young University of Paris theologian and defender of Gallican conciliarism, asserted first the general conciliarist principle that the Church is not the body of Peter, but the body of Christ alone, and that Christ had conferred supreme ecclesiastical power upon the Church before designating Peter minister of it. From this there follows that the power of binding and loosing in the sacrament of penance—the power of the keys in the penitential and secret forum—is possessed equally by all priests, and Almain denied that the papal power of jurisdiction in the exterior and public forum extended to a capacity to pass judgment on the secret sins of the heart, to grant indulgences for release of the souls suffering in purgatory, to dissolve valid but unconsummated marriages, or to dispense from the mandates of natural law. The Renaissance papacy's position on reserved sins, dispensations, and purgatorial indulgences was thus entirely dismissed.[225]

Even before the Reformation, then, indulgences and papal primacy were seen as interconnected issues. But in the cataclysmic theological and spiritual confrontation between Luther and the Roman Church it seems historically fitting that the papal indulgence prompting Luther's composition of the Ninety-Five Theses was the Jubilee pardon, promulgated initially by Julius II in 1507 to fund the rebuilding of St. Peter's, and subsequently reissued by Leo X in 1513.[226]

Thus collided head-on the Roman Renaissance exaltation of St. Peter's basilica as the pivotal sanctuary of Christendom, and all its attendant meanings for the papacy, Rome, and human destiny, with the Protestant Reformer's focus on conscience and the crucial inner experience of faith and grace. In Rome arose on the tomb of the Prince of the Apostles the sublime splendor of the vast new temple, a tabernacle embodying Christ's majesty as *sol iustitiae*.[227] In the same years the German Augustinian developed a deepening concern for the individual sinner's struggle for the certainty of faith. In Rome, the new Jerusalem, seemed manifest that treasure of merits, remittance from which afforded the dying or deceased access to the refulgent company of the blessed. In contrast, Luther suggests (Ninety-Five Theses, No. 14–16) that for a dying person defective spiritual health or love brings with it the fear and horror that by itself constitutes the penalty of purgatory, since it comes close to despair, and the difference between hell, purgatory, and heaven is the difference between despair, near despair, and assurance.

IV

The Primacy of Peter *Princeps Apostolorum* and the *Instauratio Ecclesiae Romanae*

> [Rome] . . . which from its origin has borne the
> hopes for universal dominion . . . ; whose Empire
> extended to the ocean's edge, its fame to the stars;
> illumined by the light of faith and Christian truth it
> is destined to be the firmament of religion and the
> oak of empire . . . ; it is the public Emporium of
> the whole globe, the securest haven for Christians,
> the strongest citadel, and the holiest altar.
>
> —RAFFAELE BRANDOLINI, *Oratio ad
> Lateranensem Concilium.*

> Truly, indeed, all things that are to be restored
> must hold fast to their origins.
>
> —GILES OF VITERBO, oration delivered before the
> Holy Roman Emperor Maximilian and Pope
> Julius II in S. Maria del Popolo,
> 25 November 1512.

In March 1455, Pope Nicholas V, suffering excruciating pains from the terminal stages of gout, lay dying. Realizing that the "hour" of his "calling" (*hora vocationis*) had come, he convoked the College of Cardinals to his bedside, so that *"pro majori quadam romanae Ecclesiae auctoritate, ac pro summa Sedis Apostolicae dignitate,"* he could deliver orally to them his last testament.

The scene, as recorded by Giannozzo Manetti,[1] possesses suggestive echoes of Christ's farewell discourse to His Apostles at the Last Supper, and reminds us that as pope, Nicholas was *vicarius Christi*. But more particularly, Manetti asserts that from the beginning of Nicholas's pontificate it was almost as if the humanity of Christ had appeared again on earth in the person of the pope, and his actions, beyond human means, had been guided miraculously by the Holy Spirit.[2]

Like Christ, Nicholas on the day before he died concerned himself with the nature and condition of the Church he was commending to his successors. He began, as we have seen, by discussing the sacraments, giving primary attention to penance. Then he turned to what he knew had caused considerable controversy among his contemporaries—his building program for the city of Rome. As the cardinals, Manetti notes, grew more attentive, the pope explained the two main reasons motivating his projects. These were to increase devotion and to protect the Church.

Regarding the first point, Nicholas remarked that only those who from knowledge of letters have comprehended the origin and growth of the Roman Church fully grasp its greatness and superior authority. The throngs of the unlettered hear of these matters from the erudite and seem to assent to their truth, but such a foundation lacks stability. In time, their conviction will weaken and eventually disappear altogether, unless their faith becomes aroused by extraordinary sights. This is the function of great buildings, which "as perpetual monuments and nearly eternal testimonies, almost as if made by God" provide daily corroboration and confirmation of learned truth. To beholders of these admirable constructions, both in the present and in times to come, truth is continuously proclaimed, and the populace's devotion to the Roman Church and the Apostolic See is thereby conserved, augmented, and held fast.[3] In short, Nicholas perceived the urban countenance of Rome as one vast *Biblia pauperum*, testifying to the dignity and authority of the Roman Church and arousing wonder, pious fervor, and devoted allegiance in the minds and souls of pilgrims.[4]

The second purpose of Nicholas's urban projects—to provide physical security against foreign foes and domestic enemies of the papacy—was to his mind equally important. To this end he had constructed numerous castles in the Papal States, but his main concern had been Rome itself. And rightly so, the pope declared, since this *alma Urbs*, made by omnipotent God the eternal seat of the popes, has a dignity greater than any other city and is therefore more devoutly honored and celebrated by the whole Christian populace. To make it more secure, as well as more embellished, was, then, a proper aim. Guided and assisted by the grace of God and by the Holy Apostles Peter and Paul, and trusting in their authority and power, Nicholas had repaired the walls and other collapsed fortifications of the city, restored many of the forty Station Churches, and begun to transform the Vatican Palace and the sacrosanct temple of Peter, Prince of the Apostles. In the adjacent district of the Borgo Leonino he had also begun construction of a dignified and secure setting for the offices of the Curia.

If, as the pontiff insisted they should be, his projects were completed in the future, his successors would be adored with greater veneration by all Christian peoples, and dwelling safely and securely within the city of Rome they would easily avoid persecution from both internal and external enemies. Not ambition, not pomp, not vainglory, not fame, not desire for the more enduring perpetuation of his name had led him to conceive in mind and spirit such buildings, Nicholas averred, but instead his concern for the greater authority of the Roman Church, the more illustrious dignity of the Apostolic See among Christian peoples, and the more certain avoidance of the historical pattern of persecution the Roman pontiffs had suffered.

Among recent such experiences, the pope pointed to the occupation of the city by Ladislas of Naples, the forced flight of Eugenius IV, and the conspiracy of Stefano Porcari. Seated securely in Rome with enhanced authority, power, and dignity, the Roman pontiffs can fulfill, Nicholas concluded, their charge as pastors of souls. In this way they can nourish diligently and freely, with health-giving food, the flock omnipotent God had committed to their care, and by this means lead them on the path to eternal salvation. With his final words, the dying pontiff relinquished to the cardinals, and commended to them, "this sacrosanct Roman Church, so splendid, so tranquil, and so powerful."

Nicholas V's determination to enlarge the authority of the Roman Church and to increase the dignity of the Apostolic See[5] found support from all the Renaissance popes. They were convinced that the sacredness of the Christian religion revolved around a Church centered in Rome, and that the primacy of Rome and of the Roman pontiff should be declared through especially impressive buildings and ceremonies. They repeatedly stressed, too, the unique priestly and ecclesiastical powers conferred upon Peter by Christ, and thence transmitted to all the popes as successors to the *Princeps Apostolorum*.

PAPALISM VS. CONCILIARISM

Nicholas V's pontificate proved, in fact, to be the turning point in the papacy's recovery of authority and prestige. Once again firmly established in Rome, the popes emerged as unchallenged heads of the *respublica Christiana*. Achieving both ends—staying in Rome and heading the Church—had seemed for a time beyond attainment for Nicholas's predecessor, Eugenius IV. Confronted by a rebellious Roman populace, Eugenius took flight, abandoning Rome for nearly a decade. Simultaneously, he had faced in the Council of Basel a vociferous and widely supported assault on papal ecclesiastical powers.

The general council that began its deliberations in Basel in 1431 had been convened by Martin V in accordance with the decree *Frequens* (1417) of the Council of Constance. This stipulated the regular convening of such bodies as a fundamental element of church governance. Central also to the Basel delegates' view of the Council's role was the decree *Haec Sancta* (1415) of Constance. This declared that a general council, as representative of the Church Militant, held its power directly from Christ, and that all Christians, including the pope, were subject to its decisions in matters of faith and in reform of the Church in its head and members. The Council of Basel formally affirmed this decree on a number of occasions, and in May 1439 pronounced it and the decree *Frequens* to be irrevocable articles of Catholic faith. Widespread popular antipathy to abuses of the Roman Curia, whose polices and procedures had been left unreformed at Constance, provided the groundswell of support to sustain the actions at Basel. What was really at stake, however, was not the simple redress of grievances but rather the way in which the Church was fundamentally governed. In abolishing papal reservations and annates, and in sharply curbing other papal prerogatives, the Council was, in effect, moving in the direction of transforming the papacy into a constitutional monarchy, bound strictly by the reform legislation of regularly convened general councils.[6]

Eugenius unsuccessfully resisted the tide of affairs at Basel until he obtained the agreement of the Greek Orthodox Church to meet in a long-projected Council of Union to end the schism between the Latin and Greek Churches. In 1437 the pope prorogued the Council at Basel, and transferred it to Ferrara, where the Greek delegation was to arrive the following year. In reaction, the Council of Basel, itself riven by rival factions, declared the pope contumacious, suspended him from his office, and eventually (in 1439) deposed him, electing in his stead Amadeus VIII, the Duke of Savoy, who took the name Pope Felix V.

In the meantime, at Florence, where the Council with the Greeks had been transferred in 1439, unification had been achieved. Latin representation at Florence was limited mainly to bishops from the Papal States, Tuscany, and the Venetian territories, while most other European powers, including the Duchy of Milan and the Kingdom of Aragon (both political opponents of Eugenius in Italy), continued to keep delegations at Basel. But the success of reunification with the Greeks, which ended nearly four centuries of schism, followed in the next few years by similar accords with representatives of the Armenian, Coptic, Syrian, and other Eastern Churches, acted in the pope's favor.[7] Despite this favorable turn of events, and despite Eugenius's repeated pronouncements on the illegitimacy of the Council of Basel, recognition of his papacy on the part of the European states was achieved only through intensive diplomacy and at the cost of conceding to secular rulers a large measure of control over their local churches. Not until 1449 did Felix V abdicate, and only then did the Council of Basel (having previously withdrawn to Lausanne) formally elect Nicholas V as pope and at last dissolve itself.[8]

The prolonged struggle between Eugenius IV and the Council of Basel had important consequences both for Latin Christendom and the Renaissance papacy. The Roman pontiffs appeared to emerge victorious in 1449, but the expectations of a thorough reform of the Roman Curia remained thwarted. Rankling disenchantment with the papacy deepened, especially north of the Alps, and the gulf between Rome and the rest of Latin Christendom widened. This latent anti-Roman sentiment, and the opportunity that appeals to a council gave to European rulers eager to use the ecclesiastical arena in furtherance of political interests or as a device to wrest concessions from the popes, kept conciliarism alive. Thus King Louis XI of France, citing the decree *Frequens*, repeatedly badgered Sixtus IV with the summoning of a council, as did Louis's successor Charles VIII in his dealings with Alexander VI.[9] The Venetians, too, to take an example from Italian politics, twice invoked *Frequens* and appealed to a council when the wars of Sixtus IV (1483) and Julius II (1509) threatened Venetian territory.[10]

The Renaissance popes, in turn, feared a repetition of the Basel experience and interpreted any call for a general council as an implicit attack on their authority. Pius II went further. At the close of the Council of Mantua (1460), anticipating opposition to announced new crusading taxes, he issued the bull *Execrabilis*. This declared that any appeal from a decision of the pope to a future council was null and void, and that the appellant was *ipso facto* excommunicated.[11]

In the later fifteenth and early sixteenth centuries only two attempts were actually made to convene a church council. The first was the quixotic venture of Andreas Zamometič, titular Archbishop of Krania (in Thessaly). Clapped into Castel Sant'Angelo for his outspoken opposition to Sixtus IV's policies, Zamometič, upon his release, went to Basel. From there in 1482 he issued a manifesto accusing the pope of heresy and simony, of instigating the Pazzi conspiracy, of wasting the possessions of the Church (a reference to Girolamo Riario's dynastic ambitions), and even of collusion with the Turks. On these grounds he summoned the pope to be tried by the Council of Basel, which he claimed had never gone out of existence. Zamometič, despite the notoriety of Sixtus's actions, won few supporters, and when the pope placed Basel under interdict, the city authorities, alarmed by its potential economic repercussions, arrested the archbishop. His suicide two years later ended the incident.[12]

Much more serious was the French-inspired *conciliabulum* of Pisa (1511–12). King Louis XII of France, provoked by Julius II's determination to drive the "barbarians" (i.e., the French) from Italy, responded, as his predecessors had, with plans for a council. This time threats led to action. The king found several cardinals willing to support him, and from

French-controlled Milan they convoked a general council to be held at Pisa, a city within the dominion of France's Italian ally, Florence. The Emperor Maximilian initially approved the conciliar venture, too, but Julius trumped the Pisa gathering by announcing a general council to meet under papal aegis in Rome (the Fifth Lateran Council, the sessions of which lasted from 1512 to 1517). The prelates at Pisa had already retreated to the greater safety of Milan in the spring of 1512. Then, in the aftermath of the Battle of Ravenna, which forced French military withdrawal, the *conciliabulum* moved to Asti and finally to Lyon, where it dissolved.[13]

Staunch in their opposition to conciliarist programs, vigilant in checking appeals to such assemblies, and strengthened by their successful counterattacks on the two councils which were actually declared, the Renaissance popes were sustained also in their absolutist views of their ecclesiastical authority by a massive literature in support of papal monarchy, much of it produced by intellectuals of the Roman Curia.

The starting point for all defenses of Petrine primacy and therefore of papal power was, of course, the text of Matthew 16. In response to Jesus's question as to the identity of the Son of Man, Simon had answered, "You are the Messiah, the Son of the living God." Christ replied that Simon could not have learned this from human knowledge; it was instead revealed by the Heavenly Father. He then declared:

> You are Peter [*Petrus*] and on his rock [*petram*] I will build my Church and the gates of hell will not prevail against it. I will give to you the keys of the kingdom of heaven; whatever you bind on earth will be bound in heaven, and whatever you loose on earth will be loosed in heaven. (Matthew 16: 17–19)

This text was supplemented by the thrice-repeated admonition of the resurrected Christ to Peter that if the Apostle loved him he must "feed my sheep" [*Pasce oves meas*] (John 21: 15–17). This, in turn, is closely paralleled by I Peter 5: 2, "Tend that flock of God whose shepherds you are." The Latin text of this (PASCITE QVI IN VOBIS EST GREGEM DEI) appears on the reverse of one of Julius II's medals, along with a depiction of St. Peter giving the keys to a kneeling pope and with Christ, enthroned, blessing.[14]

In the medieval ecclesiology of the Latin Church these texts meant not simply that Peter was assigned a place of special eminence among the Apostles, but rather, more fundamentally, that the transmittal of the keys and the powers of binding and loosing gave Peter and his successor Roman pontiffs ultimate legislative and judicial authority over the Church. It was the canon lawyers of the twelfth and thirteenth centuries who gave precise legal definition to these powers. Indeed, in the Decretalist formulations the pope was seen as wielding a *plenitudo potestatis*, which he exercised as vice-gerent of God, and which set him over all human law as well as assigning him absolute authority in the Church. Such absolutist concepts of papal spiritual and temporal power were embodied in Boniface VIII's Bull "*Unam Sanctam*" (1302), and received theoretical elaboration in the political writings of such early fourteenth-century figures as Augustinus Triumphus and Giles of Rome. These hierocratic theories corresponded to the historical reality of growing papal centralization, and to the extension of papal powers over such matters as appointments, appeals, and dispensations.[15] Thus a distinctively "carnal ecclesiology" came into being.

During the Renaissance period, the most outspoken and prolific defenders of papal absolutism remained the canonists of the papal court. Not surprisingly, the core of their anti-conciliar arguments continued to be derived from the hierocratic conclusions of the Decretalists and publicists of the thirteenth and fourteenth centuries. In fact, Lorenzo Aretino, an auditor of the Rota under Eugenius IV, provided an exhaustive compilation of their views in his *Liber de ecclesiastica potestate* (1440); and the absolutist tenor of the canonists' position can be readily judged from the title of Domenico di San Severino's long treatise addressed to Sixtus IV, *De Dei potentia infinita, et de Christi potentia, et Christi vicarii potestate*.[16]

Among the staunchest papal monarchists in the canonist tradition was the Castilian jurist Rodrigo Sánchez de Arévalo (1404–70). Arévalo first came to prominence in Rome through the preferment of the Spanish pope, Calixtus III, who named him to a Spanish bishopric, but his Roman career reached its apex under Paul II. Arévalo was a principal adviser to the Venetian pope and an indefatigable defender of his policies. He also held the important post of castellan of Castel Sant'Angelo, and in that capacity had custody of Leto, Platina, and other members of the Roman Academy arrested in 1468 as anti-papal conspirators. With the incarcerated Platina, Arévalo engaged in a revealing debate on the relative merits of peace and war (preserved in Arévalo's dialogue *De pace et bello*), in which the imprisoned academician stressed the horrors and cruelties of human bellicosity, while his Castilian warden argued that struggle was a law of nature and that war was not evil in itself but a necessary instrument to gain peace. Arévalo was, though, something of a humanist. He delivered orations before the papal court, composed a treatise on education, wrote a history of Spain, and published a widely disseminated work on morality, the *Speculum vitae humanae*.[17]

Arévalo had early attacked conciliarism, in works addressed to the Holy Roman Emperor Frederick III and to Pope Nicholas V, but it was under Paul II that his pro-papalist tracts reached full spate. He claimed, for instance, in his *Libellus de libera et irrefragabilii auctoritate Romani Pontificis* that the *plenitudo potestatis* meant that the pope had the same power as Peter and therefore was bound neither by election capitulations nor by any oath connected with them. He also attacked the demands of the

Fraticelli for a poor and mendicant Roman Curia in imitation of Christ's poverty (a group of Fraticelli had been arrested in Rome in 1466 and were in Arévalo's custody in Castel Sant'Angelo); defended the supreme and universal authority of the papacy against the presumed anti-clerical sentiments of the Roman Academy; justified Paul II's deposition of the Bohemian King George of Poděbrady as a heretic for his conciliarist agitation; and enlarged on a program of Church reform (*De remediis afflictae ecclesiae*, 1469), in which he attacked four groups of conciliarists (the Bohemians, the French, the Germans, and the Italians) and stressed that reform must come through papal initiative. Occasionally, certain humanist concepts prominent at the papal court appear in Arévalo's defense of papal absolutism. He drew, for instance, on the theme of God's liberality and generosity to conclude that God would thus intend to endow the Church with unrestricted authority, and he employed the Incarnationalist emphasis of the papal preachers to assert that the union with the Word gave Christ unrestricted dominion over all creation and that, as Vicar of Christ, the pope exercised the same dominion.[18]

For the most part, however, Arévalo's positions derived from the hierocratic ecclesiology of the fourteenth century. Indeed, his unswerving claims for absolute papal power, even in the temporal sphere, provoked a response from the leading fifteenth-century Thomist articulator of papal authority, Juan de Torquemada (1388–1468).[19] Arévalo, in defending Paul II's intervention in civil strife in Castile, had argued that the Church provided the only universal basis for a just human order, and that the ancient Romans had ruled only through violence and tyranny. Torquemada denied this. The Roman Empire, like the Church, was ordained by divine will, he asserted in rebuttal, and it thus exercised legitimate sovereignty; moreover, its basis was the justice and political wisdom of the ancient Romans.[20]

Torquemada thus made fewer claims for papal temporal power than did many canonists, but he remained uncompromising in his defense of the papacy as the sole repository of ecclesiastical authority. As the successor of Peter and the Vicar of Christ, all power of jurisdiction in the Church derived from the pope, he asserted. Significantly, too, Torquemada recognized a fundamental deficiency in the canonists' arguments for papal absolutism: other jurists, such as Juan de Segovia and Nicholas de Tudeschis (known as Panormitanus, and perhaps the most influential legal scholar of the century), had defended conciliarist principles, using the same medieval corpus of civil and canon law as the papal monarchists, but instead emphasizing concepts of corporation.[21] A more profound *theological*, rather than merely *legal*, basis for papal primacy thus seemed essential, and the Dominican Torquemada sought this in the writings of the great theologian of his Order, St. Thomas Aquinas.

Initial indications of this approach can be detected in Torquemada's memorandum, composed at the Council of Basel in the early 1430s, which consisted of seventy-three conclusions drawn from Aquinas. He also worked closely with Eugenius IV at the Council of Florence, and had a large share in formulating the two bulls, *Moyses vir Dei* (1439) and *Etsi non dubitemus* (1441), by which Eugenius IV attacked the doctrinal foundations of conciliar theory.[22]

The Council of Florence marked a critical juncture in theological definitions of papal primacy, too, inasmuch as the decree of union (the bull *Laetentur Coeli*) included this section:

> . . . we define the holy Apostolic See and the Roman Pontiff to hold the primacy over the whole world, and that the Roman Pontiff is the successor of blessed Peter, Prince of the Apostles, and that he is the true Vicar of Christ, head of the whole Church and father and teacher of all Christians; and to him in blessed Peter has been delivered by our Lord, Jesus Christ, the full power of feeding, ruling, and governing the universal Church. . . .[23]

For the Greeks, not the Latin doctrine of papal primacy, but instead the Procession of the Holy Spirit, proved the major stumbling block to reunification. Only in the last month of deliberations at Florence, after agreement on *Filioque* had been hammered out, did the authority of the pope, along with such matters as Purgatory and the use of leavened and unleavened bread in the Eucharist, come under discussion.[24] Nevertheless, Greek acquiescence to the supremacy of papal spiritual jurisdiction, and the fact that this was proclaimed by an ecumenical council, offered a solid base for pro-papalist arguments. As such *Laetentur coeli* was repeatedly cited in the Renaissance period.[25]

Torquemada, in his *Apparatus super decretum unionis Graecorum* (1441) was among the first to stress the theological implications of the decree for the matter of papal primacy. But for much of the 1440s and early '50s he was at work on a much more searching treatment of ecclesiology. This began as a theological commentary on the *Decretum* of Gratian, but in the years 1450–53 he set this aside to write a systematic treatise on the nature of the Church, the *Summa de Ecclesia*, dedicated to Nicholas V. Based on exhaustive patristic and scholastic citations, and encased in the rigorous dialectics of scholastic argumentation, Torquemada's *Summa* provided a powerful defense of the hierarchical ordering of the Church and of papal monarchy.[26]

Aquinas was at the core of Torquemada's work, but important also to his emphasis on the inherently hierarchical nature of the Church—which was seen as a reflection of the similar structure of the cosmos—and on a descending pattern of authority was the thought of Ps.-Dionysius the Areopagite. As the presumed expression of the Athenian convert of St. Paul (Acts 17: 34), the writings ascribed to Dionysius (now dated c. A.D. 500) were accorded enormous respect in the Middle Ages, and they had recently received renewed attention in the humanistic Latin translation of the Florentine monk and humanist, Ambrogio Traversari. The future Nicholas V had, significantly, provided the strongest encouragement to Traversari's undertaking, praised highly the results, and kept a copy of the translation in his bedroom. It is indicative, too, that when Traversari addressed the Council of Basel in 1436 as Papal Nuncio, he cited Ps.-Dionysius's authority to refute conciliarist claims that St. Paul had envisioned a Church consisting only of presbyters and deacons.[27] Other humanist defenders of papal monarchy were similarly drawn to the Ps.-Dionysius corpus. Piero da Monte, for example, cited Ps.-Dionysius in arguing that the Church Militant should conform in its hierarchical ordering to the model of the heavenly hierarchy.[28]

The renewal of Neo-Platonism in the later fifteenth and early sixteenth centuries served to strengthen further the attractiveness of the Ps.-Dionysius writings, since, in fact, their content is permeated with the thought of Plotinus, Proclus, and the whole tradition of Neo-Platonism from the late Hellenistic period. Oddly, no Italian Renaissance humanist, except Valla, doubted the authenticity of the Ps.-Dionysius corpus as the work of St. Paul's disciple.[29] Indeed, one sign of the Areopagite's stature in Rome during the early sixteenth century is that for Giles of Viterbo he was a favorite theological authority.[30] Symptomatic, too, of this same regard is the subject matter of the last tapestry in the cycle devoted to the life of St. Paul that Raphael created for the Sistine Chapel. This shows the Apostle preaching in Athens, and in the foreground the conversion of the Platonist and Areopagite Dionysius.[31]

Besides providing powerful support for the view that a hierocratic Church corresponds to the ultimate nature of the universe, Ps.-Dionysius offered the sanction of primitive Christianity—indeed, nearly Apostolic legitimacy—for a monarchical and hierarchical ecclesiology. In the context of quickening interest in Christian antiquity, to which Traversari contributed so much, the conviction that papal primacy represented the consensus of the earliest Christians made a telling argument. From this perspective, conciliarism could only appear as a dangerous and corrupting novelty.

Thomistic ecclesiology had other proponents in fifteenth-century Rome. It formed the foundation, for instance, of the *De potestate papae et termino eius*, a work of the Venetian humanist and curialist, Domenico de' Domenichi, dedicated to Calixtus III. Domenichi meant his treatise as a refutation of certain canonists' positions on the nature and scope of papal powers of dispensation, and he devoted the first book of his treatise to this topic. In later sections he discoursed on the more general issue of the relation of papal authority to that of the bishops, cardinals, and secular rulers. As a whole, however, Domenichi's tract proved neither as comprehensive nor as authoritative as Torquemada's *Summa*.[32]

The leading Thomist of the early sixteenth century, the Dominican

Cajetan (Thomas de Vio), emerged, like Torquemada, as an outspoken defender of papal primacy. As in the case of his predecessor, not just theoretical considerations but also concrete historical challenges prompted Cajetan's ecclesiological writings. The first such circumstance was the *conciliabulum* of Pisa. Cajetan's *Tractatus de comparatione auctoritatis Papae et Concilii* (1511) constituted the papacy's main theological assault on the theories of the Gallican conciliarists, and he followed it with a further exchange of treatises with the conciliarists' spokesman, Jacques Almain.[33]

Within the decade the issue of papal primacy again became a matter of contention, this time in the controversy surrounding Martin Luther. From the beginning, intellectuals in Rome perceived Luther's theological critique of the doctrine of indulgences as an implicit attack on papal authority. Hence, the initial Roman response, penned in June 1518 by Silvester Prierias, the Dominican Master of the Sacred Palace, at the request of Leo X, bore the title *In praesumptuosas Martini Lutheri conclusiones de potestate papae dialogus*. The issue of papal primacy became the clear crux of the dispute, however, only with the Leipzig Disputation a year later. As the twelfth in the series of theses for debate there, the Ingolstadt theologian Johannes Eck proposed: "We deny that the Roman Church was not superior to the other churches before the time of Silvester, but we recognize that he who has the seat and faith of blessed Peter has always been the successor to Peter and the Vicar of Christ." Luther could not resist responding with a thirteenth thesis: "That the Roman Church is superior to all Churches is indeed proved by the far-fetched decrees put out by the Roman pontiffs in the last four hundred years. But this ecclesiastical dogma is contrary to the approved histories of eleven hundred years, the plain teaching of Divine Scripture, and the decree of the Council of Nicaea, the most sacred of all councils." Luther's position that the papacy existed merely by human, not divine, right—argued both at Leipzig and in his published *Resolutio super propositione XIII de potestate papae* (1519)—provoked a fusillade of counterattacks from Rome, including works of Prierias (again), Ambrosius Catharinus, and Cristoforo Marcello. It also occasioned Cajetan's *De divina institutione Pontificatus Romani Pontificis super totam ecclesiam a Christo in Petro* (1521), six chapters of which (out of a total of fourteen) are devoted to an explication of "*Tu es Petrus*" and another four to "*Pasce oves meas*."[34]

HUMANISTS AND THE *PRIMATUS PETRI*

The hierarchical ordering of the Church under the headship of the Roman pontiffs was an unquestioned assumption, too, of the Roman humanists. Humanism as an intellectual discipline and cultural outlook lacked the systematic logical rigor of Torquemada's syllogisms and the ordered refinements of medieval canon law theory. But the humanists, as orators, were able to exploit the rhetorical resources of classical Latin, and its increasing prestige in Renaissance culture, to impress upon a different audience from the professional theologians and jurists the dignity and power of the Roman Church. If Thomas Aquinas could be triumphantly acclaimed within a Roman setting in the *encomia* at the Minerva and in the frescoes of the Carafa Chapel, so even more could St. Peter be lauded. Beyond this expertise in eloquence, the humanists contributed in another way to a defense of papal primacy. With their improved grasp of historical sources, both classical and Christian, and with their attention to archeological evidence, they were able to envision more tangibly the deeds and martyrdom of Peter. This, in turn, permitted the celebration in more potent historical and mythical terms of the link between the destiny of Rome and the destiny of the Roman Church.

The religious life of Renaissance Rome offered the humanists a number of contexts for remarks on papal primacy. The sermons for the sacred liturgies of the papal court were devoted primarily to the great mysteries of the Christian faith—Creation, the Incarnation, the immortality of the soul—but the monarchical constitution of the Church was introduced as an occasional theme. For instance, monarchy as the principle of ecclesiological order was seen as a mirror of one God in heaven. At other times the preachers stressed the pastoral role of the pope under the topic of the Church as one flock under one shepherd.[35] The Feast of Sts. Peter and Paul (29 June) would provide, one might expect, a particularly suitable occasion for humanist praise of the first pope and for the theme of papal primacy. A sermon of Sánchez de Arévalo, dating from the pontificate of Nicholas V, does just that by echoing Pope Leo the Great's sermon for the same feast; in his homily the great fifth-century pope had linked the idea of Rome as the See of Peter to Rome as head of the world.[36] But in the Renaissance period the Roman celebration of the Feast of Peter and Paul did not usually include a sermon, and thus no body of sermon literature was produced for this occasion.[37]

Where humanist treatment of the specific subject of papal primacy did repeatedly appear as a suitable rhetorical topic was in the orations "Concerning the election of the pope"—those sermons delivered just before the cardinals entered into conclave. The monarchical character of the papacy is implicit in all of these orations, but several speakers used the opportunity to provide extensive proofs of papal primacy, adduced from Scripture, the Church Fathers, and the decisions of the early Church councils.[38]

This same emphasis on Scriptural and patristic authority is present in *Contra impugnantes sedis apostolicae auctoritatem*, an extensive defense of papal primacy written in accordance with humanist precepts and addressed to Nicholas V by Piero da Monte, the Venetian humanist and jurist, whom we have met as the embattled Bishop of Brescia and ambitious curialist. Piero's treatise was the culmination of two decades of repeated articulation of papal preeminence. In 1433, as a member of the Venetian delegation, Piero had attended the Council of Basel. Prompted by his firsthand experience of the conciliar controversy, he wrote a short tract, in question and answer form, on the origin and powers of the papacy, the general Church council, and the empire. Occasional classical references spice this early work but the general scope and tone is shaped by canonist legal arguments.[39] Later, in the 1440s as a papal legate to France, Piero addressed a series of orations to the French court in defense of papal authority, and in a speech to Nicholas V he had also marshalled arguments against the rump Council of Basel.[40] At the same time, Piero became increasingly committed to humanist rhetorical principles. It is significant, for instance, that the oration he delivered before the papal court for Passion Sunday in 1450 or 1451 was the first as far as we know, "fully epideictic sermon on a Christian mystery."[41]

Hence, when Piero turned again to a more comprehensive consideration of the controverted issue of papal primacy, he was determined to present to the humanist pope, Nicholas V, a fully humanistic work. He begins the work, in characteristic humanist fashion, with remarks about the power of rhetoric to inculcate the practice of virtue, and he cites examples from Greek and Roman history, from the experience of the Old Testament patriarchs and prophets, and from the acts of the Apostles, Evangelists, and martyrs.[42] In the epilogue, he declares that his purpose has been to defend the authority of the Roman See neither with Ciceronian eloquence (a typical humanist disclaimer) nor (his real point) with the Aristotelian arguments of the dialecticians, filled as they are, he contends, with snares and deceptions, but rather solely with the authority of the Holy Scriptures and the testimony of the Church Fathers. Such an approach is dictated by his subject matter, Piero avers: since papal authority is a matter of divine power, its virtue cannot be judged, nor its magnitude grasped, nor its sublimity comprehended with the logic of the philosophers or with the charm of eloquence.[43]

The five topically organized sections of *Contra impugnantes* reflect matters that had been disputed by the Council of Basel and the popes: the Curia's practice of reservations and expectative favors in the collating of benefices, juridical powers of dispensation, the levying of first fruits and annates, ecclesiastical discipline, and the obedience of the faithful. But in accord with his announced intention, Piero buttresses his traditional pro-papalist conclusions with extensive Scriptural citations and with abundant patristic quotations. Significantly, he cites the Greek, as well as the Latin, Church Fathers, and, in particular, John Chrysostom's New Testament homilies and Cyril of Alexandria's *Thesaurus* are repeatedly quoted. For instance, in arguing the requirement of obedience to the pope, Piero notes that Cyril had declared that if we are to imitate Christ, and as His sheep hear His voice while abiding in the Church of Peter, we must not become puffed-up with pride, lest the twisting serpent tempt us to strife and lead to our being cast out, as Eve was from Paradise.[44]

Quotations from Cyril's *Thesaurus* are significant, too, inasmuch as this was one of the key Greek patristic texts that the Latin contingent at the Council of Florence had used to argue their case on the issue of the Procession of the Holy Spirit. Unknown to the Latin Middle Ages, Cyril's treatise received its first Latin translation from George of Trebizond in 1453, during the Byzantine emigré's employ at the Neapolitan court of Alfonso V.[45] The real discoverer of Cyril's *Thesaurus*, however, was Ambrogio Traversari, and he was the first to exploit Greek patristic testimony in defense of the See of Peter. In his oration to the Council of Basel, Traversari had drawn on his vast fund of patristic learning to emphasize the veneration the Greek Fathers had accorded the See of Rome, and he had used the same approach in discussions with the Greek prelates at the Council of Florence.[46]

Furthermore, Traversari was responsible for inspiring Piero da Monte's interest in the Greek Fathers. In a letter, written in 1438 to Traversari, Piero, then in England, lamented his abandonment of Greek studies, begun under Guarino da Verona, in favor of dialectics and then civil and canon law. Regretting lost time, he vowed now to resume his neglected work on the language. Over the next several years, he did just that, reaching sufficient proficiency that he could himself contribute a Latin translation of a Greek patristic work—Epiphanius's *Libellus de religione Christiana*, which he dedicated to Parentucelli's mentor, Niccolò Albergati.[47]

Piero da Monte, following Traversari's lead, thus became convinced that the early history of the Church—Greek as well as Latin—testified to the primacy of Rome. To Scripture and to the traditional citations of the Latin Fathers could now be added the testimony of the Greeks. To this end, Chrysostom proved particularly useful. Perhaps the most eloquent of the Greek Fathers, his homiletical approach to Scriptural exegesis, his Stoicizing moral concerns, his perceptions of theology shaped not by the demands of a systematizer but rather by the responsibilities of a pastor of souls, and his remarkable powers as an orator commended him to a humanist audience. He was the most frequently translated of the Greek Fathers in the Renaissance period, and probably the most admired as well.[48] Furthermore, his exegesis of Matthew 16 and John 21 sustained Petrine primacy (as Piero da Monte emphasized[49]), and he had personally appealed to the Roman pontiff to intervene in the Eastern Church to restore discipline following his imperially decreed exile from his post as Patriarch of Constantinople. Traversari had argued this point as historical confirmation from the early Church of papal preeminence, and he had also cited the similar example of Athanasius, who had sought papal support in combatting the heresy of Arius.[50] Two of the most respected Greek Fathers thus attested to the precedence accorded the See of Rome in Christian antiquity. Indeed this may explain why their portraits in particular, along with those of Aquinas, Leo the Great, and the four Latin Fathers, were included in Nicholas V's chapel in the Vatican.[51]

For humanist defenders of the papacy, then, the renewed attention to patristic sources provided the sanction of primitive Christianity for the unique dignity and authority of St. Peter's see. Increasingly, however, in the middle decades of the fifteenth century Peter was perceived by the Roman humanists not so much as an abstract principle of monarchical governance, but rather as the historical Apostle. Guided by divine will to Rome, he had made it by his martyrdom the eternal capital of Christianity. In thus shifting discussion of Petrine primacy from issues related to the definition and powers of the papal office to the personage of its founder, the humanists were able to press the unique ties that bound the Roman Church to the city of Rome. Focus on the historical foundation of the Roman Church also allowed those areas where humanists had expertise—namely the archeology and topography of ancient Rome—to come to the fore. Indeed, the first generation of Roman humanists, by dwelling on the martyrdom of Peter and the other early Christian saints, developed what might be called a "topographical mystique" of Rome as capital of Christendom. In martyrdom they also saw the key to Peter's holiness, and the virtue manifest in the lives of contemporary popes who were renewing the Roman Church.

An early expression of this general theme appears in Piero da Monte's first tract on papal power, the one written at Basel. There he asserts that it had been Christ's will to found His Church in Rome, where the *principes gentilium* dwelled, and to accomplish this through Peter's martyrdom in the city. As proof, Piero adduces the *"Quo vadis?"* encounter between Christ and the fleeing Apostle. The papacy thus rightly belongs only to the city hallowed by Peter's blood, and therefore, Piero concludes, Pope Clement V erred in moving the capital of the Roman Church beyond the Alps to Avignon.[52]

The same point is set forth more fully in Flavio Biondo's *Roma instaurata*, the work on Roman topography he composed in Rome in the mid-1440s, following his return to the Eternal City with the court of Eugenius IV. Contrasting pagan and Christian Rome, Biondo argues that not the blood poured forth by Roman armies in defense of the Roman Empire, but rather the blood of the early Christian martyrs provided the more solid foundation for the glorious majesty of the city of Rome. Through the will of God and the "true emperor" Jesus Christ, Rome became constituted the seat, citadel, and domicile of the eternal Christian religion. Its soil stained purple with the blood of the martyrs, its churches filled with innumerable relics and other signs of God's wondrous acts, and in possession of the *limina Apostolorum*, Rome has in these glorious foundations of the Faith, Biondo declares, a splendor and nobility not to be found anywhere else in the world—in particular, not Avignon, and not Bologna, Ferrara, or Florence (where the itinerant pontificate of Eugenius IV had just spent a decade). Attesting, too, Biondo continues, to the non-transferable sacredness of Rome are the pilgrims, who come not only from the whole of Latin Christendom, but also from the remote corners of Europe, and from Asia and Africa. These included the Greeks, the Armenians, the Ethiopians, and all the others, who through Eugenius's efforts had become reconciled to the Catholic faith and to the Roman Church.[53]

Among Rome's sacred sites, which provided tangible links to the deeds of the martyrs, and which Biondo was intent upon having his readers call to mind, were the place of *"Domine, quo vadis?"* and the nearby catacombs of S. Callisto with its adjoining church of the martyr St. Sebastian, recently restored by Eugenius IV; the heads of Peter and Paul in the *Sancta Sanctorum* of the Lateran; the chains that held Peter in Herod's prison in Jerusalem, now located in the church of S. Pietro in Vincoli; the ring sent from heaven to St. Agnes, preserved in her church on the Via Nomentana; the grill of St. Lawrence upon which he was burned by the Gentiles and over whom "that most stalwart athlete triumphed"; and the fountains of sweet water which burst forth from the ground where the blood from the beheading of the Apostle Paul struck.[54]

If Biondo thus underscored the continued accessibility in the Roman basilicas of relics testifying to the martyrs' heroic faith, another humanist, the Florentine Antonio Agli (c. 1400–77) labored to provide, at Nicholas V's urging, a humanistically revised version of the lives of the early Christian martyrs. In his prefatory letter to the pope,[55] Agli writes that a variety of problems had stymied his project, and except for Nicholas's insistence on its importance he would have abandoned it. One key difficulty was the expectation of all humanist historiography that history should inspire the reader to imitate in his own actions what he reads. But many of the lives of the martyrs had been presented so ineptly, so barbarously, and indeed so childishly, Agli protests, that not even silly old women would take pleasure in them or find them credible. Clumsy in their attempts at eloquence, prolix where they should be succinct, these accounts arouse mirth, where instead the effect should be *dignitas* and *gravitas*. If anyone overly attached to secular literature and knowledge, and lacking in piety, should happen to run across these saints' lives, he would jeer at the simplicity of Christians for giving credence to such puerile fables.

To avoid this, Agli says that he chose to follow Jerome, Ambrose, Eusebius of Caesarea, and other Church Fathers, whose historical treatment of the lives and deeds of Paul the monk, Antony Abbot, St. Agnes, and St. Martin of Tours were written with fidelity and with due seriousness. He had also turned to the most ancient manuscripts, both in Greek and in Latin, in order to recover the oldest and therefore most trustworthy sources of saints' lives. Such accounts were widely scattered, but he had received aid and encouragement in his quest for relevant codices from Traversari, until the Camaldolese's death. Among the soundest sources, in Agli's opinion, were those gathered at the behest of the early popes. These included in particular the deeds of the martyrs compiled under Pope Fabianus (236–50), who, Agli observes, ordered that information be sought from the inhabitants of each district of Rome and be faithfully recorded by notaries.

Troublesome to his task as the medieval form and the questionable veracity of his sources proved, Agli was convinced that his work of recovering the historical deeds of the Roman martyrs from falsity and from the accidents of dispersion had real value. Moreover, as a scholarly undertaking it belonged appropriately to Nicholas V's pontificate, inasmuch as this pope had done so much to renew the Roman Church, by rebuilding the walls of Rome and restoring (*instaurare*) its neglected and dilapidated churches.

Attention to the *acta* of the martyr saints also permitted Agli, like Piero da Monte and Flavio Biondo, to contrast the founders of classical and Christian Rome. Historians of the ancient Romans write, Agli remarks, of how much blood, toil, and sweat the Romans used, and how many wars they fought, to make Rome head of the world, to enlarge her empire, and to make their deeds eternal. His work instead dwells on those who raised up the Catholic Church, and on their struggles for the celestial kingdom, the confession of truth, and the worship of the true God. They praise Julius Caesar as the progenitor of the Roman Empire and admire the pride, might, and imperial spirit of the ancient Romans. I, Agli declares, laud to the heavens Jesus Christ Our Lord and Peter the Apostle, who established the Roman See, and I wonder at and seek to imitate the humility of Christ and His followers through which the Church endures.

Concluding his preface, Agli indicates that this first volume of his work covers the period down to the times of Marcus Aurelius and Commodus, and that wherever possible he has provided the names of the emperors and popes under whose rule the deeds of the martyrs occurred. Where such information proved unavailable, his intention is to include the account at random in subsequent volumes, or if enough instances arise, to place these separately at the end.

In fact, Agli seems subsequently to have abandoned the project altogether. Though he outlived Nicholas V by twenty years, and remained in contact with Roman circles—in 1470 Paul II named this former tutor from the days of his uncle Eugenius IV's sojourn in Florence Bishop of Volterra—only the one volume of saints' lives produced in Nicholas's pontificate remains extant.[56]

One possible explanation for Agli's failure to continue his project may lie in the changing perceptions of what saintly virtues built the Church, a subject to be explored shortly. What was not mere coincidence was the impulse Nicholas V gave to Agli's work on the early Christian martyrs. Indeed, Tertullian's famous remark that the blood of the martyrs is the seed of the Church seems to have provided a guiding conception to Nicholas's sense of the papacy's restored spiritual headship. Agli compared the pope's exertions as guardian and pastor of the Church to the blood poured forth by martyrs,[57] and Michele Canensi, Nicholas's humanist biographer, asserted that he possessed all the spiritual virtues—faith, piety, sincere love, religion, charity, holiness, and martyrdom—acclaimed in Sixtus, Urban, Silvester, Gregory, Bernard, and the other fathers of the Church. Nicholas's martyrdom, while not that of blood suffered by those whose deeds confirmed and consecrated the Catholic Church, was, Canensi argues, the no less arduous incessant cares and constant anxieties he had borne in caring for his flock.[58] Like Canensi, Manetti also regarded Nicholas V as a Christian *exemplum*. While making no overt claim for the pontiff as a martyr, Manetti did write a highly hagiographical account of the pope's life, filled with the kind of *mirabilia* present in lives of the early saints.[59]

Martyrdom as a key virtue of Christian leadership and as a primary source of Christian Rome's sacredness found prominent expression, too, in the fresco cycles Fra Angelico painted in Nicholas V's small private chapel in the Vatican Palace. The lunettes depict scenes from the life of St. Stephen, the protomartyr, but the locale of his activities has been shifted, significantly, from Jerusalem to Rome. In the first scene, he receives his ordination from St. Peter, before the ciborium-surmounted altar of the Constantinian basilica of St. Peter's. Unhistorical in itself, the didactic and exemplary intent of this rendering is further underscored by the basilica's appearance. Rather than showing St. Peter's actual mid-fifteenth century state, the painting presents, it seems, the plans then being considered for the building's remodeling. Subsequent scenes give witness to St. Stephen's distribution of alms, his preaching, and his other responsibilities as first deacon, activities also set—a-historically—in a recognizably Roman cityscape. The cycle ends with his stoning outside the walls of Jerusalem, but shown as a massive curved section of Rome's Aurelian Wall. The lower walls of the chapel are devoted to the parallel career of the Roman deacon and martyr, St. Lawrence, and again elements of a distinctly Roman setting appear, including the envisaged updated St. Peter's basilica. In the first scene, Pope Sixtus II, given the features of Nicholas V, confers the deaconate, while subsequent frescoes show Lawrence dispensing the

sacraments, receiving from Sixtus the treasure of the Church, distributing this to the poor, his summons before the emperor, his imprisonment,
and finally his martyrdom.[60]

Nicholas V viewed martyrdom as struggle and suffering on behalf
of the Church; Pius II courted martyrdom in a more literal sense. In a
lengthy speech delivered to the College of Cardinals in the secret consistory of 23 September 1463, the Piccolomini pontiff bewailed the failures
that had marked his previous attempts to launch a crusade against the
Ottomans. Efforts to raise money for this purpose had been rejected as
extortionist schemes of a greedy Curia, and his motives scorned and
derided. Corrosive distrust undermined relations between Rome and the
rest of Christendom, and, Pius admitted, the people were not entirely
wrong in seeing the cardinals and the Roman Curia as slaves to luxury and
ambition.

Given this poisoned atmosphere, a new path had to be taken to
restore confidence in the Church's leadership. This must be a return to
the long-abandoned means by which the Church had gained power:
"abstinence, purity, innocence, zeal for the faith, religious fervor, scorn of
death, and eagerness for martyrdom." The martyrdoms of Peter and
Paul, followed by the steadfast courage of the long series of martyr popes
suffering the most agonizing tortures, founded the Roman Church, Pius
asserts. In imitation of Jesus Christ, "the eternal and supreme Shepherd
who was slain for His sheep on the altar of the Cross and reconciled the
human race to the heavenly Father," these shepherds laid down their lives
for their flock. When the age of martyrdom passed, then came the time of
the holy confessors, whose teachings and pure lives bridled human vices,
and like the martyrs made the Church great. Only by imitation of their
virtues can the Church be preserved, Pius concludes. Only by setting out
personally on crusade—not to wield the sword himself, but instead imitating Moses, who stood praying on the mountain while the Israelites fought
the Amalekites—can the Lord's favor be won and other Christians roused
to war. "We too will lay down our life for our flock since in no other way
can we save the Christian religion from being trampled by the forces of
the Turk."[61]

In the end, events denied Pius a martyr's death. Wasting ill health,
compounded by fever, felled him at Ancona before the crusading fleet
had embarked, and with his death the whole expedition came to naught.

Martyrdom as the identifying sign of spiritual headship in the
Church did not find expression just in Pius's dying days. Earlier in his
pontificate the notion that the apostolate in its fullest sense embraces
martyrdom received particular emphasis in the remarkable ceremonies
accompanying the reception in Rome of the relic of St. Andrew's head. As
Pius himself records, in the detailed account in his *Commentaries* devoted
to the transfer of the head to Rome,[62] St. Andrew, the brother of St. Peter,

had become the Apostle to Greece, and there, at Patras in the Morea, he had been crucified by the Roman proconsul. Later his body had been removed to Amalfi, but his head remained at Patras until the Ottoman invasion of 1460. Thomas Paleologus, the Despot of Morea, to prevent the relic from falling into infidel hands, then took it from its sanctuary, bringing it with him into exile in Italy. Pius offered the refugee Despot a large sum for the relic, so that it could be brought to Rome to be placed beside the bones of his brother, Peter, and arranged also for the Byzantine prince to receive a pension and suitable living accommodations at the Roman Court.

The relic of the head remained temporarily at Narni until pacification of the territory around Rome permitted large crowds of pilgrims to reach the city unmolested, and until improvements to Piazza S. Pietro, aimed at accommodating the anticipated throngs, reached completion. These projects included the enlargement of the Piazza itself, restoration of the crumbling steps leading to the atrium of the basilica, and the placement there of newly commissioned statues, colossal in size, of Sts. Peter and Paul.[63]

On Palm Sunday, 1462, Bessarion, and the other two cardinals whom Pius had sent to bring the relic from Narni, reached the Ponte Molle, just outside Rome, while the pope, after first celebrating Mass in St. Peter's, proceeded to S. Maria del Popolo, where he spent the night. The next morning, which was brilliantly sun-lit in contrast to the previous month of rain, the pope passed through the Porta Flaminia to the meadows beyond, where a temporary platform had been constructed for the occasion. Bessarion placed the reliquary on the altar of the platform, and the pope, kneeling and in tears, welcomed Andrew to his brother Peter's domicile. He urged Andrew to behold the city before him, "mother Rome, hallowed by thy brother's precious blood," to which Peter and Paul had given a new birth in Christ. Who, Pius asked, would not in turn exult in the Apostle Andrew's coming? His eyes had beheld God in the flesh. His mouth had spoken to Christ. And his cheeks Jesus had surely kissed, "for we cannot doubt that thou art with thy carnal head and with it dost enter the city." Pius then called upon Andrew to intercede with God as an advocate of the holy city of Rome and to appeal to Him to transfer His anger to the impious Turks, who dishonor Christ. Then followed a hymn, composed by the humanist Agapito di Cencio de' Rustici, which supplicated Andrew to aid the cause of crusade, after which the relic was carried into the city and deposited on the main altar of S. Maria del Popolo.

The next day Pius carried the reliquary in procession to St. Peter's. So many clergy and laity marched that the head of the column reached the basilica before the pope had started, and the crowds lining the route surpassed in numbers, Pius claims, the largest that had been present

13. Pius II receiving the relic of St. Andrew's head at the Ponte Molle. Pen and ink drawing attributed to Ventura Salimbeni. Florence, Museo Horne, No. 5876. (Photo: Gabinetto Fotografico, Soprintendenza Beni Artistici e Storici di Firenze, Courtesy Fondazione Horne)

during Nicholas V's jubilee. Tapestries, gold canopies, and other lavish decorations covered the façades of the palaces, there were fountains of wine and altars with burning incense, children dressed as angels sang hymns, and the sounds of flutes and trumpets filled the air. At last the pope reached the basilica, which was filled with blazing lights. There he placed the head of St. Andrew on the high altar over the place where the bodies of Peter and Paul lay. Cardinal Bessarion, speaking for St. Andrew, then addressed the two apostolic founders of the Roman Church, urging them to heed his call for vengeance against the Turks, whose cruelty had driven him into exile; and he called on the pope, as his brother Peter's successor, to avenge the blood of Christians.

Pius responded that the bodies of Peter and Paul assuredly rejoiced at Andrew's coming, especially "the bones of thy brother Peter, whose joy is enhanced by fraternal affection." Assuredly, too, their souls in heaven, in Christ's kingdom, are invoking His aid to restore Andrew's head to its own throne. For himself, the pope promised to do all in his power "to recover thy sheep and thy home here on earth," and stressed that nothing was closer to his heart than the defense of the Faith against the Turk. Afterwards he blessed the crowds and announced a plenary indulgence for all who had come. For the remainder of Holy Week the customary rites were celebrated with particular devotion, and on Easter Sunday Pius brought both St. Andrew's head and the Veronica to the temporary loggia of benediction located at the top of the new stairs. There he gave his blessing to the crowd, and pronounced a plenary remission of sins for those who had prepared themselves through confession and contrition.

Holy Week concluded, Pius placed St. Andrew's head for temporary safekeeping in Castel Sant'Angelo. As a permanent home, he created a new chapel in Old St. Peter's, providing also a new silver reliquary for the sacred head. Within this chapel, he arranged, too, for his own burial. Pius's nephew, Cardinal Francesco Todeschini-Piccolomini, later Pope Pius III, commissioned the sculptural reliefs for his uncle's tomb, each devoted to a high point of Pius II's pontificate. One of these, appropriately, shows the pope receiving from Bessarion the reliquary of St. Andrew's head. Against a backdrop of classical Roman architecture in which Christian symbols appear triumphant over paganism—a cross surmounts an obelisk, and the processional crucifix obscures a relief of a river god in the spandrel of a triumphal arch—the pope, on bended knee, and surrounded by lay and clerical members of the Roman court, holds the relic over a Roman sarcophagus, probably intended to symbolize St. Peter's tomb.[64]

Nicholas V and Pius II, the two great humanist popes of the mid-Quattrocento, thus made the virtue of martyrdom a leitmotiv of the restored Roman papacy. Martyrdom had built the *Ecclesia Romana*, uniquely sanctified the soil of Rome, and provided the means to renew the

14. Tomb of Pius II, detail. Marble relief sculpture of the reception of St. Andrew's head. Rome, S. Andrea della Valle. (Photo: Alinari/Art Resource, NY)

Roman and Apostolic Church.[65] In particular, the reception of St. Andrew's head had focussed attention on Peter as the historical martyr whose blood consecrated the Roman Church and as the living presence within his sanctuary in the Vatican. Both aspects of St. Peter's pivotal apostolate and enduring holiness had been further developed, moreover, in the important description of the Vatican basilica written by Maffeo Vegio (1407–58). Vegio, a Lombard humanist, had, like Biondo, entered papal service under Eugenius IV. With the return of the papal court to Rome in 1443, he too became definitively established in the eternal city. He continued to serve Eugenius as *scriptor* of Apostolic briefs and *Datarius*, but the pope also named him a canon of St. Peter's, which doubtless explains much of his intense historical interest in the basilica. During his Roman period, Vegio's deepening ardor for religious matters is also apparent. In his youth he had gained fame for his Latin poetry based on classical subject matter—he composed, for instance, a thirteenth book for the *Aeneid*—but in his later hagiographical works, including lives of Pope Celestine V, St. Augustine and his mother St. Monica, S. Bernardino, and the Augustinian hermit S. Niccola da Tolentino, he celebrates the ascetic life as the means of liberation from worldly anxieties and the path to spiritual perfection.[66]

Vegio's *De rebus antiquis memorabilibus Basilicae S. Petri Romae*,[67] begun perhaps during Nicholas V's pontificate but completed only after his death, is both a pilgrim's guide to the basilica and a historical account of the church's site, of the circumstances of its construction and embellishment, and of its function as the central sanctuary of Christendom. Vegio's purpose is praise, to arouse in his reader feelings of awe and wonder. But he was concerned also for historical and archeological accuracy. At the beginning of Book I he criticizes those who accept without question accounts that are clearly fabulous or apocryphal. As an example, he cites the legend that Constantine converted to Christianity when Peter and Paul appeared to him in a dream, after he had been told that if he bathed in the blood of infants he would be cured of the leprosy which afflicted him.[68] This cannot be true, Vegio remarks, since Eusebius in his *Ecclesiastical History* states that the emperor was converted by the vision of the Cross before the Battle of Milvian Bridge. The establishment of the true circumstances of Constantine's conversion leads Vegio to digress, first, on the moral and intellectual qualities necessary for a historian—he must be well-versed in the *studia humanitatis*, be acquainted with human mores, and be attentive to source material pertinent to locating the time and place of events—and, second, to a defense of the authority and dignity of the historian against the claims of theologians and canonists.[69]

The intellectual value and moral worth of the historian thus staked out, Vegio turns to the matter at hand, the actual construction of St. Peter's basilica undertaken by Constantine. What the humanist finds particularly striking, and a clear sign of God's wisdom and goodness, is that the basilica stands on the former site of Nero's circus. What had once been a place of wantonness, evil, and atrocity, and where, as Tacitus attests, Christians were persecuted, had thus become through divine will the gateway to virtue, religion, and holiness. Where once the insane shouts of the circus mobs were heard, now sacred hymns are sung to Christ, the true God. Whereas formerly Nero staged mock sea-battles in his Vatican *naumachia*, St. Peter, the fisher of men, whom Christ called to Himself over the waters, now fights against demons in the *naumachiae* of the world. Indeed, Vegio concludes, the inscrutable and holy justice of God is made manifest in the fact that the poor fisherman prevails in the city which once reigned as the glorious and mighty ruler of the world. The ancient Romans expended incredible energy in constructing arches, baths, *fora*, sepulchers, and temples, and lavishly promoted honors, triumphs, pomp, and luxury—all in a vain attempt to make their deeds indelible and eternal. Now these monuments are thrown down, left crumbling, desolate, and decayed—a fulfillment of the prophecy that the prideful would be laid low and the humble raised up. The overrun and abandoned temples of the Emperor Augustus, such as the one to Mars Ultor in his forum, serve as signs of God's anger at human *prepotenza*, and the hand of God can be seen, too, in the destroyed temple of Jupiter on the Capitoline. Struck by lightning, it was consumed by the resulting conflagration.[70]

For Vegio, Peter's tomb within the Constantinian basilica became and will continue to endure as the sanctifying center of the Roman Church. From the high altar over his tomb archbishops and patriarchs receive the pallium of their office. Within the basilica the Holy Roman Emperors are crowned and here the saints are canonized. Here also the popes receive burial, and Vegio identifies, among numerous others, the tombs of Eugenius IV and Nicholas V, both of whom he singles out for praise. Contributing further to the basilica's function as sanctuary and shrine are the many relics, altars, and chapels, and Vegio details their location, foundation, and decoration. He does the same, too, for the various religious buildings adjacent to the church. Interspersed in his tour are accounts of the major historical events that impinged on the Vatican precinct, such as the Saracen sack during Leo IV's pontificate. In addition, he describes the many changes made over time to the building and to its decoration, including the recent alterations necessitated by Nicholas V's partial construction of a new choir. Visions, healings, and other miraculous manifestations fill his pages, the cumulative effect of which is to impress upon the reader the venerable sanctity and unparalleled spiritual dignity of the basilica. The tour concluded, Vegio, in closing his work, invites us to turn back into the basilica, in order to salute the Prince of the Apostles and to adore Him [Christ] through whose divine clemency and goodness the place of so many imperial triumphs was predestined to belong instead to St. Peter and to his successors. Until now it has been so preserved, and it will be so preserved, he asserts, in perpetuity.[71]

Besides cataloging the signs manifesting St. Peter's continued local presence within the Vatican basilica, Vegio was intent to pinpoint precisely where the Apostle was crucified and where he was buried. In so doing, he launched a topic that provoked considerable controversy among the Roman humanists.

Vegio's discussion of this matter again depends upon attentive sifting of available evidence. Several ancient traditions agree, he remarks, that Peter's body at one time lay buried in the catacombs next to S. Sebastiano. But one source—unnamed, but clearly the *Liber pontificalis*, the medieval history of the popes—states that Pope Cornelius (251–53) transferred it to Montorio on the Janiculum, "the site of the crucifixion," and from there Silvester and Constantine eventually moved it again to the Vatican basilica. Gregory the Great, on the other hand, whom Vegio regards as a more reliable source, states that the body of the Apostle was moved directly from the catacombs to the basilica. What seems certain, nevertheless, Vegio argues, is that Montorio was the site of the crucifixion. Eusebius, in his *Ecclesiastical History*, cites a certain Gaius, who speaks of a *trophaeum*, located on the Via Regalis leading *to* the Vatican, as marking the spot of Peter's martyrdom. This means, Vegio continues, the arguments of those who claim Peter met his death *within* the Vatican itself lack credence. Supporters of this view, adducing the tradition reporting the Apostle crucified between the two *metae*—one of which they identify as Hadrian's tomb—locate the site of his martyrdom at the place where now the church of S. Maria in Transpontina is situated. But, Vegio objects, Hadrian had not yet become emperor when Peter died, which means his tomb could not have existed as a topographical reference point. If the tradition is true that Peter was crucified between the two *metae*, then this must refer to the pyramid in the Vatican (Vegio means the so-called tomb of Romulus, which existed until its demolition under Alexander VI[72]) and to the similar pyramid next to the Aventine (i.e., the so-called tomb of Remus, actually the pyramid of Cestius). Precisely midway between these two *metae* lies Montorio.[73]

Vegio's Montorio hypothesis, while revealing an impressive historical awareness of Rome's ancient topography, was, in fact, a novel suggestion. No one before Vegio, it seems, considered Montorio the likely site of Peter's crucifixion.[74] The earliest Christian tradition had instead identified the great obelisk located at the side of Old St. Peter's as the place where the Apostle was martyred.[75] On the other hand, Biondo (Vegio's unnamed "they") in his *Roma instaurata* both rejected the Montorio suggestion as untenable and stated flatly that S. Maria in Transpontina stood on the spot. He did so in part because of the tradition of the two *metae*, but also because he held (wrongly) that Nero's circus was located here. According to Tacitus, Biondo observes, the Christians, whom Nero persecuted as responsible for causing the fire that devastated the city, were brought forth for sport in Nero's circus in the Vatican, or else tortured in his gardens that lay adjacent to it. This meant that Peter met his death *in* the Vatican.[76]

At an earlier point in *Roma instaurata*, Biondo, attempting to establish the ancient topography of the Vatican region, had concluded on the basis of Tacitus and on patristic testimony that the area next to St. Peter's once belonged to Nero's *naumachia*.[77] Thus he had the sites of Nero's circus and his *naumachia* precisely reversed,[78] and Vegio was indeed correct in identifying the ancient ruins next to the Vatican basilica as marking the site of his circus.

Vegio's view on the location of Nero's circus came to be the accepted one during the Renaissance period. Indeed, Biondo himself, in his *Roma triumphans*, completed in 1459, cites Pliny for the information that the great obelisk next to St. Peter's formed part of the circus.[79] This established, the Roman humanists had reached the point where they could revert to the earliest Christian tradition of the obelisk as the spot where Peter was crucified. Even so, Montorio continued to have its Renaissance defenders, a point we will return to shortly.

As to the disputed matter of Peter's bodily fate after his death, Platina, in his *Liber de vita Christi ac omnium pontificum* (1471–74), added one further piece of topographical evidence. Platina says nothing about the site of the crucifixion, but, citing St. Jerome, he states that Peter came to be buried *in* the Vatican, by the Via Aurelia, next to the gardens of Nero and not far from the Via Triumphalis that led to the ancient temple of Apollo. Like Vegio, Platina mentions in this context the testimony of Gaius, from Eusebius's *Ecclesiastical History*, but he sees Gaius's reference to a *trophaeum* as confirmation of a Vatican burial for the Apostle. He adds further that this same area of Nero's Vatican gardens contained many other bodies of the early Christian martyrs.[80]

Platina's conclusion turned out to be a correct surmise. The excavations under St. Peter's, done in the 1940s, have shown that the site next to Nero's circus was an ancient cemetery, and that an open-air monument, venerated as the spot of Peter's tomb (Gaius's "trophy"), existed long before the construction of the Constantinian basilica. Another cult center to Peter and Paul, which may have included some of their relics, also existed during the third century underneath S. Sebastiano on the Via Appia. But the prestige of the Vatican cult site determined the establishment of Constantine's basilica there. Indeed, the early Petrine shrine governed the precise location of the church. Encased with marble and surmounted by a ciborium supported by spiral columns, the former open-air monument stood at the crossing of nave and transepts.[81]

Historical and topographical considerations—the contributions of humanist methodology—aided Vegio's inquiry into the problem of Peter's crucifixion and burial. Yet his conclusions reveal, too, the influence of religiously symbolic motives. By situating Peter's crucifixion on Montorio, midway between the pyramids of Romulus and Remus, Vegio implied a link between the twin founders of ancient Rome and the founder of the Roman Church. But in contrasting the demonic depravity of Nero's circus with the heavenly portal of Peter's basilica that supplanted it, he adopted a medieval vision of the triumph of virtue over vice—like a medieval door-jamb sculpture of a saint standing victorious over the bestial embodiment of evil.

Initially, too, Biondo shared a similar point of view. In his preface to *Roma instaurata*, addressed to Eugenius IV, Biondo states that while his principal intent was to describe the magnificent buildings with which the ancient Romans had embellished the city, and to give rightful praise to their achievement even though they were idolators, nevertheless he had kept in mind the glory of the Christian martyrs, who conquered by suffering, and who in succumbing to the mad pleasures of the tyrants triumphed.[82] A decade later, however, in *Roma triumphans*, Biondo had changed his approach. Adopting the theme of *quanto magis* ("outdoing"), what he now found significant was that the exact area in the Vatican, on which Peter's basilica had subsequently arisen, in earlier times had been the *territorium triumphale*, that is the place where the ancient Romans had prepared the pomp of triumphs. From this spot, where a temple dedicated to Apollo once stood, the triumphal processions had then made their way along the Via Triumphalis, before crossing the Tiber on the Pons Triumphalis and from there proceeding to the Capitol. The bridge no longer existed, but, Biondo remarks, sections of the ancient pavement belonging to the Via Triumphalis could still be seen beneath the hospital of S. Spirito in Sassia. All this Biondo saw as an astonishing prefigurement of the Christian processions that come forth from St. Peter's basilica. The *territorium triumphale*, the Via Triumphalis, and the celebration of Roman military triumphs had mysteriously prepared the way for the greater triumph of Christianity. In testimony to the same relationship of prefigurement and fulfillment, the ancient temple of Apollo had become incorporated into the fabric of St. Peter's.[83]

In *Roma triumphans* Biondo retained the emphasis, expressed in Agli's and Vegio's works and in his own earlier *Roma instaurata*, on the uniquely sacred terrain of Rome, particularly the Vatican. The city is seen to possess a tangible holiness, which confirms, augments, and strengthens the mission of the Roman Church and the authority of its head, the

Roman pontiff. What is new in *Roma triumphans*, and of great significance for subsequent Roman Renaissance attitudes, lies in Biondo's abandoning the dichotomy of ancient Rome's pagan idolatry and Christian Rome's martyr-sanctified soil. Even before the Apostle Peter's arrival, various signs, retrospectively recognized as prophetic, pointed to the city's destined role as Christian capital. Rather than extirpating or supplanting the ancient foundations of Rome, Christianity raised these to a new level of understanding, and in so doing fulfilled the city's true meaning. From this perspective, the Eternal City, from its inception, manifested an enduring sacredness.

A notable expression of such views, from later in the fifteenth century, appears in Pomponio Leto's writings. Justifying papal authority and Rome's headship of the Catholic faith, he averred that the city, as goddess of the earth and queen of peoples, had always been the seat of the gods and the center of the empire of the human race. Thus both divine will and the logic of human reasoning, he claims, accord the Bishop of Rome authority as father and *princeps* of humanity. Who can doubt, furthermore, but that this should remain perpetually so? For Christ had declared, *"Tu es Petrus et super hanc petram aedificabo ecclesiam meam."*[84]

For Leto and his fellow Roman humanists the Church Christ built on Peter thus had distinctly Roman foundations. Increasingly, too, the Roman humanists traced back Rome's sacred origins beyond the imperial capital to the earliest Roman, and even pre-Roman Etruscan occupation. Again, Biondo seems the source for such notions. Examining in *Roma instaurata* the ancient topography of the Vatican, Biondo pointed out its pre-Christian importance as a cult site. Indeed, the name Vatican itself stemmed from such activities. According to Aulus Gellius, the word derived from the ancient custom of seeking prophecies (*vaticinii*) from the guardian deity of the site, and Festus Pompeius similarly connected it to seers (*vates*). Varro, too, Biondo states, spoke of the cult of a local god, venerated at the starting point of the Via Nova, where a voice from heaven was heard. The god was called Vaticanus because ancient Romans held he had power over the beginnings of human speech; since newborn infants are said to squall (*vagire*), a word which expresses the sound they make [!], so this explains the first syllable of the name Vaticanus.[85]

By the early sixteenth century, belief in the oracular significance of the Mons Vaticanus had become widespread. Thus Andrea Fulvio observed in his *Antiquaria Urbis* (1513) that inasmuch as in antiquity the Vatican had been a seat of oracles, it was fitting for the temple of Peter, supreme fisherman, to arise on the same site, and from here for the successors of Peter to exercise universal authority.[86]

No student of the Vatican's pre-Christian importance for cult was more ardent than Giles of Viterbo. Keenly interested in the ancient Etruscans, especially in their reputation for esoteric religious lore, Giles points out in his *Historia XX saeculorum* (1513–18) that Janus, the founder of the Etruscan religion, had been the patron deity of the Janiculum. Medieval tradition had identified Janus with Noah, or with one of Noah's sons, and Giles, too, held that after the Flood Noah's teachings had been carried into Etruria. In this way the Etruscan religion, like that of the ancient Hebrews, had its source in divine truth. Hence the ancient cult of Janus in the Vatican meant that from earliest times this Roman site had been consecrated for the true religion, Christianity. A further confirmation of this, Giles suggests, appears in the parallel of Janus and St. Peter as keybearers.[87] Nonetheless, only the coming of Peter and Paul to Rome, and their preaching and martyrdom there, made actual these earlier prefigurations of Rome as the destined center of the religious world. Through Peter's cross and blood the right bank of the Tiber became the eternal seat of the new religion. The presence of Peter's tomb actualized the Mons Vaticanus as the true holy mountain, and from this particular locus of sanctifying grace the whole world came to be governed.[88]

This growing mystique of the Vatican, developed in Roman humanist thought from Biondo onward and culminating in Giles's views of Peter's tomb as the fulcrum of the Church, has a particular relevance to contemporary decisions regarding plans for rebuilding the Vatican basilica. Indeed, Giles himself informs us that Bramante, the architect Julius II named to head the projected reconstruction, initially proposed to change the orientation of the basilica, so that it would face south, onto a large, newly created piazza that would have as its focal point the great obelisk of Nero's circus. In popular tradition the obelisk, which in fact the Emperor Caligula had brought to Rome from Egypt, was known as the "obelisk of Caesar" and was thought to contain the ashes of Julius Caesar.[89] To relate the tomb of the founder of the Roman Church to the remains of the founder of the Roman Empire in an architecturally more meaningful way thus commended itself. Indeed, half a century earlier, Pope Nicholas V, according to Manetti, had planned to have the obelisk moved from the side of the old basilica to an enlarged piazza in front of the atrium. There it would serve as a focal point to the entrance of the Apostle's sanctuary. Four bronze statues of the Evangelists were intended to replace the four ancient bronze lions on the obelisk's base, and the apex of the monument would have been surmounted in Nicholas's plans by a great bronze statue of Christ the Savior, bearing in his right hand a gold cross.[90]

Bramante's idea of using the monumental obelisk and its well-known association with Julius Caesar to enhance feelings of awe and wonder in those entering Julius II's new Templum S. Petri should, therefore, have met a favorable response from the pope, one might think, especially since Julius II was never reticent in cultivating comparisons between himself and his imperial namesake. And since Bramante judged that it would be virtually impossible to move the obelisk, the orientation of the basilica had to be shifted. To Giles's delight, however, Julius II remained adamantly opposed. To do what Bramante proposed would have necessitated the displacing of Peter's tomb, and the pope insisted the tomb of the first Roman pontiff must not be touched. The sacred must hold priority over the profane, religion over splendor, piety over ornament, Giles reports Julius declaring; the tomb was not to be placed in the temple, but rather the temple over the tomb.[91]

The new St. Peter's thus faced in the same direction as the old, but eventually what Nicholas had proposed for the obelisk was accomplished. In 1586, Domenico Fontana, at the behest of Pope Sixtus V, managed the engineering feat, regarded by contemporaries as extraordinary, of transporting the obelisk, which weights more than three hundred and fifty tons, to its present position in front of the basilica, where it stands at the center of Bernini's ellipsoid piazza.[92]

Though thwarted in his plans to move Peter's tomb and to alter the basilica's orientation, Bramante nevertheless did conceive for the new St. Peter's a building evocative in its scale and its design of Roman imperial architecture. This important project is best considered, therefore, in the context of the general renewal of Roman imperial ideas, the subject of the next chapter. To the same years, however, in which plans for the new St. Peter's were first discussed belongs another Bramante building dedicated to the Petrine cult: the Tempietto of S. Pietro in Montorio. No building project of the Roman Renaissance better exemplifies, in fact, the topographical themes of Rome's sanctity, developed in the humanist views we have been tracing.

This site on the Janiculum, pinpointed by Vegio as the exact spot of Peter's crucifixion, had been occupied from the early Middle Ages by a small monastery, long since abandoned. In 1472 Sixtus IV gave the property to Amedeo Menez da Sylva (d. 1482), a reforming Spanish Franciscan and personal confessor to the pope, with the stipulation that he arrange the reconstruction of the monastery complex. Fra Amedeo did so, beginning with the church, a project financed in large part by Ferdinand and Isabella of Spain. During his years at Montorio, Amedeo also spent much of his time praying and fasting in a small cavern, hollowed out beneath a mound in the old monastery cloister, which was believed to be the precise location of Peter's crucifixion, and therefore had become known as the *mons crucifixionis*. Since this outcropping awkwardly occupied the monastery courtyard, when rebuilding efforts turned from the church to the adjoining buildings, the *mons crucifixionis* was levelled, preserving, however, Fra Amedeo's cell beneath it as a crypt, and on this spot arose the Tempietto.[93]

The Tempietto as it stands represents only a partial realization of Bramante's plans. The small, circular, domed *martyrium*—the paleo-Christian building type for shrines to martyrs—was intended to be placed

15. Bramante, Tempietto of S. Pietro in Montorio. Rome. (Photo: Alinari/Art Resource, NY)

within a ring of columns marking an enclosing, circular portico. This architectural scheme had precedents in classical Roman architecture still extant in and around Rome, such as the *teatro marittimo* of Hadrian's villa at Tivoli. The round Tempietto, with its use of doric columns perhaps drew upon, too, the classical temples dedicated to Hercules, one of which, in the Forum Boarium, had come to light during Sixtus IV's pontificate. Such a design implied the commemoration of Peter as a hero, a kind of Christian Hercules. But Roman circular temples also were associated with the goddess Vesta, whose cult and temple type Numa Pompilius, Rome's second king, was held to have instituted. Moreover, ancient tradition connected Numa's tomb to the Janiculum. A further symbolism of Bramante's Tempietto, therefore, involved the link between Peter, the founder of the Roman Church, and Numa, the founder of the Roman religion. In this respect, Numa served as a pagan "type" of pontifical authority.[94]

In the metopes of the Tempietto appear, in fact, various liturgical and sacramental symbols of the priestly power of the Church established through Peter as Bishop of Rome and first pope. Moreover, as Arnaldo Bruschi suggests, the dark, underground crypt may be regarded as a symbol of the hidden, primitive Church of the catacombs, the columnar elevation of the Tempietto and the concentric circles of columns planned for the cloister as the terrestrial sphere to which the Church Militant ministers through its priestly offices, preserved and confirmed by the popes as successors to Peter, and the drum and cupola as the celestial spheres and the glorification of the Church Triumphant. As in the revived rhetoric of Latin epideictic employed by the Roman humanists, Bramante utilized the mode and forms of classicism to praise the dignity and authority of the Roman Church and its defining role in the cosmic destiny of the human race.

Important, also, to understanding Bramante's design is the Tempietto's function as an illusionistic image, transcending the concrete, physical boundaries of the human observer. Bramante's mastery of perspective and proportionality, and of atmospheric and luministic effects did not aim at representing the historical and political world of human society but rather at suggesting, and inspiring awe and wonder in, the supernatural grace and divine purpose mediated to mankind by the *civitas Dei*, the universal Roman Church founded through Peter.

Peter's crucifixion as sealing the divine consecration of the Roman Church thus formed a decisive element in the Roman Renaissance view of the past; and it was a perception of the origins of the Roman Church to which the Roman humanists had made fundamental contributions. Peter's martyrdom came to be conceived in topographically more concrete—and therefore historically more authentic—circumstances, and its seminal significance affirmed.

A later echo of this theme occurs, in fact, in the frescoes Michelangelo painted for Paul III's Cappella Paolina, the new chapel in the Vatican planned to hold the conclaves in which the College of Cardinals convened to elect the successor to Peter. It seems revealing that in these frescoes, dating from the 1540s, when Roman Catholicism appeared persecuted and everywhere imperilled by the Protestant challenge, the subject of Peter's crucifixion, rather than the Delivery of the Keys, should have been chosen to be paired with the Conversion of St. Paul as the appropriate visual inspiration for the cardinals' decisions. Initially, papal planners may well have intended to have the Delivery of the Keys be portrayed; usually this was paired with the Conversion of Paul, and Peter's crucifixion with Paul's beheading. But the change to the crucifixion, perhaps at Michelangelo's instigation, corresponds to the more somber and penitential mood of Counter-Reformation Rome; and his fresco, in which the site of Peter's crucifixion should in all likelihood be identified as Montorio, served as a powerful reminder that the Church gained its foundations through suffering and martyrdom.[95]

For the more confident Rome of the later fifteenth and early sixteenth centuries, however, the theme of St. Peter as martyr—so pronounced under Nicholas V and Pius II, and renewed in Michelangelo's fresco—receded. In its place emerged emphasis on the Apostle as heroic spiritual leader.

This forms the main theme, for instance, of Platina's account of Peter's life in his *Liber de vita Christi ac omnium pontificum*. Platina does not ignore the *"Quo vadis?"* story, nor Peter's crucifixion, head down, "on the same day that Paul was beheaded," but he devotes more attention to Peter's activity as Roman pontiff. In Platina's version, Peter, having received the power of the keys from Christ, and after settling the affairs of the "Asian" churches by confuting the necessity of circumcision, came to Rome, *"caput orbis terrarum."* He came, Platina states, because he determined it to be appropriate to pontifical dignity, and because he had learned Simon Magus had come there and was leading the Roman people astray with his deceptions. The contest between Simon Magus and Peter for leadership in Rome escalated, according to Platina, until Simon challenged Peter to imitate his own promised exploit of flying from the Capitoline to the Aventine. Such a feat would permit the Roman people to judge which of the two was holier, and dearer to God. As Simon flew, Peter raised his hands in prayer to the heavens asking God not to allow the people to be deluded by magic arts. Simon fell, his leg broke, and he died in ignominy shortly afterwards.[96]

Simon Magus thus vanquished, Peter then turned to propagating the Word of God by teaching and example. To this end, he called to Rome St. Mark, to whom he entrusted the task of composing the Gospel. He also ordained Linus and Cletus bishops, since they had distinguished themselves in their priestly ministrations to the Roman populace. When Peter, after his encounter with Christ, returned to Rome to face martyrdom, his last act was to consecrate Clement as bishop, and to commend to him the *cathedra Petri* and the Church of God, saying "I deliver to you the same power of binding and loosing that Christ relinquished to me; scorn and hold in contempt all matters of the flesh and of fortune, and as befits the good shepherd preach the salvation of the human race."[97] Thus were transmitted the papal powers, which, derived from Christ "our King and Priest," as from an "everflowing font," are assumed, Platina declares, by all the Roman popes in unbroken order down to the current pontiff, Sixtus IV.[98]

Platina's lives of the popes is not a work based on critical investigation of historical sources. Written quickly, it draws heavily, as Giacinto Gaida's edition shows, on the medieval *Liber pontificalis*, supplemented from Jerome, Eusebius, and Biondo's *Decades*. Platina did utilize his knowledge of the Latin classics to amplify particulars on the actions of the Roman emperors, but the biographical approach follows the *Liber pontificalis*, as does the format of including for each pope a record of papal decrees, the founding of churches, and a list of donations.[99]

In effect, Platina was simply revising according to humanistic standards the medieval *Liber pontificalis*, to the end of preserving from neglect the deeds of the Roman pontiffs "who bequeathed to us by their sweat and blood this great and splendid *respublica Christiana*."[100] But in addition, Platina, in the preface to his work, suggests that history serves a further function. As the ancients used to place statues of their most renowned and admired public figures in *fora*, before temples, and in other public places, for purposes of public utility, so much the more does history—which unlike mute statues or vain pictures presents the true image of noble men—permit us to speak with them as if they were alive, and thereby take counsel from them and be inspired to imitate their virtues. In this way posterity can learn from earlier popes what to imitate and what to avoid, and those to come will be incited *ad bene beateque vivendum*.[101]

Platina was not the only fifteenth-century humanist to choose the format of papal biography to write the history of the Roman Church. Some years before, Jacopo Zeno dedicated to his fellow Venetian, Pope Paul II, his *De vitis summorum pontificum*. Unlike Platina, Zeno begins his work not with Christ, but with Peter. This was because, Zeno explains, Christ is the eternal high-priest, to whom pontifical powers belong intrinsically, whereas the popes are called to the office of serving as His Vicar on earth and of acting in His name as minister and faithful servant over His family. Zeno's book stops in the early fourteenth century with the pontificate of Clement V, though apparently he intended eventually to extend the work down to his own time. The Venetian's *Vitae* received little attention in the Renaissance period, doubtless because of the popularity of Platina's work, but he wrote for the same purpose as his more widely read successor. In the lives of previous popes, Zeno declares, one can see "as in a mirror," the shape and likeness of those things that conduce to "good and holy living," and can discern what it is praiseworthy to imitate and what must be avoided as deserving blame. Part of his task, he goes on to say, involves expunging the false and fabulous from the history of the popes. But just as important is his responsibility to preserve for human memory in a less barbarous and more elegant literary form the lives of those who act as vice-gerents of God on earth, who through divine decree govern the whole globe, who as true fathers and shepherds are entrusted with the care and salvation of mankind, and who in all human matters act with the greatest power, the holiest majesty, and the fullest authority.[102]

Biography, in fact, dominates papal historiography in the Renaissance period. From the brief lives of early fifteenth-century popes beginning with Urban VI that Poggio Bracciolini sketched, to the individual biographies written by Manetti, Canensi, Campano, Gaspare da Verona, and Raffaele Maffei, the figure of the pope provides the organizing principle of historical presentation.[103] This reflects the humanists' defense of the inherently monarchical nature of the Church: the accomplishments of the Church as a whole depend upon the powers uniquely held by the Roman pontiffs. But the biographical approach attests, too, to the humanists' view of the foundation and destiny of Christianity as ultimately supra-historical. Each pope is called to the See of Rome by God, and, especially in Platina's work, the effect is the unfolding through time of the unbroken link of witnesses to the apostolic succession of Peter.

This same succession appears visibly in the portraits of the popes from the first three centuries of the Christian era, which form an upper register to the wall decoration of the Sistine Chapel. Their inclusion in the decoration scheme undertaken during Sixtus IV's pontificate imitates a paleo-Christian practice of Roman basilicas. Such papal portraits were present, for example, in the atrium of Old St. Peter's. Adopting this element for the Sistine Chapel thus reflects Sixtus's more general determination to impart a deliberately archaizing style, drawn from paleo-Christian precedent, to the churches he rebuilt in Rome.[104]

But in the Sistine Chapel, papal portraits underscore the overall theme of the wall decoration, which, like Platina's contemporaneous lives of the popes, is to emphasize the divinely ordained spiritual leadership of God's chosen people.[105] The Sistine Chapel served as the principal chapel of the papal palace, thus forming the setting for the important ceremonial and liturgical functions connected to the papal court. The solemnities of the papal Masses for the Sundays of Advent and Lent were celebrated here, for instance, and here the cardinals were assigned cells during the conclaves to elect the pope. Hence no place was more appropriate for a decorative scheme devoted to the *maiestas papalis.*

A later decorative addition to the Sistine Chapel, the set of tapestries Leo X commissioned from cartoons furnished by Raphael, also drew from early Christian example: the endowment Pope Leo IV made to St. Peter's basilica of eighteen golden tapestries of the life of the Apostle Peter.[106] But like the papal portraits on the upper part of the walls, the Raphael tapestries, devoted to the apostolates of Peter and Paul, emphasize the divine authority imparted to the Roman pontiffs. Moreover, they form an apex to the theme that heroic spiritual leadership built the Roman Church.

The sequence of Raphael's tapestry cycle, as reconstructed by Shearman, [107] began to the right of the altar with the *Miraculous Draft of Fishes*, proceeded to the right-hand wall with three further scenes of the life of Peter, returned to the left side of the altar wall with the *Stoning of Stephen*, continued on the left-hand wall with four scenes of the life of Paul, and concluded with *Paul Preaching at Athens*, the only tapestry placed outside the chancel. Significantly, neither apostle's martyrdom appears. Instead, St. Paul, who had initially persecuted Christians (the *Stoning of Stephen*), is converted by divine act on the road to Damascus, and becomes the divinely appointed Apostle to the Gentiles. As such he is shown converting, through his preaching, the Proconsul of Asia, Sergius Paulus, condemning at Lystra the persistent Gentile sin of idolatry, and finally evangelizing the philosophers of Athens.

Just as Paul, the *vas electionis*, fulfills his mission as *magister gentium*, so Peter, divinely called to be *Princeps apostolorum* and *Pastor ovium*, is shown establishing the Church among the Jews. In the first tapestry (the Miraculous Draft), Simon is called by Christ to be a fisher of men (Luke 5: 1–11). Forming the background setting of this important text traditionally associated with the *primatus Petri* is the city of Rome. Several of Sixtus IV's new churches, including S. Maria del Popolo and S. Maria della Pace, appear, as does the Mons Vaticanus with its Leonine wall and the new basilica of St. Peter, its southern exedra under construction. Topographical accuracy did not constitute Raphael's principal aim in this scene, since the Constantinian basilica being demolished appears without various features of the new construction, which would have obscured it. Instead, as Shearman suggests,[108] the intent was to symbolize the notion of *instauratio*, of reconstruction, and the Vatican itself is presented not at any particular historical time, but rather *sub specie aeternitatis*.

The next tapestry in the Peter cycle, the *Charge to Peter*, shows the risen Christ handing the keys to a kneeling Peter and pointing to a flock of sheep. Thus the two main Gospel texts having to do with Petrine primacy (Matthew 16 and John 21) are conflated and Christ commits to the Apostle the care of His flock. This is followed by the *Healing of the Lame Man*. Before the twisted, spiral columns, intended to symbolize the *Porta speciosa* of the Jerusalem Temple,[109] Peter, accompanied by St. John, cures

16. Tapestry, the *Charge to Peter*. Part of the tapestry-cycle for the Sistine Chapel commissioned by Leo X from cartoons furnished by Raphael. Pinacoteca Vaticana. (Photo: Alinari/Art Resource, NY)

a cripple, the first of Peter's miracles recorded in Acts (3: 1–26). In Shearman's analysis,[110] this must be seen as illustrating one aspect of the power of the keys delivered by Christ to Peter. This is the power of knowing who is to be loosed and bound (the *clavis ordinis*). The cure of the cripple is a figure for the cleansing of sinfulness, and the Beautiful Gate symbolizes the access to the heavenly Jerusalem, which Peter, as key-bearer, opens. The whole scene suggests, too (as we have previously seen[111]), the penitential forum (or the *forum conscientiae*), in which through the sacrament of penance mankind is restored to a state of grace before God. Thus Peter enacts the unique priestly powers of absolution granted to the popes.

The last tapestry shows the *Death of Ananias*, struck down for his deceit in withholding purchase-money from the Apostles (Acts 5: 1–6). Traditionally interpreted as a figure of excommunication, the depiction of the text symbolizes the other aspect of the power of the keys, the power of the pope to administer punishment in the public forum (the *clavis jurisdictionis*). This is the papal sphere of jurisdiction governing the relation of man to human society, and this meaning is underscored in the tapestry by its setting in the open cityscape that recalls the general features of a Roman forum.[112]

Using incidents described in the Gospels and in Acts, the tapestry cycle illustrates, in Shearman's words, "the complementary responsibilities, powers, or missions of the twin Founders of the Roman Church."[113] In considering the ways in which the Raphael tapestries articulate the Roman and papal-centered character of the Church, it is helpful to compare them to the influential fresco cycle of the acts of Peter, which Masaccio painted nearly a century earlier in the Brancacci Chapel of the Florentine church of S. Maria del Carmine. Here, too, Peter is shown as a heroic spiritual leader. But the scenes of him preaching and baptizing, and particularly the scenes of his raising of Tabitha and the healing of the cripple, of healing the lame with his shadow, and of the death of Ananias and the distributing of alms—all of which take place within a recognizable Florentine cityscape—suggest instead the Church's moral and social responsibilities of ministering to the material and spiritual needs of the human community in this world. It is not the death of Ananias that dominates Masaccio's fresco devoted to this incident, but rather the charitable actions of the Apostles towards the impoverished. This same socially concerned civic Christianity is present, too, in the main scene, the unusual subject of the tribute money (Matthew 17: 24–27). The precise meaning of the scene for Florentines of the late 1420s remains a matter of scholarly dispute,[114] but in general terms it appears to suggest the legitimacy of certain state demands upon the Church, a topic of lively debate among the citizens of the republic during the late fourteenth and early fifteenth centuries.

Striking in comparison to the Sistine Chapel tapestries is the absence as well in the Brancacci Chapel frescoes of any depiction of the delivery of the keys or of "feed my sheep."[115] Reference to papal primacy thus occurs only obliquely, if at all. Moreover, since Peter's miraculous healings in Masaccio's work take place in city streets and *piazze*, not before the Temple, no connection to the sacrament of penance or to the sacerdotal authority of the Church hierarchy seems to have been intended. Indeed, the one sacramental act Peter performs is baptism, which for the Florentine citizenry meant both entrance into the *respublica Christiana* and the status of native-born citizens of the republic. If the Brancacci Chapel frescoes were meant to illustrate any aspect of the theme of papal primacy, they enunciate the ideal pope's spiritual responsibility to address the moral and charitable needs of civic life within contemporary urban society rather than celebrating Peter as the founder of the Roman Church. In fact, the Roman theme is so neglected that the bishop's chair Peter occupies belongs to his first see of Antioch, not to Rome.[116]

In assessing the identity of St. Peter for the ideology of the papal court in the early sixteenth century, his depiction in an earlier Raphael commission, the Vatican Stanza d'Eliodoro, should not be overlooked. This room, part of the suite of private papal chambers, which Julius II had refurbished and redecorated when he decided to abandon the Borgia apartments, perhaps served the Della Rovere pontiff as an audience chamber. Clearly a room meant for public purposes, not for private withdrawal, its precise function remains to be conclusively demonstrated, as does the exact nature of certain details in the allegorical meaning of its fresco decoration. Two of the main paintings do include St. Peter. One, the *Repulse of Attila*, refers to the historical meeting of Leo the Great and Attila the Hun. But the setting of their encounter has been shifted from Mantua to the outskirts of Rome (the Colosseum, the *Meta Romuli*, and an aqueduct reveal this to be the case), and in a heavenly vision, which only the startled Attila can see, Peter, wielding a sword as well as the keys, and Paul, brandishing his customary sword, come to the defense of the Eternal City.[117]

The other fresco, the *Liberation of St. Peter*, shows in dramatic fashion the Apostle's release from Herod's prison in Jerusalem: through the divine intervention of the Angel of the Lord, he is set free. Both Julius II and his uncle, Sixtus IV, had, while cardinals, held S. Pietro in Vincoli as their titular church. There the chains that had bound Peter in prison were preserved as a relic. As pope, Julius retained these persistent Della Rovere connections to the Esquiline basilica. At the end of 1512, as part of the festivities celebrating the recovery of Bologna and the driving of the French from Italy, he made a pilgrimage of thanks to his former titular church.[118] The implied point thus seems to be that as God once freed the first pontiff from the bonds of his enemies, so also would He act to remove the French (or any other worldly) threat to the independence of the incumbent pontiff.

A more universal reference to the authority of Peter, and to Rome, is, I would suggest, also made in Raphael's famous Stanza della Segnatura, the middle room—between the Stanza d'Eliodoro and the Stanza dell'Incendio—of Julius II's suite of rooms in the Vatican. The Stanza della Segnatura, which almost certainly functioned under Julius as a private papal library,[119] is decorated with a fresco program, datable to 1508–11, which celebrates wisdom under the four intellectual disciplines of theology, philosophy, poetry, and jurisprudence. One of the two largest wall surfaces of the room is devoted to the *School of Athens*, in which appear the classical philosophers, headed by Plato and Aristotle, who pursued, as the *titulus* of the allegorical figure on the ceiling above them indicates, CAVSARVM COGNITIO. Facing this is the *Disputà*, or perhaps more aptly titled *Triumph of the Blessed Sacrament*. Theology, the allegorical figure above this fresco, is accompanied by cupids holding the identifying inscription, DIVINAR[VM]RER[VM]NOTITIA. The fresco itself divides horizontally into two large groupings of figures. Gathered about an open-air altar, on which stands the monstrance holding the consecrated Host (the Body of Christ), are various Fathers and Doctors of the Church, members of religious orders, bishops, and popes—including, in a prominent gold vestment, Sixtus IV. Above these theologians of the Church Militant appears the heavenly manifestation of the Church Triumphant. A semi-circular cloud, sustained by angelic cherubs, constitutes the seating for alternating Christian and Hebraic leaders of the faith, anchored at the ends by the twin apostolic founders of the Roman Church, St. Peter with the keys and St. Paul with his sword. In the center, directly above the monstrance, floats the dove of the Holy Spirit, accompanied by *putti* holding open books, on which appear the opening words of each of the four Gospels. Above them sits Christ, present not in the sacramental embodiment of the Eucharist, but in flesh and blood, marked by the stigmata. At either side are seated the Virgin Mary and John the Baptist. Directly above Christ in the golden aureole of heaven stands God the Father, holding the crystalline sphere that symbolizes the created cosmos.

Particular details of the setting for the theologians of the Church Militant seem to indicate a Roman locale. Directly behind the altar—the gold brocade antependium of which bears the inscription IVLIVS II PONT MAX, and lower within an elaborate "endless" knot design, symbolizing eternity, IVLIVS—emerges the distant skyline of a city and what appears to be the bend of a river. To the left a series of hills rises to a levelled area where a building of classicizing architecture is under construction next to a rustic *casino*, typical of the Roman suburban scene.[120] Wooden scaffolding encloses this nearly finished structure, and there bustling activity takes place with various laborers hard at their tasks, including one

17. Raphael, *Disputà*. Stanza della Segnatura, Vatican Palace. (Photo: Alinari/Art Resource, NY)

18. Raphael, *Disputà*, detail of left background. (Photo: Alinari/Art Resource, NY)

shouldering a heavy load up a ramp. The design of the building is difficult to discern, but it is clearly of a single story, with its façade defined by a series of bays consisting of round-arched recesses flanked by pilasters. These features, and the setting of the building at the top of the hill, resemble the semi-circular exedra and flanking north wall of the *cortile superiore* of Julius II's new papal palace, the Cortile del Belvedere, which was rising during these years on the Mons Vaticanus.[121] The architect of the new palace was Bramante, and his portrait appears in the foreground of Raphael's fresco,[122] just beneath the distant construction site. If the new construction belongs to the Cortile del Belvedere, then the higher wall behind it, which seems to be part of a separate building, would represent the Villa Belvedere, constructed under Innocent VIII.[123] The river and distant cityscape in the center background of the *Disputà* would, in turn, indicate the Tiber and the northern district of the city of Rome, around Porta del Popolo. And the site of the altar in the painting would then coincide with the actual site of the high altar of St. Peter's basilica!

Other considerations strengthen the hypothesis of a Roman setting for this fresco. In the first place, the view extending from the Vatican hill to the Tiber—the panoramic backdrop of the *Disputà*—would have presented itself to an observer looking north out of the window of the Stanza della Segnatura. This is significant, since, as James Ackerman has pointed out,[124] the design of the Cortile del Belvedere depends upon a perspective scheme whose point of construction is precisely the Vatican *stanze*. A deliberate relationship between Raphael's fresco decoration of the Stanza della Segnatura and the Belvedere was thus intended and created.

This is particularly true of *Parnassus*, the fresco Raphael painted around the north-facing window of the Stanza. Here, Apollo sits at the apex of Mount Helicon, surrounded by the nine muses and by classical and Renaissance poets. The Mons Vaticanus, seen through the window that opens beneath the frescoed Mt. Helicon, was believed by Roman humanists to have been sacred to Apollo. Biondo, Vegio, Albertini, and others refer to the temple of the ancient Sun-God that once stood in the Vatican.[125] Moreover, one of the most renowned ancient statues present in the sculpture garden Julius II created in the Belvedere between the *cortile superiore* and Innocent VIII's villa was the *Apollo Belvedere*, and in a contemporary Latin poem penned by the humanist Evangelista Maddaleni Fausto di Capodiferro the *Apollo Belvedere* himself addresses Julius, declaring that neither Delos nor Delphi are now his home but rather the Mons Vaticanus.[126]

That the Vatican under Julius should again be the domain of the Sun-God has a special significance in light of the Della Rovere pontiff's frequent evocation of various aspects of the god's benign powers.[127] Importantly, too, the *Apollo Belvedere* had constituted the prize piece in the collection of ancient statuary Julius had assembled before his elevation to

the papacy. At one time prominently displayed in the garden attached to
his titular church of S. Pietro in Vincoli, it had been moved to the Vatican
at Julius's behest after the 1503 election.[128] Thus besides the general
Apollonian allusions of his pontificate and the association of Apollo's cult
with the Mons Vaticanus there was the particular, long-established link
between Giuliano della Rovere and the specific manifestation of the
Sun-God in the statue of the *Apollo Belvedere*.

If, then, one can identify a precise topographical and symbolico-
political frame of reference for establishing what Raphael's fresco of
Parnassus meant for Julius II, it seems justified to search for such Roman
and Julian references in the *Disputà*. Indeed, one further element of the
painting seems to point to the other major Julian project for the Vatican.
Behind the theologians at the right of the altar projects a massive stone
block, which a number of scholars have suggested symbolizes the new St.
Peter's basilica.[129] In fact, with the demolition of large parts of the old
Constantinian structure to make way for the massive piers of the colossal
new St. Peter's, much of the sanctuary stood exposed to the elements.
Until Bramante completed his classicizing Doric *tegurio* in 1514, the high
altar was open to the air,[130] as is the altar, so pointedly decorated with
Julius's name, in Raphael's fresco. On a symbolic level, the massive foundation-stone almost certainly alludes as well to St. Peter, the "rock" on
which Christ declared he would build His Church.

In my view, then, the Church Militant of Raphael's fresco is the
Roman Church, with the basilica of St. Peter in the Vatican its sanctuary
and focal point. Established through Peter by Christ, who in the sacrament of the Eucharist is always present to it, the Roman Church has been
defended throughout its history by the theological writings of the Fathers
and Doctors. Through their divinely inspired teachings the Roman
Church has preserved unerringly the tenets of the Christian faith,[131]
including, above all, the central mystery of the Eucharist. In this way the
Roman Church has served, in one of the favorite motifs of the Roman
humanists, as a mirror (*speculum*) of the Church Triumphant. This, the
heavenly Church—the celestial Jerusalem—which so many Renaissance
preachers in Rome had urged their hearers to "look up" to, is mystically
present to the "holy Latin Jerusalem" that Christian Rome had become. It
is to this heavenly exemplar that Julius II intended to restore (*instaurare*)
the Roman Church, the work of which is suggested by the activity of
construction in the left background.[132]

It seems likely, too, that the theme of building in the fresco, and the
prominence of the massive foundation-stone and the altar set on a wide,
three-step stone pavement, echo St. Peter's own words in I Peter 2: 4–6, 9:

> So come to him, our living Stone—the stone rejected by men but
> choice and precious in the sight of God. Come, and let yourselves be
> built, as living stones, into a spiritual temple; become a holy priest-

hood, to offer spiritual sacrifices acceptable to God through Jesus Christ. For it stands written:

'I lay in Zion a choice corner-stone of great worth. The man who has faith in it will not be put to shame.'

. . . But you are a chosen race, a royal priesthood, a dedicated nation, and a people claimed by God for his own, to proclaim the triumphs of him who has called you out of darkness into his marvellous light.[133]

Another favorite "architectural" text of contemporary Roman thinkers—a passage from Paul's Letter to the Ephesians—suggests, too, a link between the theologians of the *Disputà* and the philosophers of the facing fresco of the *School of Athens*. In Ephesians 2: 13–22, Paul stresses that Christ's coming reconciled Gentiles and Jews,

. . . so as to create out of the two a single new humanity in himself, thereby making peace. . . . Thus you are no longer aliens in a foreign land, but fellow-citizens with God's people, members of God's household. You are built upon the foundation laid by the apostles and prophets, and Christ Jesus himself is the foundation-stone. In him the whole building is bonded together and grows into a holy temple in the Lord. In Him you too are being built with all the rest into a spiritual dwelling for God.[134]

In accord with this theme of *pax* and *concordia*, the philosophers of the classical tradition and the Apostles and prophets partake of the same eternal wisdom. Indeed, this divine *logos* manifests itself in the design of the building that forms the backdrop to the *School of Athens*. In appearance this most closely resembles the classical architecture of the quadrifront triumphal arch—like the Arch of Janus in Rome—and its rational intelligibility is underscored by the correspondence of its perspective construction to the geometric figure that Bramante, as Euclid, draws with his compass on the slate in the foreground of the fresco. As such, the building serves as an architectural image of the "triumph" of human reasoning, mirroring the triumphal theme of Christ as Logos in the facing *Disputà*. Certain other design features of the building depicted in the *School of Athens* resemble, however, ideas Bramante had for the new St. Peter's basilica. In its extended symbolism, therefore, the building stands for a "Temple of Philosophy," which is united in truth to the spiritual temple of the Roman Church shown on the opposite wall.[135]

MOSES, *TYPUS PAPAE*

Emphasis on the Petrine foundation of the Roman Church emerged, then, as a central intellectual theme and major artistic subject matter of the Roman Renaissance. But the humanists of the papal court were not

19. Raphael, *School of Athens*. Stanza della Segnatura, Vatican Palace. (Photo: Alinari/Art Resource, NY)

content to limit discussion of the nature of the papacy to an analysis of Peter's powers and deeds. To have relied exclusively on Peter's activities to articulate papal prerogatives and the function of Rome as Christian capital would have been problematic, for in fact the New Testament basis for Peter's career in Rome is tenuous. Indeed the absence of clear-cut Scriptural evidence for Peter's functioning as Bishop of Rome had been exploited by opponents of papal power, beginning with Marsilio of Padua, to deny that Peter was ever in the Eternal City. This anti-Petrine tradition persisted through the fifteenth and early sixteenth centuries among the Bohemian followers of Jan Hus, and the whole matter became a subject of European-wide controversy with the dissemination of the Bohemian Oldřich Velenský's polemical tract, *Petrum Romam non venisse* (1520).[136]

In defending the dignity and authority of the Roman Church and in emphasizing the powers of the papacy, the Roman humanists thus looked to additional sources. And they found in Hebraic antiquity, particularly in the religious career of Moses, prefigurements of the priestly, legislative, and governing roles of the Roman pontiffs.

A touchstone to this tendency is again Piero da Monte's treatise addressed to Nicholas V, *Contra impugnantes sedis apostolicae auctoritatem*. After presenting the customary arguments for Petrine primacy, Piero turned to other images of the Church and of the papal office. He notes that Sacred Scripture often refers to the Church as the House of the Lord, and that Pope Innocent III had said that the *domus Dei* means in different respects the whole world, the whole Church, and the souls of the faithful. In the world the pope is *imperator*, Innocent had stated, in the Church he is *paterfamilias*, and in the soul *sponsus in thalamo*. The Church, Piero continues, is also the *civitas Dei*, and indeed is properly called *domus, civitas,* and *regnum*. As the Church is called the Kingdom of Christ, so can it rightly be called the kingdom of His Vicar, who is the Roman Pontiff, and we can therefore designate the pope both King and Priest, for he is consecrated as Priest and crowned as King.[137]

But the clearest precedent for his union of priestly and regal powers lies, Piero suggests, in the Old Testament. In the section of his treatise devoted to papal powers of jurisdiction, he observes that while these stem in part from the paterfamilial role of the pope, who in this way leads men to virtue, the exercise of justice is essentially a royal power, as is clear from God's constituting Solomon king to pronounce judgment and to render justice. Yet there is a more specific Old Testament basis for papal authority over civil, criminal, and ecclesiastical justice. In Deuteronomy (17: 8–13), Piero remarks, the Israelites were enjoined, in instances where discerning a just solution proved difficult, to ascend to the place chosen by God and to obtain there true judgment from the priests of the tribe of Levi. This place elected by God, Piero asserts, must be understood as the

Apostolic See of Rome, and the levitical priests as the cardinals, who aid
the pope in rendering justice.[138]

Having thus found Old Testament support for the practice of legal
appeals to Rome, Piero similarly found an Old Testament principle to
justify papal taxation of the Church. If craftsmen working on restoring
(*instaurantes*) the Temple in Jerusalem legitimately received payments
from Temple money offered as oblations to God, according to the priestly
law (II Kings 12: 4–16), so much the more (*quanto magis*), Piero argues,
should such stipends be provided to the prelates, who act for the restoration (*instauratio*) and repair of the spiritual temple, which is the Church.
Further, the precedent of Hebraic antiquity not only justified taxation,
but showed also that just as such funds were rightly sent to Jerusalem as
the place where the divine cult was celebrated and the high-priest resided,
so now that place is the Roman Church, the mother and teacher of all, the
permanent foundation of the Christian faith, and the source, as a spring is
to streams, of rites and doctrine. In short, Piero concludes, the general
principle is that whatever belonged to the high priest in the time of the law
(*tempore legis*) is succeeded to by the Roman Pontiff in the time of grace
(*tempore gratiae*).[139]

In next discussing the necessity of obedience to the pope, Piero, in
the same way, finds arguments based in the Old Testament. That those
who speak with evil or dishonest intentions against the practices of any
pope are rightly condemned, Piero declares, and that this sin is particularly grave, is clear from God's just curse on Ham, who mocked his
drunken father Noah, instead of showing filial devotion (Genesis 9:
20–27).[140] So, too, was Miriam, the sister of Aaron, smitten—with leprosy—when she murmured against Moses (Numbers 12: 1–16). But the
most forceful admonition of the necessity of obedience to the pope is to be
found, Piero holds, in the example of Korah, Dathan, and Abiram (Numbers 16: 1–40). Haughty in spirit and swelling in pride, they schemed
against the high priest (Aaron) and attempted to shrink back from obedience to him. The earth opened and swallowed alive "the authors of such
wickedness," and celestial fire consumed their accomplices. As St. Jerome
beautifully put it, Piero remarks, the "Korists" were not punished so
severely because they violated divine law or strayed from its precepts, but
only because, motivated by pride and illicit desire for dominion, they
withdrew from true obedience. They objected to having the authority of
the high priesthood, the ultimate source of power and jurisdiction, belong to one person. To them it seemed better and more rightful instead to
establish a popular government. In our times, Piero comments, some
prelates, driven by hatred and pride, have fallen into this same error.
Lamenting that all ecclesiastical power is held rightly by the papacy, they
have scurried about to diminish, illegally, its supreme powers. These
schismatics (Piero clearly means the conciliarists) are truly Korists, for

they violate the unity of the Church. Moreover, Piero continues, the punishment of Korah and his followers shows that disobedience to and rebellion against one's superiors is the worst sin in the eyes of divine majesty. Indeed, disobedience, ingratitude, and pride were the sins that caused the expulsion of our first parents from Paradise and thus condemned the human race to eternal death.[141]

At the close of his discussion of obedience, Piero returns again to Old Testament precedent. The authority of the pope, he declares, was prefigured in Hebraic antiquity: just as all questions pertaining to the worship of God and to rites and ceremonies were resolved by the judgment of Moses, so in matters of faith they are brought to an end by the decisions of the pope, whose authority among Christians is greater even than that exercised by Moses among the Hebrews.[142]

Piero da Monte was not the first to argue that the authority of Moses and Aaron prefigured the powers of the papacy. Augustinus Triumphus, the publicist of the early fourteenth century, had also seen Old Testament figures as linear predecessors of the popes, and Juan de Torquemada made such arguments in his *Summa de Ecclesia*.[143] But in Piero's treatise these Hebraic prefigurations are given a more extended treatment. Moreover, they form the crux of his arguments from Scripture, which he was determined to make the basis of his defense of papal authority (rather than philosophical suppositions).

Piero's Old Testament arguments are echoed by other mid-fifteenth century Romans. The punishment of Korah, in particular, was one of the most frequently cited Scriptural justifications for pro-papalist condemnations of the conciliarists and of conciliar theory. Reference to the "seditious schism" of Korah, Dathan, and Abiram is made, significantly, in the opening sentence of Eugenius IV's bull *Moyses vir Dei*; Aeneas Silvius Piccolomini, in renouncing his former conciliar views in 1447, stated that he feared God's judgment and did not want to go to Hell alive with Korah and his companions; and Sánchez de Arévalo even found in the Old Testament text evidence that Korah and the other rebels had been punished both spiritually (by excommunication when they were ordered from the tabernacle) and temporally (when the earth opened up and swallowed them).[144] Sixtus IV, in his bull excommunicating Andreas Zamometič, also alluded to the punishment of Korah, and concludes his condemnation: "Nobody arrogates the honor [of the high priesthood] to himself: he is called by God, as indeed Aaron was [Hebrews 5: 4]."[145]

This passage from the Epistle to the Hebrews appears in a much more conspicuous place in the works surviving from Sixtus's pontificate. The text, in Latin (NEMO SIBI ASSVMMAT HONOREM NISI VOCATVS A DEO TANQUAM ARON), is the inscription on the attic of the otherwise faithfully reproduced Arch of Constantine, which forms the imposing backdrop in Botticelli's *Punishment of Korah*, one of the wall frescoes of the Sistine

20. Botticelli, *Punishment of Korah*. Wall fresco from the Sistine Chapel (before restoration). (Photo: Alinari/Art Resource, NY)

Chapel. At the altar in front of the arch, Aaron, wearing the triple crown, performs the priestly rite of censing, while Moses with raised rod invokes God's power against a group of figures, who, thurifers flying from their hands, are driven from the altar by heavenly fire. This scene probably represents the punishment inflicted on the sons of Aaron (Leviticus 10: 1–4), who were destroyed by God for their illicit sacrifice. At the left Moses appears again. With raised arm he stands over a chasm into which the Korists plunge to perdition, while above them two adolescents, standing on a cloud, register astonishment at what they see. These two youths are probably the sons of Korah, who by refusing to join the rebellion were miraculously saved. Both main elements of Botticelli's painting dramatically present the divine punishment accorded those who attempted to usurp priestly functions from those divinely called, and their fate confirms the commandment inscribed on the arch.[146]

Significantly, the fresco on the wall directly opposite the *Punishment of Korah* is Perugino's *Delivery of the Keys.* In the center foreground Christ hands the keys to a kneeling St. Peter, as the other Apostles, dressed in antique garb, witness the event. At a further remove appear figures in contemporary dress, who also witness the scene. Included among these are portraits of Baccio Pontelli (compass in hand), who was the architect of the Sistine Chapel, Giovannino de' Dolci (holding a carpenter's square), who supervised the actual construction of the chapel, and Perugino himself (dressed in a black robe).[147]

The delivery of the keys takes place in an enormous piazza bounded at the rear by a monumental, domed temple, central-plan in design, flanked by two triumphal arches, modelled, like the arch in the facing *Punishment of Korah*, on the Arch of Constantine. Whereas the attic of that arch, however, showed crumbling stone work, the attics of the arches in Perugino's *Delivery of the Keys* are whole and intact—suggesting the superiority of the new dispensation to the old. Again, the inscriptions on the arches provide a key to the painting's meaning: IMEMSU[M] SALAMO TEMPLVM TV HOC QVARTE SACRASTI SIXTE OPIBVS DISPAR RELIGIONE PRIOR (You, Sixtus IV, unequal in riches but superior in religion to Solomon, have consecrated this vast temple). Christ's transmittal of the keys provides the foundation for the Roman Church (symbolically rendered by the temple flanked by the triumphal arches), which is prefigured by, but surpasses, the Temple of the Hebrews.

In the middle ground on the vast piazza two other events are depicted. On the left Christ pays the taxes to a Roman soldier (not the "tribute money" of Matthew 17: 24–27 but rather the "render unto Caesar" of Matthew 22: 15–22); on the right is the stoning of Christ as he taught in the Temple (John 8: 59 and 10: 31). The stoning of Christ forms a parallel to the threatened stoning of Moses by rebellious Israelites (Numbers 4: 10), which appears in the right foreground of the *Punishment*

21. Perugino, *Delivery of the Keys*. Wall fresco from the Sistine Chapel (before restoration). (Photo: Alinari/Art Resource, NY)

of Korah. In fact, the recently uncovered original *tituli* over these two frescoes refer to these two subsidiary scenes. They read: CONTVRBATIO MOISI LEGIS SCRIPTAE LATORIS and CONTVRBATIO IESV CHRISTI LEGISLATORIS.[148] The underscored point, then, is that rebellion against God's lawmaker is divinely punished. But whereas in the foreground of the *Punishment of Korah* all is violent tumult, the attempted rebellion against Christ (the stoning) is presented by diminutive middle-ground figures totally dwarfed by the serene stability of Christ consigning the keys to Peter.[149]

Parallels between Moses and Christ provide the thematic connection not only between these two frescoes, but indeed for the entire cycle of wall paintings completed for the Sistine Chapel in the years 1481–83. The lives of Moses and Christ are presented from birth (the altar wall contained, before their replacement by Michelangelo's *Last Judgment*, the *Finding of Moses* and the *Birth of Christ*) to death and beyond (the entrance wall shows the *Archangel Michael Defending the Body of Moses against the Devil* and the *Resurrection of Christ*). Moreover, the events chosen for inclusion in the two cycles were deliberately selected, as Ettlinger has shown,[150] in order to emphasize Moses' and Christ's roles as lawgivers, rulers, and priests to their respective religious communities. Thus, for instance, the circumcision of Moses' son is placed opposite the baptism of Christ, the passage of the Red Sea with its significance for the formation of the covenant community is paired with Christ's calling of the first Apostles, the giving of the Ten Commandments is linked to the Sermon on the Mount, and the testament of Moses has its counterpart in Christ's discourse to the Apostles at the Last Supper.[151]

Throughout, Moses is presented as a *typus Christi*. It is noteworthy, however, that neither Moses nor Christ are presented primarily as miracle-workers.[152] Rather they are shown as establishing the fundamental laws, the governing order, and the priestly powers of the religious community, which existed first under the written law of Moses, and which now exists under the evangelical law of Christ. As Vicars of Christ and the historical embodiment of the Apostolic Succession of St. Peter, the portraits of the popes painted in the zone above the wall frescoes testify to the transmittal through time of the regal and sacerdotal powers of Moses and Christ. The wall decoration of the Sistine Chapel thus forms a coherent whole: the religious careers of Moses and Christ and the portraits of the early popes testify to the divine foundation and historical continuity of the *primatus papae* as the fundamental principle of God's sovereign plan for the salvation of mankind.

The prominence accorded Moses in the Sistine Chapel wall frescoes is, significantly, without precedent in the church decoration of the late Middle Ages and Renaissance.[153] The historico-theological analysis of Moses' religious role evident in the paintings clearly derives, therefore, not from previous artistic tradition, but instead from ideological themes developed at the papal court. The arguments of Torquemada, Pierŏ da Monte, and other papal defenders of papal primacy, which point to Moses as a prefigurement and lineal predecessor to Christ, provided the context for this attention to Moses.

Moreover, typological links between Moses and Christ had New Testament sanction. St. Paul, for instance, interpreted the passage through the Red Sea, the manna in the desert, and the water that gushed forth from the rock when Moses struck it with his staff as prefigurations of the sacraments established by Christ (I Corinthians 10: 1–5). But, this miracle-working and sacramental emphasis did not, as we have seen, form the thematic core of the Sistine Chapel decoration. Closer to its outlook are the general themes in the opening parts of Matthew's Gospel, in which the temptation narrative re-evokes Israel's trials in the desert and the Sermon on the Mount presents Christ in the Mosaic guise as law-giver. Indeed, the meaning of Christ's Kingdom and its significance for ecclesiology constitute fundamental Matthaean arguments.

Yet closer to the typology of the Sistine Chapel is the Epistle to the Hebrews. The author of this New Testament letter stresses that as Moses was the leader of his people, so much the greater in this capacity is Christ, just as He is a high priest superior to Aaron. The sacrificial blood of the animals in the Old Testament practice restored external purity, but the blood of Christ cleanses our conscience. Thus the Temple and its rites prefigure but serve only as shadowy copies of the heavenly sanctuary, where Christ, high priest forever, opens the way for our eternal salvation (Hebrews 3: 1–6 and 5: 1–10: 39). In Botticelli's *Temptation of Christ* these sacrificial-sacerdotal notions receive particular prominence. There an Old Testament rite of blood-sacrifice, with the high priest officiating, takes place at an altar before the Temple, a building which closely resembles Old St. Peter's.[154]

The concern shown in the Sistine Chapel to trace the roots of pontifical law-making, executive, and priestly powers to the sacred authority of Moses and Aaron must be seen also as a reflection of a more wide-ranging inquiry of the Roman humanists into Hebraic antiquity. One indication of this regard for Hebraic studies is the attention accorded the extensive commentaries, drawn from Hebrew sources, produced by Nicolaus de Lyra (d. 1349). A large number of his manuscripts were procured for the Vatican Library, and his *Espositiones in Pentateuchum* appeared in print in Rome, in an edition dated 1471 and dedicated to Sixtus IV.[155]

But Roman humanists made original contributions to Hebraic studies, too. During his sojourn at the papal court in the 1480s, Aurelio Brandolini composed *In sacram Ebreorum historiam*. In this work, Brandolini aimed not at a probing theological analysis, but instead at rewriting,

according to humanistic literary standards, the historical portions of the
Old Testament, supplemented by Josephus. In so doing he aspired to
provide a more succinct, coherent, and rhetorically polished narrative
history of the Hebrew people from Creation to the time of the
Maccabees.[156] As such, it parallels Agli's similar reworking of the lives of
the martyrs and Platina's lives of the popes.

More searching was the scholarship of Giannozzo Manetti, the leading humanist Hebraist of the mid-Quattrocento. During his stay at Nicholas V's court in the 1450s, Manetti continued work on his *Contra Iudeos et
Gentes*, an apology for Christianity against contemporary Judaism and
classical paganism, which he had begun in Florence in the later 1440s.
The work constitutes in part an incipient religious history of mankind,
and Manetti set about to trace the historical origins of both Hebraic and
pagan religious beliefs and practices. The classical authors' discussions of
ethics and their philosophical reflections on theological matters win Manetti's commendation, but he also condemns the obscenity, licentious sex-
uality, and cruel sacrificial rites of the Romans, Greeks, and other ancient
pagans. By contrast, he praises the virtue and piety of the ancient Hebrews as worshippers of the True God. Significantly, he gives particular
emphasis as well to Moses as the divinely-inspired Lawgiver and true
founder of the Jewish religion. Mosaic law, however, in contrast to
Christ's teachings is defective, Manetti holds, in its temporal concerns, in
its blood-sacrifices, and its dietary prohibitions. The latter he dismisses as
unworthy of free men. Nevertheless, the Ten Commandments, and even
more the religious history of the Hebrews from Adam to John the Baptist
(among other figures, Manetti discusses Noah, Abraham, Isaac, Joseph,
and Aaron, as well as Moses) foreshadow and mystically prefigure Christ
and the New Testament.[157]

Besides the historical reconsideration of Hebraic antiquity represented in Brandolini's history and, to a greater extent, in Manetti's treatise, the Roman Renaissance recovered from Greek patristic and from
Hellenistic Jewish sources important treatments of the figure of Moses.
One of these newly exploited sources was Gregory of Nyssa's *De vita Moysis*
(or *De vita perfecta*), which was translated into Latin by George of Trebizond in 1446 and dedicated to Cardinal Ludovico Trevisan, an influential
figure closely connected to Eugenius IV.[158] *De vita Moysis*, a late work of
this Cappadocian Father, provides both a narrative account of Moses' life,
drawn from Exodus and Numbers, which gives moral emphasis to his just
leadership of the Chosen People, and an allegorical treatment of his life as
a symbol of the mystical journey of the soul to God. Parts of Gregory's
discussion correspond to certain details of the Sistine Chapel frescoes
devoted to Moses' career. For instance, in treating the circumcision of
Moses' son (II, 37), the Greek Father suggests as an allegorical meaning
that profane culture need not be rejected, since it, too, can lead to the

generation of virtue. That the Sistine Chapel representation of this circumcision contains allusions to the Gentile roots of the Church is argued
by Ettlinger,[159] who sees in Moses' wife Zipporah, given the more active
role in the rite, a *typus Ecclesiae ex Gentilibus*. As such, her action extends,
Ettlinger suggests, the allegorical meaning of Pharaoh's daughter, whose
adoption of the infant Moses was symbolic of the *Ecclesia ex Gentilibus*.[160] In
Nyssa's *Life of Moses* (II, 12) a similar theme is advanced: he likens the
Egyptian princess's sterility to philosophy, which in itself is sterile and
must be nourished by the milk of the Church.

     None of these elements appear in George of Trebizond's brief
dedication of his translation of Nyssa's *Life of Moses*, but in praising
Cardinal Trevisan as the right hand of the pope he describes him as a
modern Joshua to Eugenius IV's Moses.[161] Parallels between Eugenius
and Moses were, in fact, a recurrent emphasis of Trebizond's thought. In
an oration before the papal court in 1437, he asserted that just as Moses
had led the Hebrews out of Egypt after four hundred years of bondage,
so would the pope bring an end to the similar period in which the Greeks
had labored in schism.[162] Four years later the same linkage appears, this
time as a reflection of the achievement of Church reunification at the
Council of Florence. Eugenius, like Moses, Trebizond writes, had
brought the Greeks to the Promised Land of the Church after five
centuries of wandering in the desert of schism.[163]

     In short, Gregory of Nyssa's *De vita Moysis* was received into papal
circles determined to exploit the *topos* of Moses as *typus papae* as a means of
enhancing the authority and prestige of the Roman pontiffs. It was this
same context that inspired papal sponsorship of the study of Philo
Judaeus (c. 30 B.C. – A.D. 45), the Alexandrian Jew whose Platonism and
allegorical exegesis of the Old Testament set such important precedents
for the Church Fathers. An apt illustration of Philo's thinking, apropos
the present discussion, is his description of human nature as twofold, part
animal (the blood in us) and part human per se (reason). But this human
part, which is also divine, consists particularly of intellect and speech, and
these, Philo suggests, are signified by Moses and Aaron, respectively.[164]

     More important, Philo had written a life of Moses. In fact, Gregory
of Nyssa's idealizing portrait of the Hebraic leader depends for many of
its particulars and for its overall themes on Philo's work.[165] In 1480 a Latin
translation of Philo's *De vita Moysis* was presented to Sixtus IV by the
Umbrian humanist, Lilio Tifernate.[166]

     Italian humanist interest in Philo actually, however, dates back to
the third decade of the fifteenth century. Among the many Greek books
that Francesco Filelfo brought back with him to Italy from Constantinople in 1428 was a manuscript of Philo's works, and at one point he
informed Traversari that he planned to make a translation of Philo's *De*

vita Moysis. Nothing came of this, however, and Traversari himself eventually gained possession of Filelfo's Philo codex.[167]

Yet interest in Philo had thus been stimulated, and acquisition of Philo's Old Testament exegesis was one of the priorities of Nicholas V's ambitious plan to recover the whole of the Greek classical and patristic heritage for Latin Christendom. In 1448, Giovanni Tortelli, who acted as coordinator of Nicholas's scholarly projects, wrote to Giannozzo Manetti in Florence, seeking the Florentine's Greek manuscript of Philo. Manetti demurred, pleading the delicate condition of the ancient manuscript, though he suggested it might be copied.[168] Despite this apparent setback, it was during Nicholas's pontificate that Tifernate began his translation of Philo. In dedicating Latin versions of four of Philo's writings to Nicholas V, the Umbrian humanist explained that both the pope and Cardinal Bessarion had encouraged his undertaking, and that his Greek source was a manuscript provided by the former Metropolitan of Nicaea.[169]

Some two decades later, in 1474, Tifernate produced another group of Philo translations, which he dedicated to Federigo da Montefeltro, Duke of Urbino.[170] But it was only in 1477, under commission to Sixtus IV, that he returned in earnest to Philo scholarship. In the course of the next eight years he produced six large volumes of translations and commentary, each handsomely written and embellished with splendid miniatures.[171]

The Greek sources for this last and most fruitful phase of Tifernate's work on Philo were, as Platina's registers indicate, manuscripts belonging to the Vatican Library.[172] His actual work of translation took place, however, not in Rome, but instead at the papal *rocca* at Ceprano, which occupied the strategic heights overlooking the Via Labicana as it crossed the border into the Kingdom of Naples.[173] The castle was far from the most amenable place to pursue scholarship and to cultivate the muses, as Tifernate complained to Sixtus,[174] and at one point an eye disease, made worse by winter dampness, threatened to halt his scholarship altogether. But he implored the intercession of St. Antony of Padua, and the affliction was cured.[175]

Ceprano did have the advantage nevertheless of presenting no competing distractions, and there Tifernate immersed himself in Philo's language and thought. Indeed his Latin version is more than a mere translation, for each Philo book is prefaced by Tifernate's commentary on its contents and marginal glosses abound. Such zeal arose in part because of Tifernate's conviction that Philo's Old Testament exegesis was particularly authoritative. He stresses that the Church Fathers had all commended Philo, and that Jerome, in particular, had regarded his knowledge as so sublime that he deserved to be enrolled in the catalogue of the saints.[176] Tifernate also cites Eusebius's *Ecclesiastical History* for the information that Philo had known the Evangelist Mark in Egypt, and he states that another ancient tradition reported that Philo had come to Rome during the time of the Emperor Claudius and had there seen Peter and heard his preaching of the Word of God.[177]

For Tifernate, Philo thus had nearly apostolic authority. From this point of view, Philo's treatment of Moses had particular significance. In the introduction to the volume which contains his translation of Philo's *De vita Moysis*, Tifernate observes that until the coming of Christ Moses had no equal in majesty and magnificence, and that, for Philo, the Hebrew leader was pre-eminent as king, lawgiver, high priest, and prophet.[178] Indeed, Tifernate points out, it is under the roles of king, lawgiver, and high priest that Philo organized his life of Moses. Moreover, the Umbrian humanist later argues, it was these same three powers of religious and secular leadership that Christ had bestowed on Sixtus as pope. Therefore what Philo says of the *regnum Moysi* is more properly said of the Church, and of Sixtus, the Roman pontiff of the *regnum Christi*.[179]

In this way, then, as Ettlinger has suggested,[180] Philo provided the thematic approach and theological authority for the idealized treatment of Moses as king, lawgiver, and high priest of the written law that appears in the Sistine Chapel. Philo, in short, suggested the aspects of Moses' sacred leadership through which he could be considered a *typus Christi* and *typus papae*. That Philo's thought was in fact discussed by the papal court in connection with the Sistine Chapel decoration seems apparent in Tifernate's comment in his fourth volume of his Philo translation. There he remarks that nowhere in *De vita Moysis*, which he had sent to the pope the previous year, did Philo refer to Moses' death or to the tradition contained in the Epistle of Jude (vs. 9) that the Archangel Michael had disputed with the devil over the body of Moses. In the meantime, however, he had come upon Philo's *De pietate et humanitate*. At the beginning of this work Philo treats of Moses' passing to the Lord, Tifernate relates, and of the succession of Joshua, who led the Hebrew people into the Promised Land.[181]

Through Tifernate's scholarship, then, Philo's allegorical exegesis of the Old Testament became accessible in Latin translation for the intellectuals of Sixtus's Rome. More pertinent to the papacy's particular concerns is that Moses, in Philo's account, could be appropriated as a prefiguration of papal powers, and, therefore as a role model for papal authority. Significantly, Sixtus had had this pointed out to him earlier— by none other than Filelfo himself. In the dedication, dated 1476, to the pope of his Latin translation of a curious Greek work, *De sacerdotio Christi*, Filelfo observes that Philo had demonstrated Moses to have been king, priest, and lawgiver to the Jewish people. As such, Filelfo notes, he had served as a harbinger of Christ. That Christ performs the functions of king and lawgiver is patently clear from the Gospels, the humanist states, but that He was actually named as a youth to the Temple priesthood in Jerusalem remained a closely guarded Jewish secret. Indeed, this recondite knowledge did not become revealed until the time of Justinian, as the work he is now presenting to the pope shows.[182]

By exploiting a variety of sources, the humanists and artists of Sixtus IV's Rome found in the figure of Moses precedents for the regal, sacerdotal, and legislative powers that comprised their image of papal authority. By the later fifteenth and early sixteenth centuries, such references to Moses and Aaron as types or prefigurements of papal powers had become commonplace. Thus in one of the triumphal arches decorating the route of Leo X's *possesso* a pope is shown censing the altar in the company of other prelates, and the inscription reads: TANQVAM AARON. The pair to this depicts a pope kneeling before an altar, an armed band standing behind him, with the identifying inscription: TANQVAM MOYSES.[183]

Some years later, Archangelus Ferrosius, in asserting that Pope Clement VII could engage in a just war against the Florentines—a reference to the papal-imperial campaign of 1529–30 to recover Florence for Medici rule—argued that just as God had constituted Moses his vicegerent on earth, conceding to him both spiritual and temporal jurisdiction, so the pope exercises these same powers, since "Peter and all his successors are said to have followed in the succession of Moses."[184]

During Alexander VI's pontificate the prayer by which Cesare Borgia was made Captain General of the papal armies cited a whole series of Old Testament precedents for God's actions on behalf of his chosen people, and beseeched God to grant to the pope's son the grace Aaron had obtained in the tabernacle and to bestow the virtue and authority Joshua and Gideon had in battle.[185]

Increasing use of the papal triple tiara for ceremonial occasions provides yet another indication of the emphasis the Roman Renaissance placed on continuities between Hebraic and Christian practices. According to Josephus, when the Jewish high priest officiated at the Temple in Jerusalem, he wore a tiara adorned with three gold rings. In the Sistine Chapel fresco of the *Punishment of Korah*, Aaron appears crowned this way, as does the high priest in the *Temptation of Christ*. The addition of a third papal crown historically dates to Boniface VIII's pontificate at the end of the thirteenth century, at which point its symbolism, however, seems to have referred not so much to Hebraic precedent as to papal hierocratic claims to wield sacerdotal, regal, and imperial power. Moreover, the popes did not wear the tiara in the celebration of the liturgy.[186]

Paul II, Sixtus IV's predecessor, was the first pontiff to break away from this medieval stricture. Not only did he commission elaborate new triple tiaras, made of gold and encrusted with gems, but he also wore the tiara, instead of the mitre, for liturgical functions. He was also the first to include an image of himself enthroned and crowned with the triple tiara on the papal seal, and the tiara appears conspicuously, too, in the coins and medals struck during his pontificate. In short, Paul II used the golden triple tiara to denote the sacred high priestly powers inherent to the papacy, along with the temporal authority the popes exercised.

This practice sparked controversy and criticism, even at the papal court. Cardinal Ammannati-Piccolomini argued that such splendor hardly accorded with the position of Gregory the Great, who had signed his apostolic letters "*Servus Servorum Dei*;" nor did it respect St. Paul's dictum: "God forbid that I should boast of anything but the Cross of Our Lord Jesus Christ, through whom the world is crucified to me and I to the world" (Galatians 6:14). Platina, too, an inveterate critic of the Barbo pope, caustically commented that the begemmed tiara made Paul II appear as a "turretted Cybele" or as a "second Aaron" of more than human aspect. Cardinal Jouffroy, on the other hand, defending Paul's usage against Fraticelli criticisms, suggested that the dazzling beauty of the jeweled tiara served as a symbol within the Church Militant of the Church Triumphant. Clearly, for Paul II, use of the triple tiara, with its evocation of Old Testament sacred ritual and its suggestions of the parallel centrality of Jerusalem and Rome as focal points for cult, contributed to the more impressive religious ceremony he was determined to create.[187]

This aim won Giles of Viterbo's retrospective approval. In the more magnificent vestments and liturgical splendor introduced by Paul II, he saw signs that the Church was approaching the culminating tenth age of ecclesiastical renovation.[188] Furthermore, Giles specifically sanctioned papal use of the splendidly begemmed triple tiara. For him, too, Hebraic precedent validated such papal practice, but rather than tracing the origins of the triple tiara to high priestly rites in the Temple, he instead saw the tiara's fundamental meaning hidden in the *arcana* of the cabala. Decipherment of this esoteric Hebrew source of divine wisdom revealed that the tiara's design depended on a complex numerological symbolism, based on the mystical meanings of the numbers three, seven, and ten. These in turn manifested the connection between high priestly (and pontifical) powers and God's sovereign majesty. [189]

Reference to Moses and Aaron as types of the Roman pontiffs thus proved recurrent in the ideology, art, and ceremony of the later Renaissance papacy. In particular, acceptance of the Jewish high priest's use of the triple tiara as a justification for papal emulation contributed to the more exultant image of pontifical sacred powers the restored papacy was determined to project. Such exploitation of Hebraic prefiguration of papal roles and powers reached its apex during the pontificate of Julius II.

Both Aaron and Moses appeared, as we have seen, in Julius's pageantry for the Festa di Agone of 1513, and contemporaries readily

22. Michelangelo, *Moses*. Part of tomb of Julius II. Rome, S. Pietro in Vincoli. (Photo: Alinari/Art Resource, NY)

perceived in the second Della Rovere pontiff's martial leadership and fierce *terribilità* an identity with Moses, the liberator of the Chosen People from bondage. From its inception, a statue of the ancient Hebraic leader figured prominently in the plans for Julius's tomb, and it has frequently been suggested that Michelangelo's *Moses* with its tremendous inner dynamic force bears an idealized likeness to the warrior pope.[190]

Not prowess in war, however, but rather vigilance in prayer constituted the Mosaic ideal Giles of Viterbo urged upon Julius in his famous opening address to the Fifth Lateran Council. Prayer, Giles asserted, expressed the pious zeal by which Moses on the mountain won God's favor and the victory over King Amalek (Exodus 17:8–13). Prayer, therefore, forms the means by which "the Church of both Moses and Christ conquers."[191]

It is precisely this attitude of prayerful vigilance that Julius II assumes in Raphael's fresco of the *Mass of Bolsena* in the Stanza d'Eliodoro. The painting's subject stems from the dramatic moment in which a thirteenth-century priest's doubts about the reality of Transubstantiation were resolved by the miracle of the bleeding Host. Julius, shown kneeling in prayer, faces across the altar to the priest and the supernatural occurrence that had initiated the feast of Corpus Domini. Just such a prayerful vigil Julius, in fact, had personally kept—before the very relic of the bloodied corporal, preserved in the cathedral of Orvieto. This came during a brief halt in the campaign of 1506, in the course of which he subsequently recovered Bologna for direct papal rule.[192]

Vigilant prayer comprises the decisive religious act also in the adjacent fresco of the *Expulsion of Heliodorus*. Raphael's painting faithfully records the events described in II Maccabees 3:1–40. Heliodorus, sent by the Seleucid monarch of Syria, enters the Jerusalem Temple, bent on seizing its treasure. The high priest Onias, kneeling before the altar, prays God to keep sacred the Temple deposits. As Heliodorus attempts to carry off his loot, there miraculously appears, in response to Onias's entreaties, a splendidly caparisoned horse, ridden by a fierce warrior in golden armor and accompanied by two youths of "surpassing strength and glorious beauty." The horse rushes upon Heliodorus, attacking him with its hooves, while the two youths scourge him. In Raphael's rendering, Onias, significantly, is given the bearded likeness of Julius II. He kneels, vested in the high priest's ephod, before an altar on which stands a scroll and behind which blazes the seven-branched candelabrum. These details serve to identify the building as the Temple in Jerusalem, but the architecture of the structure does not attempt to recreate Old Testament descriptions. Instead, the Temple appears as a splendid, classicizing Roman basilica, similar in design to some of Bramante's conceptions for the new St. Peter's. Shimmering in resplendent light gleam the gilded

23. Raphael, *Expulsion of Heliodorus*. Stanza d'Eliodoro, Vatican Palace. (Photo: Alinari/Art Resource, NY)

composite capitals and golden domes of this Temple that is also the
Roman Church, of Jerusalem that has become Rome.[193]

Like the bearded high priest Onias, Julius II, who appears in pontifical garb at the left of the fresco, witnessing from his *sedia gestatoria*
Heliodorus's expulsion, possesses a flowing white beard (he appears
similarly bearded in the *Mass of Bolsena*). Prelates of the Latin Church
traditionally were clean-shaven, but the bewhiskered portrayal of Julius
was historically accurate. While convalescing during the winter of 1510–
11, the elderly pontiff had begun to grow a beard, which he retained as
symbolic of his determination to drive the French from Italy. This motive
suggests Julius's emulation of the beard Julius Caesar grew in mourning
after his defeat by the Gauls: Suetonius reports he vowed not to cut it until
vengeance had been gained. Giles of Viterbo, however, compared Julius's
beard to Aaron's, and this high priestly identity seems uppermost in the
Heliodorus fresco.[194]

Moreover, Giles, in his 1507 *libellus* on the golden age, had previously compared the Della Rovere pontiff to the high priest Onias. In a
section of this discourse devoted to Julius's achievements as pope and to
his future tasks, Giles dwells on two Old Testament passages as prophetic
of contemporary developments. The first is Isaiah 6:1, "In the year of
King Uzziah's death I saw the Lord, seated on a throne, high and exalted.
. . ." Uzziah's death, Giles avers, must be understood as referring to
Julius's short-lived predecessor, Pius III, who was called "just as Aaron
was" to the renewal of divine things. But, in accordance with Isaiah's
prophecy, the Piccolomini pope was not created pontiff so that he might
live, but simply so that he might die, and in dying be succeeded by Julius
(who is meant by Isaiah's words "I saw the Lord seated"). And it was
Julius's destiny to undertake both the rebuilding of St. Peter's basilica
(Isaiah's "exalted throne" is to be read as prophetic of this exalted *instauratio* of the Temple of the Apostle) and the remarkable enlargement
of the Christian *imperium* through its extension to the Indian Ocean (the
meaning of the prophet's added description of the throne as "elevated.")

Even more clearly, Giles declares, does the second passage, Ecclesiasticus 50: 1–2 ("It was the high priest Simon son of Onias in whose
lifetime the house was repaired, in whose days the temple was fortified.
He laid the foundation for the high double wall, the high retaining wall of
the temple precinct. . . .), reveal the unfolding of Julius's pontifical career.
The name Simon means, Giles states (citing Jerome and Origen), "obedience," while Onias means "the affliction of God." What, Giles queries, can
more clearly be meant by obedience to God than to follow Simon Peter in
the office of pope? That Onias, in turn, also refers to Julius is clear from
the trials and tribulations the Della Rovere pontiff endured before being
called to the See of Peter. But, even more strikingly, the next lines in

Ecclesiasticus refer to the "repairs to the house" and to the fortifying and strengthening of the Temple in Jerusalem. These Giles sees as prophetic of Julius's recovery of the Papal States and of the rebuilding of St. Peter's.[195]

In Giles's approximately contemporary text on "Man's Dignity, God's Love, and the Destiny of Rome," Old Testament prefigurations of papal high priestly authority in general, and of Julius's pontifical actions in particular, are similarly identified. This time it is the prophet Elisha who is seen as a *typus* of St. Peter, and both of Julius. Just as Elijah's cloak, which Elisha took up (II Kings 2:14), symbolized the succession to prophetic leadership, so, Giles remarks, do all the Roman popes, beginning with St. Peter, take up the pontifical *pallium*. Moreover, when Elisha, to cleanse the polluted waters of Jericho, ordered its inhabitants to fetch a new bowl and put some salt in it (II Kings 2: 19–22), his actions prefigured the rejection of Jerusalem, domicile of the Old Law, and the establishment of a new seat, the Church of Rome. Peter, as the Lord ordered him to be called (Matthew 16: 18), was made the constant and immovable foundation of this new Church. Anointed high priest, just as Jacob had anointed the stone (*petram*) at Beth-El on which his head rested during his dream of the ladder to heaven (Genesis 28: 18), Peter thus became the "cup of beaten gold, decorated with every kind of precious stone" (Ecclesiasticus 50: 9–10) to which the splendidly vested high priest Simon was likened as he made his ritual entrance into the restored Temple of Jerusalem. Even more, Christ's (figurative) anointment of Peter's head— like the oil poured on the head of Aaron that flowed down over his beard (Psalm 132 [133]: 2)—was the plenitude of grace which made him the "vessel of grace." Endowed with this supernal power, Peter then instituted the new seat of grace (the Roman Church).

Exhorting the pope directly, Giles exclaims, "Hear, Holy Father; you, I say you, great Julius! For you Elisha, for you Simon Peter, labored." Both of them cast down the ranks of the Temple priesthood, despoiled them of their sacred vestments, ordered them from the Temple, "and ceded it to you, my Julius." The whole earth, all mortal men, the air, the sky, the heavens, and God Himself, whose heir the pope is, call upon Julius to take up and to devote all his mind to his pontifical duties. "Take care for the decaying, restore (*instaures*) the collapsed, castigate the erring, correct the wrong-doers, call back the ancient ways, and employ all your strength against the enemy. This Elisha, this St. Peter, this your bride [the Church] urge upon you, as, too, does the Lord Himself, who in Matthew says 'I have come not to bring peace to the world but the sword' [Matthew 10: 34]." But do this, Giles concludes, so that you may enjoy that peace which surpasses all understanding, and "as victor return in triumph to the home of Our Lord God, who lives forever and ever. Amen."[196]

SOLOMON AND THE TEMPLE

An emphasis on Moses and Aaron as prefigurements of the Roman
pontiffs gave sacred sanction to and helped in defining the leadership
role of the Renaissance popes. Like their Hebraic "types" the popes
possessed divinely ordained powers, which they were to employ actively
for defense of the liberty of the church, for its moral and spiritual
rejuvenation, and for the defeat of the infidel. As such, the revived
attention to Moses and Aaron is in accord with the stress on "princely"
virtues in the sermons delivered before the College of Cardinals just
before their entrance into conclave.[197]

Besides Moses and Aaron, the Old Testament record provided one
further Hebraic model for papal leadership. In Julius II's last bull (19
February 1513), the warrior pope thought neither of Moses' heroic guidance nor of Aaron's priestly authority, but instead of King Solomon and
his building of the Temple in Jerusalem. "That most wise King of the
Hebrews in the time of the old law"—granted, Julius states, he was
unillumined by Christian light—spared no expense to honor God by
building the lavish and magnificent Temple. In this way he furnished a
place for more decorous observance of the divine cult.

Numerous of our predecessors, Julius goes on, "illumined by the
new law of Christian light," have diligently imitated Solomon's example.
Especially is this true of Sixtus IV, "our uncle according to the flesh," who
judged nothing to be more venerable, holier, or more salubrious to the
rule of the Roman Church than the cult of Omnipotent God. In order to
celebrate these holy rites more exactly, and thus with more potency, to
impart dignity and beauty to the places of celebration, and to encourage
human piety, Sixtus restored (*instauravit*), erected, and enriched (through
provision of funds) many chapels, churches, and monasteries in the city of
Rome. Among these numerous projects, Julius continues, was his
arrangement for his funerary chapel in St. Peter's, a place he embellished
with many indulgences and where divine praises are daily uttered.

To show himself no less grateful to God than his uncle and other
predecessors, and discerning the deteriorated condition of the basilica of
the Prince of the Apostles, in danger of collapsing from age, he conceived,
the pope declares, the idea of building a more worthy temple. So that
Peter's name and divine power might be manifest on earth, and so that his
dwelling-place might surpass in dignity and beauty all others, he had laid
the foundations of a basilica of wondrous size and height. Once having
begun, he had thereafter bent all effort to the project's realization.[198]

Julius II was not the first Renaissance pontiff to link rebuilding
activities in the Vatican to Solomon's accomplishments in Jerusalem. In
fact, his uncle, Sixtus IV, had drawn a parallel, as we have seen, between
the Hebraic ruler's Temple construction and the Sistine Chapel. Even

earlier, Giannozzo Manetti, at the conclusion of his description of Nicholas V's plans to transform the Borgo Leonino, the Vatican Palace, and St. Peter's, proclaimed that the pope's plans for the Temple of the Prince of the Apostles exceeded in magnificence and splendor the seven wonders of the ancient world. If completed as intended, Nicholas's Vatican would have surpassed Egyptian Thebes with its hundred gates, the Babylon of Queen Semiramis, the pyramids, the Colossus of Rhodes, and even the Capitol of Rome, which the classical authors had extolled so highly. Indeed, the only spectacle with which it could be compared was the Temple and palace in Jerusalem, built so opulently and splendidly by King Solomon, a man whose wisdom was unmatched, Manetti states, since he judged not through the oracle of Apollo (as Socrates had done), but according to the will of omnipotent God. Wondrous as Solomon's Temple was (Manetti quotes its description from II Chronicles 3), it has nevertheless been surpassed, both in its scale and in the dignity of its architectural elements by Nicholas's conceptions for St. Peter's and the Vatican Palace, just as the old divine law has given way to the new religion of Christ.[199]

That the church as an image of the celestial Jerusalem had been prefigured in the Temple Solomon built by divine guidance was a frequent medieval *topos*: Abbot Suger, for instance, cites Solomon's Temple as the ideal prototype for his Gothic abbey church at St.-Denis.[200] This general medieval theme seems, however, to have had a more specific meaning in Old St. Peter's. Its overall dimensions, sequence of structures, and design elements corresponded closely, in fact, to Biblical descriptions of Solomon's Temple.[201] Moreover, medieval tradition held that the unusual twisted, spiral columns, which formed an iconostasis before the altar of the basilica, had formerly belonged to the Temple in Jerusalem. Indeed, Fra Mariano da Firenze states flatly in his 1517 guide to Rome that Titus and Vespasian had removed the columns from the Jerusalem Temple as part of the spoils of their conquest and had then installed them in the Templum Pacis in Rome; from there Constantine had transferred them to St. Peter's.[202] It was also widely believed during the Renaissance period that Christ had leaned against one of these columns (the "Colonna Santa") while he preached in the Temple, and that this had imparted miraculous powers to it. In actual fact, however, while the columns are of eastern Mediterranean provenance, they are Hellenistic and not Jewish in origin, and probably came from a temple devoted to the cult of Dionysus.[203]

Roman medieval tradition thus had already drawn attention to a link between the Temple and the basilica of the Prince of the Apostles. That the Temple in Jerusalem formed a typological prefiguration for the Temple in the Vatican proved particularly telling for Roman Renaissance conceptions, however, since the intellectuals of the papal court placed such stress on the transmission of high priestly authority from the

Temple priesthood, empowered by the old dispensation of the written law, to the Roman pontiff, whose sacerdotal powers derived from the new evangelical law of Christ.

Equally important was their emphasis on Rome succeeding to Jerusalem as religious cult-center and ecclesiastical capital. It is these perceptions that underlie certain features of Sixtus IV's Sistine Chapel in the Vatican, such as the fact that its overall dimensions closely resemble those of the "Holy of Holies" within the Temple.[204] A similar inspiration seems also to explain the placement of seven candelabra on the *cancellata* of the chapel: their presence echoes the seven-branched Mosaic Menorah of the Temple. For good measure, Paris de Grassis also mentions the Roman imperial custom of using seven candlesticks for processions, and he traces their association with the pope to Constantine's donation.[205]

The general idea that St. Peter's basilica "replicated" the Temple in Jerusalem took on a more precise meaning during Sixtus IV's pontificate in Lilio Tifernate's commentary on Philo. In his introduction to Bk. III of Philo's *De vita Moysis* ("De sacerdotio et prophetia"), the Umbrian humanist observes that when Moses descended from Mt. Sinai, he erected a tabernacle placed on columns. This provided the divine prototype for the design of St. Peter's, and this building in turn served as a model for many other churches.[206]

Moreover, Tifernate goes on, the sacred objects that Moses ordered made for the tabernacle, including the Ark of the Covenant and the seven-branched candelabrum, eventually came to be placed, as Philo attests, in the Temple in Jerusalem. It was precisely the history of the candelabrum that Tifernate found notable. In the first place, it had originated at Mt. Sinai, where the Old Law was established—a prefigurement of the foundation of the Church. Then it was located in Jerusalem, "where the mysteries of our salvation were consummated." Finally, the Emperor Titus brought it to Rome as part of the spoils taken from the Temple in the Roman conquest of the Jewish capital (A.D. 70).

The ancient Romans accorded the candelabrum special veneration, Tifernate states, as evidenced by its place of honor before Titus's triumphal chariot. Further, it received prominent depiction in the relief sculpted to commemorate Titus's triumph, which formed an important part of Titus's Triumphal Arch in the Roman Forum. The real significance of the candelabrum's transfer to Rome, however, was as a tangible sign that the Church of God and the dignity of His priesthood had shifted from Jerusalem to Rome.

By the same "holy power," Tifernate continues, just as he was preparing his translation of the portion of Philo's *De vita Moysis* devoted to Moses' priesthood, he discovered the relief sculpture on the Arch of Titus that showed the candelabrum, and recognized what it was. The relief had long lay forgotten and nearly buried, he states, but to the felicity of the

24. Arch of Titus, detail. Marble relief sculpture (1st century A.D.) showing the spoils from the Temple in Jerusalem, borne in Titus's triumph in Rome following his victory in the Jewish War (A.D. 70). (Photo: Alinari/Art Resource, NY)

Holy Roman Church and to the joy of the city of Rome, now, after thirteen hundred years it had again come to light. In the same way his nightly labors of scholarship were bringing Philo from the shadows of obscurity and neglect into the light of day.[207]

What might be called the theme of the *"translatio Templi"* thus assumed a fixed place in the Roman Renaissance view of the Eternal City's past. Yet Solomon provided a precedent to the Renaissance popes not so much as a divinely inspired architect—though this forms part of Manetti's praise—than as a builder on a lavish scale, who used costly and sumptuous materials. Thus Sixtus's panegyrists, for instance, in celebrating the Sistine Chapel, stress not its mystical design, but rather its splendor.[208] For Giles of Viterbo, too, the golden splendor of Solomon's Temple held the key to its prophetic meaning. When Moses, "the author of the first law," arranged for the posts and sacred vessels of the Tabernacle, he had them made of silver. But Solomon, "who manifested the nature of a second law-giver," in providing for the Temple and its furnishings, had everything made of gold. By this deed, Solomon, *Rex Pacificus*, prefigured the future founding of the Church.[209]

Similarly, what Giles finds most praiseworthy about the new St. Peter's is its splendor and soaring height. Moreover, he saw the undertaking of its construction as forming a pattern of sacred history that repeats the actions of Saul, David, and Solomon in building the Temple in Jerusalem. But whereas Solomon's Temple was destroyed even before the end of the Old Dispensation, the new St. Peter's basilica is destined to endure forever.[210]

PALEO-CHRISTIAN ANTIQUITY IN ECCLESIASTICAL ARCHITECTURE AND IN PATRISTIC SCHOLARSIHP

The underlying Roman Renaissance sense of recovery, restoration, renewal, and reaffirmation extended beyond the Petrine and Hebraic images of papal monarchy and the Roman Church to the actual rebuilding of Christian Rome and to the acquisition of the theological heritage of the early centuries of Christianity. In neither area—sacred architecture and patristic studies—did Rome initiate a trend. Instead both can be traced to Florentine developments of the first third of the fifteenth century. What was impressive about Roman accomplishments, however, was the sustained effort, persisting from the mid-Quattrocento to the early Cinquecento, and the cumulative effect of these contributions both for Roman culture itself and for the larger Renaissance world.

The Roman chronicler Sigismondo de' Conti, remarking on the spate of church-rebuilding Sixtus IV undertook in preparation for the Jubilee Year of 1475, claims there was not a chapel in the city of Rome that the pope would not have restored (*instauraverit*).[211] Sixtus's pontificate does in fact represent the high point of church construction in Rome during the fifteenth century.[212] But all the Renaissance popes expended efforts to the same end, and, in general, this was one of the most praised of their spiritual undertakings. The funeral eulogies for deceased popes, for instance, consistently remark on the rebuilding of collapsed churches. Indeed Jean Jouffroy's oration for Nicholas V summons the restored Roman churches as witnesses of the pope's activity, and in Marco Vigerio's speech for Sixtus IV Rome herself narrates the pontiff's rebuilding accomplishments.[213]

Occasionally, dissenting voices were heard. Sánchez de Arévalo, in his *De remediis Ecclesiae*, criticized the conspicuous building plans of the Renaissance popes.[214] Raffaele Maffei also considered the mania for building in Renaissance Rome as sinful luxury and ostentatious avarice. He traced the beginnings of these excesses to Paul II's Palazzo di S. Marco project, and even censured the new St. Peter's as *"non admodum necessaria."*[215] Yet even during Adrian VI's pontificate when self-criticism and self-doubt were rampant among Roman intellectuals, and when corruption was seen as the corrosive moral sickness of the Roman Church, the Dutch pope was exhorted to complete the rebuilding of St. Peter's, and he did continue work on the project.[216] Giles of Viterbo, too, though he upheld the ideal of eremitical withdrawal and nostalgically longed for the primitive Church of "caves and forests," nevertheless regarded the building of churches as one of the pope's principal spiritual duties. In particular he praised the popes of the fourth and fifth centuries for spending the Church's wealth for this purpose.[217]

Many of the Roman churches restored during the fifteenth century, such as S. Maria Maggiore and S. Stefano Rotondo, had been built during the fifth century. Awareness of the antiquity of these basilicas and titular churches seems, in fact, to have influenced the choice of a deliberately archaizing quality in Roman Quattrocento ecclesiastical architecture, evocative of Rome's paleo-Christian past. This was not an exclusive tendency, since other, divergent, stylistic impulses can be identified. The impact of Tuscan, especially Florentine, Renaissance architecture is apparent, and Lombard elements appear in S. Maria del Popolo.[218] Moreover, Paul II's rebuilt church of S. Marco (incorporated in the Palazzo di S. Marco complex) reveals the inspiration of classical Roman motifs, drawn from the nearby remains of Roman imperial architecture, such as the Colosseum and the Theater of Marcellus. As such, it points ahead to the early sixteenth century.[219]

Despite this eclecticism, the almost "anonymous" ecclesiastical architecture of Sixtus's numerous rebuilding projects seems best explained by a conscious paleo-Christian revival. As Krautheimer has pointed out,[220] S. Pietro in Vincoli, SS. Apostoli, S. Agnese f.l.m., S. Agata dei Goti, S. Cecilia, S. Eusebio, S. Croce in Gerusalemme, and other Roman basilical churches restored during and immediately after the first Della Rovere pontificate share a similar basic design. An open-timbered roof or flat ceiling covers the nave, there are groin vaults in the aisles and transepts, and a groin-vaulted portico precedes the entrance. A cloister adjoins the side of the church. As a complete entity, this was, Krautheimer concludes, "evidently the fifteenth-century conception of the appearance of an early Christian church."

The restoration of paleo-Christian antiquity striven for in the re-built sanctuaries of fifteenth-century Rome had its counterpart in papal patronage of patristic scholarship. Revival of interest in the Church Fathers formed an integral element of Italian humanism from Petrarch on, and Renaissance Rome shared in the renewed regard for the Latin patristic heritage, notably Augustine and Jerome.[221] More noteworthy, however, was the Greek patristic scholarship engaged in by Roman humanists. The antecedents for these studies can be traced to the schol-arship of the Florentine monk and humanist, Ambrogio Traversari. The most prolific translator of Greek patristic texts among Quattrocento humanists, Traversari had found in these "philosophers of Christ" a more ardent faith and a more eloquent exhortation to the *studia virtutis* and *studia pietatis* than could be gleaned from the scholastic theology of the Middle Ages.[222]

A second impetus to investigating the Greek Fathers was the Council of Florence. There a lengthy series of public debates aimed at reaching theological reconciliation between Latin and Greek Christians on the controverted matter of the Procession of the Holy Spirit. Critical to the eventual success of these discussions was a careful comparison of Greek and Latin patristic formulations—an undertaking in which Traversari assumed a key role. This served to underscore the fundamental role of the Church Fathers and of the early ecumenical councils in defining and explicating the central mysteries of the Christian faith. It also introduced to Italian humanists concerned with religious issues a substantial number of the Greek Fathers and their writings—works almost wholly neglected in the later Latin Middle Ages.[223]

One attentive witness to the disputations at Florence was Tommaso Parentucelli, the future Nicholas V. For him the centrality of the Church Fathers in the Council's deliberations served to reinforce an earlier in-terest in patristic scholarship. In fact, over the previous decade he had collaborated with Traversari, sending him various rare texts and en-couraging his undertaking a new Latin translation of the Ps.-Dionysius writings.[224] As pope, Nicholas acquired the resources to further the scho-larship pioneered by the Florentine monk, and the fall of Constantinople during his pontificate made more urgent the task of preserving Greek patristic thought from its threatened extinction.

Nicholas's first concern was the acquisition of manuscript sources.

In this his efforts produced a resounding success. During his pontificate the Vatican Library developed from a negligible repository of the Greek Fathers to the most extensive collection in Latin Europe. Most of these manuscripts came to Rome from the Greek East. One illustrative example is the important eleventh-century codex of Chrysostom's first forty-four *Homilies on Matthew* (the present BAV, ms. Vat. gr. 534). Conveyed out of Constantinople before the city's fall to Mehmed the Conqueror, the book reached Negroponte, where Francesco Griffolini, the Aretine humanist who subsequently translated a number of Chrysostom's writings, obtained it. Bringing it with him to Rome, Griffolini presented the precious volume to Nicholas V, along with a Latin poem describing the circumstances of its "rescue" from the Infidel.[225]

Besides accumulating manuscript sources, Nicholas V continued Traversari's work of making the thought of the Greek Fathers more widely accessible through humanistic Latin translations. Several humanists, drawn to Rome by prospects of Nicholas's patronage, produced such translations. Among them were Niccolò Perotti (1429–80), who paired a Latin version of Basil's homily *De invidia* with Plutarch's similarly titled moral essay, *De invidia et odio*,[226] and Lilio Tifernate, who, as we have seen, took inspiration from the 1450 Jubilee to present to Nicholas his Latin translations of various Chrysostom sermons devoted to the theme of penitence. As a translator of patristic texts for Nicholas V, no one proved more prolific than George of Trebizond. During the 1440s this Byzantine *émigré* had put into Latin Basil's *Adversus Eunomium*, a work that had figured prominently in the discussions at the Council of Florence; indeed, participants had urged Traversari to translate it, but his death in 1439 had forestalled what plans he may have entertained. Following the Basil treatise, Trebizond had then turned to Gregory of Nyssa's *De vita Moysis*, which he presented, as we have seen, to Cardinal Trevisan. His mark thus made, Trebizond became a logical choice for Nicholas V's commissions, and in the period 1447–52 he produced Latin versions of Chrysostom's *Homilies on Matthew*, Eusebius's *De praeparatione Evangelica*, Cyril of Alexandria's *Commentary on John*, and Gregory Nazianzen's orations in praise of Athanasius and Basil.[227]

Papal patronage of patristic scholarship did not cease with Nicholas V's death, and besides the popes other prelates proved instrumental in sustaining this revival of the Church Fathers. In the later 1450s Griffolini presented some short works by Chrysostom, in Latin translation, to Calixtus III's confessor and librarian, Cosma de Monteserato, a Spanish Augustinian and bibliophile.[228] The Aretine then made Latin versions of Chrysostom's *Homilies on I Corinthians* and *Homilies on John*, both undertaken for Jean Jouffroy, the French ecclesiastic and eventually cardinal, who frequently sojourned in Rome and who acquired an impressive library of classical and patristic texts.[229]

Slightly later, in the early 1460s, Pietro Balbo made a series of patristic translations for Nicolaus Cusanus, the great German thinker who had become a cardinal and lived in Rome. Balbo's most important accomplishment for Cusanus was a Latin version of Gregory of Nazianzen's profound "Theological Orations." In the same period Balbo dedicated to Pius II several translations of Greek patristic texts, and the Piccolomini pontiff rewarded him with the Bishopric of Tropea. While residing in his Calabrian diocese, Balbo continued his patristic scholarship, but eventually, it seems, he returned to Rome, where he presented a short work of Chrysostom on the virtue of patience to Sixtus IV, then bedridden with gout.[230]

This spate of humanistic Latin translations of works of the Greek Fathers continued, too, under Paul II. The outstanding achievement was the large body of Athanasius's treatises rendered into Latin and dedicated to the pope by Ognibene Lonigo, whose Greek expertise Biondo earlier had drawn upon for a translation of Herodian's account of the apotheosis of the Roman Emperor Septimius Severus.[231] In his preface to the Athanasius translations, Lonigo suggested that the Greek Father's staunch defense of orthodoxy against the Arian heresy should serve to reinforce Paul II's determination to carry on the just and necessary war against the infidel Turks.[232]

Paul II also became the recipient of a group of homilies written by Gregory of Nyssa and translated into Latin by the former Byzantine abbot Athanasius Chalcheophilos. In his dedicatory letter, this Greek scholar suggests that the brilliance of Nyssa's wisdom surpasses the splendor of the precious jewels and cameos the Barbo pontiff was so fond of collecting.[233]

In addition, Paul II commissioned a translation of Basil's important *Homilies on the Hexaemeron* (that is, on the Six Days of Creation). The translator, in this instance, was the elderly Lampugnino Birago, who in his earlier *Strategicon*, addressed to Nicholas V, had advocated the development of Greek studies as part of a comprehensive program to check the Ottoman menace.[234]

Almost immediately, Basil's exegesis of Genesis 1 received another Latin translation, this time by John Argyropoulos, the Byzantine philosopher and one of the leading intellectuals of the mid-Quattrocento, whom Sixtus IV managed to lure to Rome from Medicean Florence. While in Florence, Argyropoulos had dedicated to the Medici Latin versions of a number of Aristotle's works. In Rome, he turned to Basil, with his Latin translation of the *Homilies on the Hexaemeron* his only venture into patristic studies. He presented his text to the Della Rovere pontiff in a sumptuous dedication copy, adorned with elegant gold lettering and classical architectural motifs.[235]

To Sixtus's pontificate also belong the patristic translations produced by Cristoforo da Persona (d. 1485), a native Roman, who as a youth

FRATRIS·CHRISTOPHORI·DE·PER
SONA·ROMAN I·PRIORIS·ECCLESI
AE·SANCTE·BALBINE·DE·VRBE·IN
ATHANASII·SVPER·EPISTOLAS·PA
VLI·INTERPRETATIONEM·AD·PAP
AM·SIXTVM·QVARTVM
PREFATIO INCIPIT
FOELICITER.

VM·MECVM
animo uolutarem. B. P.
cui potissimum id opus in
scriberem: quod superiorib9
lucubraciunculis e græco
Latinum feci. Occurrit mox
Alexandri responsum: qui
ferme moriens cum quere
retur: cui nam tantum re
linqueret principatum: ei
respondit qui optimus esset. Ipse uero neminem habeo
quem tibi preponam. Quippe qui ut dignitate ceteros su
peras: ita moribus et doctrina excellis. Nam et si uiri v
doctissimi Sacrarum te litterarum et diuine scientie pe
ritissimum iudicant: non tamen negant probatiores qui
q; et sapientes. ea etiam esse mansuetudine et in omnes cle
mentia. ac tanta in deum pietate. ut non minorem ex his
q' ex summa doctrina laudem assequaris. Nec dubitant
plane id affirmare. iure te optimo ad id fastigii: tuis uir
tutibus. et deo bene iuuante fuisse euectum. non ambitio
ne ulla uel arte: quippe qui et oblatos sepe honores nil ma
gnifeceris: et ita semper ab ineunte etate te gesseris: ut quo
uis amplitudinis gradu dignus sis habitus: non ut faciut
multi. ut de se male. ita et de deo pessime meriti. qui ambi
endo et pollicitando. per dolos ac fraudes. et cupidius lon
ge q'consideratius ad dignitates nituntur: existimantes fo
tasse nihil deo esse nos cure: et iccirco prauis cupiditatib9
ut faciant satis. omni nixu contendunt. nec sentiunt hi
capti hauddubie incredibili cecitate: et presentium bono
rum auiditate precipites acti: nil quippiam fieri sine deo

25. Cristoforo da Persona presents his Latin translation of works of "Athana-sius" (i.e., Theophylact) to Sixtus IV. BAV, ms. Vat. lat. 263, fol. 1ʳ. (Photo: Biblioteca Apostolica Vaticana)

had travelled to the Greek East to learn the language, then had joined the
Roman household of Cardinal Isidore of Kiev. Through Isidore's influence Persona was named, as we have seen, Prior of the Roman monastery of S. Balbina on the Aventine, and he ended his career by serving as
Vatican librarian.[236] For Sixtus, Persona translated a large body of Chrysostom's moral homilies, a commentary on the Pauline Epistles attributed
to Athanasius (but which Erasmus later showed to be the work of the
Byzantine Theophylact [d. ca. 1107]), and, most important, Origen's
Contra Celsum. Origen's Biblical exegesis had circulated in Latin translation since the fifth century, but this extensive apology for Christianity
against the objections of classical philosophy had never appeared in Latin.
The Byzantine Theodore Gaza had stressed to Nicholas V the urgency of
acquiring a Greek text of *Contra Celsum*, and when this was accomplished
the pope had asked Gaza to translate it. Other obligations delayed his
undertaking it, however, explaining why Persona eventually, in 1477,
took on this task.[237]

Greek patristic studies receded in Rome during the weak and unin-
spired pontificate of Innocent VIII and during the dynastically ambitious
reign of Alexander VI, but they re-emerged after the turn of the century.
The leader among patristic scholars in Julian and Leonine Rome was
Raffaele Maffei. In 1515, following more than a decade's work, he pub-
lished a large volume of Basil's sermons and letters in Latin translation.
Then, in his *Stromata* (c. 1519–21)—the title derives from a work of
Clement of Alexandria—he completed a substantial compendium of
theology, begun with his earlier *De institutione Christiana*, in which the
Church Fathers, especially St. Basil's moral teachings, had a central place.
Indeed both Basil and Clement provided important precedents for Maffei's thoughts on the ways Christians might appropriate pagan wisdom,
and Basil in particular he found an inspiring exponent of the virtues of
the monk's contemplative life.[238]

To the early sixteenth century also belongs the patristic scholarship
of Zanobio Acciaiuoli (d. 1519), a Florentine Dominican whom Leo X
named Prefect of the Vatican Library in 1518. Acciaiuoli's Latin translations from the Greek included works of Eusebius, Olympiodorus, and
Theodoret. Unlike most of his predecessors among patristic scholars in
Rome, Acciaiuoli intended his studies to accomplish a deliberate objec-
tive: to counter the "errors" of Hellenism and to provide an antidote to
the "poison" of Greek wisdom. Plato he reviled for his notion of the
transmigration of souls, and even Socrates earned his scorn as a libidinous
old man. Democritus with his atomist theories, arguments for material
causation, and postulation of chance as the patterning principle of reality
Acciaiuoli perceived as particularly dangerous, and he translated
Theodoret's *On Providence* as a deliberate refutation. But the Dominican

found the whole of Greek philosophy alarming, viewing it as the seedbed of heresy.[239]

Acciaiuoli's attack on Democritus and his defense of divine providence sustained positions universally shared by Roman intellectuals.[240] Few agreed, however, with his radical separation of Christian revelation from Greek philosophy. Most Roman humanists, following the lead provided by Philo and Origen, by the Neo-Platonic notion of a *prisca theologia*, and perhaps above all by Aquinas, instead assumed a fundamental concord between theology and philosophy.[241]

In opposing the "errors" of Greek philosophy, Acciaiuoli sought to defend Christian orthodoxy against the subversive novelties of revived Greek thought. A half century earlier, Lorenzo Valla similarly had concluded that philosophy constituted a seedbed of heresy. But in contrast to the later Dominican, Valla did not seek to obviate this danger by a conservative buttressing of traditional formulations of doctrine; rather he called for a radical reform of theology. The medieval "queen of the sciences" was to be wrenched from its Aristotelian base and returned to its Scriptural and patristic foundations; and as a theological method dialectics must give way to the hermeneutical procedures of philology and rhetoric.[242]

The end results of Valla's criticism—his critique of Stoic moral idealism and his crypto-Epicureanism, his rejection of Boethius's arguments for human free will, his questioning of the Latin doctrine of the Trinity, and his pointed comments on the grammatical and theological shortcomings of Jerome's Latin translation of the Bible—made many contemporary humanists uneasy. In a stormy polemical exchange, dating from the early 1450s, Poggio Bracciolini brought these issues to the fore. Personal rancor and pent-up grievances colored their dispute, but basically Poggio accused his former colleague in the papal secretariate of willfully undermining received cultural traditions and of promoting unorthodox and even heretical doctrines. Poggio's quick temper and barbed pen had left few of his fellow humanists unscathed. Yet whatever personal antipathies they might hold towards the irascible Florentine, most shared his disquiet as to the implications of Valla's reassessments in theology.[243]

The fact of the matter was that, Valla apart, Roman humanists saw no need for doctrinal reform. An encounter with the Greek patristic tradition meant not a disturbing awareness of the discrepancies within medieval Catholic doctrine, but instead the opportunity to apply the *docta pietas* and rhetorical power of the Greek Fathers to the practical matter of Christian living.[244] What the humanists of Renaissance Rome admired most in the Greek Fathers as a whole, and in Chrysostom in particular, were their moral counsels and spiritual guidance. Chrysostom's homilies,

directed to an urban, lay audience of Antioch, reassumed direct relevance
for the restored urban context of Renaissance Italy, and this goes far in
explaining why he enjoyed overwhelming popularity as a subject for
translation. It should be remembered, too, that most Roman humanist
translators of the Greek Fathers were Greek scholars first, and in no real
sense theologians. Hence the tendency to see the writings of the Greek
Fathers as Christian "monuments" to be preserved and made known to
their fellow humanists. Certain of the Greek Fathers, notably Chrysostom
and Athanasius, had the further advantage of attesting, as we have seen,
to the spiritual primacy of the Roman pontiff. Others, especially Basil and
Gregory of Nyssa, served also to reinforce the theme, prominent among
the Roman humanists, of the goodness of Creation and the wisdom of the
Creator (a matter to be considered more closely in Chapter V).

What, then, were the real contributions of the patristic studies
undertaken by the Roman humanists? First, the cumulative efforts of the
more than a dozen humanist scholars who worked on the Greek Fathers
in Rome made a very large body of Greek patristic thought available to the
Latin West. In this regard, it is revealing that the Greek patristic editions
published in Paris by Lefèvre d'Etaples and his circle in the opening years
of the sixteenth century relied heavily on the Latin translations made by
George of Trebizond, Argyropoulos, and Acciaiuoli.[245] Even Erasmus, in
the rush to get a multi-volume Latin edition of Chrysostom to press,
resorted to using Griffolini's version of the *Homilies on I Corinthians*
despite his reservations about its quality.[246]

In fact, in terms of the persistent attention to the Greek Fathers and
the extent of what was accomplished the humanists in Renaissance Rome
did more than any other center, surpassing the work of Traversari and
Manetti in Florence, of Aldus Manutius in Venice, of Lefèvre d'Etaples in
Paris, and of Colet and his circle in Oxford. Only Erasmus's editorial work
at the Froben Press in Basel represents a similar level of achievement.

Besides this importance for Latin Christendom as a whole, the
Greek patristic revival in Rome possessed fundamental significance for
the Roman Renaissance itself. It constituted a key element in the overall
effort of cultural renewal. It enhanced the sense of Rome's intellectual
and religious centrality to the whole of mankind. Finally, this resuscitation of Greek patristic wisdom, when added to the recovery of papal
authority and the renewal of sacred architecture in the Eternal City,
convinced Renaissance Romans that their age was indeed witnessing the
restoration (*instauratio*) of pristine Christianity to the Roman Church.

V

The *Renovatio Imperii* and the *Renovatio Romae*

TOT.RVINIS.SERVATAM.IVL.CAR.SIXTI.IIII.PONT.
NEPOS.HIC.STATVIT. (This, saved from so many
ruins, Cardinal Giuliano, nephew of Pope
Sixtus IV, has placed here).

—Inscription on second-century relief sculpture of Roman imperial eagle
(symbol of Jupiter), located in the portico of SS. Apostoli, Rome.

From whom, from whom do you flee, frightened
traveller, as if the Furies or Gorgons
or the piercing basilisk were pursuing you?
Julius is not here, but rather the image of Julius.

—GIOVANNI PIERIO VALERIANO, *De imagine Iulii II P.M.*

Whoever has never been to the tavern has no idea
what paradise is. . . . And if that Caesar who
triumphed under the arches we see scattered here
and there, had triumphed by means of
well-provided taverns, his soldiers would have
adored him, as I adore these eels.

—PIETRO ARETINO, *La cortigiana*, rev. version, Act
II, Sc. 1.

On Palm Sunday (28 March) 1507, Julius II, returning to Rome as a
conqueror, celebrated an entrance emulative of the triumphs of classical
Rome. In the course of the previous summer and fall, papal armies,
commanded personally by the pope, had first forced Giampaolo Baglioni,
the tyrant of Perugia, to submit to papal overlordship, then marched on
Bologna. During the journey northward the papal forces faced a series of
human and natural obstacles. But Julius, perhaps conscious already of his
imperial destiny, exhorted his contingents, mired down near Tossignano

in the hills above Imola, by quoting to them Aeneas's words to his slackening comrades: *"Per varios casus, per tot discrimina rerum, Tendimus in Latium"* (*Aeneid*, I, ll. 204–05).[1] Despite these difficulties, the papal army enjoyed overwhelming military superiority. Rather than try his luck in battle, Giovanni Bentivoglio—whom Julius for good measure had also excommunicated—fled Bologna as papal detachments neared the city, thereby ending forty-three years of his personal rule and the century-long Bentivoglio *signoria*. In a single campaigning season the warrior pope had thus dramatically accomplished his ambition to re-establish direct papal rule to Umbria and to Emilia-Romagna. Or as the inscription read on the coins tossed to the Bolognese on 11 November 1506, while Julius was carried on his *sedia gestatoria* through thirteen hastily constructed triumphal arches to the cathedral of S. Pietro: BON[ONIAM] P[APA] IVL[IVS] A TIRANO LIBERAT.[2]

Erasmus, who witnessed Julius's entry into Bologna as its "liberator," looked askance at the pope's warrior prowess: "Pope Julius wages war, conquers, triumphs, and acts wholly like Julius [Caesar]."[3] But it was precisely as another Julius Caesar that the conquering pontiff returned to Rome. His triumphal entrance into his capital, deliberately arranged to coincide with Palm Sunday, began with Mass celebrated at S. Maria del Popolo, the church just inside the ancient Porta Flaminia that had been rebuilt by Sixtus IV and was so closely connected with the Della Rovere, then continued with a ceremonial procession to St. Peter's. The route proceeded down the Via del Corso, the long, straight street Paul II had made the focus of the Carnival races, then turned toward Ponte Sant' Angelo. At strategic points, various devices celebrated the pontifical triumph. On the Corso the ancient Arch of Domitian had been embellished with paintings and statues. When the papal cortege passed beneath it, it was as if, Albertini remarked, the Emperor Domitian himself had returned to celebrate another triumph.[4] Near Ponte Sant'Angelo stood a triumphal *carro*, drawn by four white horses in accordance with the practice of Roman triumphs. On the car was a globe (symbol of universal dominion), from which grew an oak tree with golden acorns (the Della Rovere emblem). From this ceremonial vehicle ten youths dressed as winged *genii* also waved palm branches in salute. Finally, in front of the Vatican stood a replica of the Arch of Constantine, decorated with a pictorial account of the history of Julius's military campaign.[5]

To mark his triumph, Julius issued another commemorative medal. On the obverse appears his portrait bust in profile, and an inscription explicitly linking the warrior pope to his imperial namesake: IVLIVS CAESAR PONT[IFEX] II. The reverse of the medal, however, evokes a different identity. Inscribed around the Della Rovere *impresa* surmounted by the crossed keys and tiara of the papal insignia is the legend: BENEDI[CTVS] QV[I] VENIT I[N] NO[MINE] D[OMINI].[6] This Gospel acclamation—"Blessed is

26. Medal of Julius II, issued for the triumph he celebrated in Rome, Palm Sunday
1507. Washington, D.C., National Gallery of
Art, Samuel H. Kress Collection. (Photo:
National Gallery of Art)

he who comes in the name of the Lord"—sung in various liturgical contexts including the canon of the Mass (the *"Benedictus"*), was the exultant shout of praise with which the Jerusalem crowds greeted Christ as he triumphantly entered the holy city on that first Palm Sunday.[7]

Julius II entered Rome, then, both as a second Julius Caesar, heir to the majesty of Rome's imperial glory, and in the likeness of Christ, whose Vicar the pope was, and who in that capacity governed the universal Roman Church. The things of God and Caesar, far from belonging to separate spheres, were fused in Julius's triumph. And Rome, in a similar conflation of the sacred and the secular, was both the imperial capital, the setting for so many ancient triumphs, as it was also the "holy Latin" Jerusalem, which Christ had made the capital of the *respublica Christiana*. Set aside in this quest for grandeur was the cult of martyrdom that had inspired Nicholas V and Pius II. In its stead appeared the vision of imperial *renovatio*.

THE ROMAN *IMPERIUM* AND THE POPE AS CAESAR

In the wake of the 1507 triumph, the humanists of the papal court persistently hailed Julius II as *"Divus Iulius,"* a second Julius Caesar. This is the leitmotiv, as we have seen, of the volume of verse Johannes Nagonius addressed to the pope, and in the frontispiece of the dedication copy he is depicted as a classical *triumphator*.[8]

Beyond such acclaim for the pontiff's martial exploits, the humanists of Julian Rome increasingly referred to the Roman Church as an *imperium*, a universal government, over which the pope exercises supreme power. The most extensive treatment of this theme is the oration Cristoforo Marcello delivered to the fourth session (10 December 1512) of the Fifth Lateran Council, the first presided over by Julius personally. Indeed, most of the oration is devoted to explicating the pope's responsibilities as *princeps*. Christian society, in Marcello's analysis, is a structure of government, ordered by laws and ruled by the pope as supreme monarch, whose guiding aim should be to lead his subjects *ad bene beateque vivendum*. This is accomplished in two ways. The ruler's virtues and beneficent judgment should shine forth "just as in a mirror" as an exemplary pattern to be imitated by his people. But, in addition, there is the necessity of actually exercising public power—the "imperial art" (*ars imperatoria*) proper—in which the *princeps* uses his wisdom and virtue to enact laws, make war or peace, enlarge his dominions, and administer his realm. In both these aspects, Julius, *"pontifex invictissimus,"* has been unmatched, Marcello declares, and he praises particularly the pope's "just wars" by which the *imperium* of the Church had been defended and augmented. Neither the burning heat of summer, nor winter's bitter cold, nor sleepless nights, nor ill health, nor the threat of death itself daunted his valor. In recovering Bologna, and in subduing Reggio in Emilia, Parma, and Piacenza to his most sacred Empire, Julius accomplished deeds whose glory and immortality could not be paralleled by any other pope.[9]

In reality, Julius II's Italian policies hardly had the unchecked victorious advance Marcello's remarks suggest. True, in 1511 Mirandola had been captured by a besieging papal contingent that Julius, oblivious to the bitter cold and snow of the Lombard winter and the dangers of bombardment, had lashed to victory from his headquarters in an abandoned church situated right under the town's walls.[10] But in the same year, as the French cause in Italy gained the upper hand, the Bolognese populace, incited by Bentivoglio partisans, rose up against papal rule. The more than twice life-sized bronze statue of the pope, sculpted by Michelangelo, was toppled from its niche above the central portal of S. Petronio, smashed into pieces by the mob, and eventually recast into a cannon by the pope's enemy, Alfonso d'Este, Duke of Ferrara, who mockingly named it "La Giulia." The Bolognese then placed in the niche a figure of God the Father, the inscription pointedly proclaiming: SCITOTE QVONIAM DEUS IPSE EST DOMINVS (Know that God Himself is the Lord).[11]

The papal reversals of 1511 were followed in turn, however, by the unexpected good fortune of 1512. The pyrrhic French victory at the Battle of Ravenna on Easter Sunday 1512 left French forces in Italy so decimated that Julius was able to retake Bologna, and, as Marcello relates, extend papal rule northward along the Via Emilia to Piacenza. But rather than Julius Caesar, who came, saw, and conquered,[12] Julius's rapid oscillations from adversity to success seem, in Guicciardini's apt analogy,[13] more like the struggle of Antaeus, who no matter how often apparently subdued by Hercules, as soon as he touched the earth was recharged with greater strength and vigor.

The spectacle of the white-bearded pontiff exposing his aging person and the dignity of his office to the risks of the battlefield—so Julius appears in the jaundiced cynicism of Guicciardini's history—received even less kindly treatment by Erasmus. In his scathing *Julius Exclusus*, probably composed within a few months of the pope's death, the warrior pope is portrayed as a braggart *miles gloriosus*. Surrounded by armies and vaunting his triumphs, he insists that St. Peter grant him entrance to Paradise. Far from dazzled, the heavenly gatekeeper grows increasingly dismayed as he learns of Julius's war-mongering, fiscal manipulations, despotic arrogance, and preoccupation with the material splendor of Rome and the papal court. At length he refuses the pope entry, but not before "Julius" first threatens him with excommunication, then as a parting shot warns he will return with enlarged forces to drive Peter from his post.[14]

This papal appeal to the panoply of imperial Rome must be seen, however, within the context of Italian and, subsequently, European royal ceremonial as it evolved in the Renaissance period. Naples, in particular, seems to have set an important precedent. When Alfonso the Magnanimous defeated his Angevin rival for the throne of the *Regno*, he made a triumphal entrance into the Parthenopean city in 1443—an event preserved in stone in the classical triumphal arch that forms the monumental entrance to the rebuilt Castel Nuovo. Just as Alfonso had himself represented there in the guise of a Roman *triumphator*, so his grandson, Alfonso of Calabria, repeatedly staged triumphs *all'antica* upon returning to Naples, victorious in his wars against Florence, the Turks, and the Neapolitan barons. In rebuilding the city gates, and in constructing palaces, the younger Alfonso was similarly inspired, as George Hersey has shown,[15] to evoke the monumental themes of Roman imperial architecture. The same motive can be seen in the "Triumphs of Caesar," painted by Mantegna for the Gonzaga of Mantua, and in the classical mythological themes increasingly present in the royal entrances staged in the Renaissance period.[16]

The emerging age of "gunpowder empires" provided even more sweeping ideological and propagandistic claims for monarchical rule. Thus Charles VIII of France, whose 1494 invasion unseated Alfonso II from his Neapolitan throne, was messianically portrayed by his court as *missus a Deo*; and upon entering Capua he was greeted by a populace bearing olive branches and chanting, "Blessed is he who comes in the name of the Lord."[17] Later, the Holy Roman Emperor Charles V stood forth as a new world ruler, destined to bring back Astraea, the goddess of Justice, to a dominion which because of the "providential" discovery of the New World exceeded that of the ancient Roman Empire bound by the pillars of Hercules.[18]

Within Rome itself the same appeal to the glories of Roman imperial antiquity had gradually emerged in the ceremonies of the Quattrocento. Thus, as we have seen, the fall of Granada in 1492 occasioned triumphal pageantry, echoing ancient Roman customs. Piazza Navona, the scene for this event, provided the setting, too, for the annual procession of carnival *carri*, which proclaimed papal achievements.[19] These parades of elaborate allegorical and mythological floats (called *trionfi*) first acquired prominence in the Carnival and St. John's Day spectacles of Florence,[20] but from Paul II's pontificate onwards they became a common feature of Rome also. The first Roman *trionfo* based on a pagan theme was the Barbo pope's parade of 26 April 1466, held in connection with the Feast of St. Mark. In this, nymphs, Amazons, and "Ethiopian" giants appeared, the goddess Diana praised the pontiff's *"iustum tamque sanctum imperium,"* and various rulers conquered by ancient Romans were shown, including Cleopatra subdued by Augustus.[21]

By the end of the fifteenth century in Rome, the *trionfo* as a general form of Renaissance pageantry had become fused with the historical revival of the Roman triumph itself. Typical is the triumph Cesare Borgia, following conquests of Imola and Forlì, celebrated in Rome in 1500. The spectacle centered on a procession from Piazza Navona to the Vatican in which allegorical *carri* presented the triumphs of Julius Caesar. Shortly thereafter Cesare adopted the motto "*Aut Caesar, aut nihil.*"[22]

Behind Julius II's 1507 pageantry thus lay the general imagery of Renaissance monarchy, the *trionfi*, and perhaps especially the memory of Cesare's triumph. After all, Giuliano della Rovere, an embittered Borgia rival, had been forced to the sidelines during Alexander VI's long pontificate. Yet just as important in contributing to the Palm Sunday triumph was the panegyric theme of triumph. Elaborated by Roman humanists since the mid-Quattrocento, this expressed the exalted destiny they foresaw for the restored imperial capital. The theme first appears in the concluding book of Flavio Biondo's work on ancient Roman society and culture, *Roma triumphans*. After discussing the origin, nature, and purpose of the various honors accorded victorious Roman commanders, and describing the triumphs celebrated by Manilius Volsius, Pompey, Julius Caesar, and Vespasian and Titus (among others), Biondo expresses the hope that Christian princes might perform deeds worthy of the victorious Roman consuls and emperors. But instead of a triumphal chariot decorated with Jupiter and his sceptre, Neptune and his trident, Juno with her spear, and winged Mercury, the contemporary *triumphator*'s *carro* should show, Biondo suggests, Peter with the keys, Paul with sword in hand, Michael and George slaying dragons, and Bartholomew carrying his flayed skin over his shoulder; and as Titus had replaced the traditional admonitory servant at his shoulder with a winged goddess Fortuna made of gold, so if this device were adopted it would seem an angel sent from heaven.[23]

By the closing years of the fifteenth century the Roman humanists applied the imagery of triumph to Christ himself. Pietro Marsi, in his funeral eulogy for Pomponio Leto (1497), first praised the dead humanist's services to Latin erudition and eloquence, then stressed the special value of his antiquarian researches into ancient Roman rites. It was these that had led his sodality to revive the Palilia, the festival in honor of Rome's founding. But now, Marsi declares, this triumphal pomp, lost for so long in darkness, is used to honor the image of Our Savior and *triumphator invictissimus*, Jesus Christ.[24]

Giles of Viterbo, in a paean of Rome's triumphal destiny dating from the early years of Julius II's pontificate, goes further. Christ's coming as Lord, King, and Emperor had been foreseen by the ancient Hebrew prophets, he writes ecstatically. As Isaiah had prophesied, the moon had grown red with shame and the sun was confounded when the Lord of Hosts reigned on Zion, that is when Christ, crowned with thorns, took up, by the Cross, his Kingdom. Habakkuk [3: 8], too, had spoken of the Lord's four-horse chariot (*quadrigae*) of salvation (by which, Giles asserts, he could have meant nothing other than the four evangelists). But Christ's power as King of Kings and *Princeps principum* was testified to even by the impious; for they had affixed as the inscription on his "triumphal chariot" [i.e. the Cross] *Iesus Nazarenus, Rex Iudeorum.*[25]

Christ as *triumphator* is the central image, too, of the sermon that Cristoforo Marcello delivered before the papal court for the Feast of All Saints in, probably, 1510. Here Marcello asks us to behold the triumphal epiphany, at Last Judgment, of the *Imperator Maximus* (i.e., Christ), a triumph prefigured in the fiery chariot by which Elijah was taken up to heaven. Not by armies, however, but by His voice alone, Marcello declares, does Christ compel the whole world to His will, give peace, communicate His grace, and lead humanity from death to life. Among Christ's triumphal entourage, two stand out most splendidly: Peter, the key-bearer, to whom Christ gave the power of opening and closing heaven, and Paul, the ardent defender of the faith. Christ himself, the King, enters in a golden chariot, dressed in purple raiment interlaced with gold, and crowned with a triple diadem. In his left hand he bears the standard of the Cross; with his right he extends the shining globe of the heavens. Close to his side sits the Virgin Mary, exulting in her son's triumph. Following Christ's chariot come "legions" of martyrs, "crowds" of virgins, "throngs" of priests, "cohorts" of confessors, and the kings and princes who defended the *respublica Christiana*. Among this last group is Pope Julius II himself. No one has been more vigilant, Marcello declares, in preserving ecclesiastical liberty and in augmenting the *imperium* of the Church. "Like another Julius Caesar," he has extinguished the fury of the barbarians and liberated Italy from servitude; he has raised up the falling standard of Christ, and through his auspicious and felicitous leadership he has enlarged far and wide the Roman *imperium*. "Therefore gird yourself, unconquered Pontiff," Marcello exhorts, "gird yourself to most propitious war; expel, confound, and destroy the fiercest enemies of God; . . . enlarge, unite and confirm the *imperium* of Christ Our Savior, so that . . . you may be able to rejoice perpetually in heavenly triumph."[26]

This same image of Roman triumph applied to Christ occupies an even more central place in the *Christiad*, a consciously Virgilian Christian epic poem, written in Latin by Marco Girolamo Vida (1480/85–1566). Vida, a native of Cremona, had entered the Order of Canons Regular of St. John Lateran and early in the pontificate of Julius II came to Rome to study philosophy, law, and theology. Already a poet of some note, he was, by 1511, at work on an epic *Juliad*, an account of Julius II's military exploits. The accession of Leo X seems to have forestalled completion of this project, however, and at Leo's suggestion Vida's desire to write a major Latin epic poem in the Virgilian manner came instead to be directed to the life of Christ. Vida began work on the *Christiad* about 1518; he labored at it for most of the next decade and a half, much of this time residing in a priory of his order at Frascati, in the Alban Hills above Rome; and finally presented the finished poem to Clement VII in 1532.

The poem itself opens with Christ making his way to Jerusalem for Palm Sunday. The events of the ensuing week unfold, including the Last Supper and Christ's arrest at Gethsemane. Then, in long flashbacks, Joseph and John the Evangelist recount to Pilate the Annunication, Christ's birth, and the years of His active ministry. Next follow the Crucifixion and the burial, with the climax and conclusion of the poem reached in the Resurrection, Ascension, and descent of the Paraclete.

It is Christ's Ascension that Vida likens to a Roman triumph. Just as the ancient Roman consuls, victorious in wars, returned to Rome, "most magnificent of all cities," and promulgator of laws to so many nations, and there while hearing the acclaim of the Roman people ascended the lofty Capitol, so did Christ enter heaven to the rejoicing of the heavenly angels. The Roman theme figures prominently in Vida's poem, too, inasmuch as the city is predestined to become the true earthly home of Christendom. Jerusalem and its Temple will be destroyed (like Troy); Rome will yield world dominion to Christ; and there one high priest, Christ's vicar, will lay down laws for all mankind.[27]

The idea of the Church as an *imperium* and of the pope as *princeps* did not have its origin in the works of the Roman humanists. Pope Gregory VII's *Dictatus papae* (1075) had asserted imperial claims for the papacy, and imperial notions had underpinned the legal theories of the medieval canonists in elaborating papal monarchism.[28] But the Roman humanists, possessed of superior knowledge of ancient Roman history and determined to revive the splendor of ancient Rome, made more literal the assimilation of the *respublica Christiana* to the Roman Empire. For them, the Roman Church, headed by the Roman pontiffs, and with its capital in Rome, both continued the Roman Empire and, *quanto magis*, surpassed it in universality and dominion.

Again, Flavio Biondo provides the first significant expression by a Roman humanist of this theme. At the end of *Roma instaurata*, he admits forthrightly that next to the Christian religion itself he holds the name of Rome in greatest veneration. But, he continues, it would be a mistake to see present-day Rome as merely the decayed remnant of the glory that once belonged to the city in antiquity. As the eternal capital of Christianity, Rome is reverenced in "sweet subjection" by a greater part of the globe than formerly trembled before Roman military might, and the peoples of the world now adore and revere as "perpetual dictator" not Caesar, but the Roman pontiffs, successors to the fisherman Peter and Vicars of the "Emperor" Christ.[29]

In *Roma triumphans*, Biondo further develops this fusion of Empire and Church, centered on Rome as capital. In his summation of the work, Biondo stresses that he meant his book to inspire Christian rulers to a more devoted allegiance to Rome. Just as ancient Rome formed a world community of many diverse peoples (the *patria communis* theme), from among which the most worthy individuals were drawn to Roman public service, so does this hold true for the Roman Church; and its laws and institutions merit even greater respect inasmuch as they promise the salvation and eternal glory of human souls. As this glory surpasses any achieved by ancient Rome, so even more consequential is any desertion of the Christian capital. Christian Rome is the fortress of the *respublica Christiana* founded by Peter and Paul; its praetorium is St. Peter's basilica; its consul is the Roman pontiff; its *magister militum* the Holy Roman Emperor; and its legates, quaestors, tribunes, and centurions the various Christian kings, princes, and barons.[30]

Biondo's ideas acquired a more focussed and fuller treatment in Domenico de' Domenichi's "*Oratio in laudem civitatis et civilitatis Romanae*," an epideictic oration in praise of Rome that this Venetian and long-time curialist delivered on the Capitoline Hill in June 1476 as part of the ceremonies by which he became a Roman citizen. Domenichi had been a friend and admirer of Biondo,[31] and like the Forlivesi he employed the rhetorical device of "outdoing" (*quanto magis*) to praise the superior glory and splendor of Christian over classical Rome.

The magnificence and majesty of Rome, Domenichi begins his speech, are known to all. Its divine origin, military discipline and skill, the greatness of its empire, and its virtues of fortitude, magnanimity, justice, and temperance emerge as self-evident to any reader of the ancient historians. Even the ancient Hebrews recognized Rome's superiority. Moses had foretold the destined Roman conquest of the Jews, Daniel had prophesied the greatness of the Roman Empire, and Judas Maccabeus had attested to its power. A key to Roman greatness (and one particular to the occasion) was Rome's extension of citizenship to all peoples of the Mediterranean world. Thus Trajan had come from Spain, Diocletian from Dalmatia, and Septimius Severus from Africa. Cicero stresses how valued Roman citizenship was, and Ovid, Horace, Juvenal, Seneca, Lucian, Martial, and Pliny, among so many others were all non-Romans who had been drawn to the capital and had become Roman citizens or important public servants. Turning to sacred letters, one can read in Acts, too, how much St. Paul made of Roman citizenship.

More decisive than any classical achievement, nevertheless, was that Peter and Paul made Rome head of the Church. Once the source of errors, Rome had thus become the teacher of truth and a *civitas sacerdotalis*, its citizens a holy nation and an elect people (Domenichi here paraphrases I Peter 2: 9). As the See of St. Peter, Rome became head of the whole world, and, greater still, part of the celestial kingdom. Rome's dominion thus extends farther through divine religion than it ever had through earthly domination. Victories in war had brought the rule of the Roman Empire to land and sea, but these bellicose labors accomplished less than the *pax Christiana* of Christian Rome. From all parts of the globe people converge on Rome, not, as formerly, bearing tribute, but to see the tombs of the martyrs, whose blood sanctified Roman soil, and, as adherents of the true God, Christ, to obtain remission of their sins. Here the Roman pontiff acts truly as *summus consul* and *dictator perpetuus*, since he holds both swords: to him is committed jurisdiction both on earth and over the celestial empire. From Rome legates administer papal power over all the earth "as rivers from a fountain, branches from a tree, or rays from the sun." Rome is the center and foundation of the Christian faith, and here the Faith has been, and will forever be, preserved inviolate. Whoever, therefore, sees in the present day a miserable city, partly destroyed by war and partly collapsed from the ravages of time, should instead contemplate the true glory of Rome enlarged in spiritual empire and celestial dignity.[32]

A generation later the humanists of Julian and Leonine Rome assumed an even more celebratory tone. The rebuilding of the city, a more self-conscious Ciceronianism as the distinctive mode of Roman humanism, and the extension of Christendom to the New World and to the Indies reinforced ideas of restored Rome's universal sovereignty. In a number of Inghirami's orations, notably his funeral oration for Julius II, and in the oration Blosio Palladio prepared on Rome's history for delivery on the Capitoline Hill in honor of Leo X, the theme of the triumphant Christian *imperium* received particular emphasis.[33]

The culminating expression of Roman Renaissance views belongs, however, to Giles of Viterbo. In the oration he delivered in 1507 in celebration of Portuguese successes in the Indian Ocean, he argues that these brought into Julius II's possession regions of the world unknown even to Julius Caesar; the force of Christian piety had thereby proved itself stronger even than the military might of the Romans. Returning to the same thought in a subsequent letter to the pope, Giles compares the former Julius Caesar, who believed he ruled the whole world but in fact governed only half of it, to the present Julius, who by virtue of the discovery of the New World possesses an empire that truly embraces the whole human family.[34]

But even this cannot compare with the transcendent sacred purpose for the city entailed in the structure God has established for the redemption of mankind. In the concluding section of his discourse on Rome's triumphal destiny, which dates from the early years of Julius's pontificate, Giles writes: "Listen Romans, listen seven hills, and you above all great Julius, Most Holy Father. Behold what the Spirit says: Christ is head of heaven, Rome head of earth; Rome sovereign, Christ sovereign." The heavenly bridegroom seeks his bride on earth, the sovereign leads his consort, the king his queen, the emperor of heaven and earth the empress of the earth. "You, my seven-hilled Rome, hail O happy bride! To you there is a new Romulus—so much greater than Romulus as God is than man." The Tiber, gliding past the Vatican, is the new River Jordan, the consecrated soil of Rome the new salt of the earth. "Witness you stars," Giles has Christ proclaim, "you moon, you sun, you ethereal spheres, observers of all things: I, commander of the eternal empire, have taken possession of my bride, and I make her eternal; may she live forever!" Made ruler over death, Rome's empire extends beyond land and sea to heaven. Rome takes up the keys, and has the power to open heaven or close it. And Julius as pope, the oak of whose family emblem echoes the oak of Romulus, wields through Christ's love, a power that surpasses what Augustus held—or Claudius, the Flavians, or Nero. By divine will, too, the Capitol, the former home of the *gens Iulii*, has become a divine habitation, and the land of Caesar the seedbed of God.[35]

AUGUSTUS AND CONSTANTINE

When Julius II had the medal commemorating his triumph of 1507 inscribed JVLIVS CAESAR PONT[IFEX] II, there was historical accuracy in designating his imperial namesake "pontiff." The office of Pontifex Max-imus—the headship of the college of priests that supervised various aspects of ancient Rome's state cult—was one of the public posts Julius Caesar had acquired during his career, and all the emperors had subse-quently assumed this position. As rulers, then, the emperors had exer-cised certain public religious responsibilities, which could be likened to the sacred rites performed by the popes. From the pontificate of Pius II onwards the title PONT[IFEX] MAX[IMVS] appeared regularly on papal coinage,[36] but it was under Leo X that this religious side of ancient Roman governance came particularly to be emphasized. Thus Cristoforo Mar-cello, Raffaele Brandolini, and Giles of Viterbo, among others, compared Leo's election, following Julius II's death, to Numa Pompilius's succession to Romulus.[37]

In 1515, in a similar evocation of ancient Roman *pietas*, Leo himself arranged for the transfer to the Capitoline of several marble reliefs, formerly part of a triumph arch. One, repeating the now familiar theme, shows Marcus Aurelius celebrating a triumph. But another accentuates the emperor's function as Pontifex Maximus, showing the revered Stoic ruler performing ritual sacrifices before the temple of Capitoline Jove.[38]

We have seen, too, how elements of the pictorial decoration that embellished the temporary theater constructed on the Capitoline in 1513 as the setting for Leo's brother and nephew to be created Roman citizens drew a historical parallel between the election of a Tuscan pope and the Etruscan sources of Roman religion. In a related anticipation that Julius II's belligerency would give way to Leo's munificent patronage of humanist studies, the arts, and music, contemporaries celebrated the displacement of Mars by Pallas Athena, Mercury, and Apollo.[39] In the same vein, the Roman humanists spoke of the transition from Julius Caesar to Augustus, which expressed their hopes that Leo, dedicated to *pax et concordia*, might, like Augustus, be another *pacator orbis*.[40]

In the eyes of the Roman humanists, Augustus had a further distinct virtue to commend him as an exemplar for papal emulation. In a famous passage in the *Lives of the Twelve Caesars*, Suetonius had asserted that Augustus could justly claim to have found Rome a city of brick and left it a city of marble.[41] From Nicholas V's pontificate, the humanists applied this passage to praise papal rebuilding of the capital.[42] Other emperors, too, earned the plaudits of the Roman humanists for the splendor of their building projects. Platina, for instance, declares that no one built more magnificently than Titus, who completed the Flavian amphitheater (the Colosseum), begun by his father, Vespasian,[43] and he also singles out Hadrian's undertakings: the Pons Aelius over the Tiber (Ponte Sant'Angelo), his mausoleum in the Vatican (transformed into Castel Sant'Angelo), and the villa "of amazing sumptuousness" he created at Tivoli.[44]

Both Titus and Hadrian could be admired as virtuous rulers in addition to being great builders—Platina argues that Hadrian for his liberality, splendor, magnificence, and clemency deserves to be counted among the good princes,[45] and Robert Flemmyng, the author of the *Lucubraciunculae Tiburtinae*, finds Titus the most humane and generous of the Caesars, though in these virtues he cannot be compared, he claims, to Sixtus IV.[46] Yet even Nero, who, Platina admits, was excessively libidinous, given to debauchery, cruel, and even more iniquitous and vicious than Caligula, could be at least partially rehabilitated, since "he built splendidly, both in Rome and outside it."[47] There were his baths, the Domus Aurea, and the elaborate facilities constructed at the port of Anzio, which Platina states he had recently inspected with the greatest pleasure. Thus the persecutor of Christians, the emperor responsible for St. Peter's execution, and a figure regarded by the Middle Ages as thoroughly demoniacal, had for Renaissance Romans the redeeming feature of being a builder on a lavish scale.

The emperors of the first and second centuries A.D., when Rome's power reached its zenith, had a natural appeal for members of the papal court intent on imperial renewal. But Constantine, too, occupied a prominent place in the Renaissance pantheon of great emperors. None of the popes claimed to be a second Constantine, but as the first Christian emperor he provided an exemplary model of imperial authority exercised on behalf of the Church. Moreover, Constantine's triumphal arch, the largest of ancient Rome, was associated with his providentially guided victory over Maxentius at the Battle of Milvian Bridge (it was on the eve of this battle that Constantine saw a vision of the Cross and was told "by this sign conquer!"). These connections to Christian triumph and to sovereign majesty indicate why representations of the Arch of Constantine appear in the Sistine Chapel wall frescoes and in Julius II's 1507 triumph.[48]

Roman Renaissance interest in Constantine is evinced in other ways. The Roman poet and humanist Niccolò della Valle (d. 1473)—he was a translator of Hesiod's *Works and Days*[49]—wrote an elegiac poem, inspired by Pius II's call for a crusade, in which he summons Constantine to the rescue of Rome, and the emperor replies that "pious Aeneas" would avenge her.[50] Some years later, during the Carnival of 1484, a dramatic "history of Constantine," was presented in a courtyard of the Vatican Palace, with Sixtus IV himself from an upper floor window forming part of the audience.[51] A more permanent tribute to Constantine was provided in the Sala di Costantino, the largest of the Vatican stanze. The decision to devote the decoration of this room to Constantine came from Leo X, and Raphael made some preliminary sketches, but much of the design and a large part of the execution fell to Giulio Romano, and the frescoes reached completion only during the pontificate of Clement VII. The main scene shows Constantine's victory over Maxentius at the Battle of Milvian Bridge; other paintings depict his vision of the Cross (which occurs, significantly, on the exact site of St. Peter's basilica), his baptism at the hands of Pope Silvester within the Lateran Baptistry made more classically correct in its architecture than the actual building, and the Donation. This last takes place within a classicized Old St. Peter's, where a kneeling Constantine presents to Silvester a gilded statuette symbolizing Rome.[52]

At first glance the inclusion of the Donation in the Vatican Constantine cycle seems surprising. Had not Lorenzo Valla, in his *De falso credita et ementita Constantini donatione declamatio* of 1440, demonstrated once and for all that the Donation was a forgery? With hindsight he did, but in fact the Donation continued to be cited by papal apologists right through the sixteenth century, and rather than resolving a subject of controversy, Valla's polemical diatribe became itself an issue of contention.

The Donation, or *Constitutum Constantini*, it should be remembered, claimed to be the document by which Constantine, miraculously cured of leprosy through baptism at the hands of Pope Silvester, in gratitude conferred upon the pope various imperial insignia, bestowed on him the rule of the city of Rome and of all the "western regions," and transferred his own capital to Byzantium. The document was, in fact, an eighth-century forgery, produced in the papal chancery, and created as part of the politico-legal means by which the papacy freed itself from Byzantine power and established its fateful alliance with the Carolingians.[53] A text of

27. Giulio Romano, *Vision of the Cross*. Sala di Costantino, Vatican Palace. The monuments in the background—Hadrian's tomb, the Pons Aelius over the Tiber, and the pyramid (demolished during Alexander VI's pontificate) which Renaissance Romans believed was the tomb of Romulus—indicate that Constantine receives his vision of the Cross while standing on the site where subsequently he built Old St. Peter's basilica to honor the tomb of the Apostle. The admonition to Constantine, "In this, conquer!" is rendered in Greek. (Photo: Alinari/Art Resource, NY)

the Donation later became incorporated into Gratian's *Decretum*, and thus formed part of the authoritative medieval compilation of canon law.[54]

In the later Middle Ages critics of the Church's material wealth came to focus on the Donation as a source of the Church's corruption. Thus Dante laments the evil fruit produced by Constantine's good intentions, which mired the Church in simony.[55] More vehement were Wyclif's and Hus's attacks. While not denying the authenticity of the Donation, they condemned it as an error, since the Church's temporal wealth and power led inevitably to its corruption and decadence. Hus, in fact, repeated the earlier medieval legend that at the time of the Donation a voice from heaven proclaimed a deadly poison to be poured out upon the Church of God. The Council of Constance, which burned Hus at the stake, declared heretical the Lollard-Hussite position that the Donation was an error. This action served to underscore the Donation's authenticity and tended to identify any critics as suspect of unorthodoxy.[56] A quarter century later, at the Council of Florence, the Donation gained further confirmation as a valid document, for it was included, in Greek translation, among the sources giving support to papal primacy.[57]

During the conciliar era, clamor for reform and for the eradication of simoniacal abuses persisted, however, and one form these impulses took was to focus on the ideal of the Apostolic Church. Gerson, for instance, contrasted the simplicity of the *Ecclesia primitiva*, unencumbered by material possessions, with the post-Constantine Church. Yet, while recognizing certain negative consequences of the Donation, he denied Constantine's and Silvester's actions to have been erroneous. In Hebraic history, Gerson argued, the Ark of the Covenant, which formerly had accompanied the Chosen People in their years of wanderings, came under the Kingdom to be installed amidst riches and magnificence in the Temple of Jerusalem; so, too, the Donation formed part of a divinely ordained plan. Temporalities in themselves were not evil; they became so only if they destroyed the spirit of humility and spiritual poverty.[58]

In a similar way, Giles of Viterbo, who headed the Order of Augustinian Hermits, viewed the second age of Church history—the first of eight ages of steady decline—as initiated when "pious Constantine" adorned the Church with riches. As a result, the Church abandoned the mountain caves and forsook the eremitical life. For Giles, however, this pessimistic perspective on the Church's past was counter-balanced by what the future held. His own times, he remained convinced, showed clear signs it was the Tenth Age of ecclesiastical renewal, and the center of this renewal was papal Rome.[59]

Until the 1430s, in fact, the issue was not the authenticity of the Donation—this remained unquestioned—but rather its consequences for the Church. Only during the struggle over Church reform at the Council of Basel did the denial of its historicity first appear. Nicolaus Cusanus, on the basis of a careful examination of patristic texts, concluded in his *De concordantia catholica* (1433) that the purported Donation was apocryphal, and therefore inadmissible in any discussions of the proper relations between imperial and papal power.[60]

The conciliar-papal contest of the Basel era forms the essential context, too, to Valla's *Declamatio*. Publication of Valla's diatribe formed part of the ideological offensive, of which support of the Council of Basel constituted another prong, carried on by the humanist's employer, King Alfonso of Naples, against Pope Eugenius IV. In 1440 the pope still backed, both politically and militarily, the Angevin cause. His refusal to invest Alfonso with the throne of Naples (the Kingdom as a papal fief required papal investiture of its ruler) provoked the Aragonese's attacks on Eugenius as a warmonger, whose Roman Curia was also rife with simoniacal corruption. Valla's assault on the authenticity of the Donation, questioning as it did the basis of papal temporal power in Italy, served, then, the immediate political interests of Alfonso. But Valla's ecclesiological views went beyond this. For him there was a fundamental incompatibility between the apostolic ministry of the papacy—a call to divine service—and political dominion, which required the exercise of force. Christ had declared His Kingdom was not of this world. Can it be right, then, for the pope, in order to maintain temporal power in Italy, to extort funds, raise armies, and keep the peninsula in continual strife "while Christ dies in hunger and nakedness in so many thousands of the poor?" No, Valla concludes, the Roman pontiff will truly *be* and not merely *be called* Holy Father when he serves as Vicar of Christ alone, and not also of Caesar.[61]

The very vehemence of Valla's assault on papal temporal power was one of the reasons, however, why for papal defenders the *Declamatio* had to be discredited. Thus the first direct refutation of Valla's diatribe, the *Antivalla*, begun by the long-time curialist Antonio Cortesi some time after 1464 but left unfinished on his death a decade later, focusses on the audacity, temerity, and arrogance of its author. The *Declamatio*, Cortesi asserts, was clearly the work of a madman, another Orestes, who had turned against his own mother, the Church.[62]

But other developments, too, diminished the immediate impact of Valla's attack. The Peace of Terracina of 1443, by which Eugenius recognized Alfonso as the legitimate ruler of Naples, terminated the particular circumstances that had occasioned the King's anti-papal propaganda. Moreover, at this point Valla began negotiations to return to his native Rome and to enter into papal employ (Valla did join the papal secretariate and returned definitively to Rome in 1448 following the election of Nicholas V). Valla's overtures were clouded, however, by the inquisitorial process undertaken against him in Naples. The issue that sparked this confrontation was not the attack on the Donation, but rather Valla's doubts on the historical authenticity of the Apostles' Creed: the humanist denied that it could have been produced during the Apostolic Age. Hailed before the Neapolitan tribunal, Valla extricated himself from this dangerous situation by retracting his arguments regarding the Creed. But the matter was not entirely resolved until his apology to Eugenius, written in late 1444, in which he also declared that at no time did he intend any of what he had written on behalf of the Aragonese crown to be a personal attack on the pope. He further implied, not altogether candidly, that the *Declamatio* had been produced under court pressure. In other letters to cardinals and to influential members of Eugenius's circle, Valla further admitted that he had been motivated by declamatory display and asserted that the main object of his attack was the pretentions of the canonists.[63]

Valla did not ever formally retract or suppress his diatribe against the Donation, but by his own admission it stemmed from the conjunction of particular political and personal motivations. That he spent the last years of his life in papal employ suggested to contemporaries, too, that the *Declamatio* had no practical consequences for the nature or conduct of the Renaissance papacy. Even without these mitigating factors, however, it is difficult to see how Valla's denial of the Donation's authenticity could have been regarded in Rome as the definitive argument.

In the first place, the Donation had the weight of a centuries-long tradition behind it. Thus, the popular pilgrim guides to the city of Rome, printed in such numbers from the 1470s on, frequently begin with an excerpted version of the Donation's text.[64] Similarly oblivious to any historical criticism of the text's authenticity is the treatise of Archangelus Ferrosius, which defends Pope Clement VII's 1529–30 siege of Florence as a just war. Inasmuch, Ferrosius argues, as Etruria had been included among the concessions Constantine granted to Silvester, the pope had jurisdiction over Florence. Moreover, one could cite for good measure the donation made by the Carolingian Louis the Pious, or, ignoring all else, the patent enormity of Florentine sins could not be overlooked.[65]

Valla's *Declamatio* could be dismissed, too, because for hierocratic defenders of papal temporal power, the canonists especially, papal supremacy in all matters, both spiritual and temporal, derived directly from the power of the keys Christ conceded to Peter.[66] The Thomist Juan de Torquemada found it possible to argue, furthermore, in his *Summa de Ecclesia*, that since the spirit is superior to the body, as the sun is to the moon, the power and dignity of the papal see could in no way depend on the causality of the Empire or of Constantine. Nevertheless, at times Torquemada wanted it both ways. In a subsequent dispute, the canonist Sánchez de Arévalo claimed that since the Roman Empire was based not on right but only on violence and force, universal monarchy resides legitimately solely with the Roman Pontiff as Vicar of Christ. Torquemada responded that the stress on the emperors as merely usurping tyrants was prejudicial to the Roman Church, for it would necessarily follow that the Donation of Constantine, along with many other donations and benefactions various emperors had bestowed upon the popes, would thereby be null and void.[67]

For the Roman humanists of the mid-fifteenth century only one element of the Donation seemed historically unfounded. This was the account, drawn from the *Legenda sancti Silvestri*, crediting the pope as baptizer of Constantine. Vegio, as we have seen,[68] regarded this as apocryphal, relying instead on Eusebius's account of Constantine's conversion, and Domenichi presented to Pius II a critical examination of the questions surrounding Constantine's baptism, drawn from Greek as well as Latin sources.[69]

By the end of the fifteenth century, with the conciliar threat seemingly extinguished and the papacy restored to power in Italian and European affairs, even this concession disappeared. At the same time attacks on Valla became more frequent and more vociferous. Thus the humanist Pietro Edo (1427–1504), addressing a refutation of Valla's *Declamatio* to Alexander VI, characterized it as the product of a new "heresiarch." For Edo, Christ is *"summus tum pontifex, tum imperator,"* and as *imperator* he had triumphed over the Roman Empire. Further, Rome, from its founding, had been divinely ordained to be *caput orbis terrarum* and thence the see of the Vicar of Christ. From this perspective Constantine's actions stood outside of human history and instead formed part of sacred destiny. Indeed, for Edo the problem of the Donation's historical authenticity ultimately had little import. Since Constantine became a Christian through divine grace, and since likewise he moved his capital to Byzantium as a consequence of divine intervention, then the Donation, too, belonged to the category of divine inspiration. Therefore to attack it as inauthentic or invalid smacks of heresy.[70]

In early sixteenth-century Rome the hierocratic conclusions of the canonists triumphed. Once the Donation was safely removed from the human to the divine realm, then historical and philological criticism of the document proved irrelevant. As Cardinal Domenico Iacobazzi (d. 1527/ 28) remarked, "to dispute about the said Donation seems nowadays a matter to be left to the idly curious."[71]

Even former critics of the Donation could be made to recant. In Zaccaria Ferreri's *Somnium*, the dream-vision ascent through the heavenly spheres with Dante guiding the way, which served as this former curialist's apology to Leo X for supporting the French-sponsored *conciliabulum* of Pisa and as a supplication for reconciliation with Rome, the author relates that his vision came to him one night after he had been reading late. The book calling forth such night labors was, significantly, an account of Constantine's deeds—his conquest of Rome through the power of the Cross, his cure from leprosy, and his concession to the

Roman pontiffs of Italy and all the western lands, along with the scepter, triple diadem, and other symbols of imperial sovereignty. But then sleep overcame him, and he had nodded off. During the course of his dream-vision, however, the matter of the Donation returned. When he encountered Dante, the Florentine made a telling confession. Before he had been permitted to enter Paradise he had had to spend a lengthy period in Purgatory atoning for his error in holding that the earthly *imperium* of Caesar stood independent of papal authority; instead, as Vicars of Christ the popes preside over the whole globe.[72]

On the other hand, Ulrich von Hutten's enthusiastic publication of Valla's *Declamatio* in 1517 only proved, from the Roman point of view, how questioning the Donation's authenticity aided the schismatic defamers of papal primacy. For Agostino Steuco (1497/98–1548), Vatican librarian under Paul III and enthusiast of the *philosophia perennis*, whose *Contra Laurentium Vallam de donatione Constantini* appeared in 1546, Valla's work constituted a direct assault on the *regia Pontificatus dignitas* essential to maintaining the Christian religion and was therefore tantamount to impugning the Church's *maiestas*.[73]

In short, the papal court during the pontificates of Julius II and Leo X pursued visions of imperial grandeur untrammeled by self-criticism as to the legitimacy of temporal power. Only in the aftermath of the Sack did Guicciardini, who had served both Medici popes as governor of Emilia-Romagna, passionately lament papal secular ambitions. Concluding an excursus on medieval ecclesiastical history—a section expurgated from most early editions of the *Storia d'Italia*—Guicciardini explicitly denied the historical veracity of the Donation, and charged that the popes over time had tragically diverted more and more of their energies away from salvation of souls. Shamelessly selling sacred things, they gave all their thoughts to worldly greatness.[74] In the opening years of the sixteenth century, as yet unchastened by the 1527 Sack, few Renaissance Romans even thought to ponder such matters. The *renovatio imperii* was the driving ambition.

THE CAPITOL RENEWED

Beginning with Nicholas V, the Renaissance popes gave visual expression to the imperial renewal of Rome by rebuilding the centers of sovereign power within the city—the Capitol and the Vatican complex. In antiquity the Capitoline Hill had been venerated as a religious and political focal point. There arose the important temple to Jupiter Optimus Maximus, and there, too, was the climactic goal of triumphal processions. During the Middle Ages, however, the Capitoline's function as a symbol of Roman power and majesty was largely lost. The thirteenth-century Franciscan church of S. Maria d'Aracoeli dominated the site; and its orientation toward the populated districts of the city but away from the Forum Romanum was repeated in the façade of the Palazzo del Senatore, the seat of Roman communal government built during the pontificate of Boniface VIII on the ruins of the Roman Tabularium (the archives building). The ancient urbanistic and politically symbolic link between the Capitol and the Forum was thus severed. Nonetheless the medieval Palazzo del Senatore provided the setting for the legislative and judicial enactments of Roman communal government, with the adjacent church of the Aracoeli—connected since the mid-fourteenth century to the town below by a monumental staircase—fulfilling the occasional need for a large assembly hall. In the early fifteenth century, despite sharing in the neglect and deterioration that afflicted all of Rome during the Avignonese period and the Great Schism, the Capitoline managed to preserve vestiges of its function as a center of civic governance.[75]

In 1447 the newly elected Nicholas V began the Capitol's restoration. In the first few weeks of his pontificate he concluded an accord with the officials of the Roman commune as to the rights and responsibilities of each in the governance of the city of Rome. This attained, he next was determined to embellish the Capitol as a seat of municipal government. The façade of the dilapidated Palazzo del Senatore was regularized, with emphasis placed on the new, large, square-crossed windows of the *piano nobile.* Two towers added to the rear of the building and a slender campanile arising from its center contributed to this enlarged structure's more severe and imposing mien. Indeed it now resembled a *castello* of north Italian ducal derivation, rather than a central Italian *palazzo communale.* To the right of this refurbished building, and forming an oblique angle to it, Nicholas constructed a new municipal palace. This Palazzo dei Conservatori, which housed that body of Roman councillors, was given a row of square-crossed windows on its *piano nobile,* thus repeating the dominant architectural theme of the Palazzo del Senatore façade; and by demarcating the southwest side of the Capitoline Hill the new building defined a piazza at the hill's apex.[76]

It was this new Palazzo dei Conservatori which became the recipient, in 1471, of Sixtus IV's donation of a collection of Greek and Roman bronzes. Among these were a Hellenistic sculpture of a youth pulling a thorn from his foot (the *spinario*); a Roman portrayal of a boy participating in a pagan ritual sacrifice (a *camillus*); fragments of an imperial figure, including a colossal head and an enormous arm holding a globe, popularly known as the *Palla Sansonis,* Samson's ball (some Renaissance antiquarians believed it represented Nero, but it is now thought to be the Emperor Constantius II); and, most important, the Etruscan she-wolf who nurtured Romulus and Remus and thus symbolized ancient Rome. During the Middle Ages these bronzes had stood on the top of ancient

columns outside the Lateran. There they had functioned as didactic-
moralizing emblems of papal authority and of the triumph of Christianity
over pagan idolatry. Removal to the Capitoline freed them from these
medieval meanings, and their new setting accorded with Nicholas V's
intention that this be a renewed civic center. Yet the bronzes were not to
be admired merely as museum objects, representative of the artistic
accomplishments of Greco-Roman antiquity. Whatever aesthetic value
was attached to them was superseded by their function as testaments to
Rome's ancient virtue and surpassing achievement. This, indeed, is the
motive Sixtus expresses in the inscription commemorating their "return"
to the Roman people.[77] Several of the bronzes, in fact, were not exhibited
inside the Palazzo, but rather adorned its exterior. The colossal head and
the arm holding the globe, displayed in the portico, thus provided a
visible symbol of Rome's universal dominion; and the she-wolf, positioned above the main entrance to the palace, embodied the totemic
power of Roman majesty.[78]

Subsequent papal additions to the collection of Capitoline sculpture
contributed to this same end of celebrating the glory of Rome. A larger
than life-sized statue in gilded bronze of Hercules—a figure symbolizing
for Renaissance Romans the choice of the hard, steep path to virtue—was
donated by Sixtus IV after its discovery in the ruined temple of Hercules
in the Forum Boarium. Innocent VIII removed there, too, the head and
limbs of a colossal marble statue of Constantine excavated near the
Basilica of Maxentius.[79] Later Leo X provided the marble reliefs of Marcus Aurelius and also installed before the Palazzo dei Conservatori two
antique marble river gods, which came from the ruins of the Constantinian baths on the Quirinal. One, accompanied by a sphinx, represented the
Nile; the other, with a tiger, symbolized the Tigris, but the tiger was
eventually replaced in the 1560s by a she-wolf suckling Romulus and
Remus and thus became a statue of the Tiber. More directly related to the
ancient Capitoline's political and ceremonial significance was the discovery, in 1546, of the tablets listing the consuls and the triumphs of the
ancient Roman republic. Upon exhumation, these *Fasti Consulares* and
Triumphales were affixed to the walls of the Palazzo.[80]

As these symbols of Roman triumph, power, and majesty multiplied
on the Capitoline, the Capitol's actual role in municipal government
diminished. Increasing papal control of Rome's civic affairs was apparent
already by the later years of Nicholas V's pontificate and came to be
consolidated under Sixtus IV. The papal-sponsored revival of ancient
Roman glory thus annulled traditional civic liberties; and the antique
sculpture of a lion tearing a horse—a stern reminder of communal
justice—gave way to the ascendency of the she-wolf. This transformation
of the Capitol from seat of municipal power to scenographic image and
erudite museum proceeded further under Leo X. In 1514 he stipulated

that the *Conservatori* attend lectures in Roman history before their meetings. A decade later, under Clement VII, a library was also planned for
the Palazzo dei Conservatori. More urbanistically tangible a sign of the
usurpation of former municipal liberties was the covered passageway,
elevated some thirty-five feet above the ground, Paul III constructed to
connect Palazzo Venezia, which he used as a summer palace, to the
Franciscan monastery attached to the Aracoeli on the Capitoline. At a
later point in Paul's pontificate this bridge debouched at its Capitoline end
onto the newly built Farnese Tower, where a small, enclosed garden and
large arcaded loggias offered a cool retreat from Rome's summer heat.
Romans objected that the great masonry piers of the elevated structure
impeded traffic flow; but not the least of its attractions to the pope must
have been the opportunity to pass undetected, high above the swelter and
clamor of Roman street life, to his Capitoline aerie.[81]

By the end of the Quattrocento, instead of wielding actual power,
the *Conservatori* and other Roman civic officials were assigned roles in the
increasingly elaborate ceremonies celebrating Rome's renewal. Thus, as
we have seen, the Capitoline became the starting point for the processions
of Carnival *carri*, and it became, too, the setting for the revived Palilia.
Here, also, in 1513 was created the costly temporary theater in which Leo
X's brother and nephew were made Roman citizens. Just inside the
triumphal arch entrance to this theater, which occupied the whole of the
piazza crowning the top of the Capitoline, were placed, on square pillars,
the colossal bronze hand and globe and the bronze she-wolf. In this
placement these ancient sculptures imparted the further allusion to the
now-united destinies of the Medici (the globe was seen as a reference to
the Medici *palle*) and of Rome.[82]

The linked destinies of Leo X and Rome culminated in the commissioning, by the *Conservatori*, of a colossal marble statue of Leo X, intended
for the Capitoline. The unveiling of this statue, likened by a contemporary poet to Phidias's famed sculpture of Zeus at Olympia, was planned as
the climax to extensive festivities. In this way, Leo X, Jove-like in his
lawful authority over heaven, earth, and hell, would assume permanent
command of the hill from which Jupiter once ruled the city and the world.
But just as these planned festivities neared completion, Leo suddenly
died. A lengthy oration composed for the occasion by the humanist Blosio
Palladio survives, however. Its central theme is the fusion of Roman
classical culture and Roman Christianity under the new Christian Roman Empire, ruled through the wise beneficence of the new Augustus,
Leo X.[83]

By the early Cinquecento, then, the *renovatio* of the Capitoline had
resulted not in the creation of a center for enlightened and socially
conscious public discourse, but instead in a ceremonial center, elevated
above humdrum daily life, where Rome's destiny and eternal glory could

be acclaimed.[84] In this setting, what mattered was epideictic rhetoric, the oratorical genre of praise, not the *genus deliberativum* of political decision-making.

Manifest symbol of Roman sovereignty, the Capitol attained its final form and its most far-reaching claims through the ideological assertions of Paul III and the architectural genius of Michelangelo. In 1536, when Charles V was accorded a triumphal reception in Rome in recognition of his conquest of Tunis, the Capitoline Hill, despite the previous renovations, still retained a medieval air. Contemporary drawings show, too, an unkempt rusticity: the apex of the hill was reached by a circuitous path, and the irregular dimensions of the unlevelled and unpaved piazza contributed to the sense of disorder.[85] The route of Charles's triumphal procession did not pass over the Capitoline—lack of a suitable access forced a detour around it—and the hill's dishevelled state apparently caused the pope further embarrassment. Since Paul III was making use of the hill as a summer retreat, this likely provided a further inducement to give a more imposing and majestic appearance to Rome's Capitol.

Paul's first step was to transfer to the Capitoline the gilded bronze equestrian monument of Marcus Aurelius. The only surviving example of this type of Roman imperial sculpture, this "*Caballus Constantini*," as it was popularly called, had stood during the Middle Ages with the other bronzes outside the Lateran. Although Sixtus IV removed these other ancient sculptures to the Capitol, he seems never to have entertained a similar destiny for the Marcus Aurelius; in fact, he ordered repairs to be made, and he commissioned a new pedestal, which imparted to the statue a higher and more commanding position before the Lateran Palace.[86] The first suggestion of transferral to the Capitol was a proposal of the *Conservatori*, made in 1498 to Alexander VI, who vetoed the idea.[87] By 1537, however, Paul III was determined to remove the Marcus Aurelius from its "lowly setting"—before the cathedral church of Rome, *mater et caput ecclesiarum!*—in order to make it the focal point of a renewed Piazza del Campidoglio. The Lateran canons objected, but papal will proved decisive. Michelangelo was then ordered to create a new base for the monument, and by 1539 it had been erected in the center of the Capitoline square.[88]

The significance Paul attached to a more dignified placement of the Marcus Aurelius can be seen in one of his medals, in which the statue, on its newly-inscribed base, is shown; the inscription on the medal reads: HANC. PETVNT. MIRACVLA. SEDEM. The implication is that marvels like the Marcus Aurelius have their proper setting only on the Capitol. Beyond this, the statue's grave air of authority and beneficent gesture signified the peace-making virtues of the *optimus princeps*—thus expressing Paul's own aspirations as pope. Moreover it symbolized the world-sovereignty of Roman imperial rule, to which the Roman Church was heir.[89]

28. *Marcus Aurelius,* bronze equestrian statue (2nd c. A.D.). Rome, Piazza del Campidoglio. (Photo: Alinari/Art Resource, NY)

This ideological emphasis on imperial sovereignty would have been further accentuated if Paul had fulfilled his intentions to add to the statue decoration of the Capitoline the ancient colossal marble figures of the Dioscuri, located on the Quirinal, and an ancient sculpture of Jupiter. The Quirinal *colossi* in Paul's time had not yet been correctly identified as Castor and Pollux, the twin saviors of Rome. Instead the most frequent current explanation was that both represented Alexander the Great, one statue the work of Phidias, the other produced by his "rival" Praxiteles. Besides providing a convenient allusion to the pope's given name (Alessandro), placing these images of Alexander at the top of the long ramp leading to the Piazza del Campidoglio would have suggested the Hellenistic world-empire, established by the Macedonian.[90] Alexander's achievements, in turn, served as a harbinger of the even greater universal sovereignty of Rome attained by the Antonine emperors (symbolized in the Marcus Aurelius).

The ancient statue of Jupiter was to have been placed in a niche in Michelangelo's monumental stairway to the main portal of the Palazzo del Senatore. Positioning it there would have put it directly on line with the "Alexanders" and the Marcus Aurelius, and beneath the entrance baldacchino of the palace with its ritual allusions both to imperial authority and to the altars of paleo-Christian basilicas. Providing a Jupiter image for the Capitoline formed an appropriate inclusion in any program to restore its ancient meaning, since in Roman antiquity the main temple of the hill had been devoted to this god's cult. But, as in the case of the Quirinal *colossi*, reference to Paul III was also undoubtedly implied. In Salviati's painting in Palazzo Farnese depicting the peace negotiations held at Nice in 1538, which involved Paul III, Francis I, and Charles V, the Farnese pontiff appears enthroned in the guise of Jove, the father of the gods. Jovian, too, in its symbolism is the reverse of Paul III's medal of the Marcus Aurelius monument. This shows a nude Ganymede, accompanied by a huge eagle, the symbol of Jupiter. The nude youth pours a liquid, probably nectar, from an amphora on his shoulder onto flowers in full bloom—the Farnese lily. The elliptical inscription—ΦΕΡΝΗ.ΖΗΝΟΣ-ΕΥΡΑΙΝΕΙ: "the dowry of Zeus," "he irrigates well"—constitutes in the first two Greek words a play on the Farnese name, and the implied meaning of the whole relates to the pope's paternal task of nurturing.

Contemporaries similarly understood the Farnese pontiff's adopting the bundles of lightning rods for a Farnese *impresa* as a reference to Paul III's likeness to Jove. Thus the succession Alexander-Antonine emperor-Jupiter would have symbolized the transmission of world hegemony from the empires of Greece and Rome to the *imperium* of the Roman Church governed by the Farnese pope.[91]

Paul III, who had been named a cardinal in the early years of Alexander's pontificate, lived through the Roman Renaissance heyday of

29. Medal of Paul III, by Alessandro Cesati,
called Il Grechetto. The reverse shows the
nude figure of Ganymede and the eagle
symbolizing Jupiter. Washington, D.C.,
National Gallery of Art, Samuel H. Kress Collection. (Photo: National Gallery of Art)

Julius II and Leo X, and his ambitions as pope reveal the formative influence of these earlier imperial aspirations. After 1549, however, with Spanish power entrenched on the peninsula, and Counter-Reformation impulses coming to the fore, imperial ideology in papal Rome appeared increasingly anachronistic. Thus when the statue program of the Capitoline was completed in the last third of the sixteenth century, a different emphasis developed. Instead of the Quirinal *colossi* smaller ancient statues of the Dioscuri (discovered in the Theater of Pompey) were brought to the hill—this time properly identified as Castor and Pollux—and instead of a Jupiter statue in the stairway niche there was placed an ancient sculpture of the goddess Roma. Rather than world hegemony, these sculptures symbolized, less ambitiously, the protection and preservation of Rome.[92]

Paul III's plans for renewal of the Capitol were not limited to sculptural embellishment. As the proper setting for these symbols of majesty, he conceived a comprehensive architectural transformation of the hill's apex, and it was Michelangelo who received the commission for this undertaking. Determining Michelangelo's initial plans for the hill is difficult, in part because actual work on the Capitoline progressed very slowly (it was completed only in the mid-seventeenth century). Besides this, there is the problem of Michelangelo's habitual procedure as architect, one that reveals a continual evolution in thought and design. What he eventually conceived was a trapezoidal piazza, its perimeter defined by the existing palaces (the façades of which were totally redesigned in an essentially classical idiom based on the colossal order, but with subtle chiaroscural refinements) and by the new Palazzo Nuovo. The latter had no institutional function, but served only to provide an architectural mirror image to the Palazzo dei Conservatori. The enclosed unity of this sacred space—more like a room open to the sky than a city square—was underlined by the long access ramp and the balustrade, adorned by sculpture, which demarcated the front parapet. Visitors ascended to the Piazza del Campidoglio as pilgrims to the symbolic focal point of eternal Rome, *caput mundi*.[93]

Having reached the piazza the beholder's view becomes riveted upon the Marcus Aurelius, placed at the raised center of an oval pavement inscribed within the trapezoid perimeter. Indeed the monument's potency is subtly enhanced by the optical effects of the obliquely positioned symmetrical palaces, which produce the anti-perspectival result of compressing space toward the viewer rather than the illusion of spatial depth. The convex oval pavement, divided by an elaborate curvilinear grid into twelve compartments, implies a cosmological symbolism. In fact, as Ackerman suggests,[94] it evokes the legendary shield of Achilles, which was adorned by celestial signs, and was adopted by Alexander the Great along with the epithet *Kosmokrator* (ruler of the Universe). This title and

30. Piazza del Campidoglio, Rome. (Photo: Alinari/Art Resource, NY)

the shield subsequently became emblems of the Roman emperors, so that the pavement with the idealized emperor at the center reveals the same symbolic meaning of imperial succession as Paul III's never-completed sculptural program.

The corona of sun's rays (at the pavement's center) was another attribute of the *Kosmokrator*, and this along with other motifs connected the ancient world-ruler with Apollo, the Sun-God. Greek myth associated Apollo's shrine at Delphi with the *omphalos* or *umbilicus mundi*, the navel of the cosmos. The ancient Romans figuratively moved the *umbilicus mundi* from Delphi to the Roman Forum, and medieval legend transferred this to the Capitol.[95] Thus the Marcus Aurelius as *Kosmokrator*-Apollo stands at the nodal point of the universe. The locus of power in Renaissance Rome again assumed a cosmic perspective.

THE VATICAN REBUILT

Vital as the restored Capitol was to manifesting Rome's universal sovereignty, even more fundamental for the Renaissance vision of Rome's eternal destiny was a rebuilt Vatican. Here, too, as with the Capitoline Hill, Nicholas V's plans, as recorded in Manetti's *Vita*, mark the starting point for a new conception. In essence, they specify the key elements for creating a new sacred city for the area around St. Peter's.

During the Middle Ages the frequently itinerant papacy made the Lateran Palace, not the Vatican, its principal Roman residence. Since St. John Lateran was the cathedral church of Rome, residing there emphasized the pope's authority as Bishop of Rome. When Martin V returned the papacy to Rome, he likewise gave primary attention to restoring the Lateran complex, though he mainly resided himself at the Colonna family palace next to SS. Apostoli. He did, however, choose the Lateran as his place of burial. Eugenius IV's pontificate, spent for the most part away from Rome, showed no departure from established practice.[96]

Nicholas V's decision to make the Vatican the permanent papal domicile thus pointed in a new direction. He believed that the popes, restored in their authority as successors to the priestly power of the keys uniquely given by Christ to Peter, should exercise this sacerdotal charge from the sacred precinct of the Apostle's tomb. To enhance in the public mind the dignity of the papal office, he intended the whole Borgo Leonino to be systematically rebuilt as a unified urbanistic and architectural expression of papal primacy.

In his program for refounding the Leonine city, Nicholas V first attended to rebuilding the walls. The area enclosed within them was increased slightly by including more of the slope of the Mons Saccorum, and there a great round defensive tower took shape. The intention was to

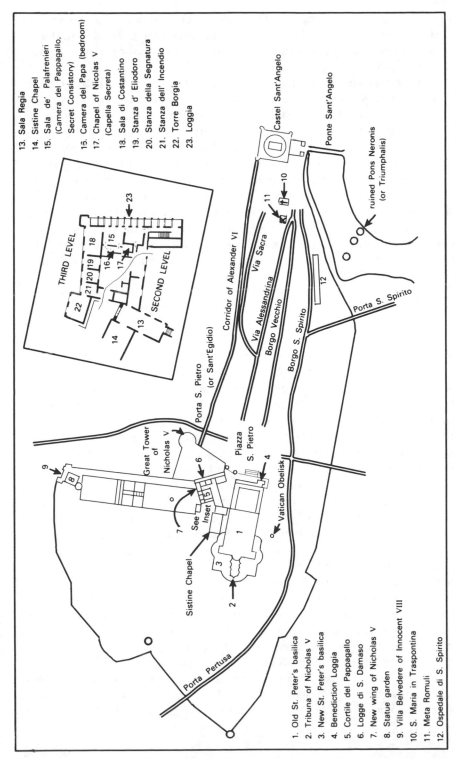

13. Sala Regia
14. Sistine Chapel
15. Sala de' Palafrenieri (Camera del Pappagallo, Secret Consistory)
16. Camera del Papa (bedroom)
17. Chapel of Nicolas V (Capella Secreta)
18. Sala di Costantino
19. Stanza d' Eliodoro
20. Stanza della Segnatura
21. Stanza dell' Incendio
22. Torre Borgia
23. Loggia

1. Old St. Peter's basilica
2. Tribuna of Nicholas V
3. New St. Peter's basilica
4. Benediction Loggia
5. Cortile del Pappagallo
6. Logge di S. Damaso
7. New wing of Nicholas V
8. Statue garden
9. Villa Belvedere of Innocent VIII
10. S. Maria in Traspontina
11. Meta Romuli
12. Ospedale di S. Spirito

The Borgo Leonino (Vatican region) in the early sixteenth century solidify defenses by connecting this new tower by means of a new wall to the Castel Sant'Angelo. The latter received improved outer defenses and in its refurbished state served as the actual and symbolic fortress-anchor for the whole sacred city.

This enclosed urban space, set off so distinctly from the disordered, mundane city across the Tiber, then became the subject of a comprehensive, rational plan. A large piazza was to be created before the *castello*, and another, centered on the repositioned Vatican obelisk, was to open out before the entrances to the basilica and Vatican palace. These two *piazze* were to be linked by three parallel streets, lined with porticoed shops, where members of the Curia could reside. This ordered arrangement of buildings, streets, and squares—their separate dignity enhanced by the intelligibility of the overall design—reveals an urbanistic conception in accordance with the architectural theories Alberti was developing in these years, and strongly suggests his collaboration in Nicholas's project. The overall scheme aimed at preparing the visitor spiritually for entrance into the basilica of the Apostle and the palace of his successor.[97]

Nicholas's second area of concern involved Old St. Peter's itself. By the middle of the fifteenth century, the Constantinian basilica had reached a seriously decayed state. Indeed, in *De re aedificatoria* Alberti states that the long walls of the nave leaned out of perpendicular nearly two meters, a situation in which the slightest earthquake could cause the whole building to collapse.[98] A major restoration thus seemed essential, though as yet no one suggested creating an entirely new building. Tall bell-towers were to be built flanking the vestibule, providing a new symmetry to the façade and also contributing to the new system of fortifications. The great Roman bronze *pigna* in the center of the atrium was also to be restored as a fountain. Nevertheless, the basic appearance of the forecourt was to remain unchanged, and the shored-up nave and aisles were also to retain their paleo-Christian basilical design.

Where Nicholas and his architectural advisers did envision major changes was at the head of the church. A new transept, domed crossing, and much enlarged choir (*tribuna*) were to be constructed there. The main impetus behind these changes stemmed from liturgical and ceremonial considerations. If the basilica was to provide the setting for the more elaborate celebration of the cult—one of Nicholas's primary concerns as pope—then this necessitated a larger and more decorous space behind the altar. Providing for the anticipated increase of clergy in attendance explains, too, the newly created side entrance into the basilica. This connected via a spiral staircase to the Vatican Palace, granting the pope and the papal court a more suitable ceremonial entrance into the church.

Attention to the crossing and apse end of Old St. Peter's is explained, too, by their greater sanctity. Here the main altar stood directly over the tomb of the Apostle, and here at the head of the choir was the intended placement for a raised papal throne, the ceremonial seat for the living occupant of St. Peter's chair. Improved illumination from the new dome and design elements derived from classical Roman architecture (four great columns were brought from the ruins of the baths of Agrippa next to the Pantheon for use in the reconstruction project) would have emphasized the more sacred nature of this space.

At Nicholas's death, however, none of these plans had come near to realization. Some older structures beyond the west end of the basilica, including the ancient mausoleum of Probus, were demolished to make way for the new *tribuna sancti Petri*, but the walls of the new choir arose only a few meters above the ground level. Work on the choir ceased upon the pontiff's death, resumed briefly under Paul II, but by the opening years of the sixteenth century still consisted merely of foundations.[99]

The third aspect of Nicholas V's rebuilding plans for the Vatican centered on the Vatican palace. Here the pope planned more extensive changes, though here, too, as in the case of the basilica, much medieval construction was to be retained. From the early Middle Ages, in fact, palace structures had adjoined the atrium of St. Peter's. In the thirteenth century, under Innocent III and Nicholas III, substantial additions appeared, to the effect that the earlier nucleus, or lower palace, became office space for Curial departments, while a new chapel, ceremonial rooms, and papal apartment came to be located further up the Mons Saccorum, thus forming an upper palace. Nicholas V preserved this basic arrangement, but gave considerable attention to refurbishing and redecorating the various public rooms of the apartment wing, which faced out towards the future Cortile di S. Damaso and beyond to Castel Sant'Angelo. In this wing he also created the small private chapel frescoed by Fra Angelico with scenes from the lives of the protomartyrs Stephen and Lawrence. At right angles to this section of the palace, Nicholas constructed a new wing. This enclosed the north side of the future Cortile del Pappagallo. The lowest (basement) level of this new projection was given over to storage rooms, while the ground floor was probably intended to house the papal library. The upper two stories (which became respectively the Appartamento Borgia and the Raphael stanze) each consisted of a series of rooms, apparently used for meetings of various tribunals and to conduct the ecclesiastical and secular governance entrusted to the pope.[100]

Nicholas V planned this refurbished palace with its new wing to be enclosed by the impressive system of fortifications connected to the great round tower. This same appearance of fortified strength was also to confront the visitor reaching the new entrance to the palace, for here he intended to insert a triumphal arch between two towers. Such a design recalls the Holy Roman Emperor Frederick II's thirteenth-century gateway to his dominions at Capua, and resembles also Alfonso of Aragon's mid-fifteenth century portal to the Castel Nuovo at Naples. Behind these walls, between the apartment wing and the Mons Saccorum, Nicholas's plans called for the creation of a lush garden, filled with fruit trees and herbs and watered by fountains. Here three new ceremonial buildings were to be built: a new *cappella palatina*, a hall for conclaves and other assemblies (to be surmounted by a benediction loggia overlooking Piazza S. Pietro), and a "theater" (*theatrum*) described by Manetti as an arcade with marble columns. Since neither the theater nor the other structures planned for the garden ever appeared, it remains uncertain whether Manetti meant by *theatrum* a place for theatrical performances. In these same years, however, Alberti discussed in *De re aedificatoria* the nature of the classical *theatrum*, making it likely that what Nicholas indeed intended was a suitable place for recitations and dramatic presentations.[101]

The theater aside, most of Nicholas's projects for the Vatican Palace, both accomplished and planned, had antecedents either in the papal palace at Avignon or in Italian princely courts.[102] Nonetheless, the pope's plans provided the basic framework for subsequent construction in the Vatican for the remainder of the fifteenth century, even if the resulting buildings emerged on different sites. Thus the Loggia of Benediction, the work of Pius II, was constructed in front of St. Peter's, where it over-looked the newly paved Piazza S. Pietro, the restored steps, and Paolo Romano's colossal statues of Peter and Paul.[103] Similarly, the Sistine Chapel, built on the site of Nicholas III's old *capella magna*, provided both a chapel for the papal court and a suitable hall for use by the cardinals during conclaves.

Nicholas V's immediate successors lacked his preoccupation with the Vatican. Pius II gave much of his attention to Pienza, and Paul II created the Palazzo di S. Marco complex in the center of Rome.[104] Sixtus IV, however, returned the principal papal residence to the Vatican Palace, Innocent VIII enlarged and modernized the lower palace and built the Villa Belvedere, and Alexander VI redecorated the second story of Nicholas V's new wing as the Borgia Apartments and added to it the fortress-like Torre Borgia.[105]

Innocent VIII's Villa Belvedere forms a departure from Nicholas V's plans. Perched on the top of Monte Sant'Egidio it faced away from the Vatican. From here a magnificent prospect opened to the north, over-looking the Prati and stretching outward to the Tiber, Monte Mario, and Monte Soracte. Removed physically and psychologically from the de-mands of the palace, this structure, the first to contain all the characteris-tics that constituted the Roman Renaissance idea of the villa, featured open-air dining in its loggia-pavilion and offered a secluded afternoon retreat for the ailing pontiff. Built in two campaigns, the asymmetrical result lacked architectural distinction, but the villa's site and orientation complied with Vitruvian (and Albertian) theories of villa construction, and the decoration program with its illusionistic landscapes of famous

Italian cities also had its basis in the artistic ideas of ancient Rome revived by the humanists.[106]

Haphazardly worked on for half a century, the Vatican Palace on Julius II's accession in 1503 comprised a disjointed assemblage of buildings, distinctly unclassical in appearance. Not without reason, military considerations had assumed first priority—even the Villa Belvedere was topped with crenellations—but Julius II was determined to change this. For the first time since Nicholas V the Vatican complex came to be subjected to a comprehensive plan.

For the new Julius Caesar, restorer of the Roman *imperium*, the persistence of medieval elements in the papal palace must have struck a discordant note. Particularly outmoded was the façade of the old thirteenth-century apartment wing, which overlooked the *giardino segreto* and faced outward toward the city of Rome. Tall, pyramid-roofed towers marked each end of this wing and the sloped roof and irregular windows of the central section added to the medieval impression. Under Bramante, succeeded by Raphael, this highly visible exterior became completely transformed. The façade was extended more than twenty meters toward Piazza S. Pietro, eliminating the medieval tower at this end and improving the overall proportions. Over the closed-in ground floor, thus made into a cryptoportico, three superimposed stories of galleries were created. In the vault of the second, Raphael's assistants provided the painted and stucco decoration, in elegantly classicizing style, of the "Vatican Loggia," devoted mainly to Old Testament scenes. Similarly Roman in its classicism is the travertine exterior of this renovated structure. Surviving examples of Roman imperial architecture in the city, notably the Colosseum, furnished design elements, and the use of Doric, Ionic, and Corinthian "orders" for the pilasters and capitals of the three loggias reflects the same impulse of Roman imperial revival. The effect of the new Logge di S. Damaso was to project from the Mons Vaticanus a new Septizonium, which would dominate the city of Rome just as Septimius Severus's palace on the Palatine had dominated it in the earlier age of Empire.[107]

The Della Rovere pontiff's imperial conception of the papacy precluded as insufficient, however, the mere refurbishing of existing medieval buildings. Not just the formal elements of decoration but also the concepts, functions, and intentions of imperial Roman architecture should assume a new life, and in Bramante Julius II found an architect of genius capable of recreating these characteristics of Roman design on a monumental scale.

Bramante's conscious revival of imperial Roman ideas for city planning can be seen in a number of projects undertaken for Julius II. One was the rebuilding of Loreto. In the colonnaded "forum," the classical façade of the domed "Temple," and the concave exedra of the Palazzo Apostolico—where the pope could stand forth like an ancient emperor for the *adoratio* of his people—appear clear echoes of Julius Caesar's Forum in Rome with its Temple of Venus Genetrix; indeed a deliberate parallel between Caesar and Venus and Julius II and the Virgin of Loreto may well have been intended. In the domed church, visible over a vast distance from its hill-top elevation, there is the likely suggestion, too, of the earthly image of Jerusalem rising on its sacred mount. But in this way, as Bruschi remarks,[108] the Virgin's humble cottage at Nazareth—the Holy House—became transformed into the imperial Jerusalem of Julius II.

A second such project to recreate an ancient Roman imperial city involved Civitavecchia. There Bramante seems to have intended, at least at one point, to restore the ancient Trajanic port as a vast, curved-mole marine amphitheater. Such a structure would permit water battles to be staged, just as in the ancient *naumachia*; in fact, one took place at Civitavecchia in honor of Julius II in 1509.[109]

Finally, in Rome itself Bramante conceived the Via Giulia-Piazza dei Tribunali plan for reconstructing the old area of Rome within the bend of the Tiber, opposite the Vatican. Here was to be established the actual and symbolic new seat of Roman justice.[110]

Each of these enormous urbanistic projects—none ever reached completion according to Bramante's intentions—reveals something of Julius II's imperial aspirations. But the most audacious of the Julian undertakings, begun at the very outset of his pontificate, was the decision to connect the old Vatican Palace nucleus to Innocent VIII's Villa Belvedere, distant some three hundred meters to the north. To do so meant spanning the intervening, upwardly sloping valley, until then given over to gardens and vineyards. In Bramante's design for this vast Cortile del Belvedere, the unevenly rising natural terrain was to be rationalized as a succession of terrace-courts, delimited at each side by corridors in the form of covered porticoes. The uppermost story would provide a level link between the second story of Nicholas V's new wing of the palace and the ground floor of the villa. The lowest court, bound on the east and west by three-story façades defined by the Doric, Ionic, and Corinthian orders, and including for the second-floor windows alternating triangular and segmental pediments taken in their design from the Pantheon, would function as a place for court spectacles. Here Nicholas V's ambition for a Vatican theater finally came to be realized. But the entertainments presented did not include classical drama. Instead, what the pope and his entourage saw staged from the windows of the Raphael stanze, and what lesser personages witnessed from the stairs doubling as theater seats that connected the lower to the intermediate terrace, were bullfights (the first took place in 1509) and knightly tournaments. In their violence and bloodshed these recall the gladiatorial games and elaborate mock battles held for the ancient emperors' pleasure. This resemblance did not escape the notice of contemporaries. In Perino del Vaga's view of the Cortile dating from the 1530s—a painting that in style assumes the guise of an ancient Roman architectural landscape—the lower Belvedere court appears as an artificial lake, in which a mock naval battle is being fought. In Perino's archaizing "reconstruction," Bramante's theater thus stands forth as the recreation of Nero's Vatican *naumachia*.[111]

The upper two terrace-courts of the Cortile Bramante designed as formal gardens, to be planted with boxtrees and parterres interspersed with fountains. Here the clamor of court spectacle would give way to the mood of restorative leisure summed up in the humanists' ideal of *otium*. Along the central axis, however, more striking architectural elements appeared. In direct line with the gigantic marble basin brought from the Baths of Titus in 1504 to serve as a fountain center for the lower court, flights of ramps framing a nymphaeum linked the second to the third court. Beyond and above this, at the rear of the upper court, rose a monumental exedra. Here a recessed hemicycle enclosed an annular raised platform, reached by a flight of eight convex and eight concave stairs. The idea for the ramps and the exedra seems to have been inspired by the remains of the ancient Roman sanctuary of the goddess Fortuna at nearby Palestrina; this, Ackerman suggests, provided Bramante with "the best preserved and most comprehensible answer to the problem of monumental construction on sharply rising ground."[112]

Behind the exedra a smaller enclosed garden, conceived as a statue court, provided the final link between the Cortile and the villa. Here were placed the *Apollo Belvedere* and other recently discovered ancient statuary, including the *Laocoön*, which made this the area of most absorbing interest to contemporary visitors.

The triumphal arch elements, the borrowings from the Pantheon and the Theater of Marcellus, the use of the nymphaeum and exedra—all evoke Roman classicism, but more truly Roman in Bramante's design are the colossal scale, the sense of grandeur, and the control of nature. As Ackerman has pointed out,[113] this sudden resurrection of a form of architecture extinct since antiquity depended upon extensive archeological research into the palace-villas of imperial antiquity. The sources for such an investigation comprised both literary sources, such as Pliny the Younger's description of his Tuscan villa, and surviving Roman ruins, notably Hadrian's Villa at Tivoli and the Palatine Hippodrome. Perhaps the most suggestive ancient sources, however, were the descriptions of Nero's Golden House (from Tacitus, *Annals*, XV, 42, and Suetonius, *De vita Caesarum: Nero*, 31). Just as the mile-long triple porticoes of Nero's fabulous city-villa spanned the valley between the Palatine and Esquiline Hills, so the second Julius Caesar's Cortile del Belvedere, with its long "*triplices porticus*," transformed the Mons Vaticanus into a vast pleasure garden and stunning manifestation of imperial power.[114]

The immensity of the Cortile del Belvedere project made completion during Julius II's pontificate impossible. Construction continued under Leo X, with particular attention to the right-hand corridor, the only convenient connection between the palace and the now-famous statue garden. The ascetic, anti-humanistic Adrian VI, however, shut off access to the Cortile, and during Clement VII's troubled reign little headway was made. Paul III redirected building energies to Bramante's plan and in the late 1530s and '40s the decoration of the corridors and exedra gradually assumed final shape. Then, with large parts of Bramante's design still unfinished, Pirro Ligorio, architect to Pope Julius III, introduced major changes. To the upper court he added a suite of rooms, transforming the garden villa into a palace, and he later replaced the exedra with the grandiose Nicchione. Under Sixtus V (1585–90) a new wing to house the Vatican Library bisected the Cortile. By this step the terrace-courts became separate enclosed courtyards, thus destroying the vast perspective space that had formed the heart of Bramante's creation.[115]

If the Cortile during Julius II's pontificate existed in the main as an unrealized concept, the statue garden between the exedra and Innocent VIII's villa reached essential completion before the pontiff's death. Contemporary accounts describe this *locus amoenus* as a classical *viridarium*, abounding in fountains and vegetation. A profusion of laurels, cypresses, and other foliage evocative of classical antiquity covered part of the enclosed space, while orange trees set in a tiled pavement occupied the rest. In the central area was placed, as part of a fountain, an ancient river-god sculpture of the Tiber, which had been excavated from the site of an ancient sanctuary of Isis in the Campus Martius and brought to the Vatican in 1512. During Leo's pontificate this was joined by a statue of the Nile, also excavated from the Iseum. Other ancient marble sculptures were arranged in niches along the sides and in the corners of the court. As a cardinal, Giuliano della Rovere already possessed some important pieces of ancient statuary, including the *Apollo Belvedere*. Hence one motive in creating the Vatican statue garden was to provide a suitable site to display the pope's collection. Placing statues in a secluded garden retreat recreated, in addition, an essential characteristic of the ancient Roman villa, as described, for instance, by Pliny the Younger. But just as sculpture on the Campidoglio conveyed symbolic content relating to Rome's power and destiny, so we can suspect, too, that the statuary of the Vatican garden carried metaphorical meaning. Unlike the public forum of the Capitol, however, this private court served no overtly political purpose. Instead the statues evoked a variety of symbolic images, some with subtle political implications, others with none, but all susceptible to emblematic elaboration or poetic conceit—a form of seeing in keeping with the mood of contemplative reverie induced by the enclosed garden setting.[116]

Guarding the entrance to the statue garden stood the so-called *Commodus*, found near the Campo de' Fiori and moved to the Vatican under Julius II. Albertini identified it in 1509 as a statue of the Roman Emperor in the guise of Hercules holding Hylas. The inscription accompanying the statue admonished: PROCUL ESTE PROPHANI. The likely source for this utterance is the Cumaean sibyl's dire warning in the *Aeneid* (VI, 258) as Aeneas completes the rites permitting him to enter the nether world. The implied meaning is that the statue garden was a sacred grove, under the protection of Hercules, symbol of virtue. This meaning was reinforced by another statue, of *Hercules and Antaeus*, interpreted by Renaissance humanists as Virtue subduing earthly lust or Reason overcoming the life of the senses. For Gianfrancesco Pico della Mirandola, writing in 1512, the whole Vatican "grove" served, in fact, in one of its guises as a place of philosophic meditation, and thus brought to mind the site by the Ilissus near Athens, the setting of Plato's *Phaedrus*, where through the influence of the nymphs and of Dionysus a state of poetic ecstasy was attained. In this manifestation, the Vatican garden became a place consecrated to philosophic contemplation, conducive to the Neo-Platonic aspiration for communion with the Beyond.[117]

Besides symbolizing virtue, Hercules also was associated with the mythical Garden of the Hesperides: in one of his labors he obtained from the dragon-guarded tree at world's end the golden apples. In the statue garden, the grove of orange trees suggests this Hesperidean setting. Under the Medici pope, Leo X, this proved indeed a particularly appropriate symbolism, since the golden apples of the Hesperides had been identified from Lorenzo the Magnificent's time with the Medici *palle*. Hesperidean golden apples suggest, too, the appearance of Aphrodite, and offer a way to understand the statue of *Venus Felix*. In part she symbolized the generative power of love, and thus provided a link to the themes of virtue and immortality embodied in Hercules.[118]

But Venus Felix also had explicit ties to the destiny of the Roman Empire. As the mother of Aeneas, Venus was the patron goddess of the Roman people (in the mythic view of Roman history put forth in Virgil's poem). Significantly, too, Julius Caesar claimed descent from the goddess, and Augustus continued the cult of this divine mother of the *gens Iulia*. Moreover, the cognomen Felix, assumed by Sulla in 81 B.C., perhaps in relation to Aphroditean associations he, too, had cultivated, conveyed the meaning of imperial victory. In this respect VENVS FELIX frequently appeared in Roman imperial inscriptions and on Roman coinage; often in fact the goddess was depicted holding apple in hand. There is a further imperial association. During the Antonine period, the celebration of

Rome's founding took place in the Templum Urbis, a sanctuary dedicated jointly to Venus Felix and Genetrix and to Roma Aeterna.[119]

Venus allusions also accompany the "*Cleopatra*," a sculpture not correctly identified as Ariadne until the eighteenth century. According to Dio Cassius, Julius Caesar placed a golden statue of Cleopatra in the temple of Venus Genetrix he built in his Forum in Rome. Installed in a fountain-grotto setting in the Vatican garden, the *Cleopatra* statue evoked as well the popular Renaissance image of the sleeping nymph. Both motifs, in fact, appear in contemporary humanist descriptions of the languorous seductress's effigy. For Evangelista Maddaleni di Capodiferro, she suggested the memory of the Egyptian queen, who seduced Julius Caesar, conqueror of the Nile; and now the second Julius Caesar, he declares, has again tamed the Nile waters in creating the fountain-sculpture in the Vatican garden. For Castiglione instead, the image of the dead queen (the figure's pose and her bracelet, thought to represent the asp, implied for Renaissance observers Cleopatra's suicidal end) served as a reminder of the temptress's dolorous fate. In historical fact, her postmortem ignominy had been vividly displayed in Rome itself, during Augustus's triumph celebrating his victory over Antony and his consort: an effigy of the defeated Egyptian queen was borne aloft in the triumphal procession.[120]

In this last guise, the *Cleopatra* forms a tie to the *Apollo Belvedere*, since Augustus, vanquisher of Cleopatra and Antony at Actium, had seen his victory over the beastly "gods of the Nile" accomplished through the aid of the Sun-God. Apollo, indeed, was the god for the new Augustan age, and Augustus strongly favored the Apollonian cult, building a temple to him on the Palatine and including the god's symbols on his coinage. Like Augustus, Julius II cultivated Apollonian ties. Among these were the Sun-God's role in poetic inspiration (as in Raphael's *Parnassus* in the Stanza della Segnatura, and the "crowning of poets" in the Cortile del Belvedere) and his martial skills: in the 1513 Festa di Agone a figure of Apollo, bow in hand, helped celebrate the pope's achievement in defending Italian "liberty." Even more, Apollo symbolized the guardian spirit and presiding genius of Rome's imperial vocation. In Capodiferro's poem, the *Apollo Belvedere*, reincarnated as a living presence in his true home, the Mons Vaticanus, addresses Julius II, through whom the laws and the works of peace have taken on new life. You, "Apollo" declares to "Julius," stand watch over the city and the world (*urbi atque orbi*); your wisdom foresees all things, nor does unbridled cupidity urge you on; you desire to create, not destroy; through you the souls of men return to me and Rome rises up again; through your deeds the splendor of a new light is coming into the world and the edge of dark night yields.[121]

If the *Apollo Belvedere*, often "reconstructed" in Renaissance sketchbooks as holding a bow, formed a symbol of victory and enlightened

31. *Apollo Belvedere* (before restoration). Vatican Museums. (Photo: Alinari/
Art Resource, NY)

power, then the *Laocoön* was an *exemplum doloris*, which Capodiferro likened to the fall of the Bentivoglio, exiled in Julius II's conquest of Bologna.[122] With this sculptural depiction of the Trojan priest's agony— one of the most acclaimed of all classical statuary—we enter once again, moreover, into a Virgilian domain. In the *Aeneid* (II, 40–56, 199–231), Laocoön, priest of Poseidon, and his two sons are ensnared by two monstrous serpents, the instruments of Pallas Athena's wrath. This was the Trojan priest's punishment for protesting the admission of the Trojan Horse within the gates of the city. Beyond contemporary political allusions and the illustration of Virgil's account, the *Laocoön*, like the other sculptures, proved capable of additional meanings. His fate could be interpreted, as it was by Capodiferro, under the theme of patriotic sacrifice. On the other hand, its realistic portrayal of human suffering made it an image of Stoic fortitude. Further, in some classical accounts Laocoön is described as a priest of Apollo, subjected to divine punishment for violating his vow of celibacy. The altar elements, and the sacrificial character of the Vatican garden niche into which the sculptural group was placed, might suggest this particular association.[123] Most important, probably, was the mere fact of its discovery and subsequent transfer to the Vatican. For Sadoleto, the finding of the *Laocoön*, which returned to the light such a remarkable example of classical genius, symbolized the dawning of a new age for Rome.[124] Long buried in the ruins of what the Renaissance called the Thermae Titi (these baths were actually the work of Trajan), in a part that once belonged to Nero's Domus Aurea, the *Laocoön* now became the most celebrated sculpture in the statue garden of the Belvedere, the domicile of the new Roman emperors.

Imperial in overall conception and in its decoration as the Cortile del Belvedere project was, even more colossal was Julius II's plan for the new St. Peter's. The sheer scale of the planned new basilica is breathtaking: not since imperial Roman times had a structure of these dimensions been envisioned. Moreover, the project entailed the destruction of the ancient Constantinian basilica, revered for more than a millennium as the sanctuary of the Apostle.

With hindsight, the decision to rebuild St. Peter's would seem to have been sooner or later inevitable. Even without taking into account its deteriorated state, the Constantinian church, venerable as it was, could not help but appear hopelessly outdated, particularly in relation to Julius's Vatican Palace projects. The grandeur in scale and design of the Cortile del Belvedere simply threatened to overshadow the aged basilica.

Yet Julius did not, it seems, begin with the idea of replacing Old St. Peter's. Initially, he planned instead to create a new funerary chapel, thus emulating the chapel his uncle Sixtus IV had made provision for in the basilica, an undertaking that Julius himself, in fact, had seen through to completion. The destined site for this new Capella Iulia was probably

32. *Laocoön*. Vatican Museums. (Photo: Alinari/Art Resource, NY)

Nicholas V's unfinished *tribuna*; besides serving as a funerary chapel for the second Della Rovere pontiff, it would thus have met the needs for increased choir space, both for liturgical functions and for the enlarged forces of papal singers. To create the new pontifical tomb for this new main chapel located behind the tomb of Peter, Julius II summoned Michelangelo to Rome in the spring of 1505. At the same time Bramante received the commission to design the chapel.[125]

Michelangelo's project for the Julius tomb and Bramante's work on the basilica were thus inter-related at their inception. Quickly, however, they became rival considerations. Bramante rapidly moved from the idea of merely completing the choir to a full-scale reconstruction of St. Peter's. In his ideas for a gigantic, central-plan Templum Iulii, the papal funerary chapel became relegated to a secondary element, and in the resulting competition between tomb and basilica Michelangelo ended up the loser. By the end of 1505 Julius had given the rebuilding of St. Peter's first priority. When Michelangelo realized that plans for the tomb were to be put off indefinitely, he fled back to Florence. The day of his unannounced departure from Rome came, in fact, the day before Julius laid the foundation stone for the new Temple of the Apostle (18 April 1506). Within a year some twenty-five hundred workers were engaged in its construction.[126]

Competitive in their claims on the pope's ambitions and financial resources, Michelangelo's tomb and Bramante's basilica nevertheless reveal striking similarities in their thematic emphasis on the *renovatio imperii*. In the project of 1505 for the Julius tomb, Michelangelo envisioned a huge, free-standing monument, some seven by eleven meters at its base. The tri-level pyramidal design called for more than forty marble statues plus several bronze reliefs depicting the pope's deeds. In the center of the ground floor was to be a door, like the "door of Hades" of Roman sarcophagi, designed to give access to the oval burial chamber. On either side of the door were to be niches, each containing a winged victory standing over a vanquished foe and flanked by herms to which nude slaves were to be chained. The second story included four seated statues, over life-sized, one of them depicting Moses. The plans for the apex of the monument remain uncertain, but probably it was to contain an effigy of the pope, crowned with triple tiara, and perhaps borne aloft on a *sedia gestatoria*.[127]

Despite the uncertainty as to various details of Michelangelo's initial plan for the Julius tomb, its overall design can be judged as unmistakably imperial in conception. Pliny the Elder's description of the Mausoleum of Halicarnassus—one of the Seven Wonders of the ancient world—doubtless provided one source of classical inspiration for the pyramidal plan and for Julius's and Michelangelo's declared intention to surpass the ancient imperial sepulchers in grandeur.[128]

33. Medal of Julius II, struck to commemorate the foundation of the new St. Peter's basilica. Created by the celebrated Renaissance medallist Cristoforo Foppa, better known as Il Caradosso. The obverse shows the bust of the pontiff, wearing cope and orphrey, with the inscription: IVLIVS.LIGVR. PAPA.SECVNDVS.MCCCCCVI. The reverse shows the new St. Peter's, according to one of Bramante's plans, and the inscription reads: TEMPLI.PETRI.INSTAVRACIO. and below, VATICANVS.M. Washington, D.C., National Gallery of Art, Samuel H. Kress Collection. (Photo: National Gallery of Art)

The three-tiered form is strongly suggestive, too, of the elaborate *rogus*, or funeral pyre, on which the corpse of the Roman emperor or his wax image was burned; by this rite of consecration the dead emperor became a *divus*. Since they were made of combustible materials, none of these pyres survived, but they were frequently depicted on the reverses of imperial coins along with the inscription CONSECRATIO. Renaissance anti-quarians mistakenly took these numismatic portrayals of the *rogus* for images of imperial mausolea. Hence reconstructions in Renaissance art of the way Hadrian's tomb originally appeared gave it the form of a *rogus*, and in Marco Fabio Calvo's representation of Augustan Rome the *rogus* served as a model for the "*Meta Pij*," which he used to symbolize the Vatican region. To the early sixteenth century, in short, the revival of the imperial "sepulcher" (the *rogus*) would suggest itself as the only appropri-ate tomb by which to commemorate the deeds of the new Julius Caesar.[129]

The winged victories and fettered slaves reveal, too, the same impe-rial notions. Whatever their allegorical meaning or meanings—some suggestions are the provinces subjugated militarily by the Della Rovere pontiff, the arts bereft by the death of so great a patron, the enemies of the Faith dominated by the power of Christianity, virtue overcoming vice, and the unregenerated soul held in bondage by natural desire—these statues in their literal sense existed as images of triumph. Further, like the crowning *quadriga* of the deified emperor atop the imperial *rogus*, Julius would have been shown entering heaven as a *triumphator*.[130]

Imperial magnificence proved likewise a prime consideration in Bramante's plans for the new St. Peter's. As with the Julius tomb, exactly what Bramante first intended for the new Templum S. Petri remains a matter of scholarly dispute, though it is clear that he produced a rapid succession of plans, and that many aspects continued in flux even while construction was under way. One early proposal, as we have seen, would have reoriented the basilica to face the great Vatican obelisk, thus creating an architecturally symbolic link between the founder of the Roman Empire and the founder of the Roman Church. But Julius vetoed this idea, since it would have meant moving the Apostle's tomb. Perhaps it was in connection with this early notion that Bramante envisioned placing the new Temple within a vast piazza, delimited at its periphery by porticoed buildings and immense exedras. Such an urbanistic conception derived probably from such surviving Roman complexes as Trajan's Forum or the Baths of Caracalla. In this way, the "holy Latin Jerusalem," which was the pope's Vatican capital, would have acquired a systematic spatial unity, surpassing both Solomon's Jerusalem and the Rome of the Caesars as an image of the heavenly city and as the axis of a cosmic empire.[131]

The colossal dimensions of this vast sacred city—its realization would have meant destroying most of the existing Vatican palace, including the Sistine Chapel, and also required altering plans for the Cortile del Belvedere[132]—make questionable whether Julius ever entertained it as a serious proposal. Yet for what Bramante did initiate for St. Peter's, the architecture and construction of the great Roman imperial baths provided key inspirations. From these buildings, and from similar imperial Roman structures, such as the Basilica of Maxentius in the Forum (the so-called Templum Pacis), Bramante learned to think of architecture not as wall-plane and decoration but instead as spatial volume. Interior space became the active principle, with walls merely the malleable surrounding mass, "excavated" by the dynamic force of the void. To conceive of architecture in this way, and to build on the gigantic scale of the new basilica's dimensions, also required the revival of Roman building techniques, especially the use of brick-faced concrete, which formed the structural basis for the domes, piers, and massive arches of the imperial baths. Both as design and structure, then, the ruins of Roman buildings in the Eternal City enabled Bramante to revolutionize architecture.[133]

At the same time, Roman imperial buildings presented a challenge: they were creations to be rivalled and even surpassed. From Vitruvius, the Renaissance learned that the temple, in Roman architectural theory, should be a central-plan domed building. This corresponded also to the circular designs of paleo-Christian *martyria* of which S. Costanza and S. Stefano Rotondo were notable surviving examples in the city of Rome. In replacing the basilical design of Old St. Peter's with a central-plan domed building, Bramante thus envisioned a vast temple-mausoleum. The greatest domed temple from Roman antiquity was the Pantheon, and Bramante designed the dome of the new St. Peter's to be comparable in its dimensions. Indeed, as has often been remarked, it was as if Bramante were raising the dome of the Pantheon over the vast, vaulted space of the Templum Pacis. The Pantheon served, moreover, as a model for certain architectural details. In 1508 Bramante ordered travertine capitals executed according to the pattern of those used in the Roman temple.[134]

When Bramante died in 1514, the new basilica was far from finished. For much of the sixteenth century its piers and coffered vaults, open to the sky in the jumble of what remained of the old basilica, seemed, in fact, more like ruins themselves than the gradually rising structure of the new temple. Not until the next century did the building reach completion. In the meantime, one architect after another modified, altered, or embellished Bramante's plans. Yet by his death the great central piers, which formed the core of the structure and governed its overall design, were in place. And though it took Michelangelo's sculptural genius to rescue the project, in part by *reducing* the overall size of the building, the essential conception remained Bramante's and Julius II's.[135]

THE VATICAN LIBRARY AND CLASSICAL STUDIES

Among the public works the Emperor Augustus undertook to adorn the city of Rome was a Greek and Latin library. As an essential part of the palace complex he created on the Palatine, the library, under its tutelary deity Apollo (to whom Augustus's Palatine temple was dedicated), provided scholars and writers of the Augustan Age access to the intellectual and literary heritage of Greco-Roman antiquity.[136]

Augustus's Palatine Library was the most important in imperial Rome, but other imperial constructions, such as Trajan's Forum and Hadrian's Villa at Tivoli, had similarly included Greek and Latin libraries. Precedent for such imperially sponsored centers of learning had, of course, been established during the Hellenistic Age, when the Ptolemies of Egypt created the great library and Museum at Alexandria, and other philhellenic monarchs had followed suit.[137]

Roman humanists were well aware of classical rulers' support for literary and philosophical studies. In a 1513 letter Pietro Bembo praised Julius II for his sustaining interest in the Vatican Library, support which he said emulated the famed devotion to the *studia litterarum* of Ptolemy Philadelphus and Attalus of Pergamum. Bembo went on to acclaim Julius's creation of another library, conveniently placed for the pope's personal use (probably the Stanza della Segnatura); this had fewer books, but was remarkable, he noted, for its beautiful paintings and delightful setting.[138] Two small *grisaille* scenes, placed beneath the *Parnassus* fresco in the Stanza della Segnatura, in fact serve as reminders of the imperial role in the preservation of great works of classical literature. One shows Augustus preventing Virgil's *Aeneid* from being cast into the flames; the other depicts Alexander the Great overseeing the deposit of Homer's *Iliad* in the coffer of Darius.[139]

This comparison of papal support for classical libraries to that of the ancient monarchs long predates Julius's pontificate. In fact, Manetti, in his *Vita Nicolai V* had likened that pontiff's zeal in creating a library in the papal palace to the achievement of Ptolemy Philadelphus, and Aurelio Brandolini had drawn an explicit parallel between Sixtus IV's founding of the Vatican Library and Augustus's creation of the Palatine Library.[140]

None of the Renaissance popes intended a literal recreation of the libraries of antiquity. They were determined, nevertheless, to make Rome a center of humanistic scholarship. When Martin V returned the papacy to Rome, the opportunities to pursue such studies were negligible. The papal library at Avignon was a sizeable collection, but there it remained despite the demands of Eugenius IV for its restitution to Rome. Not indeed until the eighteenth century were the last volumes from it joined to the Vatican Library.[141]

The upheavals of the Great Schism and the long papal absence from

Rome had, moreover, the same deleterious effects on library collections in the Eternal City as they had on churches and other buildings. When Traversari, an indefatigable searcher for classical and patristic manuscripts, was forced to spend four months in Rome in the spring of 1432 awaiting Curial processing of his appointment to be General of the Camaldolese Order, he occupied his time searching the various libraries. He did find a valuable text of Origen at the monastery of S. Cecilia, but the general situation was deplorable. The Biblioteca Capitolare of St. Peter's, a more important collection at this time than the papal library, proved unimpressive, while the library of the Basilian monastery of Grottaferrata, where he hoped to find Greek texts, had recently been pillaged by marauding troops.[142] Indeed, during Eugenius's pontificate the richest Roman library of classical and patristic manuscripts belonged to Cardinal Giordano Orsini (d. 1439), a collection he preserved in the Orsini stronghold on Monte Giordano.[143]

Eugenius tried to improve papal holdings, but he had to begin virtually from scratch. The inventory of the papal library he ordered made in 1443 upon his return to Rome shows only about three hundred forty volumes, mostly medieval theology and canon law with a smattering of classics,[144] whereas Orsini possessed more than two hundred fifty manuscripts, with a far better representation of ancient authors. The papal collection could not begin to compete with the humanist library Cosimo de' Medici had established at the Florentine monastery of S. Marco, which had as its core Niccolò Niccoli's lifetime work of manuscript purchases.[145]

The Roman situation changed dramatically with the accession of Nicholas V. On his numerous journeys within Italy and over the Alps, accompanying Cardinal Albergati as humanist secretary, the future pope had made some important manuscript finds, and he had built up a respectable personal library.[146] He had also prepared for Cosimo de' Medici a library "canon," a list of classical, patristic, and medieval *desiderata* required for a first-rate humanist collection.[147] As pope, Nicholas suddenly found himself in a position to create in the Vatican the library he had previously been able only to counsel others to establish.

Two circumstances aided Nicholas's efforts. The first was the financial windfall accruing from the success of the 1450 Jubilee. This provided surplus funds to help underwrite the quest for manuscripts, Europe-wide in scope, and to pay scribes and artisans to produce the handsomely written and sumptuously bound volumes this bibliophile pope took such delight in. The second circumstance was the fall of Constantinople. Not only did this hasten the flow of Greek manuscripts to the West, brought both by Byzantine refugees and by Latin Christians fleeing the conquering Turks, but it also made more urgent the cultivation of Greek classical and patristic studies under Latin aegis, if the cultural and intellectual heritage of Hellenism was not to be lost. With Giovanni Tortelli serving as supervisor of scholarly projects, Nicholas was able to expand rapidly the Vatican holdings: the inventories made in April 1455 just after the pope's death list over eleven hundred fifty volumes, including more than three hundred fifty in Greek.[148]

Beyond acquiring manuscripts, Nicholas provided impressive stipends to leading humanist scholars for Latin translations of classical Greek poetry, history, and philosophy. Lorenzo Valla, George of Trebizond, Guarino da Verona, Niccolò Perotti, Pier Candido Decembrio, Theodore Gaza, and Poggio Bracciolini were among those so employed; and among the Greek authors rendered into Latin were Homer, Plato, Aristotle, Theophrastus, Thucydides, Herodotus, Xenophon, Polybius, Strabo, Appian, and Epictetus.[149] The Greek Church Fathers, too, as we have seen, were made subject to the same scholarly zeal.

According to Manetti,[150] Nicholas had planned to house his library in well-lit quarters in the renovated Vatican Palace. At the time of the pope's death, however, no permanent facility had been created. In the waning months of Nicholas's pontificate, the Florentine artist Andrea del Castagno was frescoing a ground-floor room in the new wing of the Vatican Palace, a room which subsequently became the Bibliotheca Graeca under Sixtus IV, and which Nicholas may have intended as a *studiolo*. The room's painted decoration is in a distinctly classical idiom: an *all'antica* peristyle with rich Augustan frieze is illusionistically created and numerous garden motifs abound. As such it reflects Alberti's architectural theories, and it may have been inspired also by Pliny the Younger's description of the garden suite of his Tuscan villa, or even by surviving Roman mural decoration.[151]

Whether Nicholas's books were ever housed there is uncertain, however, and over the next couple of decades these ground-floor rooms were used for storage of wine and grain. Under Nicholas's immediate successors, in fact, a support for the library and for classical scholarship suffered a sharp reduction. With Calixtus III's accession many of the humanists Nicholas had brought to Rome to work on translating projects departed for more promising positions, particularly to the court of Alfonso the Magnanimous at Naples, and plans for crusades diverted energy and funds from scholarship. Nevertheless patronage of humanistic studies had become too important an aspect of a Renaissance prince's prestige for the popes to neglect it altogether. Even Paul II, who was generally rather indifferent about humanistic studies, evinced continued interest in Latin translations of the Hellenistic Greek historians, and he appointed Giovanni Andrea Bussi head of the Vatican Library, where he had access to classical and patristic manuscripts for use in publishing the first printed editions of ancient authors to appear in Rome.[152] Where more zealous involvement in humanistic scholarship might be expected,

34. Melozzo da Forlì, *Sixtus IV Appoints Platina Head of the Vatican Library*. Pina-
coteca Vaticana. The inscription, three Latin elegiac couplets written by Platina,
mentions the various projects of restoration undertaken by Sixtus IV in the city of
Rome, including churches, streets, walls, bridges, and the aqueduct of the Aqua
Virgo; now Rome owes yet more to Sixtus for the creation of the Vatican Library.
(Photo: Alinari/Art Resource, NY)

namely under Pius II, efforts were expended not for the Vatican, but instead for the pope's personal library. This was eventually installed at the end of the fifteenth century in the Cathedral of Siena; called the Libreria Piccolomini, it is famous for its Pinturicchio frescoes of the life of Pius II.[153]

The fulfillment of Nicholas V's ambition for the Vatican Library was thus left for Sixtus IV. Sixtus's own intellectual pursuits stemmed, as we have seen, from his education in scholastic theology. But establishment of a papal library, publicly accessible to humanist scholars, formed part of his overall policy of restoring Rome to its ancient grandeur. His bull of 1475, generally regarded as marking the real "founding" or "opening" of the Vatican Library, stressed its service both to the Catholic Faith and to the liberal arts. At the same time he appointed Platina head of the Library, an act commemorated in Melozzo da Forlì's famous fresco; placed, originally, opposite the entrance to the Latin reading room, the painting with its inscription written by Platina reminded each user that the foundation of the Library was Sixtus's most magnificent contribution to the renewal of Rome. Under Platina's direction, nearly a thousand additional volumes entered the Library's holdings. Just as important, the Library acquired an institutionalized administration, rules for access and usage, and a permanent location. The ground floor of Nicholas's new wing in the Vatican Palace, remodelled to improve lighting, was divided into four rooms. The largest became the Latin Library, with a smaller room behind it devoted to the Greek collection. These two rooms together comprised the Bibliotheca Communis, open to the public. Behind the Greek Library was the Bibliotheca Secreta, which held the most precious manuscripts, including some volumes in Hebrew and Arabic. The last room, the Bibliotheca Pontificum, served as an archives for registers of bulls and other papal documents.[154]

By the time of Platina's death in 1481, the Vatican Library for both the quantity and quality of its collection stood in the front rank of European libraries. Its centrality to Rome's intellectual life is clear, too—the names of leading humanists regularly appear in the lists of borrowers in Platina's registers.[155]

Particularly noteworthy were the Greek holdings. Indeed, the Vatican was rivalled as a repository of Greek manuscripts only by the Medici collections in Florence, and by the Biblioteca di S. Marco in Venice, to which Bessarion in 1468 had donated his vast Greek library. In praising Nicholas V's accomplishments in Greek studies, Filelfo argued that the volumes of Greek thought and literature brought by the pope's efforts to Rome meant not that they were lost to Greece, but rather that they had simply migrated to Magna Graecia.[156] Half a century later, Battista Casali, in a sermon preached before Julius II on the Feast of the Circumcision (1 January) 1508, advanced the theme that in the Vatican Library, established by Sixtus and further developed under Julius, Athens itself had been transferred to Rome (an echo, perhaps, of the idea of the *translatio litterarum* by which Augustus's founding of the Palatine Library had been praised by poets of the Augustan Age).[157] Casali went on, however, to make his remark more precise. The Greek learning contained in the Vatican manuscripts made it, he asserted, an "image" of Plato's Academy; and in its other holdings of Greek literature and philosophy the library represented the renewal (*instauratio*) of the Athenaeum and of Aristotle's Lyceum.[158]

This theme of Rome as the new Athens developed further under Leo X. The Medici pontiff persuaded Janus Lascaris to accept appointment to the chair of Greek studies at the Sapienza, and he established two additional faculty positions in Greek there.[159] Leo also created, with the collaboration of Angelo Colocci, a Greek *gymnasium* in Colocci's villa on the Quirinal. There under Lascaris as preceptor, and with Marcus Musurus also persuaded to come from Padua to provide instruction in Greek, some dozen young students were to immerse themselves totally in Greek language and thought. In praising Leo's project in his verse dedication to the pope of the first Greek edition of Plato's works (published in Venice in 1513), Musurus claimed that in creating the Greek Academy a new Athens was flowering on the banks of the Tiber.[160] The Greek Academy remained active during the early years of Leo's pontificate, and even published several volumes in Greek,[161] but by 1518 Lascaris had left for France, Musurus was dead, and the fledgling college was on its way to becoming defunct. Even so, the idea of Rome as a new Athens persisted. Thus a contemporary, in reference to the *Coryciana* literary circle, claimed it was as if Goritz's gardens were in the heart of Athens instead of the Imperial Fora, or that the Muses had been translated from their sanctuaries on Helicon and Parnassus to the Tarpeian and Quirinal heights![162]

Aside from the preservation of precious Greek manuscripts in the Vatican Library, Renaissance Rome contributed, it must be admitted, less to classical Greek scholarship than other Italian centers. Roman humanism, except for Valla, lacked the penetrating historico-philological inquiry brought to bear on the classics in the Venetian tradition of Ermolao Barbaro and Aldus Manutius, a critical textual approach represented also in the achievements of the Florentine Politian.[163] In Rome, moreover, no specific intellectual program or cultural ideology evolved from Greek wisdom, as happened in Florence with the civic humanists' rediscovery of the political and moral values of the Periclean *polis* and with the Platonic Academy's dedication to Neo-Platonic metaphysics and aesthetics. Roman humanists did give attention to such ancient Greek accounts of Rome's rise to imperial power as those by Polybius and Dionysius of Halicarnassus and the histories of the Gothic Wars by Procopius and

Agathias were translated.[164] Roman intellectuals were thus able to improve their grasp of their city's long history. Greek sources were also exploited for *topoi* of praise to acclaim the Roman pontiffs as ideal monarchs. Hence both Argyropoulos and Persona claimed that Sixtus IV's learning and wisdom were such that his headship of the Christian *imperium* confirmed the truth of Plato's dictum that human good and happiness required either kings to be philosophers or philosophers kings.[165] Earlier, Francesco Barbaro and Michele Canensi saw Nicholas V's elevation as similarly upholding Plato's conclusion.[166] The same impulse to associate the popes with classical ideas of the ideal ruler is detectable, too, in the popularity of Xenophon's portrait of the Persian King Cyrus as a model monarch. Poggio, with the aid of George of Trebizond, provided the first Latin translation of the *Cyropaedia* in Rome during the 1440s; Lampugnino Birago intended his translation for Pius II; and Francesco Filelfo produced a third Latin version, dedicated to Paul II.[167] In general, however, Roman humanists tended to approach Greek philosophy, history, and literature in an eclectic way, just as their favorite classical author, Cicero, had done.

In the end it was the revival of Latin, not Greek, that mattered more to Renaissance Rome. Indeed, to the extent that classicism represented a cultural program to the Roman humanists, its chief concern was with recovering the rhetorical resources of ancient Latin eloquence and restoring the purity of Ciceronian diction—the "Ciceronianism" Erasmus found so objectionable.[168] Humanism in Rome was in large part a courtier culture, finding its expression in oratory, in poetry, and in elegant and witty conversation within the setting of the *orti letterari*. This placed a premium on refinement of style.

The same impulses help explain the revival of classical Roman drama, to which Rome seems to have contributed more than any other city in Italy. Leto's Roman Academy gave emphasis to the pedagogical and literary value of performing the Latin plays of Plautus, Terence, and Seneca; and beginning in the mid-1480s Cardinal Raffaele Riario took the lead in constructing theaters and creating classical sets (following the guidelines in Vitruvius's work on architecture) for more elaborate productions, staged for the public. In one of these, the performance of Seneca's *Hippolytus* (1486), Tommaso Inghirami gained such acclaim for acting in the role of Phaedra, that he thereafter kept it as a nickname. During the early sixteenth century, Inghirami was the central figure in Rome's theatrical life, producing both performances of ancient drama and elaborate spectacles, such as the Capitoline festivities of 1513. In fact, the staging of the classical Roman plays often formed an integral part of these larger celebrations, and thus contributed to the ideological theme of imperial renewal that ran through these events. Theater doubtless had a special appeal, too, in a city where ceremony and spectacle pervaded so thoroughly its public and cultural life. Indeed, under Leo X Rome emerged as a leading center for producing new comedies, written in Italian. These included plays by Bibbiena, Ariosto, and Machiavelli. Often, as in Bibbiena's *Calandria* (1514) and Aretino's *La cortigiana* (first version 1525), Rome was the setting for the dramatic action.[169]

Latin classicism in Renaissance Rome, then, meant more than a merely literary revival. As the idiom of cultural transmission, classical Latin affected all aspects of Rome's cultural and intellectual life, including theology and religion. Indeed, John O'Malley has shown how the rediscovery of classical epideictic rhetoric as an appropriate form for the sacred oratory of the papal liturgies led also to the development of certain religious themes, such as the affirmation of human powers and the emphasis on establishing a community of peace and concord. Yet the essential aim of this *theologia rhetorica* was not the creation of new ideas nor the advancement of knowledge as such; rather it was to convey long-established truths in more persuasive ways. Thus its fundamental intent was conservative.[170]

Inasmuch, moreover, as Ciceronianism in prose and Virgilianism in poetry represented the literary apex of the Augustan Age, these reflected in a linguistic sense the same aspiration for a restored Roman imperial culture that found expression in Raphael's art and in Bramante's architecture.[171]

This imperial theme of Latin classicism, in fact, emerged at an early point in the Roman Renaissance, in the thought of Lorenzo Valla. In the "Prooemium" to the *Elegantiae*, Valla's guide to the effective use of the persuasive power of classical Latin, the Roman humanist had declared that the greatest achievement of imperial Rome, surpassing its military conquests, was the creation of the linguistic-cultural "*imperium*" of the Latin language. By this means Rome had extended the fruits of law, the liberal arts, and civilized wisdom to all peoples, liberating them from barbarism. This betterment of the human condition should be praised, he asserted, as worthy of gods rather than men. Indeed, in the diffusion of the Latin language the Romans seem almost to have left the earthly empire behind and commingled with the gods in heaven. If Ceres for discovering grain, Bacchus the vine, and Minerva the olive dwell among the gods, can it be a lesser achievement, Valla asks, to have disseminated to the nations of the world the Latin language, "that noble and nearly divine fruit, which is the food not of the body but of the mind?"[172]

The disintegration of the Roman Empire jeopardized the "sacrament" of Latin speech, however, and its survival depended on the Apostolic See of Rome. This is the central theme of Valla's "*Oratio in principio sui studii*," his inaugural lecture for the 1455–56 academic year at the University of Rome, where he held the chair of Latin eloquence. Since, Valla contends, Latin is the language of the Roman Church, both in its sacred

texts and in its administration, the Apostolic See had nourished its continual usage through the medieval centuries, and Europe thereby was
preserved from the extinction of literature, law, and philosophy that
afflicted Asia and Africa. So fused indeed had Latin language and Christian religion become in the *fides latina*, that "it seems to me that holy
religion and true literature abide together; whenever the one is absent the
other cannot exist, and because our religion is eternal, so Latin letters will
also be eternal." How much the Roman pontiffs are to be praised, then,
for cultivating the study of classical Latin, which serves also the growth of
Christian religion! To promote such study and learning, Valla concludes,
doubtless redounds to the true earthly glory of the Roman popes, but it
also is how we come to know the way that leads to celestial life.[173]

In late fifteenth and early sixteenth century Rome this notion of a
purified Latin classicism as the vehicle of a restored imperial culture had
become much more programmatic and had penetrated to the core areas
of Christianity. Thus Paolo Pompilio rewrote the Nicene Creed using
classical imagery and phrasing, and Marco Girolamo Vida conceived his
recasting of Christ's Passion in terms of Virgilian epic. Most striking of all,
perhaps, is Paolo Cortesi's systematic transformation of the language of
Lombard's *Sentences*, the medieval theological textbook. In Cortesi's work,
Ciceronian vocabulary supplants scholastic terminology, so that Adam
becomes the *Phaëthon humani generis*, a mortal sin is *capitalis tabes*, a Church
decree is *senatusconsultum*, a Christian priest is *flamen dialis* ("a priest of
Jupiter"), and St. Thomas Aquinas is *Apollo Christianorum*. In this way
even medieval scholastic theology could form part of humanist culture.
This fusion of Ciceronian classicism and Christian doctrine had the
further consequence, however, of underscoring the "Roman-ness" of
Christianity and the continuity of Empire and Church. Thus, when, in
discussing the papal power of the keys, Cortesi described it as the power
of *imperium*, he made the Roman Church (Cortesi called it the "Senate")
indistinguishable from the ancient Roman state. Similarly, when in treating the matter of indulgences, he referred to the treasure of merits
accumulated by the sacrifices of Christ and the saints by using the phrase
Reipublicae aerarium ("the treasure of the Roman state") and by adopting
the imagery of public revenue (*vectigal*) filling up a vessel (*urna*), the effect
is both to despiritualize the benefits of divine grace and also to locate these
tangible resources within the governmental functions of Rome as
capital.[174]

The integral link of classical culture and Christian religion that is
bound up in the Renaissance idea of Rome forms the core, too, of
Raffaele Maffei's *Nasi Romani in Martinum Lutherum Apologeticus*. This
tract, composed some time between the fall of 1518 and the summer of
1520, represents the earliest layman's assault on the German reformer. At
the heart of the Roman humanist's argument is, significantly, that the

Church contains more than Christian tradition: it represents also the continuation of the civilizing activity of Rome, and as such forms the basis of human culture. To challenge the authority of Rome, as Luther had done, is therefore, Maffei concludes, a treasonous act against the whole western tradition, and it threatens the unity of classical wisdom and Christian revelation—of philosophy and theology—that Basil, Jerome, and Augustine (among so many other Church Fathers) had created. It was this unity, moreover, that Rome embodied, and that the popes had defended and preserved. From Maffei's perspective, and from that of many of his Roman contemporaries, to reject Rome was tantamount to betraying civilization itself.[175]

VI

Roma Aeterna and the
Plenitudo Temporum

This is that ancient and eternal city . . . founded
during the Golden Age.

—Fra Mariano da Firenze, *Itinerarium Urbis
Romae*.

If only, Holy Father, I might witness in this age,
under your leadership—with the discords among
Christians resolved and peace at last restored to the
faithful—even the barbarian peoples and nations
made subject to you, so that the prophecy might be
fulfilled in you: 'I will make you a light to the
nations, to be my salvation to the ends of the earth'
[Isaiah 49: 6].

—Pietro Delfin, *Oratio ad Leonem X.*

ETERNAL ROME

When Renaissance Romans considered the unique majesty and splendor
of Rome's sacred *imperium*, they perceived not only its boundlessness,
transcending terrestrial limits to include heaven itself, but also its
timelessness. Thus Antonio Pucci, addressing the ninth session of the
Fifth Lateran Council (5 May 1514), described the assembled cardinals as
the immovable anchor points (*cardines*) of the whole world, the solid
columns by which the universal edifice of the Christian faith is supported
and sustained and will remain unalterable forever.[1]

Enduring stability and eternity, in fact, were recurrent leitmotivs of
Roman humanist thought. Valla argued, as we have seen, that the Latin
language, by being bound to the Roman faith, was placed beyond any
jeopardy of extinction; and Giles of Viterbo envisioned the new St. Peter's
basilica as destined to endure for all time.

Providentially founded and divinely guided, the Roman Church thereby stood apart from any merely human community. Nor was it subject, so Renaissance Romans asserted, to the caprices of fortune, as secular states were. Hence a central preoccupation of the political and historical analysis produced in early sixteenth-century Italy—the role of *fortuna* in human affairs—was regarded as inapplicable to the sacred destiny of Rome.

An early expression of such views appears in Lapo da Castiglionchio the Younger's dialogue of 1438 in praise of the Roman Curia. Many learned men, Lapo begins, have regarded ancient Athens as worthy of the highest praise, while others instead have singled out Sparta, constituted under Lycurgus's laws, or Carthage with its riches from land and sea, or especially the august Roman Empire. But none of these, Lapo maintains, can be compared with the "monarchy of Christ, called the Roman Curia," for divinity of origin, majesty of its sovereign, observance of divine things, and enduring stability. None of those ancient communities continued long in the same condition. The Roman Curia alone has conserved unchanged and uncorrupted its institutions and forms of administration for fourteen hundred years. Those ancient societies, having reached their apogee, fell through internal discord or were destroyed by their enemies. The Roman Church, though at times attacked by perfidious men, has not only not perished, but it has continued to grow in greatness, authority, and veneration, so that all Christian princes, peoples, and nations recognize it as queen and obey it as one to whom supreme power has been entrusted by divine right; and they submit to it not as to a king or tyrant but rather as to God on earth.[2]

Lapo's work, written in Ferrara during the Council with the Greek Church, five years before Eugenius IV returned to Rome, avoids connecting the divine destiny of the Roman Church to the fate of the city on the Tiber. Initially, too, other humanists tended to distinguish the timeless dominion of the *Ecclesia Romana* from *Urbs Roma* itself, which remained subject to the destructive effects of time. Thus Poggio Bracciolini, in his dedication to Nicholas V of *De varietate fortunae*, contrasts the majesty of the papacy, placed by the will of God beyond the power of fortune, with the squalor of the once beautiful ancient city, ravaged by fortune's fluctuations.[3]

With the papacy's permanent return to Rome, however, Roman humanists increasingly assimilated the transcendent historical purpose of the Roman Church to the timeless endurance of the Eternal City, its capital. In the same way they identified with ever greater frequency the *respublica Christiana* with the Roman *imperium*. The growth of these notions can be seen in the writings of Biondo and in Domenichi's oration in praise of Rome. By the early sixteenth century, not only was Giles of Viterbo able to view Christian Rome's religious centrality as prefigured in

Etruscan rites, but, as we have seen, he also has Christ himself claim Rome as his eternal bride.[4]

Striking, too, is the way Giles interpreted in the same figural fashion contemporary events. In a speech delivered in S. Maria del Popolo in November 1512 to celebrate the public proclamation of the alliance concluded between Julius II and the Holy Roman Emperor Maximilian, Giles saw the dark days that followed the crushing defeat of papal forces at the Battle of Ravenna not as the work of fate or of chance but rather as the mysterious activity of divine providence. The dark calamity of the past year's events did not signify the impending destruction of the human race, he states, but instead its divine renewal. This springing of new life from darkness, in fact, has its closest parallel in God's divine acts of Creation. Like the Almighty's calling forth light on the first day, so Julius had summoned the Fifth Lateran Council. With its announcement, hope had dawned again in the hearts of men. Then, just as on the second day God established the vault of the heavens to separate the waters, the Council, in beginning its deliberations, had clearly distinguished itself from the schismatic *conciliabulum* of Pisa. On the third day God brought forth fruit, and the Council, too, had begun to produce the rich fruit of religious reform. And now on the fourth day, when the sun was made, the treaty between pope and emperor is proclaimed in the Temple of the Virgin (S. Maria del Popolo), the Mother of that greatest Sun.

This restitution of dignity and health to the Roman Church entrusted to Julius's care was accomplished, Giles asserts, not by arms, not by legions, not by the machinery of war, not by any human action, but rather by the invincible strength of God. Victory came through piety, not by arms, through religion, not by military might, by divine power, not by human will. Moreover, Giles goes on, if God's hand is clearly detectable in the sudden transformation of the general historical situation from disaster to success, even more can Julius's particular accomplishments be seen as divinely guided. To him was providentially given not only the extension of papal dominions and the construction of eternal buildings, but more importantly the miraculous celerity by which the threat of schism in the Church was extinguished and Italy delivered from the yoke of foreign domination. Yet if Julius is to ensure the victory given him by divine grace, if he is to raise the Temple of the Apostle to the skies and preserve unchanging for posterity the monuments and memorials of "golden" Rome's eternal greatness, two further tasks remain: reform of the moral corruption that threatens Christianity from within, and the uniting of Christendom against the Ottoman threat from without. In the accomplishment of these deeds, true divine glory will redound to Julius. Just as he has overcome fortune in quelling schism and war, so the treaty with Maximilian is an auspicious sign that through God's power the liberty and "perpetual felicity" of the *respublica Christiana* will be achieved.[5]

The theme of Rome's eternity had antecedents, of course, in medieval legends, such as the proverb that as long as the Colosseum stood Rome would stand, and when it fell so would Rome and the world.[6] More important for humanist conceptions in Renaissance Rome was the ideology of the early Roman Empire. That Rome's world empire would prove of eternal duration formed a prominent panegyric theme in the Augustan Age, and this cult of Roma Aeterna had reached its apex in the early second century A.D. with the construction of the magnificent temple (the largest in Rome) dedicated to Venus Felix and Genetrix and to Roma Aeterna.[7]

Virgil's *Aeneid*, too, provided continuous inspiration for notions of the providential destiny of Rome. But the idea of Rome's eternity and transcendence over historical forces received even greater emphasis in the panegyrics of the Antonine period. Among these was Aelius Aristides's "Roman Oration," which proved so influential a source for the Roman humanists' epideictic praises.[8]

Besides this intellectual recovery of the thought-world belonging to the heyday of the Roman Empire, there were also the contributions of archeological evidence. Various marbles inscribed with the words VRBS AETERNA turned up at ancient sites. One found in 1498 had in fact once belonged to Hadrian's temple to Venus and Rome.[9]

Still more fundamental to the Roman Renaissance emphasis on timeless stability were the philosophical assumptions implicit in the religious outlook of the intellectuals attached to the papal court. For them reality was stable, ordered, coherent, and harmonious because it participated in these same qualities contained in the divine mind. Through God's providence, earth reflected—as in a mirror—heavenly immutability; hence the principle of causality was "exemplary," the correspondence of the earthly image to its heavenly pattern. Historical contingency as an explanation of causality thus had no role. Moreover, in assessing the moral value of human accomplishment the ultimate measure was enduring order (which Cajetan, for example, saw as characterizing the "new, holy Jerusalem descending from heaven," i.e., the Roman Church), just as its opposite was chaos, the confusion symbolized in Babylon (and manifest in the discord of the *conciliabulum* of Pisa).[10]

The same line of argumentation forms the crux of Marcello's speech to the Fifth Lateran Council in December 1512. The key virtue of the imperial power that Julius II exercises as *princeps* must be, Marcello declares, love. Through the virtue of love we recognize, cherish, and venerate the goodness, beauty, and power of the divine majesty and all the things set forth by Him. In the same way, love must be manifested in the actions of the pope, who is "another God on earth." The Christian *imperium* is held together far more by love than by fear (a revealing contrast to Machiavelli's opposing analysis in Chapter 17 of *The Prince*, written a year later). Fear, Marcello argues, leads to hatred, sedition, discord, and the overthrow of states. But when citizens perceive themselves loved by their prince, they will coalesce as one, readily assuming the burdens imposed upon them, and prepared to stand unflinchingly even in the face of death, no matter how terrible. This was the divine ardor that enabled the early Christian martyrs to endure the cruelest tortures; this is the supreme virtue that embraces all human and divine things, perfects them, and sustains them. By love the world was created, and through it the admirable order of the whole universe remains bound together. "Of such a nature are all the things that were brought forth out of that immense darkness and confusion into light and order—that very light which they say Prometheus took from heaven to earth, and from which all the splendor of life and wisdom proceeds." Love is the virtue, indeed the parent of all virtues, most worthy of an earthly prince. Through love God himself governs by his law the cosmos. With love, the prince is able to resist the blows of fortune; with it he will fight and conquer. The extremes of lust and hatred, joy and grief, hope and desire will be overcome. Creating harmony in himself, the prince will readily extend this to the state. He will reject pleasures, spurn riches, repulse all pomp and inane glory. In this way he will rule optimally, augment his prosperity, and preserve "in perpetuity" his enlarged *imperium*.[11]

Marcello, like Giles, thus saw Julius's activity as pope as reflective of the providential powers belonging to God the Father, in particular His acts of Creation. Order, harmony, and stability—the manifestations of God's love—constitute the elements that define the splendor of the created cosmos. In the same way these should be the enduring virtues of the universal *imperium* entrusted to the "*alter Deus in terris*."

THE GOLDEN AGE

Emphasis on Rome's eternity and on the unchanging stability of the Christian Roman *imperium* nevertheless went hand in hand with views of fulfillment and culmination. Their own time, Renaissance Romans thought, was the *plenitudo temporum*. In a repeated refrain they hailed their age as the dawn of the returning Golden Age.

In classical myth the Golden Age was the primeval period of pastoral innocence, during which the human race, under the benign rule of Saturn (and Janus) lived in tranquillity and happiness. Neither the miner's pickax nor the farmer's plow had marred the earth, money and property had not yet appeared as sources of human divisiveness, and men lived in harmony with nature, dining on natural foods, particularly the acorn, a motif Renaissance Romans linked during Julius II's pontificate to the Della Rovere *impresa* of acorn and oak tree.[12] Bucolic simplicity eventually degenerated, however, through the silver and bronze ages to the iron age of rapacity and violence; the gods no longer dwelled among men, with the virgin Astraea, the goddess of justice, the last to leave earth for heaven; and cruelty, wickedness, and endemic war marked the travail of human life.[13]

To this pessimistic scheme of the steady debasement of the human situation, Virgil introduced an important alteration, one which proved especially influential for the Roman Renaissance. In the Fourth Eclogue, the Roman poet rejoiced in the imminent fulfillment of the prophecy uttered by the Cumaean Sibyl that the iron race would cease and a new golden race would appear again. Astraea would return from the heavens, and nature, too, would experience a general rebirth, recovering its primitive fertility. Apollo would reign, with the implication that an efflorescence of literature and the arts would ensue. By connecting the mysterious boy of the Fourth Eclogue, whose birth inaugurates the new glorious age, with the underworld scene in the *Aeneid* (VI, 793 ff.) in which Anchises points out to Aeneas the divinely descended Caesar Augustus, founder of a new age of gold in the fields of Latium where Saturn once ruled, Virgil was interpreted as eulogizing the Augustan principate and the *pax Romana*. Instead of pastoral primitiveness, however, the renewed Golden Age was to be characterized by the advance of civilized institutions and by achievements in culture and the arts.[14] This was the emphasis, too, of Hadrian's proclamation of the Golden Age in A.D. 121 and of Aelius Aristides's "Roman Oration."[15]

In the general sense of bringing forth a time of peace, prosperity, and rebirth of learning and the arts, many Renaissance rulers could be celebrated. Among the most prominent was Lorenzo de' Medici, hailed by his Florentine humanist circle as restoring the Golden Age of Augustus.[16] But Virgil, after all, had been speaking of Rome and Rome's imperial destiny, and it was thus particularly appropriate, in the minds of the Roman humanists, to apply these Virgilian themes to the restored Renaissance papacy, established once again on the banks of the Tiber. Thus Canensi likened the widely shared sense of "luminous serenity" Europeans felt upon hearing the news of Nicholas V's election as pastor of the Lord's sheepfold to the coming of the Golden Age of Saturn;[17] Crivelli declared Pius II's accession to the papacy as the return of the Golden Age;[18] and Flemmyng said that with the elevation of Sixtus IV an age even more felicitous than the Golden Age had come.[19] Alessandro Cortesi and Venturino de Prioribus echoed Virgil's Fourth Eclogue more closely by seeing with Sixtus's election the return of faith, piety, probity, and the other virtues that had marked the Golden Age, and by pronouncing the return of Astraea from heaven.[20] Virgil's "now reigns Apollo" (Fourth Eclogue, v. 10) was repeatedly quoted or paraphrased, and Sixtus IV was even hailed as *"pastor Apollo."*[21] Pietro Bembo greeted the newly elected

Julius II with a poem declaring the return of the Golden Age (after the Iron Age of the Borgia pontificate); under Julius would come, too, the messianic reign of peace and the land flowing with milk and honey.[22] With even more Biblical imagery, Marcello, in the concluding remarks of his speech to the Fifth Lateran Council, declared that if Julius fulfilled the promise of the Council, if as pastor, physician, and tiller, he attended to justice, piety, concord, and peace, then the rich fruits of celestial beneficence would appear over all the earth; that with the breathing forth of Julius's spirit the waters would flow, by his besprinkling the land would grow fertile, and the Golden Age would return.[23]

Under the Medici pope, Leo X, allusions to the dawning Golden Age became torrential. This was a major theme in the pictorial decoration prepared for his *possesso*. It is alluded to also in one of the painted scenes depicting early Roman history that formed part of the temporary theater constructed on the Capitoline in 1513 as the setting for Giuliano de' Medici to be made a Roman citizen. In the scene, Janus, key in hand, cordially welcomes Saturn (with a scythe over his shoulder) to rustic Latium.[24] Indeed the pontificate of Leo X was so saturated with Golden Age imagery that Cajetan, defending the utility and antiquity of indulgences in his 1517 treatise *De indulgentiis*, was able to assert that if the Church used them properly "the Golden Age of the penitent Fathers" would return.[25]

By the early sixteenth century, the idea of the return of the Golden Age to Rome had become, in short, a commonplace of Roman humanist thought, and almost *de rigueur* in praises of the popes. But from Julius II's pontificate there survives a more extended and profound treatment of this theme. This is Giles of Viterbo's *libellus*, "*De aurea aetate*," the amplified version of the sermon he delivered in S. Maria del Popolo in December 1507 to celebrate recent Portuguese successes in the Indian Ocean. The *libellus* is not the only discussion of the Golden Age in Giles's works. He declared, for instance, that the appearance of Ficino's Platonic theology meant the providential return of the reign of Saturn and of the Golden Age foreseen by the Sibyl and the prophets.[26] But the discourse "On the Golden Age" is particularly important inasmuch as it places Rome's destiny and unfolding contemporary events within the framework of four successive Golden Ages. Indeed, it is these ages that, in Giles's view, have marked the overall course of human history.[27]

The first Golden Age, the age of Lucifer, occurred in heaven before the prideful fall of the leader of the rebel angels. The second, the age of Adam, was the state of felicity in the terrestrial paradise before the tasting of the forbidden fruit led to expulsion. These periods Giles covers quickly. Much more extensive is the discussion accorded the third Golden Age, which followed the Flood. At that point the descendents of Noah established virtuous societies in accordance with reason and with respect for the divine mysteries in Persia, Egypt, and Etruria. But especially among the ancient Etruscans under Janus did this golden life flourish: faith, concord, and peace thrived, and the Etruscans taught their young a four-stage ascent in wisdom from the investigation of nature by means of philosophy to a sublime love of the divine and celestial. At length, however, cupidity, hatred, and hostility arose, and iron war succeeded.

Then came the fourth and true Golden Age in comparison to which the previous three had been but shadows. This was the coming of Christ, the Son of God, who brought the golden light of divine truth into the world, in order to transform iron and mortal humanity into a golden and immortal race.[28] And at last under Julius II, Giles asserts, this promise is reaching its complete fulfillment. Christianity is now truly being carried to the ends of the earth, and peoples previously unknown to exist are being converted to the golden blessedness of the Faith. How clear a testimony this is to the love with which God has chosen to favor, adorn, and strengthen Julius! All his Renaissance predecessors, beginning with Eugenius IV, were forced to witness in grief the successive losses of Christian lands to the Ottoman advance. Now these calamities have given way to rejoicing. And, as a further confirmation of the eternal glory of the Christian religion under Julius, at the very time of this dramatic augmenting of the Christian *imperium* has come the renewal (*instauratio*) on a vast scale, reaching to the very heavens, of the Temple belonging to the Prince of the Apostles. Moreover, it is rising on the very site where God through Janus had inaugurated that earlier image of the Golden Age, and where, following the reigns of so many Etruscan kings, He had finally established the eternal Empire of true gold. Thus whatever over the past millenium had been lost to Latin Christendom is suddenly, in a brief moment, to be returned. And to Julius's joyful flock is to be given the golden fruit of his oak tree, and the renewal of the Golden Age in Etruria.

PAX ET CONCORDIA

Peace was a hallmark of the Golden Age, and an aspect of that epoch's proclaimed renewal for which sixteenth-century Romans fervently longed. Attend and provide, Marcello exhorts Julius II in his speech to the Fifth Lateran Council, so that concord is invigorated, discord recedes, and peace ensues—true peace, holy peace, universal and perpetual peace—so that the "kiss of justice" and the "conjugal bond of truth" will be confirmed, and the rich fruits of celestial goodness will appear over all the earth.[29]

Pax had many levels of meaning for Renaissance Romans. In the most literal sense it meant the cessation of war—in particular of the conflicts that had convulsed Italy since the 1494 French invasion, but

more generally also of the internecine quarrels that for so long had
divided Christian against Christian. To extinguish the flames of war, to
unite Christendom against the infidel Turk, and thus to create a tranquil
and stable order for the *respublica Christiana* were papal objectives repeatedly urged by humanists of the papal court. To fulfill this task, they
declared, was to emulate Augustus's *pax Romana*.[30]

But there was a religious, and even messianic, dimension to such an
accomplishment. When the Roman humanists repeatedly hailed the
newly elected Leo X as *Rex pacificus*, they evoked both Solomon (I Chronicles 22: 9) and Christ.[31] In praising peace the preachers at the papal court
also repeatedly adduced the solemn, "testamentary" words Christ had
spoken to the Apostles at the Last Supper: "Peace I leave you. My peace I
give you (John 14: 27).[32] A papal coin minted for Leo X, in fact, shows
Christ addressing the kneeling apostles, and bears the inscription: PACEM
MEAM DO VOBIS.[33]

The election of Leo X, son of Lorenzo de' Medici, whose stature as
peacemaker of Italy was already assuming mythic proportions in the
opening years of the sixteenth century,[34] did seem to contemporaries a
propitious sign. With the tumultuous career of the warrior pope Julius II
ended, now, it was hoped, a reign of peace would come. The composer
Heinrich Isaac, who had earlier enjoyed Lorenzo's patronage and then
found service at the court of the Holy Roman Emperor Maximilian, gave
expression to these longings in his remarkable six-part motet, *Optime
Pastor*. Isaac composed this composition for the ceremony of Maximilian's
"obedience" to the newly elected Medici pontiff, an act performed in
Rome by the imperial emissary Cardinal Lang in December 1513. The
double *cantus firmus* of the motet is taken from two antiphonal texts in the
Roman Missal: "*Da pacem Domine in diebus nostris: quia non est alius qui
pugnet pro nobis, nisi tu Deus noster*" (Give peace in our day Lord, for there is
no other to fight for us except Thou, Our God), and "*Sacerdos et pontifex et
virtutum artifex, bonus pastor in populo, sic placuisti Domino*" (Priest and
pontiff and author of virtue, the Good Shepherd for his people, so it
please the Lord). The Latin poetry written as the text for the interwoven
polyphony of the other four voices of this complex composition similarly
calls upon the Good Shepherd, the *Medicus*, to heal the wounds of his flock
and to return to his sheepfold *pax alma, pax aurea*. Let the soothing song of
your reed-pipe fetter your sheep to a league of concord, the singers
exhort Leo; then under the eagle (Maximilian), queen of the winged
creatures, and the true lion (Leo X), king of the beasts, the Turkish wolves
and the monsters of Canopus (the Mamluks of Egypt) can be resisted. Let
the hills exult and the pastures acclaim the *Medicus*, and let the world
rejoice in such a pope and emperor.[35]

Peace meant more to Renaissance Romans, however, than the absence of strife among Christians. Harmony was an expression of God's

providential Creation, and earth should therefore reflect the peace that reigns among Father, Son, and Holy Spirit, and the *concordantia* of the harmoniously revolving heavenly spheres.[36]

Peace, too, was the necessary condition for fulfilling Christ's words that other sheep would be brought into the fold and "there will then be one flock, one shepherd" (John 10: 16). The classical conception of Rome as *patria communis*, the common fatherland, was seen as anticipating the union of all peoples under the Roman Church. But the idea of *unum ovile, unus pastor* had the messianic sense of creating, under papal headship, the *plenitudo gentium*, a brotherhood of the whole human race. The spread of the Gospel to newly discovered parts of the globe seemed an auspicious sign that this fraternal union was indeed emerging.[37]

Peace also meant the attainment of enduring and stable doctrinal truth. For preachers at the papal court, the great heresies of the past had been refuted and a *pax theologica* reigned. Through the work of the Fathers and Doctors of the Church, all the major doctrinal questions had been resolved, and both the scholastic and patristic traditions (Greek as well as Latin) were seen as attesting to one harmonious concord of truth.[38]

Nor, in this pursuit of theological concord, did the rediscovered wisdom of the classical philosophers strike a jarring note. Roman humanists, for the most part, took up with enthusiasm Giovanni Pico della Mirandola's goal of a *pax philosophica*, the conviction that a unity of truth lay behind all theological and metaphysical systems, and that these were in fundamental accord with Christian revelation.[39] Pico, whose title *Comes Concordiae* was a nice coincidence of his family's lordship of the tiny North Italian principality of Mirandola and Concordia and of his intellectual aspiration, chose Rome, in fact, as the site for his planned disputation on his Nine Hundred Theses, drawn from his study of all the ancient and medieval philosophical traditions.[40] For this event he invited scholars from all over Italy, and to serve as an inaugural speech he penned his famous "Oration on the Dignity of Man." Appropriately, the disputation was to take place following the Feast of the Epiphany 1487. When the Theses appeared in print in Rome in December 1486, however, a number raised questions as to their agreement with Christian doctrine. Pope Innocent VIII ordered the disputation suspended and directed a commission of theologians and jurists to examine the Theses. This body reported several to be heretical and declared others of dubious orthodoxy.[41] Pico's staunch defense of the suspect theses only made matters worse, and the upshot was the issuance of formal charges of heresy and his eventual flight to France. Nonetheless, Pico retained firm supporters, among them Lorenzo de' Medici, and at length, following Innocent's death, he gained Alexander VI's pardon in 1493.

The papal pardon removed whatever restraint might have existed among Roman humanists to affirming Pico's ideas. Indeed, over the next two decades a number of preachers at the papal court paraphrased in their sermons Pico's remarks in his "Oration" on man's indeterminacy and multipotentiality.[42]

Pico was not entirely representative of Roman thought. In preparing the debate on his Nine Hundred Theses he disclaimed reliance on the elegance of the Roman tongue, preferring, he states, to follow the "Parisian" mode of disputation,[43] a theological approach out of tune with the Ciceronian tendencies favored by many Roman humanists. Paolo Cortesi, in fact, accused Pico of being overly subtle, relying too much on logic. Despite these failings, however, Cortesi and other Romans shared the synthesizing and conciliatory concerns that lay at the heart of Pico's thought.[44]

Pico, moreover, served merely as the most prominent Quattrocento advocate of the idea of theological *concordantia*. In fact, this notion was incipient already in the *theologica poetica* defended by Petrarch, Boccaccio, and Salutati. The search for accommodation between classical wisdom and Christian truth had then found further extension in the ideas propounded by Cusanus and Bessarion, and by the Florentine Neo-Platonists, particularly in Ficino's emphasis on the *prisci theologi*. For Ficino, even such mysteries as the Trinity and the Incarnation were to be found, in an approximate way, beneath the poetic veils of the esoteric writings of Orpheus, Hermes Trismegistus, Zoroaster, Pythagoras, and Plato.[45] Study of Lactantius and exploitation of the more Platonic side of St. Augustine's *corpus* aided such conceptions, as did even more the rediscovery of the Greek Church Fathers. Eusebius's *De praeparatione Evangelica*, translated by George of Trebizond for Nicholas V, the revival of Origen, including the *Contra Celsum* translated by Cristoforo da Persona and dedicated to Sixtus IV, and the writings of Ps.-Dionysius the Areopagite, translated in the fifteenth century by both Traversari and Ficino, provided patristic foundation for the concord of theology and ancient philosophy. Philo's allegorizing and Platonizing exegesis of the Old Testament, rendered into Latin by Lilio Tifernate, pointed in the same direction. Giles of Viterbo's commentary on Lombard's *Sentences* "according to the mind of Plato," which he worked on for a number of years up to 1512, suggests, too, how receptive early sixteenth-century Rome was to such tendencies.[46]

Efforts to find accommodation between ancient pagan religions and Christianity even went beyond the similarity of theological concepts to the proximity of rites and practices. Pomponio Leto, in marginal notes to his manuscript of Varro's *De lingua latina*, sees parallels between the ancient Roman priests' ritual purification of instruments used in cult ceremony and Christian priests' rites in consecrating liturgical vestments and other sacred objects. He also points out that by the term "*cella*" the ancients meant the "seat of the gods," and that this normally found placement in the middle of their temples, whereas in Christian temples this inviolable sanctuary stands at the head of the building and is called the "*Sancta Sanctorum.*"[47] Giles of Viterbo, too, was intrigued by ancient cults and religious lore, as evidenced by his careful reading and annotating of a manuscript of Pausanius's *Graeciae descriptio.*[48]

Even more striking is the fascination with the religious mythology of ancient Egypt, a trend that reached its peak in Rome in the years around 1500. An interest in things Egyptian was in part aroused by the theurgic authority of Hermes Trismegistus, the presumed ancient Egyptian sage, who was also often identified with the god-king Thoth. The Florentine Neo-Platonists regarded this Thrice-Great Hermes as the first philosopher to ascend to a contemplation of the divine. This made him, therefore, the founder of theology. Moreover, according to the ancient Neo-Platonists both Pythagoras and Plato had been initiated into Egyptian mysteries. These in turn were held to incorporate divine wisdom learned from Moses and the Hebrews. Egypt thus existed both as the progenitor of the most ancient wisdom and the fertile meeting ground of Hellenic and Hebraic profundities.[49]

The allure of the fabled land ruled by the pharaohs took on an enhanced significance for Renaissance Romans, too, from their increasing familiarity with the accounts of the ancient Romans, such as Pliny's remarks on the pyramids. Even more important was a probing of newly accessible Greek sources. Herodotus's history and Strabo's geography, both translated into Latin by orders of Nicholas V, increased humanist knowledge of ancient Egypt, as did Diodorus Siculus's *Bibliotheca* and Plutarch's *Moralia*, which contains the most detailed account of the mystery cult devoted to Isis and Osiris. Especially intriguing to Roman humanists were Egyptian hieroglyphs, many of which appeared on the obelisks the Caesars had brought to Rome. In the course of the fifteenth century several obelisks had, in fact, been unearthed from Roman soil, where they had lain neglected for centuries. What made such archeological finds even more suggestive to Renaissance humanists was the mistaken notion, derived from various classical and patristic sources, most importantly Horapollo Niliacus's second or fourth-century A.D. *Hieroglyphica*, which claimed the ancient Egyptian pictographs were cryptic images of divine ideas. By this means the sacred wisdom of Egypt had been hidden from profanation by the multitude.[50] Giles of Viterbo went further. He believed that the hieroglyphs were the means resorted to by the ancient Egyptians to protect from corruption the divine truths learned from the Hebrews. This thus served as a further testimony to the sacred character of the Hebrew language, which he believed was the actual form of discourse used by the Holy Spirit.[51]

One further stimulus to the study of Egyptian lore stemmed from Annio da Viterbo, that inventive antiquarian. In Rome in 1498, he published a collection of newly "discovered" ancient sources—actually they were Annio's forgeries—which seemed to "prove" the connection between the wisdom of ancient Egypt and the lore of the Etruscans.[52]

The most startling manifestation of Roman "Egyptology" appears in the decorative scheme of the "Room of the Saints" in the Appartamento Borgia, the series of residential and ceremonial rooms in the Vatican Palace that Pinturicchio frescoed for Alexander VI in the early years of the second Borgia pontificate. The paintings of the adjoining rooms have traditional themes—prophets and Apostles, the seven liberal arts, the Seven Joys of the Virgin—but the ceiling of the Sala dei Santi sets forth the mythology of the Borgia emblem, the ox (or bull).[53]

The ox as the heraldic device of Borgia dynasticism became ubiquitous during Alexander's pontificate, receiving prominent display both in artistic commissions, such as the ceiling of S. Maria Maggiore, and on ceremonial occasions, when bullfights were a frequent public spectacle. On the route of Alexander's *possesso*, moreover, appeared an ox fountain emitting water and wine, while another apparatus showed a gilded ox. The accompanying inscription alluded to the role of the ox in the founding of Rome—Romulus, according to legend, traced its boundaries with an ox-drawn plowshare—and proclaimed Rome now to be reborn anew through her ox, the Borgia bull. Evocative, too, of ancient Rome is Cesare Borgia's parade sword, on which a bull, sacrificed according to classical Roman practice, served as a propitiatory omen of Borgia military success. But the ox emblem could also be evoked in support of peaceful aims. In a brief discussion of hieroglyphs in *De re aedificatoria*, Alberti states that the ox stood for peace.[54] During his coronation festivities Alexander was proclaimed *Pacis Pater*, and in Pinturicchio's fresco in the Appartamento Borgia that shows St. Catherine disputing with the philosophers before the Emperor Maximian the background is dominated by a triumphal arch (modelled after the Arch of Constantine), which is surmounted by a golden bull and which is inscribed with the motto PACIS CVLTORI.

In the ceiling of the "Room of the Saints" such random allusions give way to a comprehensive celebration of the mythical genealogy of the Borgia device. The story begins with the metamorphosis of the Greek princess Io into a cow, her flight to Egypt, and her transformation there back into human shape as Isis, queen of the Nile kingdom. According to some ancient sources (e.g., Isidore of Seville's *Etymologies*), Isis taught the Egyptians the use of hieroglyphs, just as Moses was the inventer of the Hebraic script. In the Pinturicchio ceiling, Io-Isis sits enthroned, teaching the Egyptians, with Moses and Hermes Trismegistus at her side. The next scene shows her marriage to Osiris. Subsequently Osiris is shown, again in accordance with classical accounts, teaching mankind to use the plow, to grow the vine, and to gather fruit. He is, in short, the peaceful benefactor of the human race, whose divine gifts elevated humanity from the brutal

35. Pinturicchio, *The Disputation of St. Catherine of Alexandria with the Philosophers before the Emperor Maximian.* Sala dei Santi, Appartamento Borgia, Vatican Palace. (Photo: Alinari/Art Resource, NY)

state of cannibalism to benign husbandry. But then Osiris was murdered by his evil brother, and the pieces of his body scattered over all Egypt. Isis manages at length to gather the bodily parts of her former consort, and erects a pyramid over his tomb. There he reappears as Apis, the bull, and is worshipped by the Egyptians as the living image of the resurrected god. In the last scene, the bull, elevated by his priests, is borne triumphantly before the faithful, before the beginning of sacred rites. At the head of the procession appears a child blowing a horn decorated with another Borgia heraldic emblem, the double crown of the royal house of Aragon. These elements suggest a final metamorphosis of Apis-Osiris into the Borgia pope himself and have a parallel in the pope's own ceremonial appearance raised aloft on his *sedia gestatoria*. In the myth set forth in the Pinturicchio ceiling, Io-Isis, the link between Hellenic and Egyptian civilization, and Osiris-Apis, the image of the slain and resurrected divine king, are the sacred progenitors of the Borgia pontificate; and Alexander's epiphany is seen as productive of peace and the beneficent progress of humanity.

There is a revealing follow-up to this Egyptian form of Borgia glorification. Vasari, in his life of Bramante, reports that the architect had proposed to Julius II a hieroglyphic emblem for the frieze of the Cortile del Belvedere: JVLIVS II PONT. MAX. was to be pictographically rendered by the head in profile of Julius Caesar, a bridge with two arches (to indicate PONT. II.), and an obelisk (to symbolize MAX.). The pope, according to Vasari, laughed at Bramante's proposal, ordered a full-scale model to be made of it, and said that Bramante should make it known that "this folly" had been copied from a door at Viterbo—a derisive reference to Annio's forged Egyptian antiquities.[55]

Julius II, in fact, partly because of his Borgia antipathies, but also because he looked rather to Moses, Aaron, and Solomon as types of sacred authority, was less willing than Alexander VI to see in the ancient Near Eastern myths and mystery cults the prefiguration of Christian rites. Rome and Jerusalem, not Egypt, formed the foundations of Julius's sense of the papacy. One sign of this is Julius's refusal to alter the orientation of St. Peter's basilica in order to have the focal point of its forecourt be the Vatican obelisk. Another is that in Raphael's Stanza d'Eliodoro, the most personal room in terms of its decorative scheme in Julius's Vatican apartment, only Hebraic or Christian religious authority appears.[56]

It was during Julius's pontificate, moreover, that Giles of Viterbo, so often an articulator for the Della Rovere pontiff of the papacy's sacred mission and destiny, developed a deepening interest in Hebraic studies. Earlier, following Annio da Viterbo's lead, Giles had pursued Egyptian lore. But around 1507 he returned to the serious study of Hebrew and Aramaic he had begun a dozen years earlier in Florence. Giles devoted attention to Talmudic literature, but above all he cultivated the cabala, the esoteric medieval Jewish theosophy, which he and other Renaissance cabalists believed contained the hidden divine wisdom revealed to Adam, Moses, and the other patriarchs and from them descended in oral transmission down the centuries.[57]

Roman interest in the cabala did not originate with Giles. As Pico points out,[58] Julius II's uncle Sixtus IV sought to have a Latin translation made of it. To Sixtus's pontificate also belongs the Good Friday 1481 sermon of Flavius Mithridates. This converted Sicilian Jew, who had come to Rome through the patronage of Cardinal Cibo, the future Innocent VIII, dazzled his Vatican audience in the course of his two-hour oration with citations from Latin, Greek, the Hebrew "*arcana,*" and "Chaldean" to prove Christ's Passion had been foretold by prophets and rabbis. In 1486, at Perugia, this same Mithridates undertook to teach Pico the rudiments of Hebrew, and initiated him into the profundities of esoteric Jewish lore. Among the works Mithridates translated for his ardent student were a Maimonides treatise on the resurrection of the dead and Levi Gersonides's mystical commentary on the Canticles, and he collaborated with Pico also in making a new Latin translation from the Hebrew of the Book of Job, that drew extensively on Gersonides's commentary. Most important, Mithridates made accessible to Pico the cabala, translating for him the basic texts.[59]

Pico, who eventually returned to Florence after the debacle of the Nine Hundred Theses, devoted much of the last five years of his life to cabalistic studies. He thus became the pivotal figure in advocating cabalistic exegesis of the Old Testament as the key to finding a hidden concordance between Neo-Platonist metaphysics and Christian revelation. Foremost among those taking inspiration from Pico's efforts was Giles of Viterbo. Like Pico, the Roman Augustinian was drawn to the esoteric richness of the cabalistic method. By means of metaphor, number mysticism, and the riddles of acrostics, hidden depths in the Scriptural text could be revealed. For Giles, in fact, this unlocking of "*Hebraica veritas*" surpassed in significance even the recovery of the *prisci theologi*. Pagan mythical traditions bore vestiges of divine truth beneath poetic veils, but the Hebrew script and text, since this was the very language by which God spoke directly to man, carried the divine message itself.[60]

Cabalistic studies preoccupied Giles for the remainder of his life, with the final fruits of his inquiries, the *Scechina*, appearing in the 1530s. Already, however, the cabala determined the basic structure of his *Historia XX saecolorum*, the universal history he composed for Leo X in the years 1513–18. In this Giles regards the ten ages of Old Testament times and the ten ages of the Church as images of the ten Sefiroth, the emanations of the Godhead. In a letter to Gian Matteo Giberti, also dating from Leo's pontificate, Giles equates the penetration, by means of the cabala, of the treasures of secret wisdom contained in sacred Scripture with the voyages of discovery and consequent recognition of the pope as universal shepherd by all the peoples of the world. These two providential discoveries—the Hebrew *arcana* and the new lands—gave humanity deeper understanding of the divine and true knowledge of the world. Their coincidental occurrences served, moreover, as signs that the Tenth Age was dawning, the age of intellectual and religious unity of all mankind under the Roman pontiffs and the final fulfillment of Christ's words ". . . *et fiet unum ovile et unus pastor.*"[61]

THE *ECCLESIA EX JUDAEIS* AND THE *ECCLESIA EX GENTILIBUS*

Emphasis on accommodation of classical and Christian thought, and anticipation of the imminent union of all peoples in peace and concord, meant that in the minds of Renaissance Romans Christianity was neither a narrowly orthodox nor an exclusive religion. The full truth of God's nature and transcendent purpose for His Creation had indeed become embodied in Latin Christianity and the Roman Church. But a general knowledge of God had been made accessible, by His providence, to all nations from the beginning of time. The inspired wisdom of Zoroaster, Hermes Trismegistus, and the other *prisci theologi* testified to this.[62] Furthermore, the deeper mysteries of Christ's Incarnation and Resurrection had been foretold to both the ancient Hebrews, God's Chosen People, and to the Gentiles. Hosea, Isaiah, Jeremiah, Ezekiel, Zechariah, Daniel, and the other Old Testament prophets served as the means by which God had prepared the way among the Jews for the coming of Christ. Among the Gentiles prophetic preparation was accomplished through the ecstatic utterances of the sibyls.

In classical tradition the sibyls were those mantic women, dwelling at various oracular shrines—usually sacred to Apollo—who in fits of divine possession predicted the future, frequently in the form of acrostics, riddles, or other enigmatic utterance. The numbers, names, and locations of the sibyls varies—Varro provides a list of ten, which Lactantius included in his *Divinae institutiones* and thus transmitted to the Latin Middle Ages. For the Greek world, the most famous oracular shrines and female seers were those at Delphi (the Pythia) and at the oasis of Siwa in the Sahara Desert (the Egyptian or Libyan Sibyl), which Alexander the Great consulted. For the Romans, pre-eminence belonged to the Cumaean Sibyl, whose cave, sacred to Apollo, was located at the head of the Bay of Naples. In the *Aeneid*, Bk. VI, Virgil recounts Aeneas's visit to the cave of the Cumaean Sibyl; through her guidance the progenitor of Rome enters the underworld, and there learns the destiny of the city his descendents will create. Suggestive, too, of the Cumaean Sibyl's prominence is Virgil's

Fourth Eclogue. There it is her prophecy that is fulfilled in the "new progeny from heaven" and the "return of the Golden Age."[63]

The Cumaean Sibyl had a further significance in ancient Roman tradition. Written collections of prophecies, attributed to her and known as the Sibylline Books, were preserved in the Capitol. Kept under the supervision of a special priestly college, they were consulted at the command of the Senate. Renaissance Romans knew of this practice. Platina, at Sixtus IV's request, had prepared a three-volume *Liber privilegiorum*, a compilation of various bulls, donations, and other documents relating to papal powers and rights. Should anyone doubt the authenticity of this collection, let them, Platina suggests, be given papal permission to read the oldest bulls, covered with gold and encrusted with gems, which Sixtus had ordered to be preserved in Castel Sant'Angelo "as if they were another Minerva sculpted by Phidias or the books of the Sibyl Amalthea [i.e., the Cumaean Sibyl] that contained the destiny of the Roman people."[64]

Respect for the visionary powers of the sibyls explains why in the Patristic Age various apocryphal prophecies of Christ's coming were attributed to them by Christian apologists. A collection of these *Oracula Sibyllina* was preserved in Greek and in Lactantius's *Divinae institutiones*. Augustine (*City of God*, XVIII, 23) also cites the testimony of the sibyls as true foreknowledge, and he provides the text of an acrostic poem of the Erythraean Sibyl. She lived, he says, contemporaneously either with Romulus or with the Trojan War, and her rejection of false pagan idols and prediction of Last Judgment cause her to be counted among those belonging to the City of God.

The sibyls' authenticity as Christian prophetesses thus affirmed, it is not surprising that they make their appearance in medieval thought and art.[65] Generalized sibylline references were recurrent in the Middle Ages, but medieval Rome, significantly, acquired the prestige of its own particular legend. In the version included in the *Mirabilia*, the Roman senators, in gratitude for the Emperor Augustus's accomplishments, came to him, urging his worship as a divinity. Augustus initially opposed the idea, but requested a delay in his decision, and then consulted the Tiburtine Sibyl. After a three days' fast, she replied (in poetry borrowed from St. Augustine) that a king would come from heaven. Suddenly the heavens burst open, and Augustus beheld in the sky a virgin standing over an altar and holding a child in her arms. A voice proclaimed, "This is the altar of the Son of God," and the emperor immediately fell to the ground in adoration of Christ who would come. This vision took place, the *Mirabilia* goes on, in Augustus's chamber on the Capitoline Hill; hence the name of the church located there—S. Maria in Aracoeli.[66]

The legend of the Ara Coeli, like those of the fountain of oil that miraculously sprang forth on the site of S. Maria in Trastevere on the night Christ was born, or the collapse of the Templum Pacis at the same time, enabled the greatness of Rome's imperial past to participate in a direct way with Christ's coming. For Valla such fables did not hold water. In his *Declamatio* against the Donation of Constantine, he dismisses both the Ara Coeli and Templum Pacis stories as fraudulent, and argues that their falsity leads rather to the destruction of faith than to its establishment.[67] Other humanists, too, had reservations about the sibyls. In his *Rerum memorandarum libri*, Petrarch expresses skepticism, especially regarding the veracity of the Erythraean Sibyl's utterances (though in his *De otio religioso* he reverts to the customary medieval acceptance of the sibyls' authenticity).[68] More revealing as an indication of Roman Renaissance views were the doubts of Paolo Pompilio (1455–91), the humanist poet and Latin classicist who had connections with Leto's circle. Pompilio avers that various classical authorities regarded both the sibylline oracles and the verses of Orpheus as apocryphal.[69]

Leto himself thought otherwise. In his marginal commentary on Varro's *De lingua latina*, he linked the oracular powers accorded the ancient poets and seers to the role of the prophets among the Hebrews.[70] There were other humanist defenders of the sibyls. Filippo Barbieri's *Discordantiae Sanctorum Doctorum Hieronymi et Augustini*, published in Rome in 1481 and dedicated to Sixtus IV, comes down decisively in favor of Augustine (and against Jerome) on the question of the sibylline prophecies of Christ. In additon, his book included woodcuts of twelve sibyls, with texts of their prophecies taken from the inscriptions included in their depiction as part of the fresco cycle of *uomini famosi* Cardinal Giordano Orsini had painted in his Monte Giordano palace in the 1430s.[71]

In later fifteenth and early sixteenth century Rome, whatever lingering misgivings about the sibyls remained were overwhelmed by the general consensus in their favor. Thus Platina in his *Lives of the Popes* sustains the veracity of both the fountain of oil in Trastevere (a manifestation, he claims, of the extension of the grace of Christ to the Gentiles) and of the sibyls (nearly all of whom, he states, predicted Christ's advent). [72] Even the Ara Coeli legend reappears. In Raphael's *Madonna di Foligno*, commissioned by Sigismondo de' Conti (d. 1512) for S. Maria in Aracoeli, the Roman historian is shown kneeling before the heavenly vision of the Madonna and Child.[73]

Moreover, depictions of the sibyls proliferated in Roman churches and chapels: in the ceiling of the Carafa Chapel in S. Maria sopra Minerva, in the Appartamento Borgia, in the ceiling of the choir of S. Maria del Popolo, in the Chigi Chapel of S. Maria della Pace (where their prophecies are inscribed in Greek, except for the Cumaean Sibyl's IAM NO[VA] PROGE[NIES] from Virgil's Fourth Eclogue), and, most monumentally, in the Sistine Chapel ceiling.[74]

Roman enthusiasm for the sibyls, while particularly marked, partook of their widespread appeal to Renaissance Italy as a whole. Sibyls appear, among other places, in the Tempio Malatestiano in Rimini, on the pavement of the Cathedral in Siena, in the Sassetti Chapel of S. Trinita in Florence, in Perugino's Collegio del Cambio frescoes in Perugia, and in Signorelli's depiction of the *Dies irae* in the Duomo of Orvieto.[75]

Literary works, too, included the sibyls. In the Neapolitan Jacopo Sannazaro's *De partu Virginis*, the Christian epic poem inspired by a sermon of Giles of Viterbo,[76] the account of the Annunciation contains the traditional element of the Virgin Mary reading. But in this case, she peruses, significantly, the sibylline prophecies.[77]

Sibyls, as well as prophets, appear as harbingers of Christ, too, in the Florentine Matteo Palmieri's *Città di vita*, the *terza rima* poem written in imitation of Dante's *Divine Comedy*. Palmieri's poem, however, unlike Dante's, begins in heaven and ends with the ascent through the circles of Purgatory. More striking is that the Cumaean Sibyl combines the roles of Dante's Virgil and Beatrice as guide to hell and heaven.[78]

The Florentine Platonic Academy, Ficino in particular, similarly upheld the visionary powers attributed to the sibyls. Ficino's approval stemmed largely from the Neo-Platonic aspiration toward the exalted state of divine frenzy (*furor divinus*), during which knowledge of the ultimate mysteries comes to be infused into the human soul.[79]

As a Platonist, Giles of Viterbo shared this ardor for the sibyls' wisdom, "*numinis afflantis.*"[80] But as an extoller of Rome's providential destiny, he was particularly interested in the Cumaean Sibyl and her prophecies. In fact, like Palmieri and Sannazaro, he actually visited the ruins at Cumae. There he descended into the grotto on the shore of Lake Avernus the Renaissance held to be the dread cave of the Sibyl. The stale air of its depths, Giles reported, seemed particularly conducive to hallucinatory spells, and during one descent there an intense mystical experience of some sort occurred to him; in the Sibyl's honor he prostrated himself.[81]

More significant than this attempt to verify the actual site of the Sibyl's visionary utterances was Giles's conviction that she served as a true prophetess of Rome's centrality to God's plan for human redemption: she correctly foresaw, as related in Virgil's Fourth Eclogue, the coming of the Son of God, conceived by a Virgin, who would make Rome the perpetual seat of His priesthood and of His eternal empire. This prophecy the ancient Romans mistakenly applied to Romulus, the son of Mars, born of the Vestal Virgin Rhea Silvia. Despite this misapprehension, God did preserve the infant lives of the twin founders of Rome, and He did guide the city's rise in power to world dominion. In this way, Giles argues, God fulfilled his intention to make it the foundation of the Roman Church, the truly universal *imperium*. Indeed, just as God's hand can be seen in the sacred history of the ancient Hebrews—from Abraham to Moses to David to Isaiah, who prophesied the return to Jerusalem from Babylonian captivity—so from the time Janus founded Etruria on the right bank of the Tiber, God was providentially directing the course of Roman history. Thus Dardanus, exiled from Italy, went to Asia Minor, where he founded Troy. From there in turn Aeneas, after long wanderings, came back to the land of the Tiber and founded the line from which Romulus would spring.[82]

The Cumaean Sibyl, accorded oracular status by the ancient Romans, was thus, in Giles's view, the visionary *par excellence* of the Roman Church. This is her position, too, in Michelangelo's Sistine Chapel ceiling, whose overall theological program seems to reflect many of the same religious ideas advanced by Giles and other Roman humanists. Weighty with dignity and age, absorbed in her book, she sits enthroned above the scene of the creation of Eve, a foreshadowing of the birth of the Church (the second Eve) from the side of Christ (the second Adam).[83]

In Michelangelo's ceiling the Cumaean Sibyl is flanked by four other sibyls: the Delphic, Erythraean, Persian, and Libyan. Representing Greece, Ionia, Asia, and Africa respectively, they suggest the geographical expanse of the prophecies to the Gentiles. They also perhaps stand for the range of the mission of the Roman Church, in the view of early sixteenth-century Rome.[84]

Of these four sibyls, the Erythraean, however, seems especially related to the link between the Church from the Gentiles and the Church from the Jews. In the *Oracula Sibyllina*, she declares she is Noah's daughter-in-law, and in the Sistine Ceiling she sits next to the panel showing the *Sacrifice of Noah*. In this scene, moreover, the patriarch, joined by his daughter-in-law, performs a sacrifice of burnt offerings at an open-air altar placed in front of the wooden planks of the Ark. As priestess, the sibyl solemnly lights a burning brand, while at the same time shielding her face. Her gestures echo the classical representation of the death of Meleager, whose mother Althea, sacrificing her son by means of an enchanted faggot, averts her eyes in holy terror, unable to witness the import of her actions. Noah, by contrast, calmly points heavenward—a representation of prophetic assurance.[85]

St. Augustine, as Esther Dotson points out,[86] held that Noah's sacrifice upon emerging from the Ark should be understood as a "sign of regeneration," comparable to the role of circumcision for Abraham and his descendents. Circumcision, in turn, formed a typological prefigurement of baptism, and in the Sistine Chapel wall frescoes, the *Circumcision of Moses' Son* stands opposite the *Baptism of Christ*, indicating precisely this relationship. Noah belongs to sacred history *ante legem*—indeed before the division of humanity into Jew and Gentile. In fact, Noah's sons Shem and Japheth were seen as standing for the *Ecclesia Judaeorum* and the

36. Michelangelo, *Cumaean Sibyl*. Sistine Chapel ceiling. (Photo: Alinari/Art Resource, NY)

Ecclesia Gentilium, while his third son Ham, who shamefully mocked the nakedness of his drunken father (the subject of the last panel of the Sistine Ceiling) was the founder of the earthly cities of Babylon and Nineveh.[87] Noah's sacrifice was thus to be understood as anticipating circumcision and baptism, the respective "signs of regeneration" of the Chosen People first *sub lege* and then *sub gratia*. On the symbolic level, the sibyl's averted grief and Noah's heavenward gesture suggest anticipatory responses to the sacrifice of Christ's Crucifixion, the Atonement that made possible human redemption and salvation. So, too, is the Ark a type of the Church, and the adjoining scenes of the Flood and of Noah's drunkenness with their overtones of baptism and the eucharist prefigure the sacraments by which the Church transmits the salvific promises to the faithful.[88]

The Church, then, in the thematic argument set forth in the frescoes of the Sistine Chapel, has been providentially prepared for from the beginning of history as the haven and refuge for the whole of mankind.[89] In Raphael's tapestries of the careers of Peter and Paul, which completed the decoration of the Chapel, the same theme appears. Peter, the Apostle to the Jews, and Paul, the Apostle to the Gentiles, are shown as exercising complementary ministries. Appointed to their apostolates directly by Christ, they engage in the parallel tasks of healing and conversion, and of confronting the peculiar sins of each people (obstinacy or disobedience for the Jews, idolatry for the Gentiles). The whole sequence concludes with St. Paul's evangelizing of the Athenians. This forms a fitting climax to his *magisterium Gentium*, inasmuch as the conversion of the philosopher Dionysius in Athens, the center of all the ancient schools of philosophy, symbolizes the ultimate harmony between Christianity and philosophy, the highest Gentile achievement.[90]

CREATION AND ESCHATON

In the Sistine Chapel the unfolding drama of human salvation has its beginnings in God's mighty acts of Creation. Proceeding from the altar end, the first three panels of Michelangelo's ceiling show, in images of awesome mystery, God separating light from darkness, making the sun and the moon, and commanding the waters to bring forth life.[91] The whole of sacred history stems from these foundations, and it is from this vantage point that its ultimate meaning is illumined.

Divine creation of the cosmos formed the fixed anchor point not just for the decorative program of the Sistine Chapel; it was fundamental, too, to the religious outlook of the Roman humanists. Indeed, there was a tendency to explain even contemporary developments in terms of God's providential acts of Creation, a propensity apparent in those orations of

Giles of Viterbo and Cristoforo Marcello examined in the first section of this chapter. The same idea is advanced in Giles's famous inaugural speech to the Fifth Lateran Council. In it he likens the divine instruction to hold a council to the commandments in Genesis by which God created the world.[92]

Creation, moreover, was a mystery that Aurelio Brandolini, in his treatise on letter writing, which contains a passing but important description of the epideictic oratory of the papal court, recommended as particularly appropriate to the *genus demonstrativum*. Like the Trinity and the Hypostatic Union of the divine and human nature in the one person of Christ, Creation was beyond human fathoming; instead of being rationally scrutinized, it therefore should be the subject of admiration, love, and praise.[93]

In accordance with Brandolini's remarks, practitioners of the new sacred oratory did repeatedly urge their hearers to gaze upon the beauty of the universe and to behold with wonder its majestic magnitude.[94] In so doing, not only did they choose a topic suitable for rhetorical praise, but they also departed sharply from the concerns of the medieval thematic sermon with its moralistic, penitential, and often technically theological outlook.[95]

Admiration for the beauty and goodness of Creation was an attitude widespread during the Renaissance, finding early expression in the writings of Valla, Manetti, and other Quattrocento Italian humanists.[96] Support for such views could be found among the Latin Church Fathers, notably Lactantius and Augustine, but even more celebratory in their treatment of Creation were certain of the Greek Fathers, particularly Basil and Gregory of Nyssa.[97] Revival of the Greek patristic heritage assumed an important place in the intellectual culture of Renaissance Rome, as we have seen. Moreover, a revealing indication of what the Roman humanists sought in the Greek Fathers is that Basil's important *Homilies on the Hexaemeron* (i.e., on the Six Days of Creation) received two separate translations from Greek into Latin.

In the opening remarks of his *Homilies*, Basil in fact develops a theme echoed in many Roman sermons: the beauty and magnitude of Creation testify to the infinitely abounding goodness and immense wisdom of the Creator, and demonstrate the absurdity of those who suggest the universe came about by chance or fortune and not by divine will. Moreover, in prefacing his translation of this work, Argyropoulos declares that no one has surpassed Basil in elucidating the meaning of Creation and in inspiring admiration for the Creator. Basil's *Homilies on the Hexaemeron* thereby form a testament to human felicity. Inasmuch, however, as Basil died before he could treat the sixth day, the creation of man, one should, he advises, turn for the completion of the Creation account to the *De opificio hominis* of Basil's brother, Gregory of Nyssa.[98]

The Greek Fathers undoubtedly served less as an inspiration than as a confirmation of prevailing attitudes. Nonetheless the sanction of early Christian thought contributed an important element in encouraging the optimistic conclusions propounded by Roman intellectuals. Indeed, as Argyropoulos indicates, realization of the meaning of Creation remained incomplete for them without the culminating act, the divine creation of man, made in God's image and likeness. Humanity in this way was endowed with a singular dignity, and the *dignitas hominis* theme was one persistently put forth in the sermons delivered to the papal court. Among these, indeed, were three, dating from the early sixteenth century, preached on Ash Wednesday, when one might suppose an "ashes-to-ashes-and-dust-to-dust" emphasis on the evanescence of human life would instead find favor.[99] Man's dignity, for the papal orators, consisted in part in the beauty and harmony of the human body; but this was surpassed by his other endowments—memory, intellect, and will, and even more in his lordship over the rest of the cosmos, his immortal soul, and his God-like attribute of being in some measure the maker and determiner of his own existence.[100] The nobly heroic Adam of the fourth panel of Michelangelo's Sistine Chapel ceiling seems an altogether fitting visual counterpart to these ideas, so often expressed in that very setting.

Wondrous as was man's creation in divine likeness, this was surpassed in sublimity, in the minds of the papal preachers, by the mystery of the Incarnation. In this immense outpouring of divine love, Christ, by assuming human nature, made possible man's deification: "God became man, so that man might become God," as Giles of Viterbo, and other contemporaries, proclaimed.[101] When the Word became flesh, the whole universe was redeemed, reconciled, restored, and made new; and human nature acquired a dignity surpassing even Adam's original state (before the Fall). The Incarnation, in short, marked the crucial event in God's mighty deed of human redemption; as such it also formed the "cosmic" center point of all space and time.[102]

Concomitant with this Incarnational focus was a lessened emphasis on Christ's Crucifixion. In the minds of the Roman thinkers, not atonement and expiatory sacrifice with their underscoring of human sinfulness, but instead the magnitude of divine love revealed in the conjoining of divine and human natures constituted the essential core of Christianity. In seeing in the Incarnation the unmerited grace by which mankind gained salvation, they also embraced an outlook that was world-affirmative, one that legitimated human potential for activity and creativity. Furthermore, the enhanced goodness of nature and of human existence in the reconciled cosmos of the Incarnation meant that to a large extent the purpose for which God had created the universe had been fulfilled. Like St. John, whose Gospel the Roman humanists so frequently

37. Michelangelo, *Creation of Adam*. Sistine Chapel ceiling. (Photo: Alinari/Art Resource, NY)

adduced, there was a recognition of "realized eschatology": the light had come into the world (John 3: 10).[103]

Fulfillment and culmination in their manifold aspects formed the hallmarks of Roman Renaissance culture in the opening decades of the sixteenth century.[104] The myth of the Golden Age, the recovery of ancient sources of wisdom, the stimulus of European overseas expansion, the revival of classical eloquence, and the achievements in poetry and the arts contributed to this sense. Encompassing all, however, was the Christian historical framework of prophetic promise, fulfillment, and imminent transcendence.

As elsewhere in Europe, Rome at the turn into the sixteenth century did partake of apocalyptic expectations.[105] Outside Rome, such anticipations provoked dire forebodings: the final events, the unfathomable mysteries of Last Judgment and Resurrection of the Dead, were seen as hidden in the deepest recesses of the divine otherness, to be awaited in fear and trembling. In Dürer's remarkable 1498 woodcuts of the Apocalypse, for instance, the four Horsemen ride in pell-mell fury over an abjectly terrified humanity.[106] In Savonarola's millenarian preaching, too, fire and the sword predominated. To be sure, Florence, the navel of Italy, was to become the New Jerusalem, but first had to come an age of tribulation, of divine scourging, and only through repentance would the true believers enter into the shining light of the great renewal.[107]

By contrast, when Cajetan, addressing the Fifth Lateran Council, devoted his whole oration to explicating the passage from John's Apocalypse, "I saw the holy city, the new Jerusalem descending from heaven . . ." (Revelation 21: 2), he emphasized the realization of this vision in the perfection, stability, and peace of the Roman Church. The Church, he asserts, is the new Jerusalem, and in this new Jerusalem all things are made anew. In the Hebrew Synagogue had been the old man, the old law, the old leaven, but in the new Jerusalem is a new heart, new law, a bread of a new baking. But the greatest newness was that God had become man, and man in turn God. Moreover, this divine and sempiternal newness— that greatest *beneficium* of God through which we are made sons of God by perpetual adoption, and which constitutes the essential meaning of the New Testament—belongs specifically to the Church; only from the Church have the secular societies of human history received it.

Furthermore, Cajetan continues, only from heaven could this new, holy city have descended; for only from heaven could have come the surpassing newness of the partnership of the divine and human. Yet in descending, the new Jerusalem established its foundations in the "holy mountains," that is, in the miracles worked by Christ, in the preaching of the Apostles, in the sacrifices of the martyrs, and in the minds of holy and upright men cleansed of their sinfulness. The new Jerusalem did not descend, then, in a literal and material sense, but rather as an imitation and reflection of heaven. The Celestial Jerusalem, which is the Church Triumphant and has Christ as its Lord, exists, as it were, as the mother of the Church Militant, which is the Lord's sheepfold on earth, and which is governed by the Vicar of Christ.[108]

Many of Cajetan's Roman contemporaries went farther. For them the *Mons sanctus Dei* existed not just in saintly deeds and holy lives. Rather this represented the Apostolic See of Rome and had come to be realized concretely in the Vatican itself. The Roman Church was the daughter of Zion, they agreed, but in addition Rome, in supplanting the old sacred capital of Israel, became the tangible embodiment of the new Jerusalem; and the Mons Vaticanus was in a "concretized" sense the new Mt. Zion, the manifested eternal pivot upon which rested God's providential plan for human salvation.[109]

Even loftier was the vision of Giles of Viterbo. For him, Rome was the *sancta latina Ierusalem*; and as the true rather than the shadowy Mt. Zion, it was the fulfillment of all that had been foreshadowed in the "synagogue." Rome formed the center of the religious world, and at the focal point of Rome stood the tomb of the Prince of the Apostles. In the *Mons sanctificationis* of the Vatican was concentrated the wisdom, the unswerving orthodoxy, and the sanctifying grace of the Christian faith. Here Peter's eternal authority over the Church would be administered by his successors until the end of time. In his own age, Giles saw, in the pontificates of Julius II and especially Leo X, the "breaking in" of that final realization, the culminating Tenth Age of fulfillment and renewal. This renovation would not be restricted to the Church alone. Instead it would constitute a consummation cosmic in scope, a rejuvenation touching all mankind and extending to all reality. A key sign of this dawning sacralization of the universe was the new St. Peter's, the eternal Temple of the New Law rising "to the very heavens" on the Vatican Hill.[110]

VII

Epilogue:
The Sack and Its Aftermath

> With so great an alteration [the election of Adrian
> VI], I am left astounded, and in such a mentally
> confused state that I seem to be in a new world,
> and that Rome no longer is where it was.
>
> —Baldassare Castiglione, letter from Rome,
> 11 January 1522.

> See here the murders and the rapes
> That make Rome grieve in every part;
> And things both sacred and profane
> Are equally violated and put to flame.
>
> —Ludovico Ariosto, *Orlando Furioso*, Canto
> XXXIII, 55.

> O God, the heathen have set foot in thy domain
>   defiled thy holy temple
> and laid Jerusalem in ruins.
> They have thrown out the dead bodies of thy servants
>   to feed the birds of the air;
> they have made thy loyal servants carrion for wild beasts.
> Their blood is spilled all round Jerusalem like water,
>   and there they lie unburied.

To those who experienced the cataclysmic *Sacco di Roma* of 1527, these lines from Psalm 78 (79), a lamentation for the destruction of the ancient Hebraic capital, seemed an only-too-accurate account of the new Jerusalem's desecration. Indeed, following the Sack, the papal cantor, Costanzo Festa (d. 1545), used the entire Latin text of this psalm to compose a sacred motet. Festa, the first important composer of the High Renaissance native to Italy, and the only Italian before Palestrina to master fully the musical advances of the prevailing Franco-Flemish tradition of sacred polyphony, had been a member of the papal chapel since the halcyon days of Leo X. Through the compositional resources at Festa's command, the poignant outcry of the Psalmist powerfully expressed the anguish Renaissance Romans felt on seeing the *sancta latina Ierusalem* of Leonine and Clementine Rome laid to waste.[1]

Other witnesses, too, drew the parallel between Jerusalem's devastation and Rome's. A Spaniard, writing from Rome a month after the initial assault, reported this scene: "In Rome, the chief city of Christendom, no bells ring, no churches are open, no Masses are said, Sundays and feast-days have ceased." Palaces have been stripped bare, he goes on to say, houses burned to the ground, shops turned into stables, and streets into dunghills. The stench of decaying cadavers is overpowering, men and animals share common graves, all sins are openly committed, and the blasphemies of gambling soldiers ring through the air. "I know nothing to which I can compare it, except the destruction of Jerusalem."[2]

Unlike the Babylonian attack on the Hebraic capital in 586 B.C. that occasioned the writing of Psalm 78, the Sack of Rome did not occur as a result of any strategic policy. Instead, the onslaught on Rome developed as an unforeseen consequence of the continuing Habsburg-Valois rivalry for dominance in Italy and in Europe. With the utter defeat of French forces at the Battle of Pavia (24 February 1525) and the capture there of King Francis I, the Emperor Charles V appeared to have gained hegemony. Pope Clement VII, fearing the consequences to the papacy and to Medicean Florence of Spain's adding possession of Lombardy to its Neapolitan viceroyalty, saw as his only viable course the creation of an anti-imperialist alliance. The resultant League of Cognac of 1526, whose signatories were the papacy, France, Venice, and the Sforza (who hoped to regain Milan), was predicated from the papal point of view on the return of French military power to Italy. When this failed to materialize, and when imperial forces, aided by last-minute defections from the papal alliance, penetrated into papal Emilia in a winter campaign during 1526–27, Clement sought a truce. But at this point the imperial army, camped in the snows near Bologna, far in arrears in pay, and with the glittering prospect of rich booty from Florence or Rome seemingly gone a glimmer, took events into its own hands. In early April these war-hardened Spanish veterans and fearsome German *Landsknechte* crossed over the Apennines into the Casentino and on 25 April encamped near Arezzo. From there, marching with neither artillery nor baggage wagons to hamper their movement, they rushed south with lightning speed. On 2 May they were outside Viterbo, and on the evening of 5 May their campfires glowed in the *prati* and on the slopes of the Janiculum.[3]

At dawn the next morning, the imperialists, shrouded by a heavy fog, began their assault on the poorly maintained and inadequately defended walls of the Borgo Leonino. The fighting at first proved fierce, and the Duke of Bourbon, commander of the Habsburg army, was killed in the early going. But the attackers soon breached the walls near S. Spirito in Sassia, and enemy soldiers poured into Piazza S. Pietro. In the suddenness of the onslaught, Clement VII, praying in the Vatican, just had time to flee down the elevated *passetto* to Castel Sant'Angelo. There, joined by cardinals, the papal court, and terrified Roman citizens, the pope became effectively a prisoner in his own castle. Regarded as impregnable, Castel Sant'Angelo was spared direct attack, but the now leaderless army turned to gain the spoils of victory. The Ponte Sisto was quickly crossed, laying all Rome open to the whims of rampaging soldiers. For a week, while the papal court in Castel Sant'Angelo looked on in helpless anguish, the Eternal City was put to the sack.

Palaces were looted and burned, their owners subjected to enormous ransoms or murdered. Churches and monasteries were plundered, convents broken into, and nuns ravaged to sate the lust of war-maddened men. In a kind of inverse pilgrimage, soldiers furiously defiled the sacred sites and objects linked to popular devotion. Tombs were pried open, relics were stolen, even the consecrated Host on the altars of Roman churches was profaned. Looters pillaged the Sancta Sanctorum of the Lateran and reportedly played ball with the heads of Sts. Peter and Paul. Blood flowed in St. Peter's, the Veronica was reported stolen and hawked for sale about Roman hostelries, St. Andrew's head tossed to the ground, and the Sacred Lance of Longinus fastened to a *Landsknecht's* pike. Several German soldiers, affected by Lutheran anti-papal tracts, donned clerical garments, and led by one dressed in pontifical robes and the triple tiara paraded before Castel Sant'Angelo in a parody of papal processions. There before Clement's eyes they demanded the pope hand over the sails and oars of Peter's bark to Luther, and the mob hailed "*Vivat Lutherus pontifex!*" Within the Vatican Palace, the occupying imperial forces carved Lutheran graffiti into the walls of the Raphael stanze. Registers and other papal documents were strewn about, used as litter for horses, or torn up. The Raphael tapestries of the Sistine Chapel disappeared. Two of them eventually reached Venice the following year; in the meantime they had been first acquired by Isabella d'Este's agents in Rome, then seized at sea by Saracen pirates, who took them to Tunisia.[4]

Jewels, bronzes, embroidered robes, and other such precious and easily transportable art works repeatedly changed hands in makeshift art markets in the city, before vanishing altogether with the departing troops. Many humanist patrons, including Angelo Colocci, lost all their libraries. Other prominent Roman Renaissance figures, such as Cristoforo Marcello, lost their lives. For seven months, Clement remained a captive, and Rome suffered as a vanquished and occupied city. After the initial fury of pillaging spent itself, food shortages arrived, as did disease from both the rotting corpses and the plague. In all, perhaps ten thousand Romans met their death during the period of the Sack, and an equal number probably fled the city. Property losses were colossal.

The first third of the sixteenth century was not auspicious for Italian cities. Brescia (1512), Genoa (1522), and Pavia (1528) were also sacked, and Naples (1528) and Florence (1529–30) suffered serious deprivations during sieges. Violent or sudden changes of government took place frequently, too, notably in Milan and Genoa.[5] Yet amidst all the catastrophes suffered by war-torn Italy the Sack of Rome had the most profound impact and provoked the most soul-searching responses. Thus for Guicciardini, the acerbic critic of papal misuse of sacred authority for temporal ends, the destruction of Rome was nevertheless a sacrilegious act, the ultimate degradation in the downward spiral of war and devastation that had convulsed Italy and left no aspect of its society and culture unscathed. Indeed, the Sack took on the meaning for him of an "apocalyptic tragedy,"[6] and in recounting the miserable shrieks of Roman matrons and nuns, brutally raped by the invading soldiers, Guicciardini declared that one could not but say that in allowing such inhuman acts God's judgments were obscured from human comprehension.[7]

Others were not so willing to draw the conclusion of an abscondite God. Alfonso de Valdés, humanist secretary to Charles V, defended the actions of imperial troops as God's judgment on a corrupt, deceitful, and vice-ridden city. This forms the gist of the case against Rome he delivers in his lengthy *Dialogue of Lactancio and an Archdeacon*, composed in July or August 1527. He suggests further that the Sack was a divine warning to a refractory papacy and Roman clergy that had obstinately refused to be reformed.[8]

Castiglione, serving at the time as papal ambassador to the imperial court in Spain, responded, in turn, with an impassioned denunciation of Valdés's exculpatory claims. To excuse the criminal atrocities, the vilification of the pope, and the flagrant acts of sacrilege showed, he charged, utter disrespect for the Christian religion. Even the ancient Gentiles had feared to violate the sanctuaries and temples of vanquished peoples. Julius Caesar, for example, respected the temple of Osiris in Egypt, and Pompey earned praise for refusing to touch the holy of holies in Solomon's Temple in Jerusalem. When Heliodorus was sent to despoil the Temple of its treasures, a terrifying horse and rider appeared to punish his impiety (here, it seems, Castiglione recalls his friend Raphael's fresco in the Vatican Stanza d'Eliodoro). Other instances from Hebraic history reveal, too, Castiglione goes on, the punishment inflicted by God on sinners guilty of sacrilege. And yet the secretary of the Christian emperor seeks to excuse and justify the monstrous impiety, the "infernal vandalism," of imperial soldiers treading under foot the marble head of St. Andrew and the Sacred Lance that had pierced Christ's side—the deeply venerated relics of the Temple of the Apostles! Not even the Turks would countenance such desecration, and Castiglione warned that divine justice would not leave such abominations unpunished.[9]

Yet other Roman humanists, while sharing Castiglione's horror at the desecration of Rome, wondered if the city was not to blame for the evil that had befallen it. Sadoleto, who left Rome for his diocese of Carpentras just a couple of weeks before the Sack, suggested in letters written in the years immediately following that it was God's vengeful judgment on a depraved city. Yet a bewildered inconsistency runs through his explanations. At other times he invoked the cruelty of *fortuna*, the twists of fate, or the viciousness of the *Landsknechte*.[10]

Giles of Viterbo, who gathered a force of two thousand men at his own expense in order to try to free the imprisoned Clement VII in 1527, was more deeply troubled by the Sack and its meaning. The soaring optimism in imminent fulfillment and transcendence so exultantly expressed during the pontificates of Julius II and Leo X gave way to pessimistic reflections. The pride, wealth, and worldly power of the Roman clergy—the unworthiness of their lives as priests—deserved punishment. Regeneration could be accomplished only through suffering and purgation, and Charles V was the "new Cyrus," the instrument of divine wrath and God's chosen means of purging the evils of the Roman Church. Giles did not abandon his eschatological expectations, but now, significantly, Charles V became the "prince sent from heaven" and the true king of Jerusalem. Imperial messianism had replaced papal.[11]

In political terms, the Sack in fact meant the rude intrusion of geo-political reality into the grandiose papal dreams of imperial *renovatio*. When Clement VII crowned Charles V as Holy Roman Emperor at Bologna in 1530 (the basis of papal-imperial rapprochement was the imperial army that Charles had provided Clement in order to recover Florence for the Medici), what this signified was Spain's position as arbiter of Italy. Renewed Valois challenges to Habsburg peninsular dominance ensued, but the treaty of Cateau-Cambrésis of 1559 merely reconfirmed the prevailing pattern of the papacy firmly within the Spanish orbit. After the Sack, in short, the Romans were forced to recognize what level-headed political analysis had always understood: the papacy was no more than a second-class power, not the Roman Empire reborn.[12]

The Sack proved all the more devastating to the Roman Renaissance outlook, too, inasmuch as it marked just one of a series of swiftly developing crises that overtook Rome in the 1520s and '30s and that challenged the city's centrality and timeless stability. The first blow was Adrian VI's essential indifference, and at times even outright hostility, to the cultural concerns of the Roman Renaissance. Frugality proved the watchword of this Dutch pope's pontificate, and poets and artists, cut off from papal coffers, began a steady *diaspora* to Venice or to the more promising patronage of the princely courts. Under Clement the arts revived, but the leading painters, notably Rosso Fiorentino, Perino del Vaga, and the young Parmigianino, who brought to Rome artistic experiences from Tuscany and northern Italy, produced works different in character from the classical harmonies and expressive clarity of Raphael's history-painting in the Vatican. In its elegance, refinement, and sophistication this "Clementine style" reveals an inward-turning, self-conscious aestheticism. The quest for supreme elegance in form resulted in disconcerting ambiguities in the religious subject matters treated. In this proto-Mannerist art heroic grandeur gave way to refined sensuality, and noble beauty developed disturbing erotic undertones.[13]

More daunting to the preservation of Roman Renaissance views was the dawning realization that no quick solution to the Lutheran challenge existed. By the mid-1530s England, Scandinavia, and much of Germany had abandoned the Catholic fold. Rome no longer served as the spiritual capital for Europe beyond the Rhine and Danube, and thus was shattered another aspect of the city's universalism.

The somber, and even penitential, mood that overtook much of Roman culture in the 1530s has its visual counterpart in the awesome drama of the *Last Judgment*, Michelangelo's titanic fresco, completed in 1541, that covers the entire altar wall of the Sistine Chapel.[14] Michelangelo's beardless Apollonian Christ as *Sol iustitiae* shares certain earlier conceptions of the Roman Renaissance, but the tidal forces, the violently twisting figures, and the peculiar spacelessness of the composition contrast with earlier ideas. When Cristoforo Marcello, for instance, evoked the image of Last Judgment in his All Saints' sermon before the papal court, he described, as we have seen, an ordered triumphal procession in which the glory of this world finds a secure place in the next. Michelangelo's nude resurrected elect carry none of their earthly attributes with them, except for Peter with the keys and the martyrs with their instruments of torture, and even the Prince of the Apostles is subsumed beneath the inexorable command of Christ.

If the *Last Judgment* was intended as a potent warning to heretics of the destruction that awaits those outside the Roman Church, it is also a forceful reassertion of theology over philosophy, of faith over reason, of divine grace over human free will. The ineluctability of God's omniscience transcends human fathoming, and the serene confidence in human nobility expressed, for example, in the heroic deeds of Peter and Paul in Raphael's tapestry cartoons surrenders here to a sobering recognition of man's ultimate dependence on divine will. Nowhere is this clearer than in the pitiful self-portrait of Michelangelo as the flayed skin of St. Bartholomew, suspended precariously above the yawning abyss of hell. Seen from the stern vantage point of impending judgment, human dignity has a meaning more uncertain and problematic than when seen from the perspective of Creation so favored by early sixteenth-century Romans, and articulated in Michelangelo's own ceiling frescoes for the Sistine Chapel. In the same way the exultant confidence Julian and Leonine intellectuals drew from their emphasis on the eschaton at least partially realized in the Roman Church suffers a diminution when considered against the finality of the *dies irae*.

The euphoria was gone. Nevertheless, under Paul III, the Roman pope whose values and outlook absorbed so much from the culture of the early sixteenth century, a brief reprise of the ambitions of the Roman Renaissance took place. Once again the themes of *renovatio*, of *plenitudo temporum*, of Golden Age—those visions of transcendent power and mythic glory of the city of Rome and the Roman Church—appeared in the revived pageantry of Carnival and in such festive splendor as Charles V's 1536 triumph. When Paul returned in 1538 from the peace conference at Nice, where he had helped arrange a truce between Francis I and Charles V, he, too, was accorded a triumphal entry and was hailed as a peacemaker and king of kings.[15]

The rebuilding of Rome resumed also. Again work went forward on the new St. Peter's, plans for restoring the Capitoline were undertaken, and new projects conceived for the Vatican Palace. Notable among these was the Sala Regia, which served both as an atrium to the Sistine and Pauline Chapels and as a throne room for the reception of ambassadors to the papal court. In its neo-Roman architectural grandeur (the design of Antonio da Sangallo), and in the classicizing, Raphaelesque character of its stucco decoration (the work of Perino del Vaga), the Sala Regia revived the artistic values of Roman art of the early Cinquecento. This splendor, worthy of a Solomon or an Augustus, was intended to amaze its viewers and to impress upon those who came to render obedience to the Roman pontiffs the spiritual primacy and temporal majesty of the papacy. These same themes also underlie Perino's Sala Paolina in Castel Sant'Angelo with its pairing of Alexander the Great and St. Paul, Hadrian and St. Michael, as *exempla* of the temporal and spiritual mission of the *respublica Christiana*, headed by the Roman pontiffs, to pacify and reconcile all the nations of the earth.[16]

To the early years of Paul III's pontificate belongs, too, the renewed emphasis on the theme of philosophical and religious concord. This marked the main thrust of the thought of Agostino Steuco, the Augustinian from Gubbio, who came to Rome in 1534; four years later he received a bishopric and was named head of the Vatican library. Steuco's intellectual pursuits resemble those of Giles of Viterbo. Like the recently deceased former Augustinian General, Steuco studied Hebrew, Arabic, Aramaic, and other oriental languages (in addition to Greek), waxed enthusiastic over *divinus* Plato and the Neo-Platonists, and cultivated Hermes Trismegistus and the other *prisci theologi*. Like Giles, too, Steuco had a fondness for esoteric symbolism and *arcana*, and he similarly traced links between ancient Hebraic, Greek, and Etruscan religious lore. These notions appear in Steuco's *De perenni philosophia*, dedicated to Paul III in 1540, and serve to buttress his central conviction—that a single *sapientia*, knowable by all and present to mankind from earliest times, underlies all religious and philosophical truths. Revealing the same intellectual orientation, and similarly echoing earlier Roman Renaissance ideas, is Steuco's *Cosmopoeia*, a concordistic commentary on the Creation account of Genesis, published in 1535.[17]

Steuco's ideas of concord did not extend, however, to the teachings of Luther. In his 1530 *Pro religione adversus Lutheranos*, he condemned Lutheranism as a "plague," which would inevitably lead to contempt for piety and the downfall of religion.[18] Luther's disjunction of faith from reason, a position diametrically opposed to Steuco's conjoining of philosophy and theology, doubtless explains part of the vehemence of this attack, but like other Romans Steuco was a staunch defender of papal primacy, even to the point of composing, as we have seen, yet another refutation of Valla's diatribe on the Donation of Constantine.

Contemporary religious controversy only occasionally concerned Steuco, but it was the central issue that brought back to Rome many of the humanists who had joined the *diaspora* of the 1520s. In the fall of 1536, Sadoleto and Giberti, along with Federigo Fregoso, Gregorio Cortese, Reginald Pole, Tommaso Badia, Gianpietro Carafa, and Girolamo Aleandro, formed the famous ecclesiastical reform commission, headed by the Venetian humanist Gasparo Contarini, whom Paul had named a cardinal the previous year. This nine-man group was the second in the series of *ad hoc* commissions by which the Farnese pontiff, up to 1541, attempted to deal with the problem of reform. The particular impulse behind the effort in 1536 was the impending general council. Under pressure from Charles V, the pope had agreed to convene it at Mantua the following spring. Repeatedly postponed, the council at last met, under very different circumstances and with changed expectations, at Trent in 1545. Sadoleto gave the opening address to the 1536 reform commission, unleashing an unbridled attack on the avarice, luxury, and ambition of the Roman Curia. Corruption at the center had led, he charged, to loss of faith in the clergy and the consequent loss of much of Europe to the Roman obedience. What this necessitated was a return to the normative purity of the primitive Church. In this way the pristine authority of the Roman See would be renewed.[19]

Sadoleto's reproaches set down the guidelines for the commission's work, and its report, the *Consilium de emendanda Ecclesia*, dealt only with ecclesiastical abuses, not with theology or doctrine. Moreover, it suggested no new legislation was required but only strict enforcement of existing law.[20] As such the *Consilium* represents a conservative continuity with the reform proposals dating back to the fifteenth century and affirms the same principles Zaccaria Ferreri had articulated to Adrian VI in 1522: "Purge Rome, and the world will be cleansed; restore and reform Rome, and the whole world will be restored and reformed."[21] In essence, the commission held that by bringing a halt to ecclesiastical abuses and corruption, for which the Roman Curia was largely responsible, the faithful would be won back and the Protestant schism healed. When presented to the pope and the College of Cardinals in March 1537, the *Consilium* nevertheless provoked bitter controversy, and its proposals were never enacted.

Despite this setback, Contarini and his humanist allies continued for the next four years to remain at the forefront of papal reform efforts. With the naming of Sadoleto, Pole, and Carafa to the cardinalate in 1536, joined three years later by Bembo, and then in 1542 by Cortese, Badia, and Giovanni Morone, the reform party carried a certain weight against the Curialists in the College. But whereas they were united in condemning ecclesiastical abuses, they were sharply divided both as to the strategy to pursue with the Protestants and in theological matters. Sadoleto, for instance, pursued conciliatory overtures with the humanist-minded Lutherans, like Melanchthon, while Carafa opposed any such discussions. On the other hand, Sadoleto, in his commentaries on Romans, attempted to refute the Lutheran *sola fide* theology, but in the process leaned so close to Pelagianism in his neglect of prevenient grace that Badia, the Dominican Master of the Sacred Palace, forbade their publication. In contrast, Contarini was prepared to go quite far towards the Lutheran position on justification. A further division opened, too, between Pole, who by the early 1530s had given over classical scholarship entirely in favor of religious studies, and Bembo, who despite his staunch support for his fellow Venetian Contarini, remained a classicist and a theological neophyte to the end.[22]

Divergent assessments of Erasmus also stood in the way of uniting the humanist reform party. The Dutch humanist proved a controversial figure for Roman humanists. In the 1520s, he had been subjected to withering Roman humanist assault for being insufficiently Ciceronian and for harboring anti-Italian prejudices. Sadoleto and Bembo, despite their unalloyed Ciceronianism, had nonetheless desisted from joining the attack. In Sadoleto's case, this stemmed from his respect for Erasmus's Christian humanist ideas, and in this Contarini and Pole joined him. On the other hand, Aleandro, earlier an intimate of Erasmus at the Aldine Academy in Venice, from the early 1520s regarded him as a heretical precursor of Luther.[23] Troublesome, too, was Erasmus's position on papal authority. While agreeing that the papacy had divine, and not merely human, origins, he doubted whether Matthew 16 and John 21 applied to

Peter alone, and he was unconvinced that the Gospel power of the keys upheld the absolutist juridical claims made by papal monarchists.[24]

Internal conflicts thus diluted the reform party's impact in Rome. Moreover, by the late 1530s the most potent religious impulses within Italian humanist circles no longer derived from Roman Renaissance values. For the *spirituali*, who gathered about Pole and Contarini in these years, Christianity became defined in evangelical terms, sharing in the widespread European emphasis on the problem of salvation, on the quest for personal religious experience, and on the gospels as the pure expression of God's Word. In the formation of this group, student experience at the University of Padua, acquaintance with Giberti's reformed Verona, and contact with the Neapolitan circle of Juan de Valdés mattered more than Rome. Indeed, Viterbo, where Pole was cardinal legate, became the movement's principal center in the 1540s. For those *spirituali* who had known Leonine and Clementine Rome, like the Latin poet Marcantonio Flaminio, adherence to the evangelical cause meant a rejection of Roman Renaissance culture. In Rome, Flaminio wrote pastoral lyrics in echo of Catullus and Horace, rejoicing in the innocent sensuality and poignant lyricism of human love. Joined to the *spirituali*, Flaminio turned from this elegiac eroticism to religious poetry, from Tibullus to the *carmina sacra* of St. Ambrose and to Psalms.[25]

For the religious temper of the 1540s, the aspirations of the Roman Renaissance no longer seemed relevant. Figures like Sadoleto and Bembo, whose intellectual formations dated to the opening years of the Cinquecento, in fact were ill-prepared to confront the doctrinal and religious issues raised by the Reformation. The Roman humanist emphasis on human dignity, freedom, and a reconciled universe made it difficult to explore those aspects of the Christian tradition that emphasized human sinfulness and the need for atonement.[26]

Collapse of the talks at Ratisbon in 1541 signalled the end of Contarini's hopes for a negotiated settlement of the reform issues. His death the following year, combined with the spectacular apostasies of Bernardino Ochino and Peter Martyr Vermigli, left the *sprituali* on the defensive. In 1549, Pole, with Imperial backing, came within one vote of the papacy, but by 1542 initiative at Rome had already passed to the intransigents. With the re-establishment of the Holy Office of the Inquisition in that year, the *zelanti* possessed the means to force their opponents underground or into exile. At the same time, new religious energies became mobilized, notably the Jesuits, founded at Rome in 1540. The tide had turned, and with the election of the inquisitor Carafa as Pope Paul IV (1555–59), the Counter-Reformation came fully into session in Rome. Determined to eradicate the "contagion" of heresy, Carafa moved against the remaining *spirituali*. Pole, in England, remained beyond the pontiff's clutches, but Morone, not so fortunate, was imprisoned in Castel Sant'Angelo.[27]

The spirit of Counter-Reformation Rome in its negative aspects—anxious defensiveness, suspicion, and resort to repression—could hardly sustain an atmosphere congenial to Renaissance impulses. By the same token, certain of its positive aspects—the concern for dogmatic clarity, sacramentalism, organized piety, and systematic meditation—were at odds with the religious and intellectual values that had held sway earlier in the century.[28]

Yet in some of its ambitions and achievements the Counter-Reformation does reveal continuities with Renaissance aspirations. Foreign missions to Asia, Africa, and Latin America renewed the consciousness of Roman Catholicism's world-wide pastoral task, and planting the faith from Peru to the Philippines helped diminish the loss of Protestant Europe.[29]

Rome, too, experienced another renewal as a religious capital. The burgeoning population reached 100,000 by 1600, while pilgrims to that Jubilee Year probably surpassed one-half million—a quantum jump from Renaissance totals. In the same way, the pace and scale of construction after 1560 far outstripped Renaissance building. Two new *borghi* were created in the Vatican, more than a score of new streets, including Sixtus V's arterials, traversed the city, some fifty churches were built or entirely rebuilt, the same number of new palaces appeared, and the restoration of three ancient aqueducts provided water for the dozens of fountains and ornamental gardens that proliferated everywhere.[30]

An afterglow of some key ideas of the Roman Renaissance persisted in the architectural and artistic undertakings of the later sixteenth century. The humanistic themes of Golden Age, of Eternal Rome's civilizing mission, and of its spiritual centrality to the human race can be found in the iconography of the great villas created at Caprarola, Tivoli, and Bagnaia.[31] They can be found, too, in the Casino Pius IV (1559–65) built in the Vatican Gardens.[32] But the articulation of these mythic themes occurs in a more private and personal context, in the leisured recesses of Roman life, rather than at its public core. Moreover, in their pastoral and elegiac setting, in the poetically allusive nature of their iconographic programs, in the delicacy and refinement of their artistic impulses, and in their stylistic realization, from which much of early sixteenth-century individualism and naturalism has been drained away, these ideas seem less heroic, less universal, less a creative fusion of Christian and classical values than their complex intermingling.[33]

Priestly and sacramental concerns, furthermore, became preeminent. Thus in the decoration of Pius IV's Casino, Moses as *typus Christi* is depicted not as lawgiver and king, but instead as striking the rock at

Horeb and gathering manna, prefigurements of Christ's institution of the sacraments of baptism and the eucharist.[34] Baptismal, too, is the new setting provided for the *Cleopatra* statue. Removed from the Vatican statue court by order of Julius III (1550–55) and installed in the Stanza della Cleopatra at the end of the eastern corridor of the Belvedere, the antique sculpture no longer alluded to the vanquished Egyptian queen. Rather, as a nymph, she belonged to the overall symbolism of the nymphaeum setting, while the ceiling frescoes provided pointed references to the baptismal waters of regeneration administered by the Roman Church.[35]

By 1600, Rome had again become a center of the arts. The pomp of papal liturgies, the splendor of Roman spectacles, the magnificence of the city's new vistas, and the sumptuousness of its new churches and palaces again set standards for taste and style. But Baroque Rome was a capital more narrowly religious and propagandistic than its Renaissance predecessor. Through the sheer grandeur of outward forms, orthodox religion manifested its power, and it relied more on the emotionally volatile joining of sensuality to mysticism. The inhuman violence of torture and martyrdom alternated with ineffable visionary transports. Exuberant theatricality and a taste for the marvellous replaced the Renaissance emphasis on Apollonian virtues.[36]

The monolithic orthodoxy of Tridentine faith also intruded into the former humanistic fields of antiquarian studies, history, and oratory. Rome's antiquarians continued to collect artifacts and amass epigraphic evidence, but the Christian, not the classical, city tended to become uppermost in their thoughts. Onofrio Panvinio thus produced a large volume on Rome's seven basilicas, and Pompeo Ugonio did the same for the station churches. In this way they met pilgrim desires for details about the sites they visited. To serve much the same end, Antonio Gallonio described the deaths of the Roman martyrs, organizing his information according to the instruments by which they were tortured and put to death.[37]

In history, the most important work of Counter-Reformation Rome was Cesare Baronio's *Annales Ecclesiasticae*, begun in the 1570s as the Catholic reply to the Lutheran *Magdeburg Centuries*. Baronio's massive work of scholarship, which began with the Incarnation and reached into the twelfth century, remaining incomplete at its author's death in 1607, became the definitive ecclesiastical history for Roman Catholicism. Yet the purpose of sacred history, for Baronio, was to affirm the unchanging orthodoxy of the Church. Sacred history, the record of God acting through men, could not deviate from sacred truth. Therefore, what post-Tridentine Catholicism upheld as orthodox must have been orthodox for the early centuries of Christianity as well. History thus served theology. Abandoned as irrelevant, both for perceiving the nature of the Roman Church and for understanding its mission were the Renaissance interests in Hebraic and Greco-Roman antiquity.[38]

In sacred oratory, much the same picture emerges. Counter-Reformation preachers continued to exploit the resources of classical Latin rhetoric, including epideictic. But for them, Latin represented more the language of faith than the language of culture. In the funeral oratory for the popes, Roman preachers emphasized almost exclusively the priestly virtues of Christ's vicars, whose efforts had made Rome the model of the Tridentine ideal. As the *exemplum* of faith and morals for the whole world, Rome had truly become *the* Holy City. Not so much Rome, the wonder of antiquity, but rather the renewed Rome, "the theater of unheard-of piety," caused the multitudes to marvel, and as the showcase of holiness it had brought back the Golden Age.[39]

In May 1597 a triumphal procession mounted the Capitoline Hill, passed along the route of the ancient Via Sacra through the arches of Septimius Severus and Titus in the Forum Romanum and through the Arch of Constantine, then proceeded out the Via Appia. What this ceremony celebrated was not military victory, however, but rather the return of the relics of the Roman martyr saints Domitilla, Nereus, and Achilleus to the basilica of SS. Nereo ed Achilleo, newly restored by Cardinal Cesare Baronio as his titular church. The translation took place the evening of 11 May, the vigil of the saints' feastday. In the inscriptions placed for this occasion on the ancient Roman arches and on the temporary triumphal arches, decorated with the martyrs' trophies and placed before their church, what received acclaim was the glory of the martyrs' victory over Roman paganism. Through their blood shed in sacrifice, the martyrs triumphed over those who pursued the path of worldly glory; in defeating false religion they made Rome a Christian city; and the return of their intercessory power to their restored *titulus* exemplified the regeneration of the Apostolic Church, the work of the Counter-Reformation.[40]

Maffeo Vegio would have understood and approved celebrating how the martyrs' holiness extirpated demonic depravity. Doubtless he would have applauded, too, Sixtus V's placing statues of Sts. Peter and Paul atop the ancient triumphal columns erected in honor of the Emperors Trajan and Marcus Aurelius. Flavio Biondo and his intellectual heirs of the Roman Renaissance would have found this reversion to the medieval view of Christianity triumphing over paganism a diminution of their vision of reborn Rome fulfilling its classical heritage.

VIII

Conclusion

Rome in 1521 no longer impressed its beholders as being the same city that Eugenius IV had seen upon his return in 1443 or that Pius II had journeyed to in 1460. The Eternal City, which in the mid-fifteenth century still remained a decayed medieval municipality marked by decades of neglect, squalor, depopulation, and the melancholy presence of the ancient ruins, had by the time of Leo X's death in 1521 emerged once more as a capital. The new arteries, like the Via Giulia and the Ponte Sisto, the dozens of new and rebuilt churches, like S. Maria del Popolo, Sant'Agostino, S. Pietro in Montorio, and S. Maria della Pace, each embellished with tomb sculpture and altar paintings, the many cardinals' palaces, the villas and gardens with their collections of antiquities, the restoration of the Capitol, and, above all, the colossal projects in the Vatican provided physical testimony to a renewed urban vitality. No other Italian city in the Renaissance period had experienced so extensive a transformation. Once more, as in antiquity, Rome had become *the* City. A true cosmopolis, again the *patria communis* to Western Civilization, Rome's new marvels had also made it the focal point for High Renaissance achievements in urban planning, in architecture, in sculpture, and in painting.

Similar transformations distinguished Rome's cultural and intellectual life. Rome had succeeded Florence as the foremost humanist center. Classical studies flourished in the Vatican Library, at the Sapienza, and in the informal academies of the city's *orti letterari*. Rome's humanists had made significant contributions to archeology, epigraphy, numismatics, patristics, Greek scholarship, and Roman drama. Neo-Latin literature thrived in the poetry and oratory of the papal court. Nor was theology neglected. Renewed attention to St. Thomas Aquinas, and to the Greek Fathers, helped give shape to the Roman humanist emphasis on the religious themes of Creation, Incarnation, divine providence, and human dignity.

Under Leo's patronage, Rome had become a leading center for Renaissance sacred music as well, and no city could match the dazzling round of theatrical presentations, pageantry, and ceremony, those *gesamtkunst* displays of intellectual and artistic virtuosity. In these cultural manifestations, seemingly god-like in their grandeur, heroic nobility, and brilliance, there seemed fulfilled that exalted heritage Valla had praised in Rome's civilization.

The accomplishments of Renaissance Rome deserve underscoring, for too often both the city and the Renaissance papacy have evoked the image of quagmire—of corruption, cynicism, hypocrisy, depravity, and decadence. This image has a certain warrant. Tensions indeed existed, as we have seen, between the secular and spiritual aspirations of the Renaissance popes, and these competing claims did not often reach satisfactory resolution. Yet to stop here is to overlook so much that was creative in the cultural world of the city belonging to the popes. The central argument of this book is that the Renaissance in Rome elaborated a persistent vision of religious and cultural renewal. Expressed in humanist writings, manifested in the arts, and realized in the rebuilt city itself, these themes of *instauratio* and *renovatio* had drawn upon the precedents of both the Greco-Roman and Judaeo-Christian past. In Rome and in the Roman Church the humanists and artists of the Eternal City saw fused the civilizing wisdom and the sanctifying power of the *fides latina*. To them, Rome, under the authority of Roman pontiffs restored to their rightful primacy in ecclesiastical and temporal matters, represented the culmination of human history. The capital of the world, Rome was also the cosmic center point, and the entrance to the heavenly kingdom.

Such ideas of Rome's imperial vocation and of its apostolic mission were not altogether new in the Renaissance period, nor did they entirely disappear after the middle of the sixteenth century. Certain elements of these notions proved recurrent in the long medieval and early modern history of Rome and the papacy. Readers of this book, in fact, may well have noted resemblances to the aspirations of an Innocent III or a Boniface VIII and detected similarities to the cultural world of a Sixtus V or Urban VIII. Yet, I am convinced the period 1443 to 1527 does constitute a distinct epoch, which deserves to be called Renaissance. What sets Renaissance Rome apart from the high medieval or baroque periods is less the utter novelty of its basic ideology—much of this had patristic or scholastic precedent—than the breadth of its vision, the passion with which these ideas were articulated, and their realization in the physical and cultural renewal of the city. The humanists' image of Rome tended to be presented in rhetorical, not philosophical or legal, garb. Moreover, their inquiry into Rome's past and their assessment of the meaning of Greco-Roman, Christian, and Hebraic antiquity related the city and the papacy to a larger constellation of cultural ideals, more universal in their import, purpose, and consequence.

If the cultural ideology of papal Rome in this period was Renaissance, it was nevertheless Renaissance in a different sense from what came forth from Florence earlier in the fifteenth century. In Rome, a different cultural and political setting meant a different intellectual focus, and even a different mode of seeing and thinking. To review briefly the Roman outlook in comparison with that of Florentine civic humanism, the most comprehensive, creative, and familiar achievement of early Florentine humanism, may serve to highlight what was distinctive in Rome and to underscore the way in which attention to the Renaissance in Rome forces us to extend our understanding of the Italian Renaissance as a whole.

Florentine civic humanism found inspiration in the recovered ideals of the Roman Republic and of the Athenian *polis*. From this ancient republican thought-world, Leonardo Bruni and his Florentine contemporaries acquired the intellectual resources by which to assess in more pragmatic, realistic terms the political and historical forces shaping the secular existences of autonomous city-state polities. They also affirmed anew the Periclean ideal of the individual as citizen, morally and intellectually committed to the civic life of the *polis*.

The humanists of the papal court, instead, looked to the civilizing achievements of capitals and empires—to the vast Hellenistic world created in the wake of Alexander the Great's conquests, to the Roman Mediterranean *oikoumene* established by the Caesars, and especially to the *imperium* of the Roman Church, headed by the popes, which they were convinced was destined to endure for all time in the Eternal City, and which would eventually incorporate the whole globe. Within this court-dominated Roman culture, the intellectual's task was correspondingly altered: not the shrewd and level-headed analysis of the politico-historical realities essential to the responsible citizen's deliberations, but rather the acclaiming of Rome's mythic past and its providential mission, which transcended the dimensions of mere human history and of *polis*-defined civic space.

As in intellectual commitments, so in aesthetic values similar distinctions emerged. Florentine civic humanism, marked by a sober definition of the citizen's public responsibilities has its counterpart in the human measure of Brunelleschi's architecture. Conceptually transparent in overall design, the sharply etched outlines of smooth, gray *pietra serena* columns, capitals, and moldings accentuate its lucidity. Renaissance Roman architecture was not scaled to a human measure, and the favored building stone there was travertine. Rough-textured, straw-colored, this pock-marked, porous stone facilitated, as Paolo Portoghesi has pointed out,[1] the illusionistic intentions of Bramante and other Roman architects. These same ambiguous edges, and the contrast of sun-suffused surfaces with deeply-shadowed recesses, appear, too, in the mythic perceptions of Rome conjured forth by the Roman humanists.

A further difference between Florentine and Roman Renaissance culture appears essential. If the Florentine civic humanists were lay intellectuals, more often than not the humanists in Rome were also clerics. Many of these Curial humanists, furthermore, whether by formal education or by administrative function had a grounding in theology and canon law. This meant that the antagonism between humanism and the medieval university world, and the tension between secular ambitions and the Church, detectable in some aspects of Florentine culture, proved far more muted in Rome. Humanists of the papal court, while finding much of scholastic style repugnant, in fact shared the basic conclusions of the canonists and medieval theologians on such matters as papal primacy, a hierarchically structured Church and society, a universe ordered by divine intelligence, and a harmony between nature and grace. In their eclecticism, they also tended not so much to press differences as to incorporate all received and rediscovered ideas into larger syntheses.

Finally, Rome in the period 1443 to 1527 avoided the series of political crises and ensuing intellectual changes that marked Florence in the fifteenth and early sixteenth centuries. Until the Sack, no external threat or single papal accession affected Rome so decisively as the Medici rise to power, Savonarola's prophetic preaching, and the succession of French and Spanish incursions from 1494 to 1530 affected Florence. Instead it is the continuity of basic outlook and the persistent elaboration of basic themes that dominate the Roman scene.

In short, Roman Renaissance culture differed from Florentine because it stemmed from a different political, economic, and social context, because humanists addressed different issues and concerns, and, perhaps most of all, because the basic nature of the two cities was so different.

If recognition of the Renaissance in Rome enlarges our awareness of the Italian Renaissance in general, it helps to explain, too, why Luther's criticisms in the early years of the Reformation fell upon such deaf ears in the city of the popes. Inspired by visions of the dawning Golden Age and convinced the Vatican was the fulcrum of the universe, intellectuals at the papal court believed they resided at the center of civilization. What significance could fulminations have, no matter how vehement, when they emanated from Wittenberg, that small Saxon town contemporaries described as situated "*in termino civilitatis*" (at the edge of civilization)?[2]

Then, too, Luther and his opponents in Rome perceived Christianity in strikingly different terms. Roman humanists gave serious attention to religious matters, but they saw no sharp disjunction between the truths revealed in Christ and the wisdom of human civilization. For them Christianity had Hellenistic—and even Etruscan and Egyptian—roots, and emphasis on the Incarnation and the Ascension affirmed the possibilities for human activity and creativity. Human nature, or at least human culture as informed by classical antiquity, somehow related to divine grace, so that Christianity represented the culmination rather than the antithesis of Greco-Roman experience.

For the Roman humanists also the Church Militant, while mirroring the Church Triumphant, was a highly visible Church, with the pope—the Vicar of Christ and successor to Peter, Moses, Solomon, and Caesar—its monarchical head. The Gospel constituted a "second law," and Christ had assumed the role of a new Moses, as lawgiver to His people. In the sacraments, especially penance, He had as "*Medicus*" instituted the healing powers bestowed upon His sacred priesthood, the clergy, by which Christians became cleansed of their sins and gained egress to heaven.

Luther instead saw the meaning of Christianity, accessible only by faith, as revealing the hidden ways of God, who works contrary to human reason and expectation. Luther's God was the Old Testament Yahweh, the Hebraic God of awesome mystery and power. He warned also against conflating Law and Gospel, and pointed out the dangers of seeing Christ as a second Moses. In his Theology of the Cross, Christ's Crucifixion forms the crux of Christianity, and it is passive righteousness—what the grace of Christ works in our consciences—that results in justification and redemption. The Church of Christ is not the Roman Church, where Luther became convinced Antichrist dwelled, but rather the invisible, spiritual community of believers, where all true Christians were equally priests and kings. He denied, too, that the papacy had divine foundation, and he repudiated as contrary to Scripture the view that the papal power of the keys granted remission from sin.[3]

A further basic difference isolated Luther and Renaissance Romans from each other. Luther with his Hebraic sense of God who speaks and calls, and his emphasis on hearing the Word of God in conscience, stressed the essentially auditory nature of religious experience. In Rome emphasis fell on the visual. Much of Roman religious and ceremonial life revolved around spectacular feasts for the eye, and the visual image, symbol, and pictorial device constituted key elements of Roman Renaissance culture. Encouraged, too, by the expectations of revived epideictic rhetoric—the display oratory of antiquity—Roman humanists urged their audiences to gaze upon, admire, and wonder at the images evoked by their words. Use of ekphrasis, the extended visual description, as a rhetorical device further contributed to the aim of bringing about "seeing through hearing." Indeed, the way Hellenistic and Byzantine orators had frequently employed ekphrasis to describe buildings or works of art induced Roman humanists to make frequent analogies between the art of words and the plastic arts. A striking instance is the sermon Hieronymus Scoptius delivered to the papal court for the Feast of All Saints during the pontificate of Sixtus IV. He spoke of Christ in preaching the Sermon on the Mount as if He were an expert in the art of painting, renewing our sin-soiled souls according to the form of their original beauty; Christ restored us to this "new portrait" by "painting" in His Sermon all the individual elements that lead the way to beatitude.[4]

The world indeed looked different when perceived from Rome, and to share the Renaissance Romans' vision required, it seems, residing in the Eternal City itself. Only on those who stood in the presence of the tombs, relics, monuments, and ruins, and who beheld the new splendors of the Vatican, could the mythic Rome of its humanists and artists work its spell. As one distanced oneself from the city on the Tiber, the vision dissipated. Yet, for those who found in Rome an intellectual and spiritual home, its images proved a powerfully creative impulse.

In the end, nonetheless, certain aspects of the Renaissance in Rome remain unsettling. The megalomaniac element, the grandiosity, and the dreamlike unreality in Roman High Renaissance style, which Frederick Hartt argued still required interpretation,[5] perhaps should be defined as the capacity for self-delusion. The *speculum* (mirror) motif in humanist writings, and the emphasis on a figural or typological relationship between past and present (Moses is a "type" of Christ, Julius II is the "second Julius Caesar," Apollo's "new home" is the Mons Vaticanus) inhibited a sober and measured assessment of reality. The city of Rome itself, I have suggested, with its many layers and its alternating demonic and celestial faces, bore major responsibility for this lessened capacity to view the contemporary world with level-headed dispassion. The Sack of Rome in 1527 forcibly dispelled Roman illusions.

To destroy myths nevertheless confines as well as liberates. The impartial witness cannot regret the Romans' awakening, however rude, from the narcissistic trance into which many of them had fallen. But he can see loss in the failure of Western Civilization in succeeding eras to sustain their efforts at a creative fusion of Christianity and civilization, and to forge a world community in which the things of God might also be those of Caesar. The Roman Renaissance aspired to a world in which religion and culture would not be at odds, and where intellectual and artistic creativity would enlarge the meaning of each.

What Bramante, Raphael, and Michelangelo conceived while inspired by this ideal still arouses our wonder and admiration. In the new St. Peter's, in the Stanza della Segnatura, and in the Sistine Chapel ceiling, classical and Christian stand conjoined. The truths of poetry, philosophy, and theology are one. And the human race, created in God's image and embodied in the idealized forms of classical beauty, manifests with solemn dignity, heroic strength, and spiritual wholeness its restoration to divine likeness.

NOTES

I. Introduction

1. For the significance of this Curial connection, see John F. D'Amico, *Renaissance Humanism in Papal Rome: Humanists and Churchmen on the Eve of the Reformation* (Baltimore: Johns Hopkins U. Pr., 1983), pp. 4–8.

2. See pp. 73–75.

3. Kathleen Weil-Garris and John F. D'Amico, "The Renaissance Cardinal's Ideal Palace: A Chapter from Cortesi's *De Cardinalatu*," in Henry A. Millon, ed., *Studies in Italian Art and Architecture 15th through 18th Centuries* [Memoirs of the American Academy in Rome, 35] (Rome: Ed. dell'Elefante, 1980), pp. 91–97.

4. Loren W. Partridge, "Divinity and Dynasty at Caprarola: Perfect History in the Room of the Farnese Deeds," *AB*, LX (1978), pp. 494–96.

5. See pp. 89, 214, 264–66, 97–98.

6. See pp. 200–01.

7. Weil-Garris and D'Amico, "Renaissance Cardinal's Ideal Palace," p. 91.

8. See pp. 201–26.

9. See pp. 96–97, 158–60.

10. George Holmes, *The Florentine Enlightenment, 1400–50* (N.Y.: Pegasus, 1969), pp. 48–105.

11. The fullest account of the Council is Joseph Gill, S.J., *The Council of Florence* (Cambridge: Cambridge U. Pr., 1959). For Eugenius's pontificate, note *id.*, *Eugenius IV: Pope of Christian Union* (Westminster, Md.: Newman Pr., 1961). A major *desideratum* is new biographical treatment of the Renaissance popes. Except for Eugenius IV, Pius II, and Alexander VI, recent book-length biographies are lacking. The following notes will indicate which existing works should be consulted for material on pontifical careers. Still essential in this regard is Ludwig von Pastor, *History of the Popes*, ed. and trans. F. I. Antrobus *et al.*, vols. 1–8 (St. Louis: Herder, 1891–1910). More recent references, particularly in relation to papal temporal policy, can be found in Kenneth M. Setton, *The Papacy and the Levant (1204–1571), Vol. II: The Fifteenth Century* (Philadelphia: American Philosophical Society, 1978). Note also D'Amico, *Renaissance Humanism in Papal Rome*, pp. 8–12.

12. For discussion of this work, see pp. 62–63, 170–71, 183.

13. See pp. 166–201.

14. For the circumstances of Nicholas's election, see pp. ooo–ooo. For a recent sketch of Nicholas V's life, see Cesare Vasoli, "Profilo di un Papa umanista: Tommaso Parentucelli," in *Studi sulla cultura del Rinascimento* (Manduria: Lacaita, 1968), pp. 69–121; note also John B. Toews, "Formative Forces in the Pontificate of Nicholas V," *CHR*, LIV (1968–69), pp. 261–84.

15. Michael Mallett devotes a chapter to Calixtus III in his *The Borgias: The Rise and Fall of a Renaissance Dynasty* (London: Paladin, 1972), pp. 60–78.

16. Pius II has received more scholarly attention than any other Renaissance pope. In English there is R. J. Mitchell, *The Laurels and the Tiara: Pope Pius II, 1405–1464* (Garden City, N.Y.: Doubleday, 1962). For a full bibliography, see Setton, *Papacy and the Levant*, II, p. 200, n. 10. To this should be added G. Paparelli, *Enea Silvio Piccolomini: L'Umanesimo sul soglio di Pietro*, 2nd ed. (Ravenna: Longo, 1978).

17. For the reception of St. Andrew's head, see pp. 174–77.

18. For a sympathetic treatment, with particular emphasis on Paul's antiquarian interests, see Roberto Weiss, *Un umanista veneziano: Papa Paolo II* (Venice: Istituto per la collaborazione culturale, 1958).

19. Several recent studies have looked closely at the suppression of Leto's Roman Academy: D'Amico, *Renaissance Humanism in Papal Rome*, pp. 91–97; A. J. Dunston, "Pope Paul II and the Humanists," *The Journal of Religious History*, VII (1972–73), pp. 287–306; and

Richard J. Palermino, "The Roman Academy, the Catacombs, and the Conspiracy of 1468," *AHP*, XVIII (1980), pp. 117–55.

20. Egmont Lee introduces his book on the classical studies undertaken during Sixtus's pontificate with a chapter on the pope's life: *Sixtus IV and Men of Letters* [Temi e Testi, 26] (Rome: Edizioni di storia e letteratura, 1978), pp. 11–45.

21. For a fuller discussion, see pp. 95–96, 105, 114–15.

22. For the role of the cardinals' *familia* in the cultural life of Renaissance Rome, see esp. D'Amico, *Renaissance Humanism in Papal Rome*, pp. 45–56.

23. Mallett, *The Borgias*, pp. 79–227, offers a balanced and judicious examination of Alexander VI's life.

24. For Castellesi, see D'Amico, *Renaissance Humanism in Papal Rome*, pp. 16–19, 169–95.

25. Howard Hibbard, *Michelangelo* (N.Y.: Harper & Row, 1974), pp. 36–48.

26. For the cloister, see Arnaldo Bruschi, *Bramante architetto* (Bari: Laterza, 1969), pp. 245–90. I discuss the Tempietto on pp. 186–88 herein.

27. See pp. 92–93.

28. Alfred A. Strnad, "Francesco Todeschini-Piccolomini: Politik und Mäzenarentum im Quattrocento," *Römishe Historische Mitteilungen*, VIII-IX (1964/65–1965/66), pp. 101–425.

29. For a recent, fascinating consideration of the "Julian image," and for references to earlier studies on Julius II's pontificate, see Loren Partridge and Randolph Starn, *A Renaissance Likeness: Art and Culture in Raphael's 'Julius II'* (Berkeley and Los Angeles: U. of California Pr., 1980).

30. For the popes as caesars, see pp. 235–47. Bonner Mitchell discusses the scholarship devoted to Leo X's life in his *Rome in the High Renaissance: The Age of Leo X* (Norman: U. of Oklahoma Pr., 1973), pp. 149–51.

31. Robert E. McNally, S.J., "Pope Adrian VI (1522–23) and Church Reform," *AHP*, VII (1969), pp. 253–85.

32. For a fuller treatment of these developments, see the Epilogue, pp. 320–32.

II. Urbs Roma

1. *The Commentaries of Pius II*, trans. Florence A. Gragg, historical notes by Leona C. Gabel, *SCSH*, XXX (1947), pp. 310–12, 326–29, 344. For Pienza, see *ibid.*, XXV (1940), p. 147, XXXV (1951), pp. 546, 597–606; Leonardo Benevolo, *Storia dell'architettura del Rinascimento* (Bari: Laterza, 1968), I, pp. 233–45; and Crivelli's contemporary poetic description, in Leslie F. Smith, "Lodrisio Crivelli of Milan and Aeneas Silvius, 1457–1464," *SR*, IX (1962), pp. 37–38, 56–63. For the nature and circumstances of Pius's *Commentaries*, see Setton, *The Papacy and the Levant*, II, pp. 201–03.

2. *Commentaries*, *SCSH*, XXX (1947), pp. 335–46. For the general character of the region traversed by the Via Cassia in the fifteenth century, see Mallett, *The Borgias*, pp. 28–29.

3. Jean Delumeau, *Vie économique et sociale de Rome dans la seconde moitié du XVIᵉ siècle* [BEFAR, 184] (Paris: E. de Boccard, 1957), pp. 521–29, 566–78, 583–89; see also Peter Partner, *The Lands of St. Peter: The Papal State in the Middle Ages and the Early Renaissance* (Berkeley and Los Angeles: U. of California Pr., 1972), pp. 420–27; *id.*, "Papal Financial Policy in the Renaissance and Counter-Reformation," *Past & Present*, LXXXVIII (1980), pp. 40–46; T. W. Potter, *The Changing Landscape of South Etruria* (N.Y.: St. Martin's Pr., 1979); and Paolo Brezzi, "Il sistema agrario nel territorio romano alla fine del Medio Evo," *Studi romani*, XXV (1977), pp. 153–68. Melissa Meriam Bullard has analyzed how the low agricultural productivity of the Roman Campagna, combined with the exploitative and corrupt provisioning procedures of the Renaissance papacy provoked bread riots at the end of Clement VII's pontificate: "Grain Supply and Urban Unrest in Renaissance Rome: The Crisis of 1533–34," in P. A. Ramsey, ed., *Rome in the Renaissance: The City and the Myth. Papers of the Thirteenth Annual Conference of the Center for Medieval and Early Renaissance Studies* [Medieval and Renaissance Texts and Studies, 18] (Binghamton, N.Y.: Center for Medieval and Early Renaissance Studies, 1982), pp. 279–92.

4. Avery Andrews, "The 'Lost' Fifth Book of the Life of Paul II by Gaspar of Verona," *SR*, XVII (1970), pp. 26–35.

5. *Ibid.*, pp. 12–13.

6. Jacopo Gherardi da Volterra, *Il diario romano*, ed. Enrico Carusi, *RIS²*, Vol. XXIII, Pt. III (Città di Castello: S. Lapi, 1904), pp. 107–09; P. J. Jones, *The Malatesta of Rimini and the Papal State* (Cambridge: Cambridge U. Pr., 1974), p. 250; Michael Mallett, *Mercenaries and their Masters: Warfare in Renaissance Italy* (London: Bodley Head, 1974), pp. 159, 197.

7. Pastor, *The History of the Popes from the Close of the Middle Ages*, IV, pp. 427–28; for Estensi hydraulic projects, see Werner L. Gundersheimer, *Ferrara: The Style of a Renaissance Despotism* (Princeton: Princeton U. Pr., 1973), pp. 135–38.

8. Delumeau, *Vie économique et sociale*, pp. 578–83.

9. Fernand Braudel, *The Mediterranean and the Mediterranean World in the Age of Phillip II*, trans. Sian Reynolds (N.Y.: Harper & Row, 1972), I, pp. 61–62, 72–75, 78–82.

10. Jean Delumeau, *L'alun de Rome, XVᵉ-XIXᵉ siècle* (Paris: S.E.V.P.E.N., 1962), pp. 13–24; Pius II, *Commentaries*, *SCSH*, XXXV (1951), pp. 505–07; Setton, *Papacy and the Levant*, II, pp. 239–40.

11. The 1480–81 "anticipatory" budget of Sixtus IV set the alum revenue at an exaggerated 50,000 ducats; Clement VII's budget of 1525 pegged it at a more realistic 18,750 ducats: Peter Partner, "The 'Budget' of the Roman Church in the Renaissance Period," in E. F. Jacob, ed., *Italian Renaissance Studies* (London: Faber, 1960), p. 269; for details of the contractual arrangements and estimated profits, see Delumeau, *L'alun de Rome*, pp. 79–96, 147–58.

12. Delumeau, *L'alun de Rome*, pp. 97, 103–06; Ottorino Montenovesi, "Agostino Chigi, banchiere e appaltatore dell'allume di Tolfa," *ARSRSP*, LX (n.s. III)(1937), pp. 107–47; Felix Gilbert, *The Pope, his Banker, and Venice* (Cambridge: Harvard U. Pr., 1980), pp. 37–42, 59–62, 72–85, 92–93, 105–110.

13. *L'alun de Rome*, p. 318.

14. *Commentaries*, *SCSH*, XLIII (1957), pp. 753–55.

15. Poggio, *The Facetiae (or Jocose Tales)* (Paris: Liseux, 1879), II, Tale CLXVIII, pp. 72–74.

16. Andrews, "'Lost' Fifth Book," pp. 44–45.

17. Kenneth M. Setton, "Pope Leo X and the Turkish Peril," *PAPS*, CXIII (1969), p. 392.

18. *The Autobiography of Benvenuto Cellini*, trans. George Bull (Harmondsworth: Penguin, 1956), pp. 57–58.

19. Gherardi, *Diario romano*, pp. 13–14.

20. David R. Coffin, *The Villa in the Life of Renaissance Rome* (Princeton: Princeton U. Pr., 1979), pp. 111–45; for Castellesi's *Venatio* note also D'Amico, *Renaissance Humanism in Papal Rome*, p. 187.

21. Coffin, p. 123.

22. E. Delaruelle, E.-R. Labande, and Paul Ourliac, *L'Église au temps du Grand Schisme et de la crise conciliaire (1378–1449)* [Augustin Fliche and Victor Martin, eds. *Histoire de l'Église*, XIV] (Paris: Bloud & Gay, 1964), p. 1141.

23. Francesco Petrarca, *Le familiari*, ed. Vittorio Rossi, II [Edizione nazionale delle opere di Francesco Petrarca, XI] (Florence: Sansoni, 1934), Bk. VI, Ep. 2, pp. 56–58; note Ernest H. Wilkins, "On Petrarch's *Ep. Fam.* VI 2," *Speculum*, XXXVIII (1963), pp. 620–22, and Roberto Weiss, *The Renaissance Discovery of Classical Antiquity* (Oxford: Blackwell, 1969), pp. 32–35. For the appearance of medieval Rome, see Robert Brentano, *Rome before Avignon: A Social History of Thirteenth-Century Rome* (N.Y.: Easic Books, 1974), pp. 13–24, and Richard Krautheimer, *Rome: Profile of a City, 312–1308* (Princeton: Princeton U. Pr., 1980), pp. 231–326; for fifteenth-century Rome, see Torgil Magnuson, *Studies in Roman Quattrocento Architecture* (Stockholm: Almquist & Wiksell, 1958), pp. 11–34, 41–51. Especially useful for its numerous maps and contemporary depictions of Rome is Italo Insolera, *Roma: Immagini e realtà dal X al XX secolo* (Bari: Laterza, 1980), pp. 12–130.

24. Franco Borsi, *Leon Battista Alberti* (N.Y.: Harper & Row, 1977), pp. 38–39.

25. Delumeau, *Vie économique et sociale*, pp. 225–26, 327–53.

26. Gherardi, *Diario romano*, pp. 31–32; for a recent discussion of Gherardi's career and of the nature of his diary, see Egmont Lee, "Jacopo Gherardi and the Court of Sixtus IV," *CHR*, LXV (1979), pp. 221–37.

27. Bartolomeo Nogara, *Scritti inediti e rari di Biondo Flavio* [Studi e Testi, 48] (Rome, 1927), p. 156; Partner, *Papal State*, p. 419. Contemporary drawings and paintings give the same impression: note the view from the Aventine made c. 1495, contained in the *Codex Escurialensis*, fol. 56ᵛ (reproduced in Krautheimer, *Rome*, p. 274), and the general panorama of Rome painted by Masolino in 1435 for the baptistry of Castiglione d'Olona (*ibid.*, p. 303).

28. Emilio Re, "Maestri di strada," *ARSRSP*, XLIII (1920), pp. 5–102; Camillo Scaccia-Scarafoni, "L'antico statuto dei *Magistri stratarum* e altri documenti relativi a quella Magistratura," *ARSRSP*, L (1927), pp. 239–308; Magnuson, pp. 34–41; Carroll William Westfall, *In this Most Perfect Paradise: Alberti, Nicholas V, and the Invention of Conscious Urban Planning in Rome, 1447–55* (University Park: Pennsylvania St. U. Pr., 1974), pp. 78–84; Egmont Lee, *Sixtus IV and Men of Letters* (Rome: Edizioni di storia e letteratura, 1978), pp. 125–35.

29. Gherardi, *Diario romano*, p. 92.

30. For the urban planning of the Tuscan city-states, see John Larner, *Culture and Society in Italy, 1290–1420* (London: Batsford, 1971), pp. 86–96.

31. Westfall, pp. 68–71, 92–100, 107. For Florence, see Richard A. Goldthwaite, *The Building of Renaissance Florence: An Economic and Social History* (Baltimore: Johns Hopkins U. Pr., 1980), pp. 4–9; for Piazza S. Marco and its adjoining structures, see John McAndrew, *Venetian Architecture of the Early Renaissance* (Cambridge: MIT Pr., 1980), pp. 378–425. Bruni's remarks appear in his *Laudatio Florentinae Urbis*, ed. Baron, pp. 237–40 (for the full citation, and for studies relating to the *Laudatio*, see below n. 217).

32. Peter Partner, *Renaissance Rome, 1500–1559: A Portrait of a Society* (Berkeley and Los Angeles: U. of California Pr., 1976), pp. 150–51; Delumeau, *Vie économique et sociale*, pp. 457–85; Pio Paschini, *Roma nel Rinascimento* [*Storia di Roma*, XII] (Bologna: Cappelli, 1940), pp. 341–43, 351–52, 357–59, 362–66, 393–96.

33. *Commentaries*, *SCSH*, XXV (1940), p. 118, XXX (1947), pp. 342–43.

34. Delumeau, *Vie économique et sociale*, pp. 138–44; Partner, *Renaissance Rome*, pp. 87–88.

35. Delumeau, *Vie économique et sociale*, pp. 416–24.

36. Georgina Masson, *Courtesans of the Italian Renaissance* (London: Secker & Warburg, 1975).

37. Delumeau, *Vie économique et sociale*, pp. 207–11; Paschini, pp. 444–45; and esp. Melissa M. Bullard, "*Mercatores Florentini Romanam Curiam Sequentes* in the Early Sixteenth Century," *JMRS*, VI (1976), pp. 51–71. Egmont Lee, similarly, has noted the ethnic diversity of Rome's working class. German immigrants, for instance, were prominent in the baking and cobbler trades and among the managers of inns. Lee suggests further that the role of small businesses in the trades and in retail sales constituted a more important element in Rome's economy than is usually recognized. Yet he admits that the guild structure remained weaker in Rome than in other Quattrocento Italian cities. On balance, the world of work seems to have been less decisive in shaping Renaissance Rome than in other contemporary urban societies. For Lee's discussion, see his "Workmen and Work in Quattrocento Rome," in Ramsey, ed., *Rome in the Renaissance*, pp. 141–52. Note also Clifford W. Maas, *The German Community in Renaissance Rome, 1378–1523* [*Römische Quartalschrift, Supplementheft 39*] (Freiburg: Herder, 1981), pp. 1–29.

38. The Latin text of Lapo's *Dialogus super excellentia et dignitate Curiae Romanae* was published by Richard Scholz: "Eine humanistische Schilderung der Kurie aus dem Jahre 1438," *QFIAB*, XVI (1913–14), pp 108–53; a partial Latin text with Italian trans. also appears in Eugenio Garin, ed., *Prosatori latini del Quattrocento* (Milan-Naples: Ricciardi, 1952), pp. 170–211. Note discussion of this work in D.S. Chambers, "The Economic Predicament of Renaissance Cardinals," *SMRH*, III (1966), p. 291; Hans Baron, "Franciscan Poverty and Civic Wealth in Humanistic Thought," *Speculum*, XIII (1938), pp. 29–30; Leona C. Gabel, "The First Revival of Rome, 1420–84," in *The Renaissance Reconsidered: A Symposium* [*SCSH*, XLIV (1964)], p. 22; and D'Amico, *Renaissance Humanism in Papal Rome*, pp. 117–18. For Lapo's career, see Riccardo Fubini, "Castiglionchio, Lapo da, detto il Giovane, *DBI* XXII, pp. 44–51.

39. Chambers, pp. 291–94; Carlo Dionisotti, "Chierici e laici," in *Geografia e storia della letteratura italiana* (Turin: Einaudi, 1967), pp. 80–86; and, most recently, D'Amico, *Renaissance Humanism in Papal Rome*, pp. 49–53, 78–80, 226–36.

40. *Commentaries*, SCSH, XXXV (1951), pp. 535–36. For a reconstruction of the original appearance of Borgia's palace, see Magnuson, *Roman Quattrocento Architecture*, pp. 230–41.

41. D.S. Chambers, "The Housing Problems of Cardinal Francesco Gonzaga," *JWCI*, XXXIX (1976), pp. 21–58. Note also Weil-Garris and D'Amico, "The Renaissance Cardinal's Ideal Palace: A Chapter from Cortesi's *De Cardinalatu*," in Millon, ed., *Studies in Italian Art and Architecture 15th through 18th Centuries*, pp. 45–123; and D'Amico, *Renaissance Humanism in Papal Rome*, pp. 45–56.

42. Magnuson, pp. 217–349; Staale Sinding-Larsen, "A Tale of Two Cities: Florentine and Roman Visual Context for Fifteenth-Century Palaces," *Institutum Romanum Norvegiae: Acta ad archaeologiam et artium historiam pertinentia*, VI (1975), pp. 195–207.

43. Paolo Portoghesi, *Roma del Rinascimento* (Venice: Electa, 1970), pp. 39–41; the most recent study of early sixteenth-century Roman palaces is Christoph Luitpold Frommel, *Der Römische Palastbau der Hochrenaissance*, 3 vols. [Römische Forschungen der Bibliotheca Hertziana, 21] (Tübingen: Wasmuth, 1973). For Cortesi's advice, see Weil-Garris and D'Amico, "Renaissance Cardinal's Ideal Palace," pp. 76–89 *passim*.

44. Francesco Albertini includes the cardinals' palaces among the new "wonders" of the city of Rome in his *Opusculum de mirabilibus novae et veteris Urbis Romae* (Rome: Mazocchio, 1510); the section of Albertini's text devoted to "new Rome" has been published by August Schmarsow (Heilbronn: Henninger, 1886).

45. For the text of Sixtus's bull, see Eugene Müntz, *Les arts à la cour des papes pendant le XVᵉ e le XVIᵉ siècles*, III [BEFAR, 28] (Paris, 1881), pp. 182–87; note discussion in Delumeau, *Vie économique et sociale*, pp. 232–34, and Lee, *Sixtus IV*, p. 131.

46. The text is in Müntz, *Les arts*, III, pp. 180–81; note Partner, *Renaissance Rome*, pp. 17, 163.

47. *Vie économique et sociale*, pp. 514–17.

48. *The Mediterranean*, I, pp. 344–52.

49. Pio Pecchiai, "Il secolo XVI," in Luigi Fiorani, *et al., Rite, ceremonie, feste, e vita di popolo nella Roma dei Papi* [*Roma cristiana*, XII] (Bologna: Cappelli, 1970), pp. 132–34; note also Delumeau, *Vie économique et sociale*, p. 180; Partner, *Renaissance Rome*, p. 54.

50. For estimates of the number of pilgrims in Rome during the fifteenth and sixteenth centuries, see Delumeau, *Vie économique et sociale*, pp. 169–74.

51. Müntz, *Les arts*, III, p. 182.

52. Mark S. Weil, *The History and Decoration of the Ponte S. Angelo* (University Park: Pennsylvania St. U. Pr., 1974), pp. 23–24.

53. Lee, *Sixtus IV*, p. 127.

54. There is thus a continuity between the urbanism of the Renaissance popes and the more comprehensive network of rectilinear arteries connecting the major basilicas created by Sixtus V (1585–90): see Delumeau, *Vie économique et sociale*, pp. 288–327. For Bramante's urban planning, see Bruschi, *Bramante architetto*, pp. 625–47, and Agnoldomenico Pica, "Cittá di Bramante," in *Studi Bramanteschi: Atti del Congresso internazionale, Milano-Urbino-Roma, 1970* (Rome: De Luca, 1974), pp. 131–36. Note also Luigi Salerno, Luigi Spezzaferro, and Manfredo Tafuri, *Via Giulia: Una utopia urbanistica del '500* (Rome: Aristide Staderini, 1975). For an overview of the whole topic, see James S. Ackerman, "The Planning of Renaissance Rome, 1450–1580," in Ramsey, ed., *Rome in the Renaissance*, pp. 3–18.

55. Delumeau, *Vie économique et sociale*, pp. 408–09. For S. Maria dell'Anima, see Maas, *German Community in Renaissance Rome*, pp. 70–114.

56. For medieval pilgrimages to Rome, see Peter Llewellyn, *Rome in the Dark Ages* (N.Y.: Praeger, 1971), pp. 173–98; R.W. Southern, *The Making of the Middle Ages* (New Haven: Yale U. Pr., 1953), pp. 134–39; Brentano, *Rome before Avignon*, pp. 53–55; and Jonathan Sumption, *Pilgrimage: An Image of Mediaeval Religion* (Totowa, N.J.: Rowman and Littlefield, 1975), pp. 217–56.

57. Iohannes Burchardus, *Liber notarum*, ed. Enrico Celani, *RIS²*, Vol. XXXII, Pt. I (Città di Castello: S. Lapi, 1906), I, pp. 198–201; Gundersheimer, *Ferrara*, pp. 75, 219.

58. Llewellyn, p. 174.

59. Maffeo Vegio, *De rebus antiquis memorabilibus Basilicae S. Petri Romae* in *Acta Sanctorum, Junii*, Vol. VII (Supplementi Pars II), (Antwerp, 1717), pp. 73–74. For Vegio, note Bruno Vignati, *Maffeo Vegio, umanista cristiano (1407–1458)* (Bergamo, 1959), and *id.*,

"Alcune note ed osservazioni sul *De rebus memorabilibus Basilicae S. Petri Romae*," in Socrate Corvi, ed., *Studi su Maffeo Vegio* (Lodi: Archivio storico lodigiano, 1959), pp. 58–69.

60. Vignati, *Maffeo Vegio*, pp. 27–31; Pius II, *Commentaries, SCSH*, XLIII (1957), p. 751; Diana Webb, "Eloquence and Education: A Humanist Approach to Hagiography," *Journal of Ecclesiastical History*, XXXI (1980), pp. 19–39.

61. Llewellyn, pp. 183–90, and esp. Patrick J. Geary, *Furta Sacra: Thefts of Relics in the Central Middle Ages* (Princeton: Princeton U. Pr., 1978), pp. 47–59, 63–67, 143–46.

62. Gherardi, *Diario romano*, p. 120. Convinced of their curative powers, Louis XI sought relics from all over Europe and even from Istanbul, where the Sultan still preserved a collection: J. Huizinga, *The Waning of the Middle Ages* (N.Y.: Doubleday, 1954), pp. 186–87.

63. Günter Urban, "Die Kirchenbaukunst des Quattrocento in Rom," *Römishes Jahrbuch für Kunstgeschichte*, IX–X (1961–62), pp. 176–77.

64. Ruth W. Kennedy, "The Contribution of Martin V to the Rebuilding of Rome, 1420–1431," in *The Renaissance Reconsidered: A Symposium* [*SCSH*, XLIV (1964)], p. 34; John White, *The Birth and Rebirth of Pictorial Space* (N.Y.: Harper & Row, 1972), pp. 142–43. For the foundation of the basilica, an ex-voto gift to the Virgin Mary by Sixtus III after the Council of Ephesus declared (through the urging of papal representatives) the doctrine of Theotokos, see Richard Krautheimer, "The Architecture of Sixtus III: A Fifth-Century Renaissance?" in *Studies in Early Christian, Medieval, and Renaissance Art* (N.Y.: New York U. Pr., 1969), pp. 181–96. The legend of the miraculous snow grew increasingly popular in the thirteenth century, when feast-days, indulgences, and mosaic decoration gave testimony to it: Brentano, p. 87. Flavio Biondo mentions the basilica "*cuius fundamenta aestivae nivis indicio fuerunt iacta*" as among the objects which testify to the sacred character of Rome: *Roma instaurata*, in *Opera omnia* (Basil: Froben, 1531), p. 272.

65. Weil, *Ponte S. Angelo*, pp. 21–22, 92–93; Westfall, *In this Most Perfect Paradise*, p. 100; Charles Burroughs, "Below the Angel: An Urbanistic Project in the Rome of Pope Nicholas V," *JWCI*, XLV (1982), pp. 114–19.

66. Ludwig Schudt, *Le guide di Roma: Materialen zu einer Geschichte der römischen Topographie* (Vienna: B. Filser, 1971; first. publ. 1930), pp. 19–26, 185–232. A reproduction of one of these guidebooks is Christian Hülsen, ed., *Mirabilia Romae. Rom Stephan Planck 20 Nov. MCCCCLXXXIX: Ein römisches Pilgerbuch des 15. Jahrhunderts in deutscher Sprache* (Berlin, 1925).

67. Schudt, pp. 135–36.

68. Fra Mariano da Firenze, *Itinerarium Urbis Romae*, ed. P. Enrico Bulletti (Rome, 1931). Cf. the guide to Rome written by the English Augustinian friar, who came as a pilgrim to the city in 1450: John Capgrave, *Ye Solace of Pilgrimes: A Description of Rome, circa A.D. 1450*, ed. C.A. Mills (London: Oxford U. Pr., 1911). Note discussion of these works in Weiss, *Renaissance Discovery*, pp. 74–75, 86.

69. Giovanni Rucellai, *Giovanni Rucellai ed il suo zibaldone*, Vol. I: '*Il zibaldone quaresimale*', ed. Alessandro Perosa (London: Warburg Institute, 1960), pp. 67–78; a substantial portion of the text appears also in Roberto Valentini and Giuseppe Zucchetti, eds., *Codice topografico della Città di Roma* (Rome: Tipografia del Senato, 1946), IV, pp. 399–419. For discussion of Rucellai's perception of Rome, see Weiss, pp. 73–74, and, for a different view, Westfall, pp. 174–79. For the changing identifications of the Basilica of Maxentius in the Middle Ages, see Louis Duchesne, "Notes sur la topographie de Rome au Moyen-Age, I: *Templum Romae, Templum Romuli*," in *Scripta minora: Études de topographie romaine et de géographie ecclésiastique* [Collection de l'École Française de Rome, XIII] (Rome, 1973), pp. 3–15.

70. Hans Baron, *The Crisis of the Early Italian Renaissance*, 2nd ed. (Princeton: Princeton U. Pr., 1966), pp. 126–34; David Robey, "P.P. Vergerio the Elder: Republicanism and Civic Values in the Work of an Early Humanist," *Past & Present*, LVIII (1973), pp. 3–37.

71. Valentini and Zucchetti, *Codice topografico*, IV, pp. 89–100. The early fifteenth-century Curial humanist Cencio de' Rustici similarly accuses contemporary Romans of destroying Latin and Greek libraries "partly through ignorance, partly through neglect, and partly so that the divine face of the Veronica might be painted." For an English translation of the text of Rustici's 1416 diatribe, see Phyllis Walter Goodhart Gordan, ed. and trans., *Two Renaissance Book Hunters: The Letters of Poggius Bracciolini to Nicolaus de Niccolis* (N.Y.: Columbia U. Pr., 1974), pp. 187–90; note discussion of Vergerio's and Rustici's remarks in Weiss, *Renaissance Discovery*, pp. 56–58.

72. *Diario romano*, p. 52.
73. Relevant portions of Castiglione's letter are quoted by Portoghesi, *Roma del Rinascimento*, p. 22; for the complete text, see Baldassar Castiglione, *Lettere inedite e rare*, ed. Guglielmo Gorni (Milan: Ricciardi, 1969), pp. 41–44.
74. Burchard, *Liber notarum*, II, pp. 135–36, 446–47.
75. Lucien Febvre, "The Origins of the French Reformation: A Badly-Put Question?" in *A New Kind of History and Other Essays*, ed. Peter Burke, trans. K. Folca (N.Y.: Harper & Row, 1973), pp. 60–65.
76. Brentano, pp. 19, 54, 86, 175, 272. Note also André Chastel, "La Véronique," *Revue de l'Art*, XL (1978), pp. 71–82.
77. *Roma instaurata* in *Opera omnia*, p. 272.
78. *De rebus antiquis*, p. 66.
79. Burchard, *Liber notarum*, II, pp. 202, 234, 235, 246–47; Gherardi, *Diario romano*, p. 116.
80. Heinrich Wölflin, *The Art of Albrecht Dürer* (London: Phaidon, 1971), p. 194; Erwin Panofsky, *The Life and Art of Albrecht Dürer*, 4th ed. (Princeton: Princeton U. Pr., 1955), p. 150. Indulgences could be obtained by reciting specified prayers before reproductions of devotional images, the most popular of which in the fifteenth century was the Veronica: Sixten Ringborn, *Icon to Narrative: The Rise of the Dramatic Close-up in Fifteenth-Century Devotional Painting* (Åbo: Åbo Akademi, 1965), pp. 23–24. A depiction of the Veronica appears also in the painted architectural frieze of the Carafa Chapel in S. Maria sopra Minerva, frescoed by Filippino Lippi (1488-93): Bruschi, *Bramante architetto*, pp. 447–48.
81. Ringborn, pp. 25–26; Carlo Bertelli, "The 'Image of Pity' in Santa Croce in Gerusalemme," *Essays in the History of Art Presented to Rudolf Wittkower*, eds. Douglas Fraser, Howard Hibbard, and Milton J. Lewine (London: Phaidon, 1967), pp. 40–55.
82. John Shearman, *Raphael's Cartoons in the Collection of Her Majesty the Queen and the Tapestries for the Sistine Chapel* (London: Phaidon, 1972), pp. 50–51.
83. Biondo, *Roma instaurata*, in *Opera omnia*, p. 272; Vegio, *De rebus antiquis*, pp. 66–67.
84. Burchard mentions seeing and touching the relic during a ceremonial visit to the basilica made by Innocent VIII on 12 March 1492: *Liber notarum*, I, pp. 339–41. An inscription recording the discovery was placed in the basilica by Cardinal Carvajal in the early sixteenth century: Ilaria Toesca, "A Majolica Inscription in Santa Croce in Gerusalemme," in *Essays in the History of Art Presented to Rudolf Wittkower*, pp. 102–05.
85. Burchard, *Liber notarum*, I, pp. 356–57, 362–68; Setton, *Papacy and the Levant*, II, pp. 427–29.
86. Burchard, I, p. 420.
87. *Ibid.*, I, pp. 154–55, II, pp. 101–13.
88. Pius II, *Commentaries*, *SCSH*, XXXV (1951), pp. 551–56.
89. *Roma instaurata*, in *Opera omnia*, p. 272.
90. Febvre, "Origins," pp. 61–62; Ringborn, *Icon to Narrative*, pp. 26–28.
91. Gherardi, *Diario romano*, p. 79.
92. Urban, "Die Kirchenbaukunst," pp. 154–76; Enzo Bentivoglio and Simonetta Valtieri, *Santa Maria del Popolo a Roma* (Rome: Bardi, 1976); Partridge and Starn, *A Renaissance Likeness*, pp. 75–103.
93. Burchard, *Liber notarum*, II, pp. 504–06; Gherardi, *Diario romano*, pp. 35–36.
94. Burchard, II, pp. 21, 325, 507; Gherardi, pp. 130–31.
95. Albertini, *Opusculum de mirabilibus*, in Valentini and Zucchetti, *Codice topografico*, IV, p. 489. For this and other sixteenth-century processions involving venerated images of the Virgin, see Pecchiai, "Il Secolo XVI," in Fiorani, *et al.*, *Rite*, pp. 167–69. Note also E. Rodocanachi, *Rome au temps de Jules II et de Léon X* (Paris: Hachette, 1912), pp. 304–06.
96. Febvre, "Origins," p. 62; Bruschi, *Bramante architetto*, pp. 652–67, 960–79; Kathleen Weil-Garris Posner, "Cloister, Court and City Square," *Gesta*, XII (1973), pp. 123–32; *id.*, "Alcuni progetti per piazze e facciate di Bramante e di Antonio da Sangallo a Loreto," in *Studi Bramanteschi*, pp. 313–38.
97. Pastor, *History of the Popes*, VI, p. 332.
98. *Autobiography*, p. 186.
99. Staale Sinding-Larsen, "Some Functional and Iconographical Aspects of the Centralized Church in the Italian Renaissance," *Institutum Romanum Norvegiae: Acta ad*

archaeologiam et artium historiam pertinentia, II (1965), pp. 243–51; Portoghesi, *Roma del Rinascimento*, pp. 432–33.

100. Bentivoglio and Valtieri, p. 108; for detailed analysis of the chapel, see John Shearman, "The Chigi Chapel in S. Maria del Popolo," *JWCI*, XXIV (1961), pp. 129–60.

101. *Roma instaurata*, in *Opera omnia*, p. 245.

102. For the reliquary, see Bruschi, *Bramante architetto*, p. 482; for the rebuilding of the church, see Urban, *Die Kirchenbaukunst*, pp. 104–08, 269, Portoghesi, *Roma del Rinascimento*, p. 429, and Richard Krautheimer, "S. Pietro in Vincoli and the Tripartite Transept in the Early Christian Basilica," *PAPS*, LXXXIV (1941), pp. 364–66.

103. See pp. 186–88.

104. See pp. 276–81.

105. Herbert Thurston, S.J., *The Holy Year of Jubilee: An Account of the History and Ceremonial of the Roman Jubilee* (London: Sands, 1900); Antonio Samoré, "Aspetti caratteristici degli Anni Santi: Dalla documentazione dell'Archivio Segreto Vaticano," *Studi romani*, XXIII (1975), pp. 419–41. For discussion of the date of Martin's Jubilee, see Gordan, *Two Renaissance Book Hunters*, pp. 108, 295.

106. Westfall, *In this Most Perfect Paradise*, pp. 21–24 (where relevant portions of the bull are quoted). For other contemporary references to the Jewish precedent, see Vegio, *De rebus antiquis*, p. 75, Platina, *Liber de vita Christi ac omnium pontificum*, ed. Giacinto Gaida, *RIS²*, Vol. III, Pt. I (Città di Castello, 1913–32), p. 260, and Burchard, *Liber notarum*, II. p. 190.

107. Roberto Weiss, "Andrea Fulvio antiquario romano (c. 1470–1527)," *Annali della Scuola Normale Superiore di Pisa—Lettere, storia e filosofia*, 2nd ser., XXVIII (1959), pp. 14, 26–29.

108. Eva-Maria Jung-Inglessis, "La Porta Santa," *Studi romani*, XXIII (1975), pp. 473–85; Thurston, pp. 405–10.

109. Burchard, *Liber notarum*, II, pp. 179–92; Jung-Inglessis, pp. 476–79.

110. Gherardi, *Diario romano*, pp. 27–29; Enrico Carusi, "L'instrumento di assoluzione dei Fiorentini dalle censure di Sisto IV," *Archivio Muratoriano*, II, No. 16 (1915), pp. 286–92.

111. For contemporary descriptions of the pope's blessing, see Gherardi, *Diario romano*, p. 116, and Burchard, *Liber notarum, I*, pp. 201–02, 267, 309, 420, etc. For the construction of the Loggia of Benediction, see Ruth Olitsky Rubinstein, "Pius II's Piazza S. Pietro and St. Andrew's Head," *Essays in the History of Architecture Presented to Rudolf Wittkower*, ed. Douglas Fraser, Howard Hibbard, and Milton J. Lewine (London: Phaidon, 1967), pp. 23, 32.

112. John W. O'Malley, *Praise and Blame in Renaissance Rome: Rhetoric, Doctrine, and Reform in the Sacred Orators of the Papal Court, c. 1450–1521* (Durham: Duke U. Pr., 1979), pp. 10–11, 130–31, 201–03.

113. Nelson H. Minnich and Heinrich W. Pfeiffer, S.J., "De Grassi's 'Conciliabulum' at Lateran V: The De Gargiis Woodcut of Lateran V Re-examined," *AHP*, XIX (1981), p. 154.

114. O'Malley, *Praise and Blame*, pp. 202–03; note also John M. McManamon, "The Ideal Renaissance Pope: Funeral Oratory from the Papal Court," *AHP*, XIV (1976), p. 12.

115. Giannozzo Manetti, *Vita Nicolai V summi pontificis*, *RIS*, Vol. III, Pt. 2 (Milan, 1734), cols. 923, 941, 953. For corrections to the error-filled Muratori text, see Francesco Pagnotti, "La vita di Niccolò V scritta da Giannozzo Manetti: Studio preparatorio alla nuova edizione critica," *ARSRSP*, XIV (1891), pp. 411–36.

116. Léonce Celier, "L'idée de réforme à la cour pontificale du Concile de Bâle au Concile de Latran," *Revue des questions historiques*, LXXXVI (n.s. XLII) (1909), pp. 418–35; *id.*, "Alexandre VI et la réforme de l'Église," *MAHEFR*, XXVII (1907), pp. 65–124; O'Malley, *Praise and Blame*, p. 7.

117. Bernardo Morsolin, *Zaccaria Ferreri, Episodio biografico del secolo decimosesto* (Vicenza, 1877), pp. 86–91.

118. Joaquim Nabuco, *Le Cérémonial Apostolique avant Innocent VIII: Texte du manuscrit Urbinate Latin 469 de la Bibliothèque Vaticane établi par Dom Filippo Tamburini* [Bibliotheca "Ephemerides Liturgicae" Sectio historica, XXX] (Rome: Edizioni liturgiche, 1966), pp. 15*–22*; Marc Dykmans, S.J., "Le Cérémonial de Nicholas V," *RHE*, LXIII (1968), pp. 365–78; Bernhard Schimmelpfennig, *Die Zeremonienbücher der Römischen Kurie im Mittelalter* [Bibliothek des Deutschen Historischen Instituts in Rom, XL] (Tübingen: Niemeyer, 1973), pp. 134–36.

119. J. Lesellier, "Les mefaits du Cérémoniaire Jean Burckard," *MAHEFR*, XLIV (1927), pp. 11–34. Burchard's collections of documents are preserved in BAV, mss. Vat. lat. 5633, 12343, 12348.

120. Morsolin, pp. 97–107; note also John Sparrow, "Latin Verse of the High Renaissance," in Jacob, ed., *Italian Renaissance Studies*, pp. 384, 401 n. 2.

121. Nabuco, pp. 26*–28*, 33*–34*. For Burchard's career, see also Lesellier; Burchard, *Liber notarum*, pp. xi–xxviii; and Setton, *Papacy and the Levant*, II, pp. 388–90. A list of Masters of Ceremonies in the Renaissance period and the dates covered by their diaries is provided by Leone Caetani, "Vita e diario di Paolo Alaleone de Branca, Maestro delle Ceremonie Pontificie 1582–1638," *ARSRSP*, XVI (1893), pp. 6–7.

122. e.g. Vegio, *De rebus antiquis,* p. 75, and Manetti, *Vita*, in Magnuson, *Studies in Roman Quattrocento Architecture*, p. 352 (Magnuson, pp. 351–62 contains cols. 929–40 of the Muratori text of Manetti's *Vita* corrected according to Pagnotti's revisions). For the history of the Roman Stations, see Giuseppe Mantovano, "Il Medioevo," in Fiorani, *et al.*, *Rite*, pp. 61–72, and Johann Peter Kirsch, *Die Stationskirchen des Missale Romanum* (Freiburg im Breisgau, 1926).

123. Platina, *Liber de vita Christi*, p. 334.

124. Manetti, *Vita*, col. 950.

125. Urban, *Die Kirchenbaukunst*, pp. 264–81, and esp. pp. 125–54 (S. Marco) and pp. 219–32 (S. Lorenzo in Damaso); Krautheimer, "S. Pietro in Vincoli," pp. 364-66.

126. The text of Albertini's work is now lost, but its existence is indicated in the preface to his *De mirabilibus . . . Urbis Romae:* Valentini and Zucchetti, *Codice topografico*, IV, pp. 462–63. Note also Cesare Olschki, "Francesco Albertini," *Roma: Rivista di studi e di vita romana*, II (1924), p. 483, and J. Ruysschaert, "Albertini, Francesco," *DBI*, I, pp. 724–25. For the text of Leto's poem, see D.G. Morin, "Les distiques de Pomponio Leto sur les stations liturgiques du Carême," *Revue Bénédictine*, XXXV (1923), pp. 20–23.

127. Burchard, *Liber notarum*, I, pp. 400–01.

128. The text of the diary was published by Dykmans, "Le Cérémonial de Nicholas V," pp. 785–825; an example of the non-observance of the Stations is the following: "*Dominica in ramis* [Palm Sunday] *anno 1452, papa non ivit ad Sanctum Johannem Lateranensem* [the Station church for that day] *sed dixit missam in ecclesia Sancti Petri . . .*": p. 813.

129. For the innovative character of the 1488 Ceremonial, see Nabuco, pp. 28*–33*, and Dykmans, p. 366. For the liturgical setting of the sermons *coram papa inter missarum solemnia*, see O'Malley, *Praise and Blame*, pp. 7–28.

130. Nabuco, p. 32*.

131. F. Wasner, "Fifteenth-Century Texts on the Ceremonial of the *Legatus a latere*," *Traditio*, XIV (1958), pp. 295–338, and "Addenda Varia," *Traditio*, XVI (1960), pp. 405–16.

132. Jörg Traeger, *Der reitende Papst: Ein Beitrag zur Ikonographie Papsttums* (Munich: Schnell & Steiner, 1970), pp. 13ff. For performance of this ceremony in 1499 and 1500, see Burchard, *Liber notarum*, II, pp. 153, 235. Leo X included the tribute of these horses in his entourage when he entered his native city in November 1515: John Shearman, "The Florentine *Entrata* of Leo X, 1515," *JWCI*, XXXVIII (1975), p. 150.

133. Rodocanachi, *Rome au temps de Jules II et de Léon X*, pp. 294–96; Elisabeth Cornides, *Rose und Schwert im päpstlichen Zeremoniell: Von den Anfängen bis zum Pontifikat Gregors XIII* (Vienna: Geyer, 1967).

134. Burchard, *Liber notarum*, II, pp. 208–12.

135. Gordon Rupp, *Luther's Progress to the Diet of Worms* (N. Y.: Harper & Row, 1964), pp. 63–65; Barbara McClung Hallman, "Practical Aspects of Roman Diplomacy in Germany, 1517–1541," *JMRS*, X (1980), p. 195.

136. *Liber notarum*, II, pp. 448–49; for other celebrations of this feast, see *ibid.*, I, pp. 193–95, and Gherardi, *Diario romano*, p. 51.

137. Rodocanachi, pp. 153–60; Domenico Gnoli, *La Roma di Leone X* (Milan: Hoepli, 1938), pp. 166–76.

138. Rab Hatfield, "The Compagnia de' Magi," *JWCI*, XXXIII (1970), pp. 107–61; for public ceremony, note also Richard C. Trexler, *The Libro Cerimoniale of the Florentine Republic* [Travaux d'humanisme et Renaissance, 165] (Geneva: Droz, 1978); and *id.*, *Public Life in Renaissance Florence* (N.Y.: Academic Pr., 1980), esp. pp. 213–364.

139. "Florentine Religious Experience: The Sacred Image," *SR*, XIX (1972), pp. 7–41.

140. For Dati's account of the Feast of St. John the Baptist, see Gene Brucker, ed.,

The Society of Renaissance Florence: A Documentary Study (N.Y.: Harper & Row, 1971), pp. 75–78; for his participation in the *pratiche*, see *id.*, *The Civic World of Early Renaissance Florence* (Princeton: Princeton U. Pr., 1977), p. 301.

141. Brian Pullan, *Rich and Poor in Renaissance Venice: The Social Institutions of a Catholic State, to 1620* (Cambridge: Harvard U. Pr., 1971), pp. 127–31. For the political function of pageantry in Venice, see Edward Muir, "Images of Power: Art and Pageantry in Renaissance Venice," *AHR*, LXXXIV (1979), pp. 16–52; and *id.*, *Civic Ritual in Renaissance Venice* (Princeton: Princeton U. Pr., 1981).

142. See pp. 96–99, 256–58.

143. Burchard, *Liber notarum*, I, pp. 336–38; Setton, *Papacy and the Levant*, II, pp. 422–24; Paschini, *Roma del Rinascimento*, pp. 445–46. For S. Giacomo degli Spagnoli, see Urban, *Die Kirchenbaukunst*, pp. 266–67.

144. Franciscus Novellus Romanus, *Compendium vitae Leonis Papae X* (Rome: ?, 1536), p. 119ᵛ. For Paris de Grassis's account of the concluding procession and ceremony at the Minerva, see Pastor, VII, Appendix 40, pp. 492–93. Note also Richard M. Douglas, *Jacopo Sadoleto, 1477–1547: Humanist and Reformer* (Cambridge: Harvard U. Pr., 1959), pp. 23–24; Setton, "Leo X and the Turkish Peril," p. 406, and Pecchiai, "Il secolo XVI," in Fiorani, *et al.*, *Rite*, pp. 169–70.

145. Pecchiai, p. 170; for Panvinio, see Eric Cochrane, *Historians and Historiography in the Italian Renaissance* (Chicago and London: U. of Chicago Pr., 1981), pp. 398–99, 439, 458.

146. Gherardi, *Diario romano*, pp. 53–54; Stefano Infessura, *Diario della città di Roma*, ed. Oreste Tommasini [Fonti per la storia d'Italia, 5] (Rome, 1890), pp. 86–87.

147. John W. O'Malley, S.J., "Fulfillment of the Christian Golden Age under Pope Julius II: Text of a Discourse of Giles of Viterbo, 1507," *Traditio*, XXV (1969), pp. 266–67.

148. Francesco Cancellieri, *Storia de' solenni possessi de' Sommi Pontefici da Leone III a Pio VII* (Rome, 1802); Brentano, *Rome before Avignon*, pp. 60–62.

149. For the papal *possesso* during the Renaissance, see Mark Dykmans, "D'Avignon à Rome: Martin V et le cortege apostolique," *Bulletin de l'Institut Historique Belge de Rome*, XXXIX (1968), pp. 203–309; Nabuco, *Le Cérémonial apostolique*, pp. 31–33; Schimmelpfennig, *Die Zeremonienbücher*, pp. 338–49; *id.*, "Die Krönung des Papstes im Mittelalter dargestellt am Beispiel der Krönung Pius II (3. 9. 1458)," *QFIAB*, LIV (1974), pp. 192–270; Burchard, *Liber notarum*, I, pp. 59–84, II, pp. 417–20; Giovanni Jacopo Penni, *Chronica delle magnifiche et honorate pompe fatte in Roma per la creatione et incoronatione di Papa Leone X, Pont. Opt. Max.*, published in Guglielmo Roscoe, *Vita e pontificato di Leone X*, ed. Luigi Bossi (Milan: Sonzogno, 1816–17), V, pp. 192–231.

150. See esp. Burchard, I, p. 67, and Penni, p. 207. Celani notes in his edition of Burchard's *Liber notarum* (p. 67, n. 2) that the first occasion on which the pope was presented the Mosaic Law occurred in the coronation rites of Eugenius III in 1145.

151. The text of Angeli's comments is in Cancellieri, pp. 36–37.

152. *Ibid.*, pp. 36–37; Burchard, I, p. 82 mentions that money was thrown not only at the places designated in the ceremonial books, but also in Innocent VIII's *possesso* "*et alibi, ubi populi oppressionem videbat.*"

153. Luigi Frati, "Delle monete gettate al popolo nel solenne ingresso in Bologna di Giulio II per la cacciata di Gio. II Bentivoglio," *Atti e memorie della R. deputazione di storia patria per le provincie di Romagna*, 3rd ser., I (1883), pp. 474–87.

154. Shearman, "Florentine *Entrata*," p. 152.

155. Burchard, I, p. 82 notes that the tumult of the crowd around the Lateran prevented Innocent VIII from performing this rite.

156. Besides Penni's firsthand account, see Shearman's analysis of its themes in *Raphael's Cartoons*, pp. 13–20.

157. Frances Ames-Lewis, "Early Medicean Devices," *JWCI*, XLII (1979), pp. 122–43; Marilyn Perry, "'Candor Illaesvs': The 'Impresa' of Clement VII and other Medici Devices in the Vatican Stanze," *Burlington Magazine*, CXIX (1977), pp. 676–86.

158. Shearman, *Raphael's Cartoons*, pp. 17–18.

159. Mantovano, "Il Medioevo," in Fiorani, *et al.*, *Rite*, pp. 115–16.

160. *Le vite di Paolo II di Gaspare da Verona e Michele Canensi*, ed. Giuseppe Zippel, *RIS²*, Vol. III, Pt. XVI (Città di Castello: S. Lapi, 1904–11), pp. 115–17. For the Roman Carnival during the Renaissance, see Mantovano, pp. 117–20; Pecchiai, pp. 162–64; Paschini, *Roma nel Rinascimento*, pp. 446–48; Rodocanachi, *Rome au temps de Jules II et de Léon X*,

pp. 325–36; Burchard, *Liber notarum*, I, pp. 182–84; and esp. A. Ademollo, *Alessandro VI, Giulio II e Leone X nel Carnevale di Roma* (Rome: A. Borzi, 1967; first publ. Florence, 1891).

161. *Roma instaurata*, in *Opera omnia*, p. 270.

162. Ademollo, pp. 67–71.

163. The most precise contemporary description is an anonymous letter, the text of which is to be found in Alessandro Luzio, "Federico Gonzaga ostaggio alla corte di Giulio II," *ARSRSP*, IX (1886), pp. 577–82. Another firsthand account is the *ottava rima* poem of Giovanni Jacopo Penni, *La magnifica et sumptuosa festa . . . per el Carnovale, MDXIII* (?, n.d.). Note also Ademollo, pp. 21–53 and Bonner Mitchell, *Italian Civic Pageantry in the High Renaissance: A Descriptive Bibliography of Triumphal Entries and Selected Other Festivities for State Occasions* [Biblioteca di bibliografia italiana, 89] (Florence: Leo S. Olschki, 1979), p. 116.

164. "La Festa de Agoni facta in tempo de papa Leone decimo . . . ordinata per T. Phaedro Vulterrano," BAV, ms. Vat. lat. 3351, fol. 171ᵛ. Note also Hubert Janitschek, "Über einige bisher unbekannte Künstler, die unter Leo X in Rom arbeiteten," *Reportorium für Kunstwissenschaft*, II (1879), pp. 416–17; Fabrizio Cruciani, *Il teatro del Campidoglio e le feste romane del 1513* (Milan: Il Polifilo, 1968), pp. lxxv, xciii–xciv.

165. Krautheimer, *Rome*, pp. 203, 319.

166. An English translation of Raphael's letter appears in Elizabeth G. Holt, *A Documentary History of Art* (Garden City, N.Y.: Doubleday, 1957), I, pp. 289–96; for the destroyed monuments, see Weiss, *Renaissance Discovery*, pp. 98–101.

167. Müntz, *Les arts*, III, p. 15.

168. *Ibid.*, I, pp. 266–69.

169. Note the typical remarks of Traversari, who was guided by Poggio through the ruins during his first trip to Rome in 1432: see my "Ambrogio Traversari and the 'Tempio degli Scolari' at S. Maria degli Angeli in Florence," in Sergio Bertelli and Gloria Ramakus, eds., *Essays Presented to Myron P. Gilmore* (Florence: La Nuova Italia, 1978), I, p. 278.

170. Poggio Bracciolini, *De varietate fortunae* [Collana di studi e testi diretta da Giuseppe Vecchi. B. Scriptores, Vol. CII] (Bologna: Forni, 1969; reprint of edition of Dominicus Gcorgius Lutetiae Parisiorum, 1723), pp. 5–7; extracts from Bk. I of Poggio's dialogue appear in Valentini and Zucchetti, *Codice topografico*, IV, pp. 223–45. For the nature and circumstances of Poggio's work, see Weiss, *Renaissance Discovery*, pp. 63–66, and Richard Krautheimer with Trude Krautheimer-Hess, *Lorenzo Ghiberti*, 2nd ed. (Princeton: Princeton U. Pr., 1970), I, pp. 294–305.

171. Valentini and Zucchetti, IV, pp. 237–38; note also Gordan, *Two Renaissance Book Hunters*, pp. 146–47.

172. Valentini and Zucchetti, IV, p. 233.

173. Gordan, pp. 167–70.

174. *Ibid.*, pp. 127–30.

175. *Opera omnia*, p. 222. For discussion of Biondo's treatise, see Weiss, *Renaissance Discovery*, pp. 66–70; *id.*, "Biondo Flavio archeologo," *Studi romagnoli*, XIV (1963), pp. 335–41; Nogara, *Scritti inediti*, pp. xcvi–cii; Riccardo Fubini, "Biondo, Flavio," *DBI*, X, pp. 547–48; and Dorothy M. Robathan, "Flavio Biondo's *Roma instaurata*," *MH*, n.s. I (1970), pp. 203–16.

176. Gustina Scaglia, "The Origin of an Archeological Plan of Rome by Alessandro Strozzi," *JWCI* (1964), pp. 142–43, 153–54.

177. *Roma instaurata*, in *Opera omnia*, p. 258.

178. Weiss, *Renaissance Discovery*, pp. 73–89. André Chastel argues that archeological studies were of fundamental importance in shaping the cultural character of Leonine and Clementine Rome: *The Sack of Rome, 1527*, trans. Beth Archer [A.W. Mellon Lectures in the Fine Arts, 26] (Princeton: Princeton U. Pr., 1983), pp. 140–48.

179. Weiss, *Renaissance Discovery*, pp. 145–66.

180. E.g. BAV, ms. Vat. lat. 214, containing the *Peri Archon* and other works of Origen, produced for Sixtus IV; for the impact of the Roman environment on the classicizing taste of the miniaturist of this ms., see Maurizio Bonicatti, "Aspetti dell'illustrazione del libro nell' ambiente padano del secondo '400," *Rivista d'arte*, XXXII (3rd s. VII) (1957), pp. 107–49; for the coronation medal of Sixtus IV reproduced on the arch (fol. 1ʳ), see Roberto Weiss, *The Medals of Sixtus IV (1471–1484)* (Rome: Edizioni di storia e letteratura, 1961), p. 17.

181. See, in general, Weiss, *Renaissance Discovery*, pp. 162–63. The most detailed

recent study is Iiro Kajanto, *Classical and Christian: Studies in the Latin Epitaphs of Medieval and Renaissance Rome* [Annales Academia Scientiarum Fennica, Ser. B, Vol. 203] (Helsinki: Suomalainen Tiedeakatemia Pr., 1980).

182. Note Albertini, *De mirabilibus*, in Valentini and Zucchetti, IV, pp. 492–93.

183. Weiss, *Renaissance Discovery*, pp. 167–79, 186–95.

184. Samy Lattès, "A proposito dell'opera incompiuta *De ponderibus et mensuris* di Angelo Colocci," in *Atti del Convegno di studi su Angelo Colocci, Jesi, 13–14 settembre 1969* (Jesi: Amministrazione comunale, 1972), pp. 97–108.

185. Antonio di Tuccio Manetti, *The Life of Brunelleschi*, ed. Howard Saalman, trans. Catherine Enggass (University Park: Pennsylvania St. U. Pr., 1970), pp. 52–53.

186. For Ciriaco's account of his 1433 visit with Sigismund, see Kyriacus Anconitanus, *Itinerarium*, ed. Laurentius Mehus (Bologna: Forni, 1969; reprint of edition of Florence: Giovanelli, 1742), pp. 21–22. For Ciriaco, see Bernard Ashmole, "Cyriac of Ancona," *PBA*, XLV (1959), pp. 25–41, and Charles Mitchell, "Archeology and Romance in Renaissance Italy," in Jacob, *Italian Renaissance Studies*, pp. 455–83.

187. Joan Gadol, *Leon Battista Alberti: Universal Man of the Early Renaissance* (Chicago: U. of Chicago Pr., 1969), pp, 98–99, 104–06.

188. For Giuliano making measurements of the Colosseum, see Cruciani, *Teatro del Campidoglio*, p. lviii.

189. Gadol, p. 94; Pius II, *Commentaries*, *SCSH*, XLIII (1957), p. 762.

190. Gadol, pp. 70–74, 157–95; Samuel Y. Edgerton, Jr., *The Renaissance Rediscovery of Linear Perspective* (N.Y.: Basic Books, 1975), pp. 91–123. For maps, views, and plans of Rome in the medieval and Renaissance periods, see Camillo Scaccia-Scarafoni, *Le piante di Roma* (Rome: R. Istituto di Archeologia e Storia dell'Arte, 1939); Amato Pietro Frutaz, *Le piante di Roma* (Rome: Istituto di Studi Romani, 1962); Scaglia, "Origin," pp. 137–59; Weiss, *Renaissance Discovery*, pp. 90–98; Westfall, *In this Most Perfect Paradise*, pp. 85–92.

191. Jürgen Schulz, "Jacopo de' Barbari's View of Venice: Map Making, City Views, and Moralized Geography Before the Year 1500," *AB*, LX (1978), pp. 456–58.

192. Frutaz, *Piante*, pp. 51–54; Weiss, *Renaissance Discovery*, pp. 94–98.

193. Frutaz, pp. 168–70; note also, in general, John A. Pinto, "Origins and Development of the Ichnographic City Plan," *JSAH*, XXXV (1976), pp. 34–50.

194. Weiss, *Renaissance Discovery*, pp. 33–34, 61–62.

195. *Roma instaurata*, pp. 261–62; *Roma triumphans*, in *Opera omnia*, pp. 30–53.

196. Weiss, *Renaissance Discovery*, pp. 65, 80.

197. *Ibid.*, pp. 35, 69, 86.

198. *Ibid.*, p. 88.

199. *Ibid.*, pp. 85–86, 94, 125–26, 154. Note also Roberto Weiss, "Traccia per una biografia di Annio da Viterbo," *Italia medioevale e umanistica*, V (1962), pp. 425–41.

200. The text of Leto's *Excerpta* is in Valentini and Zucchetti, IV, pp. 423–36. For Leto's antiquarianism, see Weiss, *Renaissance Discovery*, pp. 76–78 and esp. Vladimiro Zabughin, *Giulio Pomponio Leto* (Rome: La vita letteraria, 1909–12), I, p. 225–26.

201. Denys Hay, "Flavio Biondo and the Middle Ages," *PBA*, XLV (1959), pp. 97–128; Cochrane, *Historians and Historiography*, pp. 34–40.

202. "*Itaque coepimus tentare, si speculum, exemplar, imaginem, doctrinam omnis virtutis et bene sancte ac foeliciter vivendi rationis, Urbem Romam florentem ac qualem beatus Aurelius Augustinus triumphatem videre desideravit: nostrorum hominum ingenio et doctrina valentium oculis et menti subjicere ac proponere poterimus.*" Biondo, *Roma triumphans*, in *Opera omnia*, p. 2. For discussion of the nature of this work, see Nogara, pp. cxlix-xlv, and Fubini, *DBI*, X, pp. 552–53. Note also A. Mazzocco, "Some Philological Aspects of Biondo Flavio's *Roma triumphans*," *Humanistica Lovaniensia*, XXVIII (1979), pp. 1–26.

203. BAV, ms. Reg. lat. 1882, fol. 2ʳ, dated 1456: see Francesco Ehrle, S.J., "Due nuove vedute di Roma del secolo XV," *Atti del IIᵒ Congresso internazionale di archeologia cristiana, tenuto in Roma nell'aprile 1900* (Rome: Spithöver, 1902), pp. 257–63.

204. "*Quod si quis cuncta, quae a Graecis, Latinisque scriptoribus traduntur imitaturus observet, proponatque sibi ut in aedificando formulam, exemplar Romanae civitatis, profecto ingenue fateatur necesse est, qualem Respublicam prisci habuerint, se satis percipere non potuisse. Haec nos, ut videmur, adsequuti, dum opitulandi nostrae civitati studio veterum monumenta prosequimur, opus ipsum adgrediemur, si prius de situ Urbis, deque ipsius moenibus, de pomerio, de regionibus, de aedificiis ceterisque generis eiusdem disseruerimus. Nam permagni interest in percipienda civitatis forma, et illud*"

antea cognovisse, prolata saepius ab Regibus primo deinde a Principibus moenia, inductas aquas, cloacas exaedificatus: ac denique singula singulis regionibus cum publice, tum privatim constructa aedificia, quae sacris, profanisque, vel commodis, vel voluptatibus inservirent." Bernardus Oricellarius, De Urbe Roma, RIS, II (Florence, 1770), cols. 783–84. For the circumstances in which Rucellai wrote this work, see Felix Gilbert, "Bernardo Rucellai and the Orti Oricellari: A Study on the Origin of Modern Political Thought," JWCI, XII (1949), pp. 122–23.

205. Valentini and Zucchetti, Codice topografico, IV, pp. 462–63.

206. Olschki, "Albertini," p. 487.

207. Baron, Crisis, esp. pp. 47–62, 409–30; Felix Gilbert, Machiavelli and Guicciardini: Politics and History in Sixteenth-Century Florence (Princeton: Princeton U. Pr., 1965), esp. pp. 153–200. For an overview of the changing perceptions of Rome, from Petrarch to Machiavelli, see Franco Gaeta, "Sull'idea di Roma nell'Umanesimo e nel Rinascimento (Appunti e spunti per una ricerca)," Studi romani, XXV (1977), pp. 169–86.

208. A contemporary account is Leon Battista Alberti, De Porcaria conjuratione, in Opera inedita, ed. Girolamo Mancini (Florence: Sansoni, 1890), pp. 257–66; English trans. by Renée Neu Watkins, Humanism and Liberty: Writings on Freedom from Fifteenth-Century Florence (Columbia: U. of South Carolina Pr., 1978), pp. 107–15. See also Roberto Cessi, "La congiura di Stefano Porcari," in Saggi romani [Storia e letteratura: Raccolta di studi e testi, LXII] (Rome, 1956), pp. 65–112; Massimo Miglio, "'Viva la libertà et popolo de Roma': Oratoria e politica a Roma, Stefano Porcari," ARSRSP, XCVII (1974), pp. 5–37; Baron, Crisis, pp. 434–35.

209. Roma triumphans, in Opera omnia, p. 1.

210. Gherardi, Diario romano, p. 117.

211. Liber notarum, II, pp. 278–80.

212. Arturo Graf, Roma nella memoria e nelle immaginazioni del Medio Evo (Turin: Chiantore, 1923); Luigi Salerno, Roma Communis Patria (Bologna: Cappelli, 1968); Nancy Lenkeith, Dante and the Legend of Rome (London: Warburg Institute, 1952), pp. 8–26, 76–95; Charles Till Davis, Dante and the Idea of Rome (Oxford: Clarendon Pr., 1957), pp. 1–138.

213. Signorili's Descriptio appears in Valentini and Zucchetti, Codice topografico, IV, pp. 151–208 (see p. 163 for the laudatory appellations).

214. The Latin translation, by Francesco Aleardo da Verona, is in BAV, ms. Reg. lat. 807, fols. 24ᵛ–59ʳ (dated 14 May 1444); the theme of Rome as part of heaven is developed in fols. 29ᵛ–30ᵛ. Brief mention of Chrysoloras's work appears in O'Malley, Praise and Blame, p. 79, and in Andrew Martindale, The Triumphs of Caesar by Andrea Mantegna in the Collection of Her Majesty the Queen at Hampton Court (London: Harvey Miller, 1979), pp. 51–52; for a fuller discussion, including Chrysoloras's classical and Byzantine sources, see Helene Homeyer, "Zur Synkrisis des Manuel Chrysoloras, einem Vergleich zwischen Rom und Konstantinopel: Ein Beitrag zum italienischen Frühhumanismus," Klio, LXII (1980), pp. 525–34.

215. For the Greek text, English translation, and extensive commentary on the "Roman Oration," see James H. Oliver, "The Ruling Power: A Study of the Roman Empire in the Second Century after Christ through the 'Roman Oration' of Aelius Aristides," TAPS, n.s. XLIII (1953), pp. 871–1003.

216. Valentini and Zucchetti, IV, p. 231.

217. Note esp. Theodore C. Burgess, "Epideictic Literature," Studies in Classical Philology, III (1902), pp. 89–263; particularly helpful is the succinct discussion in O'Malley, Praise and Blame, pp. 36–41. Praise of cities was one of the classical topoi of epideictic rhetoric (Burgess, pp. 110–12), and such panegyrics became a common form of Italian humanist oratory. The most famous, undoubtedly, is Leonardo Bruni's Laudatio Florentinae urbis, the Latin text of which Hans Baron published in his From Petrarch to Leonardo Bruni: Studies in Humanistic and Political Literature (Chicago: U. of Chicago Pr., 1968), pp. 219–63, and which Baron discusses extensively in his Crisis, pp. 191–224 and again in From Petrarch to Bruni, pp. 151–71. For an English translation and recent scholarship on Bruni's Laudatio, see Benjamin G. Kohl and Ronald G. Witt, eds., The Earthly Republic: Italian Humanists on Government and Society (Philadelphia: U. of Pennsylvania Pr., 1978), pp. 121–75. The model for Bruni's Laudatio was Aristides's panegyric on Athens: for this work, see James H. Oliver, "The Civilizing Power: A Study of the Panathenaic Discourse of Aelius Aristides against the Background of Literature and Cultural Conflict, with Text, Translation, and Commentary," TAPS, n.s. LVIII (1968), pp. 3–223. For the relation of Bruni's Laudatio to other humanist panegyrics of cities, note O'Malley, Praise and Blame, pp. 77–79, and Hermann Goldbrun-

ner, "*Laudatio urbis*: Zu neueren Untersuchungen über das humanistische Städtelob," *QFIAB*, LXIII (1983), pp. 313–28.
218. Note, in particular, the "Conclusion" of *Praise and Blame*, pp. 238–43.
219. O'Malley, *Praise and Blame*, pp. 63–66, 79. For the place of ekphrasis in the Byzantine tradition, see George L. Kustas, *Studies in Byzantine Rhetoric* (Thessalonica: Patriarchal Institute for Patristic Studies, 1973), pp. 57–61.
220. Chrysoloras's description of the Arch of Constantine proved influential, Michael Baxandall argues, for subsequent Italian humanist treatments of the visual arts: *Giotto and the Orators: Humanist Observers of Painting in Italy and the Discovery of Pictorial Composition, 1350–1450* (Oxford: Clarendon Pr., 1971), pp. 78–87.
221. Kohl and Witt, *Earthly Republic*, p. 243.
222. Coffin, *Villa in the Life of Renaissance Rome*, pp. 64–66.
223. *Opera omnia*, p. 240; for the location of the Colonna villa, see Krautheimer, *Rome*, p. 255.
224. *Opera omnia*, pp. 179–80, 191–92.
225. Coffin, *Villa in the Life of Renaissance Rome*, pp. 182–83; for the various Roman academies and their garden settings, see D'Amico, *Renaissance Humanism in Papal Rome*, pp. 89–112; note also T. C. Price Zimmerman, "Renaissance Symposia," in Sergio Bertelli and Gloria Ramakus, eds., *Essays Presented to Myron P. Gilmore* (Florence: La Nuova Italia, 1978), I, pp. 363–74.
226. For Goritz, see Phyllis Pray Bober, "The *Coryciana* and the Nymph Corycia," *JWCI*, XL (1977), pp. 223–39. Goritz commissioned Sansovino and Raphael to design and execute the St. Anne altar in the Roman church of Sant'Agostino. This ensemble of architecture, sculpture, and painting (Raphael's *Isaiah*) was dedicated by Goritz in 1512 and intended as his tomb. The ensemble has now been restored to its original conception, and Virginia Anne Bonito has shown how its form and content, in particular the text in Hebrew of Isaiah's scroll, reflect the religious and humanistic interests of Goritz's circle: "The Saint Anne altar in Sant'Agostino: restoration and interpretation," *Burlington Magazine*, CXXIV (1982), pp. 268–76. For Colocci, see Federico Ubaldini, *Vita di Mons. Angelo Colocci*, ed. Vittorio Fanelli [Studi e Testi, 256] (Vatican, 1969), pp. 38–75; Coffin, *Villa in the Life of Renaissance Rome*, pp. 164, 197; Elisabeth B. MacDougall, "The Sleeping Nymph: Origins of a Humanist Fountain Type," *AB*, LVII (1975), pp. 357–65.
227. Coffin, p. 192; Douglas, *Sadoleto*, pp. 18–19.
228. Gilbert, "Bernardo Rucellai and the Orti Oricellari," pp. 101–31.
229. Coffin, pp. 96–97; Eugenio Battisti, "*Natura Artificiosa* to *Natura Artificialis*," in David R. Coffin, ed., *The Italian Garden: First Dumbarton Oaks Colloquium on the History of Landscape Architecture* (Washington: Dumbarton Oaks, 1972), p. 33.
230. Pius II, *Commentaries*, *SCSH*, XLIII (1957), p. 763.
231. Battisti, pp. 31–33; MacDougall, "Sleeping Nymph," p. 363.
232. Coffin, *Villa*, p. 252.
233. *Ibid.*, p. 255.
234. Elisabeth B. MacDougall, "*Ars Hortulorum*: Sixteenth-Century Garden Iconography and Literary Theory in Italy," in Coffin, ed., *Italian Garden*, pp. 37–59; *id.*, "*L'Ingegnoso Artifizio*: Sixteenth Century Garden Fountains in Rome," in Elisabeth B. MacDougall, ed., *Fons Sapientiae: Renaissance Garden Fountains. Fifth Dumbarton Oaks Colloquium on the History of Landscape Architecture* (Washington, D. C.: Dumbarton Oaks, 1978), pp. 87–99.
235. Battisti, p. 30.
236. *Roma instaurata*, in *Opera omnia*, p. 266.
237. Nicole Dacos, *La découverte de la Domus Aurea et la formation des grotesques à la Renaissance* [Studies of the Warburg Institute, 31] (London-Leiden, 1969); J. Schulz, "Pinturicchio and the Revival of Antiquity," *JWCI*, XXV (1962), pp. 46–50; Mario Salmi, "Bernardo Dovizi e l'arte," *Rinascimento*, 2nd ser., IX (1969), pp. 12–15.
238. Hans Henrik Brummer, *The Statue Court of the Vatican Belvedere* [Stockholm Studies in the History of Art, 20] (Stockholm: Almquist & Wiksell, 1970), pp. 75–119.
239. Weiss, *Renaissance Discovery*, p. 191.
240. James S. Ackerman, *The Architecture of Michelangelo* (Harmondsworth: Penguin, 1971), p. 193.
241. Weiss, *Renaissance Discovery*, p. 102; Giovanni Mercati, *Opere minori*, IV [Studi e Testi, 79] (Vatican, 1937), pp. 268–83.

242. Platina, *Liber de vita Christi*, p. 33; for earlier visits to the catacombs, see Delaruelle, *et al.*, *L'Église au temps du Grand Schisme*, p. 1146.

243. Weiss, *Renaissance Discovery*, p. 162; Lee, *Sixtus IV*, pp. 7, 61; Dunston, "Pope Paul II and the Humanists," pp. 288–89; Palermino, "The Roman Academy, the Catacombs and the Conspiracy of 1468," pp. 117–55.

244. See p. 257.

245. Ackerman, *Architecture of Michelangelo*, pp. 192–96; Coffin, pp. 89–90.

246. See p. 271.

247. David R. Coffin, *The Villa d'Este at Tivoli* (Princeton: Princeton U. Pr., 1960), pp. 23–28.

248. Schulz, "Barbari's View of Venice," p. 467; Coffin, *Villa in the Life of Renaissance Rome*, pp. 101–03.

249. Note esp. Marcello's sermon for the Feast of All Saints, discussed on p. 242.

250. See respectively Manetti, *Vita Nicolai V*, col. 928; Gherardi, *Diario Romano*, pp. 96–97; and Rodocanachi, *Rome au temps de Jules II et de Léon X*, pp. 320–21.

251. Note the speeches of Cajetan (17 May 1512) and Stefano Taleazzi (4 May 1515), in Johannes Dominicus Mansi, *Sacrorum Conciliorum nova et amplissima collectio* (Graz: Akademische Druck- u. Verlaganstalt, 1961; first publ. Paris, 1901), XXXII, cols. 719–27, 920. A portion of Cajetan's speech is missing from the Mansi edition; for the missing text, see Nelson H. Minnich, S.J., "Concepts of Reform Proposed at the Fifth Lateran Council," *AHP*, VII (1969), pp. 239–41; note also Minnich's discussion of these two speeches, pp. 175–79, 198–201. For the long career in Rome of Taleazzi (Stephanus Thegliatius, d. 1515), note Setton, "Leo X and the Turkish Peril," pp. 378–79. For futher consideration of the theme of the Roman Church as the new Jerusalem descending from heaven, see pp. 318–19.

252. Zaccaria Ferreri, *Lugudunense somnium* ... (?, 1513?). For discussion of this work, see Morsolin, *Zaccaria Ferreri*, pp. 61–63; *id.*, "Un latinista del Cinquecento imitatore di Dante," *Atti del R. Istituto Veneto di scienze, lettere, ed arti*, 7th ser., V (1893–94), pp. 1429–46; and Shearman, *Raphael's Cartoons*, pp. 1-2.

253. For relevant portions of the text and discussion, see Pica, "Città di Bramante," pp. 117–25; there is also a recent edition: Andrea Guarna da Salerno, *Scimmia*, ed. and trans. E. and G. Battisti (Rome: Istituto grafico tiberino, 1970). For Bramante's Belvedere staircase, see Bruschi, pp. 417–33.

254. For Acciaiuoli's *Oratio in laudem Urbis Romae* (Rome: J. Mazochius, 1518), I have drawn on the remarks of Eugene F. Rice, Jr., "Zanobio Acciaiuoli, O.P., Prefect of the Vatican Library under Leo X," a paper presented to the conference "Rome in the Renaissance: The City and the Myth," Center for Medieval and Renaissance Studies, State University of New York at Binghamton, 18–20 October 1979.

255. Francis Morgan Nichols, ed. and trans., *Mirabilia Urbis Romae: The Marvels of Rome* (London: Ellis and Elvey, 1889), pp. 97–98.

256. *Itinerarium*, p. 26.

257. *Diario*, p. 78.

258. Valentini and Zucchetti, *Codice topografico*, IV, p. 403.

259. Graf, *Roma nella memoria* ... *del Medio Evo*, pp. 262–84.

260. Pius II, *Commentaries*, *SCSH*, XXX (1947), p. 346; Albertini, *De mirabilibus*, in Valentini and Zucchetti, IV, p. 495. Note also Bentivoglio and Valtieri, *Santa Maria del Popolo*, pp. 9–10.

261. *Excerpta*, in Valentini and Zucchetti, IV, p. 431.

262. Rome as Babylon, or the Great Whore of Babylon, stems ultimately from I Peter 5:13 and Revelation 16:19 and 17:1–19:2, texts to which Domenichi refers in acknowledging the just criticisms by the European princes of the Roman Curia as the "mother of all fornications and abominations of the earth:" see the passage from his *Tractatus de reformationibus Romanae Curiae* quoted in O'Malley, *Praise and Blame*, p. 211. Humanists who refer to Rome as Babylon include Traversari [see Charles L. Stinger, *Humanism and the Church Fathers: Ambrogio Traversari (1386–1439) and Christian Antiquity in the Italian Renaissance* (Albany: SUNY Pr., 1977), p. 176], Poggio [his *De avaritia* cites with approval Petrarch's condemnation of the Avignonese papacy as a greedy Babylon: see the text in Kohl and Witt, *Earthly Republic*, p. 273], and Giles of Viterbo [John W. O'Malley, *Giles of Viterbo on Church and Reform: A Study in Renaissance Thought* [Studies in Medieval and Reformation Thought, V] (Leiden: Brill, 1968), p. 132]. Note also the Prologue to Pietro Aretino, *La Cortigiana*, ed.

Giuliano Innamorati [Collezione di teatro, 137] (Turin: Einaudi, 1970), p. 35: ". . . e mi vien da ridere perch'io penso che inanzi che questa tela si levassi dal volto di questa città, vi credevate che ci fussi sotto la torre de Babilonia, e sotto ci era Roma." Benozzo Gozzoli, in a scene in the Camposanto of Pisa depicting the construction of the tower of Babel, shows Babylon with clearly identifiable Roman monuments, including the Pantheon: Frutaz, Piante, pp. 136–37. For the theme of Rome as Babylon during the Middle Ages, see Charles Pietri, Roma Christiana: Recherches sur l'Église de Rome, son organisation, sa politique, son idéologie de Miltiade à Sixte III (311–440) [BEFAR, 224] (Paris: de Boccard, 1976), pp. 1636–45; Brentano, Rome before Avignon, pp. 88–89; Davis, Dante and the Idea of Rome, pp. 195–235; and id., "Rome and Babylon in Dante," in Ramsey, ed., Rome in the Renaissance, pp. 19–40. For the theme's continuation in the sixteenth century, note Hubert Jedin, "Rom und Romidee im Zeitalter der Reformation und Gegenreformation," in Kirche des Glaubens, Kirche der Geschichte: Ausgewählte Aufsätze und Vorträge, I (Vienna: Herder, 1966), pp. 143–52, and Chastel, Sack of Rome, pp. 67–78.

263. The Latin text is in O'Malley, Praise and Blame, p. 215, n. 79. Note also McManamon, "Ideal Renaissance Pope," pp. 16–17, 45.

264. Pius II, Commentaries, SCSH, XXX (1947), pp. 374–76, XXXV (1951), pp. 504–05.

265. Roma instaurata, in Opera Omnia, p. 262.

266. Francesco Fabi Montani, Feste e spettacoli di Roma dal secolo X a tutto il XVI particolarmente nel Carnevale e nel maggio (Rome, 1861), pp. 51–53; Cruciani, Teatro del Campidoglio, xcii, n. 48.

267. Autobiography, pp. 120–23.

III. The Renaissance Papacy and the Respublica Christiana

1. The conclaves of 1431 and 1447 were held in this Dominican monastery. From 1455 until the end of the Renaissance period voting took place in the Vatican Palace, in the Capella Parva of St. Nicholas, also known as the Chapel of the Sacrament. For the decade 1549–59 conclaves met in the Cappella Paolina, completed during Paul III's pontificate, but thereafter the Sistine Chapel was used. During the Renaissance period the old Capella Magna of the Vatican Palace at first served as a dormitory for cardinals during conclave. When this was replaced by the Sistine Chapel, it was here that the cardinals slept, until finally in the 1560s and thereafter they were assigned rooms in the papal apartments. When the Sistine Chapel functioned as a cardinals' dormitory, temporary wooden-framed cubicles, covered with cloth, were constructed to form a cell for each cardinal: see D. S. Chambers, "Papal Conclaves and Prophetic Mystery in the Sistine Chapel," JWCI, XLI (1978), pp. 322–23.

2. RIS, III, Pt. 2, col. 917. The Muratori edition deletes Manetti's lengthy and revealing discussion of the importance dreams had in Greek and Roman history, literature, and philosophy (Aeneas, Sophocles, Socrates, etc.) and also in sacred history (Joseph and Pharaoh's dream, Daniel and the dream of Nebuchadnezzar). This portion of Manetti's Vita is published as an appendix to Laura Onofri's important analysis of this work: "Sacralità, immaginazione e proposte politiche: La Vita di Niccolò V di Giannozzo Manetti," Humanistica Lovaniensia, XXVIII (1979), pp. 27–77. Vespasiano da Bisticci, drawing heavily on Manetti's account, also stresses this "mirabile visione:" "La vita di Nicolao P.P. V," in Le vite, ed. Aulo Greco (Florence: Istituto Nazionale di Studi sul Rinascimento, 1970), I, pp. 54–55. The Florentine book-dealer adds also (ibid., pp. 56, 61) that Nicholas's divine election was further demonstrated by his bringing peace to Italy not by force of arms but by the Cross. Pius II, Commentaries, SCSH, XXII (1936–37), pp. 63–64, records Nicholas V describing to the Holy Roman Emperor Frederick III a different version of this episode: the dream occurred not while the cardinals were in conclave, but rather the night before Eugenius died. There is no mention of any dream in the Viterbese humanist Michele Canensi's Ad Beatissimum D.N. Nicolaum V Pontificem Maximum . . . de ipsius laudibus et divina electione (datable to 1451 or early 1452). Less hagiographical in approach than Manetti's Vita, Canensi nevertheless, as his title suggests, sees revealed in the pope's life his "pre-election" to Peter's see, and stresses that the cardinals in the conclave with one voice "by divine inspiration" elected Nicholas pope, which

thus confirmed God's will: "*Ipse enim Deus. . . . dixit et factus es, ipse idem mandavit et es creatus pontifex summus. . . .*" For this text, see Massimo Miglio, *Storiografia pontificia del Quattrocento* (Bologna: Pàtron, 1975), pp. 225–26 (note also Miglio's discussion of the biographies of Canensi and Manetti, pp. 71–111). Platina, *Liber de vita Christi ac omnium pontificum*, likewise makes no mention of an oracular dream, but he does cite the Cardinal of Portugal as stating when he came forth from the conclave: "*Non nos Nicolaum, sed Deus pontificem designavit.*" The theme of divine election to the papcy was a general one: Poggio Bracciolini, in the introduction to his brief sketches of early fifteenth-century popes, indicates as the purpose of his narrative to show ". . . *quo Dei providentia non hominum prudentia palam sit regi pontificatum.*" For this text, see Miglio, *Storiografia*, p. 175. For review of, and useful supplements to, Miglio's book, see Riccardo Fubini, "Papato e storiografia nel Quattrocento: Storia biografia e propaganda in un recente studio," *Studi medievali*, 3rd ser., XVIII, Pt. I (1977), pp. 321–51.

3. Joachim W. Stieber, *Pope Eugenius IV, the Council of Basel, and the Secular and Ecclesiastical Authorities in the Empire: The Conflict over Supreme Authority and Power in the Church* [Studies in the History of Christian Thought, ed. Heiko A. Oberman, XIII] (Leiden: Brill, 1978), Appendix C, pp. 375–77.

4. Manetti, *Vita Nicolai V*, col. 909.

5. *Ibid.*, cols. 909–10.

6. *Ibid.*, col. 918.

7. Onofri, "Sacralità," pp. 36–37, 51.

8. Mallett, *The Borgias*, pp. 62, 66, 69; Pius II, *Commentaries, SCSH*, XXII (1936–37), p. 76.

9. BAV, ms. Vat. lat. 3646, pp. 9ᵛ–11ᵛ, 27ʳ⁻ᵛ. Raffaele Brandolini makes the same point in his *Dialogus Leo nuncupatus*, ed. Francesco Fogliazzi (Venice: Occhi, 1753), p. 100: ". . . *sed quum rerum initia progressusque mecum animo revolverem, id non fato, Philosophorum ritu, sed Dei unius voluntati, nutuque tribuebam.*" For this work, written 1513–14, note Shearman, *Raphael's Cartoons*, pp. 12, 14. An idealized life of Leo X, including the events immediately before his election, forms the subject matter of the border "reliefs" of the Raphael tapestries for the Sistine Chapel: *ibid.*, pp. 84–89.

10. Pius II, *Commentaries, SCSH*, XXII (1936–37), pp. 93–105; for the expurgation of this passage from the first published edition of 1584, see Eugenio Garin, *Portraits from the Quattrocento*, trans. Victor A. and Elizabeth Velen (N.Y.: Harper & Row, 1972), pp. 31–32.

11. Pius II, *Commentaries, SCSH*, XXII (1936–37), pp. 62–63; note also *ibid.*, p. 84 where King Alfonso of Naples prophesied that Aeneas Silvius is "destined by God to succeed Calixtus III as pope."

12. *RIS²*, III, Pt. I, p. 399; for this and other hagiographic treatments of Sixtus's early life, see Lee, *Sixtus IV and Men of Letters*, pp. 11–12, and Dino Cortese, "Sisto Quarto Papa Antoniano," *Il Santo*, XII (1972), pp. 211–71.

13. Federigo Patetta, *Venturino de Prioribus: Umanista ligure del secolo XV* [Studi e Testi, 149] (Vatican, 1950), pp. 315–16.

14. Vincenzo Pacifici, *Un carme biografico di Sisto IV del 1477* (Tivoli, 1921), p. 8; for the identification of the author of this work, see Augusto Campana, "Roma di Sisto IV: Le *Lucubraciunculae Tibertinae* di Robert Flemmyng," *Strenna dei Romanisti*, IX (1948), pp. 88–98.

15. Weiss, *Medals of Sixtus IV*, pp. 13–18.

16. Cortese, "Sisto Quarto Papa Antoniano," pp. 233–37.

17. *Collectionis Bullarum, Brevium aliorumque Diplomatum sacrosanctae Basilicae Vaticanae*, Vol II: *Ab Urbano V ad Paulum III* (Rome: Archigymnasio Sapientiae, 1750), pp. 205–06.

18. L.D. Ettlinger, "Pollaiuolo's Tomb of Sixtus IV," *JWCI*, XVI (1953), pp. 268–70.

19. Pietro de Angelis, *L'architetto e gli affreschi di Santo Spirito in Saxia* (Rome, 1961); Lee, *Sixtus IV*, pp. 137–42.

20. Elisabetta Mayer, *Un umanista italiano della corte di Mattia Corvino: Aurelio Brandolini Lippo* [Biblioteca dell'Accademia d'Ungheria di Roma, 14] (Rome, 1938), pp. 17–27; Giuseppe de Luca, "Un umanista fiorentino e la Roma rinnovata da Sisto IV," *Rinascita*, I (1938), pp. 74–90. For other aspects of Brandolini's career in Rome, see Charles Trinkaus, *In Our Image and Likeness: Humanity and Divinity in Italian Renaissance Thought* (Chicago: U. of

Chicago Pr., 1970), pp. 297–321, 601–13; and O'Malley, *Praise and Blame*, pp. 44–50, 113–14.

21. BAV, ms. Urb. lat. 739, fols. 18^v–32^v.

22. Manetti, *Vita Nicolai V*, col. 921; Platina, *Liber de vita Christi ac omnium pontificum*, p. 328.

23. Pastor, *History of the Popes*, IV, p. 201; Flemmyng, *Lucubraciunculae Tiburtinae*, in Pacifici, *Un carme biografico*, p. 12.

24. Pius II, *Commentaries*, SCSH, XXII (1936–37), pp. 104–05; Garin, *Portraits from the Quattrocento*, p. 30.

25. Partridge and Starn, *A Renaissance Likeness*, pp. 62–63.

26. Setton, *Papacy and the Levant*, II, pp. 435–36; Burchard, *Liber notarum*, I, p. 376.

27. Shearman, *Raphael's Cartoons*, pp. 15–20, and *id.*, "The Vatican Stanze: Functions and Decoration," *PBA*, LVII (1971), pp. 384–89. Begnius's remarks appear in Mansi, *Collectio*, XXXII, cols. 803–04; for further discussion of his speech, see Minnich, "Concepts of Reform," pp. 185–89.

28. McManamon, "Ideal Renaissance Pope," pp. 33–54.

29. The text appears in *ibid.*, pp. 62–70; note also McManamon's discussion of it, pp. 54–59.

30. Mallett, *The Borgias*, pp. 60–66.

31. *Ibid.*, pp. 82–83.

32. Mitchell, *Rome in the High Renaissance*, pp. 126–28; Pastor, IX, pp. 1–230.

33. Denys Hay, *The Church in Italy in the Fifteenth Century: The Birkbeck Lectures, 1971* (Cambridge: Cambridge U. Pr., 1977), pp. 33–38; for the transformation of the College of Cardinals in this period, see also Hubert Jedin, *A History of the Council of Trent*, trans. Dom Ernest Graf, O.S.B., Vol. I (St. Louis: Herder, 1949), pp. 76–92; and esp. John A.F. Thomson, *Popes and Princes, 1417–1517: Politics and Polity in the Late Medieval Church* (London: Allen & Unwin, 1980), pp. 57–77.

34. O'Malley, *Giles of Viterbo*, p. 111.

35. Richard B. Hilary, "The Nepotism of Pope Pius II, 1458–1464," *CHR*, LXIV (1978), pp. 33–35; for a general overview of this issue, see Wolfgang Reinhard, "Nepotismus: Der Funktionswandel einer päpstgeschichtlichen Konstanten," *Zeitschrift für Kirchengeschichte*, LXXXVI (1975), pp. 145–85.

36. Niccolò Machiavelli, *De principatibus*, in *Opere politiche*, ed. Mario Puppo (Florence: Le Monnier, 1969), p. 108; Lee, *Sixtus IV*, pp. 11–45; Mallett, *The Borgias*, pp. 56–57.

37. Paschini, *Roma nel Rinascimento*, pp. 59–157; Partner, *Lands of St. Peter*, pp. 366–419; Jean Guiraud, *L'État Pontifical après le Grand Schisme: Étude de géographie politique* [BEFAR, 73] (Paris, 1896); and Thomson, *Popes and Princes*, pp. 119–26. For the *condottieri* in the Papal States, note esp. Mallett, *Mercenaries and their Masters*, pp. 66–75.

38. Mallett, *The Borgias*, pp. 40–41; Westfall, *In this Most Perfect Paradise*, pp. 71–84; Jean Delumeau, "Rome: Political and Administrative Centralization in the Papal State in the Sixteenth Century," in Eric Cochrane, ed., *The Late Italian Renaissance, 1525–1630* (N.Y.: Harper & Row, 1970), p. 294.

39. Cruciani, *Il teatro del Campidoglio*, esp. pp. 48–50, 83–85; note also Bonner Mitchell, "The S.P.Q.R. in Two Roman Festivals of the Early and Mid-Quattrocento," *The Sixteenth Century Journal*, IX/4 (1978), pp. 95–99; and *id.*, *Italian Civic Pageantry*, pp. 119–24.

40. Garrett Mattingly, *Renaissance Diplomacy* (Baltimore: Penguin, 1964), pp. 67–86.

41. Partner, "The 'Budget' of the Roman Church," pp. 256–64; Thomson, *Popes and Princes*, pp. 78–85. Partner provides a more comprehensive discussion in "Papal Financial Policy in the Renaissance and Counter-Reformation," pp. 17–62. No study of papal finances in the Renaissance period is as exhaustive as that of Jean Favier for the period preceding: *Les finances pontificales a l'époque du Grand Schisme d'Occident, 1378–1409* [BEFAR, 211] (Paris, 1966). For the growth of territorial bureaucracy, see Peter Partner, *The Papal State under Martin V: The Administration and Government of the Temporal Power in the Early Fifteenth Century* (London: The British School at Rome, 1958).

42. These ideas underlie, for instance, Raphael's frescoes of the *Repulse of Attila* and the *Liberation of St. Peter*, painted in the Vatican Stanza d'Eliodoro, and discussed on p. 195.

43. Partner, *Lands of St. Peter*, pp. 420–40; Mallett, *The Borgias*, pp. 28–36. For Ancona, note esp. Peter Earle, "The Commercial Development of Ancona, 1479–1551," *Economic History Review*, XXII (1969), pp. 28–44.

44. P. J. Jones's studies provide the best picture of a fifteenth-century Romagnol *signoria: The Malatesta of Rimini*, pp. 149–261, 289–338, and *id.*, "The End of Malatesta Rule in Rimini," in Jacob, *Italian Renaissance Studies*, pp. 217–55. Note also John Larner, "Order and Disorder in Romagna, 1450–1500," in Lauro Martines, ed., *Violence and Civil Disorder in Italian Cities 1200–1500* (Berkeley and Los Angeles: U. of California Pr., 1972), pp. 38–71.

45. Delumeau, "Rome: Political and Administrative Centralization," pp. 287–304; *id., Vie économique et sociale de Rome*, pp. 756–58, 824–43. For the whole issue of papal "state-building" in the period from Eugenius IV to Urban VIII, see Paolo Prodi, *Il sovrano pontefice. Un corpo e due anime: la monarchia papale nella prima età moderna* (Bologna: Il Mulino, 1982).

46. Partner, "'Budget'," p. 263; Mallett, *Mercenaries*, p. 228 notes that Paul II's siege of Rimini in 1469 cost half a million ducats, approximately double the total papal income for that year.

47. Gherardi, *Diario romano*, pp. 107–09.

48. For a general discussion of these developments, see J.R. Hale, "The Early Development of the Bastion: An Italian Chronology c. 1450 - c. 1534," in J. R. Hale, J. R. L. Highfield, and B. Smalley, *Europe in the Late Middle Ages* (Evanston: Northwestern U. Pr., 1965), pp. 466–94, and *id., Renaissance Fortification: Art or Engineering?* (London: Thames & Hudson, 1977). Note Pius II, *Commentaries, SCSH*, XXX (1947), p. 394 for construction of the *Arx Pia* at Tivoli.

49. Manetti, *Vita Nicolai V*, in Magnuson, *Roman Quattrocento Architecture*, p. 352.

50. Touring Club Italiano, *Guida d'Italia: Roma* (Milan, 1965), pp. 188, 310.

51. Magnuson, pp. 68–71, 115–16, 127–29; Westfall, *In this Most Perfect Paradise*, pp. 143–49; Johannes Wilde, "The Decoration of the Sistine Chapel," *PBA*, XLIV (1958), pp. 63–64.

52. Simon Pepper, "Planning versus Fortification: Sangallo's Project for the Defense of Rome," *The Architectural Review*, CLIX (1976), pp. 162–69.

53. For Lucrezia's marriages, see Mallett, *The Borgias*, pp. 99, 116, 137–38, 144–46, 159, 170–71, 232–38; for the pageantry of her wedding to Alfonso d'Este, see Mitchell, *Italian Civic Pageantry*, pp. 113–14, and *id.*, "Les intermèdes au service de l'état," in Jean Jacquot, ed., *Les fêtes de la Renaissance*, III (Paris: Éditions du Centre National de la Recherche Scientifique, 1975), pp. 119–20.

54. Mallett, *The Borgias*, pp. 199–203.

55. The End of Malatesta Rule," p. 217.

56. Lee, *Sixtus IV*, pp. 38–40; Ernst Breisach, *Caterina Sforza: A Renaissance Virago* (Chicago: U. of Chicago Pr., 1967), pp. 18–24, 42–47, 96–100, 193–246.

57. J.R. Hale, *Florence and the Medici: The Pattern of Control* (London: Thames & Hudson, 1977), pp. 95–106; Paschini, *Roma nel Rinascimento*, pp. 418–20. For the disruptive effect of this dynastic war on Leo's efforts to promote crusade, see Setton, "Leo X and the Turkish Peril," pp. 392–93.

58. See respectively, Brentano, *Rome before Avignon*, pp. 163–64; Delumeau, "Rome: Political and Administrative Centralization," pp. 290–91; and Francis Haskell, *Patrons and Painters: Art and Society in Baroque Italy* (N.Y.: Harper & Row, 1971), pp. 58–59, 146.

59. Hay, *Church in Italy*, p. 36; note Machiavelli's analysis in *The Prince*, Chap. XI "On Ecclesiastical Principalities."

60. Garin, *Portraits from the Quattrocento*, pp. 38–39; Samuel Eliot Morison, *Admiral of the Ocean Sea: A Life of Christopher Columbus* (Boston: Little, Brown, 1942), pp. 92–95.

61. Karl H. Dannenfeldt, "The Humanists' Knowledge of Arabic," *SR*, II (1955), pp. 102–03. Among Leo Africanus's Roman pupils of Arabic was Giles of Viterbo.

62. Mattingly, *Renaissance Diplomacy*, pp. 91–92, 125–39 *passim*; Setton, "Leo X and the Turkish Peril," p. 390.

63. De Angelis, *Santo Spirito in Saxia*, pp. 189–276 *passim*.

64. Marc Dykmans, "Du Monte Mario à l'escalier de Saint-Pierre de Rome," *MAHEFR*, LXXX (1968), pp. 547–94; *id.*, "Le cérémonial de Nicholas V," pp. 785–90, 798–812; Franz Wasner, "Tor der Geschichte: Beitrage zum päpstlichen Zeremonienwesen im 15. Jahrhundert," *AHP*, VI (1968), pp. 142–53; Manetti, *Vita Nicolai V*, cols. 940–42.

65. For the circumstances of Charles's coronation, see Francesco Guicciardini, *Storia d'Italia*, ed. Silvana Seidel Menchi (Turin: Einaudi, 1971), pp. 2029–2041.

66. Steven Runciman, *A History of the Crusades* (N.Y.: Harper & Row, 1964), I, pp.

107–08. In an oration delivered before King Alfonso I at Naples in 1452, Flavio Biondo stressed the example of Pope Urban II and the contributions of southern Italy to the First Crusade in arguing the necessity of relying on God's power: as He did then, so would He now find a way to bring peace to Italy and effective collaboration in war against the Turks. See Nogara, *Scritti inediti*, pp. cxxix-cxliv.

67. McManamon, "Ideal Renaissance Pope," pp. 52–53.

68. Clare O'Reilly, "'Without Councils We Cannot Be Saved . . .': Giles of Viterbo Addresses the Fifth Lateran Council," *Augustiniana*, XXVII (1977), pp. 172–74, 198–201. For Giles's preoccupation with the Turkish threat, note also *id.*, "'Maximus Caesar et Pontifex Maximus': Giles of Viterbo Proclaims the Alliance between Emperor Maximilian I and Pope Julius II," *Augustiniana*, XXII (1972), pp. 92–93, 108–12. For a recent consideration of the works of and about this central figure of the Roman Renaissance, see Francis X. Martin, O.S.A., "The Writings of Giles of Viterbo," *Augustiniana*, XXIX (1979), pp. 141–93. To this should be added *Egidio da Viterbo, O.S.A. e il suo tempo: Atti del V Convegno dell'Istituto Storico Agostiniano, Roma—Viterbo, 20–23 ottobre 1982* [Studia Augustiniana Historica, 9] (Rome: Ed. "Analecta Augustiniana," 1983). Especially helpful for grasping Giles's place within the intellectual and cultural currents of early sixteenth-century Rome is John O'Malley's paper in this volume, "Egidio da Viterbo and Renaissance Rome," pp. 67–84.

69. O'Malley, *Giles of Viterbo*, p. 127.

70. *Ibid.*, pp. 128–29.

71. Mansi, *Collectio*, XXXII, col. 804; note Setton, "Leo X and the Turkish Peril," pp. 372–73.

72. BAV, ms. Vat. lat. 1682, fols. 6ʳ–7ᵛ. Nagonius's volume remained in Julius II's private library: see the inventory of books taken after the pontiff's death (BAV, ms. Vat. lat. 3966, fols. 111ʳ–114ʳ), reproduced in Léon Dorez, "La bibliothèque privée du Pape Jules II," *Revue des bibliothèques*, VI (1896), pp. 109 ff. For a brief consideration of some important themes in Nagonius's volume, see Elisabeth Schröter, "Der Vatikan als Hügel Apollons unter den Musen: Kunst und Panegyrik von Nikolaus V. bis Julius II.," *Römische Quartalschrift*, LXXV (1980), pp, 227–29. For what is known of Nagonius's life and works, see Francis Wormald, "An Italian Poet at the Court of Henry VII," *JWCI*, XIV (1951), pp. 118–19. To Wormald's list of Nagonius's works should be added BAV, ms. Vat. lat. 5213, six books of poems in praise of Venice and of Doge Leonardo Loredan, addressed to the Senate of Venice.

73. BAV, ms. Vat. lat. 1682, fol. 8ᵛ; for the miniature, see Ernst Steinmann, *Die Sixtinische Kapelle* (Munich, 1901–06), II, pp. 18–19.

74. *La exortatione de la crutiata a la Sanctita del nostro Signore Papa Leone X e a tucti li signori e principi christiani de la impresa contra Turchi* (Rome?, ?); I have used the copy in the Vatican: BAV, Stamp. Chigi IV, 2204, int. 3.

75. Huizinga, *Waning of the Middle Ages*, pp. 92–93.

76. Donald Weinstein, *Savonarola and Florence: Prophecy and Patriotism in the Renaissance* (Princeton: Princeton U. Pr., 1970), pp. 113–14. Anne Denis, *Charles VIII et les Italiens: Histoire et mythe* [Travaux d'humanisme et Renaissance, CLXVII] (Geneva: Droz, 1979), pp. 64–66.

77. William H. McNeill, *Venice: The Hinge of Europe, 1081–1797* (Chicago: U. of Chicago Pr., 1974), pp. 1–3, 38–39; for Nicopolis, see Aziz S. Atiya, "The Crusade in the Fourteenth Century," in Kenneth M. Setton, ed., *A History of the Crusades*, III: *The Fourteenth and Fifteenth Centuries* (Madison: U. of Wisconsin Pr., 1975), pp. 21–26.

78. Marshall G. S. Hodgson, *The Venture of Islam: Conscience and History in a World Civilization* (Chicago: U. of Chicago Pr., 1974), II, pp. 559–61.

79. Setton, *Papacy and the Levant*, II, pp. 58–94; note also Giuseppe Valentini, S.J., "La crociata da Eugenio IV a Callisto III (dai documenti d'Archivio di Venezia)," *AHP*, XII (1974), pp. 91–123.

80. Setton, *Papacy and the Levant*, II, p. 150 (quoting a letter of Aeneas Silvius Piccolomini to Pope Nicholas V, dated 12 July 1453, six weeks after the fall of Constantinople).

81. *Ibid.*, p. 137. For an overview of papal-Ottoman relations in the Renaissance and Counter-Reformation periods, see Charles A. Frazee, *Catholics and Sultans: The church and the Ottoman Empire, 1453–1923* (Cambridge: Cambridge U. Pr., 1983), pp. 5–150.

82. Frederic C. Lane, *Venice: A Maritime Republic* (Baltimore: Johns Hopkins U. Pr., 1973), pp. 234–37; Setton, *Papacy and the Levant*, II, pp. 271–363.

83. Setton, *Papacy and the Levant*, II, pp. 149–51, 154–57.

84. *Ibid.*, pp. 159–60.

85. Pius II, *Commentaries*, SCSH, XXV (1939–40), pp. 115–18, 191–279; Setton, *Papacy and the Levant*, II, pp. 200–18.

86. Setton, "Leo X and the Turkish Peril," pp. 401–20.

87. Setton, *Papacy and the Levant*, II, pp. 261–70.

88. *Ibid.*, pp. 99–103, 192–95.

89. *Ibid.*, pp. 271–313; for Paul II's policies, see also Giuseppe Valentini, S.J., "La sospensione della crociata nei primi anni di Paolo II (1464–1468)," *AHP*, XIV (1976), pp. 71–101.

90. Setton, *Papacy and the Levant*, II, pp. 279–82.

91. John Francis Guilmartin, Jr., *Gunpowder and Galleys: Changing Technology and Mediterranean Warfare at Sea in the Sixteenth Century* (Cambridge: Cambridge U. Pr., 1974), pp. 253–73.

92. Setton, *Papacy and the Levant*, II, pp. 163–71, 184–90; Mallett, *The Borgias*, pp. 70–72.

93. Setton, *Papacy and the Levant*, II, pp. 316–18.

94. Gherardi, *Diario romano*, pp. 53–54, 58–60; Setton, *Papacy and the Levant*, II, pp. 340–45, 367–71.

95. Setton, *Papacy and the Levant*, II, pp. 371–73; Gherardi, *Diario romano*, p. 70.

96. Bruschi, *Bramante*, pp. 938–45; Delumeau, *L'alun de Rome*, pp. 183–88; for Julius II's foundation medal, see Roberto Weiss, "The Medals of Julius II (1503–1513)," *JWCI*, XXVIII (1965), p. 177.

97. Ludwig H. Heydenreich, "The Military Architect," in Ladislao Reti, ed., *The Unknown Leonardo* (N.Y.: McGraw-Hill, 1974), p. 163.

98. Guilmartin, *Gunpowder and Galleys*, pp. 42–56; Braudel, *The Mediterranean*, pp. 906–07.

99. Guilmartin, pp. 221–52; Braudel, pp. 1088–1106.

100. Calixtus III denounced as traitors the commanders of the papal fleet of 1455, which instead of defending the islands and shores of the Ionian and Aegean Seas preyed on Venetian and Genoese shipping: Setton, *Papacy and the Levant*, II, pp. 166–67; for the expenses of naval war, see Braudel, *Mediterranean*, pp. 840–42, 1096–97.

101. Ettore Rossi, "The Hospitallers at Rhodes, 1421–1523," in Setton, *A History of the Crusades*, III, pp. 314–39; Braudel, pp. 1014–26; Guilmartin, pp. 176–93.

102. Braudel, pp. 657–703, 904–06.

103. Mitchell, "The S.P.Q.R. in Two Roman Festivals," pp. 99–102; *id.*, *Italian Civic Pageantry*, pp. 125–29.

104. Braudel, pp. 1125–42.

105. Setton, *Papacy and the Levant*, II, pp. 381–485 *passim*.

106. Hodgson, *Venture of Islam*, III, pp. 113–19.

107. Robert Schwoebel, *The Shadow of the Crescent: The Renaissance Image of the Turk (1453–1517)* (N.Y.: St. Martin's Pr., 1967), pp. 214–15 stresses the negative effects which failure of the papal crusade had on the late fifteenth-century papacy.

108. Setton, *Papacy and the Levant*, II, pp. 454–58, 536–37; Mallett, *The Borgias*, pp. 158–59, 200–01.

109. John Monfasani, *George of Trebizond: A Biography and a Study of his Rhetoric and Logic* (Leiden: Brill, 1976), pp. 130–36, 184–94.

110. Franco Gaeta, "Sulla Lettera a Maometto di Pio II," *Bullettino dell'Istituto Storico Italiano per il Medio Evo e Archivio Muratoriano*, LXXVII (1965), pp. 127–227.

111. Setton, "Leo X and the Turkish Peril," p. 410.

112. Luis Weckmann-Munoz, "The Alexandrine Bulls of 1493: Pseudo-Asiatic Documents," in Fredi Chiappelli, ed., *First Images of America: The Impact of the New World on the Old* (Berkeley and Los Angeles: U. of California Pr., 1976), I, pp. 201–09.

113. Miguel Batllori, S.J., "The Papal Division of the World and its Consequences," in Chiappelli, I, pp. 211–20; James Muldoon, "Papal Responsibility for the Infidel: Another Look at Alexander VI's *Inter Caetera*," *CHR*, LXIV (1978), pp. 168–84; for a fuller discus-

sion, see *id.*, *Popes, Lawyers, and Infidels: The Church and the Non-Christian World, 1250–1550* (Philadelphia: University of Pennsylvania Pr., 1979).

114. John W. O'Malley, "The Discovery of America and Reform Thought at the Papal Court in the Early Cinquecento," in Chiappelli, I, pp. 190–91, note also John F. D'Amico, "Papal History and Curial Reform in the Renaissance: Raffaele Maffei's *Brevis Historia* of Julius II and Leo X," *AHP*, XVIII (1980), pp. 179–80.

115. O'Malley, "Fulfillment of the Christian Golden Age," pp. 333–38; note also *id.*, "Discovery of America," pp. 186–87, 191–94.

116. O'Malley, *Giles of Viterbo*, pp. 109–16.

117. *Ibid.*, pp. 116–17, 175–78.

118. Setton, *Papacy and the Levant*, II, p. 150.

119. For Birago's advocacy of Greek learning in the *Strategicon*, see BAV, ms. Vat. lat. 3423, fols. 52ᵛ–54ʳ; note Setton, *Papacy and the Levant*, II, p. 156, for discussion of this work. For Birago's career, see M. Miglio, "Lampugnino Birago," *DBI*, X (1968), pp. 595–97.

120. Setton, *Papacy and the Levant*, II, p. 131.

121. Giovanni Mercati, *Scritti d'Isidoro il Cardinale Ruteno* [Studi e Testi, 46] (Rome, 1926), pp. 128–32; Girolamo Mancini, *Francesco Griffolini, cognominato Francesco Aretino* (Florence: Carnesecchi, 1890), pp. 22–45.

122. Pio Paschini, "Un ellenista romano del Quattrocento e la sua famiglia," *Atti dell'Accademia degli Arcadi*, XXI (1939–40), pp. 45–56; Jeanne Bignami Odier, *La Bibliothèque Vaticane de Sixte IV à Pie XI* [Studi e Testi, 272] (Vatican, 1973), p. 25.

123. Monfasani, *George of Trebizond*, pp. 201–29; Deno J. Geanakoplos, *Greek Scholars in Venice: Studies in the Dissemination of Greek Learning from Byzantium to Western Europe* (Cambridge: Harvard U. Pr., 1962), pp. 85–92.

124. The standard account is W. von Hofmann, *Forschungen zur Geschichte der Kurialen Behörden vom Schisma bis zur Reformation* [Bibliothek des Deutschen Historischen Instituts in Rom, XII] (Rome: Von Loescher, 1914; reprinted Turin: Bottega d'Erasmo, 1971). Note also Niccolò del Re, *La Curia Romana: Lineamenti storico-giuridici*, 3rd ed., (Rome: Edizioni di storia e letteratura, 1972); and the briefer discussions in Mallett, *The Borgias*, pp. 45–59; Hay, *Church in Italy*, pp. 41–48; Thomson, *Popes and Princes*, pp. 95–113; and D'Amico, *Renaissance Humanism in Papal Rome*, pp. 19–35. For an overview of the Curia's development since the eleventh century, see Lajos Pásztor, "L'histoire de la Curie Romaine, Problème d'histoire de l'Église," *RHE*, LXIV (1969), pp. 353–66. A survey of sources and studies of papal administration in the fifteenth century is provided by Stieber, *Pope Eugenius IV, the Council of Basel . . .*, Appendix A, pp. 351–69. Detailed studies of individual Curial departments include Adolf Gottlob, *Aus der Camera Apostolica des 15. Jahrhunderts* (Innsbruck: Wagner, 1889); B. Katterbach, O.F.M., *Referendarii utriusque Signaturae a Martino V ad Clementem IX et Praelati Signaturae Supplicationum a Martino V ad Leonem XIII* [Studi e Testi, 55] (Vatican, 1931); and Brigide Schwarz, *Die Organisation kurialer Schreiberkollegien von ihrer Entstehung bis zur Mitte des 15. Jahrhunderts* (Tübingen: Niemeyer, 1972). Note also Ernst Pitz, "Die römische Kurie als Thema des vergleichenden Sozialgeschichte," *QFIAB*, LVIII (1978), pp. 216–359.

125. There is a superb recent study of the administrative history of the Avignonese papacy: Bernard Guillemain, *La Cour Pontificale d'Avignon, 1300–1376: Étude d'une société*, 2nd ed. (Paris: de Boccard, 1966).

126. Mallett, *The Borgias*, pp. 206–07.

127. Pius II, *Commentaries, SCSH*, XXXV (1951), p. 571.

128. Von Hofmann, I, pp. 288–89.

129. Bruschi, *Bramante architetto*, pp. 593–608, 946–59; Stanislaus von Moos, "The Palace as a Fortress: Rome and Bologna under Pope Julius II," in Henry A. Millon and Linda Nochlin, eds., *Art and Architecture in the Service of Politics* (Cambridge: MIT Pr., 1978), pp. 47–57.

130. Domenico de' Domenichi, serving at the time as a *referendarius* to the *Signatura*, addressed a treatise, *De episcopali dignitate* (1461) to Pius II, in which he attacks the precedence accorded Apostolic Protonotaries over bishops at the opening of the Council of Mantua: see Hubert Jedin, "Studien über Domenico de' Domenichi (1416–78)," *Akademie der Wissenschaften und der Literatur in Mainz. Abhandlungen der Geistes- und Sozialwissenschaftlichen Klasse* (1957, Nr. 5) (Wiesbaden: F. Steiner, 1958), pp. 251–57; for the general issue of precedence, see Hay, *Church in Italy*, p. 45.

131. Léonce Celier, *Les Dataires du XV siècle et les origines de la Daterie* [BEFAR, 103] (Paris, 1910). Also useful for the Renaissance period, despite its title is Felice Litva, "L'attività finanziaria della Dataria durante il periodo tridentino," *AHP*, V (1967), pp. 79–174.

132. Geoffrey Barraclough, *Papal Provisions: Aspects of Church History—Constitutional, Legal, and Administrative—in the Later Middle Ages* (Oxford: Blackwell, 1935), pp. 8–9.

133. Chambers, "Economic Predicament of Renaissance Cardinals," pp. 300–02; A.V. Antonovics, "A Late Fifteenth-Century Division Register of the College of Cardinals," *Papers of the British School at Rome*, XXXV (n.s. XXII) (1967), pp. 87–101.

134. Raymond de Roover, *The Rise and Decline of the Medici Bank, 1397–1494* (Cambridge: Harvard U. Pr., 1963), p. 201.

135. Jean Gérardin, *Étude sur les bénéfices ecclésiastiques aux XVIe et XVIIe siècles* (Geneva: Slatkine Reprints, 1971; first publ. Nancy, 1897), pp. 75–77. For a survey of scholarship on papal reservations, see Stieber, *Pope Eugenius IV*, Appendix B, pp. 370–74.

136. Celier, *Les Dataires*, p. 155.

137. Guillemain, *La Cour Pontificale d'Avignon*, p. 105.

138. Hay, *Church in Italy*, pp. 18–19.

139. Peter Desa Wiggins, *The Satires of Ludovico Ariosto: A Renaissance Autobiography* (Athens: Ohio U. Pr., 1976), pp. 25–48.

140. Gérardin, pp. 55–62.

141. Celier, *Les Dataires*, pp. 143–44; for the work of the 1497 reform commission, see *id.*, "Alexandre VI et la réforme de l'Église," *MAHEFR*, XXVII (1907), pp. 65–124, and *id.*, "L'idée de réforme à la cour pontificale du Concile de Bâle au Concile de Latran," *Revue des questions historiques*, LXXXVI (n.s. XLII) (1909), pp. 418–35.

142. Marcel Bataillon, "La chasse aux bénéfices vue de Rome par Juan Páez de Castro," in *Histoire économique du monde méditerranéen 1450–1650: Mélanges en l'honneur de Fernand Braudel* (Toulouse: Privat, 1973), pp. 81–93; for the use of special couriers in the quest for benefices, note also Delumeau, *Vie économique et sociale de Rome*, pp. 55–57.

143. Celier, *Les Dataires*, pp. 87–102.

144. Gabriel Ardant, "Financial Policy and Economic Infrastructure of Modern States and Nations," in Charles Tilly, ed., *The Formation of National States in Western Europe* (Princeton: Princeton U. Pr., 1975), p. 188.

145. Partner, "The 'Budget'," pp. 257–58, 266–74; *id.*, "Papal Financial Policy," pp. 21–25; Delumeau, *Vie économique*, pp. 772–77; von Hofmann, I, pp. 159–61, II, pp. 53–54, 149–52.

146. Celier, "L'idée de réforme;" *id.*, "Alexandre VI et la réforme;" von Hofmann, II, pp. 227–52; Nelson H. Minnich, "*Incipiat judicium ad Domo Domini*: The Fifth Lateran Council and the Reform of Rome," in Guy Fitch Lytle, ed., *Reform and Authority in the Medieval and Reformation Church* (Washington, D.C.: Catholic U. of America Pr., 1981), pp. 127–42; John C. Olin, *The Catholic Reformation: Savonarola to Ignatius Loyola—Reform in the Church 1495–1540* (N.Y.: Harper & Row, 1969), pp. 54–64, 183–97.

147. Delumeau, *Vie économique*, pp. 783–824; Partner, "Papal Financial Policy," pp. 25–29.

148. Celier, *Les Dataires*, pp. 156–60.

149. *Ibid.*, pp. 160–62.

150. Partner, "The 'Budget'," pp. 262–63, 266–72, 278.

151. De Roover, *Medici Bank*, pp. 47–48, 136, 194–224. For a detailed analysis of the fiscal policies and banking practices of Leo X and Clement VII, see Melissa M. Bullard, *Filippo Strozzi and the Medici: Favor and Finance in Sixteenth-Century Florence and Rome* (Cambridge: Cambridge U. Pr., 1980), pp. 91–172. For Agostino Chigi's role in the financial world of Rome, see most recently, Gilbert, *The Pope, his Banker, and Venice*, pp. 63–93.

152. O'Malley, *Giles of Viterbo*, p. 171; Roger Aubenas and Robert Ricard, *L'Église et la Renaissance* [Augustin Fliche and Victor Martin, eds., *Histoire de l'Église*, XV] (Paris: Bloud & Gay, 1951), pp. 87–88. Raffaele Maffei makes the same charges: D'Amico, *Renaissance Humanism in Papal Rome*, pp. 221–26.

153. John Dillenberger, ed., *Martin Luther: Selections from his Writings* (Garden City, N.Y.: Doubleday, 1961), pp. 428–30; for the *gravamina*, see Gerald Strauss, *Manifestations of Discontent in Germany on the Eve of the Reformation* (Bloomington: Indiana U. Pr., 1971), pp. 35–63.

154. Barraclough, *Papal Provisions*, pp. 71–90.

155. Hay, *Church in Italy*, pp. 10–11, 110–22; Delaruelle, *et al.*, *L'Église au temps du Grand Schisme*, pp. 298–306.
156. For the extent of this practice, see Hay, p. 44.
157. David Herlihy, *Medieval and Renaissance Pistoia: The Social History of an Italian Town, 1200–1430* (New Haven: Yale U. Pr., 1967), pp. 241–58; Marvin B. Becker, *Medieval Italy: Constraints and Creativity* (Bloomington: Indiana U. Pr., 1981), esp. pp. 99–134.
158. Ernest Hatch Wilkins, *Life of Petrarch* (Chicago: U. of Chicago Pr., 1961), pp. 10–11, 32, 56–57, 82, 197.
159. Pio Paschini, "Una famiglia di curiali: I Maffei di Volterra," *RSCI*, VII (1953), pp. 337–76; D'Amico, *Renaissance Humanism in Papal Rome*, pp. 81–88.
160. Lee, *Sixtus IV and Men of Letters*, pp. 66–70.
161. Flavio di Bernardo, *Un vescovo umanista alla Corte Pontificia: Giannantonio Campano (1429–1477)* [Miscellanea Historiae Pontificiae, 39] (Rome: Università Gregoriana, 1975); Lee, pp. 91–99; D'Amico, pp. 14–15; and the review article of Riccardo Fubini, "Umanesimo curiale del Quattrocento: Nuovi studi su Giovann'Antonio Campano," *Rivista storica italiana*, LXXXVIII (1976), pp. 745–55.
162. Pio Paschini, "Tre illustri prelati del Rinascimento: Ermolao Barbaro, Adriano Castellesi, Giovanni Grimani," *Lateranum*, n.s. XXIII (1957), pp. 43–130; D'Amico, *Renaissance Humanism in Papal Rome*, pp. 16–18. For bio-bibliographic information on an extensive group of Curial humanists in the Renaissance period, see *ibid.*, pp. 3–112; for Sixtus IV's pontificate, see Lee, *Sixtus IV*, pp. 47–122.
163. For the increasing "clericalization" of the Roman Curia, see Hay, pp. 102–05; and Dionisotti, "Chierici e laici," pp. 66–77. For the situation of Curial humanists under the Medici popes, see Vincenzo De Caprio, "Intellettuali e mercato del lavoro nella Roma medicea," *Studi romani*, XXIX (1981), pp. 29–46, and *id.*, "L'area umanistica romana (1513–1527)," *ibid.*, pp. 321–35.
164. Douglas, *Sadoleto*, pp. 1–93.
165. Agostino Zanelli, *Pietro del Monte* (Milan: Cogliati, 1907); Johannes Haller, *Piero da Monte: Ein Gelehrter und päpstlicher Beamter des 15. Jahrhunderts. Seine Briefsammlung* [Bibliothek des Deutschen Historischen Instituts in Rom, XIX] (Rome, 1941). Note also Agostino Sottili, *Studenti tedeschi e umanesimo italiano nell' Università di Padova durante il Quattrocento*, I: *Pietro del Monte nella società accademica padovana (1430–33)* [Contributi alla storia dell'Università di Padova, 7] (Padua: Antenori, 1971); and O'Malley, *Praise and Blame*, pp. 81–83.
166. H. Outram Evennett, *The Spirit of the Counter-Reformation* (Notre Dame: U. of Notre Dame Pr., 1970), pp. 96–102; Adriano Prosperi, *Tra Evangelismo e Controriforma: G.M. Giberti (1495–1543)* [Uomini e dottrine, 16] (Rome: Edizioni di storia e letteratura, 1969).
167. Thomas N. Tentler, *Sin and Confession on the Eve of the Reformation* (Princeton: Princeton U. Pr., 1977), pp. 304–07.
168. Chambers, "Economic Predicament," p. 299; the fullest account of this tribunal is Emil Göller, *Die päpstliche Pönitentiarie von ihrem Ursprung bis zu ihrer Umgestaltung unter Pius V* [Bibliothek der königlichen Preussischen Historischen Instituts in Rom, Vols. 3–4, 7–8] (Rome, 1907–11).
169. Von Hofmann, II, pp. 97–98; Rodocanachi, *Pontificat de Léon X*, pp. 63, 151, 249–50; Guicciardini, *Storia d'Italia*, pp. 1371–72; J.J. Scarisbrick, *Henry VIII* (Berkeley and Los Angeles: U. of California Pr., 1968), pp. 203–07, 220, 222.
170. Guillemain, *La Cour Pontificale d'Avignon*, pp. 345–56; von Hofmann, I, pp. 131–32; F.E. Schneider, *Die Römische Rota: Nach geltendem Recht auf geschichtlicher Grundlage*, Vol. I: *Die Verfassung der Rota* (Paderborn, 1914). For the Audientia, a tribunal that also exercised ecclesiastical jurisdiction, see Peter Herde, *Audientia litterarum contradictarum: Untersuchungen über die päpstlichen Justizbriefe und die päpstliche Delegationsgerichtsbarkeit vom 13. bis zum Beginn des 16. Jahrhunderts*, 2 vols. (Tübingen: Niemeyer, 1970).
171. Strauss, *Manifestations of Discontent*, pp. 43, 53.
172. Dieter Brosius, "Eine Reise an die Kurie im Jahre 1462: Der Rechenschaftsbericht des Lübecker Domherrn Albert Krummediek," *QFIAB*, LVIII (1978), pp. 411–40.
173. Robert E. McNally, S.J., "Pope Adrian VI (1522–23) and Church Reform," *AHP*, VII (1969), pp. 266–69.
174. Von Hofmann, I, pp. 77–79; Chambers, "Economic Predicament," p. 300.

175. Shearman, "Vatican Stanze," pp. 377–79.

176. Celier, Les Dataires, pp. 163–64.

177. Richard C. Trexler, The Spiritual Power: Republican Florence under the Interdict [Studies in Medieval and Reformation Thought, IX] (Leiden: Brill, 1974), pp. 170–73.

178. Ibid., pp. 173–78; Weinstein, Savonarola and Florence, pp. 281–88.

179. Mallett, The Borgias, p. 153.

180. See pp. 235–36.

181. William J. Bouwsma, Venice and the Defense of Republican Liberty: Renaissance Values in the Age of the Counter Reformation (Berkeley and Los Angeles: U. of California Pr., 1968), pp. 98–99.

182. Storia d'Italia, pp. 425–28.

183. Trexler, Spiritual Power, pp. 20–28.

184. Strauss, Manifestations of Discontent, p. 59; note Luther's more vehement objections in his Appeal to the German Nobility, in Dillenberger, p. 454.

185. Tentler, Sin and Confession, pp. 302–04.

186. Bouwsma, Venice, pp. 5–8, 48.

187. O'Malley, Giles of Viterbo, p. 66. Raffaele Maffei and Paolo Cortesi reached similar conclusions: see D'Amico, Renaissance Humanism in Papal Rome, pp. 226, 235.

188. For Giles's views, see O'Malley, Giles, pp. 144–46, 163–64, 186; for others', see D'Amico, Renaissance Humanism in Papal Rome, pp. 212–37.

189. Gordon Griffiths, "Leonardo Bruni and the Restoration of the University of Rome (1406)," RQ, XXVI (1973), pp. 1–10.

190. D.S. Chambers, "Studium Urbis and gabella studii: The University of Rome in the Fifteenth Century," in Cecil H. Clough, ed., Cultural Aspects of the Italian Renaissance: Essays in Honour of Paul Oskar Kristeller (Manchester: Manchester U. Pr., 1976), pp. 68–110. For the Sapienza under Sixtus IV, see Lee, pp. 150–92.

191. Chambers, "Studium Urbis," pp. 83–84; for the impressive number of medieval, classical, and especially patristic volumes with which Capranica endowed his Collegio, see A.V. Antonovics, "The Library of Cardinal Domenico Capranica," in Clough, Cultural Aspects, pp. 141–59.

192. Chambers, "Studium Urbis," p. 84; O'Malley, Praise and Blame, pp. 17–19; id., "The Feast of Thomas Aquinas in Renaissance Rome: A Neglected Document and its Import," RSCI, XXXV (1981), pp. 17–19.

193. O'Malley, "Feast of Aquinas," pp. 12–14, 18–19.

194. Ibid., pp. 14–25.

195. These are the motives Paris de Grassis ascribes to Nicholas's devotion to Aquinas: see ibid., p. 26.

196. The Jerome figure was later changed to St. Bonaventura. For the decoration of the chapel, see John Pope-Hennessy, Fra Angelico, 2nd ed. (London: Phaidon, 1974), pp. 29–33, 212–14.

197. John W. O'Malley, "Some Renaissance Panegyrics of Aquinas," RQ, XXVII (1974), pp. 174–92; id., Praise and Blame, p. 15. For Valla's panegyric, see also Hanna H. Gray, "Valla's Encomium of St. Thomas Aquinas and the Humanist Conception of Christian Antiquity," in Heinz Bluhm, ed., Essays in History and Literature Presented by the Fellows of the Newberry Library to Stanley Pargellis (Chicago: Newberry Library, 1965), pp. 37–51; Mario Fois, S.J., Il pensiero cristiano di Lorenzo Valla nel quadro storico-culturale del suo ambiente [Analecta Gregoriana, 174] (Rome: Università Gregoriana, 1969), pp. 464–69; Salvatore I. Camporeale, Lorenzo Valla: Umanesimo e teologia (Florence: Istituto Nazionale di Studi sul Rinascimento, 1972), pp. 3–5, 141–42, 302–11; and id., "Lorenzo Valla tra Medioevo e Rinascimento: Encomium S. Thomae, 1457," Memorie Domenicane, n.s. VII (1976), pp. 11–194. For the reaction to Valla's oration, see Gaspare da Verona, De gestis tempore Pontificis Maximi Pauli Secundi, in RIS², III, 16, p. 33. For Thomism in general in the Renaissance period, see Paul Oskar Kristeller, Le Thomisme et la pensée italienne de la Renaissance (Montreal: Institut d'Études Médiévales, 1967); an English translation (but without the supporting Latin texts) appears in id., Medieval Aspects of Renaissance Learning, ed. and trans. Edward P. Mahoney (Durham: Duke U. Pr., 1974), pp. 29–91.

198. For Carafa's support of Thomism, see O'Malley, "Feast of Aquinas," pp. 11–14. Analysis of the Carafa Chapel is the subject of Gail L. Geiger, "Filippino Lippi's Carafa

Annunciation: Theology, Artistic Conventions and Patronage," *AB*, LXIII (1981), pp. 62–75, and *id.*, "Filippino Lippi's *Triumph of Saint Thomas Aquinas*," in Ramsey, ed., *Rome in the Renaissance*, pp. 223–36.

199. Some Roman Renaissance panegyrics of Augustine survive, but his feast day (28 August) was infrequently commemorated, and poorly attended: O'Malley, "Feast of Aquinas," p. 8; *id.*, *Praise and Blame*, pp. 14–15.

200. D'Amico, *Renaissance Humanism in Papal Rome*, pp. 148–68.

201. *Ibid.*, pp. 192–99. In contrast, Castellesi, in his fideistic and skeptical *De vera philosophia* (1507), rejected a reliance on Aristotelian dialectics in theology. In attacking scholasticism, he turned instead to the four Latin Church Fathers, and especially to Scripture, which he regarded as the sole source of religious truth: *ibid.*, pp. 169–88.

202. See p. 233.

203. O'Malley, *Praise and Blame*, pp. 61–62.

204. *Ibid.*, pp. 237–41.

205. Ettlinger, "Pollaiuolo's Tomb of Sixtus IV," pp. 239–65; Erwin Panofsky, *Tomb Sculpture: Four Lectures on its Changing Aspects from Ancient Egypt to Bernini* (N.Y.: Abrams, 1964), pp. 87–88.

206. Pius II, *Commentaries, SCSH*, XLIII (1957), pp. 704–29; Lee, *Sixtus IV*, pp. 19–20.

207. For a summary of Sixtus's position, see L. D. Ettlinger, *The Sistine Chapel before Michelangelo: Religious Imagery and Papal Primacy* (Oxford: Clarendon Pr., 1965), pp. 83–84.

208. For Sixtus's Mariology, see Aubenas and Ricard, *L'Église et la Renaissance*, pp. 339–41; for the doctrine of the Immaculate Conception in late medieval theology, see Heiko A. Oberman, *The Harvest of Medieval Theology: Gabriel Biel and Late Medieval Nominalism* (Grand Rapids: Eerdmans, 1967), pp. 283–98. For Sixtus's celebration of the Feast of the Immaculate Conception, see Gherardi, *Diario romano*, pp. 29, 82.

209. Gherardi, pp. 95–97.

210. John Moorman, *A History of the Franciscan Order from its Origins to the Year 1517* (Oxford: Oxford U. Pr., 1968), pp. 487–88, 513.

211. Oberman, *Harvest*, pp. 404–05.

212. *Ibid.*, pp. 146–60; Tentler, *Sin and Confession*, pp. 233–301.

213. Manetti, *Vita Nicolai V*, cols. 947–49. The description of penance as the "second plank" originated with Jerome and was a theological commonplace: Tentler, p. 65. Note Luther's objections to this metaphor as dangerous and misleading: *the Babylonian Captivity of the Church*, in Dillenberger, *Martin Luther: Selections*, p. 292. The sacrament of penance was among the topics included in the religious writings of the fifteenth-century humanists: for the views of Sicco Polenton and Bartolomeo della Fonte, see Trinkaus, *In Our Image*, pp. 616–33.

214. Tentler, pp. 318–39.

215. For a general discussion of the development of the doctrine of indulgences in the fourteenth and fifteenth centuries, see Delaruelle, *et al.*, *L'Église au temps du Grand Schisme*, pp. 810–20, and Aubenas and Ricard, *L'Église et la Renaissance*, pp. 183–87. Note in particular Juan de Torquemada's reference, in his *Commentary on Penance* addressed to Nicholas V, to the overflowing treasury stored up as a result of devotion to the Apostolic See of Rome; it is on this which the pope draws in granting the Jubilee indulgences: Westfall, *In this Most Perfect Paradise*, p. 21.

216. *Sin and Confession*, pp. 327–31.

217. Gene Brucker, ed., *Two Memoirs of Renaissance Florence: The Diaries of Buonaccorso Pitti and Gregorio Dati* (N.Y.: Harper & Row, 1967), p. 132.

218. BAV, ms. Vat. lat. 406, fols. 18r-v. By contrast, the evangelical reformer Wolfgang Capito complained in his preface to his Latin translation of Chrysostom's *Paraenesis ad Theodorum lapsum* that the Greek Father's treatment of repentance had been misused by defenders of the late medieval sacrament of penance. According to Capito, Chrysostom, far from upholding the "puerile doctrine" that after forgiveness a debt of sinfulness remains to be discharged, maintains the paradoxical nature of the restoration of sinful man to a state of grace. From unrepentant sin follows total damnation, but from repentance comes total remission at once. God is neither irascible and avenging, nor on the other hand does He accept with impunity evil deeds or recognize their gradual removal through penance. The preface, addressed to Albert, Archbishop of Mainz and Margrave of Brandenburg, appears

in Divi Io. Chrysostomi *Homilia*, trans. V. Fabritius Capito (Basel: Froben, 1519), pp. 11–16. For Capito, see James M. Kittelson, *Wolfgang Capito: From Humanist to Reformer* [Studies in Medieval and Reformation Thought, XVII] (Leiden: Brill, 1975). John Calvin, early in his career as a reformer, planned a French edition of Chrysostom homilies. Nothing came of the project, but his Latin preface to the planned edition is extant. After much praise of Chrysostom as a Biblical exegete and preacher, Calvin remarks that in one area the Greek Father lapsed: he spoke excessively of the merit of works and obscured somewhat the grace of God in our election and calling. Calvin suggests that Chrysostom could hardly have been ignorant of this central Christian doctrine and that he modified Scripture's teaching on the blindness of human genius, the perversity of the heart, the impotence of the soul, and the corruption of all nature lest it be abhorrent to common opinion or give an occasion for philosophers to trap men with their malicious cavillings. He thus spoke obscurely regarding predestination and conceded too much to free will. Yet, Calvin argues, these concerns were hardly sufficient cause for Chrysostom to stray from the simple truth of Scripture. All human thought should be captive to it, rather than ceding to human judgment. The preface appears in Johannis Calvini, *Opera quae supersunt omnia. Corpus Reformatorum* (Braunschweig and Berlin: 1863 ff), IX, cols. 831–38. Note François Wendel, *Calvin: The Origins and Development of his Religious Thought* (London: Collins, 1963; first publ. Paris, 1959), p. 124.

219. I follow here the interpretation of Shearman, *Raphael's Cartoons*, pp. 49–50, rather than the Eucharistic emphasis of Ettlinger, *Sistine Chapel*, pp. 78–88. Note also Eunice D. Howe, "A Temple Façade Reconsidered: Botticelli's 'Temptation of Christ'," in Ramsey, ed., *Rome in the Renaissance*, pp. 209–21.

220. Shearman, *Raphael's Cartoons*, pp. 66–67, 77–78.

221. Mansi, *Sacrorum Conciliorum collectio*, XXXII, cols. 759–61; for the speech, see Minnich, "Concepts of Reform," pp. 181–83. For the *Christus Medicus* motif, see Shearman, *Raphael's Cartoons*, p. 17.

222. Shearman, *Raphael's Cartoons*, pp. 15, 77–78. The same theme appears in an anonymous six-part motet composed in honor of Clement VII's election in 1523. The text reads (in part): "*Letare sancta mater ecclesia et exultate vos medicos in honore medicorum Cosmi et Damiani quibus spiritus sanctus tantam gratiam conferre dignatus est ut omnem egritudinem expellerent. . . . Gaudeat medicum nobilissima familia que contra fidelium mortiferos morbos Clementem medicum simul et medellam nobis contulit suavem. . . .*" For the complete text and a brief discussion of this motet, see Edward E. Lowinsky, "A Newly Discovered Sixteenth-Century Motet Manuscript at the Biblioteca Vallicelliana in Rome," *JAMS*, III (1950), pp. 197, 203.

223. Vegio, *De rebus antiquis memorabilibus Basilicae S. Petri Romae*, p. 64.

224. Oberman, *Harvest*, p. 405.

225. Francis Oakley, "Conciliarism in the Sixteenth Century: Jacques Almain Again," *ARG*, LXVIII (1977), pp. 111–27.

226. For the financing of new St. Peter's, see Christoph Luitpold Frommel, "Die Peterskirche unter Papst Julius II, im Licht neuer Dokumente," *Römisches Jahrbuch für Kunstgeschichte*, XVI (1976), pp. 81–84 (the significant parts of Julius's 1507 bull appear as document 54, pp. 97–98).

227. These are the terms with which Giles of Viterbo discusses Julius II's intentions for the basilica in his *Historia XX saeculorum* (the relevant text appears as document 8 in Frommel, "Die Peterskirche," pp. 89–90).

IV. The Primacy of Peter *Princeps Apostolorum* and the *Instauratio Ecclesiae Romanae*

1. Nicholas V's last testament forms the major part of Book III of Manetti's *Vita Nicolai V* (in the *RIS* ed., cols. 947–56). Manetti (col. 957) states that his account repeats faithfully what eyewitnesses recounted to him. For discussion of the authenticity of the last testament, see Miglio, *Storiografia pontificia*, pp. 107–08, and Onofri, "Sacralità," pp. 37–40.

2. *Vita Nicolai V*, col. 922. Manetti had said much the same thing in his 1447 oration congratulating Nicholas V on his election, which he delivered as Florentine ambassador to the papal court: "*Nos itaque, Beatissime Pater, Florentini populi nomine legati, audita promotione tua, confestim ad novam Christi humanitatem et . . . non secus ac Magi, quos Matthaeus evangelista, visa stella itineris sui duce, cum gaudio magno valde ex oriente usque ad Hierosolymam venisse testur, ut*

Iesum imprime natum adorarent, e Florentia moventes Romam venerandi et adorandi gratia contendimus." See Onofri, pp. 33–34, 42.

    3. Manetti, *Vita Nicolai V*, cols. 949–50.

    4. Miglio, *Storiografia*, p. 109; note also Westfall, *In this Most Perfect Paradise*, pp. 33–34.

    5. Manetti, *Vita Nicolai V*, col. 923, declares that Nicholas V "*semper omnia cogitabat, atque animo et mente volvebat, quae ad exaugendam Romanae Ecclesiae auctoritatem, atque ad amplificandam Sedis Apostolicae dignitatem ullatenus pertinere arbitrabatur.*"

    6. The most recent discussion of the Council of Basel is Stieber, *Pope Eugenius IV and the Council of Basel.* A helpful collection of documents in English translation related to the conciliar controversy is provided by C. M. D. Crowder, *Unity, Heresy, and Reform, 1378–1460* (N.Y.: St. Martin's Pr., 1977). Note also Thomson, *Popes and Princes*, pp. 3–28.

    7. Gill, *The Council of Florence.*

    8. Stieber, pp. 331–47.

    9. Hubert Jedin, *A History of the Council of Trent*, Vol. I: *The Struggle for the Council* (St. Louis: B. Herder, 1957), pp. 54–59.

    10. *Ibid.*, p. 59.

    11. *Execrabilis's* condemnations of conciliar appeals was not consistently invoked by the Renaissance popes, and thus did not constitute the definitive papal statement on conciliarism, as it often has been claimed to be. Nevertheless, Sixtus IV did cite Pius's bull in 1483 during the War of Ferrara. Part of the pretext for excommunicating the Doge of Venice and other Venetian leaders was that appeals to a council, traceable to Venetian activity, had been found posted on St. Peter's, Ponte Sant'Angelo, and the Pantheon. Similarly, Julius II reaffirmed *Execrabilis* in 1509, in condemning Venetian calls for a council during the War of the League of Cambrai: see G.B. Picotti, "La publicazione e i primi effetti della *Execrabilis* di Pio II," *ARSRSP*, XXXVII (1914), pp. 5–56.

    12. Jedin, *Council of Trent*, I, pp. 101–06.

    13. *Ibid.*, pp. 106–16; despite the political motive for convening the Fifth Lateran Council, the number of prelates who attended and their internationality is greater than often recognized: see Nelson H. Minnich, "The Participants at the Fifth Lateran Council," *AHP*, XII (1974), pp. 157–206.

    14. Weiss, "Medals of Julius II," p. 171.

    15. Walter Ullmann, *Medieval Papalism: The Political Theories of the Medieval Canonists* (London: Methuen, 1949); Brian Tierney, *Foundations of Conciliar Theory: The Contribution of the Medieval Canonists from Gratian to the Great Schism* (Cambridge: Cambridge U. Pr., 1955); William D. McCready, "Papalists and Antipapalists: Aspects of the Church-State Controversy in the Later Middle Ages," *Viator*, VI (1975), pp. 241–73; *id.*, "The Papal Sovereign in the Ecclesiology of Augustinus Triumphus," *Mediaeval Studies*, XXXIX (1977), pp. 177–205. For early medieval development of the doctrine of papal primacy, see Ullmann, *The Growth of Papal Government in the Middle Ages: A Study in the Ideological Relation of Clerical to Lay Power*, 2nd ed., (London: Methuen, 1962); and Pietri, *Roma Christiana*, pp. 1413–1651.

    16. Michele Maccarrone, *Vicarius Christi: Storia del titolo papale* [Lateranum, n.s. XVIII, No. 1–4 (1952)], pp. 235–80; Martin Grabmann, *Studien über den Einfluss der aristotelischen Philosophie auf die mittelalterlichen Theorien über das Verhältnis von Kirche und Staat* [Sitzungsberichte der Bayerischen Akademie der Wissenschaften philosophisch-historische Abteilung, Heft 2 (1934)], pp. 72–76, 101–06, 134–44; Jedin, *Council of Trent*, I, pp. 25–26, 92–100. For a survey of fifeenth- and sixteenth-century theologians' and canonists' discussions of the relative authority of the pope and the general council, see Remigius Bäumer, *Nachwirkungen des konziliaren Gedankens in der Theologie und Kanonistik des frühen 16. Jahrhunderts* [Reformationsgeschichtliche Studien und Texte, 100] (Münster: Aschendorff, 1971).

    17. Richard H. Trame, S.J., *Rodrigo Sánchez de Arévalo (1404–1470): Spanish Diplomat and Champion of the Papacy* [The Catholic University of America Studies in Mediaeval History, n.s. XV] (Washington, D.C., 1958); Grabmann, pp. 114–29; Hubert Jedin, "Sánchez de Arévalo und die Konzilsfrage unter Paul II," *Historisches Jahrbuch*, LXXIII (1954), pp. 95–119; O'Malley, *Praise and Blame*, pp. 90–92, 204–06.

    18. O'Malley, *Praise and Blame*, p. 219.

    19. Juan de Torquemada is not to be confused with his nephew, Tomás de Torquemada, the infamous inquisitor.

20. Hubert Jedin, "Juan de Torquemada und das Imperium Romanum," *Archivum Fratrum Praedicatorum*, XII (1942), pp. 247–78; Trame, pp. 151–59.

21. Antony Black, *Monarchy and Community: Political Ideas in the Later Conciliar Controversy, 1430–1450* (Cambridge: Cambridge U. Pr., 1970), pp. 7–52; for scholarship on Juan de Segovia and Panormitanus, see Stieber, pp. 379–80, 397, 401; for the medieval background to corporation theory, see Tierney, pp. 96–153.

22. Vicente Betran de Heredia, O.P., "Noticias y documentos para la biografia del Cardinal Juan de Torquemada," *Archivum Fratrum Praedicatorum*, XXX (1960), pp. 53–148; Black, pp. 53–84; Grabmann, pp. 130–33.

23. Gill, *Council of Florence*, pp. 414–15.

24. Joseph Gill, S.J., *Personalities of the Council of Florence and Other Essays* (N.Y.: Barnes & Noble, 1964), pp. 264–86.

25. Jedin, *Council of Trent*, I, pp. 19–20.

26. Heredia, pp. 83–88.

27. Black, pp. 57–67; note Stinger, *Humanism and the Church Fathers*, pp. 158–62.

28. Piero da Monte, *Contra impugnantes sedis apostolicae auctoritatem*, BAV, ms. Vat. lat. 4145, fols. 21ᵛ-22ʳ.

29. Camporeale, *Lorenzo Valla*, pp. 428–30.

30. O'Malley, *Giles of Viterbo*, p. 58.

31. Shearman, *Raphael's Cartoons*, pp. 70–73.

32. Grabmann, pp. 106–14; Jedin, "Studien über Domenico de' Domenichi," pp. 234–36. Domenichi's treatise has recently received a modern edition: Heribert Smolinsky, *Domenico de' Domenichi und seine Schrift 'De potestate pape et termino eius.' Edition und Kommentar* (Münster: Aschendorff, 1977).

33. Cajetan's ecclesiological tracts are discussed by Friedrich Lauchert in his introduction to his edition of Cajetan's *De divina institutione Pontificatus Romani Pontificis (1521)* [Corpus Catholicorum, 10] (Münster: Aschendorff, 1925), pp. ix–xxiv. For a recent discussion of Cajetan's thought, see Jared Wicks, "Thomism between Renaissance and Reformation: The Case of Cajetan," *ARG*, LXVIII (1977), pp. 9–32.

34. A useful survey of the impact of Luther's thought at the papal court is Elisabeth Gregorich Gleason, "Sixteenth-Century Italian Interpretations of Luther," *ARG*, LX (1969), pp. 160–73. For a more detailed consideration of Rome's initial responses to Luther, which involved legal, theological, and diplomatic activity, see Jared Wicks, "Roman Reactions to Luther: The First Year (1518)," *CHR*, LXIX (1983), pp. 521–62. The key Counter-Reformation sourcebook for arguments for Petrine primacy was Eck's *Enchiridion*, first published in 1525, many times reprinted, and now available in the edition of Pierre Fraenkel: Johannes Eck, *Enchiridion locorum communionem adversus Lutherum et alios hostes Ecclesiae (1525–1543)* [Corpus Catholicorum, 34] (Münster: Aschendorff, 1979). The first four chapters are devoted to the nature of the Church, and the lengthy third chapter, "De primatu sedis apostolicae et Petri" (pp. 48–75) emphasizes patristic consensus on the meaning of Matthew 16:17–19 and John 21:15–17. For Eck, the *testimonia patrum et historiae* confirm Petrine primacy, and it is from this belief that the Prostestant innovators had diverged. Eck's treatment draws upon his own earlier (1520–21) *De primatu Petri*, and in general upon the whole tradition of pro-papalist ecclesiology as it developed in the fifteenth and early sixteenth centuries.

35. O'Malley, *Praise and Blame*, pp. 220–21.

36. *Ibid.*, pp. 14, 92, 210.

37. *Ibid.*, p. 15.

38. McManamon, "Ideal Renaissance Pope," pp. 27, 40–42.

39. *De summi pontificis generalis concilii et imperialis maiestatis origine et potestate*, BAV, ms. Vat. lat. 4134, fols. 21ʳ-67ᵛ and ms. Vat. lat. 4136, fols. 48ʳ-92ᵛ. For the date of the work see Haller, *Piero da Monte*, p. 25. Ms. Vat. lat. 4134, a collection of various texts on papal authority, was compiled for Juan de Torquemada, and Piero's text contains a number of glosses in Torquemada's hand: Jürgen Miethke, "Eine unbekannte Handschrift vom Petrus de Paludes Traktat *De potestate Papae* aus dem Besitz Juan de Torquemadas in den Vatikanischen Bibliothek," *QFIAB*, LIX (1979), pp. 468–75.

40. Zanelli, *Pietro del Monte*, pp. 53–66; Haller, pp. 97–98. These orations are present in BAV, ms. Vat. lat. 2694.

41. O'Malley, *Praise and Blame*, pp. 81–83.

42. BAV, ms. Vat. lat. 4145, fols. 1ʳ–4ᵛ; the text of the preface and epilogue only of *Contra impugnantes* are present in BAV, ms. Vat. lat. 2694, fols. 297ᵛ–300ʳ.

43. BAV, ms. Vat. lat. 4145, fol. 118ᵛ.

44. *Ibid.*, fols. 104ʳ⁻ᵛ. Note also Piero's list of patristic authorities, including Cyril and Chrysostom, cited with regard to the power of the keys: *ibid.*, fols. 12ʳ-15ᵛ.

45. Monfasani, *George of Trebizond*, p. 118.

46. See Stinger, *Humanism and the Church Fathers*, pp. 190–92, 203–22.

47. Haller, *Piero da Monte*, pp. 79–83, 87. Piero's translation appears in BAV, ms. Vat. Lat. 1694, fols. 49ᵛ–59ᵛ.

48. For Traversari's regard for Chrysostom, see Stinger, *Humanism and the Church Fathers*, pp. 108–09, 130–33. For the Roman humanists' Chrysostom scholarship, see pp. 229–34 herein.

49. BAV, ms. Vat. lat. 4145, fols. 12ʳ-15ᵛ.

50. Stinger, *Humanism and the Church Fathers*, pp. 190, 207–08.

51. Pope-Hennessy, *Fra Angelico*, pp. 212–14.

52. BAV, ms. Vat. lat. 4134, fols. 25ʳ-27ʳ.

53. *Roma instaurata*, pp. 271–72.

54. *Ibid.*

55. The text of the preface of Agli's *De vitis et gestis sanctorum* appears in Miglio, *Storiografia pontificia*, pp. 177–80. For Agli, see *ibid.*, pp. 16–17, and A. d'Addario, "Antonio Agli," *DBI*, I (Rome, 1960), pp. 400–01.

56. The copy of Agli's work presented to Nicholas V was among the manuscripts of the Vatican Library heavily damaged during the 1527 Sack: note Giovanni Mercati, *Opere minori*, III [Studi e Testi, 78] (Vatican, 1937), pp. 131–34; for a continuation of some of Agli's humanistic concerns in the hagiography written by the Florentine canon Francesco da Castiglione in the 1460s, see Fubini, "Papato e storiografia," pp. 338–40.

57. Miglio, *Storiografia*, pp. 178–79.

58. *Ibid.*, pp. 79, 210–11.

59. *Ibid.*, pp. 99–101.

60. Pope-Hennessy, *Fra Angelico*, pp. 31–33; Stefano Orlandi, O.P., *Beato Angelico* (Florence: Olschki, 1964), pp. 97–103. Richard Krautheimer, "Fra Angelico and— Perhaps—Alberti," in Irving Lavin and John Plummer, eds., *Studies in Late Medieval and Renaissance Painting in Honor of Millard Meiss* (N.Y.: New York U. Pr., 1977), pp. 290–96. In Giulio Romano's *Stoning of St. Stephen*, a painting done for Gian Matteo Giberti and intended for the church of S. Stefano in Genoa, where Giberti had a benefice, the saint's martyrdom also appears within a Roman setting, which includes the theater of Marcellus, and the column and market of Trajan: Frederick Hartt, *Giulio Romano* (New Haven: Yale U. Pr., 1958), pp. 55–56.

61. Pius II, *Commentaries*, *SCSH*, XLIII (1957), pp. 817–27; Setton, *Papacy and the Levant*, II, p. 261. Cf. Pius's remarks of 1460 that military threats would not prevent his return to Rome. Where could a pope die more honorably than in Rome, he asks; what tomb is more fitting than the Vatican? "We do not shrink from dying by an impious sword; to die for Rome and in Rome, to meet death for the patrimony of St. Peter is glorious:" *Commentaries*, *SCSH*, XXX (1947), p. 344.

62. The account forms the first half of book VIII, *SCSH*, XXXV (1951), pp. 523–42 and may originally have existed as a work independent of the *Commentaries*: see Rubinstein, "Pius II's Piazza S. Pietro and St. Andrew's Head," p. 29, n. 81. For the St. Andrew's head ceremony, see also Setton, *Papacy and the Levant*, II, pp. 228–30.

63. Rubinstein, pp. 22–29.

64. *Ibid.*, pp. 31–32. In 1964, five centuries after the relic of St. Andrew's head was brought to Rome, Pope Paul VI returned it to Patras: *ibid.*, p. 33. That the Roman Renaissance continued an interest in St. Andrew is shown by Ghirlandajo's *The Calling of the First Apostles*, one of the wall frescoes commissioned by Sixtus IV for the Sistine Chapel. The background of this painting follows Matthew 4: 18–22 in showing Christ at the Sea of Galilee calling first Peter and his brother Andrew from their fishing nets, then James and John. But in the foreground Christ addresses only Peter and Andrew, Peter kneeling closer to Christ, Andrew kneeling more modestly next to his brother. The founding Apostles of the two great branches of Christendom, Roman and Greek, are thus shown in their proper relationship (from the papal point of view). For the fresco, see Ettlinger, *Sistine Chapel*. p. 90.

65. The theme of martyrdom occasionally appears in later Renaissance pontificates. A dying Julius II, for instance, spoke of his "martyrdom" as pope: Partridge and Starn, *A Renaissance Likeness*, p. 68. Images of imperial majesty, however, as will be discussed in Chapter IV, tended to outrival these penitential notions.

66. For Vegio's career, see the studies cited in Chapter II, notes 59 and 60; note also Anna Cox Brinton, *Maphaeus Vegius and his Thirteenth Book of the Aeneid* (Stanford: Stanford U. Pr., 1930).

67. The text appears in *Acta Sanctorum. Junii,* t. VII (Supplementi Pars II) (Antwerp, 1717). pp. 61–85. Parts of it appear in Valentini and Zucchetti, *Codice topografico,* IV, pp. 377–98. For mss. note Weiss, *Renaissance Discovery,* p. 72; for discussion of its composition and contents, see Vignati, "Alcune note," pp. 58–69.

68. For this legend, which dates from at least the fifth-century *Life of St. Sylvester,* see John Holland Smith, *Constantine the Great* (N.Y.: Scribner's, 1971), pp. 310–15. The legend was also incorporated in the "Donation of Constantine" (see pp. 247–54 herein). The Oratorio di S. Silvestro of the Roman church of SS. Quattro Coronati contains a thirteenth-century fresco cycle of the life of Constantine which includes his dream of Peter and Paul and his cure from leprosy through baptism at Silvester's hands. Hartt, *Giulio Romano,* pp. 42–51, notes that during an initial stage of planning the decoration of the Sala di Costantino in the Vatican Palace it was proposed to include a depiction of the slaughter of children to provide blood for Constantine's cure from leprosy; this did not, however, form part of the final design.

69. *De rebus antiquis,* pp. 62–63.

70. *Ibid.,* pp. 64–69.

71. *Ibid.,* p. 85.

72. B.M. Peebles, "La *Meta Romuli* e una lettera di Michele Ferno," *Rend Pont Acc,* 3rd Ser., XII (1936), pp. 21–63.

73. The section of Vegio's text which discusses Peter's martyrdom can be found in J.M. Huskinson, "The Crucifixion of St. Peter: A Fifteenth-Century Topographical Problem," *JWCI,* XXXII (1969), pp. 160–61.

74. *Ibid.,* pp. 154–56; Huskinson here suggests also that the site of Peter's crucifixion depicted on the Porta Argentea of St. Peter's (a work Eugenius IV commissioned Filarete to sculpt some time before 1434, though it was completed only in 1445) was Montorio. That this is so, he argues, suggests as well Vegio's likely involvement in the program of the door.

75. *Ibid.,* p. 136.

76. Huskinson, pp. 158–59, provides the text of the relevant passages of *Roma instaurata.*

77. The relevant text is quoted and discussed by James S. Ackerman, *The Cortile of the Belvedere.* [Studi e documenti per la storia del Palazzo Apostolico Vaticano, III] (Vatican, 1954), pp. 128–29; note also *id.,* "The Belvedere as a Classical Villa," *JWCI,* XIV (1951), pp. 81–82.

78. Ackerman, *Cortile,* p. 129.

79. *Roma triumphans,* p. 212.

80. *RIS²,* III, Pt. I, p. 12.

81. Ferdinando Castagnoli, "Il Circo di Nerone in Vaticano," *Rend Pont Acc,* 3rd ser., XXXII (1959–60), pp. 97–121; George H. Forsyth, Jr., "The Transept of Old St. Peter's at Rome," in *Late Classical and Mediaeval Studies in Honor of Albert Mathias Friend, Jr.,* ed. Kurt Weitzman (Princeton: Princeton U. Pr., 1955), pp. 56–70; J.B. Ward Perkins, "The Shrine of St. Peter and its Twelve Spiral Columns," *Journal of Roman Studies,* XLII (1952), pp. 21–33; José Ruysschaert, "La Tomba di Pietro: Nuove considerazioni archeologiche e storiche," *Studi romani,* XXIV (1976), pp. 322–30; and Krautheimer, *Rome,* pp. 19–20. A helpful guide to the enormous bibliography on the excavations is Angelus A. de Marco, O.F.M., *The Tomb of St. Peter: A Representative and Annotated Bibliography* [Supplements to Novum Testamentum, VIII] (Leiden: Brill, 1964). For early Christian treatments of Peter in Rome, see Pietri, *Roma Christiana,* pp. 51–69, 357–401, 1537–96.

82. *Roma instaurata,* p. 222. The same emphasis on the substitution of Christian supernatural grace for pagan Roman glory occurs in Biondo's discussion, also in *Roma instaurata* (pp. 229, 245), regarding the chains which once had bound St. Peter in Herod's prison in Jerusalem and from which he was miraculously freed by the Angel of the Lord (Acts 12: 1–19). The chains, when brought to Rome by the Empress Eudoxia, resulted,

Biondo notes, in substituting for the traditional celebration of the Emperor Augustus's victory over Antony and Cleopatra at Actium (held annually on 1 August) a feast day in honor of St. Peter's liberation from prison. Thus, Biondo declares, a day formerly marked by games and dissipation had become through papal concession a time for receiving the body and blood of Our Lord and an occasion for the remission of the sins of the penitent.

83. *Roma triumphans*, pp. 212–14. There was an ancient Via triumphalis in the Vatican, but the route of the ancient Roman triumphs did not start here; instead it originated across the Tiber in the Campus Martius: Martindale, *Triumphs of Caesar*, pp. 60–62. In *De rebus antiquis*, pp. 75–76, Vegio also relates the triumphs of the ancient Romans to later Christian processions. He observes that Pope Honorius was accustomed to perform litanies at the church of S. Apollinare and that a procession would then go from there to St. Peter's. The church of S. Apollinare, Vegio goes on, was formerly a temple of Apollo and was dedicated to St. Apollinaris so that the similarity of the two names might draw to Christianity the large crowds which frequented the pagan temple. The ruined foundations of this temple can still be seen, he says, next to the church of S. Agostino, and also marks an area, known as the *prata Flaminea*, where later the circus Flaminius was built. To this, according to Livy, the Roman consuls came in the celebration of triumphs. But this conjunction of classical and Christian elements leads Vegio to conclude: "*Mirum certe in hoc videmus Dei judicium, qui eodem in templo postea ad celebrandos melius caelestes triumphos, decantandasque divinas laudes, jubente Romano Pontifice, sacerdotum conventum fieri voluerit.*" Where Biondo eventually came to see precedent and prefigurement in the ancient triumphs, Vegio saw instead the extirpation of pagan rites by Christian liturgy.

84. Zabughin, *Leto*, I, p. 229.

85. *Roma instaurata*, p. 229.

86. Shearman, *Raphael's Cartoons*, p. 64, n. 114; for other aspects of the mystique of the Mons Vaticanus during Leo X's pontificate, see *ibid.*, pp. 64–65.

87. Janus is shown holding a key in one of the scenes painted for the 1513 Capitoline pageantry in which Leo X's brother, Giuliano, was made a Roman citizen: Cruciani, *Teatro del Campidoglio*, p. 26. Note also herein, Chapter VI, n. 24.

88. O'Malley, *Giles of Viterbo*, pp. 123–24. The continuity between Etruscan Rome and Christian Rome, between Janus and Peter, was earlier expressed in Giles's 1507 discourse on the golden age: O'Malley, "Fulfillment of the Christian Golden Age," esp. pp. 272–73, 285–86, 295, 331–32.

89. John Capgrave, for instance, in his *Ye Solace of Pilgrimes* (see Chapter II, n. 68), describes the Vatican obelisk thusly: "Ther is a piler fast by seynt peter cherch all of o ston a grete merueyle for to be hold for as the elde writeris sey that had experiens of the mesur the piler is in heith cc. feet and ii. Up on this pilere is a grete ball of copir or brasse whech was sumtyme gilt and fretted with precious stones in whech was julius caesar body put rith for this cause. For as he was lord a boue alle men that wer olyue whil he regned her so schuld his body rest a boue all bodies that wer byried be for him." Biondo, *Roma instaurata*, p. 229, also describes the Vatican obelisk as the "obelisk of Caesar" and states that "*cineres C. Caesaris Obelisco insigni positos.*" The inscription at the base of the obelisk, however, records its dedication to the Emperors Augustus and Tiberius, as Vegio and subsequent Roman humanists noted, and Bernardo Rucellai wonders in *De Urbe Roma*, pp. 1126–27, why St. Jerome had described it as the obelisk of Nero, when the inscription indicates otherwise. For the history of the Vatican obelisk, see Erik Iversen, *Obelisks in Exile*, Vol. I: *The Obelisks of Rome* (Copenhagen: G.E.C. Gad, 1968), pp. 19–46.

90. Magnuson, *Roman Quattrocento Architecture*, pp. 80–81, quotes the relevant text from Manetti's life of Nicholas V and discusses the architectural significance of the projected site. Note also Westfall, *In this Most Perfect Paradise*, p. 113.

91. Giles's remarks appear in his *Historia XX saeculorum*. Relevant portions of this text appear in O'Malley, *Giles of Viterbo*, p. 125, and in Frommel, "Die Peterskirche," document no. 8, pp. 89–90.

92. Fontana's accomplishment required, however, the simultaneous pulling power of nine hundred men and seventy-five horses applied to five levers and forty windlasses, and the cost of the operation approached 40,000 scudi: William Barclay Parsons, *Engineers and Engineering in the Renaissance* (Cambridge, Mass., and London: MIT Pr., 1968), pp. 155–67.

93. For the church of S. Pietro in Montorio, see Urban, "Die Kirchenbaukunst," pp. 277–79, and Bruschi, *Bramante architetto*, pp. 986–89.

94. *Bramante architetto*, pp. 470–81. For the sources, function, and design of the Tempietto, see besides *ibid.*, pp. 463–527, 989–1035, E. Rosenthal, "The Antecedents of Bramante's Tempietto," *JSAH*, XXIII (1964), pp. 55–74; Portoghesi, *Roma del Rinascimento*, pp. 51–55, 433–34; Sinding-Larsen, "Some Functional and Iconographical Aspects of the Centralized Church," pp. 219–20, 236–37; and Wolfgang Lotz, *Studies in Italian Renaissance Architecture* (Cambridge, Mass. and London: MIT Pr., 1977), pp. 70–71. For Numa's tomb on the Janiculum, see Coffin, *Villa in the Life of Renaissance Rome*, pp. 262–64.

95. Leo Steinberg, *Michelangelo's Last Paintings: The Conversion of St. Paul and the Crucifixion of St. Peter in the Cappella Paolina, Vatican Palace* (N.Y.: Oxford U. Pr., 1975), pp. 42–55; Philipp Fehl, "Michelangelo's *Crucifixion of St. Peter*: Notes on the Identification of the Locale of the Action," *AB*, LIII (1971), pp. 327–43.

96. The ultimate source for this legend of the contest between Simon Magus and St. Peter, and of Simon's fall on the Via Sacra, is Justin Martyr (2nd c.): see Christian Hülsen, "The Legend of the Aracoeli" (Paper read before the British and American Archeological Society of Rome, 14 February 1907) (Rome: G. Bertero, 1907), p. 7.

97. RIS², III, Pt. I, pp. 10–12. It is instructive to compare Platina's account and the representation of Peter and Paul on the ciborium which Sixtus IV commissioned for the high altar of old St. Peter's. The sculpted reliefs do show Peter and Paul's condemnation before Nero and their martyrdom, but they also show Peter's healing of the lame man at the Jerusalem Temple and the defeat of Simon Magus. For the ciborium, see Müntz, *Les arts à la cour des papes*, III, pp. 148–49; P. Giordani, "Studii sulla scultura romana del Quattrocento: I bassorilievi del tabernacolo di Sisto IV," *L'arte*, X (1907), p. 271; and Shearman, *Raphael's Cartoons*, pp. 74–75.

98. *Liber de vita Christi*, p. 8.

99. *Ibid.*, pp. xxxv–lxxii.

100. *Ibid.*, p. 3.

101. *Ibid.*

102. Zeno's prefatory letter appears in Miglio, *Storiografia pontificia*, pp. 181–83. Note also *ibid.*, pp. 17–19; and for Zeno's career, Ludovico Bertalot and Augusto Campana, "Gli scritti di Iacopo Zeno e il suo elogio di Ciriaco d'Ancona," *La bibliofilia*, XLI (1939), pp. 356–76.

103. Miglio, *Storiografia*, pp. 7–30. Note also Carlo da Capidimonte, O.F.M., "Poggio Bracciolini autore delle anonome *Vitae quorundam pontificium*," *RSCI*, XIV (1960), pp. 27–47; Fubini, "Papato e storiografia," pp. 321–51; D'Amico, "Papal History and Curial Reform," pp. 157–90; and, for a general survey of historiography at the Roman Curia, Cochrane, *Historians and Historiography*, pp. 34–58.

104. See pp. 227–28. Vegio, *De rebus antiquis*, p. 72 mentions the portraits of the popes in the atrium of old St. Peter's.

105. Ettlinger, *Sistine Chapel*, pp. 12, 102–03. When Michelangelo painted his fresco of the *Last Judgment* on the altar wall the papal portraits there were destroyed. Ettlinger argues, pp. 22–23, that the altar wall contained portraits only of Linus and Cletus, thus matching the series in S. Paolo f.l.m., which began with Linus. Wilde, "Decoration of the Sistine Chapel," pp. 69–70, suggests that in addition to Linus and Cletus portraits of Christ with Peter on his right hand and Paul on his left were also present.

106. Shearman, *Raphael's Cartoons*, p. 7.

107. *Ibid.*, pp. 21–44.

108. *Ibid.*, pp. 50–55, 63–65. The lake in this tapestry, set as it is before the Mons Vaticanus, may perhaps recall, Shearman postulates (p. 65, n. 114) Nero's Vatican *naumachia*. Raphael in that case would have echoed Vegio's stress on Peter called by Christ as the fisher of men to combat evil in the *naumachiae* of the world.

109. For the Renaissance understanding of the origin and meaning of these columns, see p. 223.

110. *Raphael's Cartoons*, pp. 65–68.

111. See p. 152.

112. Shearman, *Raphael's Cartoons*, p. 67.

113. *Ibid.*, p. 75.

114. Frederick Hartt, "Art and Freedom in Quattrocento Florence," in Lucy Freeman Sandler, ed., *Essays in Memory of Karl Lehmann* [*Marsyas: Studies in the History of Art*, Supplement 1] (N.Y.: Institute of Fine Arts, New York U., 1964), pp. 128–29, sees the fresco

as connected to the Florentine imposition of the *catasto* and it "announces taxation as a civic duty divinely revealed." Millard Meiss, "Masaccio and the Early Renaissance: The Circular Plan," in *The Painter's Choice: Problems in the Interpretation of Renaissance Art* (N.Y.: Harper & Row, 1976), pp. 64–65, draws on St. Augustine's exegesis of the Matthew text in seeing it as a symbol of redemption, which is accomplished through the Church: "Thus it conveys in a different guise the idea normally expressed by the Gift of the Keys." Anthony Molho, "The Brancacci Chapel: Studies in its Iconography and History," *JWCI*, XL (1977), pp. 50–98, interprets the whole decoration of the chapel as underscoring papal primacy, and the *Tribute Money* as the Church's *voluntary* contribution to the civic needs in opposition to contemporary Florentine demands to *impose* yet greater exactions on an already heavily-taxed Florentine Church.

115. Molho suggests that reference to these texts was omitted, since the medieval hierocratic doctrine of papal primacy, which these texts had been used to sustain, was too sensitive and controversial a matter to present in a Florentine chapel in the Conciliar Age. Meiss, p. 72, proposes that Donatello's relief of the *Ascension of Christ and the Gift of the Keys to St. Peter* was the original altarpiece for the Brancacci Chapel.

116. Meiss, p. 72.

117. The painting was unfinished at Julius's death, and the figures of the pope and his entourage were moved from the distance to a more prominent foreground position in order to allow Leo X to appear prominently as his illustrious forebear of the same name: Shearman, "Vatican Stanze," pp. 383–84; *id.*, "Raphael's Unexecuted Projects for the Stanze," *Walter Friedlander zum 90. Geburtstag: Eine Festgabe seiner europäischen Schüler, Freunde und Verehrer* (Berlin: de Gruyter, 1965), pp. 170–73; for another recent analysis of the decorative scheme of this stanza, see Jörg Traeger, "Raffaels Stanza d'Eliodoro und ihr Bildsprogramm," *Römisches Jahrbuch für Kunstgeschichte*, XIII (1971), pp. 29–99.

118. Traeger, p. 36.

119. Shearman, "Vatican Stanze," pp. 379–83. There is a massive literature on the Stanza della Signatura. Useful recent discussions include: G.I. Hoogewerff, "La Stanza della Segnatura: Osservasioni e commenti," *Rend Pont Acc*, 3rd ser., XXIII-XXIV (1949), pp. 317–56; André Chastel, *Art et humanisme à Florence au temps de Laurent le Magnifique: Études sur la Renaissance et l'humanisme platonicien* (Paris: Presses universitaires de France, 1959), pp. 469–84; E. H. Gombrich, *Symbolic Images: Studies in the Art of the Renaissance, II* (Oxford: Phaidon, 1972), pp. 85–101; Herbert von Einem, "Das Programm der Stanza della Segnatura im Vatikan," *Rheinisch-Westfälische Akademie der Wissenschaften: Geisteswissenschaften* [Vörtrage G 169] (Opladen, 1971); Heinrich Pfeiffer, S.J., *Zur Ikonographie von Raffaels Disputà: Egidio da Viterbo und die christlich-platonische Konzeption der Stanza della Segnatura* [Miscellanea Historiae Pontificiae, 37] (Rome: Università Gregoriana, 1975); Nancy Rash-Fabbri, "A Note on the Stanza della Segnatura," *Gazette des Beaux-Arts*, XCIV (1979), pp. 97–104.

120. Raphael included a similarly rustic group of houses in the view of the Vatican, which forms the background in his cartoon for the Sistine Chapel tapestry of the *Miraculous Draft*: Shearman, *Raphael's Cartoons*, p. 51. Coffin, *Villa*, pp. 16–19, notes that numerous rustic *vigne* existed just outside Renaissance Rome, especially in the Prati, which abut the Vatican hill.

121. Bruschi, *Bramante*, pp. 373–416. Bruschi (p. 373, n. 119) notes that the preliminary work of levelling the ground and building sustaining walls for the *cortile superiore* was substantially complete by 1509, at which point Bramante could refine his plans for this part of the palace.

122. Pfeiffer, pp. 94–95.

123. Coffin, *Villa*, pp. 69–74.

124. *Cortile del Belvedere*, p. 125; note also Bruschi, p. 320, von Einem, pp. 34–35, and Shearman, "Vatican Stanze," p. 382.

125. See pp. 183, 274. For other contemporary references, note Shearman, "Vatican Stanze," p. 414, n. 105, and Brummer, *Statue Court of the Vatican Belvedere*, p. 226, n. 39. In Giulio Simone's *Oratio de poetice et musarum triumpho* (1517), Leo X is hailed as Apollo Musagetes and the Vatican hill is called a new Parnassus: MacDougall, "Sleeping Nymph," p. 363. For further discussion, see esp. Schröter, "Der Vatikan als Hügel Apollons," pp. 208–40.

126. The relevant text is quoted by Brummer, p. 225.

127. According to Paris de Grassis, when Julius II in 1512 entertained Matthaeus Lang, the imperial ambassador, with a banquet in the garden of the Belvedere, part of the post-prandial diversions was a dramatic skit in which youths dressed as Apollo and the Muses and as Orpheus declaimed verses in praise of Julius and Maximilian. Afterwards Julius crowned two of the poets with laurel crowns provided by Inghirami: Cruciani, *Teatro di Campidoglio*, p. xciii, n. 50; Coffin, *Villa in the Life of Renaissance Rome*, p. 83; Schröter, pp. 237–39. For the political symbolism of Apollo for Julius's pontificate, see pp. 274–76 herein, and for the association of Apollo with other Renaissance pontiffs, note also pp. 56, 247, 297.

128. Brummer, pp. 44–71.

129. Chastel, pp. 460, 476; von Einem, p. 35; Bruschi, p. 485.

130. Shearman, *Raphael's Cartoons*, p. 9, and *id.*, "Il 'Tiburio' di Bramante in San Pietro," in *Studi Bramanteschi*, pp. 567–73.

131. That the Roman Church could not err was part of the medieval pro-papalist tradition. In sustaining this view, Piero da Monte, in *Contra impugnantes*, BAV, ms. Vat. lat. 4145, fol. 25ᵛ, attributes to St. Sixtus (Pope Sixtus II, 257–58) the statement that the faith of the Roman Church had never supported heresy, but rather that heresies, whenever they had arisen, had been extinguished with the light of its doctrine. Platina, in *Liber de vita Christi ac omnium pontificum*, pp. 42–43, had also taken note of Sixtus II's fight against the Sabellians and other heretics. In Raphael's *Sistine Madonna*, painted sometime between June 1512 and Julius II's decease in February 1513, Julius appears in the guise of St. Sixtus kneeling before a celestial vision of the Madonna and Child. The painting was commissioned by the pope for the rebuilt Benedictine Abbey of S. Sisto in Piacenza, a city which as a result of papal successes in 1512 adhered voluntarily to papal rule: John Pope-Hennessey, *Raphael: The Wrightsman Lectures* (N.Y.: New York U. Pr., 1970), pp. 209 ff. To the motives of the name of the rebuilt monastery, and of St. Sixtus as a prominent early defender of Roman inerrancy, should also be added Julius II's persistent evocation of his uncle Sixtus IV's achievements. The conclusion to be drawn is that when considering the constellation of ideas and themes associated with Julian commissions the universal and the personal are often conjoined. Thus Raphael's *Disputà* should be seen as expressing general conceptions of the Roman Church while at the same time specifically glorifying the Della Rovere. In this way, then, Sixtus IV, splendidly arrayed in golden vestments, is given a prominent position among the theologians of the Church.

132. For the theme of Rome as "*sancta Latina Ierusalem*," see pp. 318–19. Julius II himself officiated for the ceremonies held in connection with placing the first stone for the foundation of the great piers that marked the crossing of the new St. Peter's. The commemorative medals laid down with the foundation stone bore the inscription TEMPLI PETRI INSTAVRACIO: Weiss, "Medals of Julius II," p. 170. For the texts of Burchard's and Paris de Grassis's accounts of the ceremony, see Frommel, "Die Peterskirche," Appendices 25 and 26, pp. 94–95.

133. I Peter 2: 9 (". . . for you are a chosen race, a royal priesthood," etc.) was frequently cited by Roman humanists in celebrating the destiny of Rome. For Domenichi's use of it, see pp. 244–45. Allusions to Peter's imagery of "living stones" was also frequent, particularly in the early sixteenth century. Cajetan, in his speech before the Fifth Lateran Council (17 May 1512), described the Roman Church in these terms: "*Illorum est haec sanctissima Ierusalem, quae ex vivis lapidibus construitur. . . .*" (Mansi, *Collectio*, XXXII, col. 723). Similarly, Stefano Taleazzi, in his address to the Council (4 May 1515), stated: ". . . *verum etiam et mysterium incarnationis Verbi Dei pro civitate magni domini in caelis et in terris ex lapidibus vivis construenda prae se ferre invenitur, pro qua Rex magnus ab initio et ante saecula praeparaverat terram immaculatam, in qua aedificaret sibi domum, de qua gloriose educeret immaculatam, aeternam sponsam, matrem justorum laetantem, et non minus in posterum fidem catholicam et apostolicam suam, juxta decretum sacrosancti consistorii Trinitatis et unitatis divinae, pro communi salute per orbem universum promulgandam esse statuerit. . . .*" (*ibid.*, col. 918). For Renaissance Romans' emphasis on the Mons Vaticanus as the true Mt. Zion, see pp. 318–19 herein. S.J. Freedberg, *Painting of the High Renaissance in Rome and Florence* (Cambridge: Harvard U. Pr., 1961), pp. 118–19, suggests that the sequence of semicircles, each populated with figures, which provides the underlying pictorial design of Raphael's *Disputà*, creates the architectural effect of an apsidal half-dome of a church—"a church more perfect in its substance than any architecture of

stone." While not excluding the idealizing characteristics of Raphael's painting, I would argue instead that it is precisely the "living stones" that are emphasized, and that it is the Roman Church rather than "an ideal council of the Church" that is depicted.

134. Allusions to this text occur in the speeches of Giovanni Battista da Gargha and Antonio Pucci to the Fifth Lateran Council, and in Giles of Viterbo's *Historia XX saeculorum*. A conflation of Paul's remarks with the text of I Peter 2 occurs in Zaccaria Ferreri's *Somnium*, p. 101ᵛ:

> *Maximus ipse etenim pater* [i.e. Leo X] *immortalia tecta*
> *Construet aetherio regi de marmore vivo*
> *Efficiens utraque esse unum: divisaque sicut*
> *Angulus annectet, dispersaque colliget: aegra*
> *Curabit medica ipse manu: convertet in aurum*
> *Ferrea saecla: hominum fera pectora molliet: atque*
> *Ambrosiam nectarque omnem diffundet in orbem.*

For the significance of these two Pauline and Petrine texts in interpreting the meaning of Raphael's tapestries for the Sistine Chapel, see Shearman, *Raphael's Cartoons*, pp. 1, 74 n. 170, 78–82.

135. Bruschi, *Bramante architetto*, pp. 718–19, 1036–39.

136. Remigius Bäumer, "Die Auseinandersetzungen über die römische Petrustradition in den ersten Jahrzehnten der Reformationszeit," *Römische Quartalschrift*, LVII (1962), pp. 20–57; A.J. Lamping, *Ulrichus Velenus (Oldřich Velenský) and his Treatise against the Papacy* [Studies in Medieval and Reformation Thought, XIX] (Leiden: Brill, 1976). A refutation of Velenský, stemming from Roman circles, is the *Tractatus adversus negantem Petrum Apostolum Romae fuisse*, written by the Benedictine humanist Gregorio Cortese (1482–1548) in 1523 and dedicated to Adrian VI: Lamping, p. 166.

137. BAV, ms. Vat. lat. 4145, fols. 17ʳ-18ᵛ.

138. *Ibid.*, fols. 39ʳ, 45ᵛ.

139. *Ibid.*, fols. 65ᵛ-66ᵛ.

140. The same analogy is made by Angelo of Vallombrosa in his attack on supporters of the *conciliabulum* of Pisa. He calls them imitators of Ham for their disobedience to the *Vicarius Dei*: *Apologeticum Angeli Anachoritae Vallisumbrosae pro Julio Papa contra consilium Decii* (?, 1511), fol. 3ʳ.

141. BAV, ms. Vat. lat. 4145, fols, 71ʳ⁻ᵛ, 108ʳ-110ʳ.

142. *Ibid.*, fol. 114ʳ.

143. M.J. Wilks, *The Problem of Sovereignty in the Later Middle Ages* (Cambridge: Cambridge U. Pr., 1962), pp. 538–47; Ettlinger, *Sistine Chapel*, pp. 110–16; Bouwsma, *Venice and the Defense of Republican Liberty*, pp. 44–48. Piero da Monte, in his earlier treatise, *De summi pontificis . . . origine et potestate* (BAV, mss. Vat. lat. 4134, fol. 22ʳ and 4136, fol. 49ᵛ), had argued, in answer to the question as to the source of the Roman pontiff's power, that he held it immediately from God, but also that the priesthood had been transferred from Aaron to Christ, and from Christ to Peter. Old Testament arguments prove much more extensive and more crucial to Piero's case, however, in his later *Contra impugnantes*.

144. Ettlinger, *Sistine Chapel*, pp. 104–06.

145. *Ibid.*, pp. 107–08.

146. *Ibid.*, pp. 66–70. Interestingly, Zaccaria Ferreri, in his *De reformatione Ecclesiae suasoria*, addressed to Adrian VI in 1522, cites this passage from Hebrews to stress the urgent need to end the abuse of prelates appointing their own relatives to the priesthood; this office should be conferred only "on those called by God." For the relevant text, see McNally, "Pope Adrian VI (1522–23) and Church Reform," pp. 272–75.

147. D. Redig de Campos, "L'architetto e il costruttore della Cappella Sistina," *Palatino: Rivista romana di cultura*, 3rd ser. IX (1965), pp. 90–93.

148. D. Redig de Campos, "I 'tituli' degli affreschi del Quattrocento nella Cappella Sistina," *Rend Pont Acc*, XLII (1970), pp. 299–314; for the meaning of the fresco, see Ettlinger, *Sistine Chapel*, pp. 90–93.

149. During the Renaissance it was popular tradition that whichever cardinal would be elected pope would have as his assigned cell in the Sistine Chapel (distributed by lottery) the space beneath the *Delivery of the Keys*. Pius III, Julius II, Clement VII, and Paul III were

all elected popes from this auspicious position: see Chambers, "Papal Conclaves and Prophetic Meaning," pp. 323–26.

150. *Sistine Chapel*, pp. 104–19; for substantial agreement, despite some differences in details, see Roberto Salvini, "The Sistine Chapel: Ideology and Architecture," *Art History*, III (1980), pp. 144–57.

151. The typological relationship between Moses and Christ is made explicit in the *tituli*, in which correspondences in word order and repetition of key words are readily apparent; the texts of the *tituli*, as given by Redig de Campos, "I 'tituli'," pp. 306–08, are as follows:

Circumcison of Moses' Son: OBSERVATIO ANTIQVE REGENERATIONIS A MOISE PER CIRCONCISIONEM, and *Baptism of Christ*: INSTITVTIO NOVAE REGENERATIONIS A CHRISTO IN BAPTISMO.

Trials of Moses: TEMPTATIO MOISI LEGIS SCRIPTAE LATORIS, and *Temptation of Christ*: TEMPTATIO IESV CHRISTI LATORIS EVANGELICAE LEGIS.

Crossing of the Red Sea: CONGREGATIO POPVLI A MOISE LEGEM SCRIPTAM ACCEPTVRI, and *Calling of the First Apostles*: CONGREGATIO POPVLI LEGEM EVANGELICAM RECEPTVRI.

Delivery of the Tablets of the Law: PROMVLGATIO LEGIS SCRIPTAE PER MOISEM, and *Sermon on the Mount*: PROMVLGATIO EVANGELICAE LEGIS PER CHRISTVM.

Punishment of Korah: CONTVRBATIO MOISI LEGIS SCRIPTAE LATORIS, and *Delivery of the Keys*: CONTVRBATIO IESV CHRISTI LEGISLATORIS.

Testament of Moses: REPLICATIO LEGIS SCRIPTAE A MOISE, and *Last Supper*: REPLICATIO LEGIS EVANGELICAE A CHRISTO.

Archangel Michael Defending the Body of Moses (inscription lost), and *Resurrection of Christ*: RESURRECTIO ET ASCENSIO CHRISTI EVANGELICAE LEGIS LATORIS.

152. This contrasts to the usual early Christian and medieval treatments of Moses, where the miracles in the desert are given prominence: Ettlinger, *Sistine Chapel*, pp. 100–03. Pietri, *Roma Christiana*, pp. 315–56, 1437–42, notes that in third- and early fourth-century Rome Moses was depicted as a type of Peter by stressing the miracle of the rock in the desert; after the middle of the fourth century, however, a typological connection between Moses and Peter was made on the basis of their role as promulgators of the written and evangelical law. Perhaps, as in other aspects of Sixtus IV's artistic and scholarly policies, there was recognition of, and deliberate revival of, a paleo-Christian *Roman* tradition (although in the Sistine Chapel the typological link is made between Moses and Christ, rather than Moses and Peter). Nevertheless, Ettlinger is certainly right in asserting that no living artistic tradition related to Moses could have suggested his treatment in the Sistine Chapel.

153. Ettlinger, *Sistine Chapel*, pp. 7, 100, 102.

154. *Ibid.*, pp. 68–69, 79–81, 94.

155. *Ibid.*, pp. 69–70. Julius II gave to King Manuel of Portugal an illuminated Bible with the commentary of Nicolaus de Lyra: Dorez, "La bibliothèque privée du Pape Jules II," p. 100. Giles of Viterbo made marginal annotations in his copy of Lyra's Old Testament notes and he singled him out as an important earlier Christian Hebraist, but he held him to be deficient, like Jerome, in failing to penetrate to the mystical kernel of Scripture by means of the cabala: O'Malley, *Giles*, pp. 73–74, 193.

156. Trinkaus, *In Our Image and Likeness*, pp. 601–13.

157. *Ibid.*, pp. 726–34; Alfonso De Petris, "*L'Adversus Judeos et Gentes* di Giannozzo Manetti," *Rinascimento*, 2nd ser., XVI (1976), pp. 193–205.

158. Monfasani, *George of Trebizond*, p. 57.

159. *Sistine Chapel*, pp. 60–61, 71–73.

160. *Ibid.*, pp. 58, 60–61.

161. Monfasani, p. 57.

162. *Ibid.*, p. 35.

163. *Ibid.*, pp. 49–50.

164. Philo, *De incorruptione mundi*: see the Latin translation of this passage in the version presented by Lilio Tifernate to Sixtus IV in 1479 (BAV, ms. Vat. lat. 180. fol. 32ʳ).

165. For the sources of Nyssa's work, see Jean Daniélou, S.J.'s introduction (pp. 7–42) to his edition, Gregoire de Nysse, *La vie de Moïse* [Sources Chretiennes, Vol. I] 3rd ed. (Paris: Les editions du Cerf, 1968). For Philo's life of Moses, see Erwin R. Goodenough, "Philo's Exposition of the Law and his *De vita Mosis*," *Harvard Theological Review*, XXVI

(1933), pp. 109–25, and *id.*, *An Introduction to Philo Judaeus*, 2nd ed. (Oxford: Basil Blackwell, 1962), pp. 33–35, 144–53.

166. Tifernate came from Città di Castello (the classical name of the city was Tifernum). In BAV, ms. Vat. lat. 180, fol. 1ʳ he gives his name as Lilius Aegidius Libellius Tyfernatis. When borrowing a ms. of Philo from the Vatican Library on 22 May 1477 he signed his name as Lilius de Archilibellis legum doctor de Civitate Castelli: Maria Bertola, *I due primi registri di prestito della Biblioteca Apostolica Vaticana: Codici Vaticani latini 3964, 3966* (Vatican, 1942), p. 10. A son, Iohannes Baptista, is subsequently listed as borrowing and returning books for his father: *ibid.*, pp. 10, 15. No modern study of Tifernate exists. There is a short (19 pp.) booklet: F.M. Staffa, *Delle traduzioni dal greco in latino fatte da Gregorio e da Lilio Tifernati* (Gubbio, 1758). More useful is Joannes Baptista Card. Pitra, *Analecta sacra spicilegio solesmensi*, Vol. II: *Patres antenicaeni* (Tusculanis, 1884), pp. 315–34. Note also Charles L. Stinger, "Greek Patristics and Christian Antiquity in Renaissance Rome," in Ramsey, ed., *Rome in the Renaissance*, pp. 155–56.

167. See Stinger, *Humanism and the Church Fathers*, pp. 39, 145.

168. BAV, ms. Vat. lat. 3908, fol. 178ʳ. For Tortelli's role under Nicholas V, see Mariangela Regoliosi, "Nuove ricerche intorno a Giovanni Tortelli. 2. La vita di Giovanni Tortelli," *Italia medioevale e umanistica*, XII (1969), pp. 172–75.

169. BAV, ms. Barb. lat. 662 (XIV, 35), fols. 125ʳ⁻ᵛ; the text appears in Pitra, p. 333. The dedication copy of the translation presented to Nicholas has disappeared: Maria Bertola, "Codici latini di Niccolò V perduti o dispersi," *Mélanges Eugène Tisserant*, Vol. VI [Studi e Testi, 236] (Vatican, 1964), p. 139. In BAV, ms. Vat. lat. 180, fols. 1ʳ⁻ᵛ Tifernate also states that he had begun his Philo translation project during the pontificates of Nicholas V and Calixtus III. Only one of Philo's works, his *Liber quaestionum et solutionum in Genesim* was available in Latin translation during the Middle Ages. There is a fifteenth-century copy of this in the old Vatican fondo (BAV, ms. Vat. lat. 488, fols. 129ʳ ff.); Nicolaus Cusanus also owned a copy (Cues 16, dated 1451): see Françoise Petit, *L'ancienne version latine des questions sur la Genèse de Philon d'Alexandrie* [Text und Untersuchungen zur Geschichte der Altchristlichen Literatur, 113–114] (Berlin: Akademie Verlag, 1973), Vol. I, pp. vii–43.

170. The prefatory letter appears in BAV, ms. Urb. lat. 227, fols. 19ʳ⁻ᵛ; the text of the translations follows on fols. 19ᵛ-54ᵛ, 72ᵛ-110ᵛ. Another copy exists in BAV, ms. Vat. lat. 11600.

171. BAV, mss. Vat. lat. 180 (dedicated to Sixtus IV, dated 1479), 181 (to Sixtus, 1481), 182 (to Sixtus, 1480), 183 (to Sixtus, 1481–82), 184 (to Innocent VIII, 1484), 185 (to Innocent, 1485?). Parts of these translations also appear in BAV, mss. Vat. lat. 11577 and Barb. lat. 662.

172. The first loan was made 22 May 1477; other loans were made in October 1478 and January 1480. This last volume was returned by Tifernate himself in July 1485: Bertola, *I due registri*, pp. 10, 15, 19. Bertola identifies the borrowed Greek Philo codices as the present BAV, mss. Vat. gr. 381 and 382.

173. The colophons of Tifernate's translations state they were made "*Ex arce tuae Sanctitatis Ceperanensi.*" For the strategic importance of Ceprano, see Partner, *Lands of St. Peter*, p. 424.

174. BAV, ms. Vat. lat. 181, fol. 5ᵛ.

175. Tifernate composed a Greek poem of thanks to the saint: for this and his account of the eye disease, see BAV, ms. Vat. lat. 181, fol. 163ʳ; the texts also appear in Pitra, p. 334.

176. BAV, ms. Vat. lat. 180, fol. 1ᵛ.

177. BAV, ms. Urb. lat. 227, fol. 19ʳ. Platina, *De vita Christi ac omnium pontificum*, p. 11, also cites Philo's regard for Mark's character and for his teachings in Alexandria.

178. BAV, ms. Vat. lat. 182, fol. 4ᵛ.

179. *Ibid.*, fol. 68ʳ; see also fol. 120ᵛ, and fol. 72ʳ.

180. *Sistine Chapel*, pp. 116–17.

181. BAV, ms. Vat. lat. 183, fol. 119ᵛ; cf. Ettlinger, *Sistine Chapel*, pp. 74–75.

182. BAV, ms. Vat. lat. 3654, fols, 2ᵛ-3ʳ; note also Ettlinger, *Sistine Chapel*, pp. 85–86. Robert Grosseteste had made a Latin translation of *De sacerdotio Christi* in the thirteenth century, and besides Filelfo's there were at least three other Quattrocento Latin versions made. One was attributed to Traversari, and another Lauro Quirini dedicated to Nicholas V

in 1452: see Giovanni Card. Mercati, *Ultimi contributi alla storia degli umanisti*, Fasc. I: *Traversariana* [Studi e Testi, 90] (Vatican, 1939), pp. 70–85.
    183. Penni, *Chronica*, in Roscoe, *Vita e pontificato di Leone X*, Vol. V, pp. 219–20; note also Shearman, *Raphael's Cartoons*, pp. 48–49.
    184. *De potestate summi Pontificis, eius veneratione, et cognominatione, ac de justo bello Clem. vii contra Florentinas*, BAV, ms. Vat. lat. 4125, fols. 183ᵛ-185ʳ.
    185. Burchard, *Liber notarum*, II, p. 209.
    186. Eugene Müntz, "La tiare pontificale du VIIIᵉ au XVIᵉ siècle," *Mémoires de l'Institut national de France*, XXXVI (1898), pp. 235–324; P. Bernhard Sirch, O.S.B., *Der Ursprung der bischöflichen Mitra und päpstlichen Tiara* [Kirchengeschichtliche Quellen und Studien, 8] (St. Ottilien: Eos Verlag der Erzabtei, 1975), pp. 109–87; Krautheimer, *Rome*, p. 151.
    187. Miglio, *Storiografia pontificia*, pp. 121–53. Note Platina's praise of Pope Sylvester for rejecting the pomp of the bejeweled golden diadem conceded to him by Constantine: *Liber de vita Christi*, p. 53.
    188. O'Malley, *Giles of Viterbo*, p. 113.
    189. F. Secret, "Notes sur Egidio da Viterbo," *Augustiniana*, XXVII (1977), pp. 226–30; O'Malley, *Giles*, p. 80. For Giles's cabalistic studies, see pp. 306–08 herein.
    190. Herbert von Einem, *Michelangelo* (London: Methuen, 1973; first publ. Stuttgart, 1959), pp. 81–82, 172–73; Hibbard, *Michelangelo*, p. 158.
    191. O'Reilly, "'Without Councils We Cannot Be Saved'," pp. 199–200.
    192. Traeger, "Raffaels Stanza d'Eliodoro," pp. 34–36.
    193. For the architecture and pictorial design of the fresco, see Shearman, "Raphael's Unexecuted Projects for the Stanze," pp. 169–70. For various interpretations of the fresco's meaning, see Shearman, *Vatican Stanze*, pp. 384–85; and Traeger, pp. 31–34, 57. Edgar Wind, "Maccabean Histories in the Sistine Ceiling: A Note on Michelangelo's Use of the Malermi Bible," in Jacob, ed., *Italian Renaissance Studies*, p. 318, suggests that the coincident feast-days of St. Peter in Prison and the Maccabean Martyrs in the liturgical calendar, and the fact that relics of the martyrs were preserved in the crypt of S. Pietro in Vincoli, directly beneath Peter's chains, may have influenced the juxtaposition of the Heliodorus incident and St. Peter's miraculous delivery in the program of the Stanza d'Eliodoro. The divine chastisement of Heliodorus in answer to the high priest's prayers appears in another commission of Julius II: as one of the ten gold medallions in Michelangelo's Sistine Chapel ceiling. Another of the medallions also emphasizes the authority of the Jewish high priest. This scene, taken from an interpolation of I Maccabees, depicts an encounter between Alexander the Great and the high priest near Jerusalem. Upon their meeting, Alexander, as a sign of respect, descended from his horse, and knelt before the high priest, adoring the Name of God on his vestments and venerating the pontiff's person. For interpretation of these and the other gold medallions, see Wind, "Maccabean Histories," pp. 319–27, and Esther Gordon Dotson, "An Augustinian Interpretation of Michelangelo's Sistine Ceiling," *AB*, LXI (1979), pp. 421–24. The encounter of Alexander and the high priest is also one of the ceiling scenes of the Sala Paolina in Castel Sant'Angelo, which dates from the last years of Paul III's pontificate. The whole cycle of paintings in the room is devoted to the lives of Alexander the Great and of St. Paul (these allude to the pope's given name—Alessandro Farnese—and to his chosen name as pope), and the underlying theme is the divinely ordained mission to establish the universal temporal and spiritual sovereignty of the *respublica Christiana*. The meaning of the vault scene of Alexander kneeling before the high priest is thus the proper relation (from the papal point of view) between *imperium* and *sacerdotium*. The same idea appears in a contemporary medal struck for Paul III. The reverse shows Alexander kneeling before the high priest, with the Temple of Jerusalem in the background; the inscription states pointedly: OMNES REGES SERVIENT EI. The Sala Paolina and the medal are discussed by Richard Harprath, *Papst Paul III. als Alexander der Grosse: Das Freskenprogramm der Sala Paolina in der Engelsburg* [Beiträge zur Kunstgeschichte, 13] (Berlin and New York: de Gruyter, 1978), esp. pp. 27–29. For the meaning of the Sala Paolina cycle, see the important criticisms of Harprath's theses and the suggested alternatives made by Loren Partridge in his review, *AB*, LXII (1980), pp. 661–63. Note also Elisabeth Schröter, "Zur Inhaltsdeutung des Alexander-Programms der Sala Paolina in der Engelsburg," *Römische Quartalschrift*, LXXV (1980), pp. 76–99.

194. Mark J. Zucker, "Raphael and the Beard of Julius II," *AB*, LIX (1977), pp. 524–33; Partridge and Starn, *A Renaissance Likeness*, pp. 43–46, 124–25.

195. O'Malley, "Fulfillment of the Christian Golden Age," pp. 320–22. Traeger, "Raffaels Stanza d'Eliodoro," pp. 66–70, argues the case (for different reasons) of Giles's involvement in the artistic program of this room.

196. John W. O'Malley, S.J., "Man's dignity, God's Love, and the Destiny of Rome: A Text of Giles of Viterbo," *Viator*, III (1972), pp. 411–12, 415–16. Given Giles's remarks, it is noteworthy that a depiction of Jacob's dream of the ladder to heaven is depicted above the *Liberation of St. Peter* in the Stanza d'Eliodoro; in the painting the dreaming patriarch rests his head on a prominent stone.

197. See p. 92.

198. *Collectionis Bullarum*, II, pp. 348–51; relevant excerpts of this bull are provided by Frommel, "Die Peterskirche unter Papst Julius II," Appendix No. 382, pp. 126–27; for Julius II as Solomon, see also *id.*, " 'Capella Iulia': Die Grabkapelle Papst Julius II in Neu-St. Peter," *Zeitschrift für Kunstgeschichte*, XL (1977), pp. 30, 60–61.

199. Manetti, *Vita Nicolai V*, cols. 938–40 (in the text revised by Magnuson, *Roman Quattrocento Architecture*, pp. 360–62). Note the discussion of Onofri, "Sacralità," pp. 49–50, 56–70; Westfall, *In this Most Perfect Paradise*, pp. 124–25, 150–51, 172–73, 180–83; and *id.*, "Biblical Typology in the *Vita Nicolai V* by Giannozzo Manetti," in J. IJsewijn and E. Kessler, eds., *Acta Conventus Neo-Latini Lovaniensis: Proceedings of the First International Congress of Neo-Latin Studies, Louvain 23–28 August 1971* (Munich: Wilhelm Fink, 1973), pp. 701–09. Manetti's praise of Nicholas V's projects for the Vatican should be compared to his earlier (1436) *Oratio* in celebration of the Florentine *duomo* and its consecration by Eugenius IV. There he asserts that the magnificence of S. Maria del Fiore merits its ranking among the seven wonders of the world, and that, like the ancient Athenians, Florentines can glory in the admirable elegance of their temple. No mention is made, however, of Solomon or the Temple in Jerusalem. For the text of Manetti's *Oratio* and a brief discussion of its themes, see Eugenio Battisti, "Il mondo visuale della fiabe," in Enrico Castelli, ed., *Umanesimo e esoterismo: Atti del V Convegno internazionale di studi umanistici, Oberhofen, 16–17 settembre 1960* (Padua: Dott. Antonio Milani, 1960), pp. 308–20.

200. Otto von Simson, *The Gothic Cathedral: Origins of Gothic Architecture and the Medieval Concept of Order* (Princeton: Princeton U. Pr., 1962), pp. 11, 37–38, 95–96, 196; note also Carol Herselle Krinsky, "Representations of the Temple of Jerusalem before 1500," *JWCI*, XXXIII (1971), pp. 1–19.

201. Turpin C. Bannister, "The Constantinian Basilica of Saint Peter at Rome," *JSAH*, XXVII (1968), pp. 3–32.

202. Shearman, *Raphael's Cartoons*, p. 80, n. 202 (citing *Itinerarium*, p. 82). For other Renaissance references to the spiral columns, see Capgrave, *Solace of Pilgrimes*, pp. 61–66 and Giovanni Rucellai (in Valentini and Zucchetti, *Codice topografico*, IV, p. 402).

203. Ward Perkins, "The Shrine of St. Peter and its Twelve Spiral Columns," pp. 21–33; for Renaissance references to the healing powers of the "Colonna Santa," see Shearman, *Raphael's Cartoons*, pp. 56–57.

204. Eugenio Battisti, *Rinascimento e Barocco* (Florence: Einaudi, 1960), pp. 87–95.

205. Shearman, *Raphael's Cartoons*, pp. 7–8.

206. BAV, ms. Vat. lat. 182, fols. 128ᵛ-129ᵛ; note Ettlinger, *Sistine Chapel*, pp. 79–80.

207. Vat. lat. 182, fols. 1ʳ-5ᵛ. Tifernate's thematic emphasis on the candelabrum is highlighted by the miniature of it on fol. 1ʳ. The Umbrian humanist's claim to have "discovered" the relief on the Arch of Titus (fol. 5ᵛ) seems unsubstantiated, however. Platina, in his *Liber de vita Christi ac omnium pontificum* (completed by 1474), describes Titus's conquest of Jerusalem and subsequent triumph in Rome; he goes on to say (p. 15): "*Extant adhuc in via Nova huius triumphi monimenta: apparent insculpta candelabra, apparent tabulae veteris legis e templo ablatae et in triumphum ductae.* Moreover, the "Arch of the Seven-Armed Candlestick" appears as a reference point in a medieval deed describing a cottage located near S. Maria Nova: see Krautheimer, *Rome*, p. 290. For patristic typological treatment of various sacred objects in the Temple (notably Clement of Alexandria, *Stromata*, V, 6) and the influence of Philo's discussion of these matters, see Jean Danielou, S.J., "Aux sources de l'esoterisme Judeo-chretien," in Enrico Castelli, ed., *Umanesimo e esoterismo: Atti del V Convegno internazionale di studi umanistici, Oberhofen, 16–17 settembre 1960* (Padua: Dott. Antonio Milani, 1960), pp. 39–46.

208. Battisti, *Rinascimento e barocco*, pp. 88–89 (citing Aurelio Brandolini and Robert Flemmyng). The same theme of splendor appears, too, in Maffeo Vegio's observation that emulation of Solomon's Temple inspired Pope Honorius to have the doors to St. Peter's basilica plated with silver and the middle door (the Porta Argentea) decorated with silver reliefs: *De rebus antiquis*, p. 84. The general Roman Renaissance aesthetic of splendor was given definition by the Augustinian Ambrogio Massari (1432–85), a prominent court preacher during the 1460s and '70s, who became prior general of the Augustinian Order during Sixtus IV's lifetime, and who resided at the Augustinian church of S. Maria del Popolo during its reconstruction. In his life of St. Augustine, published in Rome in 1481, Massari argues that beauty conduces to the acquisition of virtue, and that beauty consists of *pulchritudo, decor, dulcedo, odor, splendor (in quo lux illa ineffabilis suam recognovit similitudinem)*, and *candidulus ornatus: quo nos ille est candor lucis aeternae, speculum sine macula Dei maiestatis*. For this passage, see Battisti, *Rinascimento e barocco*, p. 85, and Bentivoglio and Valtieri, *Santa Maria del Popolo a Roma*, p. 18, n. 4. For Massari's career, note O'Malley, *Praise and Blame*, pp. 101–04.

209. O'Malley, "Fulfillment of the Christian Golden Age," pp. 308–09.

210. *Ibid.*, pp. 322–23; Giles extends these ideas in his later *Historia XX saeculorum*: for the text of relevant passages, see Frommel, "Die Peterskirche," Appendix 8, pp. 89–90; for discussion see O'Malley, *Giles of Viterbo*, pp. 125, 136, and *id.*, "Giles of Viterbo: A Reformer's Thought on Renaissance Rome," pp. 10–11. Note also Traeger, "Raffaels Stanza d'Eliodoro," pp. 57–59.

211. The passage is cited in Lee, *Sixtus IV*, p. 143, n. 86. A number of Roman churches retain inscriptions attesting to Sixtus's rebuilding activity; one of these is S. Vitale, the entrance portal of which is inscribed "SIXTVS IIII PON. MAX. A FVNDAMENTIS RESTAVRAVIT ANNO IVBILEI MCCCCLXXV." See Urban, "Die Kirchenbaukunst," p. 214.

212. Urban, p. 75; for a list of repairs, restorations, and rebuilding efforts regarding the Roman churches in the period 1418–1500, see *ibid.*, pp. 263–81. For sixteenth-century church construction, see Portoghesi, *Roma del Rinascimento*, pp. 409–94 passim.

213. McManamon, "The Ideal Renaissance Pope," p. 50. Similarly, Raffaele Brandolini, directing his remarks specifically to Pope Leo X in part of his *Oratio ad Lateranensem Concilium* (BAV, ms. Ottob. lat. 813, fols. 56ᵛ-57ᵛ), calls upon the pontiff to reform first Rome. He then lists the measures required: "*Huius mores, instituta, ritus disciplinasque ad verterem integritatem, ad pristinam severitatem, ad pietatem, ad innocentiam revocatae. Amplissimos hanc (ut caepistis) aedificiis decorate.* For the oration, note O'Malley, *Praise and Blame*, pp. 171–72.

214. Jedin, "Sánchez de Arévalo und die Konzilsfrage unter Paul II," p. 111.

215. D'Amico, *Renaissance Humanism in Papal Rome*, p. 222.

216. McNally, "Pope Adrian VI (1522–23) and Church Reform," p. 272.

217. O'Malley, "Giles of Viterbo: A Reformer's Thought on Renaissance Rome," p. 5; *id.*, *Giles of Viterbo*, pp. 137–38.

218. Bentivoglio and Valtieri, *Santa Maria del Popolo*, pp. 15–22, argue for the Lombard elements present in its Quattrocento reconstruction. The most complete analysis of fifteenth-century Roman ecclesiastical architecture and its sources is Urban, "Die Kirchenbaukunst;" note esp. his conclusion, pp. 232–44.

219. Urban, pp. 125–54.

220. Krautheimer, "S. Pietro in Vincoli," pp. 364–66. James Ackerman in remarks to the conference "Rome in the Renaissance: The City and the Myth," Center for Medieval and Early Renaissance Studies, State Unversity of New York at Binghamton, 18–20 October 1979, also emphasized the paleo-Christian inspiration for Sixtus IV's church reconstruction projects.

221. For the patristic studies of the Italian humanists, see in general Trinkaus, *In Our Image and Likeness*, and Stinger, *Humanism and the Church Fathers*. Note also August Buck, "Der Rückgriff des Renaissance-Humanismus auf die Patristik," in Kurt Baldinger, ed., *Festschrift Walther von Wartburg zum 80. Geburtstag* (Tübingen: Niemeyer, 1968), Vol. I, pp. 153–75, and Riccardo Fubini, "Intendimenti umanistici e riferimenti patristici dal Petrarca al Valla," *Giornale storico della letteratura italiana*, CLI (1974), pp. 520–78. One indication of Roman Renaissance regard for Augustine is the panegyrics delivered in his honor, including two by Ambrogio Massari: see O'Malley, *Praise and Blame*, pp. 14, 102–03; for the frequent citation of Augustine and Jerome in the sermons delivered before the papal court *inter*

missarum solemnia, see *ibid.*, p. 56. For Jerome in the Renaissance, see Eugene F. Rice's forthcoming book (Johns Hopkins U. Pr.).

222. Stinger, *Humanism and the Church Fathers*, pp. 84, 124–66, 198–202. For the Italian humanists' study of the Greek Fathers, note also Deno J. Geanakoplos, *Interaction of the "Sibling" Byzantine and Western Cultures in the Middle Ages and Italian Renaissance (330–1600)* (New Haven: Yale U. Pr., 1976), pp. 265–80.

223. Stinger, *Humanism and the Church Fathers*, pp. 203–23; Camporeale, *Lorenzo Valla*, pp. 235–76, has shown how attentive Valla was to the Greek prelates' discussions of the nature of the Trinity, presented in their speeches to the Council of Florence, and how this encounter with Greek patristic thought proved a decisive step in the Roman humanist's commitment to restructure theology according to *graeca veritas*, and on the basis of philology and rhetoric instead of dialectics.

224. Stinger, *Humanism and the Church Fathers*, pp. 115, 120–22, 143–44, 147, 159–61; George of Trebizond, in the dedication to Nicholas V of his translation of Cyril's *In Ioannem*, remarks on the pope's role in inspiring Traversari's Dionysius translation: BAV, ms. Vat. lat. 525, fols. 2^r-v (for this, note also Monfasani, *George of Trebizond*, p. 60). For a more detailed consideration of the Roman humanist study of the Greek Fathers, see Stinger, "Greek Patristics and Christian Antiquity in Renaissance Rome," in Ramsey, ed., *Rome in the Renaissance*, pp. 153–69.

225. The text of the poem and discussion of the circumstances of its composition appear in Mercati, *Scritti d'Isidoro il Cardinale Ruteno*, pp. 128–32. The inventory of the papal library holdings taken after Nicholas V's death shows forty mss. of Chrysostom, nineteen of Basil, sixteen of Gregory Nazianzen, and a large number of other Greek Fathers: Eugene Müntz and Paul Fabre, *La Bibliothèque du Vatican au XVe siècle* [BEFAR, Vol. 48] (Paris: Thorin, 1887), pp. 34–114, 314–44.

226. Giovanni Mercati, *Per la cronologia della vita e degli scritti di Niccolò Perotti Arcivescovo di Siponto* [Studi e Testi, 44] Rome, 1925, pp. 34–43; Revilo Pendleton Oliver, *Niccolò Perotti's Version of the Enchiridion of Epictetus* (Urbana: U. of Illinois Pr., 1954), pp. 1–34, 139. For Perotti's career in Rome, note also Lee, *Sixtus IV and Men of Letters*, pp. 87–91.

227. Monfasani, *George of Trebizond*, pp. 47–49, 57, 71–79. For Traversari's interest in Basil's *Adversus Eunomium* and Chrysostom's *Homilies on Matthew*, see Stinger, *Humanism and the Church Fathers*, pp. 154–56, 214–18. After his abrupt departure from the papal Curia, Trebizond gained a place at the court of King Alfonso of Naples, and for him he translated Cyril's *Thesaurus*: Monfasani, p. 118. BAV, ms. Vat. lat. 529 contains a Latin translation of Cyril's commentary on Genesis; no date is indicated in the ms., and the translator identifies himself only as Joseph (fol. 1^r), but the translation was probably done for Nicholas V since Vespasiano (ed. Greco, p. 69) includes this work as among those commissioned by Nicholas V, and Platina's index of the Vatican holdings made in 1475 lists a Latin version of the work (Müntz and Fabre, p. 187).

228. The Vatican ms. of the translations is BAV, ms. Vat. lat. 390, fols. 249^r-264^v; for Cosma, see Anselmo M. Albareda, O.S.B., "Il bibliotecario di Callisto III," *Miscellanea Giovanni Mercati*, vol. IV [Studi e Testi, 124] (Vatican, 1946), pp. 178–208. Griffolini should not be confused with another "Francesco d'Arezzo," Francesco Accolti (1416–88), who was also a humanist Greek scholar: for Accolti, see Michele Messina, "Francesco Accolti di Arezzo," *Rinascimento*, I (1950), pp. 293–321; for Griffolini, see Mancini, *Francesco Griffolini*.

229. For these translations, see Mancini, pp. 23–34, and Mercati, *Scritti d'Isidoro*, p. 129. Jouffroy possessed a number of volumes of Latin translations of Chrysostom's works, including those made by Traversari, George of Trebizond, and Pietro Balbo, as well as Griffolini: see Giovanni Card. Mercati, "Una lettera di Vespasiano da Bisticci a Jean Jouffroi e la biblioteca romana del Jouffroi," in *Mélanges dédiés à la mémoire de Félix Grat* (Paris, 1946), Vol. I, pp. 357–66. For Jouffroy's career, see the discussion and references cited in Monfasani, p. 171; Miglio, *Storiografia pontificia*, pp. 135–47; O'Malley, *Praise and Blame*, pp. 7, 87, 202–03; and McManamon, "Ideal Renaissance Pope," pp. 12, 33–54 *passim*.

230. A. Pratesi, "Balbo, Pietro," *DBI*, V (1963), pp. 378–79; Sister Agnes Clare Way, "Gregorius Nazianzenus," in Paul Oskar Kristeller and F. Edward Cranz, eds., *Catalogus translationum et commentariorum: Medieval and Renaissance Latin Translations and Commentaries*, Vol. II (Washington, D.C., 1971), pp. 138–40. For Balbo's translation of Proclus's *Platonic Theology* for Cusanus, see Stinger, *Humanism and the Church Fathers*, pp. 43–44. Balbo's Latin version of Chrysostom's homily *De patientia et longanimitate* is in BAV, ms. Vat. lat. 3660, fol. 1^r ff.

231. Nogara, *Scritti inediti*, pp. xxx-xxxiii.
232. BAV, ms. Vat. lat. 261, fols. I^r-II^r. Lonigo also translated a short Chrysostom work, *De virtute et vitio*, which he dedicated to Isotta Nogarola and her sister: BAV, ms. Vat. lat. 409, fols. 60^v-64^v.
233. BAV, ms. Vat. lat. 256. For Chalcheophilos, see Zippel, ed., *Vite di Paolo II*, p. 59, n. 4, and Andrews, "'Lost' Fifth Book of the Life of Paul II," p. 45.
234. Birago's Basil translation is in BAV, ms. Vat. lat. 302, fols. 1^r ff. For the *Strategicon*, see pp. 121–22.
235. BAV, ms. Vat. lat. 301, fols. 1^r ff. That Basil's *Homilies on the Hexaemeron* should have received two successive humanistic Latin translations is particularly noteworthy inasmuch as there already existed the late classical Latin translation of the work made by Eustathius: see Stinger, *Humanism and the Church Fathers*, p. 8. For Argyropoulos's translations from the Greek, see Giuseppe Cammelli, *I dotti bizantini e le origine dell'Umanesimo*, Vol. II *Giovanni Argiropulo* (Florence, 1941), pp. 183–84.
236. Note p. 122.
237. Persona's Chrysostom translations are in BAV, ms. Vat. lat. 408, and his "Athanasius" in BAV, ms. Vat. lat. 263, the title page of which contains a splendid miniature of Persona presenting his translation to the pope: see Alfonso M. Stickler, *Quinto Centenario della Biblioteca Apostolica Vaticana, 1475–1975, Catalogo della mostra* (BAV, 1975), p. 24 and plate VIII. For Erasmus's identification of the Greek author of the Pauline commentary as Theophylact, see P.S. Allen, *Opus epistolarum Des. Erasmi Roterodami* (Oxford: 1906–58), Vol. III, p. 339; Vol. VI, pp. 467–70. The published edition of Persona's translation of Origen's *Contra Celsum* (Rome: Georgius Herolt, 1481) is prefaced by a letter of Theodore Gaza in which he praises Persona's previous translations from the Greek, explains his own earlier involvement with the Origen work, and encourages Persona's undertaking, declaring that the Greek ms. of it was preserved intact in the Vatican Library precisely for someone of Persona's scholarly skills. Gaza's prefatory letter appears also in Apostolo Zeno, *Dissertazioni Vossiane* (Venice, 1753), Vol. II, pp. 139–40. Mercati, *Opere minori*, IV, pp. 89–93, 174, has shown that the Greek ms. Persona used as the source for his translation is the present BAV, ms. Vat. gr. 387. That Persona began the translation in 1477 is indicated by the record of the loan made to him of the Origen codex in January of that year; he returned it five months later: Bertola, *I due primi registri*, p. 8. For Persona's Greek patristic scholarship, note also Paschini, "Un ellenista romano," pp. 45–56. For Renaissance study of Origen, see Stinger, *Humanism and the Church Fathers*, pp. 83–100 *passim*, 151–52; Edgar Wind, "The Revival of Origen," in Dorothy Miner, ed., *Studies in Art and Literature for Belle da Costa Greene* (Princeton: Princeton U. Pr., 1954), pp. 412–24; and esp. Max Schär, *Das Nachleben des Origenes im Zeitalter des Humanismus* [Basler Beiträge zur Geschichtswissenschaft, 140] (Basel and Stuttgart: Helbing & Lichtenhahn, 1979), (pp. 112–26 for Persona).
238. D'Amico, *Renaissance Humanism in Papal Rome*, pp. 189–208.
239. Rice, "Zanobio Acciaiuoli," paper to "Rome in the Renaissance" Conference (cited above, Chap. II, n. 254).
240. Note, for example, Marcello's oration to Leo X, cited on p. 85.
241. Castellesi was an exception: what has Aristotle to do with Paul, he asks in his *De vera philosophia*, or Plato with Peter? See D'Amico, *Renaissance Humanism in Papal Rome*, pp. 169–88.
242. Camporeale, *Lorenzo Valla*, esp. pp. 211–33, 344–45; Trinkaus, *In Our Image and Likeness*, pp. 103–70, 571–78.
243. The Poggio-Valla has been exhaustively explored by Camporeale, *Valla*; note esp. his concluding comments, pp. 401–02.
244. Birago, in translating Basil's *Homilies on the Hexaemeron*, did encounter the troubling problem of the differing Greek and Latin wording of the text of Genesis 1–2, and he devotes much of his prefatory letter to Paul II to a justification of his departures from Jerome's Vulgate; these alterations were required, he states, lest Basil's discussion seem "ridiculous": see BAV, ms. Vat. lat. 302, fols. 1^r-5^r. For Manetti's similar caution and defensiveness in suggesting revisions to Jerome's Latin text of the Bible, see Trinkaus, *In Our Image*, pp. 595–601. Only Valla pressed home the point that varying textual readings of Scripture entailed doctrinal implications.
245. Eugene F. Rice, Jr., ed., *The Prefatory Epistles of Jacques Lefèvre d'Étaples and Related Texts* (N.Y.: Columbia U. Pr., 1972), pp. 182, 283–84, 333–34, 412, 419.
246. Allen, *Opus epistolarum Des. Erasmi*, IX, p. 5.

V. The *Renovatio Imperii* and the *Renovatio Romae*

1. Pastor, *History of the Popes*, VI, p. 279.
2. A detailed account of Julius's triumphs in Bologna and Rome appears in Paris de Grassis's diaries, the relevant portions of which were published by Luigi Frati, *Le due spedizioni militari di Giulio II tratte dal Diario di Paride Grassi Bolognese* [Documenti e studi pubblicati per cura della R. deputazione di storia patria per le provincie di Romagna, I] (Bologna: Regia Tip., 1886). For other sources and studies, see Mitchell, *Italian Civic Pageantry*, pp. 15–17. Adriano Castellesi's Latin poem, *Iter Julii II*, celebrates the pontiff's triumphal journey to the conquest of Bologna, concluding with an account of Julius's ceremonial entrance into the conquered city: note Jacob Burckhardt, *The Civilization of the Renaissance in Italy* (N.Y.: Harper & Row, 1958), p. 136. For the coins tossed to the Bolognese, see Frati, "Delle monete gettate," pp. 474–87, and Weiss, "Medals of Julius II," p. 179. For the conquest, note also Cecilia M. Ady, *The Bentivoglio of Bologna: A Study in Despotism* (London: Oxford U. Pr., 1969; first publ. 1937), pp. 130–33, 198. For Perugia, see C. F. Black, "The Baglioni as Tyrants of Perugia, 1488–1540," *English Historical Review*, LXXXV (1970), pp. 245–81.
3. *"Summus Pontifex Iulius belligeratur, vincit, triumphat, planeque Iulium agit."* Desiderius Erasmus Roterodami, *Opera omnia*, Ordinis primi, Tomus primus (Amsterdam: North-Holland Publishing, 1969), p. 573; cf. Allen, *Opus epistolarum*, I, pp. 434–35.
4. Albertini's remark appears in the chapter *"De nonnullis triumphantibus"* in his *Opusculum de mirabilibus novae et veteris Urbis Romae*, the 1510 guidebook to Rome dedicated to Julius II: see Bruschi, *Bramante architetto*, pp. 638–39.
5. For the manifold symbolism of Julius's 1507 triumph, note esp. Partridge and Starn, *A Renaissance Likeness*, pp. 57–58, 63, 143. Chastel, *Art et humanisme*, pp. 456–57, sees Julius II as cultivating a "triumphal" style." For other sources and further bibliography, see Mitchell, *Italian Civic Pageantry*, pp. 114–15; and Schröter, "Der Vatikan als Hügel Apollons," pp. 229–30.
6. Weiss, "Medals of Julius II," p. 180.
7. The acclamation, recorded by all the Evangelists (Matthew 21:9, Mark 11:9, Luke 19:38, and John 12:3), has as its source Psalm 118, an ancient Hebraic hymn of thanksgiving for military victory, in which the king, rejoicing in Yahweh's wondrous power, enters through the gates of Jerusalem in triumphal procession and passes exultingly into the Temple: note Mitchell Dahood, S.J., *Psalms III, 101–150* [Anchor Bible, 17A] (Garden City, N.Y.: Doubleday, 1970), pp. 154–60. For the *"Benedictus,"* see Joseph A. Jungmann, S.J., *The Mass of the Roman Rite: Its Origins and Development* (N.Y.: Benziger Bros., 1951), II, pp. 136–38. The *Benedictus* acclamation also has important precedents in the Hellenistic and Roman *Adventus* rites welcoming monarchs. These often had messianic implications and were closely associated with the imperial theology of triumph and victory. For this, and for the fusion of classical and Christian elements in medieval royal and ecclesiastical entrance ceremonials, see Ernst H. Kantorowicz, "The 'King's Advent' and the Enigmatic Panels in the Doors of Santa Sabina," *AB*, XXVI (1944), pp. 207–31. For the *Adventus* in late antiquity and its politico-cultural significance for Constantine and the early Byzantine emperors, see Sabine G. MacCormack, *Art and Ceremony in Late Antiquity* (Berkeley and Los Angeles: U. of California Pr., 1981), pp. 15–89.
8. See p. 109. For other references of Nagonius and of other contemporaries to the pope as a second Julius Caesar, see Schröter, "Der Vatikan als Hügel Apollons," pp. 225–33. Raffaele Maffei, on the other hand, likened Julius II to Tiberius, on the grounds of their similar cruelties and excesses: D'Amico, "Papal History and Curial Reform," pp. 174, 197. Note also Partridge and Starn, pp. 52–53, 137–40.
9. Mansi, *Collectio*, XXXII, cols. 755–62. Note also the oration that Massimo Corvino (d. 1522) delivered in S. Maria del Popolo on 5 October 1511 to celebrate the promulgation of the Holy League of the Papacy, Spain, and Venice. Corvino repeatedly refers to "this sacrosanct Apostolic *Imperium*," and likens the virtuous purpose of the Holy League in defending it to the valor of the ancient Greek city-states, led by Sparta, in confronting the Persian challenge: *Oratio Maximi Corvini Partenopei episcopi Eserniensis sanctissimo Iulio II Pontifici Maximo dicta* (Rome: ?, 1513), fols. 2ʳ-3ᵛ. For Corvino, note Minnich, "Concepts of Reform," pp. 205–06. Marcello's remarks reveal similarities to the "mirror-for-princes" literature that came increasingly to the fore in the late fifteenth and early sixteenth

centuries in Italy as princely government triumphed on the peninsula. Among the most elaborate and influential of these humanist tracts was Francesco Patrizi's *De regno et regis institutione*, dedicated to Sixtus IV in the 1470s. For the development in general, see Quentin Skinner, *The Foundations of Modern Political Thought*, Vol. I: *The Renaissance* (Cambridge: Cambridge U. Pr., 1978), pp. 113–28.

10. Guicciardini, *Storia d'Italia*, pp. 897–901. Dispatches from the battle at Mirandola are recorded in the Venetian Sanudo's diaries: for a revealing selection of texts, showing Julius's coarseness in the heat of battle, see Frederick Hartt, *"Lignum vitae in medio paradisi*: The Stanza d'Eliodoro and the Sistine Ceiling," *AB*, XXXII (1950), p. 118, n. 14.

11. Pastor, VI, p. 509; von Einem, *Michelangelo*, p. 48.

12. One of the triumphal arches for Julius's 1507 Palm Sunday Triumph in Rome carried this inscription:

> *Virtuti et Gloriae Sancti Pontificis*
> *auctoris pacis libertatisque: Veni, vidi, vici.*

See Schröter, "Der Vatikan als Hügel Apollons," pp. 229–30.

13. *Storia d'Italia*, p. 870.

14. *The 'Julius Exclusus' of Erasmus*, trans. Paul Pascal, intro. and critical notes by J. Kelly Sowards (Bloomington and London: Indiana U. Pr., 1968). For recent scholarship on Erasmus's work, see James K. McConica, "Erasmus and the *Julius Exclusus*: A Humanist Reflects on the Church," in Charles Trinkaus and Heiko A. Oberman, eds., *The Pursuit of Holiness in Late Medieval and Renaissance Religion: Papers from the University of Michigan Conference* [Studies in Medieval and Reformation Thought, X] (Leiden: Brill, 1974), pp. 444–71; and Marcia L. Colish, "Seneca's *Apocolocyntosis* as a Possible Source for Erasmus' *Julius Exclusus*," *RQ*, XXIX (1976), pp. 361–68. Note also Gilbert, *The Pope, his Banker, and Venice*, pp. 111–17.

15. George L. Hersey, *Alfonso II and the Artistic Renewal of Naples 1485–1495* (New Haven: Yale U. Pr., 1969). esp. pp. 2–4, 11, 50–57, 58–81.

16. A useful introduction to this whole subject is Roy Strong, *Splendor at Court: Renaissance Spectacle and the Theater of Power* (Boston: Houghton Mifflin, 1973), pp. 19–76; for detailed studies, see Josephe Chartrou, *Les entrées solennelles et triomphales à la Renaissance (1448–1551)* (Paris: P.U.F., 1928), and Jacquot, ed., *Les fêtes de la Renaissance*. Note also Martindale, *Triumphs of Caesar by Mantegna*, esp. pp. 47–55.

17. Denis, *Charles VIII et les Italiens*, pp. 50–51. Robert W. Scheller, "Imperial Themes in Art and Literature of the Early French Renaissance: the Period of Charles VIII," *Simiolus: Netherlands Quarterly for the History of Art*, XII (1981–82), pp. 5–69, points to the evocation of Christ-like and imperial images in the eulogies addressed to Charles VIII during his 1494–95 Italian campaign.

18. Frances A. Yates, *Astraea: The Imperial Theme in the Sixteenth Century* (London: Routledge & Kegan Paul), pp. 20–28.

19. See pp. 58–59.

20. Note Walter H. Rubsamen, "The Music for 'Quant'e bella giovinezza' and Other Carnival Songs by Lorenzo de' Medici," in Charles S. Singleton, ed., *Art, Science, and History in the Italian Renaissance* (Baltimore: Johns Hopkins U. Pr., 1967), pp. 163–84; and Trexler, *Public Life in Renaissance Florence*, pp. 414–17. In the Festa di S. Giovanni of 1491, Lorenzo de' Medici recreated the triumph of the Roman consul Aemilius Paullus: *ibid.*, pp. 450–51.

21. Canensi, *De vita et pontificatu Pauli II P.M.*, ed. Zippel, pp. 135–37.

22. Sarah Bradford, *Cesare Borgia: His Life and Times* (London: Weidenfeld and Nicolson, 1976), pp. 114–16.

23. Biondo, *Opera omnia*, pp. 215–16; note also Vegio's and Biondo's comments on the archeology of the Vatican region, discussed on pp. 179–84. For further discussion of the Roman humanists' treatment of the triumphal theme, see Charles L. Stinger, "*Roma triumphans*: Triumphs in the Thought and Ceremonies of Renaissance Rome," *MH*, n.s. X (1981), pp. 189–201.

24. *Funebris oratio in obitu Pomponii Laeti* (Rome: E. Silber, 1497), fols. 1ᵛ, 4ᵛ. For Marsi, see O'Malley, *Praise and Blame*, pp. 104–05.

25. O'Malley, "Man's Dignity, God's Love, and the Destiny of Rome," pp. 411–16. For a similar treatment of the Cross, note the oration of the Hospitaler Johannes Baptista de Gargiis to the eighth session of the Fifth Lateran Council (19 Dec. 1513): "*Victorem Christum*

regem sequamur, qui nos vult victoriae suae habere participes. Crux illius nostra est victoria, cujus patibulum noster est triumphus. Terra non nobis patria est, sed caelum nos cives et incolas expectat." Mansi, *Collectio,* XXXII, col. 853.

26. *Oratio in die omnium sanctorum* (Rome: M. Silber?, after 1 Nov. 1511), fols. 5ʳ-6ᵛ. For the oration, see O'Malley, *Praise and Blame,* p. 66.

27. Mario A. Di Cesare, *Vida's 'Christiad' and Vergilian Epic* (N.Y.: Columbia U. Pr., 1964), pp. 202–79. The most recent edition of the text is Marco Girolamo Vida, *The Christiad: A Latin-English Edition,* ed. and trans. Gertrude C. Drake and Clarence A. Forbes (Carbondale-Edwardsville: Southern Illinois U. Pr., 1978).

28. Ullmann, *Growth of Papal Goverment,* pp. 276, 310.

29. Biondo, *Opera omnia,* p. 271. Chrysoloras's *Laudatio* may have suggested panegyric themes to Biondo and later Roman humanists: see pp. 73–74.

30. Biondo, *Opera omnia,* p. 216.

31. Nogara, *Scritti inediti,* pp. clxxiii-clxxiv.

32. BAV, ms. Ottob. lat. 83ʳ-87ᵛ. Note O'Malley, *Praise and Blame,* pp. 208–10. As part of his *De laudibus Sixti IIII,* Aurelio Brandolini included a section comparing his own age with the ancient Roman past; he concludes, like Domenichi, that the spiritual empire of the pope surpasses that of the Roman Empire: the relevant text appears in De Luca, "Un umanista fiorentino," p. 78.

33. O'Malley, "Discovery of America," pp. 190–92; D'Amico, *Renaissance Humanism in Papal Rome,* pp. 132, 134–37, 207–08. For Inghirami's funeral oration for Julius II, see McManamon, "Ideal Renaissance Pope," pp. 30–32, 42. Note also the same ideas in Raffaele Brandolini, *Dialogus Leo nuncupatus,* pp. 69, 89, 95, etc.

34. O'Malley, "Fulfillment of the Christian Golden Age," p. 269; *id., Giles of Viterbo,* p. 127.

35. O'Malley, "Man's Dignity," pp. 411–16.

36. Weiss, *Medals of Sixtus IV,* p. 19.

37. Marcello, *Oratio ad Leonem X Pont. Max.,* BAV, ms. Vat. lat. 3646, fol. 27ʳ; Raffaele Brandolini, *Dialogus Leo nuncupatus,* p. 124; note other references in Shearman, *Raphael's Cartoons,* p. 15, and D'Amico, "Papal History," pp. 176–77.

38. Herbert Siebenhüner, *Das Kapitol in Rom: Idee und Gestalt* (Munich: Kösel, 1954), p. 73; Tilmann Buddensieg, "Zum Statuenprogramm in Kapitolsplan Pauls III," *Zeitschrift für Kunstgeschichte,* XXXII (1969), pp. 182–86.

39. Note esp. Marcello, *Oratio ad Leonem X Pont. Max.,* BAV, ms. Vat. 3646, fol. 17ᵛ: *"Te tanquam ad alterum Apollinem confluebant omnes.... Tot artibus insignitus, tot virtutibus ornatus, tanta sapientia preditus nunquam alias visus alter a deo datus in terris Mercurius videbaris."* For use of this theme in Leo's *possesso,* see pp. 56–57 herein. Praise of the popes as Apollo is a panegyric theme which can be traced back to Nicholas V's pontificate, as Schröter, "Der Vatikan als Hügel Apollons," has shown. One interesting work (not discussed by Schröter) is an oration of the Florentine humanist and poet Naldo de' Naldi (1436—after 1513), who compares Sixtus IV to the Greek Sun-God: all Rome had turned, "just as to another Apollo," to the pontiff whose philosophic wisdom illuminates the nature of all things; moreover, if Orpheus with his theology based on false gods had such power that he could soften the hardest oaks and have them follow him, so much the more *(quanto magis)* does Sixtus, with true divine wisdom, in the same way move oaks, stones, and all things. The text of Naldi's *Oratio ad Sixtum IIII Pont. Max.* (which, however, seems not to have actually been delivered) appears in Cortese, "Sisto Quarto Papa Antoniano," pp. 255–60. Naldi had earlier compared Nicholas V to Phoebus Apollo: Schröter, p. 211.

40. Shearman, *Raphael's Cartoons,* p. 15.

41. Platina, *Liber de vita Christi ac omnium pontificum,* p. 6, completes his laudatory sketch of Augustus's career by paraphrasing Suetonius: *"Urbem Romam ita exornavit, ut gloriatus sit se urbem lateritiam invenisse marmoream relinquere."*

42. Francesco Griffolini, in dedicating his Latin translation of Chrysostom's *Homilies on John* to Cosimo de' Medici (1462), praised the achievements of a number of contemporary Italian statesmen, including Nicholas V: *"Quid ad clarissimum Principem Nicolao V defuit? Cuius tempora etsi brevissima, quantulocumque tamen, in hac nostra inferiore Italia, Augusti paci contulerim, cuius ductu, et auspicio, ut urbs Roma, itaque Romana lingua renovata est; quem nisi invida tam repente mors e medio sustulisset, non minus quam Augustus, urbem e lateritia marmoream reliquisse gloriari potuisset."* For the text, see Angelo Maria Bandini, *Catalogus Codicum Latino-*

rum Bibliothecae Mediceae Laurentianae (Florence, 1774–77), Vol IV, col. 443 (from ms. Plut. XIV, dext. 2). For this same theme used in praise of Sixtus IV, see Lee, *Sixtus IV and Men of Letters*, pp. 123–24. Albertini, *Opusculum de mirabilibus novae et veteris urbis Romae* (in Valentini and Zucchetti, *Codice topografico*, IV, p. 497), argues that just as Julius II was another Caesar in enlarging the Empire, so he was like Augustus in adorning the city of Rome.

43. *Liber de vita Christi*, p. 15.

44. *Ibid.*, p. 21.

45. *Ibid.*, p. 22; in Paul III's Sala Paolina in Castel Sant'Angelo, Hadrian is portrayed as a symbol of the temporal authority of the Church, just as St. Michael the Archangel is shown opposite as the image of its spiritual dominion: Harprath, *Papst Paul III als Alexander der Grosse*, pp. 58–59, and Partridge, review of same, *AB*, LXII (1980), p. 663.

46. Pacifici, *Un carme biografico*, pp. 31–32.

47. *Liber de vita Christi*, p. 13. On the other hand, Stefano Infessura, a Roman municipal official whose allegiance to republican traditions placed him at odds with papal autocracy, charged Sixtus IV with being a second Nero: "*Gaude, prisce Nero, superat te crimine Xystus/hic scelus omne simul clauditur et vitium.*" Cited by Massimo Miglio, "Il leone e la lupa: Dal simbolo al pasticcio alla francese," *Studi romani*, XXX (1982), p. 184.

48. Partridge and Starn, *A Renaissance Likeness*, pp. 53, 138–39.

49. Lee, *Sixtus IV*, p. 106, n. 95.

50. Ferdinand Gregorovius, *History of the City of Rome in the Middle Ages*, trans. from the 4th Ger. ed. by Annie Hamilton, Vol. VII, Pt. II (London: George Bell & Sons, 1909), p. 643.

51. Gherardi, *Diario romano*, p. 130.

52. Hartt, *Giulio Romano*, pp. 42–52; Weil, *Ponte S. Angelo*, p. 90. For the depiction of the Donation and use of other Constantinian imagery in the Roman art of the early sixteenth century, see Traeger, "Raffaels Stanza d'Eliodoro," pp. 46–49. André Chastel includes a brief discussion of the thematic content of the Sala di Costantino in his *The Sack of Rome*, pp. 50–67. The most complete account is Rolf Quednau, *Die Sala di Costantino im Vatikanischen Palast: zur Dekoration der beiden Medici-Päpste Leo X. und Clemens VII.* [Studien zur Kunstgeschichte, 13] (Hildesheim: Georg Olms, 1979).

53. Ullmann, *Growth of Papal Government*, pp. 74–86.

54. Domenico Maffei, *La Donazione di Costantino nei giuristi medievali* (Milan: Giuffrè, 1964), pp. 27–29.

55. *Inferno*, Canto XIX, LL. 115–17, *Paradiso*, Canto XX, LL. 55–60; note also *Purgatorio*, Canto XXXII, LL. 124–29, and Davis, *Dante and the Idea of Rome*, pp. 177–87. In his earlier *De monarchia*, III, 10, Dante argued it was not legally possible for Constantine to alienate, nor for the Church to accept, imperial authority; the Donation was therefore invalid: Dante Alighieri, *Monarchia*, ed. Pier Giorgio Ricci [*Le opere* di Dante Alighieri, Edizione Nazionale a cura della Società Dantesca Italiana, V] (Verona: Arnaldo Mondadori, 1965), pp. 256–61.

56. Louis B. Pascoe, S.J., "Gerson and the Donation of Constantine: Growth and Development with the Church," *Viator*, V (1974), pp. 477–78.

57. Fois, *Il pensiero cristiano di Lorenzo Valla*, p. 343.

58. Pascoe, pp. 469–85; cf. Salutati's comments quoted in Trinkaus, *In Our Image*, p. 668.

59. O'Malley, *Giles of Viterbo*, pp. 106–07, 130.

60. Fois, pp. 325–27.

61. Lorenzo Valla, *De falso credita et ementita Constantini donatione*, ed. Wolfram Setz [Monumenta Germaniae historica: Quellen zur Geistesgeschichte des Mittelalters, 10] (Weimar: Hermann Böhlaus Nachfolger, 1976), pp. 81, 174, 176. For recent considerations of the *Declamatio*, see Fois, pp. 296–350; Camporeale, *Lorenzo Valla*, pp. 10–11; Prodi, *Il sovrano pontefice*, pp. 32–33; and Wolfram Setz, *Lorenzo Vallas Schrift gegen die Konstantinische Schenkung* [Bibliothek des Deutschen Historischen Instituts in Rom, 44] (Tübingen, 1975). Note also Joseph M. Levine, "Reginald Pecock and Lorenzo Valla on the Donation of Constantine," *SR*, XX (1973), pp. 118–43; and Heiko A. Oberman, "The Shape of Late Medieval Thought: The Birthpangs of the Modern Era," *ARG*, LXIV (1973), p. 26.

62. Giovanni Antonazzi, "Lorenzo Valla e la Donazione di Costantino nel secolo XV con un testo inedito di Antonio Cortesi," *RSCI*, IV (1950), pp. 186–234.

63. Fois, pp. 359–94; Camporeale, *Lorenzo Valla*, pp. 227–28, 235, 267–73; Gianni

Zippel, "L'autodifesa di Lorenzo Valla per il processo dell'Inquisizione napoletana (1444)," *Italia medioevale e umanistica*, XIII (1970), pp. 59–94.

64. Schudt, *Le guide di Roma*, pp. 19–26; *Mirabilia Romae. Rom Stephan Planck*, p. 1.

65. *De potestate summi Pontificis, eius veneratione, et cognominatione, ac de justo bello Clem. VII contra Florentinas*, BAV, ms. Vat. lat. 4125, fols. 55ᵛ-68ᵛ; note also Ferrosius's appended "*Epithemata opusculi*," fols. 187ʳ-189ᵛ.

66. Maffei, *Donazione di Costantino*, pp. 276–318. The anonymous refutation of Valla's work present in Bibl. Capitolare, Lucca, ms. 582, fols. 270–74, an oration delivered before the papal court, states this argument in typical fashion: ". . . *docent dicente beatissimo pontificie Nicolao quod Christus apostolo Petro aeterne vite clavigero terreni simul et celestis imperii iura remisit.*" See Franco Gaeta, "Una polemica quattrocentesca contro la *De falso credita et ementita Constantini declamatio* di Lorenzo Valla," *Rivista storica italiana*, LXIV (1952), p. 398. Similarly, Domenichi, in his *De potestate pape et termino eius*, regarded the Donation as irrelevant, since the pope is *dominus mundi* anyway: see Prodi, *Il sovrano pontefice*, pp. 39–40.

67. Jedin, "Juan de Torquemada und das Imperium Romanum," pp. 247–78.

68. See p. 179. Francesco da Castiglione also thought Silvester's baptism of Constantine apocryphal: Fubini, "Papato e storiografia," p. 339.

69. Jedin, *Studien über Domenico de' Domenichi*, pp. 264–68.

70. Massimo Miglio, "L'umanista Pietro Edo e la polemica sulla Donazione di Costantino," *Bullettino dell'Istituto Storico Italiano per il Medio Evo e Archivio Muratoriano*, LXXIX (1968), pp. 167–232. The same emphasis on "*Constantinus a divina gratia afflatus*" ceding universal imperial dominion to Silvester as Vicar of Christ is made in the speech of the Archbishop of Patras, Stefano Taleazzi (d. 1515), to the Tenth Session (4 May 1515) of the Fifth Lateran Council: Mansi, *Collectio*, XXXII, cols. 923–24, and Minnich, "Concepts of Reform," pp. 198–201. In defending Paul II's use of the tiara against the Fraticelli, Jean Jouffroy also refers to Constantine's Donation as motivated "*divino instinctu*" and argues that Silvester would not have accepted it if he had not held it to be useful and necessary "*ecclesiasticae maiestati:*" Miglio, *Storiografia pontificia*, pp. 139–40.

71. Maffei, *Donazione di Costantino*, p. 332.

72. *Lugdunense Somnium*, pp. 66ʳ-ᵛ, 91ᵛ.

73. M.T. Graziosi, "Agostino Steuco e il suo *Antivalla*," *L'Umanesimo umbro: Atti del IX Convegno di Studi Umbri, Gubbio, 22–23 sett. 1974* (Perugia: Univ., 1977), pp. 511–23; note also Fois, p. 344. For Steuco's life and thought, see Karl H. Dannenfeldt, "The Pseudo-Zoroastrian Oracles in the Renaissance," *SR*, IV (1957), pp. 17–18, and Charles B. Schmitt, "Perennial Philosophy: From Agostino Steuco to Leibniz," *JHI*, XXVII (1966), pp. 505–32.

74. Guicciardini, *Storia d'Italia*, pp. 417–28; note Bouwsma, *Venice*, pp. 34–35. In short, those who rejected papal claims to temporal dominion (like Mario Salamonio, see n. 81 below) were convinced by Valla's arguments that the Donation was a forgery; defenders of papal temporal power, on the other hand, discredited Valla.

75. Westfall, *In this Most Perfect Paradise*, pp. 92–94; Siebenhüner, *Das Kapitol*, pp. 17–36. For an overview of the Capitol in this period, see Fritz Saxl, "The Capitol during the Renaissance: A Symbol of the Imperial Idea," in *Lectures* (London: Warburg, 1957), pp. 200–14.

76. Westfall, *In this Most Perfect Paradise*, pp. 74–76, 94–100.

77. The inscription reads: SIXTUS IIII. PONT. MAX. OB IMMENSAM BENIGNITATEM AENEAS INSIGNES STATUAS PRISCAE EXCELLENTIAE VIRTUTISQUE MONUMENTUM ROMANO POPULO UNDE EXORTAE FUERE RESTITUENDAS CONDONANDASQUE CENSUIT . . . (see Lee, *Sixtus IV*, p. 148, n. 111).

78. W.S. Hecksher, *Sixtus IIII aeneas insignes statuas romano populo restituendas censuit* (The Hague, 1955); Lee, *Sixtus IV*, pp. 148–50; Siebenhüner, *Das Kapitol*, pp. 37–45; Ackerman, *Architecture of Michelangelo*, pp. 163–64.

79. Siebenhüner, pp. 43–44, 46; note also Weiss, *Renaissance Discovery*, pp. 102, 191; and Brummer, *Statue Court in the Vatican Belvedere*, pp. 243–44.

80. Siebenhüner, pp. 46–53, 91; Buddensieg, "Zum Statuenprogramm in Kapitolsplan Pauls III," p. 182. For the discovery of the *Fasti* tablets, see Cochrane, *Historians and Historiography*, p. 425.

81. For the ways in which papal restoration of the Capitoline extirpated its function as a focal point for communal liberties, I am indebted to Miglio's "Il leone e la lupa," pp. 177–86. For Paul III's bridge and the Farnese Tower, see Coffin, *Villa in the Life of*

Renaissance Rome, pp. 31–34. An analogous rear-guard defense of eroding noble position in Renaissance Rome appears in the dialogue, *Li nuptiali*, written shortly after 1500 by Marcantonio Altieri, member of the Roman baronage and a humanist participant in Leto's Roman Academy. In this work on the marriage rites of the Roman aristocracy, Altieri traces their origin to classical practices and attributes the contemporary decay of the Roman nobility to the abandonment of these ancient mores. See Christiane Klapisch-Zuber, "Une ethnologie du mariage au temps de l'Humanisme," *Annales: Économies, Sociétés, Civilisations*, XXXVI (1981), pp. 1016–27. For Altieri, see also Cruciani, *Il teatro del Campidoglio*, pp. xxxiv-xxxvii, xlv-xlvi, 3–20, 127–30, and Miglio, "Il leone e la lupa," pp. 182–83. A more extensive defense of the historical rights of the Roman populace appears in Mario Salamonio's *Patritii Romani de principatu*. Salamonio, who belonged to one of Rome's most ancient noble families, had studied under Pomponio Leto at the Sapienza and acquired from him a familiarity with the laws and magistracies of ancient Rome. He was a leading jurist as well, and an active participant in Rome's legal and political life. His work, a dialogue among a philosopher, a historian, a theologian, and a jurist, was written in the wake of the abortive Colonna uprising against Julius II in 1511, and he intended it as a theoretical support for the ultimate sovereignty of the Roman people over and against papal usurpation: see Skinner, *Foundations of Modern Political Thought*, I, pp. 148–52.

    82. Cruciani, *Teatro di Campidoglio*, pp. lxiii-lxiv, 151.

    83. A brief mention of the statue appears in Novellus, *Compendium vitae Leonis Papae X*, pp. 119^{r-v}. For stylistic analysis of the statue, the work of the little-known Bolognese sculptor Domenico Amio, and of C. Silvanus Germanicus's poem describing it, which imitates in several passages Statius's *Silva* written in praise of an equestrian statue of the Roman Emperor Domitian, see Hans Henrik Brummer and Tore Janson, "Art, Literature and Politics: An Episode in the Roman Renaissance," *Konsthistorisk Tidskrift*, XLV (1976), pp. 79–93. For the content of Palladio's *Oratio totam fere Romanum historiam complectens*, see D'Amico, *Renaissance Humanism in Papal Rome*, pp. 134–37.

    84. For a comparison of various *piazze* in Renaissance Italian cities, see Wolfgang Lotz, *Studies in Italian Renaissance Architecture* (Cambridge, Mass.: MIT Pr., 1977), pp. 74–116.

    85. See Siebenhüner, *Das Kapitol*, illus. 7–9, 28, 29, 33; for Charles V's triumph, see Mitchell, "The S.Q.P.R. in Two Roman Festivals," pp. 99–101, and Chastel, *Sack of Rome*, pp. 207–15.

    86. Philipp Fehl, "The Placement of the Equestrian Statue of Marcus Aurelius in the Middle Ages," *JWCI*, XXXVII (1974), pp. 362–67; for medieval legends of the statue, note also James S. Ackerman, "*Marcus Aurelius* on the Capitoline Hill," *Renaissance News*, X (1957), pp. 69–75.

    87. Siebenhüner, p. 54.

    88. The inscription on Michelangelo's base refers to Paul III transferring the statue EX HVMILIORI LOCO IN AREAM CAPITOLINAM: see Buddensieg, pp. 188, 219.

    89. *Ibid.*, pp. 188–92; note also Harprath, *Papst Paul III als Alexander der Grosse*, pp. 68–71.

    90. Partridge, review of Harprath, *Papst Paul III*, in *AB*, LXII (1980), p. 663, sees as one of the underlying themes of the Sala Paolina in Castel Sant'Angelo the "unbroken historical continuity" from Alexander the Great to St. Paul to Paul III, an idea in general accord with the Capitoline program, but with the inclusion in addition of the origin of Rome's spiritual sovereignty. For the importance of Alexandrian motifs in Paul III's pontificate, see also Bernice Davidson, "The Decoration of the Sala Regia under Paul III," *AB*, LVIII (1976), p. 418; note also Chapter IV, n. 193, herein.

    91. In interpreting the meaning of Paul III's sculptural program for the Capitoline, I am convinced by Buddensieg's revisions of Ackerman's exegesis: see "Zum statuenprogramm," pp. 192–204, 214–16. For the medal of the Marcus Aurelius monument, see also Harprath, p. 19.

    92. Buddensieg, pp. 205–14.

    93. Ackerman, *Architecture of Michelangelo*, pp. 144–63; for Michelangelo's design intentions, note also Portoghesi, *Roma del Rinascimento*, pp. 201–08, 470–72; Siebenhüner, *Das Kapitol*, pp. 64–119; and Guglielmo de Angelis d'Ossat and Carlo Pietrangeli, *Il Campidoglio di Michelangelo* (Rome: "Silvana" Editoriale d'Arte, 1965).

    94. Ackerman, *Architecture of Michelangelo*, pp. 169–72.

95. *Ibid.*, pp. 172–73; for the *omphalos-umbilicus* motif, note also Siebenhüner, pp. 91–92.

96. Westfall, *In this Most Perfect Paradise*, pp. 4–7.

97. Nicholas's plans for the Vatican must be reconstructed primarily from Manetti's *Vita Nicolai V*; relevant portions of the text are edited by Magnuson, *Roman Quattrocento Architecture*, pp. 351–62. For discussion of Alberti's role, see *ibid.*, pp. 85–97; Westfall, *In this Most Perfect Paradise*, pp. 167–84; and Borsi, *Leon Battista Alberti*, pp. 50–58. For interpretation of the Borgo Leonino project, see Magnuson, pp. 65–85, and Westfall, pp. 100–16. Charles Burroughs, "A Planned Myth and a Myth of Planning: Nicholas V and Rome," in Ramsey, ed., *Rome in the Renaissance*, pp. 197–207, argues that the Borgo scheme dates only from late in Nicholas's pontificate and was essentially a literary construct, rather than an actual building campaign; see also *id.*, "Below the Angel," pp. 94–124.

98. Magnuson, p. 164.

99. *Ibid.*, pp. 163–214; Westfall, pp. 116–127; Günter Urban, "Zum Neu-bau Projekt von St. Peter unter Nikolaus V," *Festschrift für Harald Keller* (Darmstadt: Eduard Roether, 1963),pp. 131–73.

100. Magnuson, pp. 98–162; Westfall, pp. 128–65.

101. Westfall's interpretation (pp. 152–54) of the planned Vatican *theatrum* as merely a ceremonial reception area is shown to be suspect by Elisabeth B. MacDougall in her review of Westfall's book, *AB*, LXI (1979), pp. 309–12.

102. Westfall, pp. 132–43, describes the traditional character of the decorative schema for the apartment wing, while stressing the originality of the ceremonial structures planned for the "paradise" setting in the Vatican garden. Indeed he sees these aspects of Nicholas's Vatican palace plans as establishing precedents for Federigo da Montefeltro's palace in Urbino: "Chivalric Decoration: The Palazzo Ducale in Urbino as a Political Statement," in Henry A. Millon and Linda Nochlin, eds., *Art and Architecture in the Service of Politics* (Cambridge, Mass.: MIT Pr., 1978), pp. 20–45. For the tenuousness of Westfall's chain of reasoning regarding the paradise *topos* and acts of government, see MacDougall's review, esp. pp. 311–12.

103. Rubinstein, "Pius II's Piazza S. Pietro," pp. 23–29, 32–33.

104. For Palazzo di S. Marco, see Magnuson, pp. 245–96.

105. Ackerman, *Cortile del Belvedere*, pp. 5–9.

106. Coffin, *Villa in the Life of Renaissance Rome*, pp. 69–81.

107. Deoclecio Redig de Campos, "Bramante e il Palazzo Apostolico Vaticano," *RendPontAcc*, 3rd ser. XLIII (1970–71), p. 283–99; Bruschi, *Bramante architetto*, pp. 294–95, 931–37; Ackerman, *Cortile del Belvedere*, pp. 10–12, 137.

108. *Bramante architetto*, pp. 655–57. Similarly, Blosio Palladio, in concluding the oration he prepared for the unveiling of Leo X's statue on the Capitoline, invoked the "Capitoline Virgin" as protectress of the Capitoline Hill, and of Rome; as such she succeeded to and preserved much of the imperial meaning associated with the ancient cult of Capitoline Jupiter: see D'Amico, *Renaissance Humanism in Papal Rome*, p. 137.

109. Note the revised English ed., Arnaldo Bruschi, *Bramante* (London: Thames & Hudson, 1977), pp. 119–23.

110. Bruschi, *Bramante architetto*, pp. 593–603, 609–47; note also the works cited in Chapter II, n. 54, herein.

111. Ackerman, *Cortile*, pp. 126–30; for the architecture of the Cortile, see also Bruschi, *Bramante architetto*, pp. 291–434.

112. Ackerman, *Cortile*, pp. 132–34.

113. *Ibid.*, pp. 130–38.

114. *Ibid.*, p. 131. The gigantic dimensions of the Cortile are indicated in the inscription of a medal of Julius II, dating from the period 1504–08. The reverse depicts the Belvedere, with the inscription: VIA.IVL.III.ADIT.LON.M.ALTI.LXX.P. and below VATICANVS.M. Weiss, "Medals of Julius II," pp. 180–81, deciphers this as: VIA IVLIA TRIVM ADITVM LONGITVDINIS MILLE ALTITVDINIS SEPTVAGINTA PEDVM.

115. Ackerman, *Cortile*, pp. 52–109, 138–40.

116. The most extensive treatment of the statue garden is Brummer, *The Statue Court in the Vatican Belvedere*; note also Ackerman, *Cortile*, pp. 32–37, and Terry Comito, *The Idea of the Garden in the Renaissance* (New Brunswick: Rutgers U. Pr., 1978), pp. 164–67.

117. Brummer, pp. 234–41; for the text of Pico's remarks, see *ibid.*, pp. 273–74.

118. *Ibid.*, pp. 227–34; for a different emphasis, note E.H. Gombrich, "The Belvedere Garden as a Grove of Venus," in *Symbolic Images*, pp. 104–08.

119. Brummer, pp. 125–26; Oliver, "The Ruling Power," p. 887; Lidia Storoni Mazzolani, *The Idea of the City in Roman Thought: From Walled City to Spiritual Commonwealth* (Bloomington: Indiana U. Pr., 1970), pp. 107–08; Kenneth J. Pratt, "Rome as Eternal," *JHI*, XXVI (1965), pp. 27–28.

120. Brummer, pp. 182, 220–22 (where the relevant texts of Capodiferro and Castiglione are quoted); for the complete text of Castiglione's "Cleopatra," see Alessandro Perosa and John Sparrow, *Renaissance Latin Verse: An Anthology* (Chapel Hill: U. of N. Carolina Pr., 1979), pp. 193–95. For the statue, see also MacDougall, "Sleeping Nymph," pp. 357–65.

121. Capodiferro's poem, the text of which appears in Brummer, p. 225, also makes mention of Apollo's role at Actium. For Augustus's cult of Apollo, see Mazzolani, pp. 150–52, and esp. Jean Gagé, *Apollon Romain: Essais sur le culte d'Apollon et le développement du 'ritus Graecus' à Rome des origines à Auguste* (Paris: de Boccard, 1955), pp. 479–682. Aeneas's shield, the ekphrasis of which appears in the *Aeneid*, VIII, 626–731, portrays Apollo routing Anubis and other monstrous gods of the East at Actium. Augustus's victory at Actium may have had a more particular meaning for the Della Rovere pontiff, whose titular church as a cardinal had been S. Pietro in Vincoli. As Biondo had noted in *Roma instaurata* (see above, Chapter IV, n. 82), the 1 August ancient Christian *festa* for the liberation of St. Peter from prison, initiated when the relics of the chains were brought to Rome, coincided with the traditional Roman festival honoring Augustus's victory over Antony and Cleopatra. For discussion of Capodiferro's poem, note, besides Brummer, pp. 222–26, Schröter, "Der Vatikan als Hügel Apollons," pp. 232–33. For Julius II's links to Apollo, note also pp. 000–000 herein.

122. Brummer, p. 226; L.D. Ettlinger, "*Exemplum Doloris*: Reflections on the Laocoön Group," in M. Meiss, ed., *De artibus opuscula XL: Essays in Honor of Erwin Panofsky* (N.Y.: New York U. Pr., 1961), Vol. I, pp. 121–26.

123. Brummer, pp. 114–19.

124. For the text of Sadoleto's poem, see Perosa and Sparrow, *Renaissance Latin Verse*, pp. 185–86; note also Brummer, pp. 219–20, and Douglas, *Sadoleto*, pp. 9–10.

125. For the most recent discussion of the circumstances in which the new St. Peter's was conceived, see Frommel, "'Capella Iulia'," pp. 26–35, 43–62.

126. For the early stages of the basilica's reconstruction, see Frommel, "Die Peterskirche," pp. 59–84, and Bruschi, *Bramante architetto*, pp. 905–07.

127. The basic study remains Erwin Panofsky, "The First Two Projects of Michelangelo's Tomb of Julius II," *AB*, XIX (1937), pp. 561–79; note additional discussion in *id.*, *Tomb Sculpture*, pp. 88–90, and *id.*, *Studies in Iconology* (N.Y.: Harper & Row, 1967), pp. 187–99. See also Hibbard, *Michelangelo*, pp. 86–92; von Einem, *Michelangelo*, pp. 39–45; and esp. Frommel, "'Capella Iulia'," pp. 36–43.

128. Frommel, "'Capella Iulia'," pp. 38–39.

129. Alfred Frazer, "A Numismatic Source for Michelangelo's First Design for the Tomb of Julius II," *AB*, LVII (1975), pp. 53–57. For the meaning of imperial *consecratio* in late antiquity and in early Byzantium, see MacCormack, *Art and Ceremony in Late Antiquity*, pp. 91–158.

130. Panofsky, *Studies in Iconology*, p. 190; Chastel, *Art et humanisme*, pp. 464–65. For Julius II entering heaven as a triumphator, see Marcello's sermon for All Saints, discussed on p. 242 herein. The peroration of Inghirami's funeral oration for Julius II suggests, too, the idea of the Roman Emperor's apotheosis: Julius's great deeds will immortalize him. See McManamon, "Ideal Renaissance Pope," p. 32.

131. Bruschi, *Bramante architetto*, pp. 546–72, 619–25; cf. however, Frommel, "Die Peterskirche," pp. 72–74.

132. Bruschi, *Bramante architetto*, p. 621.

133. *Ibid.*, pp. 549–67; Ackerman, *Architecture of Michelangelo*, pp. 27–29.

134. Bruschi, *Bramante architetto*, pp. 535–37, 540, 580–82, 906.

135. For the history of the new St. Peter's in the sixteenth century, see Portoghesi, *Roma del Rinascimento*, pp. 64–67, 87–88, 191–94, 209–15, 409–16. For Michelangelo's work, see Ackerman, *Architecture of Michelangelo*, pp. 199–225.

136. Suetonius, *De vita Caesarum: Augustus*, xxix; Horace, *Epistolae*, I, iii; Gagé,

Apollon Romain, pp. 523–31. That the Renaissance Romans were aware of Augustus's creation is indicated by the identification of the Mons Palatinus as the location of the *"Templum Apollonis cum Bibliotheca"* in Marco Fabio Calvo's schematic map of ancient Rome: note Schröter, "Der Vatikan als Hügel Apollons," p. 214, n. 33.

137. F. E. Peters, *The Harvest of Hellenism: A History of the Near East from Alexander the Great to the Triumph of Christianity* (N.Y.: Simon & Schuster, 1970), pp. 193–94, 314–15.

138. Shearman, "Vatican Stanze," pp. 382–83, and p. 410, n. 85.

139. Chastel, *Art et humanisme*, p. 483. A scene of Alexander the Great preserving the works of Homer also appears in the Alexander cycle in Paul III's Sala Paolina in Castel Sant'Angelo; see Harprath, *Papst Paul III als Alexander der Grosse*, pp. 37–39.

140. Manetti, *Vita Nicolai V*, col. 926; for Brandolini's observations, see Schröter, p. 215.

141. Müntz and Fabre, *Bibliothèque du Vatican au XVe siècle*, pp. 1–9.

142. Stinger, *Humanism and the Church Fathers*, pp. 53, 83, 141.

143. Müntz and Fabre, pp. 7–8.

144. The text of the inventory appears in Müntz and Fabre, pp. 9–32.

145. Berthold L. Ullman and Philip A. Stadter, *The Public Library of the Renaissance: Niccolò Niccoli, Cosimo de' Medici and the Library of San Marco* [Medioevo e Umanesimo, 10] (Padua: Antenori, 1972).

146. Remigio Sabbadini, *Le scoperte dei codici latini e greci ne' secoli XIV e XV*, 2nd ed. (Florence: Sansoni, 1967), vol. I, pp. 89–91, 106–07, 115.

147. The text of the "canon" appears in G. Sforza, *La patria, la famiglia, e la giovinezza di Papa Niccolò Quinto*, (Lucca, 1884), pp. 359–81. Note also Vespasiano da Bisticci, "Vita di Nicolao P.P. V," in *Le Vite*, ed. Greco, pp. 46–47.

148. For the inventories, see Müntz and Fabre, p. 34–114, 315–44. Both Manetti, *Vita Nicolai V*, cols. 924–25, and Vespasiano, "Vita di Nicolao P.P. V," pp. 63–64, connect funds generated from the Jubilee with Nicholas's library projects. For Tortelli's role, see Chap. IV, n. 168, herein.

149. Vespasiano, "Vita di Nicolao P.P. V," pp. 65–68; Vasoli, *Studi sulla cultura del Rinascimento*, pp. 105–06. Trebizond's translating activity has been analyzed by Monfasani, pp. 71–79; for Perotti, see Oliver, *Perotti's Version of the Enchiridion*. For the translations of Strabo's *Geography* and of the ancient Greek historians, see E. B. Fryde, *Humanism and Renaissance Historiography* (London: Hambledon Pr., 1983), pp. 55–113.

150. *Vita Nicolai V*, in Magnuson, *Roman Quattrocento Architecture*, p. 355.

151. Toby Yuen, "The 'Bibliotheca Graeca': Castagno, Alberti, and Ancient Sources," *The Burlington Magazine*, CXII (1970), pp. 725–36.

152. Weiss, *Un umanista veneziano: Papa Paolo II*, pp. 16–22; M. Miglio, "Bussi, Giovanni Andrea," *DBI*, XV (Rome, 1972), pp. 565–72; Lee, *Sixtus IV and Men of Letters*, pp. 105–10.

153. Müntz and Fabre, pp. 121–22.

154. *Ibid.*, pp. 135–306; Paul Fabre, "La Vaticane de Sixte IV," *MAHEFR*, XV (1895), pp. 455–83; John Willis Clark, "On the Vatican Library of Sixtus IV," *Proceedings of the Cambridge Antiquarian Society*, X (n.s. IV) (1904), pp. 11–61; Deoclecio Redig de Campos, *I Palazzi Vaticani* [Roma christiana, 18] (Bologna: Cappelli, 1967), pp. 57–63; *id.*, "Testimonianze del primo nucleo edilizio dei Palazzi Vaticani e restauro delle pitture delle stanze della 'Bibliotheca Latina' e 'Bibliotheca Graeca'," *Il restauro delle aule di Niccolò V e di Sisto IV nel Palazzo Apostolico Vaticano* (Vatican, 1967); José Ruysschaert, "Sixte IV, Fondateur de la Bibliothèque Vaticane (15 Juin 1475)," *AHP*, VII (1969), pp. 513–24; Odier, *Bibliothèque Vaticane*, pp. 2–25; Lee, *Sixtus IV*, pp. 110–22.

155. Bertola, *I due primi registri*, provides a facsimile edition of Platina's registers.

156. Filelfo's remarks are quoted in Müntz and Fabre, pp. 37–38.

157. Schröter, "Vatikan als Hügel Apollons," pp. 216–17.

158. John W. O'Malley, "The Vatican Library and the Schools of Athens: A Text of Battista Casali, 1508," *JMRS*, VII (1977), pp. 271–87.

159. Vittore Fanelli, "Il ginnasio greco di Leone X a Roma," *Studi romani*, IX (1961), pp. 379–80. For Leo X's success in attracting Greek-born scholars to Rome and their role in furthering Greek scholarship in the Eternal City, see Geanakoplos, *Greek Scholars in Venice*, pp. 184–87, 213–21. As early as 1406, Leonardo Bruni, while serving as Papal Secretary, had

persuaded Innocent VII to include an appointment in Greek studies as part of his planned re-establishment of the University of Rome: see Griffiths, "Leonardo Bruni and the Restoration of the University of Rome," pp. 3–4, 9–10. These plans remained in abeyance, however, and it was Sixtus IV's appointment of Argyropoulos to teach Greek literature and philosophy at the Sapienza which firmly established Greek studies there: Lee, *Sixtus IV*, pp. 171–77.

160. Fanelli, "Ginnasio greco," pp. 381–82; for Musurus's career, see Geanakoplos, *Greek Scholars in Venice*, pp. 111–66.

161. Francesco Barberi and Emidio Cerulli, "Le edizioni greche in Gymnasio Mediceo ad Caballinum Montem," in *Atti del Convegno di studi su Angelo Colocci, Jesi, 13–14 settembre 1969* (Jesi: Amministrazione comunale, 1972), pp. 61–76; note also Luigi Michelini Tocci, "Dei libri a stampa appartenuti al Colocci," in *ibid.*, pp. 77–96.

162. Bober, "Coryciana," pp. 237–39.

163. Vittore Branca, "Ermolao Barbaro and Late Quattrocento Venetian Humanism," in J.R. Hale, ed., *Renaissance Venice* (London: Faber & Faber, 1973), pp. 218–43; Eugenio Garin, "The Cultural Background of Politian," in *Portraits from the Quattrocento*, pp. 161–89.

164. A Latin version of Polybius was made by Perotti for Nicholas V (see Fryde, *Humanism and Renaissance Historiography*, pp. 99–102); Dionysius of Halicarnassus's *Antiquitates Romanae* was translated by Birago for Paul II (Miglio, "Birago, Lampugnino," in *DBI*, X, pp. 595–97); Procopius and Agathias were translated by Persona (Paschini, "Un ellenista romano," p. 48; Bertola, *I due primi registri*, pp. 23–24). Other scholarship devoted to ancient Roman history includes Poggio's translation, with George of Trebizond's help, of Diodorus Siculus's *Bibliotheca Historica*, completed in 1449 for Nicholas V (Monfasani, *George of Trebizond*, p. 70); Decembrio's translation of Appian for Nicholas V, done 1452–54 (Fryde, pp. 102–07); Politian's translation at the request of Innocent VIII of Herodian's history of the Roman Emperors after Marcus Aurelius to A.D. 238 (Fryde, pp. 107–13; Dominique de Menil, ed., *Builders and Humanists: The Renaissance Popes as Patrons of the Arts*, Catalogue of the exhibition, University of St. Thomas Art Dept. Houston, March-May 1966, pp. 236–37); Leto's *Romanae Historiae Compendium*, which covers the period 244–711 A.D. and was dedicated to Francesco Borgia, a relative of Alexander VI (de Menil, pp. 240–41); and Filippo Beroaldo the Younger's 1515 edition of Tacitus, commissioned by Leo X, which included previously lost parts of the *Annals* and of the *History* contained in a manuscript the Medici pope had acquired from a German monastery in 1509 (*ibid.*, pp. 250–51; Kenneth C. Schellhase, *Tacitus in Renaissance Political Thought* [Chicago: U. of Chicago Pr., 1976], pp. 12–15; Else-Lilly Etter, *Tacitus in der Geistesgeschichte des 16. und 17. Jahrhunderts* [Basler Beiträge zur Geschichtswissenschaft, Vol. 103] [Basel and Stuttgart: Helbing und Lichtenhahn, 1966], pp. 26–27). Mention should be made, too, of the editorial work of Campano and Bussi for early printed editions of Livy, Caesar's *Bellum Gallicum*, Suetonius, and Plutarch's *Lives* (in Latin translation): see Flavio di Bernardo, *Giannantonio Campano*, pp. 233–44, and Lee, *Sixtus IV*, pp. 99–109.

165. See Argyropoulos's dedication to Sixtus of his translation of Basil's *Homilies on the Hexaemeron*, BAV, ms. Vat. lat. 301, fol. 4ʳ. Persona, in dedicating his translation of "Athanasius" (i.e. Theophylact) to Sixtus, wrote: ". . . et ita ut non immerito illud asseveraverim, quod est a Platone dictum, et a multis iam usurpatum, tunc beatam fore rem publicam, cum vel regnare philosophi ceperint, vel reges philosophari. Cui igitur B.P. id opus vel rectius ipse dicaverim ulli inscripserim dignius quam tibi, qui princeps sis et philosophus, et ceteris quidem eo prestantior, quo et christi vicem nunc geris, et ad philosophiam accedat, rerum divinarum summa cognitio, et optimarum artium altarum peritia non mediocris." BAV, ms. Vat. lat. 263, fol. 1ᵛ.

166. Onofri, "Sacralità," p. 40; Miglio, *Storiografia pontificia*, p. 222.

167. For Poggio's translation, dedicated to King Alfonso the Magnanimous of Naples, see Monfasani, *George of Trebizond*, p. 53; for Birago's, see Miglio's article in *DBI*, X, pp. 595–97; for Filelfo's see de Menil, ed., *Builders and Humanists*, pp. 230–31.

168. Ciceronianism is a central concern of D'Amico's *Renaissance Humanism in Papal Rome*; note esp. pp. 115–43. See also O'Malley's discussion on the "new rhetoric" in *Praise and Blame*, pp. 36–76. For Erasmus's criticisms (expressed in his 1528 dialogue, *Ciceronianus*), see *ibid.*, pp. 29–31, 51–52, 114; D'Amico, *Renaissance Humanism*, pp. 138–42, 167–68; and Myron P. Gilmore, "Italian Reactions to Erasmian Humanism," in Heiko A. Oberman with Thomas A. Brady, Jr., eds., *Itinerarium Italicum: The Profile of the Italian Renaissance in the*

Mirror of its European Transformations (Dedicated to Paul Oskar Kristeller on the Occasion of his 70th Birthday) [Studies in Medieval and Reformation Thought, XIV] (Leiden: Brill, 1975), pp. 107–110.

169. Aulo Greco, "Roma e la commedia del Rinascimento," Studi romani, XXII (1974), pp. 25–35; Fabrizio Cruciani, "Il teatro dei Ciceroniani: Tommaso 'Fedra' Inghirami," Forum Italicum, XIV (1980), pp. 356–77.

170. O'Malley, Praise and Blame, pp. 238–42. D'Amico, Renaissance Humanism in Papal Rome, pp. 238–40, draws much the same conclusion.

171. Note D'Amico's perceptive remarks, in Renaissance Humanism in Papal Rome, pp. 125, 159.

172. Garin, ed., Prosatori latini del Quattrocento, pp. 594–610; Biondo expresses similar ideas in his preface to Roma triumphans, in Opera omnia, p. 2. For Valla's views, note D'Amico, Renaissance Humanism in Papal Rome, pp. 118–19, and Lawrence J. Johnson, "The 'Linguistic Imperialism' of Lorenzo Valla and the Renaissance Humanists," Interpretation, VII (1978), pp. 29–49.

173. Laurentius Valla, Opera omnia, ed. Eugenio Garin (Turin: Bottega d'Erasmo, 1962), II, pp. 281–86; note discussion in Trinkaus, In Our Image, p. 765; and Fois, Il pensiero cristiano di Lorenzo Valla, pp. 441–48.

174. D'Amico, Renaissance Humanism in Papal Rome, pp. 156–58.

175. John F. D'Amico, "A Humanist Response to Martin Luther: Raffaele Maffei's Apologeticus," Sixteenth Century Journal, VI/2 (1975), pp. 37–56. Note also O'Malley, Praise and Blame, p. 241. A similarly positive religious affirmation of civilization, and an emphasis on the Logos as a civilizing agent, appears in the writings of Eusebius of Caesarea, whose works were widely read in Renaissance Rome. Note Robert M. Grant, "Civilization as a Preparation for Christianity in the Thought of Eusebius," in F. Forrester Church and Timothy George, eds., Continuity and Discontinuity in Church History: Essays Presented to George Huntston Williams on the Occasion of his 65th Birthday [Studies in the History of Christian Thought, XIX] (Leiden: Brill, 1979), pp. 62–70. Grant also points out (p. 64) that Eusebius probably drew upon the ideas of the cooperation of human minds with the divine expressed in Origen's Contra Celsum, a work which, as we have seen, Cristoforo da Persona translated in Rome in 1477.

VI. Roma Aeterna and the Plenitudo Temporam

1. Mansi, Collectio, XXXII, col. 896; Minnich, "Concepts of Reform," pp. 192–98.
2. Garin, Prosatori latini, p. 170.
3. De varietate fortunae, p. 3.
4. See pp. 245–46.
5. O'Reilly, "'Maximus Caesar et Pontifex Maximus'," pp. 80–117; note also Partridge and Starn, A Renaissance Likeness, pp. 79–81. Giles's remarks form the greatest possible contrast with the famous opening page of Guicciardini's Storia d'Italia (Menchi ed., p. 5), in which the Florentine historian emphasizes the calamities to which miserable mortals had been subjected, the frequent shifts of fortune, and the instability of human affairs, "not unlike a sea whipped by winds."
6. Davis, Dante and the Idea of Rome, p. 3.
7. Oliver, "The Ruling Power," p. 887.
8. Ibid., p. 875; note also Mazzolani, Idea of the City in Roman Thought, pp. 119–20, 174–75; Salerno, Roma Communis Patria, p. 15; Pratt, "Rome as Eternal," pp. 25–30.
9. Pratt, p. 35.
10. For this outlook in general, see O'Malley, Praise and Blame, pp. 125–31, 201–03, 210–11, 220–22; and id., "Historical Thought and the Reform Crisis of the Early Sixteenth Century," Theological Studies, XXVIII (1967), pp. 531–48. For the telling lack of a sense of historical process in Giles's thought in particular, see id., Giles of Viterbo, pp. 180–85. Cajetan's remarks appear in his address to the Fifth Lateran Council, in Mansi, Collectio, XXXII, col. 725. For the theme of providentially created order in Vida's Christiad, see Di Cesare, pp. 271–75. For notions of "exemplary causality" in Biondo and Bernardo Rucellai, see pp. 69–71 herein. To grasp Roman Renaissance views, it is useful to compare Venetian attitudes. Renaissance Venetians were also convinced that the uniqueness of the most serene republic was expressed in its historical duration. Duration, however, did not

depend on notions of divine providence or cosmic order, but rather on the indissoluble link in Venice's secular civilization between its existence as a human community and liberty: note the insightful remarks of Alberto Tenenti, "The Sense of Space and Time in the Venetian World of the Fifteenth and Sixteenth Centuries," in Hale, ed., *Renaissance Venice*, pp. 33–37.

11. Mansi, *Collectio*, XXXII, col. 757.

12. Partridge and Starn, *A Renaissance Likeness*, pp. 56–59, 142–43; Hartt, *"Lignum vitae in medio paradisi,"* pp. 133–34.

13. Harry Levin, *The Myth of the Golden Age in the Renaissance* (Bloomington: Indiana U. Pr., 1969), pp. 13–27.

14. Harold Mattingly, "Virgil's Fourth Eclogue" *JWCI*, X (1947), pp. 14–19; see also Yates, *Astraea*, p. 4.

15. Oliver, "The Ruling Power," pp. 887, 906–07, 949–50.

16. E.H. Gombrich, "Renaissance and Golden Age," in *Norm and Form: Studies in the Art of the Renaissance* (London: Phaidon, 1971), pp. 29–34; Gerhart B. Ladner, "Vegetation Symbolism and the Concept of the Renaissance," in Meiss, ed., *De artibus opuscula XL*, I, pp. 315–17. For the Renaissance in general note, besides Levin, Henry Kamen, "Golden Age, Iron Age: A Conflict of Concepts in the Renaissance," *JMRS*, IV (1974), pp. 135–55.

17. Miglio, *Storiografia pontificia*, p. 225; Manetti says much the same thing in his 1447 oration to Nicholas V: Onofri, "Sacralità," p. 57.

18. Smith, "Lodrisio Crivelli," p. 50.

19. Pacifici, *Un Carme biografico di Sisto IV*, p. 15.

20. Alessandro Cortesi, *Carmen in laudem pontificatus Sixti IV (1475)*, ed. Dino Cortese (Padua, 1971), pp. 8, 15–19; Patetta, *Venturino de Prioribus*, pp. 142–43, 382.

21. Schröter, "Vatikan als Hügel Apollons," p. 220; this article is fundamental for any consideration of the Golden Age theme in Renaissance Rome.

22. *Ibid.*, pp. 221–22; Rash-Fabbri, "A Note on the Stanza della Segnatura," p. 102.

23. Mansi, *Collectio*, XXXII, col. 762. Gargha's oration to the Fifth Lateran Council (19 December 1513) also spoke of the reform of religion (under the recently elected Leo X) as ushering in the Golden Age and the return of justice from heaven: *ibid*, col. 854. For other early sixteenth-century Roman humanist references to the Golden Age, note O'Malley, "Discovery of America and Reform Thought at the Papal Court," p. 191 and 198, n. 35.

24. Cruciani, *Teatro del Campidoglio*, p. 26. A more elaborate treatment of the same theme, including the *Meeting of Janus and Saturn*, formed part of the ceiling decoration for the Villa Lante, constructed on the Janiculum by Baldassare Turini, who served Leo X as *datarius* and later, under Clement VII, held the post of papal secretary: Coffin, *Villa in the Life of Renaissance Rome*, pp. 257–65. Similar ideas appear in the Florentine *trionfo* of 1513, which celebrated the resumption of Medici rule in that city as the return of the Golden Age: Gilbert, *Machiavelli and Guicciardini*, pp. 142–43.

25. O'Malley, *Praise and Blame*, p. 184.

26. O'Malley, *Giles of Viterbo*, pp. 49–50.

27. The text of Giles's *libellus* appears in O'Malley, "Fulfillment of the Christian Golden Age," pp. 278–338.

28. Vida's *Christiad* advances the same idea: Di Cesare, pp. 254, 271–72, 284.

29. Mansi, *Collectio*, XXXII, col. 761. For the prevalence of the theme of *pax et concordia* among the Roman humanists, see O'Malley, *Praise and Blame*, pp. 228–32; note also D'Amico, *Renaissance Humanism in Papal Rome*, p. 225. The longing for peace and concord did not originate in the Roman Renaissance. Oberman, for instance, in his "Shape of Late Medieval Thought," pp. 24–25, notes the prominence of aspirations for peace and concord in the reform proposals of the Conciliar period. In later fifteenth and early sixteenth century Rome, however, not only was the *pax et concordia* motif ubiquitous, but it also represented the enlarged expectations for the providential role of the Roman Church in human history and the new political and cultural ideals of the mature Renaissance world.

30. In the same way the Roman humanists hailed Julius II with Julius Caesar's title, *Pacator Orbis*: Schröter, "Vatikan als Hügel Apollons," p. 229.

31. Shearman, *Raphael's Cartoons*, pp. 17, 74–76.

32. E.g., Cajetan, addressing the Fifth Lateran Council, describes the Church as ". . . *illa Ierusalem, . . . in qua . . . rex pacificus pacem relinquit nobis, pacem suam dat nobis:*" Mansi, *Collectio*, XXXII, col. 723. For other citations of this passage in the works of Roman intellectuals, see O'Malley, *Praise and Blame*, p. 229, and Di Cesare, *Vida's 'Christiad'*, p. 255.

"*Pacem meam do vobis*" was, of course, also a prominent liturgical text, recited in every Mass, just before communion.

33. Shearman, *Raphael's Cartoons*, p. 19.

34. Gilbert, *Machiavelli and Guicciardini*, pp. 105–23.

35. For the score of Isaac's motet, see Albert Dunning, ed., *Vier Staatsmotetten des 16. Jahrhunderts*, in Friedrich Blume and Kurt Gudewill, eds., *Das Chorwerk*, Vol. CXX (Wolfenbuttel: Möseler, 1977), pp. 1–22. For the historical circumstances of the motet, see also Albert Dunning, *Die Staatsmotette, 1480–1555* (Utrecht: A. Oosthoek's Uitgeversmaatschappij N.V., 1969), pp. 45–53. For Giovanni de' Medici's praise of Isaac as a composer of motets, see the remarks Paolo Cortesi attributes to him in *De Cardinalatu*: for the text, English trans., and commentary on the relevant passage, see Nino Pirotta, "Music and Cultural Tendencies in Fifteenth Century Italy," *JAMS*, XIX (1966), pp. 147–61. For expectations of Leo's pontificate similar to those voiced by Isaac, see Marcello, "*Oratio ad Leonem X. Pont. Max.*," BAV, ms. Vat. lat. 3646, fols. 30^{r-v}; Raffaele Brandolini, *Dialogus Leo nuncupatus*, pp. 105–07; and the sources cited in Shearman, *Raphael's Cartoons*, pp. 14–17, 74–78.

36. O'Malley, *Praise and Blame*, pp. 129–32, 222.

37. *Ibid.*, pp. 196, 208–09; *id.*, *Giles of Viterbo*, pp. 115, 168–69; *id.*, "Discovery of America," pp. 189–95; Shearman, *Raphael's Cartoons*, pp. 78–83.

38. O'Malley, *Praise and Blame*, pp. 161–63.

39. In a letter to Benivieni, Pico writes that he was inspired to pursue the ideal of a *pax philosophica* by Christ's words in John 14: 27: "*Pacem meam do vobis, pacem relinquo vobis.*" See Ernst Cassirer, "Giovanni Pico della Mirandola: A Study in the History of Renaissance Ideas," *JHI*, III (1942), pp. 126–27. For Pico's ideas of theological concord, note also Trinkaus, *In Our Image*, pp. 753–60.

40. Eugenio Garin, *Portraits from the Quattrocento*, pp. 200–06. For the text of the Theses and discussion of the events surrounding their composition and partial condemnation, see Giovanni Pico della Mirandola, *Conclusiones sive Theses DCCCC*, ed. Bohdan Kieszkowski [Travaux d'humanisme et Renaissance, CXXXI] (Geneva: Droz, 1973). Pico notes (*ibid.*, p. 6) that he raised the number of his theses from 700 to 900 ". . . *in eo numero, utpote mistico, pedam sistere.*" For Pico's preoccupation with the idea of a universal concord of doctrines, for his stress on a *pax unifica*, and for the place of the planned Roman disputation in promoting this end, see esp. Giovanni Di Napoli, *Giovanni Pico della Mirandola e la problematica dottrinale del suo tempo* (Rome: Desclée, 1965), Ch. 2 and 3.

41. One of Pico's objectionable theses—and one he seemed particularly determined to defend—was the greater likelihood of Origen's salvation (whereas the Middle Ages had considered him a heresiarch); for Pico's defense of Origen, see Wind, "Revival of Origen," pp. 412–16. For the whole matter of the condemnation, note esp. William G. Craven, *Giovanni Pico della Mirandola, Symbol of his Age: Modern Interpretations of a Renaissance Philosopher* [Travaux d'humanisme et Renaissance, CLXXXV] (Geneva: Droz, 1981), pp. 47–75.

42. O'Malley, *Praise and Blame*, pp. 112, 132–36; *id.*, "An Ash Wednesday Sermon on the Dignity of Man for Pope Julius II, 1513," in Sergio Bertelli and Gloria Ramakus, eds., *Essays Presented to Myron P. Gilmore* (Florence: La Nuova Italia, 1978), I, pp. 193–207.

43. "*In quibus recitandis non Romanae linguae nitorem, sed celebratissimorum Parisiensium disputatorum dicendi genus est imitatus.*" Pico, *Conclusiones*, ed., Kieszkowski, p. 27.

44. *Ibid.*, pp. 21–22; John F. D'Amico, "Paolo Cortesi's Rehabilitation of Giovanni Pico della Mirandola," *Bibliothèque d'humanisme et Renaissance*, XLIV (1982), pp. 37–51.

45. Trinkaus, *In Our Image*, pp. 683–753; D.P. Walker, *The Ancient Theology: Studies in Christian Platonism from the Fifteenth to the Eighteenth Century* (Ithaca: Cornell U. Pr., 1972), pp. 1–41.

46. For Giles's ideas of a *pax philosophica* and their intellectual antecedents, see O'Malley, *Giles of Viterbo*, pp. 19–33, 55–63; and Wind, "Revival of Origen," pp. 416–18.

47. Zabughin, *Giulio Pomponio Leto*, I, pp. 223–24 (citing BAV, ms. Vat. lat. 3415, fols. 93^{r}, 102^{r}).

48. John Whittaker, "Greek Manuscripts from the Library of Giles of Viterbo at the Biblioteca Angelica in Rome," *Scriptorium*, XXXI (1977), pp. 221–22.

49. Walker, *Ancient Theology*, pp. 17–21; Karl H. Dannenfeldt, "Egypt and Egyptian Antiquities in the Renaissance," *SR*, VI (1959), p. 10.

50. Dannenfeldt, "Egypt," pp. 8–11, 23–24; Jean Seznec, *The Survival of the Pagan Gods: The Mythological Tradition and its Place in Renaissance Humanism and Art* (N.Y.: Harper &

Row, 1961), pp. 99–100; Edgar Wind, *Pagan Mysteries in the Renaissance*, 2nd ed. (N.Y.: Norton, 1968), pp. 206–08; Rudolf Wittkower, "Hieroglyphics in the Early Renaissance," in Bernard S. Levy, ed., *Developments in the Early Renaissance* (Albany: SUNY Pr., 1972), pp. 58–97.

51. O'Malley, *Giles of Viterbo*, p. 81.

52. Dannenfeldt, "Egypt," pp. 9–10.

53. For what follows, see Fritz Saxl, "The Appartamento Borgia," in *Lectures*, pp. 174–88; and N. Randolph Parks, "On the Meaning of Pinturicchio's *Sala dei Santi*," *Art History*, II (1979), pp. 291–317.

54. Wittkower, "Hieroglyphics," p. 69.

55. Gombrich, *Symbolic Images*, pp. 102–04.

56. Traeger, "Raffaels Stanza d'Eliodoro," pp. 57–59, sees the fusion in the person of the Roman pontiff of the priestly authority of Jerusalem with the political authority of Rome as a key theme of Raphael's frescoes for this room.

57. O'Malley, *Giles of Viterbo*, pp. 84–91; note also Wind, *Pagan Mysteries*, pp. 18–21.

58. "Oration on the Dignity of Man," in Ernst Cassirer, *et al.*, *The Renaissance Philosophy of Man* (Chicago: U. of Chicago Pr., 1948), p. 252; note Trinkaus, *In Our Image*, pp. 756–58, and Kieszkowski's edition of Pico's *Conclusiones*, p. 18.

59. Flavius Mithridates, *Sermo de Passione Domini*, ed. Chaim Wirszubski (Jerusalem: Israel Academy of Science and Humanities, 1963); note also Gherardi, *Diario romano*, p. 49, O'Malley, *Praise and Blame*, p. 23, and Pico, *Conclusiones*, ed. Kieszkowski, pp. 17–19. For Mithridates' relations with Pico, see G. Dell'Acqua and L. Münster, "I rapporti di Giovanni Pico della Mirandola con alcuni filosofi ebrei," in *L'Opera e il pensiero di Giovanni Pico della Mirandola nella storia dell'Umanesimo: Convegno internazionale (Mirandola: 15–18 settembre 1963)* (Florence: Istituto Nazionale di Studi sul Rinascimento, 1965), Vol. II: *Comunicazioni*, pp. 149–68; François Secret, "Nouvelles precisions sur Flavius Mithridates maitre de Pic de la Mirandole et traducteur de commentaires de Kabbale," *ibid.*, pp. 169–87; Chaim Wirszubski, "Giovanni Pico's Book of Job," *JWCI*, XXXII (1969), pp. 171–99.

60. O'Malley, *Giles of Viterbo*, pp. 77–82; for the relationship between Pico and Giles, see also Secret, "Notes sur Egidio da Viterbo," pp. 205–12. For the importance of Hebrew learning to Giles's Biblical scholarship, see F. X. Martin, O.S.A., "Giles of Viterbo as Scripture Scholar," in *Egidio da Viterbo, O.S.A., e il suo tempo*, pp. 191–222.

61. O'Malley, *Giles of Viterbo*, pp. 74, 97–101; *id.*, "Giles of Viterbo: A Reformer's Thought on Renaissance Rome," pp. 7–8.

62. For the meaning of orthodoxy in Giles of Viterbo's thought and its relationship to aspirations for concord, see O'Malley, *Giles*, pp. 33–39.

63. For a general background to the sibyls, see Edgar Wind, "Michelangelo's Prophets and Sibyls," *PBA*, LI (1965), pp. 57–60.

64. Miglio, *Storiografia pontificia*, p. 185.

65. Seznec, *Survival of the Pagan Gods*, pp. 16–17, 128.

66. Hülsen, "Legend of the Aracoeli," pp. 1–11; Giuseppe Giannelli, "La leggenda dei *Mirabilia* e l'antica topografia dell'Arce Capitolina," *Studi romani*, XXVI (1978), pp. 60–71; Brentano, *Rome before Avignon*, pp. 78–79.

67. Valla, *De falso credita et ementita Constantini donatione*, ed. Setz, pp. 141–42.

68. Francesco Petrarca, *Rerum memorandarum libri*, ed. Giuseppe Billanovich (Florence, 1943), pp. 210–14; *id.*, *De otio religioso*, ed. Giuseppe Rotondi [Studi e Testi, 195] (Vatican, 1958), pp. 26–29. Note Fubini, "Intendimenti umanistici e riferimenti patristici," p. 547.

69. Giovanni Mercati, *Opere minori*, IV, pp. 275–76.

70. Zabughin, *Leto*, I, pp. 225–26.

71. Dotson, "An Augustinian Interpretation of Michelangelo's Sistine Ceiling," pp. 407–08.

72. *Liber de vita Christi ac omnium pontificum*, pp. 6–7. A further indication of Roman humanist curiosity about the sibyls is Castiglione's request, datable to the first decade of the sixteenth century, of a certain "Messer Paolo" for information on the specifics of time and place of the sibyls, their prophecies, and who has written about them: Castiglione, *Lettere rare e inedite*, p. 109.

73. Pope-Hennessy, *Raphael*, pp. 207–09; Herbert von Einem, "Bemerkungen zu Raffaels *Madonna di Foligno*," in *Studies in Honor of Millard Meiss*, pp. 131–42.

74. Michael Hirst, "The Chigi Chapel in S. Maria della Pace," *JWCI*, XXIV (1961), pp. 169–70; L.D. Ettlinger, "A Note on Raphael's Sibyls in S. Maria della Pace," *ibid.*, pp. 322–23.

75. Chastel, *Art et humanisme*, pp. 236–40.

76. Martin, "Writings of Giles of Viterbo," p. 174.

77. Wind, "Michelangelo's Prophets and Sibyls," p. 60, n. 1.

78. A modern edition of Palmieri's poem was published by Margaret Rooke, *Smith College Studies in Modern Languages*, VIII–IX (1927–28). For the sibylline and other Gentile prophecies of Christ, see Bk. III, Chaps, 26–27 (IX, pp. 216–25).

79. Wind, "Michelangelo's Prophets and Sibyls," p. 58, n. 2, 70–74; and *id.*, *Pagan Mysteries*, p. 175.

80. "*Easdem distinxit Platonicus Latinus, cum ad aurum et beatam vitam assequendam mortales instituit; Sibyllae ducentis scientia prius, deinde numinis afflantis sapientia institui nos oportere significavit.*" Giles of Viterbo, *Libellus*, "*De aurea aetate*," in O'Malley, "Fulfillment," p. 292. This recalls the Virgilian description, "*Adflata est numine*," of the Cumaean Sibyl's divine possession (*Aeneid*, VI, 50), which is echoed, too, as Wind, *Pagan Mysteries*, p. 175, points out, by the inscription NVMINE AFFLATVR that identifies the personification of poetry in the medallion above Raphael's *Parnassus* in the Stanza della Segnatura.

81. Wind, "Michelangelo's Prophets and Sibyls," p. 83, n. 2; John Whittaker, "Giles of Viterbo as Classical Scholar," in *Egidio da Viterbo, O.S.A. e il suo tempo*, pp. 86–92. For Palmieri's visit, see *Città di vita*, Bk. I, Ch. I (*Smith College Studies in Modern Languages*, VIII, pp. 1–5); for Sannazaro's, see his Latin poem "Cumae" in Perosa and Sparrow, eds., *Renaissance Latin Verse*, pp. 149–50.

82. *Libellus* "*De aurea aetate*," in O'Malley, "Fulfillment," pp. 296, 331–32.

83. Wind, "Michelangelo's Prophets and Sibyls," pp. 69–70; Dotson, "Augustinian Interpretation," pp. 412–13. To my mind Dotson provides the most convincing interpretation of the Sistine Chapel ceiling to date, though I am not as persuaded as she that Giles likely took a hand in devising its theological program. I believe instead that the ceiling reflects views generally held in Rome and therefore that other humanists could be suitable candidates for involvement in the project. For a thoughtful criticism of Dotson's approach, see Thomas Martone's letter to the editor, *AB*, LXIV (1982), pp. 484–85; note Dotson's reply, *AB*, LXIV (1982), pp. 655–57.

84. Wind, "Michelangelo's Prophets and Sibyls," p. 58; Dotson, p. 426.

85. Wind," Michelangelo's Prophets and Sibyls," pp. 61–63; *id.*, "The Ark of Noah: A Study in the Symbolism of Michelangelo," *Measure*, I (1950), pp. 414–16.

86. Dotson, p. 234.

87. Wind, "Ark of Noah," p. 413; Dotson, p. 247. Note above, p. 204, for Piero da Monte's and Angelo of Vallombrosa's remarks on Ham.

88. Wind, "Ark of Noah," pp. 417–21; Manetti, in his *Life of Nicholas V*, had argued the similarity of the proportions of St. Peter's basilica to Noah's Ark: Battisti, *Rinascimento e Barocco*, pp. 79–81.

89. Dotson, pp. 426–29, stresses the importance of the ecclesiological theme to the overall meaning of the Sistine Chapel ceiling.

90. Shearman, *Raphael's Cartoons*, pp. 61–82.

91. Which aspects of Creation are included in the second and third panels has been a subject of scholarly disagreement; I follow Dotson's persuasive analysis, pp. 235–39.

92. "*Quae quidem omnia (nisi ferrei simus) quidnam aliud quam caelitus missae voces sunt? Voces namque Dei (ut Proclus ait) facta sunt, de quo uno aiunt oraculo, quod dixit et facta sunt. Et in arcanis Hebreorum legimus, decem dictis quae in Genesi leguntur, orbem universum esse conditum. Voces igitur sunt quae cernimus, voces monentis Dei ac praecipientis ut Synodum habeas, ut Ecclesiam emendes. . . .*" O'Reilly, "'Without Councils We Cannot Be Saved. . .'," p. 202. For Giles's perception of all sacred history as the *providentiae imago*, see O'Malley, *Giles*, pp. 181–84.

93. O'Malley, *Praise and Blame*, p. 49.

94. *Ibid.*, pp. 126, 132–33; the same perspective appears in Vida's *Christiad*: see Di Cesare, p. 274.

95. O'Malley, *Praise and Blame*, pp. 68–70.

96. Trinkaus, *In Our Image and Likeness*, Pts. I-II.

97. *Ibid.*, pp. 181–88; Eugenio Garin, "La *dignitas hominis* e la letteratura patristica," *Rinascita*, I (1938), pp. 112–13, 125–29.

98. BAV, ms. Vat. lat. 301, fols. 6ʳ-7ʳ. Gregory of Nyssa's work had been translated into Latin twice in the Middle Ages, and had previously been cited by Giannozzo Manetti in his *De dignitate et excellentia hominis*: Trinkaus, *In Our Image*, pp. 185–86, 239.

99. O'Malley, *Praise and Blame*, p. 137; *id.*, "An Ash Wednesday Sermon."

100. O'Malley, *Praise and Blame*, pp. 133–37. For Luther's divergent conclusions, see Charles Trinkaus, "Luther's Hexameral Anthropology," in Church and George, eds., *Continuity and Discontinuity in Church History*, pp. 150–68.

101. O'Malley, "Man's Dignity, God's Love, and the Destiny of Rome," pp. 398–401; both Cajetan and Taleazzi also proclaim this in their addresses to the Fifth Lateran Council: Mansi, *Collectio*, XXXII, cols. 723, 920. As O'Malley, *Praise and Blame*, p. 150, points out, this assertion has patristic precedent.

102. This is the perspective, for instance, of Vida's *Christiad*: Di Cesare, pp. 222–23, 253, 278–79; in Staale Sinding-Larsen's view, this is part of the meaning, too, of Michelangelo's Sistine frescoes: "A Re-Reading of the Sistine Ceiling," *Institutum Romanum Norvegiae: Acta ad archaeologiam et artium historiam pertinentia*, IV (1969), p. 151.

103. O'Malley, *Praise and Blame*, pp. 137–50; for the theme of realized eschatology in the fourth Gospel, see Raymond E. Brown, *The Gospel According to John (I-XII)* [The Anchor Bible, Vol. 29] (Garden City, N.Y.: Doubleday, 1966), pp. cxvi-cxxi.

104. This has been remarked by a number of scholars, based on a variety of evidence: Chastel, *Art et humanisme*, pp. 453–55; Portoghesi, *Roma del Rinascimento*, pp. 16–17; O'Malley, *Praise and Blame*, pp. 163, 240; Partridge and Starn, *A Renaissance Likeness*, pp. 68–73, 104–16. Note also Onofri, "Sacralità," p. 57, for Manetti's similar remarks on the Rome of Nicholas V.

105. Romans did not always agree on the signs of the impending end. The Neo-Platonist Giles of Viterbo saw the consummation of the tenth age as involving the purgation from the Church of the Peripatetics' errors (O'Malley, *Giles*, p. 110); the Aristotelian George of Trebizond had identified the resurgence of Platonism in Rome as the great final Apostasy prophesied by St. Paul (II Thessalonians 2: 7) and a sign of the Last Days (note Monfasani, pp. 133, 212–15, 224–25).

106. Panofsky, *Life and Art of Albrecht Dürer*, pp. 51–59; for apocalyptic expectation north of the Alps, see, in general, Oberman, *Harvest*, p. 77, and *id.*, *Forerunners of the Reformation: The Shape of Late Medieval Thought* (N.Y.: Holt, Rinehart & Winston, 1966), pp. 12–14.

107. Weinstein, *Savonarola and Florence*, pp. 138–84.

108. Mansi, *Collectio*, XXXII, cols. 723–24. The theme of the Church as the new Jerusalem descending from heaven had appeared in St. Bernard's *De consideratione*, and had been invoked earlier in the Roman Renaissance in a sermon by Lodovico da Ferrara: O'Malley, *Praise and Blame*, pp. 107, 201–02.

109. E.g., Stefano Taleazzi's sermon to the Fifth Lateran Council: "'Vidi civitatem sanctam novam Ierusalem descendentem de coelo, a Deo paratam sicut sponsam ornatam viro suo.' In hac ergo tali ac tanta civitate Dei, sancta videlicet Romana ecclesia, magnus dominus nimium laudabilis etiam invenitur, et in monte sancto apostolicae sedis eius pro secunda sabbati, plus solito exaltari et magnificari jure aeterno reperitur." Mansi, *Collectio*, XXXII, col. 920; note also Leo X's 1514 Bull *Posteaquam ad universalis ecclesiae curam*, cited (along with other similar statements from other sources) in Shearman, *Raphael's Cartoons*, p. 64, n. 114.

110. O'Malley, *Giles of Viterbo*, pp. 113–14, 122–26, 161–62, 188–90; and *id.*, "Giles of Viterbo: A Reformer's Thought on Renaissance Rome," pp. 7–11.

VII. Epilogue: The Sack and Its Aftermath

1. Lowinsky, "A Newly Discovered Sixteenth-Century Motet Manuscript," pp. 180–82, argues convincingly for the dating of this composition to the time of the Sack. For what occasion and in what circumstances the work was first performed are unknown. Its inclusion in the manuscripts of the Capella Sistina indicate it was written for the official use of the papal chapel. In setting the entire text of Psalm 78 (79), Festa created a five-voice motet of extraordinary size. For the complete score, which bears the title *Deus venerunt gentes*, see Costanzo Festa, *Opera omnia*, ed. Albert Seay, Vol. III (*Motetti*, I) [Corpus mensurabilis musicae, XXV³] (American Institute of Musicology, 1977), pp. 63–78. The *prima pars* is

written over an *ostinato* on vs. 6 of this psalm: *"Effunde iram tuam in gentes quae te non noverunt, Et in regna quae nomen tuum non invocaverunt."* The *seconda pars* contains an *ostinato* on vs. 9 (which is also the antiphon to this psalm): *"Adiuva nos, Deus, salutaris noster; Et propter gloriam nominis tui, Domine, libera nos, Et propitius esto peccatis nostris, propter nomen tuum."* Festa entered the papal chapel in 1517 and remained attached to it until his death in Rome in 1545. Throughout this period he was closely connected to Medicean circles, composing for Clement VII a politically motivated motet, *Florentia tempus est penitentiae* (1527–29), calling upon Florentines to return to papal obedience, and later, in 1539, composing some of the music for Cosimo I's wedding. Contemporaries recognized Festa as a follower of the great Josquin Desprez (d. 1521), but his formation as a composer is still subject to dispute. For recent discussion, see David Crawford, "A Review of Costanzo Festa's Biography," *JAMS*, XXVIII (1975), pp. 102–11, and Lowinsky's rejoinder, "On the Presentation and Interpretation of Evidence: Another Review of Costanzo Festa's Biography," *JAMS*, XXX (1977), pp. 106–28. Festa also composed in the new secular genre of the madrigal: Hans Musch, *Costanzo Festa als Madrigalkomponist* [Sammlung Musikwissenschaftlicher Abhandlungen, 61] (Baden-Baden: Koerner, 1977); pp. 16–23 contain a helpful sketch of Festa's career. Another early madrigalist, Philippe Verdelot, a Northern composer who resided in Florence in the 1520s, composed a madrigal to the words of a sonnet, *Trist'Amarilli mia*, which seems to refer allegorically to the Sack: Don Harran, "The 'Sack of Rome' Set to Music," *RQ*, XXIII (1970), pp. 412–21.

2. Pastor, *History of the Popes*, IX, pp. 426–27.

3. The Sack, its antecedents, and its consequences are treated at length in Pastor, IX, pp. 272–467; see also Judith Hook, *The Sack of Rome, 1527* (London: Macmillan, 1972), E.R. Chamberlin, *The Sack of Rome* (London: Batsford, 1979), and M.L. Lenzi, *Il sacco di Roma del 1527* (Florence: Nuova Italia, 1978). For its cultural impact, see Chastel, *Sack of Rome*.

4. For the Lutheran graffiti, see Deoclezio Redig de Campos, "Il nome di Martin Lutero graffito sulla Disputà del Sacramento," *Ecclesia*, VI (1947), pp. 648–49, and *id.*, "Un altro graffito del Sacco nelle Stanze di Raffaello," *Ecclesia*, XIX (1960), pp. 552–54. For the theft of the Raphael tapestries, see Shearman, *Raphael's Cartoons*, pp. 140–41. Chastel, *Sack of Rome*, pp. 91–108, discusses the atrocities and profanations.

5. Lauro Martines, *Power and Imagination: City-States in Renaissance Italy* (N.Y.: Knopf, 1979), pp. 284–85, 295–96; Braudel, *The Mediterranean*, p. 390. For the impact of these calamities on contemporary historians, see Cochrane, *Historians and Historiography*, pp. 163–97.

6. Roberto Ridolfi, *The Life of Francesco Guicciardini*, trans. Cecil Grayson (N.Y.: Knopf, 1968), pp. 174–75; note also Gilbert, *Machiavelli and Guicciardini*, pp. 287–89.

7. Guicciardini, *Storia d'Italia*, ed. Menchi, p. 1859.

8. John E. Longhurst, trans. and ed., with Raymond R. MacCurdy, *Alfonso de Valdés and the Sack of Rome: Dialogue of Lactancio and an Archdeacon* (Albuquerque: U. of New Mexico Pr., 1952); note also Yates, *Astraea*, pp. 24–25.

9. *Alfonso de Valdés and the Sack of Rome*, Appendix III, pp. 101–17.

10. Douglas, *Sadoleto*, pp. 54–57.

11. O'Malley, *Giles of Viterbo*, pp. 7, 110–16, 133–34, 176. For the Sack's disruptive impact on Roman humanism and on the cultural ideology of the Leonine period, see De Caprio, "Intellettuali e mercato del lavoro nella Roma medicea;" note esp. pp. 29–33 for discussion of Giovanni Pierio Valeriano's *De litteratorum infelicitate*, a dialogue written in the wake of the Sack, in which the author sees in this "cruel tragedy" the destruction of the eighty-year period of humanism's ascendency in Rome. For Valeriano, note also Charles Trinkaus, *Adversity's Noblemen: The Italian Humanists on Happiness* (N.Y.: Octagon Books, 1965; first publ. N.Y.: Columbia U. Pr., 1940), pp. 137–38.

12. For a brief sketch of the political repercussions of the events of 1527–30, see Martines, *Power and Imagination*, pp. 285–87. I am convinced these were the watershed years, not the pontificate of Paul IV (1555–59), as Partner, *Renaissance Rome*, pp. 30–46, argues.

13. Among those who left were Bembo (for Padua, 1521), Pietro Aretino (after several abrupt departures and returns in the years 1522–25, he left for Venice in 1525, never to return), and Giulio Romano (to Mantua, 1524, but plans were already afoot for his departure to the Gonzaga court almost immediately after Leo's death). For Adrian's impact and for the Clementine style, see Chastel, *Sack of Rome*, pp. 136–39, 149–78.

14. For a recent analysis of this work, see Marcia B. Hall, "Michelangelo's *Last Judgment*: Resurrection of the Body and Predestination," *AB*, LVIII (1976), pp. 85–92. The thesis of Leo Steinberg, "Michelangelo's *Last Judgment* as Merciful Heresy," *Art in America*, LXIII, No. 6 (Nov.-Dec. 1975), pp. 48–63, that the theological content of the fresco is unorthodox, seems hardly plausible. Is this a tenable conclusion for the altar-wall decoration of the main chapel of the papal palace in Rome? Nevertheless, Steinberg provides a sensitive reading of certain elements in the work, e.g., the representation of the Virgin, the corporeality of the saved, and the personifications of the mortal sins. For Michelangelo's own spiritual anxieties during the 1530s and '40s, note *id.*, *Michelangelo's Last Paintings*, pp. 39–41.

15. For Paul III's triumphal entry in 1538, see Mitchell, *Italian Civic Pageantry*, pp. 129–30. In the Carnival of 1536, the first in many years to emulate the pomp of the early sixteenth-century *Festa di Agone*, the theme of the triumphal *carri* focussed on the triumphs of the ancient Roman consul, Aemilius Paullus. Not only the identity of names with the reigning pontiff but also the evocation of the Roman hero's justice as an administrator, his stern support for religion, and his victories in battle were meant in praise of the person and policies of the Farnese pope. As such, it echoed the propagandistic purposes to which the procession was put by Alexander VI and Julius II. Fundamental for the meaning and purpose of public festivities during Paul's pontificate remains V. Forcella, *Tornei e giostre, ingressi trionfali e feste carnevalesche in Roma sotto Paolo III* (Rome, 1885). For the revival of Roman High Renaissance values under Paul III, note the succinct but perceptive analysis of Davidson, "The Decoration of the Sala Regia," pp. 418–21, and also Portoghesi, *Roma del Rinascimento*, pp. 167–72.

16. Davidson, "Sala Regia," pp. 395–423; Harprath, *Papst Paul III. als Alexander der Grosse*; Partridge, review of Harprath, *AB*, LXII (1980), pp. 661–63; and Schröter, "Zur Inhaltsdeutung des Alexander-Programms der Sala Paolina," esp. pp. 88–92.

17. Schmitt, "Perennial Philosophy: From Agostino Steuco to Leibniz," pp. 515–27; Secret, "Notes sur Egidio da Viterbo," pp. 230–33.

18. Schmitt, p. 516.

19. Douglas, *Sadoleto*, pp. 99–103.

20. *Ibid.*, pp. 106–09; for a brief discussion and English trans. of the *Consilium*, see Olin, ed., *Catholic Reformation*, pp. 183–97.

21. Ferreri's *De reformatione Ecclesiae suasoria*, in typical Roman Renaissance fashion, contrasts the Babylon of the present age of the Roman Church with the purity and beauty of the "former Zion," when hearts and minds were one with the Lord. He continues, "*Porro cum Romana ecclesia sit caput, mater et magistra omnium ecclesiarum, ea infecta et reliquiae facile inficiuntur ecclesiae, et ea purgata praeclarisque virtutibus, et moribus instaurata et reformata, reliquiae instaurantur et reformantur ecclesiae. Purga Romam, purgatur mundus. Instaura, reforma Romam, instauratur, reformatur orbis universus. . . .*" For discussion of this work and relevant citations from the text, see McNally, "Pope Adrian VI and Church Reform," pp. 272–75.

22. Douglas, *Sadoleto*, pp. 72–162. Note also Marvin W. Anderson, "Biblical Humanism and Roman Catholic Reform (1501–42): Contarini, Pole, and Giberti," *Concordia Theological Monthly*, XXXIX (1968), pp. 686–707. For Contarini, see J. B. Ross, "Gasparo Contarini and his Friends," *SR*, XVII (1970), pp. 192–232; *id.*, "The Emergence of Gasparo Contarini: A Bibliographic Essay," *Church History*, XLI (1972), pp. 22–45; Felix Gilbert, "Religion and Politics in the Thought of Gasparo Contarini," in Theodore K. Rabb and Jerrold E. Seigel, eds., *Action and Conviction in Early Modern Europe: Essays in Memory of E. H. Harbison* (Princeton: Princeton U. Pr., 1969), pp. 90–116; and Peter Matheson, *Cardinal Contarini at Regensburg* (Oxford: Clarendon Pr., 1972). For Pole, see Dermot Fenlon, *Heresy and Obedience in Tridentine Italy: Cardinal Pole and the Counter Reformation* (Cambridge: Cambridge U. Pr., 1972).

23. Myron P. Gilmore, "Anti-Erasmianism in Italy: The Dialogue of Ortensio Lando on Erasmus' Funeral," *JMRS*, IV (1974), pp. 1–14; and *id.*, "Italian Reactions to Erasmian Humanism," pp. 61–115.

24. Harry J. McSorley, "Erasmus and the Primacy of the Roman Pontiff: Between Conciliarism and Papalism," *ARG*, LXV (1974), pp. 37–54.

25. There is an enormous recent literature on the *spirituali*: note esp. Elisabeth G. Gleason, "On the Nature of Sixteenth-Century Italian Evangelism: Scholarship, 1953–1978," *Sixteenth Century Journal*, IX/3 (1978), pp. 3–25, to which should be added Paolo

Simoncelli, *Evangelismo italiano del Cinquecento* (Rome, 1979). For Flaminio, see Carol Maddison, *Marcantonio Flaminio: Poet, Humanist and Reformer* (Chapel Hill: U. of N. Carolina Pr., 1965).

26. Note Douglas's perceptive comments: *Sadoleto*, pp. 86, 92–93. In accounting for Contarini's failure at Ratisbon, Matheson comments, p. 180, "his heritage was that of the Mediterranean. He was a Latin through and through. His ideals were the Classical ones. He still believed in the triumph of reason and order and harmony. His world remained fundamentally intact." One further difficulty in negotiation with the Protestants was that papal representatives sent to Germany in the early Reformation period lacked knowledge of German: see Barbara McClung Hallman, "Italian 'Natural Superiority' and the Lutheran Question: 1517–1546," *ARG*, LXXI (1980), pp. 134–48.

27. Two recent articles treat aspects of these developments: Massimo Firpo, "Sulla legazione di pace di Reginald Pole (1553–1556)," *Rivista storica italiana*, XCIII (1981), pp. 821–37, and Massimo Firpo and Dario Marcatto, "il primo processo inquisitoriale contro il Cardinale Giovanni Morone (1552–1553)," *Rivista storica italiana*, XCIII (1981), pp. 71–142.

28. Evennett, *Spirit of the Counter-Reformation*, pp. 23–42.

29. Jean Delumeau, *Catholicism between Luther and Voltaire: A New View of the Counter-Reformation* (Philadelphia: Westminster Pr., 1977), pp. 60–95. For recent approaches to the whole issue of the Counter-Reformation, see John W. O'Malley, "Catholic Reform," in Steven Ozment, ed., *Reformation Europe: A Guide to Research* (St. Louis: Center for Reformation Research, 1982), pp. 297–319.

30. Delumeau, *Vie économique et sociale de Rome*, pp. 223–339.

31. Coffin, *Villa in the Life of Renaissance Rome*, pp. 281–362; Partridge, "Divinity and Dynasty at Caprarola," pp. 494–530; Claudia Lazzaro-Bruno, "The Villa Lante at Bagnaia: An Allegory of Art and Nature," *AB*, LIX (1977), pp. 553–60.

32. Graham Smith, *The Casino of Pius IV* (Princeton: Princeton U. Pr., 1977); note also M. Fagiolo and M.L. Madonna, "La Roma di Pio IV: la *Civitas Pia*, la *Salus Medica*, la *Custodia Angelica*," *Arte illustrata*, V (1972), pp. 383–402, and Coffin, *Villa*, pp. 267–78.

33. Smith, pp. 107–12, stresses the qualities of intimacy and introspection present in the Casino of Pius IV; note also esp. Partridge, "Divinity and Dynasty at Caprarola," p. 528, for the differences in style between the frescoes in the Room of the Farnese Deeds and Roman art of the early Cinquecento.

34. Smith, pp. 91–92.

35. Brummer, *Statue Court*, pp. 254–64; MacDougall, "Sleeping Nymph," p. 365.

36. Haskell, *Patrons and Painters*, pp. 3–93; Victor-L. Tapie, *The Age of Grandeur: Baroque Art and Architecture* (N.Y.: Praeger, 1966), pp. 3–66.

37. Cochrane, *Historians and Historiography*, pp. 452–53.

38. *Ibid.*, pp. 457–71.

39. Frederick J. McGinness, "The Rhetoric of Praise and the New Rome of the Counter Reformation," in Ramsey, ed., *Rome in the Renaissance*, pp. 355–70; *id.*, "Preaching Ideals and Practice in Counter-Reformation Rome," *Sixteenth Century Journal*, XI/2 (1980), pp. 109–27.

40. Richard Krautheimer, "A Christian Triumph in 1597," in *Essays in the History of Art Presented to Rudolf Wittkower*, pp. 174–78.

VIII. Conclusion

1. Portoghesi, *Roma del Rinascimento*, pp. 14–15.

2. Steven Ozment, *The Age of Reform, 1250–1550: An Intellectual and Religious History of Late Medieval and Reformation Europe* (New Haven: Yale U. Pr., 1980), p. 309.

3. Scott H. Hendrix, *Luther and the Papacy: Stages in a Reformation Conflict* (Philadelphia: Fortress Pr., 1981).

4. O'Malley, *Praise and Blame*, p. 65.

5. Hartt, "Art and Freedom," p. 117, n. 7.

BIBLIOGRAPHY

Abbreviations

AB	*The Art Bulletin*
AHP	*Archivum historiae pontificiae*
AHR	*American Historical Review*
ARG	*Archiv für Reformationsgeschichte*
ARSRSP	*Archivio della R. Società Romana di Storia Patria*
BAV	Biblioteca Apostolica Vaticana
BEFAR	Bibliothèque des Écoles Françaises d'Athènes et de Rome
CHR	*Catholic Historical Review*
DBI	*Dizionario biografico degli Italiani* (Rome, 1960–)
JAMS	*Journal of the American Musicological Society*
JHI	*Journal of the History of Ideas*
JMRS	*The Journal of Medieval and Renaissance History*
JSAH	*Journal of the Society of Architectural Historians*
MAHEFR	*Melanges d'archéologie et d'histoire de l'École Française de Rome*
MH	*Medievalia et Humanistica*
PAPS	*Proceedings of the American Philosophical Society*
PBA	*Proceedings of the British Academy*
QFIAB	*Quellen und Forschungen aus italienischen Archiven und Bibliotheken*
RendPontAcc	*Atti della Pontificia Accademia Romana di Archeologia, Rendiconti*
RHE	*Revue d'histoire ecclésiastique*
RIS	*Rerum italicarum scriptores*, ed. Muratori
RIS²	*Rerum italicarum scriptores*, 2nd ed.
RQ	*Renaissance Quarterly*
RSCI	*Rivista di storia della Chiesa in Italia*
SCSH	*Smith College Studies in History*
SMRH	*Studies in Medieval and Renaissance History*
SR	*Studies in the Renaissance*
TAPS	*Transactions of the American Philosophical Society*

Primary Sources

Acciaiuoli, Zanobio. *Oratio in laudem Urbis Romae.* Rome: J. Mazochius, 1518.

Alberti, Leon Battista. *De Porcaria conjuratione.* In *Opera inedita*, ed. Girolamo Mancini, pp. 257–66. Florence: Sansoni, 1890.

Albertini, Francesco. *Opusculum de mirabilibus novae et veteris Urbis Romae.* Rome: Mazocchio, 1510. Text of *Opusculum de mirabilibus novae Urbis Romae* (only), ed. August Schmarsow. Heilbronn: Henniger, 1886.

Alighieri, Dante. *Monarchia*, ed. Pier Giorgio Ricci. *Le opere di Dante Alighieri*, Edizione nazionale a cura della Società Dantesca Italiana, Vol. V. Verona: Arnaldo Mondadori, 1965.

Anconitanus, Kyriacus (Ciriaco d'Ancona). *Itinerarium*, ed. Laurentius Mehus. Bologna: Forni, 1969; reprint edition of Florence: Giovanelli, 1742.

Anon. Latin trans. of Cyril of Alexandria, *Commentary on Genesis*. BAV, ms. Vat. lat. 529.

Aretino, Pietro. *La Cortigiana*, ed. Giuliano Innamorati. Collezione di teatro, 137. Turin: Einaudi, 1970.

Argyropoulos, John, trans. Latin trans. of Basil, *Homilies on the Hexaemeron*. BAV, ms. Vat. lat. 301.

Ariosto, Ludovico. *The Satires of Ludovico Ariosto: A Renaissance Autobiography*, trans. Peter Desa Wiggins. Athens: Ohio U. Pr., 1976.

Augustine. *De civitate Dei*. BAV, ms. Reg. lat. 1882.

Balbo, Pietro, trans. Latin trans. of John Chrysostom homily, *De patientia et longanimitate*. BAV, ms. Vat. lat. 3660.

Bardoni, Girolamo. *La exortatione de la crutiata a la Sanctita del nostro Signore Papa Leone X e a tucti li signori e principi christiani de la impresa contra Turchi*. Rome?, ?.

Bertola, Maria. *I due primi registri di prestito della Biblioteca Apostolica Vaticana: Codici Vaticani latini 3964, 3966*. Vatican, 1942.

Biondo, Flavio. *Opera omnia*. Basel: Froben, 1531.

———. *Scritti inediti e rari di Biondo Flavio*, ed. Bartolomeo Nogara. Studi e Testi, 48. Rome, 1927.

Birago, Lampugnino. *Strategicon*. BAV, ms. Vat. lat. 3423.

———, trans. Latin trans. of Basil, *Homilies on the Hexaemeron*. BAV, ms. Vat. lat. 302.

da Bisticci, Vespasiano. *Le vite*, ed. Aulo Greco. Vol. I. Florence: Istituto Nazionale di Studi sul Rinascimento, 1970.

Brandolini, Aurelio Lippo. *De laudibus et de rebus gestis Sixti IIII Pont. Max.* BAV, ms. Urb. lat. 739, fols. 18^v-32^v.

Brandolini, Raffaele. *Dialogus Leo nuncupatus*, ed. Francesco Fogliazzi. Venice: Occhi, 1753.

———. *Oratio ad Lateranensem Concilium*. BAV, ms. Ottob. lat. 813.

Brucker, Gene, ed. *The Society of Renaissance Florence: A Documentary Study*. N.Y.: Harper & Row, 1971.

———. *Two Memoirs of Renaissance Florence: The Diaries of Buonaccorso Pitti and Gregorio Dati*. N.Y.: Harper & Row, 1967.

Burchardus, Iohannes. *Liber notarum*, ed. Enrico Celani. RIS², Vol. XXXII, Pt. I. Città di Castello: S. Lapi, 1906.

Cajetan (Tommaso de Vio). *De divina institutione Pontificatus Romani Pontificis (1521)*, ed. Friedrich Lauchert. Corpus Catholicorum, 10. Münster: Aschendorff, 1925.

Calvin, Iohannes. *Opera quae supersunt omnia*. Corpus Reformatorum. 59 vols. Braunschweig and Berlin, 1863–1900.

Canensi, Michele. *Le vite di Paolo II di Gaspare da Verona e Michele Canensi*, ed. Giuseppe Zippel. RIS², Vol. III, Pt. XVI. Città di Castello: S. Lapi, 1904–11.

Capgrave, John. *Ye solace of Pilgrimes: A Description of Rome, circa A.D. 1450*, ed. C. A. Mills. London: Oxford U. Pr., 1911.

Capito, V. Fabritius, trans. Latin trans. of John Chrysostom, *Homilia*. Basel: Froben, 1519.

Cassirer, Ernst, *et al*. *The Renaissance Philosophy of Man*. Chicago: U. of Chicago Pr., 1948.

Castiglione, Baldassare. *Lettere inedite e rare*, ed. Guglielmo Gorni. Milan: Ricciardi, 1969.

Cellini, Benvenuto. *The Autobiography of Benvenuto Cellini*, trans. George Bull. Harmondsworth: Penguin, 1956.

Chalcheophilos, Athanasius, trans. Latin trans. of Gregory of Nyssa, *Homilies*, BAV, ms. Vat. lat. 256.

Chrysoloras, Manuel. *Laudatio Urbis Romae et Constantinopolis*, trans. Francesco Aleardo da Verona. BAV, ms. Vat. lat. 807, fols. 24^v-59^r.

Collectionis Bullarum, Brevium aliorumque Diplomatum sacrosanctae Basilicae Vaticanae, Vol. II: *Ab Urbano V ad Paulum III*. Rome: Archigymnasio Sapientiae, 1750.

Cortesi, Alessandro. *Carmen in laudem pontificatus Sixti IV (1475)*, ed. Dino Cortese. Padua, 1971.

Corvinus, Maximus. *Oratio Maximi Corvini Partenopei episcopi Eserniensis sanctissimo Iulio II Pontifici Maximo dicta*. Rome: ?, 1513.

Domenichi, Domenico de'. "Oratio in laudem civitatis et civilitatis Romanae." BAV, ms. Ottob. lat. 83^r-87^v.

———. *Domenico de' Domenichi und seine Schrift 'De potestate pape et termino eius'. Edition und Kommentar*, ed. Heribert Smolinsky. Münster: Aschendorff, 1977.

Dunning, Albert, ed. *Vier Staatsmotetten des 16. Jahrhunderts*. Das Chorwerk, eds. Friedrich Blume and Kurt Gudewill, Vol. CXX. Wolfenbuttel: Möseler, 1977.

Eck, Johannes. *Enchiridion locorum, communionem adversus Lutherum et alios hostes Ecclesiae*

(1525–1543), ed. Pierre Fraenkel. Corpus Catholicorum, 34. Münster: Aschendorff, 1979.

Erasmus, Desiderius. *The 'Julius Exclusus' of Erasmus*. Translated by Paul Pascal, intro. and critical notes by J. Kelly Sowards. Bloomington: Indiana U. Pr., 1968.

———. *Opera omnia*. Ordinis primis, Tomus primus. Amsterdam: North-Holland Publishing, 1969.

———. *Opus epistolarum Des. Erasmi Roterodami*, ed. P. S. Allen. 12 vols. Oxford: Clarendon Pr., 1906–58.

Ferreri, Zaccaria. *Lugudunense Somnium*. ?. 1513?.

Ferrosius, Archangelus. *De potestate summi Pontificis, eius veneratione, et cognominatione, ac de justo bello Clem. vii contra Florentinus*. BAV, ms. Vat. lat. 4125, fols. 1ᵛ-182ᵛ.

Festa, Costanzo. *Opera omnia*, ed. Albert Seay, Vol. III (Motetti, I). Corpus mensurabilis musicae, XXV³. American Institute of Musicology, 1977.

"La Festa de Agoni facta in tempo de papa Leone decimo . . . ordinata per T. Phaedro Vulterrano." BAV, ms. Vat. lat. 3351, fol. 171ᵛ.

Filelfo, Francesco, trans. Latin trans. of *De sacerdotio Christi*. BAV, ms. Vat. lat. 3654.

da Firenze, Mariano, Fra. *Itinerarium Urbis Romae*, ed. P. Enrico Bulletti. Rome, 1931.

Garin, Eugenio, ed. *Prosatori latini del Quattrocento*. Milan-Naples: Ricciardi, 1952.

Gherardi da Volterra, Jacopo. *Il diario romano*, ed. Enrico Carusi. RIS², Vol. XXIII, Pt. III. Città di Castello: S. Lapi, 1904.

Griffolini, Francesco, trans. Latin trans. of miscellaneous works of John Chrysostom. BAV, ms. Vat. lat. 390, fols. 249ʳ-264ᵛ.

Guarna da Salerno, Andrea. *Scimmia*, ed. and trans. E. and G. Battisti. Rome: Istituto grafico tiberino, 1970.

Guicciardini, Francesco. *Storia d'Italia*, ed. Silvana Seidel Menchi. 3 vols. Turin: Einaudi, 1971.

Holt, Elizabeth G. *A Documentary History of Art*. 2 vols. Garden City, N.Y.: Doubleday, 1957.

Hülsen, Christian, ed. *Mirabilia Romae: Rom Stephen Planck 20 Nov. MCCCCLXXXIX. Ein römisches Pilgerbuch des 15. Jahrhunderts in deutscher Sprache*. Berlin, 1925.

Infessura, Stefano. *Diario della città di Roma*, ed. Oreste Tommasini. Fonti per la storia d'Italia, 5. Rome, 1890.

Kohl, Benjamin G., and Witt, Ronald G., eds. *The Earthly Republic: Italian Humanists on Government and Society*. Philadelphia: U. of Pennsylvania Pr., 1978.

Lefèvre d'Étaples, Jacques. *The Prefatory Epistles of Jacques Lefèvre d'Étaples and Related Texts*, ed. Eugene F. Rice, Jr. N.Y.: Columbia U. Pr., 1972.

Lonigo, Ognibene, trans. Latin trans. of works of Athanasius. BAV, ms. Vat. lat. 261.

———. Latin trans. of John Chrysostom, *De virtute et vitio*. BAV, ms. Vat. lat. 409, fols. 60ᵛ-64ᵛ.

Luther, Martin. *Martin Luther: Selections from his Writings*, ed. John Dillenberger. Garden City, N.Y.: Doubleday, 1961.

Machiavelli, Niccolò. *Opere politiche*, ed. Mario Puppo. Florence: Le Monnier, 1969.

Manetti, Antonio di Tuccio. *The Life of Brunelleschi*, ed. Howard Saalman, trans. Catherine Enggass. University Park: Pennsylvania St. U. Pr., 1970.

Manetti, Giannozzo. *Vita Nicolai V summi pontificis*. RIS, Vol. III, Pt. II, cols. 907–60. Milan, 1734.

———. Letter to Giovanni Tortelli. BAV, ms. Vat. lat. 3908, fol. 178ʳ

Mansi, Johannes Dominicus. *Sacrorum Conciliorum nova et amplissima collectio*. 53 vols. Graz: Akademische Druck- u. Verlaganstalt, 1960–61; reprint edition of Paris, 1901–27.

Marcello, Cristoforo. "Oratio ad Leonem X Pont. Max." BAV, ms. Vat. lat. 3646, fols. 1ʳ-31ʳ.

———. *Oratio in die omnium sanctorum*. Rome: M. Silber?, after 1 Nov. 1511.

Marsi, Pietro. *Funebris oratio in obitu Pomponii Laeti*. Rome: E. Silber, 1497.

Mithridates, Flavius. *Sermo de Passione Domini*, ed. Chaim Wirszubski. Jerusalem: Israel Academy of Science and Humanities, 1963.

da Monte, Piero. *Contra impugnantes sedis apostolicae auctoritatem*. BAV, ms. Vat. lat. 4145.

———. *De summi generalis concilii et imperialis maiestatis origine et potestate*. BAV, ms. Vat. lat. 4134, fols. 21ʳ-67ᵛ; another copy in BAV, ms. Vat. lat. 4136, fols 48ʳ-92ᵛ.

———. Orations, Latin trans. of Epiphanius's *Libellus de religione Christiana*, and other works. BAV, ms. Vat. lat. 2694.

————. *Piero da Monte: Ein Gelehrter und päpstlicher Beamter des 15. Jahrhunderts, Seine Brief-sammlung*, ed. Johannes Haller. Bibliothek des Deutschen Historischen Instituts in Rom, XIX. Rome, 1941.

Nagonius, Johannes Michael. *Ad divum Iulium II et Franciscum Mariam nepotem libri I-VIII.* BAV, ms. Vat. lat. 1682.

Nichols, Francis Morgan, ed. and trans. *Mirabilia Urbis Romae: The Marvels of Rome.* London: Ellis & Elvey, 1889.

Novellus Romanus, Franciscus. *Compendium vitae Leonis Papae X.* Rome: ?, 1536.

Nyssa, Gregory of. *La vie de Moïse*, ed. Jean Daniélou, S.J. 3rd ed. Sources Chrétiennes, Vol. I. Paris: Les editions du Cerf, 1968.

Olin, John C. *The Catholic Reformation: Savonarola to Ignatius Loyola—Reform in the Church, 1495–1540.* N.Y.: Harper & Row, 1969.

Oricellarius, Bernardus (Bernardo Rucellai). *De Urbe Roma.* RIS, Vol. II, cols. 755–1132. Florence, 1770.

Origen. *Peri Archon*, and other works. BAV, ms. Vat. lat. 214.

Palmieri, Matteo. *Città di vita*, ed. Margaret Rooke. *Smith College Studies in Modern Languages*, Vols. VIII-IX (1927–28).

Penni, Giovanni Jacopo. *Chronica delle magnifiche et honorate pompe fatte in Roma per la creatione et incoronatione di Papa Leone X, Pont. Opt. Max.*, in Guglielmo Roscoe, *Vita e pontificato di Leone X*, ed. Luigi Bossi. Vol. V, pp. 192–231. Milan: Sonzogno, 1816–17.

————. *La magnifica et sumptuosa festa . . . per el Carnovale MDXIII.* ? , n.d.

Perosa, Alessandro, and Sparrow, John. *Renaissance Latin Verse: An Anthology.* Chapel Hill: U. of N. Carolina Pr., 1979.

da Persona, Cristoforo, trans. Latin trans. of Chrysostom homilies, BAV, ms. Vat. lat. 408.

————. Latin trans. of Origen, *Contra Celsum.* Rome: Georgius Herolt, 1481.

————. Latin trans. of Theophylact, *Commentaries on St. Paul's Epistles.* BAV, ms. Vat. lat. 263.

Petrarca, Francesco. *De otio religioso*, ed. Giuseppe Rotondi. Studi e Testi, 195. Vatican, 1958.

————. *Le familiari*, ed. Vittorio Rossi. 4 vols. Edizione nazionale delle opere di Francesco Petrarca, Vols. X-XIII. Florence: Sansoni, 1933.

————. *Rerum memorandarum libri*, ed. Giuseppe Billanovich. Florence, 1943.

Pico della Mirandola, Giovanni. *Conclusiones sive Theses DCCCC*, ed. Bohdan Kieszkowski. Travaux d'humanisme et Renaissance, CXXXI. Geneva: Droz, 1973.

Pius II. *The Commentaries of Pius II*, trans. Florence A. Gragg, historical notes by Leona C. Gabel. *SCSH*, XXII (1936–37), XXV (1939–40), XXX (1947), XXXV (1951), XLIII (1957).

Platina. *Liber de vita Christi ac omnium pontificum*, ed. Giacinto Gaida. RIS², Vol. III, Pt. I. Città di Castello, 1913–32.

Poggio Bracciolini. *De varietate fortunae.* Collana di studi e testi diretta da Giuseppe Vecchi. B. Scriptores, Vol. CII. Bologna: Forni, 1969; reprint ed. of Paris: Dominicus Georgius Lutetiae, 1723.

————. *The Facetiae (or Jocose Tales).* 2 vols. Paris: Liseux, 1879.

————. *Two Renaissance Book Hunters: The Letters of Poggius Bracciolini to Nicolaus de Niccolis*, ed. and trans. Phyllis Walter Goodhart Gordan. N.Y.: Columbia U. Pr., 1974.

Rucellai, Giovanni. *Giovanni Rucellai ed il suo zibaldone, I: 'Il zibaldone quaresimale'*, ed. Alessandro Perosa. London: Warburg Institute, 1960.

Tifernate, Lilio, trans. Latin trans. of John Chrysostom, homilies *De poenitentia*, and Ps.-Chrysostom sermon *In iustum et beatum Job de patientia.* BAV, ms. Vat. lat. 406.

————. Latin trans. of works of Philo. BAV, mss. Vat. lat. 180–185, Barb. lat. 662 (XIV, 35), Urb. lat. 227, fols. 19ᵛ-54ᵛ, 72ᵛ-110ᵛ.

Trebizond, George of, trans. Latin trans. of Cyril of Alexandria, *In Ioannem.* BAV, ms. Vat. lat. 525.

Ubaldini, Federico. *Vita di Mons. Angelo Colocci*, ed. Vittorio Fanelli. Studi e Testi, 256. Vatican, 1969.

de Valdés, Alfonso. *Alfonso de Valdés and the Sack of Rome: Dialogue of Lactancio and an Archdeacon.* Translated by John E. Longhurst and edited with Raymond R. MacCurdy. Albuquerque: U. of New Mexico Pr., 1952.

Valentini, Roberto, and Zucchetti, Giuseppe, eds. *Codice topografico della Città di Roma.* 4 vols. Rome: Tipografia del Senato, 1946.

Valla, Laurentius. *Opera omnia*, ed. Eugenio Garin. 2 vols. Turin: Bottega d'Erasmo, 1962.

Valla, Lorenzo. *De falso credita et ementita Constantini donatione*, ed. Wolfram Setz. Monumenta Germaniae historica: Quellen zur Geistesgeschichte des Mittelalters, 10. Weimar: Hermann Böhlaus Nachfolger, 1976.

da Vallombrosa, Angelo. *Apologeticum Angeli Anachoritae Vallisumbrosae pro Julio Papa contra consilium Decii*. ?, 1511.

Vegio, Maffeo. *De rebus antiquis memorabilibus Basilicae S. Petri Romae*. In *Acta Sanctorum, Junii*, Vol. VII (Supplementi, Pars II), pp. 61–85. Antwerp, 1717.

da Verona, Gaspare. *Le vite di Paolo II di Gaspare da Verona e Michele Canensi*, ed., Giuseppe Zippel. RIS², Vol. III, Pt. XVI. Città di Castello: S. Lapi, 1904–11.

Vida, Marco Girolamo. *The Christiad: A Latin-English Edition*, ed. and trans. Gertrude C. Drake and Clarence A. Forbes. Carbondale-Edwardsville: Southern Illinois U. Pr., 1978.

Watkins, Renée Neu. *Humanism and Liberty: Writings on Freedom from Fifteenth-Century Florence*. Columbia: U. of S. Carolina Pr., 1978.

Secondary Sources

Ackerman, James S. *The Architecture of Michelangelo*. Harmondsworth: Penguin, 1971.
———. "The Belvedere as a Classical Villa," *JWCI*, XIV (1951), pp. 70–91.
———. *The Cortile of the Belvedere*. Studi e documenti per la storia del Palazzo Apostolico Vaticano, Vol. III. Vatican, 1954.
———. "*Marcus Aurelius* on the Capitoline Hill," *Renaissance News*, X (1957), pp. 69–75.
———. "The Planning of Renaissance Rome, 1450–1580." In P. A. Ramsey, ed., *Rome in the Renaissance: The City and the Myth. Papers of the Thirteenth Annual Conference*, pp. 3–18. Medieval and Renaissance Texts and Studies, 18. Binghamton, N.Y.: Center for Medieval and Early Renaissance Studies, 1982.

d'Addario, A. "Agli, Antonio," *DBI*, I, pp. 400–01.

Ademollo, A. *Alessandro VI, Giulio II e Leone X nel Carnevale di Roma*. Rome: A. Borzi, 1967; first publ. Florence, 1891.

Ady, Cecilia M. *The Bentivoglio of Bologna: A Study in Despotism*. London: Oxford U. Pr., 1969; first publ. 1937.

Albareda, Anselmo M. O.S.B. "Il bibliotecario di Callisto III." In *Miscellanea Giovanni Mercati*, Vol. IV, pp. 178–208. Studi e Testi, 124. Vatican, 1946.

Ames-Lewis, Frances. "Early Medicean Devices," *JWCI*, XLII (1979), pp. 122–43.

Anderson, Marvin W. "Biblical Humanism and Roman Catholic Reform (1501–42): Contarini, Pole, and Giberti," *Concordia Theological Monthly*, XXXIX (1968), pp. 686–707.

Andrews, Avery. "The 'Lost' Fifth Book of the Life of Paul II by Gaspar of Verona," *SR*, XVII (1970), pp. 26–35.

de Angelis, Pietro. *L'architetto e gli affreschi di Santo Spirito in Saxia*. Rome, 1961.

de Angelis d'Ossat, Guglielmo, and Pietrangeli, Carlo. *Il Campidoglio di Michelangelo*. Rome: "Silvana" Editoriale d'Arte, 1965.

Antonazzi, Giovanni. "Lorenzo Valla e la Donazione di Costantino nel secolo XV con un testo inedito di Antonio Cortesi," *RSCI*, IV (1950), pp. 186–234.

Antonovics, A.V. "A Late Fifteenth-Century Division Register of the College of Cardinals," *Papers of the British School at Rome*, XXXV (n.s. XXII) (1967), pp. 87–101.
———. "The Library of Cardinal Domenico Capranica." In Cecil H. Clough, ed., *Cultural Aspects of the Italian Renaissance: Essays in Honour of Paul Oskar Kristeller*, pp. 141–59. Manchester: Manchester U. Pr., 1976.

Ardant, Gabriel. "Financial Policy and Economic Infrastructure of Modern States and Nations." In Charles Tilly, ed., *The Formation of National States in Western Europe*, pp. 164–242. Princeton: Princeton U. Pr., 1975.

Ashmole, Bernard. "Cyriac of Ancona," *PBA*, XLV (1959), pp. 25–41.

Atiya, Aziz S. "The Crusade in the Fourteenth Century." In Kenneth M. Setton, ed., *A History of the Crusades*, Vol. III: *The Fourteenth and Fifteenth Centuries*, pp. 3–26. Madison: U. of Wisconsin Pr., 1975.

Aubenas, Roger, and Ricard, Robert. *L'Église et la Renaissance*. Augustin Fliche and Victor Martin, eds., *Histoire de l'Église*, Vol. XV. Paris: Bloud & Gay, 1951.

Bandini, Angelo Maria. *Catalogus Codicum Latinorum Bibliothecae Mediceae Laurentinae.* 4 vols. Florence, 1774–77.
Bannister, Turpin C. "The Constantinian Basilica of Saint Peter at Rome," *JSAH*, XXVII (1968), pp. 3–32.
Barberi, Francesco, and Cerulli, Emidio. "Le edizioni greche in Gymnasio Mediceo ad Caballinum Montem." In *Atti del Convegno di studi su Angelo Colocci, Jesi, 13–14 settembre 1969*, pp. 61–76. Jesi: Amministrazione comunale, 1972.
Baron, Hans. *The Crisis of the Early Italian Renaissance.* 2nd ed. Princeton: Princeton U. Pr., 1966.
————. "Franciscan Poverty and Civic Wealth in Humanistic Thought," *Speculum*, XIII (1938), pp. 1–38.
————. *From Petrarch to Leonardo Bruni: Studies in Humanistic and Political Literature.* Chicago: U. of Chicago Pr., 1968.
Barraclough, Geoffrey. *Papal Provisions: Aspects of Church History—Constitutional, Legal, and Administrative—in the Later Middle Ages.* Oxford: Blackwell, 1935.
Bataillon, Marcel. "La chasse aux bénéfices vue de Rome par Juan Páez de Castro." In *Histoire économique du monde méditerranéen 1450–1650: Mélanges en l'honneur de Fernand Braudel*, pp. 81–93. Toulouse: Privat, 1973.
Batllori, Miguel, S.J. "The Papal Division of the World and its Consequences." In Fredi Chiappelli, ed., *First Images of America: The Impact of the New World on the Old*, Vol. I, pp. 211–20. Berkeley and Los Angeles: U. of California Pr., 1976.
Battisti, Eugenio, "Il mondo visuale della fiabe." In Enrico Castelli, ed., *Umanesimo e esoterismo: Atti del V Convegno internazionale di studi umanistici, Oberhofen, 16–17 settembre, 1960*, pp. 308–20. Padua: Dott. Antonio Milani, 1960.
————. "*Natura Artificiosa to Natura Artificialis.*" In David R. Coffin, ed., *The Italian Garden: First Dumbarton Oaks Colloquium on the History of Landscape Architecture*, pp. 1–36. Washington: Dumbarton Oaks, 1972.
————. *Rinascimento e Barocco.* Florence: Einaudi, 1960.
Bäumer, Remigius. "Die Auseinandersetzungen über die römische Petrustradition in den ersten Jahrzehnten der Reformationszeit," *Römische Quartalschrift*, LVII (1962), pp. 20–57.
————. *Nachwirkungen des konziliaren Gedankens in der Theologie und Kanonistik des frühen 16. Jahrhunderts.* Reformations-geschichtliche Studien und Teste, 100. Münster: Aschendorff, 1971.
Baxandall, Michael. *Giotto and the Orators: Humanist Observers of Painting in Italy and the Discovery of Pictorial Composition, 1350–1450.* Oxford: Clarendon Pr., 1971.
Becker, Marvin B. *Medieval Italy: Constraints and Creativity.* Bloomington: Indiana U. Pr., 1981.
Benevolo, Leonardo. *Storia dell'architettura del Rinascimento.* Bari: Laterza, 1968.
Bentivoglio, Enzo, and Valtieri, Simonetta. *Santa Maria del Popolo a Roma.* Rome: Bardi, 1976.
di Bernardo, Flavio. *Un vescovo umanista alla Corte Pontificia: Giannantonio Campano (1429–1477).* Miscellanea Historiae Pontificiae, 39. Rome: Università Gregoriana, 1975.
Bertalot, Ludovico, and Campana, Augusto. "Gli scritti di Iacopo Zeno e il suo elogio di Ciriaco d'Ancona," *La bibliofilia*, XLI (1939), pp. 356–76.
Bertelli, Carlo. "The 'Image of Pity' in Santa Croce in Gerusalemme." In Douglas Fraser, Howard Hibbard, and Milton J. Lewine, eds., *Essays in the History of Art Presented to Rudolf Wittkower*, pp. 40–55. London: Phaidon, 1967.
Bertola, Maria. "Codici latini di Niccolò V perduti o dispersi." In *Mélanges Eugène Tisserant*, Vol. VI, pp. 129–40. Studi e Testi, 236. Vatican, 1964.
Betran de Heredia, Vicente, O.P. "Noticias y documentos para la biografia del Cardinal Juan de Torquemada," *Archivum Fratrum Praedicatorum*, XXX (1960), pp. 53–148.
Black, Antony. *Monarchy and Community: Political Ideas in the Later Conciliar Controversy, 1430–1450.* Cambridge: Cambridge U. Pr., 1970.
Black, C. F. "The Baglioni as Tyrants of Perugia, 1488–1540," *English Historical Review*, LXXXV (1970), pp. 245–81.
Bober, Phyllis Pray. "The *Coryciana* and the Nymph Corycia," *JWCI*, XL (1977), pp. 223–39.
Bonicatti, Maurizio. "Aspetti dell'illustrazione del libro nell' ambiente padano del secondo '400," *Rivista d'arte*, XXXII (3rd ser., VII) (1957), pp. 107–49.

Bonito, Virginia Anne. "The Saint Anne altar in Sant'Agostino: Restoration and interpretation," *The Burlington Magazine*, CXXIV (1982), pp. 268–76.
Borsi, Franco. *Leon Battista Alberti*. N.Y.: Harper & Row, 1977.
Bouwsma, William J. *Venice and the Defense of Republican Liberty: Renaissance Values in the Age of the Counter Reformation*. Berkeley and Los Angeles: U. of California Pr., 1968.
Bradford, Sarah. *Cesare Borgia: His Life and Times*. London: Weidenfeld and Nicolson, 1976.
Branca, Vittore. "Ermolao Barbaro and Late Quattrocento Venetian Humanism." In J. R. Hale, ed., *Renaissance Venice*, pp. 218–43. London: Faber & Faber, 1973.
Braudel, Fernand. *The Mediterranean and the Mediterranean World in the Age of Phillip II*, trans. Siân Reynolds. 2 vols. N.Y.: Harper & Row, 1972.
Brcisach, Ernst. *Caterina Sforza: A Renaissance Virago*. Chicago: U. of Chicago Pr., 1967.
Brentano, Robert. *Rome before Avignon: A Social History of Thirteenth-Century Rome*. N.Y.: Basic Books, 1974.
Brezzi, Paolo. "Il sistema agrario nel territorio romano alla fine del Medio Evo," *Studi romani*, XXV (1977), pp. 153–68.
Brinton, Anna Cox. *Maphaeus Vegius and his Thirteenth Book of the Aeneid*. Stanford: Stanford U. Pr., 1930.
Brosius, Dieter. "Eine Reise an die Kurie im Jahre 1462: Der Rechenschaftsbericht des Lübecker Domherrn Albert Krummediek," *QFIAB*, LVIII (1978), pp. 411–40.
Brown, Raymond E. *The Gospel According to John (I-XII)*. The Anchor Bible, Vol. 29. Garden City, N.Y.: Doubleday, 1966.
Brucker, Gene. *The Civic World of Early Renaissance Florence*. Princeton: Princeton U. Pr., 1977.
Brummer, Hans Henrik. *The Statue Court of the Vatican Belvedere*. Stockholm Studies in the History of Art, 20. Stockholm: Almquist & Wiksell, 1970.
Brummer, Hans Henrik, and Janson, Tore. "Art, Literature and Politics: An Episode in the Roman Renaissance," *Konsthistorisk Tidskrift*, XLV (1976), pp. 79–93.
Bruschi, Arnaldo. *Bramante architetto*. Bari: Laterza, 1969. Shorter, revised English version: *Bramante*. London: Thames & Hudson, 1977.
Buck, August. "Der Rückgriff des Renaissance-Humanismus auf die Patristik." In Kurt Baldinger, ed., *Festschrift Walter von Wartburg zum 80. Geburtstag*, Vol. I, pp. 153–75. Tübingen: Niemeyer, 1968.
Buddensieg, Tilmann. "Zum Statuenprogramm in Kapitolsplan Pauls III," *Zeitschrift für Kunstgeschichte*, XXXII (1969), pp. 177–228.
Bullard, Melissa M. *Filippo Strozzi and the Medici: Favor and Finance in Sixteenth-Century Florence and Rome*. Cambridge: Cambridge U. Pr., 1980.
———. "Grain Supply and Urban Unrest in Renaissance Rome: The Crisis of 1533–34." In P. A. Ramsey, ed., *Rome in the Renaissance: The City and the Myth. Papers of the Thirteenth Annual Conference of the Center for Medieval and Early Renaissance Studies*, pp. 279–92. Medieval and Renaissance Texts and Studies, 18. Binghamton, N.Y.: Center for Medieval and Early Renaissance Studies, 1982.
———. "*Mercatores Florentini Romanam Curiam Sequentes* in the Early Sixteenth Century," *JMRS*, VI (1976), pp. 51–71.
Burckhardt, Jacob. *The Civilization of the Renaissance in Italy*. N.Y.: Harper & Row, 1958.
Burgess, Theodore C. "Epideictic Literature," *Studies in Classical Philology*, III (1902), pp. 89–263.
Burroughs, Charles. "Below the Angel: An Urbanistic Project in the Rome of Pope Nicholas V," *JWCI*, XLV (1982), pp. 94–124.
———. "A Planned Myth and a Myth of Planning: Nicholas V and Rome." In P. A. Ramsey, ed., *Rome in the Renaissance: The City and the Myth. Papers of the Thirteenth Annual Conference of the Center for Medieval and Early Renaissance Studies*, pp. 197–207. Medieval and Renaissance Texts and Studies, 18. Binghamton, N.Y.: Center for Medieval and Renaissance Studies, 1982.
Caetani, Leone. "Vita e diario di Paolo Alaleone de Branca, Maestro delle Ceremonie Pontificie 1582–1638," *ARSRSP*, XVI (1893), pp. 5–39.
Cammelli, Giuseppe. *I dotti bizantini e le origine dell'Umanesimo*. Vol. II: *Giovanni Argiropulo*. Florence, 1941.
Campana, Augusto. "Roma di Sisto IV: Le *Lucubraciunculae Tiburtinae* di Robert Flemmyng," *Strenna dei Romanisti*, IX (1948), pp. 88–98.

Camporeale, Salvatore I. "Lorenzo Valla tra Medioevo e Rinascimento: *Encomium S. Thomae*, 1457," *Memorie Domenicane*, n.s. VII (1976), pp. 11–194.
———. *Lorenzo Valla: Umanesimo e teologia*. Florence: Istituto Nazionale di Studi sul Rinascimento, 1972.
Cancellieri, Francesco. *Storia de' solenni possessi de' Sommi Pontefici da Leone III a Pio VII*. Rome, 1802.
da Capodimonte, Carlo, O.F.M. "Poggio Bracciolini autore delle anonome *Vitae quorundam pontificium*," *RSCI*, XIV (1960), pp. 27–47.
Carusi, Enrico. "L'instrumento di assoluzione dei Fiorentini dalle censure di Sisto IV," *Archivio Muratoriano*, II, No. 16 (1915), pp. 286–92.
Cassirer, "Giovanni Pico della Mirandola: A Study in the History of Renaissance Ideas," *JHI*, III (1942), pp. 123–44, 319–46.
Castagnoli, Ferdinando. "Il Circo di Nerone in Vaticano," *RendPontAcc*, 3rd ser., XXXII (1959–60), pp. 97–121.
Celier, Léonce. "Alexandre VI et la réforme de l'Église," *MAHEFR*, XXVII (1907), pp. 65–124.
———. *Les Dataires du XV siècle et les origines de la Daterie*. BEFAR, 103. Paris, 1910.
———. "L'idée de réforme à la cour pontificale du Concile de Bâle au Concile de Latran" *Revue des questions historiques*, LXXXVI (n.s. XLII) (1909), pp. 418–35.
Cessi, Roberto. "La congiura di Stefano Porcari." In *Saggi romani*, pp. 65–112. Storia e letteratura: Raccolta si studi e testi, LXII. Rome, 1956.
Chamberlin, E. R. *The Sack of Rome*. London: Batsford, 1979.
Chambers, D.S. "The Economic Predicament of Renaissance Cardinals," *SMRH*, III (1966), pp. 287–313.
———. "The Housing Problems of Cardinal Francesco Gonzaga," *JWCI*, XXXIX (1976), pp. 21–58.
———. "Papal Conclaves and Prophetic Mystery in the Sistine Chapel," *JWCI*, XLI (1978), pp. 322–26.
———. "*Studium Urbis* and *gabella studii*: The University of Rome in the Fifteenth Century." In Cecil H. Clough, ed., *Cultural Aspects of the Italian Renaissance: Essays in Honour of Paul Oskar Kristeller*, pp. 68–110. Manchester: Manchester U. Pr., 1976.
Chartrou, Josephe. *Les entrées solennelles et triomphales à la Renaissance (1448–1551)*. Paris: P. U. F., 1928.
Chastel, André. *Art et humanisme à Florence au temps de Laurent le Magnifique: Études sur la Renaissance et l'humanisme platonicien*. Paris: P. U. F., 1959
———. *The Sack of Rome, 1527*, trans. Beth Archer. A. W. Mellon Lectures in the Fine Arts, 26. Bollingen Series XXXV, 26. Princeton: Princeton U. Pr., 1983.
———. "La Véronique," *Revue d l'Art*, XL (1978), pp. 71–82.
Clark, John Willis. "On the Vatican Library of Sixtus IV," *Proceedings of the Cambridge Antiquarian Society*, X (n.s. IV) (1904), pp. 11–61.
Cochrane, Eric. *Historians and Historiography in the Italian Renaissance*. Chicago and London: U. of Chicago Pr., 1981.
Coffin, David R. *The Villa d'Este at Tivoli*. Princeton: Princeton U. Pr., 1960.
———. *The Villa in the Life of Renaissance Rome*. Princeton: Princeton U. Pr., 1979.
Colish, Marcia L. "Seneca's *Apocolocyntosis* as a Possible Source for Erasmus' *Julius Exclusus*," *RQ*, XXIX (1976), pp. 361–68.
Comito, Terry. *The Idea of the Garden in the Renaissance*. New Brunswick, N.J.: Rutgers U. Pr., 1978.
Cornides, Elisabeth. *Rose und Schwert im päpstlichen Zeremoniell: Von den Anfängen bis zum Pontifikat Gregors XIII*. Vienna: Geyer, 1967.
Cortese, Dino. "Sisto Quarto Papa Antoniano," *Il Santo*, XII (1972), pp. 211–71.
Craven, William G. *Giovanni Pico della Mirandola, Symbol of his Age: Modern Interpretations of a Renaissance Philosopher*. Travaux d'humanisme et Renaissance, CLXXXV. Geneva: Droz, 1981.
Crawford, David. "A Review of Costanzo Festa's Biography," *JAMS*, XXVIII (1975), pp. 102–11.
Crowder, C. M. D. *Unity, Heresy, and Reform, 1378–1460*. N.Y.: St. Martin's Pr., 1977.
Cruciani, Fabrizio. "Il teatro dei Ciceroniani: Tommaso 'Fedra' Inghirami," *Forum Italicum*, XIV (1980), pp. 356–77.

————. *Il teatro del Campidoglio e le feste romane del 1513*. Milan: Il Polifilo, 1968.

Dacos, Nicole. *La découverte de la Domus Aurea et la formation des grotesques à la Renaissance*. Studies of the Warburg Institute, 31. London-Leiden, 1969.

Dahood, Mitchell, S.J. *Psalms III, 101–150*. Anchor Bible 17A. Garden City, N.Y.: Doubleday, 1970.

D'Amico, John F. "A Humanist Response to Martin Luther: Raffaele Maffei's *Apologeticus*," *Sixteenth Century Journal*, VI/2 (1975), pp. 37–56.

————. "Paolo Cortesi's Rehabilitation of Giovanni Pico della Mirandola," *Bibliothèque d'humansime et Renaissance*, XLIV (1982), pp. 37–51.

————. "Papal History and Curial Reform in the Renaissance: Raffaele Maffei's *Brevis Historica* of Julius II and Leo X," *AHP*, XVIII (1980), pp. 157–210.

————. *Renaissance Humanism in Papal Rome: Humanists and Churchmen on the Eve of the Reformation*. Baltimore: Johns Hopkins U. Pr., 1983.

Daniélou, Jean, S. J. "Aux sources de l'esoterisme Judeo-chretien." In Enrico Castelli, ed., *Umanesimo e esoterismo: Atti del V Convegno internazionale di studi umanistici, Oberhofen, 16–17 settembre 1960*, pp. 39–46. Padua: Dott. Antonio Milani, 1960.

Dannenfeldt, Karl H. "Egypt and Egyptian Antiquities in the Renaissance," *SR*, VI (1959), pp. 7–27.

————. "The Humanists' Knowledge of Arabic," *SR*, II (1955), pp. 96–117.

————. "The Pseudo-Zoroastrian Oracles in the Renaissance," *SR*, IV (1957), pp. 7–27.

Davidson, Bernice. "The Decoration of the Sala Regia under Paul III," *AB*, LVIII (1976), pp. 395–423.

Davis, Charles Till. *Dante and the Idea of Rome*. Oxford: Clarendon Pr., 1957.

De Caprio, Vincenzo. "L'area umanistica romana (1513–1527)," *Studi romani*, XXIX (1981), pp. 321–35.

————. "Intellettuali e mercato del lavoro nella Roma medicea," *Studi romani*, XXIX (1981), pp. 29–46.

Delaruelle, E.; Labande, E.-R.; and Ourliac, Paul. *L'Église au temps du Grand Schisme et de la crise conciliaire (1378–1449)*. Augustin Fliche and Victor Martin, eds., *Histoire de l'Église*, XIV. Paris: Bloud & Gay, 1964.

Dell'Acqua, G. and Münster, L. "I rapporti di Giovanni Pico della Mirandola con alcuni filosofi ebrei." In *L'Opera e il pensiero di Giovanni Pico della Mirandola nella storia dell'Umanesimo: Convegno internazionale (Mirandola: 15–18 settembre 1963)*, Vol. II: *Comunicazioni*, pp. 149–68. Florence: Istituto Nazionale di Studi sul Rinascimento, 1965.

Delumeau, Jean. *L'alun de Rome, XVe-XIXe siècle*. Paris: S.E.V.P.E.N., 1962.

————. *Catholicism between Luther and Voltaire: A New View of the Counter-Reformation*. Philadelphia: Westminster Pr., 1977.

————. "Rome: Political and Administrative Centralization in the Papal State in the Sixteenth Century." In Eric Cochrane, ed., *The Late Italian Renaissance, 1525–1630*, pp. 287–304. N.Y.: Harper & Row, 1970.

————. *Vie économique et sociale de Rome dans la seconde moitié du XVIe siècle*. BEFAR, 184. Paris: E. de Boccard, 1957.

Denis, Anne. *Charles VIII et les Italiens: Histoire et mythe*. Travaux d'humanisme et Renaissance, CLXVII. Geneva: Droz, 1979.

De Petris, Alfonso. "L'*Adversus Judeos et Gentes* di Giannozzo Manetti," *Rinascimento*, 2nd ser., XVI (1976), pp. 193–205.

Di Cesare, Mario A. *Vida's 'Christiad' and Vergilian Epic*. N.Y.: Columbia U. Pr., 1964.

Di Napoli, Giovanni. *Giovanni Pico della Mirandola e la problematica dottrinale del suo tempo*. Rome: Desclée, 1965.

Dionisotti, Carlo. "Chierici e laici." In *Geografia e storia della letteratura italiana*, pp. 55–88. Turin: Einaudi, 1967.

Dorez, Léon. "La bibliothèque privée du Pape Jules II," *Revue des bibliothèques*, VI (1896), pp. 109ff.

Dotson, Esther Gordon. "An Augustinian Interpretation of Michelangelo's Sistine Ceiling," *AB*, LXI (1979), pp. 223–56, 405–29.

Douglas, Richard M. *Jacopo Sadoleto, 1477–1547: Humanist and Reformer*. Cambridge: Harvard U. Pr., 1959.

Duchesne, Louis. "Notes sur la topographie de Rome au Moyen-Age, I: *Templum Romae*,

Templum Romuli." In *Scripta minora: Études de topographie romaine et de géographie ecclésiastique*, pp. 3–15. Collection de l'École Française de Rome, XIII. Rome, 1973.

Dunning, Albert. *Die Staatsmotette, 1480–1555.* Utrecht: A. Oosthoek's Uitgeversmaatschappij N. V., 1969.

Dunston, A. J. "Pope Paul II and the Humanists," *The Journal of Religious History*, VII (1972–73), pp. 287–306.

Dykmans, Marc, S.J. "Le Cérémonial de Nicholas V," *RHE*, LXIII (1968), pp. 365–78.

———. "D'Avignon à Rome: Martin V et le cortege apostolique," *Bulletin de l'Institut Historique Belge de Rome*, XXXIX (1968), pp. 203–309.

———. "Du Monte Mario à l'escalier de Saint-Pierre de Rome," *MAHEFR*, LXXX (1968), pp. 547–94.

Earle, Peter. "The Commercial Development of Ancona, 1479–1551," *Economic History Review*, XXII (1969), pp. 28–44.

Edgerton, Samuel Y., Jr. *The Renaissance Rediscovery of Linear Perspective.* N.Y.: Basic Books, 1975.

Ehrle, Francesco, S.J. "Due nuove vedute di Roma del secolo XV." In *Atti del II° Congresso internazionale di archeologia cristiana, tenuto in Roma nell'aprile 1900*, pp. 257–63. Rome: Spithöven, 1902.

von Einem, Herbert. "Bemerkungen zur Raffaels *Madonna di Foligno.*" In Irving Lavin and John Plummer, eds., *Studies in Late Medieval and Renaissance Painting in Honor of Millard Meiss*, pp. 131–42. N.Y.: New York U. Pr., 1977.

———. *Michelangelo.* London: Methuen, 1973; first publ. Stuttgart, 1959.

———. "Das Programm der Stanza della Segnatura im Vatikan," *Rheinisch-Westfälische Akademie der Wissenschaften: Geisteswissenschaften.* Vörtrage G 169. Opladen: 1971.

Etter, Else-Lilly. *Tacitus in der Geistesgeschichte des 16. und 17. Jahrhunderts.* Basler Beiträge zur Geschichtswissenschaft, 103. Basel and Stuttgart: Helbing und Lichtenhahn, 1966.

Ettlinger, L. D. "*Exemplum Doloris*: Reflections on the Laocoön Group." In M. Meiss, ed., *De artibus opuscula XL: Essays in Honor of Erwin Panofsky*, Vol. I, pp. 121–26. N.Y.: New York U. Pr., 1961.

———. "A Note on Raphael's Sibyls in S. Maria della Pace," *JWCI*, XXIV (1961), pp. 322–23.

———. "Pollaiuolo's Tomb of Sixtus IV," *JWCI*, XVI (1953), pp. 239–74.

———. *The Sistine Chapel before Michelangelo: Religious Imagery and Papal Primacy.* Oxford: Clarendon Pr., 1965.

Evennett, H. Outram. *The Spirit of the Counter-Reformation.* Notre Dame: U. of Notre Dame Pr., 1970.

Fabre, Paul. "La Vaticane de Sixte IV," *MAHEFR*, XV (1895), pp. 455–83.

Fagiolo M., and Madonna, M. L. "La Roma di Pio IV: la *Civitas Pia*, la *Salus Medica*, la *Custodia Angelica*," *Arte illustrata*, V (1972), pp. 383–402.

Fanelli, Vittore, "Il ginnasio greco di Leone X a Roma," *Studi romani*, IX (1961), pp. 379–93.

Favier, Jean. *Les finances pontificales à l'époque du Grand Schisme d'Occident, 1378–1409.* BEFAR, 211. Paris, 1966.

Febvre, Lucien. *A New Kind of History and Other Essays*, ed. Peter Burke, trans. K. Folca. N.Y.: Harper & Row, 1973.

Fehl, Philipp. "Michelangelo's *Crucifixion of St. Peter*: Notes on the Identification of the Locale of the Action," *AB*, LIII (1971), pp. 327–43.

———. "The Placement of the Equestrian Statue of Marcus Aurelius in the Middle Ages," *JWCI*, XXXVII (1974), pp. 362–67.

Fenlon, Dermot. *Heresy and Obedience in Tridentine Italy: Cardinal Pole and the Counter Reformation.* Cambridge: Cambridge U. Pr., 1972.

Fiorani, Luigi, *et al. Rite, ceremonie, feste, e vita di popolo nella Roma dei Papi.* Roma cristiana, XII. Bologna, Cappelli, 1970.

Firpo, Massimo. "Sulla legazione di pace di Reginald Pole (1553–1556)," *Rivista storica italiana*, XCIII (1981), pp. 821–37.

Firpo, Massimo, and Marcatto, Dario. "Il primo processo inquisitoriale contro il Cardinale Giovanni Morone (1552–1553)," *Rivista storica italiana*, XCIII (1981), pp. 71–142.

Fois, Mario, S.J. *Il pensiero cristiano di Lorenzo Valla nel quadro storico-culturale del suo ambiente.* Analecta Gregoriana, 174. Rome: Università Gregoriana, 1969.

Forcella, V. *Tornei e giostre, ingressi trionfali e feste carnevalesche in Roma sotto Paolo III.* Rome, 1885.

Forsyth, George H., Jr. "The Transept of Old St. Peter's at Rome." In Kurt Weitzman, ed., *Late Classical and Medieval Studies in Honor of Albert Mathias Friend, Jr.*, pp. 56–70. Princeton: Princeton U. Pr., 1955.

Frati, Luigi. "Delle monete gettate al popolo nel solenne ingresso in Bologna di Giulio II per la cacciata di Gio. II Bentivoglio," *Atti e memorie della R. deputazione di storia patria per le provincie di Romagna*, 3rd ser., I (1883), pp. 474–87.

———. *Le due spedizioni militari di Giulio II tratte dal Diario di Paride Grassi Bolognese.* Documenti e studi pubblicati per cura della R. deputazione di storia patria per le provincie di Romagna, I. Bologna: Regia Tip., 1886.

Frazee, Charles A. *Catholics and Sultans: The Church and the Ottoman Empire, 1453–1923.* Cambridge: Cambridge U. Pr., 1983.

Frazer, Alfred. "A Numismatic Source for Michelangelo's First Design for the Tomb of Julius II," *AB*, LVII (1975), pp. 53–57.

Freedberg, S. J. *Painting in the High Renaissance in Rome and Florence.* Cambridge: Harvard U. Pr., 1961.

Frommel, Christoph Luitpold. "'Capella Iulia': Die Grabkapelle Papst Julius II in Neu-St. Peter," *Zeitschrift für Kunstgeschichte*, XL (1977), pp. 26–62.

———. "Die Peterskirche unter Papst Julius II, im Licht neuer Dokumente," *Römisches Jahrbuch für Kunstgeschichte*, XVI (1976), pp. 57–136.

———. *Der Römische Palastbau der Hochrenaissance.* 3 vols. Römische Forschungen der Bibliotheca Hertziana, 21. Tübingen: Wasmuth, 1973.

Frutaz, Amato Pietro. *Le piante di Roma.* Rome: Istituto di Studi Romani, 1962.

Fryde, E. B. *Humanism and Renaissance Historiography.* London: Hambledon Pr., 1983.

Fubini, Riccardo. "Biondo, Flavio." *DBI*, X, pp. 536–59.

———. "Castiglionchio, Lapo da, detto il Giovane," *DBI*, XXII, pp. 44–51.

———. "Intendimenti umanistici e riferimenti patristici dal Petrarca al Valla," *Giornale storico della letteratura italiana*, CLI (1974), pp. 520–78.

———. "Papato e storiografia nel Quattrocento: Storia, biografia e propaganda in un recente studio," *Studi medievali*, 3rd ser., XVIII, Pt. I (1977), pp. 321–51.

———. "Umanesimo curiale del Quattrocento: Nuovi studi su Giovann'Antonio Campano," *Rivista storica italiana*, LXXXVIII (1976), pp. 745–55.

Gabel, Leona C. "The First Revival of Rome, 1420–84." In *The Renaissance Reconsidered: A Symposium*, pp. 13–25. *SCSH*, XLIV (1964).

Gadol, Joan. *Leon Battista Alberti: Universal Man of the Early Renaissance.* Chicago: U. of Chicago Pr., 1969.

Gaeta, Franco. "Una polemica quattrocentesca contro la *De falso credita et ementita Constantini declamatio* di Lorenzo Valla," *Rivista storica italiana*, LXIV (1952), pp. 383–98.

———. "Sull'idea di Roma nell'Umanesimo e nel Rinascimento (Appunti e spunti per una ricerca)," *Studi romani*, XXV (1977), pp. 169–86.

———. "Sulla lettera a Maometto di Pio II," *Bullettino dell'Istituto Storico Italiano per il Medio Evo e Archivio Muratoriano*, LXXVII (1965), pp. 127–227.

Gagé, Jean. *Apollon Romain: Essais sur le culte d'Apollon et le développement du 'ritus Graecus' à Rome des origines à Auguste.* Paris: de Boccard, 1955.

Garin, Eugenio. "La *dignitas hominis* e la letteratura patristica," *Rinascita*, I (1938), pp. 102–46.

———. *Portraits from the Quattrocento*, trans. Victor A. and Elizabeth Velen. N.Y.: Harper & Row, 1972.

Geanakoplos, Deno J. *Greek Scholars in Venice: Studies in the Dissemination of Greek Learning from Byzantium to Western Europe.* Cambridge: Harvard U. Pr., 1962.

———. *Interaction of the "Sibling" Byzantine and Western Cultures in the Middle Ages and Italian Renaissance (330–1600).* New Haven: Yale U. Pr., 1976.

Geary, Patrick J. *Furta Sacra: Thefts of Relics in the Central Middle Ages.* Princeton: Princeton U. Pr., 1978.

Geiger, Gail L. "Filippino Lippi's Carafa *Annunciation*: Theology, Artistic Conventions and Patronage," *AB*, LXIII (1981), pp. 62–75.

———. "Filippino Lippi's *Triumph of Saint Thomas Aquinas*." In P. A. Ramsey, ed., *Rome in the Renaissance: The City and the Myth. Papers of the Thirteenth Annual Conference of the Center for Medieval and Early Renaissance Studies*, pp. 223–36. Medieval and Renaissance

Texts and Studies, 18. Binghamton, N.Y.: Center for Medieval and Early Renaisance Studies, 1982.

Gerardin, Jean. *Étude sur les bénéfices ecclésiastiques aux XVIᵉ et XVIIᵉ siècles*. Geneva: Slatkine Reprints, 1971; first publ. Nancy, 1897.

Giannelli, Giuseppe. "La leggenda dei *Mirabilia* e l'antica topografia dell'Arce Capitolina," *Studi romani*, XXVI (1978), pp. 60–71.

Gilbert, Felix. "Bernardo Rucellai and the Orti Oricellari: A Study on the Origin of Modern Political Thought," *JWCI*, XII (1949), pp. 101–31.

———. *Machiavelli and Guicciardini: Politics and History in Sixteenth-Century Florence*. Princeton: Princeton U. Pr., 1965.

———. *The Pope, his Banker, and Venice*. Cambridge: Harvard U. Pr., 1980.

———. "Religion and Politics in the Thought of Gasparo Contarini." In Theodore K. Rabb and Jerrold E. Seigel, eds., *Action and Conviction in Early Modern Europe: Essays in Memory of E. H. Harbison*, pp. 90–116. Princeton: Princeton U. Pr., 1969.

Gill, Joseph, S.J. *The Council of Florence*. Cambridge: Cambridge U. Pr., 1959.

———. *Eugenius IV: Pope of Christian Union*. Westminster, Md.: Newman Pr., 1961.

———. *Personalities of the Council of Florence and Other Essays*. N.Y.: Barnes & Noble, 1964.

Gilmore, Myron P. "Anti-Erasmianism in Italy: The Dialogue of Ortensio Lando on Erasmus' Funeral," *JMRS*, IV (1974), pp. 1–14.

———. "Italian Reactions to Erasmian Humanism." In Heiko A. Oberman with Thomas A. Brady, Jr., eds., *Itinerarium Italicum: The Profile of the Italian Renaissance in the Mirror of its European Transformations (Dedicated to Paul Oskar Kristeller on the Occasion of his 70th Birthday)*, pp. 61–115. Studies in Medieval and Reformation Thought, XIV. Leiden: Brill, 1975.

Giordani, P. "Studi sulla scultura romana del Quattrocento: I bassorilievi del tabernacolo di Sisto IV," *L'arte*, X (1907), pp. 271ff.

Gleason, Elisabeth G. "On the Nature of Sixteenth-Century Italian Evangelism: Scholarship, 1953–1978," *Sixteenth Century Journal*, IX/3 (1978), pp. 3–25.

———. "Sixteenth Century Italian Interpretations of Luther," *ARG*, LX (1969), pp. 160–73.

Gnoli, Domenico. *La Roma di Leone X*. Milan: Hoepli, 1938.

Goldbrunner, Hermann. "*Laudatio urbis*: Zu neueren Untersuchungen über das humanistische Städtelob," *QFIAB*, LXIII (1983), pp. 313–28.

Goldthwaite, Richard A. *The Building of Renaissance Florence: An Economic and Social History*. Baltimore: Johns Hopkins U. Pr., 1980.

Göller, E. *Die päpstliche Pönitentiarie von ihrem Ursprung bis zu ihrer Ungestaltung unter Pius V*. Bibliothek des königlichen Preussischen Historischen Instituts in Rom, Vols. 3–4, 7–8. Rome, 1907–11.

Gombrich, E. H. *Norm and Form: Studies in the Art of the Renaissance*. London: Phaidon, 1971.

———. *Symbolic Images: Studies in the Art of the Renaissance, II*. London: Phaidon, 1972.

Goodenough, Erwin R. *An Introduction to Philo Judaeus*, 2nd ed. Oxford: Blackwell, 1962.

———. "Philo's Exposition of the Law and his *De vita Mosis*," *Harvard Theological Review*, XXVI (1933), pp. 109–25.

Gottlob, Adolf. *Aus der Camera Apostolica des 15. Jahrhunderts*. Innsbruck: Wagner, 1889.

Grabmann, Martin. *Studien über den Einfluss der aristotelischen Philosophie auf die mittelalterlichen Theorien über das Verhältnis von Kirche und Staat*. Sitzungsberichte der Bayerischen Akademie der Wissenschaften philosophisch-historische Abteilung, Vol. 2 (1934).

Graf, Arturo. *Roma nella memoria e nelle immaginazioni del Medio Evo*. Turin: Chiantore, 1923.

Grant, Robert M. "Civilization as a Preparation for Christianity in the Thought of Eusebius." In F. Forrester Church and Timothy George, eds., *Continuity and Discontinuity in Church History: Essays Presented to George Huntston Williams on the Occasion of his 65th Birthday*, pp. 62–70. Studies in the History of Christian Thought, XIX. Leiden: Brill, 1979.

Gray, Hanna H. "Valla's *Encomium of St. Thomas Aquinas* and the Humanist Conception of Christian Antiquity." In Heinz Bluhm, ed., *Essays in History and Literature Presented by the Fellows of the Newberry Library to Stanley Pargellis*, pp. 37–51. Chicago: Newberry Library, 1965.

Graziosi, M. T. "Agostino Steuco e il suo *Antivalla*." In *L'Umanesimo umbro: Atti del IX Convegno di Studi Umbri, Gubbio, 22–23 sett. 1974*, pp. 511–23. Perugia: Univ., 1977.

Greco, Aulo. "Roma e la commedia del Rinascimento," *Studi romani*, XXII (1974), pp. 25–35.

Gregorovius, Ferdinand. *History of the City of Rome in the Middle Ages*, trans. from the 4th Ger. ed. by Annie Hamilton. Vols. 7–8. London: George Bell & Sons, 1900–02.

Griffiths, Gordon. "Leonardo Bruni and the Restoration of the University of Rome (1406)," *RQ*, XXVI (1973), pp. 1–10.

Guillemain, Bernard. *La Cour Pontificale d'Avignon 1300–1376, Étude d'une société*, 2nd ed. Paris: de Boccard, 1966.

Guilmartin, John Francis, Jr. *Gunpowder and Galleys: Changing Technology and Mediterranean Warfare at Sea in the Sixteenth Century*. Cambridge: Cambridge U. Pr., 1974.

Guiraud, Jean. *L'État Pontifical après le Grand Schisme: Étude de géographie politique*. BEFAR, 73. Paris, 1896.

Gundersheimer, Werner L. *Ferrara: The Style of a Renaissance Despotism*. Princeton: Princeton U. Pr., 1973.

Hale, J. R. "The Early Development of the Bastion: An Italian Chronology c. 1450 – c. 1534." In J. R. Hale, J. R. L. Highfield, and B. Smalley, eds., *Europe in the Late Middle Ages*, pp. 466–94. Evanston: Northwestern U. Pr., 1965.

———. *Florence and the Medici: The Pattern of Control*. London: Thames & Hudson, 1977.

———. *Renaissance Fortification: Art or Engineering?* London: Thames & Hudson, 1977.

Hall, Marcia B. "Michelangelo's *Last Judgment*: Resurrection of the Body and Predestination," *AB*, LVIII (1976), pp. 85–92.

Hallman, Barbara McClung. "Italian 'Natural Superiority' and the Lutheran Question: 1517–1546," *ARG*, LXXI (1980), pp. 134–48.

———. "Practical Aspects of Roman Diplomacy in Germany, 1517–1541," *JMRS*, X (1980), pp. 193–206.

Harprath, Richard. *Papst Paul III. als Alexander der Grosse: Das Freskenprogramm der Sala Paolina in der Engelsburg*. Beiträge zur Kunstgeschichte, 13. Berlin and N.Y.: de Gruyter, 1978.

Harran, Don. "The 'Sack of Rome' Set to Music," *RQ*, XXIII (1970), pp. 412–21.

Hartt, Frederick. "Art and Freedom in Quattrocento Florence." In Lucy Freeman Sandler, ed., *Essays in Memory of Karl Lehmann*, pp. 114–31. Marsyas: Studies in the History of Art, Supplement 1. N.Y.: Institute of Fine Arts, New York U., 1964.

———. *Giulio Romano*. New Haven: Yale U. Pr., 1958.

———. "*Lignum vitae in medio paradisi*: The Stanza d'Eliodoro and the Sistine Ceiling," *AB*, XXXII (1950), pp. 115–45, 181–218.

Haskell, Francis. *Patrons and Painters: Art and Society in Baroque Italy*. N.Y.: Harper & Row, 1971.

Hatfield, Rab. "The Compagnia de' Magi," *JWCI*, XXXIII (1970), pp. 107–61.

Hay, Denys. *The Church in Italy in the Fifteenth Century: The Birkbeck Lectures, 1971*. Cambridge: Cambridge U. Pr., 1977.

———. "Flavio Biondo and the Middle Ages," *PBA*, XLV (1959), pp. 97–128.

Hecksher, W. S. *Sixtus IIII aeneas insignes statuas romano populo restituendas censuit*. The Hague, 1955.

Hendrix, Scott H. *Luther and the Papacy: Stages in a Reformation Conflict*. Philadelphia: Fortress Pr., 1981.

Herde, Peter. *Audientia litterarum contradictarum: Untersuchungen über die päpstlichen Justizbriefe und die päpstliche Delegationsgerichtsbarkeit vom 13. bis zum Beginn des 16. Jahrhunderts*. 2 vols. Tübingen: Niemeyer, 1970.

Herlihy, David. *Medieval and Renaissance Pistoia: The Social History of an Italian Town, 1200–1430*. New Haven: Yale U. Pr., 1967.

Hersey, George L. *Alfonso II and the Artistic Renewal of Naples 1485–1495*. New Haven: Yale U. Pr., 1969.

Heydenreich, Ludwig H. "The Military Architect." In Ladislao Reti, ed., *The Unknown Leonardo*, pp. 136–65. N.Y.: McGraw-Hill, 1974.

Hibbard, Howard. *Michelangelo*. N.Y.: Harper & Row, 1974.

Hilary, Richard B. "The Nepotism of Pope Pius II, 1458–1464," *CHR*, LXIV (1978), pp. 33–35.

Hirst, Michael. "The Chigi Chapel in S. Maria della Pace," *JWCI*, XXIV (1961), pp. 161–85.

Hodgson, Marshall G. S. *The Venture of Islam: Conscience and History in a World Civilization*. 3 vols. Chicago: Chicago U. Pr., 1974.

von Hofmann, W. *Forschungen zur Geschichte der Kurialen Behörden vom Schisma bis zur*

Reformation. 2 vols. Bibliothek des Deutschen Historischen Instituts in Rom, XII. Rome: von Loescher, 1914; reprinted Turin: Bottega d'Erasmo, 1971.

Holmes, George. *The Florentine Enlightenment, 1400–50*. N.Y.: Pegasus, 1969.

Homeyer, Helene. "Zur *Synkrisis* des Manuel Chrysoloras, einem Vergleich zwischen Rom und Konstantinopel: Ein Beitrag zum italienischen Frühhumanismus," *Klio*, LXII (1980), pp. 525–34.

Hoogewerff, G. I. "La Stanza della Segnatura: Osservazioni e commenti," *RendPontAcc*, 3rd ser., XXIII-XXIV (1949), pp. 317–56.

Hook, Judith. *The Sack of Rome, 1527*. London: Macmillan, 1972.

Howe, Eunice D. "A Temple Façade Reconsidered: Botticelli's 'Temptation of Christ'." In P. A. Ramsey, ed., *Rome in the Renaissance: The City and the Myth. Papers of the Thirteenth Annual Conference of the Center for Medieval and Early Renaissance Studies*, pp. 209–21. Medieval and Renaissance Texts and Studies, 18. Binghamton, N.Y.: Center for Medieval and Early Renaissance Studies, 1982.

Huizinga, J. *The Waning of the Middle Ages*, Garden City, N.Y.: Doubleday, 1954.

Hülsen, Christian. "The Legend of the Aracoeli" (Paper read before the British and American Archeological Society of Rome, 14 February 1907). Rome: G. Bertero, 1907.

Huskinson, J. M. "The Crucifixion of St. Peter: A Fifteenth-Century Topographical Problem," *JWCI*, XXXII (1969), pp. 135–61.

Insolera, Italo. *Roma: Immagini e realtà dal X al XX secolo*. Bari: Laterza, 1980.

Iversen, Erik. *Obelisks in Exile*, Vol. I: *The Obelisks of Rome*. Copenhagen: G. E. C. Gad, 1968.

Janitschek, Hubert. "Über einige bisher unbekannte Künstler die unter Leo X in Rom arbeiteten," *Reportorium für Kunstwissenschaft*, II (1879), pp. 416–17.

Jedin, Hubert. *A History of the Council of Trent*, trans. Dom Ernest Graf, O.S.B., Vol. I: *The Struggle for the Council*. St. Louis: Herder, 1957.

———. "Juan de Torquemada und das Imperium Romanum," *Archivum Fratrum Praedicatorum*, XII (1942), pp. 247–78.

———. "Rom und Romidee im Zeitalter der Reformation und Gegenreformation." In *Kirche des Glaubens, Kirche der Geschichte: Ausgewählte Aufsätze und Vorträge*, Vol. I, pp. 143–52. Vienna: Herder, 1966.

———. "Sánchez de Arévalo und die Konzilsfrage unter Paul II," *Historisches Jahrbuch*, LXXIII (1954), pp. 95–119.

———. "Studien über Domenico de' Domenichi (1416–78)," *Akademie der Wissenschaften und der Literatur in Mainz. Abhandlungen der Geistes- un Sozialwissenschaftlichen Klasse*, 1957, No. 5, pp. 177–300. Wiesbaden: F. Steiner, 1958.

Johnson, Lawrence J. "The 'Linguistic Imperialism' of Lorenzo Valla and the Renaissance Humanists," *Interpretation*, VII (1978), pp. 29–49.

Jones, P. J. "The End of Malatesta Rule in Rimini." In E. F. Jacob, ed., *Italian Renaissance Studies*, pp. 217–55. London: Faber & Faber, 1960.

———. *The Malatesta of Rimini and the Papal State*. Cambridge: Cambridge U. Pr., 1974.

Jung-Inglessis, Eva-Maria. "La Porta Santa," *Studi romani*, XXIII (1975), pp. 473–85.

Jungmann, Joseph A., S.J. *The Mass of the Roman Rite: Its Origins and Development*. 2 vols. N.Y.: Benziger Bros., 1951.

Kajanto, Iiro. *Classical and Christian: Studies in the Latin Epitaphs of Medieval and Renaissance Rome*. Annales Academia Scientiarum Fennica, Ser. B, Vol. 203. Helsinki: Suomalainen Tiedeakatemia Pr., 1980.

Kamen, Henry. "Golden Age, Iron Age: A Conflict of Concepts in the Renaissance," *JMRS*, IV (1974), pp. 135–55.

Kantorowicz, Ernst H. "The 'King's Advent' and the Enigmatic Panels in the Doors of Santa Sabina," *AB*, XXVI (1944), pp. 207–31.

Katterbach, B., O.F.M. *Referendarii utriusque Signaturae a Martino V ad Clementem IX et Praelati Signaturae Supplicationum a Martino V ad Leonem XIII*. Studi e Testi, 55. Vatican, 1931.

Kennedy, Ruth W. "The Contribution of Martin V to the Rebuilding of Rome, 1420–31." In *The Renaissance Reconsidered: A Symposium*, pp. 27–52. SCSH, XLIV (1964).

Kirsch, Johann Peter. *Die Stationskirchen des Missale Romanum*. Freiburg im Breisgau, 1926.

Kittelson, James M. *Wolfgang Capito: From Humanist to Reformer*. Studies in Medieval and Reformation Thought, XVII. Leiden: Brill, 1975.

Klapisch-Zuber, Christiane. "Une ethnologie du mariage au temps de l'Humanisme," *Annales: Économies, Sociétés, Civilisations,* XXXVI (1981), pp. 1016–27.
Krautheimer, Richard. "A Christian Triumph in 1597." In Douglas Fraser, Howard Hibbard, and Milton J. Lewine, eds., *Essays in the History of Art Presented to Rudolf Wittkower,* pp. 174–78. London: Phaidon, 1967.
———. "Fra Angelico and—Perhaps—Alberti." In Irving Lavin and John Plummer, eds., *Studies in Late Medieval and Renaissance Painting in Honor of Millard Meiss,* pp. 290–96. N.Y.: New York U. Pr., 1977.
———. *Rome: Profile of a City, 312–1308.* Princeton: Princeton U. Pr., 1980.
———. "S. Pietro in Vincoli and the Tripartite Transept in the Early Christian Basilica," *PAPS,* LXXXIV (1941), pp. 353–429.
———. *Studies in Early Christian, Medieval, and Renaissance Art.* N.Y.: New York U. Pr., 1969.
Krautheimer, Richard, with Krautheimer-Hess, Trude. *Lorenzo Ghiberti.* 2 vols. 2nd ed. Princeton: Princeton U. Pr., 1970.
Krinsky, Carol Herselle. "Representations of the Temple of Jerusalem before 1500," *JWCI,* XXXIII (1971), pp. 1–19.
Kristeller, Paul Oskar. *Medieval Aspects of Renaissance Learning,* ed. and trans. Edward P. Mahoney. Duke Monographs in Medieval and Renaissance Studies, 1. Durham: Duke U. Pr., 1974.
———. *Le Thomisme et la pensée italienne de la Renaissance.* Montreal: Institut d'Études Médiévales, 1967.
Kustas, George L. *Studies in Byzantine Rhetoric.* Thessalonica: Patriarchal Institute for Patristic Studies, 1973.
Ladner, Gerhart B. "Vegetation Symbolism and the Concept of the Renaissance." In M. Meiss, ed., *De artibus opuscula XL: Essays in Honor of Erwin Panofsky,* I, pp. 303–22. N.Y.: New York U. Pr., 1961.
Lamping, A. J. *Ulrichus Velenus (Oldřich Velenský) and his Treatise against the Papacy.* Studies in Medieval and Reformation Thought, XIX. Leiden: Brill, 1976.
Lane, Frederic C. *Venice: A Maritime Republic.* Baltimore: Johns Hopkins U. Pr., 1973.
Larner, John. *Culture and Society in Italy, 1290–1420.* London: Batsford, 1971.
———. "Order and Disorder in Romagna, 1450–1500." In Lauro Martines, ed., *Violence and Civil Disorder in Italian Cities, 1200–1500,* pp. 38–71. Berkeley and Los Angeles: U. of California Pr., 1972.
Lattès, Samy. "A proposito dell'opera incompiuta *De ponderibus et mensuris* di Angelo Colocci." In *Atti del Convegno di studi su Angelo Colocci, Jesi, 13–14 settembre 1969,* pp. 97–108. Jesi: Amministrazione comunale, 1972.
Lazzaro-Bruno, Claudia. "The Villa Lante at Bagnaia: An Allegory of Art and Nature," *AB,* LIX (1977), pp. 553–60.
Lee, Egmont. "Jacopo Gherardi and the Court of Sixtus IV," *CHR,* LXV (1979), pp. 221–37.
———. *Sixtus IV and Men of Letters.* Temi e Testi, 26. Rome: Edizioni di storia e letteratura, 1978.
———. "Workmen and Work in Quattrocento Rome." In P. A. Ramsey, ed., *Rome in the Renaissance: The City and the Myth. Papers of the Thirteenth Annual Conference of the Center for Medieval and Early Renaissance Studies,* pp. 141–52. Medieval and Renaissance Texts and Studies, 18. Binghamton, N.Y.: Center for Medieval and Early Renaissance Studies, 1982.
Lenkeith, Nancy. *Dante and the Legend of Rome.* London: Warburg Institute, 1952.
Lenzi, M.L. *Il Sacco di Rome del 1527.* Florence: La Nuova Italia, 1978.
Lesellier, J. "Les mefaits du Cérémoniaire Jean Burckard," *MAHEFR,* XLIV (1927), pp. 11–34.
Levin, Harry. *The Myth of the Golden Age in the Renaissance.* Bloomington: Indiana U. Pr., 1969.
Levine, Joseph M. "Reginald Pecock and Lorenzo Valla on the Donation of Constantine," *SR,* XX (1973), pp. 118–43.
Litva, Felice. "L'attività finanziaria della Dataria durante il periodo tridentino," *AHP,* V (1967), pp. 79–174.
Llewellyn, Peter. *Rome in the Dark Ages.* N.Y.: Praeger, 1971.
Lotz, Wolfgang. *Studies in Italian Renaissance Architecture.* Cambridge: MIT Pr., 1977.

Lowinsky, Edward E. "A Newly Discovered Sixteenth-Century Motet Manuscript at the Biblioteca Vallicelliana in Rome," *JAMS*, III (1950), pp. 173–232.

――――. "On the Presentation and Interpretation of Evidence: Another Review of Costanzo Festa's Biography," *JAMS*, XXX (1977), pp. 106–28.

de Luca, Giuseppe. "Un umanista fiorentino e la Roma rinnovata da Sisto IV," *Rinascita*, I (1938), pp. 74–90.

Luzio, Alessandro. "Federico Gonzaga ostaggio alla corte di Giulio II," *ARSRSP*, IX (1886), pp. 577–82.

Maas, Clifford W. *The German Community in Renaissance Rome, 1378–1523*. Römische Quartalschrift, Supplementheft 39. Freiburg: Herder, 1981.

McAndrew, John. *Venetian Architecture of the Early Renaissance*. Cambridge: MIT Pr., 1980.

Maccarrone, Michele. *Vicarius Christi: Storia del titolo papale*. Lateranum, n.s. XVIII, No. 1–4 (1952).

McConica, James K. "Erasmus and the *Julius Exclusus*: A Humanist Reflects on the Church." In Charles Trinkaus and Heiko A. Oberman, eds., *The Pursuit of Holiness in Late Medieval and Renaissance Religion: Papers from the University of Michigan Conference*, pp. 444–71. Studies in Medieval and Reformation Thought, X. Leiden: Brill, 1974.

MacCormack, Sabine G. *Art and Ceremony in Late Antiquity*. Berkeley and Los Angeles: U. of California Pr., 1981.

McCready, William D. "The Papal Sovereign in the Ecclesiology of Augustinus Triumphus," *Mediaeval Studies*, XXXIX (1977), pp. 177–205.

――――. "Papalists and Antipapalists: Aspects of the Church-State Controversy in the Later Middle Ages," *Viator*, VI (1975), pp. 241–73.

MacDougall, Elisabeth B. "*Ars Hortulorum*: Sixteenth-Century Garden Iconography and Literary Theory in Italy." In David R. Coffin, ed., *The Italian Garden: First Dumbarton Oaks Colloquium on the History of Landscape Architecture*, pp. 37–59. Washington, D. C.: Dumbarton Oaks, 1972.

――――. "*L'Ingegnoso Artifizio*: Sixteenth Century Garden Fountains in Rome." In Elisabeth B. MacDougall, ed., *Fons Sapientiae: Renaissance Garden Fountains. Fifth Dumbarton Oaks Colloquium on the History of Landscape Architecture*, pp. 87–113. Washington, D. C.: Dumbarton Oaks, 1978.

――――. "The Sleeping Nymph: Origins of a Humanist Fountain Type," *AB*, LVII (1975), pp. 357–65.

――――. Review of Carroll William Westfall, *In this Most Perfect Paradise: Alberti, Nicholas V, and the Invention of Conscious Urban Planning in Rome, 1447–55. AB*, LXI (1979), pp. 309–12.

McGinness, Frederick J. "Preaching Ideals and Practice in Counter-Reformation Rome," *Sixteenth Century Journal*, XI/2 (1980), pp. 109–27.

――――. "The Rhetoric of Praise and the New Rome of the Counter Reformation." In P. A. Ramsey, ed., *Rome in the Renaissance: The City and the Myth. Papers of the Thirteenth Annual Conference of the Center for Medieval and Early Renaissance Studies*, pp. 355–70. Medieval and Renaissance Texts and Studies, 18. Binghamton, N.Y.: Center for Medieval and Early Renaissance Studies, 1982.

McManamon, John M. "The Ideal Renaissance Pope: Funeral Oratory from the Papal Court," *AHP*, XIV (1976), pp. 9–70.

McNally, Robert E., S.J. "Pope Adrian VI (1522–23) and Church Reform," *AHP*, VII (1969), pp. 253–85.

McNeill, William H. *Venice: The Hinge of Europe, 1081–1797*. Chicago: U. of Chicago Pr., 1974.

McSorley, Harry J. "Erasmus and the Primacy of the Roman Pontiff: Between Conciliarism and Papalism," *ARG*, LXV (1974), pp. 37–54.

Maddison, Carol. *Marcantonio Flaminio: Poet, Humanist and Reformer*. Chapel Hill: U. of N. Carolina Pr., 1965.

Maffei, Domenico. *La Donazione di Costantino nei giuristi medievali*. Milan: Giuffrè, 1964.

Magnuson, Torgil. *Studies in Roman Quattrocento Architecture*. Stockholm: Almquist & Wiksell, 1958.

Mallett, Michael. *The Borgias: The Rise and Fall of a Renaissance Dynasty*. London: Paladin, 1972.

————. *Mercenaries and their Masters: Warfare in Renaissance Italy.* London: Bodley Head, 1974.

Mancini, Girolamo. *Francesco Griffolini, cognominato Francesco Aretino.* Florence: Carnesecchi, 1890.

de Marco, Angelus A., O.F.M. *The Tomb of St. Peter: A Representative and Annotated Bibliography.* Supplements to Novum Testamentum, VIII. Leiden: Brill, 1964.

Martin, Francis X., O.S.A. "Giles of Viterbo as Scripture Scholar." In *Egidio da Viterbo, O.S.A. e il suo tempo: Atti del V Convegno dell'Istituto Storico Agostiniano, Roma—Viterbo, 20–23 ottobre 1982*, pp. 191–222. Studia Augustiniana Historica, 9. Rome: "Analecta Augustiniana," 1983.

————. "The Writings of Giles of Viterbo," *Augustiniana*, XXIX (1979), pp. 141–93.

Martindale, Andrew. *The Triumphs of Caesar by Andrea Mantegna in the Collection of Her Majesty the Queen at Hampton Court.* London: Harvey Miller, 1979.

Martines, Lauro. *Power and Imagination: City-States in Renaissance Italy.* N.Y.: Knopf, 1979.

Masson, Georgina. *Courtesans of the Italian Renaissance.* London: Secker & Warburg, 1975.

Matheson, Peter. *Cardinal Contarini at Regensburg.* Oxford: Clarendon Pr., 1972.

Mattingly, Garrett. *Renaissance Diplomacy.* Baltimore: Penguin, 1964.

Mattingly, Harold. "Virgil's Fourth Eclogue," *JWCI*, X (1947), pp. 14–19.

Mayer, Elisabetta. *Un umanista italiano della corte di Mattia Corvino: Aurelio Brandolini Lippo.* Biblioteca dell'Accademia d'Ungheria di Roma, 14. Rome, 1938.

Mazzocco, A. "Some Philological Aspects of Biondo Flavio's *Roma triumphans*," *Humanistica Lovaniensia*, XXVIII (1979), pp. 1–26.

Mazzolani, Lidia Storoni. *The Idea of the City in Roman Thought: From Walled City to Spiritual Commonwealth.* Bloomington: Indiana U. Pr., 1970.

Meiss, Millard. *The Painter's Choice: Problems in the Interpretation of Renaissance Art.* N.Y.: Harper & Row, 1976.

de Menil, Dominique, ed. *Builders and Humanists: The Renaissance Popes as Patrons of the Arts.* Catalogue of the exhibition, University of St. Thomas Art Dept., Houston, March-May 1966.

Mercati, Giovanni Card. "Una lettera di Vespasiano da Bisticci a Jean Jouffroi e la biblioteca romana del Jouffroi." In *Mélanges dédiés à al mémoire de Félix Grat*, Vol. I, pp. 357–66. Paris, 1946.

————. *Opere minori*, Vols. 3–4. Studi e Testi, 78–79. Vatican, 1937.

————. *Per la cronologia della vita e degli scritti di Niccolò Perotti Arcivescovo di Siponto.* Studi e Testi, 44. Rome, 1925.

————. *Scritti d'Isidoro il Cardinale Ruteno.* Studi e Testi, 46. Rome, 1926.

————. *Ultimi contributi alla storia degli umanisti*, Fasc I: *Traversariana.* Studi e Testi, 90. Vatican, 1939.

Messina, Michele. "Francesco Accolti di Arezzo," *Rinascimento*, I (1950), pp. 293–321.

Meithke, Jürgen. "Eine unbekannte Handschrift vom Petrus de Paludes Traktat *De potestate Papae* aus dem Besitz Juan de Torquemadas in den Vatikanischen Bibliothek," *QFIAB*, LIX (1979), pp. 468–75.

Miglio, Massimo. "Birago, Lampugnino," *DBI*, X, pp. 595–97.

————. "Bussi, Giovanni Andrea," *DBI*, XV, pp. 565–72.

————. "Il leone e la lupa: Dal simbolo al pasticcio alla francese," *Studi romani*, XXX (1982), pp. 177–86.

————. *Storiografia pontificia del Quattrocento.* Bologna: Pàtron, 1975.

————. "L'umanista Pietro Edo e la polemica sulla Donazione di Costantino," *Bullettino dell'Istituto Storico Italiano per il Medio Evo e Archivio Muratoriano*, LXXIX (1968), pp. 167–232.

————. "'Viva la libertà et popolo de Roma': Oratoria e politica a Roma, Stefano Porcari," *ARSRSP*, XCVII (1974), pp. 5–37.

Minnich, Nelson H., S.J. "Concepts of Reform Proposed at the Fifth Lateran Council," *AHP*, VII (1969), pp. 163–251.

————. "*Incipiat judicium ad Domo Domini*: The Fifth Lateran Council and the Reform of Rome." In Guy Fitch Lytle, ed., *Reform and Authority in the Medieval and Reformation Church*, pp. 127–42. Washington: Catholic U. of America Pr., 1981.

————. "The Participants at the Fifth Lateran Council," *AHP*, XII (1974), pp. 157–206.

Minnich, Nelson H., S.J., and Pfeiffer, Heinrich W., S.J. "De Grassi's 'Conciliabulum' at
    Lateran V: The De Gargiis Woodcut of Lateran V Re-examined," *AHP*, XIX (1981),
    pp. 147–72.
Mitchell, Bonner, *Italian Civic Pageantry in the High Renaissance: A Descriptive Bibliography of
    Triumphal Entries and Selected Other Festivities for State Occasions.* Biblioteca di biblio-
    grafia italiana, 89. Florence: Leo S. Olschki, 1979.
————. "Les intermèdes au service de l'état." In Jean Jacquot, ed., *Les fêtes de la Renaissance*,
    Vol. III, pp. 117–31. Paris: Éditions du Centre National de la Recherche Scientifique,
    1975.
————. *Rome in the High Renaissance: The Age of Leo X.* Norman: U. of Oklahoma Pr., 1973.
————. "The S.P.Q.R. in Two Roman Festivals of the Early and Mid-Quattrocento," *Six-
    teenth Century Journal*, IX/4 (1978), pp. 95–102.
Mitchell, Charles. "Archeology and Romance in Renaissance Italy." In E. F. Jacob, ed.,
    Italian Renaissance Studies, pp. 455–83. London: Faber & Faber, 1960.
Mitchell, R. J. *The Laurels and the Tiara: Pope Pius II, 1405–1464.* Garden City, N.Y.:
    Doubleday, 1962.
Molho, Anthony. "The Brancacci Chapel: Studies in its Iconography and History," *JWCI*,
    XL (1977), pp. 50–98.
Monfasani, John. *George of Trebizond: A Biography and a Study of his Rhetoric and Logic.* Leiden:
    Brill, 1976.
Montani, Francesco Fabi. *Feste e spettacoli di Roma dal secolo X a tutto il XVI particolarmente nel
    Carnevale e nel maggio.* Rome, 1861.
Montenovesi, Ottorino. "Agostino Chigi, banchiere e appaltatore dell'allume di Tolfa,"
    ARSRSP, LX (n.s. III) (1937), pp. 107–47.
Moorman, John. *A History of the Franciscan Order from its Origins to the Year 1517.* Oxford:
    Oxford U. Pr., 1968.
von Moos, Stanislaus. "The Palace as a Fortress: Rome and Bologna under Pope Julius II."
    In Henry A. Millon and Linda Nochlin, eds., *Art and Architecture in the Service of Politics*,
    pp. 46–79. Cambridge: MIT Pr., 1978.
Morin, D. G. "Les distiques de Pomponio Leto sur les stations liturgiques du Carême," *Revue
    Bénédictine*, XXXV (1923), pp. 20–23.
Morison, Samuel Eliot. *Admiral of the Ocean Sea: A Life of Christopher Columbus.* Boston: Little,
    Brown, 1942.
Morsolin, Bernardo. "Un latinista del Cinquecento imitatore di Dante," *Atti del R. Istituto
    Veneto di Scienze, Lettere, ed Arti*, 7th ser., V (1893–94), pp. 1429–46.
————. *Zaccaria Ferreri, Episodio biografico del secolo decimosesto.* Vicenza, 1877.
Muir Edward. *Civic Ritual in Renaissance Venice.* Princeton: Princeton U. Pr., 1981.
————. "Images of Power: Art and Pageantry in Renaissance Venice," *AHR*, LXXXIV
    (1979), pp. 16–52.
Muldoon, James. "Papal Responsibility for the Infidel: Another Look at Alexander VI's *Inter
    Caetera*," *CHR*, LXIV (1978), pp. 168–84.
————. *Popes, Lawyers, and Infidels: The Church and the Non-Christian World, 1250–1550.*
    Philadelphia: U. of Pennsylvania Pr., 1979.
Müntz, Eugene. *Les arts à la cour des papes pendant le XVe et le XVIe siècles.* 3 vols. BEFAR, 26–28.
    Paris, 1881.
————. "La tiare pontificale du VIIIe au XVIe siècle," *Mémoires de l'Institut National de France*,
    XXXVI (1898), pp. 235–324.
Müntz, Eugene, and Fabre, Paul. *La Bibliothèque du Vatican au XVe siècle.* BEFAR, 48. Paris:
    Thorin, 1887.
Musch, Hans. *Costanzo Festa als Madrigalkomponist.* Sammlung Musikwissenschaftlicher
    Abhundlungen, 61. Baden-Baden: Koerner, 1977.
Nabuco, Joaquim. *Le Cérémonial Apostolique avant Innocent VIII: Texte du manuscrit Urbinate
    Latin 469 de la Bibliothèque Vaticane établi par Dom Filippo Tamburini.* Bibliotheca
    "Ephemerides Liturgicae" Sectio historica, XXX. Rome: Edizioni liturgiche, 1966.
Oakley, Francis. "Conciliarism in the Sixteenth Century: Jacques Almain Again," *ARG*,
    LXVIII (1977), pp. 111–27.
Oberman, Heiko. *Forerunners of the Reformation: The Shape of Late Medieval Thought.* N.Y.:
    Holt, Rinehart, & Winston, 1966.

———. *The Harvest of Medieval Theology: Gabriel Biel and Late Medieval Nominalism.* Grand Rapids: Eerdmans, 1967.

———. "The Shape of Late Medieval Thought: The Birthpangs of the Modern Era," *ARG,* LXIV (1973), pp. 13–33.

Odier, Jeanne Bignami. *La Bibliothèque Vaticane de Sixte IV à Pie XI.* Studi e Testi, 272. Vatican, 1973.

Oliver, James H. "The Civilizing Power: A Study of the *Panathenaic Discourse* of Aelius Aristides against the Background of Literature and Cultural Conflict, with Text, Translation, and Commentary," *TAPS,* n.s. LVIII (1968), pp. 3–223.

———. "The Ruling Power: A Study of the Roman Empire in the Second Century after Christ through the 'Roman Oration' of Aelius Aristides," *TAPS,* n.s. XLIII (1953), pp. 871–1003.

Oliver, Revilo Pendleton. *Niccolò Perotti's Version of the Enchiridion of Epictetus.* Urbana: U. of Illinois Pr., 1954.

Olschki, Cesare. "Francesco Albertini," *Roma: Rivista di studi e di vita romana,* II (1924), pp. 483–90.

O'Malley, John W. "An Ash Wednesday Sermon on the Dignity of Man for Pope Julius II, 1513." In Sergio Bertelli and Gloria Ramakus, eds., *Essays Presented to Myron P. Gilmore,* Vol. I, pp. 193–207. Florence: La Nuova Italian, 1978.

———. "Catholic Reform." In Steven Ozment, ed., *Reformation Europe: A Guide to Research,* pp. 297–319. St. Louis: Center for Reformation Research, 1982.

———. "The Discovery of America and Reform Thought at the Papal Court in the Early Cinquecento." In Fredi Chiappelli, ed., *First Images of America: The Impact of the New World on the Old,* Vol. I, pp. 185–200. Berkeley and Los Angeles: U. of California Pr., 1976.

———. "Egidio da Viterbo and Renaissance Rome." In *Egidio da Viterbo, O.S.A. e il suo tempo: Atti del V Convegno dell'Istituto Storico Agostiniano, Roma—Viterbo, 20–23 ottobre 1982,* pp. 67–84. Studia Augustiniana Historica, 9. Rome: Ed. "Analecta Augustiniana," 1983.

———. "The Feast of Thomas Aquinas in Renaissance Rome: A Neglected Document and its Import," *RSCI,* XXXV (1981), pp. 1–27.

———. "Fulfillment of the Christian Golden Age under Pope Julius II: Text of a Discourse of Giles of Viterbo, 1507," *Traditio,* XXV (1969), pp. 265–338.

———. *Giles of Viterbo on Church and Reform: A Study in Renaissance Thought.* Studies in Medieval and Reformation Thought, V. Leiden: Brill, 1968.

———. "Historical Thought and the Reform Crisis of the Early Sixteenth Century," *Theological Studies,* XXVIII (1967), pp. 531–48.

———. "Man's Dignity, God's Love, and the Destiny of Rome: A Text of Giles of Viterbo," *Viator,* III (1972), pp. 389–416.

———. *Praise and Blame in Renaissance Rome: Rhetoric, Doctrine, and Reform in the Sacred Orators of the Papal Court, c. 1450–1521.* Duke Monographs in Medieval and Renaissance Studies, 3. Durham: Duke U. Pr., 1979.

———. "Some Renaissance Panegyrics of Aquinas," *RQ,* XXVII (1974), pp. 174–92.

———. "The Vatican Library and the Schools of Athens: A Text of Battista Casali, 1508," *JMRS,* VII (1977), pp. 271–87.

Onofri, Laura. "Sacralità, immaginazione e proposte politiche: La *Vita* di Niccolò V di Giannozzo Manetti," *Humanistica Lovaniensia,* XXVIII (1979), pp. 27–77.

O'Reilly, Clare. "'Maximus Caesar et Pontifex Maximus': Giles of Viterbo Proclaims the Alliance between Emperor Maximilian I and Pope Julius II," *Augustiniana,* XXII (1972), pp. 80–117.

———. "'Without Councils We Cannot Be Saved . . .': Giles of Viterbo Addresses the Fifth Lateran Council," *Augustiniana,* XXVII (1977), pp. 166–204.

Orlandi, Stefano, O.P. *Beato Angelico.* Florence: Leo S. Olschki, 1964.

Ozment, Steven. *The Age of Reform, 1250–1550: An Intellectual and Religious History of Late Medieval and Reformation Europe.* New Haven: Yale U. Pr., 1980.

Pacifici, Vincenzo. *Un carme biografico di Sisto IV del 1477.* Tivoli, 1921.

Pagnotti, Francesco. "La vita di Niccolò V scritta da Giannozzo Manetti: Studio preparatorio alla nuova edizione critica," *ARSRSP,* XIV (1891), pp. 411–36.

Palermino, Richard J. "The Roman Academy, the Catacombs, and the Conspiracy of 1468," *AHP*, XVIII (1980), pp. 117–55.

Panofsky, Erwin. "The First Two Projects of Michelangelo's Tomb of Julius II," *AB*, XIX (1937), pp. 561–79.

——. *The Life and Art of Albrecht Dürer.* 4th ed. Princeton: Princeton U. Pr., 1955.

——. *Studies in Iconology.* N.Y.: Harper & Row, 1967.

——. *Tomb Sculpture: Four Lectures on its Changing Aspects from Ancient Egypt to Bernini.* N.Y.: Abrams, 1964.

Paparelli, G. *Enea Silvio Piccolomini: L'Umanesimo sul soglio di Pietro.* 2nd ed. Ravenna: Longo, 1978.

Parks, N. Randolph. "On the Meaning of Pinturicchio's *Sala dei Santi*," *Art History*, II (1979), pp. 291–317.

Parsons, William Barclay. *Engineers and Engineering in the Renaissance.* Cambridge, Mass., and London: MIT Pr., 1968.

Partner, Peter. "The 'Budget' of the Roman Church in the Renaissance Period." In E. F. Jacob, ed., *Italian Renaissance Studies*, pp. 256–78. London: Faber & Faber, 1960.

——. *The Lands of St. Peter: The Papal State in the Middle Ages and the Early Renaissance.* Berkeley and Los Angeles: U. of California Pr., 1972.

——. "Papal Financial Policy in the Renaissance and Counter-Reformation," *Past & Present*, LXXXVIII (1980), pp. 17–62.

——. *The Papal State under Martin V: The Administration and Government of the Temporal Power in the Early Fifteenth Century.* London: The British School at Rome, 1958.

——. *Renaissance Rome, 1500–1559: A Portrait of a Society.* Berkeley and Los Angeles: U. of California Pr., 1976.

Partridge, Loren W. "Divinity and Dynasty at Caprarola: Perfect History in the Room of the Farnese Deeds," *AB*, LX (1978), pp. 494–530.

——. Review of Richard Harprath, *Papst Paul III. als Alexander der Grosse: Das Freskenprogramm der Sala Paolina in der Engelsburg. AB*, LXII (1980), pp. 661–63.

——, and Starn, Randolph. *A Renaissance Likeness: Art and Culture in Raphael's 'Julius II'.* Berkeley and Los Angeles: U. of California Pr., 1980.

Paschini, Pio. "Un ellenista romano del Quattrocento e la sua famiglia," *Atti dell'Accademia degli Arcadi*, XXI (1939–40), pp. 45–56.

——. "Una famiglia di curiali: I Maffei di Volterra," *RSCI*, VII (1953), pp. 337–76.

——. *Roma nel Rinascimento.* Storia di Roma, XII. Bologna: Cappelli, 1940.

——. "Tre illustri prelati del Rinascimento: Ermolao Barbaro, Adriano Castellesi, Giovanni Grimani," *Lateranum*, n.s. XXIII (1957), pp. 43–130.

Pascoe, Louis B., S.J. "Gerson and the Donation of Constantine: Growth and Development with the Church," *Viator*, V (1974), pp. 469–85.

von Pastor, Ludwig. *History of the Popes*, ed. and trans. F. I. Antrobus, *et al.* Vols. 1–8. St. Louis: Herder, 1891–1910.

Pásztor, Lajos. "L'histoire de la Curie Romaine, Problème d'histoire de l'Église," *RHE*, LXIV (1969), pp. 353–66.

Patetta, Federigo. *Venturino de Prioribus: Umanista ligure del secolo XV.* Studi e Testi, 149. Vatican, 1950.

Peebles, B. M. "La *Meta Romuli* e una lettera di Michele Ferno," *RendPontAcc*, 3rd ser., XII (1936), pp. 21–63.

Pepper, Simon. "Planning versus Fortification: Sangallo's Project for the Defense of Rome," *The Architectural Review*, CLIX (1976), pp. 162–69.

Perry, Marilyn. "'Candor Illaesvs': the 'Impresa' of Clement VII and other Medici Devices in the Vatican Stanze," *The Burlington Magazine*, CXIX (1977), pp. 676–86.

Peters, F. E. *The Harvest of Hellenism: A History of the Near East from Alexander the Great to the Triumph of Christianity.* N.Y.: Simon & Schuster, 1970.

Petit, Françoise. *L'ancienne version latine des questions sur la Genèse de Philon d'Alexandrie.* 2 vols. Text und Untersuchungen zur Geschichte der Altchristlichen Literatur, 113–114. Berlin: Akademie Verlag, 1973.

Pfeiffer, Heinrich, S.J. *Zur Ikonographie von Raffaels Disputà: Egidio da Viterbo und die christlich-platonische Konzeption der Stanza della Segnatura.* Miscellanea Historiae Pontificiae, 37. Rome: Università Gregoriana, 1975.

Pica, Agnoldomenico. "Città di Bramante." In *Studi Bramanteschi: Atti del Congresso internazionale, Milano-Urbino-Roma, 1970*, pp. 117–36. Rome: De Luca, 1974.

Picotti, G. B. "La publicazione e i primi effetti della *Execrabilis* di Pio II," *ARSRSP*, XXXVII (1914), pp. 5–56.

Pietri, Charles. *Roma Christiana: Recherches sur l'Église de Rome, son organisation, sa politique, son idéologie de Miltiade à Sixte III (311–440)*. BEFAR, 224. Paris: de Boccard, 1976.

Pinto, John A. "Origins and Development of the Ichnographic City Plan," *JSAH*, XXXV (1976), pp. 34-50.

Pirotta, Nino. "Music and Cultural Tendencies in Fifteenth Century Italy," *JAMS*, XIX (1966), pp. 147–61.

Pitra, Joannes Baptista, Card. *Analecta sacra spicilegio Solesmensi*. Vol. II: *Patres Antenicaeni*. Tusculanis, 1884.

Pitz, Ernst. "Die römische Kurie als Thema des vergleichenden Sozialgeschichte," *QFIAB*, LVIII (1978), pp. 216–359.

Pope-Hennessy, John. *Fra Angelico*. 2nd ed. London: Phaidon, 1974.

———. *Raphael: The Wrightsman Lectures*. N.Y.: New York U. Pr., 1970.

Portoghesi, Paolo. *Roma del Rinascimento*. 2 vols. Venice: Electa, 1970.

Potter, T. W. *The Changing Landscape of South Etruria*. N.Y.: St. Martin's Pr., 1979.

Pratesi, A. "Balbo, Pietro," *DBI*, V, pp. 378–79.

Pratt, Kenneth, Jr. "Rome as Eternal," *JHI*, XXVI (1965), pp. 25–44.

Prodi, Paolo. *Il sovrano pontefice. Un corpo e due anime: La monarchia papale nella prima età moderna*. Bologna: Il Mulino, 1982.

Prosperi, Adriano. *Tra Evangelismo e Controriforma: G. M. Giberti (1495–1543)*. Uomini e dottrine, 16. Rome: Edizioni di storia e letteratura, 1969.

Pullan, Brian. *Rich and Poor in Renaissance Venice: The Social Institutions of a Catholic State, to 1620*. Cambridge: Harvard U. Pr., 1971.

Quednau, Rolf. *Die Sala di Costantino im Vatikanischen Palast: zur Dekoration der beiden Medici-Päpste Leo X. und Clemens VII*. Studien zur Kunstgeschichte, 13. Hildesheim: Georg Olms, 1979.

Quondam, Amedeo. "Un'assenza, un progetto: Per una ricerca sulla storia di Roma tra 1465 e 1527," *Studi romani*, XXVII (1979), pp. 166–75.

Rash-Fabbri, Nancy. "A Note on the Stanza della Segnatura," *Gazette des Beaux-Arts*, XCIV (1979), pp. 97–104.

Re, Emilio. "Maestri di strada," *ARSRSP*, XLIII (1920), pp. 5–102.

del Re, Niccolò. *La Curia Romana: Lineamenti storico-giuridici*. 3rd ed. Rome: Edizioni di storia e letteratura, 1972.

Redig de Campos. Deoclezio. "Un'altro graffito del Sacco nelle Stanze di Raffaello," *Ecclesia*, XIX (1960), pp. 552–54.

———. "L'architetto e il costruttore della Cappella Sistina," *Palatino: Rivista romana di cultura*, 3rd ser. IX (1965), pp. 90–93.

———. "Bramante e il Palazzo Apostolico Vaticano," *RendPontAcc*, 3rd ser., XLIII (1970–71), pp. 283–99.

———. "Il nome di Martin Lutero graffito sulla Disputà del Sacramento," *Ecclesia*, VI (1947), pp. 648–49.

———. *I Palazzi Vaticani*. Roma cristiana, 18. Bologna: Cappelli, 1967.

———. "Testimonianze del primo nucleo edilizio dei Palazzi Vaticani e restauro delle pitture delle stanze della 'Bibliotheca Latina' e 'Bibliotheca Greca'." In *Il restauro delle aule di Niccolò V e di Sisto IV nel Palazzo Apostolico Vaticano*. Vatican, 1967.

———. "I 'tituli' degli affreschi del Quattrocento nella Cappella Sistina," *RendPontAcc*, XLII (1970), pp. 299–314.

Regoliosi, Mariangela. "Nuove ricerche intorno a Giovanni Tortelli. 2. La vita di Giovanni Tortelli," *Italia medioevale e umanistica*, XII (1969), pp. 129–96.

Reinhard, Wolfgang. "Nepotismus: Der Funktionswandel einer päpstgeschichtlichen Konstanten," *Zeitschrift für Kirchengeschichte*, LXXXVI (1975), pp. 145–85.

Ridolfi, Roberto. *The Life of Francesco Guicciardini*, trans. Cecil Grayson. N.Y.: Knopf, 1968.

Ringborn, Sixten. *Icon to Narrative: The Rise of the Dramatic Close-up in Fifteenth-Century Devotional Painting*. Åbo: Åbo Akademi, 1965.

Robathan, Dorothy M. "Flavio Biondo's *Roma instaurata*," *MH*, n.s. I (1970), pp. 203–16.

Robey, David. "P. P. Vergerio the Elder: Republicanism and Civic Values in the Work of an Early Humanist," *Past & Present*, LVIII, (1973), pp. 3–37.

Rodocanachi, E. *Rome au temps de Jules II et de Léon X.* Paris: Hachette, 1912.

de Roover, Raymond. *The Rise and Decline of the Medici Bank, 1397–1494.* Cambridge: Harvard U. Pr., 1963.

Rosenthal, E. "The Antecedents of Bramante's Tempietto," *JSAH*, XXIII (1964), pp. 55–74.

Ross, J. B. "The Emergence of Gasparo Contarini: A Bibliographic Essay," *Church History*, XLI (1972), pp. 22–45.

———. "Gasparo Contarini and his Friends," *SR*, XVII (1970), pp. 192–232.

Rossi, Ettore. "The Hospitallers at Rhodes, 1421–1523." In Kenneth Setton, ed., *A History of the Crusades*, Vol. III: *The Fourteenth and Fifteenth Centuries*, pp. 314–39. Madison: U. of Wisconsin Pr., 1975.

Rubinstein, Ruth Olitsky. "Pius II's Piazza S. Pietro and St. Andrew's Head." In Douglas Fraser, Howard Hibbard, and Milton J. Lewine, eds., *Essays in the History of Architecture Presented to Rudolf Wittkower*, pp. 22–33. London: Phaidon, 1967.

Rubsamen, Walter H. "The Music for 'Quant'e bella giovinezza' and Other Carnival Songs by Lorenzo de' Medici." In Charles S. Singleton, ed., *Art, Science, and History in the Italian Renaissance*, pp. 163–84. Baltimore: Johns Hopkins U. Pr., 1967.

Runciman, Steven. *A History of the Crusades.* 3 vols. N.Y.: Harper & Row, 1964.

Rupp, Gordon. *Luther's Progress to the Diet of Worms.* N.Y.: Harper & Row, 1964.

Ruysschaert, José. "Albertini, Francesco." *DBI*, I, pp. 724–25.

———. "Sixte IV, Fondateur de la Bibliothèque Vaticane (15 Juin 1475)," *AHP*, VII (1969), pp. 513–24.

———. "La tomba di Pietro: Nuove considerazioni archeologiche e storiche," *Studi romani*, XXIV (1976), pp. 322-30.

Sabbadini, Remigio. *Le scoperte dei codici latini e greci ne' secoli XIV e XV.* 2nd ed. 2 vols. Florence: Sansoni, 1967.

Salerno, Luigi. *Roma Communis Patria.* Bologna: Cappelli, 1968.

Salerno, Luigi; Spezzaferro, Luigi; and Tafuri, Manfredo. *Via Giulia: Una utopia urbanistica del '500.* Rome: Aristide Staderini, 1975.

Salmi, Mario. "Bernardo Dovizi e l'arte," *Rinascimento*, 2nd ser., IX (1969), pp. 3–50.

Salvini, Roberto. "The Sistine Chapel: Ideology and Architecture," *Art History*, III (1980), pp. 144–57.

Samoré, Antonio. "Aspetti caratteristici degli Anni Santi: Dalla documentazione dell'Archivio Segreto Vaticano," *Studi romani*, XXIII (1975), pp. 419-41.

Saxl, Fritz. *Lectures.* London: Warburg, 1957.

Scaccia-Scarafoni, Camillo. "L'antico statuto dei *Magistri stratarum* e altri documenti relativi a quella magistratura," *ARSRSP*, L (1927), pp. 239–308.

———. *Le piante di Roma.* Rome: R. Istituto di Archeologia e Storia dell'Arte, 1939.

Scaglia, Gustina. "The Origin of an Archeological Plan of Rome by Alessandro Strozzi," *JWCI*, XXVII (1964), pp. 137–59.

Scarisbrick, J. J. *Henry VIII.* Berkeley and Los Angeles: U. of California Pr., 1968.

Schär, Max. *Das Nachleben des Origines im Zeitalter des Humanismus.* Basler Beiträge zur Geschichtswissenschaft, 140. Basel and Stuttgart: Helbing & Lichtenhahn, 1979.

Scheller, Robert W. "Imperial Themes in Art and Literature of the Early French Renaissance: the Period of Charles VIII," *Simiolus: Netherlands Quarterly for the History of Art*, XII (1981–82), pp. 5–69.

Schellhase, Kenneth C. *Tacitus in Renaissance Political Thought.* Chicago: U. of Chicago Pr., 1976.

Schimmelpfennig, Bernhard. "Die Krönung des Päpstes im Mittelalter dargestellt am Beispiel der Krönung Pius II (3. 9. 1458)," *QFIAB*, LIV (1974), pp. 192–270.

———. *Die Zeremonienbücher der Römischen Kurie im Mittelalter.* Bibliothek des Deutschen Historischen Instituts in Rom, XL. Tübingen: Niemeyer, 1973.

Schmitt, Charles B. "Perennial Philosophy: From Agostino Steuco to Leibniz," *JHI*, XXVII (1966), pp. 505–32.

Schneider, F. E. *Die Römische Rota: Nach geltendem Recht auf geschichtlicher Grundlage.* Vol. I: *Die Verfassung der Rota.* Paderborn, 1914.

Scholz, Ricard. "Eine humanistische Schilderung der Kurie aus dem Jahre 1438," *QFIAB*, XVI (1913–14), pp. 108–53.

Schröter, Elisabeth. "Der Vatikan als Hügel Apollons unter der Musen: Kunst und Panegyrik von Nikolaus V. bis Julius II.," *Römische Quartalschrift*, LXXV (1980), pp. 208–40.

———. "Zur Inhaltsdeutung des Alexander-Programms der Sala Paolina in der Engelsburg," *Römisches Quartalschrift*. LXXV (1980), pp. 76–99.

Schudt, Ludwig. *Le guide di Roma: Materialen zu einer Geschichte der römischen Topographie*. Vienna: B. Filser, 1971; first publ. 1930.

Schulz, Jürgen. "Jacopo de' Barbari's View of Venice: Map Making, City Views, and Moralized Geography Before the Year 1500," *AB*, LX (1978), pp. 425–74.

———. "Pinturicchio and the Revival of Antiquity," *JWCI*, XXV (1962), pp. 35–55.

Schwarz, Brigide. *Die Organisation Kurialer Schreiberkollegien von Enstehung bis zur Mitte des 15. Jahrhunderts*. Tübingen: Niemeyer, 1972.

Schwoebel, Robert. *The Shadow of the Crescent: The Renaissance Image of the Turk (1453–1517)*. N.Y.: St. Martin's Pr., 1967.

Secret, François. "Notes sur Egidio da Viterbo," *Augustiniana*, XXVII (1977), pp. 205–37.

———. "Nouvelles precisions sur Flavius Mithridates maitre de Pic de la Mirandole et traducteur de commentaires de Kabbale." In *L'Opera e il pensiero di Giovanni Pico della Mirandola nella storia dell'Umanesimo: Convegno internazionale (Mirandola: 15–18 settembre 1963)*, Vol. II: *Comunicazioni*, pp. 169–87. Florence: Istituto Nazionale di Studi sul Rinascimento, 1965.

Setton, Kenneth M. *The Papacy and the Levant (1204–1571)*. Vols. 1–2. Philadelphia: American Philosophical Society, 1976–78.

———. "Pope Leo X and the Turkish Peril," *PAPS*, CXIII (1969), pp. 367–424.

Setz, Wolfram. *Lorenzo Vallas Schrift gegen die Konstantinische Schenkung*. Bibliothek des Deutschen Historischen Instituts in Rom, 44. Tübingen, 1975.

Seznec, Jean. *The Survival of the Pagan Gods: The Mythological Tradition and its Place in Renaissance Humanism and Art*. N.Y.: Harper & Row, 1961.

Sforza, G. *La patria, la famiglia, e la giovinezza di Papa Niccolò Quinto*. Lucca, 1884.

Shearman, John. "The Chigi Chapel in S. Maria del Popolo," *JWCI*, XXIV (1961), pp. 129–60.

———. "The Florentine *Entrata* of Leo X, 1515," *JWCI*, XXXVIII (1975), pp. 136–54.

———. *Raphael's Cartoons in the Collection of Her Majesty the Queen and the Tapestries for the Sistine Chapel*. London: Phaidon, 1972.

———. "Raphael's Unexecuted Projects for the Stanze." In *Walter Friedlander zum 90. Geburtstag: Eine Festgabe seiner europäischen Schüler, Freunde und Verehrer*, pp. 158–80. Berlin: de Gruyter, 1965.

———. "Il 'Tiburio' di Bramante in San Pietro." In *Studi Bramanteschi: Atti del Congresso internazionale, Milano-Urbino-Roma, 1970*, pp. 567–73. Rome: De Luca, 1974.

———. "The Vatican Stanze: Functions and Decoration," *PBA*, LVII (1971), pp. 369–424.

Siebenhüner, Herbert. *Das Kapitol in Rom: Idee und Gestalt*. Munich: Kösel, 1954.

Simoncelli, Paolo. *Evangelismo italiano del Cinquecento*. Rome, 1979.

von Simson, Otto. *The Gothic Cathedral: Origins of Gothic Architecture and the Medieval Concept of Order*. Princeton: Princeton U. Pr., 1962.

Sinding-Larsen, Staale. "A Re-Reading of the Sistine Ceiling," *Institutum Romanum Norvegiae: Acta ad archaeologiam et artium historiam pertinentia*, IV (1969), pp. 143–57.

———. "Some Functional and Iconographical Aspects of the Centralized Church in the Italian Renaissance," *Institutum Romanum Norvegiae: Acta ad archaeologiam et artium historiam pertinentia*, II (1965), pp. 203–52.

———. "A Tale of Two Cities: Florentine and Roman Visual Context for Fifteenth-Century Palaces," *Institutum Romanum Norvegiae: Acta ad archaeologiam et artium historiam pertinentia*, VI (1975), pp. 163–212.

Sirch, P. Bernhard, O.S.B. *Der Ursprung der bischöflichen Mitra und päpstlichen Tiara*. Kirchengeschichtliche Quellen und Studien, 8. St. Ottilien: Eos Verlag der Erzabtei, 1975.

Skinner, Quentin. *The Foundations of Modern Political Thought*. Vol. I: *The Renaissance*. Cambridge: Cambridge U. Pr., 1978.

Smith, Graham. *The Casino of Pius IV*. Princeton: Princeton U. Pr., 1977.

Smith, John Holland. *Constantine the Great*. N.Y.: Scribner's, 1971.

Smith, Leslie F. "Lodrisio Crivelli of Milan and Aeneas Silvius, 1457–1464," *SR*, IX (1962), pp. 31–63.

Sottili, Agostino. *Studenti tedeschi e Umanesimo italiano nell'Università di Padova durante il Quattrocento, I: Pietro del Monte nella società accademica padovana (1430–33)*. Contributi alla storia dell'Università di Padova, 7. Padua: Antenori, 1971.

Southern, R. W. *The Making of the Middle Ages*. New Haven: Yale U. Pr., 1953.

Sparrow, John. "Latin Verse of the High Renaissance." In E. F. Jacob, ed., *Italian Renaissance Studies*, pp. 354–409. London: Faber & Faber, 1960.

Staffa, F. M. *Delle traduzioni dal greco in latino fatte da Gregorio e da Lilio Tifernati*. Gubbio, 1758.

Steinberg, Leo. "Michelangelo's *Last Judgment* as Merciful Heresy," *Art in America*, LXIII, No. 6 (Nov.–Dec. 1975), pp. 48–63.

———. *Michelangelo's Last Paintings: The Conversion of St. Paul and the Crucifixion of St. Peter in the Cappella Paolina, Vatican Palace*. N.Y.: Oxford U. Pr., 1975.

Steinmann, Ernst. *Die Sixtinische Kapelle*. 2 vols. Munich, 1901–06.

Stickler, Alfonso M. *Quinto Centenario della Biblioteca Apostolica Vaticana, 1475–1975. Catalogo della mostra*. Vatican, 1975.

Stieber, Joachim W. *Pope Eugenius IV, the Council of Basel, and the Secular and Ecclesiastical Authorities in the Empire: The Conflict over Supreme Authority and Power in the Church*. Studies in the History of Christian Thought, XIII. Leiden: Brill, 1978.

Stinger, Charles L. "Ambrogio Traversari and the 'Tempio degli Scolari' at S. Maria degli Angeli in Florence." In Sergio Bertelli and Gloria Ramakus, eds., *Essays Presented to Myron P. Gilmore*, Vol. I, pp. 271–86. Florence: La Nuova Italia, 1978.

———. "Greek Patristics and Christian Antiquity in Renaissance Rome." In P. A. Ramsey, ed., *Rome in the Renaissance: The City and the Myth. Papers from the Thirteenth Annual Conference of the Center for Medieval and Early Renaissance Studies*, pp. 153–69. Medieval and Renaissance Texts and Studies, 18. Binghamton, N.Y.: Center for Medieval and Early Renaissance Studies, 1982.

———. *Humanism and the Church Fathers: Ambrogio Traversari (1386–1439) and Christian Antiquity in the Italian Renaissance*. Albany: SUNY Pr., 1977.

———. "*Roma triumphans*: Triumphs in the Thought and Ceremonies of Renaissance Rome," *MH*, n.s. X (1981), pp. 189–201.

Strauss, Gerald. *Manifestations of Discontent in Germany on the Eve of the Reformation*. Bloomington: Indiana U. Pr., 1971.

Strnad, Alfred A. "Francesco Todeschini-Piccolomini: Politik und Mäzenarentum im Quattrocento," *Römische Historische Mitteilungen*, VIII-IX (1964/65–1965/66), pp. 101–425.

Strong, Roy. *Splendor at Court: Renaissance Spectacle and the Theater of Power*. Boston: Houghton Mifflin, 1973.

Sumption, Jonathan. *Pilgrimage: An Image of Mediaeval Religion*. Totowa, N.J.: Rowman & Littlefield, 1975.

Tapié, Victor-L. *The Age of Grandeur: Baroque Art and Architecture*. N.Y.: Praeger, 1966.

Tenenti, Alberto. "The Sense of Space and Time in the Venetian World of the Fifteenth and Sixteenth Centuries." In J. R. Hale, ed., *Renaissance Venice*, pp. 17–46. London: Faber & Faber, 1973.

Tentler, Thomas N. *Sin and Confession on the Eve of the Reformation*. Princeton: Princeton U. Pr., 1977.

Thomson, John A. F. *Popes and Princes, 1417–1517: Politics and Polity in the Late Medieval Church*. London: Allen & Unwin, 1980.

Thurston, Herbert, S.J. *The Holy Year of Jubilee: An Account of the History and Ceremonial of the Roman Jubilee*. London: Sands, 1900.

Tierney, Brian. *Foundations of Conciliar Theory: The Contribution of the Medieval Canonists from Gratian to the Great Schism*. Cambridge: Cambridge U. Pr., 1955.

Tocci, Luigi Michelini. "Dei libri a stampa appartenuti al Colocci." In *Atti del Convegno di studi su Angelo Colocci, Jesi, 13–14 settembre 1969*, pp. 77–96. Jesi: Amministrazione comunale, 1972.

Toesca, Ilaria. "A Majolica Inscription in Santa Croce in Gerusalemme." In Douglas Fraser, Howard Hibbard, and Milton J. Lewine, eds., *Essays in the History of Art Presented to Rudolf Wittkower*, pp. 102–05. London: Phaidon, 1967.

Toews, John B. "Formative Forces in the Pontificate of Nicholas V," *CHR*, LIV (1968–69), pp. 261–84.

Touring Club Italiano. *Giuda d'Italia: Roma*. Milan: 1965.

Traeger, Jörg. "Raffaels Stanza d'Eliodoro und ihr Bildsprogramm," *Römisches Jahrbuch für Kunstgeschichte*, XIII (1971), pp. 29–99.

———. *Der reitende Papst: Ein Beitrag zur Ikonographie Papsttums.* Munich: Schnell & Steiner, 1970.

Trame, Richard H., S.J. *Rodrigo Sánchez de Arévalo (1404–1470): Spanish Diplomat and Champion of the Papacy.* The Catholic University of America Studies in Mediaeval History, n.s. XV. Washington, D. C.: Catholic U. Pr., 1958.

Trexler, Richard C. "Florentine Religious Experience: The Sacred Image," *SR*, XIX (1972), pp. 7–41.

———. *The Libro Cerimoniale of the Florentine Republic.* Travaux d'Humanisme et Renaissance, 165. Geneva; Droz, 1978.

———. *Public Life in Renaissance Florence.* N.Y.: Academic Pr., 1980.

———. *The Spiritual Power: Republican Florence under the Interdict.* Studies in Medieval and Reformation Thought, IX. Leiden: Brill, 1974.

Trinkaus, Charles. *Adversity's Noblemen: The Italian Humanists on Happiness.* N.Y.: Octagon Books, 1965; first publ. N.Y.: Columbia U. Pr., 1940.

———. *In Our Image and Likeness: Humanity and Divinity in Italian Renaissance Thought.* 2 vols. Chicago: U. of Chicago Pr., 1970.

———. "Luther's Hexameral Anthropology." In F. Forrester Church and Timothy George, eds., *Continuity and Discontinuity in Church History: Essays Presented to George Huntston Williams on the Occasion of his 65th Birthday*, pp. 150–68. Studies in the History of Christian Thought, XIX. Leiden: Brill, 1979.

Ullman, Berthold L., and Stadter, Philip A. *The Public Library of the Renaissance: Niccolò Niccoli, Cosimo de' Medici and the Library of San Marco.* Medioevo e Umanesimo, 10. Padua: Antenori, 1972.

Ullmann, Walter. *The Growth of Papal Government in the Middle Ages: A Study in the Ideological Relation of Clerical to Lay Power.* 2nd ed. London: Methuen, 1962.

———. *Medieval Papalism: The Political Theories of the Medieval Canonists.* London: Methuen, 1949.

Urban, Günter. "Die Kirchenbaukunst des Quattrocento in Rom," *Römisches Jahrbuch für Kunstgeschichte*, IX-X (1961–62), pp. 75–287.

———. "Zum Neu-bau Projekt von St. Peter unter Nikolaus V." In *Festschrift für Harald Keller*, pp. 131–73. Darmstadt: Eduard Roether, 1963.

Valentini, Giuseppe, S.J. "La crociata da Eugenio IV a Callisto III (dai documenti d'Archivio di Venezia)," *AHP*, XII (1974), pp. 91–123.

———. "La sospensione della crociata nei primi anni di Paolo II (1464–1468)," *AHP*, XIV (1976), pp. 71–101.

Vasoli, Cesare. "Profilo di un Papa umanista: Tommaso Parentucelli." In *Studi sulla cultura del Rinascimento*, pp. 69–121. Manduria: Lacaita, 1968.

Vignati, Bruno. "Alcune note ed osservazioni sul *De rebus memorabilibus Basilicae S. Petri Romae*." In Socrate Corvi, ed., *Studi su Maffeo Vegio*, pp. 58–69. Lodi: Archivio storico lodigiano, 1959.

———. *Maffeo Vegio, Umanista cristiano (1407–1458)*. Bergamo, 1959.

Walker, D. P. *The Ancient Theology: Studies in Christian Platonism from the Fifteenth to the Eighteenth Century.* Ithaca: Cornell U. Pr., 1972.

Ward Perkins, J. B. "The Shrine of St. Peter and its Twelve Spiral Columns," *Journal of Roman Studies*, XLII (1952), pp. 21–33.

Wasner, Franz. "Addenda Varia," *Traditio*, XVI (1960), pp. 405–16.

———. "Fifteenth-Century Texts on the Ceremonial of the *Legatus a latere*," *Traditio*, XIV (1958), pp. 295–338.

———. "Tor der Geschichte: Beitrage zum päpstlichen Zeremonienwesen im 15. Jahrhundert," *AHP*, VI (1968), pp. 142–53.

Way, Sister Agnes Clare. "Gregorius Nazianzenus." In Paul Oskar Kristeller and F. Edward Cranz, eds. *Catalogus translationum et commentariorum: Medieval and Renaissance Latin Translations and Commentaries*, Vol. II, pp. 43–192. Washington, D.C., 1971.

Webb, Diana. "Eloquence and Education: A Humanist Approach to Hagiography," *Journal of Ecclesiastical History*, XXXI (1980), pp. 19–39.

Weckmann-Munoz, Luis. "The Alexandrine Bulls of 1493: Pseudo-Asiatic Documents." In

Fredi Chiappelli, ed., *First Images of America: The Impact of the New World on the Old*, Vol. I, pp. 201–09. Berkeley and Los Angeles: U. of California Pr., 1976.

Weil, Mark S. *The History and Decoration of the Ponte S. Angelo*. University Park: Pennsylvania St. U. Pr., 1974.

Weil-Garris Posner, Kathleen. "Alcuni progetti per piazze e facciate di Bramante e di Antonio da Sangallo a Loreto." In *Studi Bramanteschi: Atti del Congresso internazionale, Milano-Urbino-Roma, 1970*, pp. 313–38. Rome: De Luca, 1974.

———. "Cloister, Court and City Square," *Gesta*, XII (1973), pp. 123–32.

Weil-Garris, Kathleen, and D'Amico, John F. "The Renaissance Cardinal's Ideal Palace: A Chapter from Cortesi's *De Cardinalatu*." In Henry A. Millon, ed., *Studies in Italian Art and Architecture 15th through 18th Centuries*, pp. 45–123. Memoirs of the American Academy in Rome, 35. Rome: Ed. dell'Elefante, 1980.

Weinstein, Donald. *Savonarola and Florence: Prophecy and Patriotism in the Renaissance*. Princeton: Princeton U. Pr., 1970.

Weiss, Roberto. "Andrea Fulvio antiquario romano (c. 1470–1527)," *Annali della Scuola Normale Superiore di Pisa—Lettere, storia e filosofia*, 2nd ser., XXVIII (1959), pp. 1–44.

———. "Biondo Flavio archeologo," *Studi romagnoli*, XIV (1963), pp. 335–41.

———. "The Medals of Julius II (1503–1513)," *JWCI*, XXVIII (1965), pp. 163–82.

———. *The Medals of Sixtus IV (1471–1484)*. Rome: Edizioni di storia e letteratura, 1961.

———. *The Renaissance Discovery of Classical Antiquity*. Oxford: Blackwell, 1969.

———. "Traccia per una biografia di Annio da Viterbo," *Italia medioevale e umanistica*, V (1962), pp. 425–41.

———. *Un umanista veneziano: Papa Paolo II*. Venice: Istituto per la collaborazione culturale, 1958.

Wendel, François. *Calvin: The Origins and Development of his Religious Thought*. London: Collins, 1963; first publ. Paris, 1959.

Westfall, Carroll William. "Biblical Typology in the *Vita Nicolai V* by Giannozzo Manetti." In J. IJsewijn and E. Kessler, eds., *Acta Conventus Neo-Latini Lovaniensis: Proceedings of the First International Congress of Neo-Latin Studies, Louvain, 23–28 August 1971*, pp. 701–09. Munich: Wilhelm Fink, 1973.

———. "Chivalric Decoration: The Palazzo Ducale in Urbino as a Political Statement." In Henry A. Millon and Linda Nochlin, eds., *Art and Architecture in the Service of Politics*, pp. 20–45. Cambridge, Mass.: MIT Pr., 1978.

———. *In this Most Perfect Paradise: Alberti, Nicholas V, and the Invention of Conscious Urban Planning in Rome, 1447–55*. University Park: Pennsylvania St. U. Pr., 1974.

White, John. *The Birth and Rebirth of Pictorial Space*. N.Y.: Harper & Row, 1972.

Whittaker, John. "Giles of Viterbo as Classical Scholar." In *Egidio da Viterbo, O.S.A. e il suo tempo: Atti del V Convegno dell'Istituto Storico Agostiniano, Roma—Viterbo, 20–23 ottobre 1982*, pp. 85–105. Studia Augustiniana Historica, 9. Rome: Ed. "Analecta Augustiniana," 1983.

———. "Greek Manuscripts from the Library of Giles of Viterbo at the Biblioteca Angelica in Rome," *Scriptorium*, XXXI (1977), pp. 212–39.

Wicks, Jared. "Roman Reactions to Luther: The First Year (1518)," *CHR* LXIX (1983), pp. 521–62.

———. "Thomism between Renaissance and Reformation: The Case of Cajetan," *ARG*, LXVIII (1977), pp. 9–32.

Wilde, Johannes. "The Decoration of the Sistine Chapel," *PBA*, XLIV (1958), pp. 61–81.

Wilkins, Ernest Harch. *Life of Petrarch*. Chicago: U. of Chicago Pr., 1961.

———. "On Petrarch's *Ep. Fam.* VI 2," *Speculum*, XXXVIII (1963), pp. 620–22.

Wilks, M. J. *The Problem of Sovereignty in the Later Middle Ages*. Cambridge: Cambridge U. Pr., 1962.

Wind, Edgar. "The Ark of Noah: A Study in the Symbolism of Michelangelo," *Measure*, I (1950), pp. 411–21.

———. "Maccabean Histories in the Sistine Ceiling: A Note on Michelangelo's Use of the Malermi Bible." In E. F. Jacob, ed., *Italian Renaissance Studies*, pp. 312–27. London: Faber & Faber, 1960.

———. "Michelangelo's Prophets and Sibyls," *PBA*, LI (1965), pp. 47–84.

———. *Pagan Mysteries in the Renaissance*. 2nd ed. N.Y.: Norton, 1968.

———. "The Revival of Origen." In Dorothy Miner, ed., *Studies in Art and Literature for Belle da Costa Greene*, pp. 412–24. Princeton: Princeton U. Pr., 1954.

Wirszubski, Chaim. "Giovanni Pico's Book of Job," *JWCI*, XXXII (1969), pp. 171–99.

Wittkower, Rudolf. "Hieroglyphics in the Early Renaissance." In Bernard S. Levy, ed., *Developments in the Early Renaissance*, pp. 58–97. Albany: SUNY Pr., 1972.

Wölfflin, Heinrich. *The Art of Albrecht Dürer*. London: Phaidon, 1971.

Wormald, Francis. "An Italian Poet at the Court of Henry VII," *JWCI*, XIV (1951), pp. 118–19.

Yates, Frances A. *Astraea: The Imperial Theme in the Sixteenth Century*. London: Routledge & Kegan Paul, 1975.

Yuen, Toby. "The 'Bibliotheca Greca': Castagno, Alberti, and Ancient Sources," *The Burlington Magazine*, CXII (1970), pp. 725–36.

Zabughin, Vladimiro. *Giulio Pomponio Leto*. 3 vols. Rome: La vita letteraria, 1909.

Zanelli, Agostino. *Pietro del Monte*. Milan: Cogliati, 1907.

Zeno, Apostolo. *Dissertazioni Vossiane*. 2 vols. Venice, 1753.

Zimmerman, T. C. Price. "Renaissance Symposia." In Sergio Bertelli and Gloria Ramakus, eds., *Essays Presented to Myron P. Gilmore*, Vol. I, pp. 363–74. Florence: La Nuova Italia, 1978.

Zippel, Gianni. "L'autodifesa di Lorenzo Valla per il processo dell' Inquisizione napoletana (1444)," *Italia medioevale e umanistica*, XIII (1970), pp. 59–94.

Zucker, Mark J. "Raphael and the Beard of Julius II," *AB*, LIX (1977), pp. 524–33.

INDEX

CHARLES L. STINGER is Professor of History at the State University of New York at Buffalo. He is author of *Humanism and the Church Fathers: Ambrogio Traversari* and *Christian Antiquity in the Italian Renaissance.*